THE STATES OF THE MANORS OF WESTMINSTER ABBEY
*c.*1300–1422
Part 1

Records of Social and Economic History is a British Academy Research Project.

The British Academy, established by Royal Charter in 1902, is the national academy for the humanities and social sciences, promoting, sustaining and representing advanced research. As an academy composed of senior scholars throughout the UK, it gives recognition to academic excellence and achievement, and plays a leadership role in representing the humanities and social sciences nationally and internationally. As a learned society, the British Academy facilitates the research of individuals and groups of scholars.

More information can be found at *www.britishacademy.ac.uk*

RECORDS OF SOCIAL AND ECONOMIC HISTORY
NEW SERIES 57

THE STATES OF THE MANORS OF WESTMINSTER ABBEY *c*.1300–1422

Part 1

Introduction
Method of Editing
Word List and Glossary
Texts: The Abbot's Estates
Texts: The Convent's Estates

EDITED BY
BARBARA F. HARVEY
AND
CHRISTOPHER M. WOOLGAR

Published for THE BRITISH ACADEMY
by OXFORD UNIVERSITY PRESS

Oxford University Press, Great Clarendon Street, Oxford OX2 6DP

First edition published in 2019

British Library Cataloguing in Publication Data
Data available

Library of Congress Cataloging in Publication Data
Data available

Typeset by
New Leaf Design, Malton, North Yorkshire

ISBN 978–0–19–726662–5

Foreword

Westminster Abbey was one of the great landowners of medieval England. Given the pivotal role of agriculture at the time, this gave it considerable secular power—social and economic, political and legal. It owned dozens of estates, mainly in the Home Counties and the West Midlands, and how it ran them directly affected those working on the estates, while influencing wider markets for labour and goods. Historians have long been concerned with these themes in relation to metanarratives about feudalism, commercialisation and Malthusian constraints. Managing estates for the benefit of the Abbey, in cash and in kind, was a major administrative challenge, requiring information to be gathered with which to make decisions about possible changes. In these two volumes (Records of Social and Economic History, new series, 57 and 58) Barbara Harvey, the leading authority on the estates of Westminster Abbey before the Dissolution, and Christopher Woolgar have painstakingly transcribed and edited key accounts from the period 1300 to 1422 which saw the Abbey shift away from some direct management ('demesne' farming) towards tenancies. These seventy-five 'states' show the resources of the Abbey's individual estates and what it knew of them, before, during and after the Black Death. As such, they provide rich evidence of the agricultural economy of medieval England and of the men who decided on its form.

The Records of Social and Economic History committee are very grateful to Professor Woolgar for bringing this edition to completion after ill health slowed and then halted Miss Harvey's labours. Professor Harding, the general editor of the series, also deserves our thanks for guiding the final text through to publication.

Julian Hoppit, Chair, Records of Social and Economic History Committee
February 2019

Contents

Part 2

Editorial Preface and Acknowledgements

These volumes bring to publication those documents that the monks of Westminster produced to provide an overview of their extensive estates in the fourteenth century. Barbara Harvey began this edition in the early 2000s, a continuation of her work on the Abbey and its estates over many years. She was unable to complete it, but she had done a very great deal to prepare it by the time, in 2016, that she passed it to Christopher Woolgar to bring to a conclusion. The division of labour has been roughly as follows: initial transcription, annotation and checking of all material except the convent's states after 1400 was done by Barbara Harvey. She was also able to prepare the appendix on the abbot's manorial and estate officials. Christopher Woolgar has completed the transcription, checked the material and prepared descriptions of the manuscripts; he has written the introduction and prepared the Word List and Glossary, and brought the text as a whole to its final form.

Both Barbara Harvey and Christopher Woolgar have incurred a great many debts in the preparation of these volumes. Firstly, we wish to thank the Dean and Chapter of Westminster for permission to publish the documents from their muniments. We are both grateful, for their continued interest and support, to successive Keepers of the Muniments, Dr Richard Mortimer and Mr Matthew Payne, to Miss Christine Reynolds, the Assistant Keeper, and to Dr Tony Trowles, the Librarian, who have made our visits to the Abbey a pleasure. We are also grateful to the Essex Record Office for their assistance with our work on the items from the Mildmay family archive which are calendared in the second volume and for their permission to reproduce an image of one of the states of the convent's manors. The research for this edition has, over the years, taken us to other archives and we are happy to acknowledge in particular the assistance of the staff of the National Archives, the British Library, Cambridge University Library, Gloucestershire Archives, Hertfordshire Archives and Local Studies, and the former Guildhall Library Manuscripts Division, now part of London Metropolitan Archives.

We also wish to thank the British Academy and the members of its Records of Social and Economic History Committee for their support for the work on this edition.

Barbara Harvey
Christopher Woolgar
23 September 2018

Abbreviations

The following abbreviations are used in the text:

AND	*Anglo-Norman Dictionary*, 2nd edn., at www.anglo-norman.net/
BL	London, British Library
Br.	Brother
BRUO	A. B. Emden, *A Biographical Register of the University of Oxford to A.D. 1500* (3 vols., Oxford, 1957–9)
Campbell, *English Seigniorial Agriculture*	B. M. S. Campbell, *English Seigniorial Agriculture 1250–1450* (Cambridge, 2000)
CUL	Cambridge University Library
Customary	*Customary of the Benedictine Monasteries of Saint Augustine, Canterbury, and Saint Peter, Westminster*, ed. E. M. Thompson (2 vols., Henry Bradshaw Society, 23, 28; 1902, 1904)
DMLBS	*Dictionary of Medieval Latin from British Sources*, ed. R. E. Latham, D. R. Howlett and others (London, 1975–2013)
EconHR	*Economic History Review*
ERO	Chelmsford, Essex Record Office
Flete, *History*	John Flete, *The History of Westminster Abbey*, ed. J. Armitage Robinson (Cambridge, 1909)
GRO	Gloucester, Gloucestershire Record Office (now Gloucestershire Archives)
HALS	Hertford, Hertfordshire Archives and Local Studies
Harvey, *Estates*	B. F. Harvey, *Westminster Abbey and Its Estates in the Middle Ages* (Oxford, 1977)
Harvey, *Living and Dying*	B. F. Harvey, *Living and Dying in England 1100–1540: The Monastic Experience* (Oxford, 1993)
Harvey, *Medieval Oxfordshire Village*	P. D. A. Harvey, *A Medieval Oxfordshire Village: Cuxham 1240 to 1400* (Oxford, 1965)
Harvey, *Obedientiaries*	B. F. Harvey, *The Obedientiaries of Westminster Abbey and Their Financial Records, c.1275 to 1540* (Westminster Abbey Record Series, 3; 2002)
LMA	London Metropolitan Archives
LNQ	Liber Niger Quaternus (WAM Muniment Book 1)
LS	*A Latin Dictionary*, ed. C. T. Lewis and C. Short (Oxford, 1879)
Manorial Records of Cuxham, ed. Harvey	*Manorial Records of Cuxham, Oxfordshire, c.1200–1359*, ed. P. D. A. Harvey (Historical Manuscripts Commission, Joint Publications series, 23; 1976)
MED	*Middle English Dictionary*, ed. H. Kurath, S. M. Kuhn and others (Ann Arbor, 1956–2001)

Neilson, *Customary Rents*	N. Neilson, *Customary Rents*, in *Oxford Studies in Social and Legal History*, vol. 2, ed. P. Vinogradoff (Oxford, 1910)
OED	*Oxford English Dictionary*
OLD	*Oxford Latin Dictionary*, ed. P. G. W. Glare (2nd edn., 2 vols., Oxford, 2012)
Pearce, *Monks*	E. H. Pearce, *The Monks of Westminster, Being a Register of the Brethren of the Convent from the Time of the Confessor to the Dissolution* (Cambridge, 1916)
RO	Record Office
Stern, *Hertfordshire Demesne*	D. V. Stern, *A Hertfordshire Demense of Westminster Abbey: Profits, Productivity and Weather*, ed. C. Thornton (Hertford, 2000)
TPN	*Taxatio ecclesiastica Angliae et Walliae auctoritate P. Nicholai IV, c.A.D. 1291*, ed. S. Ayscough and J. Caley (London, 1802)
VCH	*Victoria Histories of the Counties of England*, with county abbreviation and volume number
Walter de Wenlok, ed. Harvey	*Documents Illustrating the Rule of Walter de Wenlok, Abbot of Westminster, 1282–1307*, ed. B. F. Harvey (Camden 4th series, 2; 1965)
WAM	Westminster Abbey Muniments
WD	Westminster Domesday, a cartulary, now WAM Muniment Book 11

Editorial Conventions, Weights and Measures

The following abbreviations and conventions have been used throughout the volume for all forms of the words noted below.

bus. *bussellus*, bushel
d. *denarius* (penny)
di. *dimidius*, *-a*, *-um* (half)
lb. pound (weight)
li. *libra* (pound sterling)
lib. *libra* (weight) in Latin forms
mem. membrane
ob. *obolus* (halfpenny)
p. *pecia*, peck (dry capacity)
qr. *quarterium*, quarter (dry capacity)
qua. *quadrans* (farthing)
quart. *quatrona* (a quarter of a hundred, or of a hundredweight)
rot. rotulet
s. *solidus* (shilling)
st. stone (weight)

Measures of wool

1 clove = 7 or 8 lb. (here usually 7 lb.)
1 sack = 26 st. or 364 lb.
1 stone = 14 lb.
1 todd = 2 st.

Measures of dry capacity

1 qr. = 8 bus.
1 bus. = 4 p.

Note different customs on different manors which affect calculation of capacity, such as the use of heaped or struck measure, e.g. II 33, Launton, 6 qr. wheat with the eighth bushel heaped, and conventions about whether a grain has been winnowed or not.

Measures of area

1 acre = 4 roods
1 rood = 40 [square] perches (statute measure)

A perch was a rod of 16½ feet, but there were also customary perches and customary acres of varying size. Customary acres might be defined as acres 'as they lie' in the fields, referring to the cultivated strips.

Currency

£1 (pound) = 20s. (shillings) = 240d. (pence) 1s. = 12d. 1 mark = 13s. 4d. = 160d.

Reconstructions of text

Wholly editorial reconstructions of parts of texts that are missing have been placed in square brackets [ ]. Missing areas are represented by three points, where there is a space that would allow up to three letters and abbreviations to be written. Five points have been employed for more extensively damaged passages and where the damaged passage continues onto a further line, the five points have been repeated.

Layout

The layout of the original documents has been maintained as far as possible, but the manuscripts are not always consistent; at the same time, some of the practices, with long lists of entries one under the other in columns, are not easy to use and consume a great deal of space in print. Significant changes to the layout made in print are noted in the descriptions and footnotes.

Conventions for dates and numbers in the calendared documents

In preparing the English calendar, the descriptions of rents and farms use the phrase 'at the four usual terms'. This means the payments that were due at Michaelmas (29 September), Christmas (25 December), Easter (varying dates in March/April) and the nativity of St John the Baptist (24 June). Beyond this rents and farms were often paid at Martinmas (11 November) and the Purification of the Blessed Virgin Mary (2 February). Other dates are identified in footnotes.

In the absence of evidence for customary usages of numbers—such as long hundreds—to imply different quantities, in the calendared texts it has been assumed that C = 100 and M = 1,000.

Counties

References to counties in England and Wales are to those obtaining immediately prior to the changes made in 1974 under the Local Government Act 1972.

Introduction

The documents edited in these volumes are witnesses to the administration of one of the country's great monastic estates, that of Westminster Abbey, in the period from around 1300 to 1422. Landed property formed a substantial, but not the only, basis for Westminster's income. At the start of the fourteenth century, it is probable that the Abbey had some 38,000 acres of land, of which about 21,000 acres were held by tenants on customary tenures, with 17,000 acres held in demesne.[1] The revenues from these lands were equally impressive in their scale. At the Dissolution, Westminster had a net income that exceeded £2,800 p.a., placing the house second only to Glastonbury Abbey in its wealth.[2]

The primary purpose of these assets was the support of monastic life. Whether and to what extent there was a monastery at Westminster prior to 959, when St Dunstan was able to establish a Benedictine house on the site, is a debated question. What is certain is that the attachment of Edward the Confessor to Westminster was pivotal in establishing its long-term importance —as his burial place, subsequently as his shrine, and also as the coronation church of the kings of England. The Confessor endowed the monastery which accompanied the newly rebuilt Romanesque church with sufficient resources to support a community of some eighty monks. Henry III rebuilt the Abbey again, this time as a major Gothic church, the focus of the cult of Edward the Confessor, in which he had a special interest, and with a view too that it should be his own burial place. In the early years of the fourteenth century the numbers of monks are less certain: there may have been a little over fifty. In 1398, towards the end of the period covered by this edition, the monastic community comprised the abbot and fifty-eight professed monks, and a few more or less in surrounding years—but the decrease in monks was matched by an increase in the numbers of their servants.[3] The extensive estate that supported this community is the focus of these books; and the documentary record that helps us understand the decisions the monks made about its management is of far-reaching importance for our knowledge of the economy and society of late medieval England.

[1] For the Abbey's estates in general, see Harvey, *Estates*; here, in particular, pp. 127–8.

[2] Harvey, *Estates*, pp. 26, 63.

[3] Harvey, *Estates*, pp. 22–5; Harvey, *Living and Dying in England*, pp. 2–3. Harvey, *Estates*, p. 67, n. 1, for numbers in 1398; isolated figures for numbers of monks in the early fourteenth century give 55 in 1305 and 1306, and 50 in 1307.

Since the Norman Conquest, most land in England has been managed indirectly, by landlords leasing out their property. There is one significant exception, however: for a period of two hundred years from approximately 1170, many chose to manage their lands directly, in a system known as demesne farming. The reasons for this, as far as monastic estates were concerned, were in part to do with developments in land law. At Westminster, the Abbey had lost estates to those tenants in fee whose tenancies had effectively become perpetual. Another part of the rationale for the change to direct management was common to secular estates as well. A period of significant inflation from 1180 onwards led to the loss of opportunity and revenue where long-term leases were employed, and short-term leasing was less attractive to many of the more important leaseholders.[4] The monks of Westminster maintained the system of direct management into the early fourteenth century, when some properties were put back on lease; but they continued to manage the great majority of their estates directly for a much longer period—it was not until the 1360s and 1370s, after the Black Death, that there was significant change, returning many estates to leaseholds of different forms and characteristics.[5] The typical leaseholds of this new period of management were of the demesne farms—that is the home farms of manors—rather than the whole of an estate, with its customary lands and appurtenances; and there were also leases of smaller holdings and livestock. This led the abbot and convent into the necessity of collecting a range of rents and dues, in different forms, some in cash, some in kind, some managed through the manorial court, others by formal indentures of lease.

These volumes publish seventy-five documents providing overviews of the Westminster estate and its revenues, as administered in its two principal parts, by the abbot on the one hand, and by the convent on the other. The documents fall into two types, although both are called 'states' (from the Latin *status*) at different points and both are intimately linked to the system of manorial accounts and accounting that the Abbey employed. These records are, firstly, views of account, that is, estimates of the corn, stock and cash on the manors, made partway through the financial year (which usually started at Michaelmas, 29 September), often at a mid-point, in late March. The survival of views for substantial parts of an estate is unusual, and the second group of documents, the 'states' or 'dockets', also has little by way of parallel. In the developed form in which they appear, the states of the manors

[4] P. D. A. Harvey, 'The Pipe Rolls and the Adoption of Demesne Farming in England', *EconHR*, 2nd series, 27 (1974), pp. 345–59; R. H. Britnell, *The Commercialisation of English Society, 1000–1500* (2nd edn., Manchester, 1996), pp. 108–11. See also P. D. A. Harvey, 'The English Inflation of 1180–1220', *Past and Present* 61 (Nov. 1973), pp. 3–30; P. Latimer, 'The English Inflation of 1180–1220 Reconsidered', *Past and Present* 171 (May 2001), pp. 3–29.
[5] Harvey, *Estates*, pp. 130–1, 148–51.

presented a docket: a summary of key elements of the manorial account, made after the final audit usually around Michaelmas, with information about the management of the estate, its value, arrears and so on.[6] Together the documents printed comprise all the views of the estate for the convent beyond those for individual manors, and all the states and dockets for the estates of both the abbot and the convent that survive between *c.*1300 and 1422.[7] After this date, the information in the documents of this type is reduced in scale, and the level of repetition from year to year increases. That notwithstanding, the states—and the views before them—provided information which allowed the head of the house and the convent to follow the overall fortunes of their estates and to use this documentation to make decisions about management of the property.

The Westminster estates

A formal division of the resources of the Abbey was made in 1225 into two portions, one for the abbot, the other for the convent, with the intention that the activities of the abbot would be supported by the one entirely, and that the convent, its religious life and activities would be supported in large part by the other. All the properties were assigned to one portion or the other: none was held to provide for both, and the arrangement also reallocated properties to the convent so that there was sufficient to cover the expected costs. From this point onwards, the convent was responsible for the appointment (and dismissal) of the obedientiaries who were to administer the monastic offices or 'obediences'.[8]

The abbot's manors were divided for administrative purposes into two groups, those in the Eastern Parts, and those in the Western Parts, each overseen by a collector. Those in the Eastern Parts were the manors closer to London: in Middlesex—Eye, Laleham, Staines and Yeoveney—with Denham and Denham Durdent's in Buckinghamshire; Islip in Oxfordshire; and Pyrford in Surrey. From time to time, however, Denham and Islip were administered as part of the manors of the receiver of the Western Parts.[9] Those manors principally the purview of the receiver or collector of the Western Parts were an important group in Gloucestershire: Bourton-on-the-Hill,

[6] *OED* docket *sb.*[1], 2., first citation from 1485, but on the evidence of these Westminster documents the term was in use earlier, as *dogerelli* from 1362–3 (II 16) and *dogettus* from 1366–7 (II 20); and possibly from 1353: II 11, p. 333, n.25.

[7] One badly damaged fragment, from the early fourteenth century, covering parts of the manors of Amwell, Stevenage and Wheathampstead, BL, Add. Roll 66773, has not been included.

[8] Harvey, *Estates*, pp. 64, 85–91; the properties are listed in detail at pp. 335–64.

[9] Harvey, *Obedientiaries*, p. 218.

Deerhurst, Hardwicke, Sutton-under-Brailes and Todenham; a further group in Worcestershire: Birlingham, Castlemorton, Chaceley, Longdon, Pensham, Pershore and its borough, Pinvin and Wick; and the abbey's liberties in these two counties.[10]

If the abbot had the lands most distant from the Abbey, in Gloucestershire and Worcestershire, the most likely reason is that it was considered important that the monks and those of them who acted as obedientiaries providing direct supervision of the convent's manors should be closer to Westminster, to minimise travel and absence from the house.[11] The convent administered a group of properties in Essex: Beckswell, Benfleet, Fanton, Feering (and its rectory), Kelvedon (and its rectory) and Moulsham; in Hertfordshire, Aldenham, [Great] Amwell, Ashwell (and its rectory), Kinsbourne, Sayesbury and Sawbridgeworth rectory, Stevenage and Wheathampstead (and Harpenden and its church); in Kent, Combe in Greenwich; in Middlesex, Ashford (and its rectory), Chelsea, Greenford with Hanwell, Halliford, Hampstead, Hendon with Frith and Newhall, Knightsbridge, Paddington and Teddington; the manor of Launton in Oxfordshire; the manor and rectory of Oakham in Rutland; and, in Surrey, Allfarthing in Wandsworth, Battersea, Morden (and its rectory) and Wandsworth and Downe.

In the period up to 1420, two further groups of manors—the 'royal manors'—fell broadly under the convent's administrative arrangements, although they had a different position. At this date, the royal manors supported two foundations, that for Eleanor of Castile, and that for Anne of Bohemia and her husband, Richard II. Eleanor's foundation, a grant to the Abbey from Edward I for the good of her soul, comprised manors acquired in part in her lifetime: Birdbrook in Essex, Turweston in Buckinghamshire, Knowle and Grafton in Warwickshire, Westerham in Kent, with the addition of Stangraves and Edenbridge, both also in Kent, in 1381, and administered closely with Westerham.[12] The endowment provided for the commemoration of Eleanor's anniversary, for the poor, and for pittances for the prior and convent. It had a special status within the monastery, with its own warden and arrangements for auditing.[13] Anne of Bohemia's anniversaries were initially supported by an Exchequer grant from 1394, but this was followed by an endowment in 1398–9 to provide for the good of her soul and that of her husband, Richard II, based on the manors of Holme with Langford in Bedfordshire; in Middlesex, Hodford (in Hendon), and Northolt and Down; along with Steventon and its rectory in Berkshire and Westbury in Wiltshire.

[10] Harvey, *Obedientiaries*, pp. 3, 222–3.
[11] Harvey, *Estates*, pp. 87–8.
[12] Stangraves first appears in the state for 1391–2: II 35.
[13] Harvey, *Obedientiaries*, p. 139.

As well as providing support for liturgical arrangements, provision was also made for pittances for the monks.[14] The manors of Eleanor of Castile appear from the start of the documents edited in this volume; those for Anne of Bohemia and Richard II from 1399.[15]

The division of the estate also reflected to some degree the different needs of the abbot and convent. By 1225, the abbot was largely absent from the liturgical life of Westminster and lived apart from the community while still maintaining authority over aspects of monastic life. He had his own great household, which was peripatetic round his estates, living on the manors for much of the year; even when the abbot came to the capital, he had a residence close to Westminster but separate from the Abbey, at La Neyte on his manor at Eye.[16] The extent of the abbot's absence from Westminster was less from the time of Abbot Litlyngton, who had a new house built within the monastery itself.[17] This style of living allowed the abbot to provide hospitality on behalf of the house, to conduct business for the community and to sustain a political presence. An abbot of a house of the stature of Westminster was expected to live in a manner appropriate and requisite for the dignity of his monastery; this role, more open to the life of the world, was accepted by most contemporaries as fitting for heads of greater monastic houses generally.[18] The abbot could draw directly on the produce of his lands when living on his manors. This was particularly important for corn (the household of Abbot Litlyngton received grain worth in excess of £90 p.a. in this way),[19] but also for other commodities at other times.[20] The connection to the estates was managed by the steward of the abbot's household—sometimes referred to as a warden or treasurer, who was down to the 1370s normally a monk—and there were also separate receivers for the estates. The revenues of the abbot's estates amounted to about one third of those of the monastery as a whole: in the 1360s, the net income that Abbot Litlyngton received was some £600 p.a., and the abbot's

[14] Harvey, *Obedientiaries*, pp. 154–5.

[15] II 41.

[16] For the abbot and great household living, see the ordinances for the household of Abbot Wenlok: *Walter de Wenlok*, ed. Harvey, pp. 241–8.

[17] Harvey, *Obedientiaries*, p. 2; J. A. Robinson, *The Abbot's House at Westminster* (Cambridge, 1911), pp. 9–13, 16–22.

[18] Harvey, *Estates*, p. 131; M. Heale, *The Abbots and Priors of Late Medieval and Reformation England* (Oxford, 2016); M. Heale, 'Abbots' Households in Late Medieval England', in *The Elite Household in England, 1100–1550*, ed. C. M. Woolgar (Donington, 2018), pp. 258–76.

[19] Harvey, *Estates*, p. 137.

[20] At several periods in the 1290s and then again from the 1370s, stock and goods for the abbot's household drawn directly from the demesnes were managed by accountants as a series of fictitious sales entered in the manorial accounts: *Walter de Wenlok*, ed. Harvey, pp. 242–3.

portion had probably been worth that amount since the start of the fourteenth century.[21]

The economy of the estate allocated to the monks at Westminster had a slightly different rationale, although there were many points in common with that of the abbot. Beyond support for the Abbey's spiritual life and commemorations, the monks needed provisions, but they were wanted at Westminster rather than wherever a travelling household might be located. Those provisions might be corn delivered directly to Westminster, or the revenues of the estate might come by some other arrangement, especially the delivery of cash to the Abbey. Around 1400, it is likely that the income of the convent—with the royal manors—was of the order of £1,600 p.a.[22] The revenues, beyond provisions, were applied to all the needs of the house, albeit some of the estates were allocated to particular obedientiaries of the monastery.

The division of the estate in 1225 also spoke to a wider concern among monastic communities that their economies should be planned and carefully managed. At Westminster, therefore, an estimate was made of the principal provisions that would be required by the convent on a daily basis. An underlying market rate was assumed, that a quarter of wheat would cost 5s., a quarter of barley 3s. and a quarter of oats 2s.—and the notion was that each day the cellarer would need 2½ quarters of wheat for bread, and that 3 quarters of barley and 6 quarters of oats would be needed for brewing every other day.[23] The arrangement, however, made no provision for a rise in the price of these grains above these levels. It is indicative, though, of the engagement of the convent with the market. There was significant change here during the fourteenth century. Around 1300, it is likely that the convent's demesnes and rectories supplied about 40% by cash value of their needs in corn in kind; by the 1360s that proportion had risen to 84% either directly drawn from the demesnes and tithes, or from corn rents.[24]

The principal monastic official concerned in the administration of the convent's estate was the monk-bailiff, in the Abbey's accounts most often called simply 'the bailiff'. The post can be traced back to the mid-thirteenth century: his main role was oversight of the convent's estates, involving near continuous contact with manorial officials as well as, in due course, supervision of the Abbey's counsellors, legal and more general. By the mid-fourteenth century the post was usually held by the senior of the two treasurers of the convent. The royal manors were overseen by a warden, but

[21] Harvey, *Estates*, pp. 60–1, 134–7.
[22] For a discussion and estimates, see Harvey, *Estates*, pp. 55–63.
[23] *Customary*, ii, pp. 102–3; Harvey, *Estates*, p. 141. See also below, p. 11.
[24] Harvey, *Estates*, pp. 142–8. That is, rents to be delivered in corn not cash, as a hedge against volatility in price, but also as an assured source of provisions, sometimes incorporating too arrangements for delivery to Westminster.

he was often the same person as the monk-bailiff. Equally the rectories and ecclesiastical property held by the convent were overseen by the warden of the churches—and at some points at least this was also the same person as the monk-bailiff. Many of the convent's documents published in this edition, the states of the manors, must have had a close connection with this official: even if he was not directly named as their originator or compiler, the monk-bailiff, or his office, must have provided much of the information required in their preparation.[25]

Monastic accounting systems

If accounts were not essential for the change in the way land was managed from a system of leasing to direct farming, they would at the very least have facilitated the supervision that was a necessary concomitant of the new practice. At the same time, they spoke to the moral obligation of those entrusted with estates, the reeves and bailiffs, to respond to the charge they had been given.[26] There were good reasons for monasteries in particular to have accounting systems—and in the first half of the thirteenth century the monastic reform movement reiterated their importance. As monks held all property in common, it was not permissible for anyone to appropriate anything to himself or his office (*proprietas*). Beyond this, the system of endowments dedicated to particular offices had resulted in the obedientiaries of many monasteries controlling their own revenues and their disbursement. In consequence there had developed a patchwork of small administrative systems, with nobody possessing a coherent overview of the monastery's finances.

There are references from *c.* 1170 onwards to the use of accounts in English monasteries, but there is no evidence that a formal written document or statement was envisaged at this stage. At St Swithun's Cathedral Priory, Winchester, Bishop Henry of Blois, who had earlier been responsible for financial reforms at Cluny, ordered the account of the priory and of all the obedientiaries to be audited (or 'heard') each year by twelve senior monks of the house: any surplus was to be held for the common use of the community.[27] In the 1190s,

[25] Harvey, *Obedientiaries*, pp. 104–5; see also II 49, n. 1.

[26] P. D. A. Harvey, 'Agricultural Treatises and Manorial Accounting in Medieval England', *Agricultural History Review* 20 (1972), pp. 170–82; J. Sabapathy, *Officers and Accountability in Medieval England 1170–1300* (Oxford, 2014), pp. 25–82.

[27] R. A. L. Smith, 'The *Regimen scaccarii* in the English Monasteries', *Transactions of the Royal Historical Society*, 4th series, 24 (1942), pp. 74–5; *Registrum Johannis de Pontissara, episcopi Wyntoniensis, 1282–1304*, ed. C. Deedes (2 vols., Canterbury and York Society, 19, 30; 1915–24), ii, pp. 622–3.

Abbot Samson of Bury centralised business in his monastery to combat the tendency to fragmentation and appropriation.[28] At Waltham Abbey, by 1191, an account of all expenses was given at quarterly intervals by the obedientiaries before an auditing committee of senior monks[29]—and it is at this point that the first written accounts appear among the internal records of English monastic houses. The treasurers' accounts for Canterbury Cathedral Priory provide an overview of the house's finances for 1198–9, starting a sequence that still survives to 1384, albeit with some gaps.[30] Pope Innocent III (1198–1216) was also anxious to reform the financial organisation of monasteries, encouraging attempts to centralise control of finance.[31] It is no surprise therefore to find in the statutes of English Benedictine monks injunctions about accounting. In the province of Canterbury, 1218–19, their general chapter demanded that no monk give or receive anything without licence from his superior, that all, especially obedientiaries, observe this, on pain of excommunication; all was to be disbursed faithfully for the benefit of the Church, and a faithful account was to be rendered to the abbot or prior, joined with the more discreet members of the house according to their number.[32] This instruction was repeated: accounting had become an essential part of monastic management. Archbishop Stephen Langton in the statutes of the council held at Oxford in 1222 required all obedientiaries of a monastery and the greater prelates to render an account of receipts and expenses preferably four times a year, but at least twice, before monks deputed by the convent or before superiors, according to the custom of the house.[33] The legatine visitation of Bury St Edmunds in 1234 required the obedientiaries to render their accounts twice a year, keeping their rolls of all receipts and expenses to the end of the year so that the improved or worsening financial position of the house could be determined.[34] In 1235 and 1237, Pope Gregory IX (1227–41) enjoined the preparation of a *status*, giving the totals of income and expenditure for each

[28] *The Chronicle of Jocelin of Brakelond Concerning the Acts of Samson Abbot of the Monastery of St Edmund*, ed. H. E. Butler (London, 1949), pp. 2, 38, 41–2, 87–90.
[29] Smith, '*Regimen scaccarii*', p. 76.
[30] R. A. L. Smith, 'The Central Financial System of Christ Church, Canterbury, 1186–1512', *English Historical Review* 55 (1940), pp. 353–69, with the account for 1198–9 printed at pp. 368–9; *idem*, *Canterbury Cathedral Priory: A Study in Monastic Administration* (Cambridge, 1943), pp. 14–28, sequence of accounts described at p. 15.
[31] U. Berlière, 'Innocent III et la réorganisation des monastères bénédictins', *Revue bénédictine* 32 (1920), pp. 22–42, 145–50.
[32] *Documents Illustrating the Activities of the General and Provincial Chapters of the English Black Monks 1215–1540*, ed. W. A. Pantin (3 vols., Camden 3rd series, 45, 47, 54; 1931–7), i, p. 12.
[33] *Councils and Synods with Other Documents Relating to the English Church: II. A.D. 1205–1313*, ed. F. M. Powicke and C. R. Cheney (2 vols., Oxford, 1964), i, p. 118, cap. 38.
[34] R. Graham, 'A Papal Visitation of Bury St Edmunds and Westminster in 1234', *English Historical Review* 27 (1912), pp. 728–39, at p. 735.

office of the monastery, to be available at episcopal visitations.[35] In the Benedictine statutes of 1249, all heads of houses were expected to read out (this is probably the sense of *recitent*) once a year before the convent the state of the house (*status domus*)—an injunction repeated in 1277.[36]

These injunctions tell us obliquely about the form of the account, in that rendering a report of receipts and expenses suggests a charge/discharge account—like manorial accounts or, indeed, like the earliest individual obedientiary accounts to survive, those for Kingswood Abbey, a cellarer's account for 1240–1, and a bursar's roll for the following year.[37] They also mention the presentation of a *status*, by which we should understand a description of the overall financial position of the house in a summary—and intelligible—form. The notion that there was a standard form of account, common to all, is something which should be quickly dispensed with, however. Firstly, a good deal of accounting in the thirteenth century was carried out in oral form: the heads of monastic houses probably did this, presenting an oral report on the overall finances of their convent. The requirement to account did not, of itself, require a written document, although some written materials, or aides-mémoire, would doubtless have been a useful development.[38] The statutes of the Benedictines for the northern province for 1221 required the obedientiaries of the house to show the state of their office (*statum officii sui*) faithfully to the head of the house when requested. Beyond this, bursars, cellarers and grangers were to give an account of their receipts and expenses 'in the due and accustomed form' (*modo debito et consueto*), that is, there was no prescribed form, but each house had a usual way for doing this.[39] Secondly, although few accounts have survived for this early period, what there is

[35] *Les registres de Grégoire IX: recueil des bulles de ce pape publiées ou analysées d'après les manuscrits originaux du Vatican*, ed. L. Auvray (4 vols., Paris, 1896–1955), ii, p. 325; C. R. Cheney, *Episcopal Visitation of Monasteries in the Thirteenth Century* (Manchester, 1931), pp. 72, 160–7. For an overview of injunctions, papal, episcopal and monastic, relating to accounting in monasteries, see H. Dewez, 'Connaître par les nombres. Cultures et écritures comptables au prieuré cathédral de Norwich (1256–1344)' (Thèse de doctorat d'histoire médiévale, Université Paris I, 2014), pp. 173–251. Professor Woolgar is grateful to Dr Dewez for allowing him to consult her thesis.

[36] *Documents Illustrating the Activities of the General and Provincial Chapters*, ed. Pantin, i, pp. 36, 84–5, also repeating points about the periodicity of accounting, and its importance for determining the improving—or deteriorating—position of the house.

[37] Bristol University Library, MSS DM 104/12–13, printed in translation by V. R. Perkins, 'Documents Relating to the Monastery of St Mary, Kingswood', *Transactions of the Bristol and Gloucestershire Archaeological Society* 22 (1899), pp. 193–201.

[38] Cf. for the development of oral accounting, *Manorial Records of Cuxham*, ed. Harvey, pp. 14–15; for household accounts, *Household Accounts from Medieval England*, ed. C. M. Woolgar (2 vols., British Academy, Records of Social and Economic History, new series, 17–18; 1992–3), i, pp. 10–12; and, in monasteries, Harvey, *Obedientiaries*, pp. xvi–xvii.

[39] *Documents Illustrating the Activities of the General and Provincial Chapters*, ed. Pantin, i, p. 238.

suggests variety and experimentation, rather than the adoption of a standard form. At the same time, the approach in monasteries was concerned with establishing the overall financial picture of the house.

Accounting for manorial revenues was as important to monasteries as the management of the internal offices of the house: these were two parts of the same process, and documents like a *status* encouraged this overview. The *status*, however, might be shaped in different ways: it might cover the internal offices of the house, a *status obedientiariorum*, or it might cover the manors, a *status maneriorum*, or they might be combined in some guise. The purpose of all, however, was to facilitate an overview of the economy. Monastic houses often drew provisions, especially corn and malt, direct from their estates, and a combined form of accounting was necessary to reflect this. A fragment of a mid-thirteenth-century account from Bury St Edmunds contains part of the subcellarer's accounts and also an account for the corn of the abbey's estates. This latter has entries for each manor giving the quantities of wheat received, wheat baked, wheat sold, the value of wheat sold, the amount of wheat remaining on the manor, the value of that remaining and the price per seam. There is a similar account for malt. The subcellarer at Bury, besides superintending the provision of bread and ale for the domestic needs of the monastery, was presumably responsible in addition for the corn on the manors, keeping an account of its movement and value.[40] The injunctions of 1234 for Bury had enjoined a state of the manors, rents and goods belonging to the cellarer be prepared by estimate, dividing the year into four parts, to ensure that there was no shortfall in any quarter—and that there should equally be a state of the farms. Bailiffs and bedels were to give surety, as well as swearing to serve prudently and faithfully, that they would answer fully for all receipts and expenses, of goods as well as cash, at the account and as often as they were asked.[41] This holistic approach to the economy can be seen in later accounting records—across monastic orders—which deal with both the internal and external finances and provisions of the house in one document. It appears at the Gilbertine house of Malton Priory in accounts for 1244–57; at Beaulieu Abbey, a Cistercian house, in its account book of 1269–70; among the Benedictines, at Peterborough Abbey—in the accounts for the bakehouse, enrolled alongside the manorial accounts as in 1300–1 and 1309–10 (and possibly also *c.*1289); and at Oseney Abbey, a house of Augustinian canons, for the year ending at Michaelmas 1280.[42]

[40] Now re-used as the outer wrapper to one of the first parts of the *Liber albus* of the monastery: BL, Harley MS 1005, ff. 2, 41.

[41] Graham, 'Papal Visitation of Bury St Edmunds and Westminster', p. 734.

[42] R. Graham, 'The Finances of Malton Priory, 1244–1257', *Transactions of the Royal Historical Society*, 2nd series, 18 (1904), pp. 132–56; *The Account-Book of Beaulieu Abbey*, ed. S. F. Hockey (Camden 4th series, 16; 1975); Northamptonshire RO, enrolled manorial accounts, Fitzwilliam

The financial overview, encouraged by the *status*, reflects something beyond the documents we now have—the ways in which institutions might plan and manage their economy as a whole. The use of charge/discharge accounts in planning appears more often to have been oblique rather than direct. On the one hand, what was sought related to the 'profit' (*proficuum*) or 'value' (*valor*) of manors; on the other it was connected to consumption—and the ways in which a house could estimate what its needs were in terms of provisions. In some form this must have underlain the estimate of foodstuffs Westminster made in 1225. Although charge/discharge accounts were employed for the obedientiaries across a wide range of monasteries, there were additions to these or direct calculations on central accounts that were focused on questions of consumption: the amount of corn or ale needed each week, for example. At Durham Cathedral Priory, between 1307 and 1339, the cellarer's summary cash account had calculations of monthly and weekly averages of cash expenditure. The calculations reached their most elaborate on the 1339 account, which gave, in addition to the two cash averages, the average weekly expenditure of each commodity in the larder for which the cellarer was responsible, together with a note of the number of portions (*fercula*) consumed, the total number given to strangers and an estimated average for each flesh day.[43] These entries are the counterpart to the planning that is implicit in the states of manors.[44]

The production of states, both of the internal offices of the house and of the manors, required more detailed accounting as its foundation. The advent of manorial accounts, therefore, is a touchstone of the potential an institution had for managing its affairs, especially in terms of agricultural production. Accounts made it possible to compare production from year to year, and to use that information to make decisions. The earliest manorial accounts for individual manors held by monasteries that now survive as separate

(Milton) MSS 2388, for 1300–1, with the bakehouse account on mem. 24, calculating weekly rates of consumption of wheat by the convent, and MS 2389, for 1309–10, with bakehouse account on mem. 31r, both printed in *The Accounts of Godfrey of Crowland, Abbot of Peterborough 1299–1321*, ed. S. Raban (Northamptonshire Record Society, 45; 2011), pp. 210–13, 637–40; Fitzwilliam (Milton) Rolls 265, mem. 1, bakehouse account *c*.1289, filed with a survey of the Abbey's arable and meadow; *Cartulary of Oseney Abbey*, ed. H. E. Salter (6 vols., Oxford Historical Society, 89–91, 97–8, 101; 1926–36), vi, pp. 184–207. A further Augustinian example comes from Bolton Priory: *The Bolton Priory Compotus 1286–1325, Together With a Priory Account Roll for 1377–78*, ed. I. Kershaw and D. M. Smith (Yorkshire Archaeological Society, Record Series, 154; 2000).

[43] The averages are present on Durham University Library, Special Collections, Archives of the Dean and Chapter of Durham, cellarers' accounts: 1307–8 (A); 1311–12 (A); 1317–18; 1319–20, mem. 2; 1324, mem. 2; 1324–5 (A); 1326 (A); 1326–7 (A); 1327–8; 1328–9 (A); 1338; 1339.

[44] For examples of other calculations on obedientiary accounts, see *Household Accounts from Medieval England*, ed. Woolgar, i, pp. 44–6.

documents date from the 1230s, for the manor of Froyle in Hampshire, belonging to the abbey of St Mary's, in Winchester.[45] It is likely that Westminster Abbey also used written accounts on its estates and for its monastic obediences in the 1240s.[46] A composition between the abbot of Westminster, Richard de Crokesley, and the convent, from August 1252, echoes the injunctions that had been given to the Benedictine general chapter in 1249 about obedientiaries accounting—but here, it reshapes that injunction, that once a year, or more often if it seemed expedient, not only the obedientiaries but also the ministers looking after the manors, the reeves and bailiffs, should give the abbot and convent an account of their charge.[47] The first surviving accounts for the Westminster Abbey estates are for the manor of Todenham with Sutton-under-Brailes, for 1252–3—and they were clearly not the earliest to have been prepared for that manor.[48] There are also accounts for Knightsbridge, from 1257–8,[49] and for Launton, from 1268.[50] Another ten Westminster manors have runs of accounts starting in the 1270s: Aldenham, from 1279; Ashford, from 1278; Ashwell, from 1275; Battersea, from 1277; Eye, from 1274; Feering, from 1272; Islip, from 1277; Laleham, from 1276; Oakham, from 1275; and Stevenage, from 1270.[51] The earliest obedientiary account from Westminster is a draft for the cellarer's office, for 1282—and there is a suggestion that it reflects the earlier monastic practice of keeping integrated accounts, covering the charges of more than one obedientiary.[52] These start dates demonstrate a commitment to written accounts on the part of both the abbot and the convent: adopting them in the 1250s—if not earlier—places Westminster among a comparatively small group of institutions

[45] BL, Add. Rolls, 13338–9, 17457–78, cited in *Manorial Records of Cuxham*, ed. Harvey, pp. 21–2 and n. 28

[46] Harvey, *Obedientiaries*, p. xxxix, argues that they were probably adopted no later than the abbatiate of Richard de Berking (1222–46), who may have been a baron of the Exchequer. The papal visitation in 1234 enjoined obedientiaries to render accounts at least once a year, or as instructed by the abbot and the more discreet monks. Although the statutes asked for all the rents of the monastery, of both the abbot's and the convent's portions, to be recorded in three rolls, there is no mention of manorial accounts or of auditing the records of the estates other than as might be implicit in the records of the obedientiaries. Graham, 'Papal Visitation of Bury St Edmunds and Westminster', pp. 738–9.

[47] *Walter de Wenlok*, ed. Harvey, pp. 228–9: 'Et semel in anno vel pluries si visum fuerit expedire tam ipsi [obedientiarii] quam ministri maneriorum prepositi et ballivi de suis obedientiis et administrationibus reddent abbati et conventui rationem.'

[48] WAM 25900; Harvey, *Obedientiaries*, p. xxxix.

[49] WAM 16367.

[50] WAM 15286.

[51] Respectively, WAM 26016, 26655, 26248, 27494, 26848, 25572, 14776, 27105, 20218, 26339.

[52] Harvey, *Obedientiaries*, p. xxxix: it includes a panel for the expenses of the monk-bailiff, and other accounts for the treasurers for 1302–3 also include material relating to the hosteller.

using these processes at this date.[53] The survival of accounts from the 1270s is probably a wider reflection of the take-up of written accounts across the Westminster estates. It is likely that these are simply the earliest of their sequences to have survived, rather than a witness to the introduction of written accounts piecemeal on the manors over some two to three decades.

These manorial accounts were important in the overall management of Westminster's estates, but they were not the only records or practices to be used there or elsewhere. Manorial accounts were typically documents produced at the end of an accounting year that concluded at Michaelmas (29 September). As early as the statutes of Gregory IX of 1235 and 1237, it had been the ambition that the state of a monastic house should be produced twice a year, once after harvest in the Kalends of October (14 September to 1 October), and secondly in the Kalends of April (16 March to 1 April).[54] This mirrored practice on some English estates in the thirteenth century, where it had become usual—and was advocated by Walter of Henley and other authors of agricultural treatises—to hold what was known as a view of account (*visus compoti*) partway through the year, as an additional check on local agents. It was also a way of understanding the position of the manor on the ground at a key point in the year.[55] The injunctions about the view of account and audit made for the abbey of Bury St Edmunds in 1298 advocated at least three views each year by two monks and a trustworthy clerk, firstly, immediately after the barns had been filled after harvest, secondly after the Purification (2 February), and thirdly after Easter, when all the seed would have been sown.[56] On some estates, these visits were used for the preparation of drafts of the annual manorial accounts, making entries for what had already transpired, as an aid in preparing the final document for the auditors

[53] Institutions and seigneurial administrations where accounts dating before 1250 have been found are listed in P. D. A. Harvey, *Manorial Records* (London, 1984), p. 25. To these, Durham may now be added: A. J. Piper, 'Evidence of Accounting and Local Estate Services at Durham, *c.*1240', *Archives* 20, no. 87 (1992), pp. 36–40.

[54] *Les registres de Grégoire IX*, ed. Auvray, ii, p. 325.

[55] *Walter of Henley and Other Treatises on Estate Management and Accounting*, ed. D. Oschinsky (Oxford, 1971), pp. 187–8, 340–1.

[56] *Walter of Henley*, ed. Oschinsky, pp. 468–9. Some of this may have been foreshadowed in 1234, when the visitors' injunctions for the monastery had asked that the state of all the Bury manors should be known at harvest, in the 15 days before 1 August, so that the Abbey was clear how things might be managed in the following year; and that nothing was to be drawn from the estates until Michaelmas unless it was necessary for the immediate provisioning of the house and the manors: Graham, 'Papal Visitation of Bury St Edmunds and Westminster', p. 734. Whether a view was held—and how often—depended on the estate: a version of the text of Walter advocated two views a year, a practice also proposed in the treatise edited by L. Lacour, 'Traité d'économie rurale composé en Angleterre au XIIIe siècle', *Bibliothèque de l'École des Chartes*, 17 (1856), pp. 123–41, 367–81, at pp. 374–5.

later in the year.[57] Estimating amounts of corn on the manors was often part of the view, especially if the corn was kept in barns, in stacks, unthreshed. The results of the view, however, were often scrappy pieces of documentation —and views may have been taken without creating a written document, or at least one in a standard form.[58] That said, some estates took great care to gather together estimates of corn on their manors, and some monasteries produced rolls summarising the position on every property. To this end, Norwich Cathedral Priory produced rolls of *Estimacio grangiarum*, listing stacks of corn and legumes in their barns, the estimated contents and, in many cases, as a comparison, a note of the quantities that in fact resulted from threshing.[59] There are similar records of *Estimaciones bladorum* for Worcester Cathedral Priory, with one example from 1289, and a further seventeen rolls for dates between 1400 and 1462, many listing tithe corn. The Worcester rolls were the result of a *tourn* made by a chosen official, skilled in estimating corn in stacks, just after Michaelmas each year.[60] This practice of estimating corn—with or without a view of account, and with or without a record engrossing all the estimates across the estate—was an important feature of seigneurial administration across the demesnes and rectories of England from the thirteenth century on.[61] Bishop Grosseteste, in his *Rules*, composed for the countess of Lincoln probably between 1245 and 1253, proposed that at the audit of manorial accounts her trusted servants should compare these rolls with others containing estimates of corn and stock which her steward had been instructed to prepare after the previous harvest.[62]

[57] *Manorial Records of Cuxham*, ed. Harvey, p. 60.

[58] *Manorial Records of Cuxham*, ed. Harvey, p. 60.

[59] Norfolk RO, Archives of the Dean and Chapter of Norwich, DCN 66/1–20. Extracts from DCN 66/12, a roll for 1299, and DCN 66/18, for 1334, are edited in Dewez, 'Connaître par les nombres', pp. 483–6.

[60] Discussed in C. Dyer, 'Peasant Farming in Late Medieval England: Evidence from the Tithe Estimations by Worcester Cathedral Priory', in *Peasants and Lords in the Medieval English Economy: Essays in Honour of Bruce M. S. Campbell*, ed. M. Kowaleski, J. Langdon and P. R. Schofield (Turnhout, 2015), pp. 83–109. It is impossible to know how many other institutions prepared records like this, but there is at least a suspicion that the practice was much more widespread, e.g. Oseney Abbey, early fourteenth century, before 1337: D. Postles, 'Estimates of Harvest on Some Oseney Abbey Properties', in *idem*, *Oseney Abbey Studies* (Leicester, 2008), pp. 75–80.

[61] See, for example, references to it on the estates of Elizabeth de Burgh, Lady of Clare: J. Ward, 'The Great Household on the Move: Travel Among the Servants of Elizabeth de Burgh (d. 1360)', in *Elite Household in England*, ed. Woolgar, pp. 277–94, at p. 287.

[62] *Walter of Henley*, ed. Oschinsky, pp. 392–5. Rather than estimating by size of stack, the *Rules* advocated threshing every twentieth sheaf: pp. 390–3. For the date, L. J. Wilkinson, 'The Rules of Robert Grosseteste Reconsidered: the Lady as Estate and Household Manager in Thirteenth-Century England', in *The Medieval Household in Christian Europe, c.850–c.1550: Managing Power, Wealth, and the Body*, ed. C. Beattie, A. Maslakovic and S. Rees Jones (Turnhout, 2003), pp. 293–306, at pp. 299–300.

If the first ambition of the manorial account was to set out the position between an accountant and his lord in terms of who owed what to whom, landlords also wanted to know how well their properties were doing, what their profit (*proficuum*) or value (*valor*) was. Notes of profit or value appear on the earliest separate manorial accounts to survive for individual manors, from the 1230s. These notes are usually additions to the account, made at the close of the auditing process, and where they occur—these statements are only present on a minority of accounts—they often appear right at the foot of a roll. They can be assumed to have been made at the very close of the auditing process, and they are often in different hands and inks to the rest of the account.[63] They can be shown to be the results of calculations of some sophistication, the profit including not only cash liveries to the lord, but also valuations of corn and stock delivered to the lord's household or the institution holding the property, along with other transfers out of the property. The components varied from estate to estate, and some even took into consideration seasonal variations in prices. It has been argued that these calculations were significant in assisting lords in decisions about whether to continue to run a manor in demesne, or whether to lease it out.[64] They were used on the estates of some of the major Benedictine houses and, at Westminster, from the evidence of the accounts that have survived, they had been adopted on the convent's lands from 1267–8, and on the abbot's manors by 1291–2.[65] This information was in turn to form an integral part of the documents edited in these volumes: the *valor*, manor by manor, appears on a great many of the states. Westminster was not the only estate to use this information on documents relating to the overall management of properties. Indeed, the *valor* was to become a separate class of document, presenting this information alongside more detailed reckonings of the position of each property across an estate. In the longer term, into the fifteenth century, it was an essential tool of landed administration at the highest level, along with related material, such as listings of debts and arrears.[66]

[63] *Manorial Records of Cuxham*, ed. Harvey, pp. 15–16, 56–7; Harvey, *Manorial Records*, pp. 28–9.

[64] E. Stone, 'Profit and Loss Accountancy at Norwich Cathedral Priory', *Transactions of the Royal Historical Society*, 5th series, 12 (1962), pp. 25–48; D. Postles, 'The Perception of Profit Before the Leasing of Demesnes', *Agricultural History Review* 34, no. 2 (1985), pp. 12–28; D. Stone, *Decision-Making in Medieval Agriculture* (Oxford, 2005), pp. 199–201, 211; Dewez, 'Connaître par les nombres', pp. 411–62, 493–9.

[65] Convent: e.g. WAM 15286; abbot: WAM 26856; Postles, 'Perception of Profit', p. 22; *Walter de Wenlok*, ed. Harvey, p. 242, n. 1. For a discussion of the components of the calculation on the convent's manor of Kinsbourne in the latter part of the fourteenth century, Stern, *Hertfordshire Demesne*, pp. 145–56.

[66] *The Grey of Ruthin Valor: The Valor of the English Lands of Edmund Grey, Earl of Kent, Drawn Up From the Ministers' Accounts of 1467–8*, ed. R. I. Jack (Sydney, 1965), pp. 8–27. The abbot of Westminster had enrolments of debts of officials in 1349–50 (I 1, n. 39), if not earlier.

The Westminster views of account

At Westminster, the views of account all come from the convent's estates—with two exceptions (I 3 and I 15)—and are the earliest documents edited here. Confusingly, they are called 'states' in their headings, e.g. 'Status maneriorum domine regine visus per fratres .....' (II 1), that is, 'the state of the manors of the queen [the royal manors] viewed by brothers ...'. The monks involved usually held a supervisory function in relation to the estates concerned; but it was not always monks who did this work. The estimates made in 1321–3 (II 7–8, 10) were given on oath by groups of four or five individuals, some of whom had been or were currently manorial reeves or serjeants. The views were taken partway through the year: II 1–2 contain the view of the manors of Eleanor of Castile, taken from 21 March to 26 March 1300, and those for the pittancer's manors, taken 21 March to 3 April, and one can see a sequence, as the viewing party moved from manor to manor. The common factor here was the monk leading the view, Alexander de Neuport, the warden of Eleanor of Castile's manors, who was also the pittancer. Like other documents of their type, they record the cash arrears from the previous final account, rents owing, corn in the granary, an estimate of corn to be threshed, other potential cash receipts, corn to be sold, notes of livestock and of land sown. They also note respites—allowances to be made to the accountant—and points for discussion. II 3, from around 25 March 1305, includes statements of what cash the manor might produce *de claro* ('clear', free from any further charges), along with any caveats. II 4, which includes views dating from 2 December 1312 to 19 December 1312, and 31 December 1312, works through each type of corn, estimating how much was in the barns, what might be sown, what was needed for the manorial servants (*famuli*), and whether there was a surplus that might be sent to Westminster or whether additional corn was required on the manor. There is then a statement of livestock. The calculation passes to cash, examining receipts up to the view and the potential for rents, other dues and charges that might be raised; it notes what prospective charges there were—leaving a statement of the cash that might be remitted to Westminster. The notes of financial responsibility, of what the reeves, bedels and other officials owed at the view, and of their *superplusagium* or otherwise, suggest that these events were like audits, but carried out on the manor rather than at Westminster. In their work, those taking the view had access to documentation from earlier years: those making the estimates for Stevenage in December 1323 had the view of the reeve's account from the previous accounting year, which was then attached to the roll of estimates (II 8). The latest view for the convent's properties, from December 1334 (II 9), is an indenture made on the transfer of office between wardens of the royal manors, but is similar in content and form to the earlier views. Two further views relate to the abbot's lands. I 3 covers three-quarters of the year, 29 September 1349 to 24 June 1350. Again, it is a fair copy, in this case linked to the view of account that was expected to have been taken at 25 March, but running on from then until May, estimating corn across the estate, as well as noting cash receipts, cash expenses, and a cash balance in a year when the estate, in the immediate aftermath of the Black Death, was in a parlous condition. I 15 is an outlier chronologically: it is the latest view we have for a group of properties, either for the abbot or for the convent, and its survival argues for the preparation of this documentation over a longer timespan than might otherwise have been suspected. The two membranes refer to different years, 1379–80 for the Eastern Parts and 1380–1 for the Western. Both membranes contain views taken at the mid-point of the year; and they are in the typical form of the view, noting the cash debt or excess of the reeves, and then providing estimates for the corn.

The Westminster views of account are unusual, for their detail, their systematisation and because the documents as we have them are mainly fair copies—that is, they are engrossments, even though the information they contained was less definitive and more speculative than the final accounts and most documents rendered fair in this way. Some of these engrossments are elaborate: II 4 is especially well written. The estimates for the manors made in November to December 1321, 1322 and 1323 (II 7–8, 10) are the remaining sections of documents which presumably once covered the whole estate and which were well laid out fair copies. There is no evidence on these documents of their use at the audit of the manorial accounts at the end of the year, yet as they were produced year after year in clean form, they were intended as items of record. There seems to have been a disjuncture between these rolls as working documents—or at least the point at which they served that function—and the form in which we now have them, as fair copies. II 4 has copyist's mistakes which suggest that an omission at an earlier stage of producing the roll was passed over and that the clerk did not, in making his fair copy, understand the document as it was in front of him. One may speculate therefore that however interesting the information the views contain, it had largely lost its pragmatic, working value at the point of engrossment; yet it was considered a record of importance for preservation and may have been used in a formal context, perhaps in presenting the information to the convent. As we shall see, the same was true of the states and dockets.

The Westminster states and dockets

The Westminster states, or dockets, differ from the views in important ways, although they may have been derived from them.[67] The view came at a point during the accounting year, often a mid-point, and was taken on the manor itself, whereas the states and dockets are documentation from the end of the financial year, produced at Westminster after the conclusion of the audit of the manorial accounts.[68] The views and manorial accounts were charge/discharge accounts which set out the cash receipts and expenses, and then struck a balance. Manorial accounts did the same for corn and then for stock in separate accounts normally on the dorse of the rolls.[69] The states, for both abbot and convent, were different in purpose.

The earliest documents we might regard as states appear as a series of systematic memoranda about the remainders—of cash, corn and stock—at the conclusion of the auditing of the manorial accounts, noting the debts and arrears and profits—or *valor*—of the manors (I 1). While the states of the abbot and convent differ in form and content to a greater or lesser extent, they have important points in common. In 1348, the abbot's documentation was prepared at or immediately after the audit of the manorial accounts, giving memoranda of cash liveries, and of debts manor by manor. Beyond this, it provides a series of remainders at the audit of the account: these list out the stock remaining, the debt for each manor (i.e. the arrears), the *valor* of the manor, and the rents and farms. This information is available for 1348 (I 1) and 1349 (I 2)—although there are no entries for the *valor* on the latter, rather statements of the financial position *de claro* or a note of debt.

The convent's documents from the 1350s are also cast as remainders at the audit. The roll for 1351–2 (II 10) gives the remainders at 1 August 1352, lists stock, the excess or debt of each serjeant, rents, corn in hand and notes of what was sown that year. The roll for 1352–3 (II 11) is similar in form, but has totals and sections for estimates for corn in a second hand and ink—one must imagine these additions being made to the document once the audit of

[67] It is important to distinguish these states from other documents that are called a *status*, not necessarily at Westminster, but elsewhere, as at Durham: these states were essentially inventories of an office, initially made on its transfer from one official to another, and they might take the form of indentures, like II 9. In time their compilation might become an annual process. For Durham, see A. Dobie, *Accounting at Durham Cathedral Priory: Management and Control of a Major Ecclesiastical Corporation, 1083–1539* (Basingstoke, 2015), pp. 142–3.

[68] Usually Michaelmas. The accounting year on the estates of the convent concluded on 1 August in 1351, 1352 and 1353, but reverted to Michaelmas for 1354: II 10–12. The estates of the manors of Queen Eleanor of Castile's foundation initially used an accounting year beginning on 30 November, that is, two days after her anniversary.

[69] For an introduction to the development of manorial accounts, *Manorial Records of Cuxham*, ed. Harvey, pp. 12–71.

the manorial accounts was complete. The corn estimates—*estimacio manerii*—are for corn harvested but, given the date, not yet threshed—and this practice makes an important link to the supervision implied by the view. From this point the rolls identify leviable rents—*redditus levabilis*—which become before the end of the decade *denarii levabiles*, a precursor of the entries for the *valor* of the manor in the 1360s. In 1354–5 (II 13), the entries for these sums have been added in a second ink, that is, this is something that happened late in the process of producing this documentation after the audit.

The pattern of these entries allows us to describe the compilation of the state. The first stage was to take the manorial accounts as they came to hand after the auditing work. The sequence of manors may not have mattered much at first, and there is some variability in the order of the properties as they appear on the earlier states; but almost all the abbot's states from 1366–7 (I 7) onwards start with a sequence of manors from Islip, Sutton-under-Brailes, Todenham, Bourton-on-the-Hill, Pershore, Pensham and so on.[70] The convent's states come to a stable order a little later, and from 1380–1 (II 29) start with a sequence of manors from Aldenham, Kinsbourne, Stevenage, Wheathampstead, Ashwell and Launton. A separate section for the convent's rectories appears from 1391–2 (II 35), formalising an arrangement that can first be seen in the preceding year (II 34). This variability may reflect the progress of the auditing process itself, but it is more likely that the progression to systematisation was a reflection of a wider sense of bureaucractic orderliness: it would be easier to prepare a state, to avoid omission, if there were a regular pattern—clerks going through all the manorial accounts to extract a particular piece of information from each, such as cash deliveries to Westminster, would be less likely to overlook information.[71] This is readily apparent in cases like the state of the abbot's manors for 1381–2 (I 16), where the document was prepared—and copied fair—before the information about wool valuations had come to hand, and the totals for that therefore needed to be added. Something similar happened with the convent's documentation too: in the state for 1355 (II 13), otherwise a fair copy in a single hand, the entries of cash sums for *redditus levabilis* are all in a second ink.

The manorial accounts provided information in the following ways: the corn and stock account on the dorse of the manorial account supplied the figures for the remainders of grain and livestock at the end of the year. The

[70] There are exceptions, however: I 22, for example, has quite a different order of estates.

[71] That said, there is still variability. In some years, there is more than one version of the dockets, with the manors in a different order, and with different information. In 1365–6 (II 18), there are two rolls, whose dockets vary in wording and arrangement, but not in factual detail—i.e. they have been drawn from a common source. In 1374–5 (II 24), one of the rolls, WAM 6178, omits cash deliveries to Westminster. In 1378–9 (II 28), when there are also two rolls, the information and order of the manors are duplicated.

notes of cash deliveries to Westminster (either to a member of the abbot's household or another of his officials, in the case of his estates, or to the monk-bailiff of Westminster in the case of the convent) were taken from one of the last entries on the front of the manorial account, at the end of the cash discharge section, for *liberaciones denariorum*. Deliveries of goods in kind to the abbot's household and of corn to Westminster came from the stock and corn accounts on the dorse of the manorial accounts. The Westminster estates normally sent wool from the manors to collecting points for sale: the manorial accounts usually record the transfer of fleeces in the stock accounts, but not always the details of the sale—and this information the administrators would have needed to collate at the audit if they were to understand the position of each manor and its contribution to the economy. Notes of funds from the sale of wool were therefore incorporated from other sources when it came to preparing the state. This was important if there was to be an assessment of the profit (*proficuum*) or value (*valor*) of individual manors. The *valor* was a figure that did not derive immediately from the manorial account, although in some instances it was noted on it and it was calculated from at least some of the information the account contains. The addition of the *valor* came at the final stage of the audit, the production of an overall assessment of the estate's value. Information about rents and farms must usually have come from another source, a rental and/or custumal: these were not added to the convent's dockets until 1370–1 (II 23), although they had appeared on the abbot's documents from the earliest we now have (I 1). The states usually include a statement about either the debt or the clear value of the manor, and of arrears owed there—and this information also came from the manorial account.

The direct link between the states and dockets and the auditing of the manorial accounts is well illustrated by entries for the *valor*. The final section of the cash account for each manorial account sets out the balance—and this section was usually entered at the audit. At Hendon, one of the convent's estates, in 1368–9, the end of the recto of the manorial account rendered by the reeve, John Godhywe, had a statement entered at the audit of the cash balance, noting an initial debt of £19 17s. 5¾d. Allowances were then made to the reeve which reduced the debt to a clear £13. This debt was then divided between what he owed, and what was owed by others, introduced by the phrase *unde super*—which left him with an excess on his account. Finally, a further hand added a statement of the *valor*: £71 8s. 7d., including the charges of felling/gathering wood, carrying it and a value for the wood in hand.[72] It was this additional statement that was copied onto the docket (II 21). Similarly, at Bourton-on-the-Hill, one of the abbot's estates, in 1376–7 the

[72] WAM 32585, mem. 5r.

manorial account noted a cash debt of the reeve of £27 2s. 10½d. It then proceeded to analyse this debt further: the reeve was allowed £1 10s. 'by special grace of the lord [the abbot]' for 10 quarters of barley surcharged to him by the auditor. He was then allowed, by similar grace, for his assiduous labour that year and for various items disallowed on the account, a further £1 13s. 0½d. This reduced his debt to £24 18s 10d. Two other steps appear on this account: firstly, a further note, in small handwriting in the left margin—we must imagine this as another review by the auditors—reduced his debt to a sum of £1 10s. clear. It was this sum that appeared as the clear debt on the state for the year (I 13). There was then a statement in another hand, at the very foot of the roll: 'Valet manerium hoc anno cum lana xxxv li.'[73] This statement coincides exactly with the wording of the *valor* section on the state for 1376–7 (I 13).

As we have seen, notes of profit or *valor* can be found on the manorial accounts of the estates of both the convent and the abbot from the second half of the thirteenth century. The states and dockets edited here show that they were considered systematically as part of the auditing process from the mid-fourteenth century up to the 1420s—exactly the period when the question of whether to continue to run estates in demesne or to lease the land and/or stock was to the fore. There is no evidence, however, that this consideration of the *valor* was a novelty, even if engrossing the information in fair copy rolls was new. One feature, however, tells us more about those making the calculations. The entries of the *valor* on Westminster's manorial accounts do not appear on every roll. On the abbot's estates, the accounts for Bourton-on-the-Hill, for example, have in 1360–1 a statement in an additional hand of the *valor*, with wool;[74] the account for following year has no *valor*;[75] but the one for 1362–3 does. This is made in a new hand, close to the bottom of the account in the margin, and in this case it in part employs Arabic numerals, a rare occurrence within this accounting system: 'Valet 13 li. v s. preter 58 petras viij lb. lane.'[76] However slight this evidence may seem, it points to the calculation of these sums by an official versed in mathematics and able to work on a wider and more imaginative scale in understanding the finances of the estates. These traces can be paralleled in the handling of audit and budgetary information at a high level at other monastic houses—the most senior auditors and officials had a wider facility for computation and thinking about its

[73] WAM 8305, mem. 3r.
[74] WAM 8289, mem. 2r.
[75] WAM 8290.
[76] WAM 8291, mem. 4r.

consequences for management than is apparent from the vast bulk of the documentation, which has nothing beyond Roman numerals.[77]

The reasoning behind the calculation of profit and value on some estates is often opaque, but the states cumulatively give us information about what the Westminster managers thought this should comprise. Firstly, the Westminster states use the terms *proficuum* and *valor* interchangeably, albeit in different documents—but there can be no doubt that the same calculation was intended.[78] In some instances (II 20), we have a grand total for the *valor* of the whole of the convent's estate, even though there survive on the dockets no entries for the *valor* manor by manor. Secondly, the statements of value sometimes go beyond a cash sum, demonstrating what it comprised. At the core of this was always a calculation of the value of husbandry (although we may not now be able to reconstruct how it was reached) and rents and farms paid to the abbot or convent. That the profits of husbandry were included can be demonstrated in those instances where surplus corn was sent to Westminster, and where we can see what value was set on it.[79] At the convent's manor of Birdbrook, in 1368–9, the manorial account (in a section copied onto the state as well: II 21) has a statement of the *valor*, with the profit of stock and a new millstone—and in this case the *valor* was divided into what was 'leviable' beyond lands, meadows, pasture, wool and profits of stock, and what came from husbandry.[80] Where the demesne was at farm, as at Yeoveney in 1370–1 (I 9), the *valor* was the rent specified in the lease of the manor. At Denham in 1366–7 (I 7), the value was to include wool and a new building, hay sent to the abbot's household and the profit of a tenement that had belonged to James Andrew—that is, elements beyond the demesne husbandry. At Ebury in 1370–1 (I 9), the *valor* was to include hay sent to the abbot's household and the value of pasture used for the household's animals. These are commonly

[77] Cf. H. Dewez, 'The Writing of the Obedientiary Account Rolls at Norwich Cathedral Priory (1256–1344)', in *Ruling the Script in the Middle Ages: Formal Aspects of Written Communication (Books, Charters, and Inscriptions)*, ed. S. Barret, D. Stutzmann and G. Vogeler (Turnhout, 2016), pp. 197–225, at pp. 219–25; H. W. Saunders, *An Introduction to the Obedientiary and Manor Rolls of Norwich Cathedral Priory* (Norwich, 1930), pp. 154–5. Arabic numerals can also be found when averages are calculated on obedientiary accounts at other houses: they are associated with most of the computations of averages at Boxley Abbey, for example, in the account for the subcellarer and provisor, 1376–7: TNA, SC 6/1254/6; for the subcellarer and provisor, 1378: SC 6/1254/15; and on the sacrist's account for Selborne Priory in 1399–1400: Magdalen College, Oxford, Archives: Estate Paper 55/18.

[78] II 24. There are two versions of the convent's dockets for this year, 1374–5: WAM 6178 uses 'valor manerii', WAM 6181 'proficuus manerii'. Postles, 'Perception of Profit', pp. 14–15.

[79] e.g. Kinsbourne, in 1373–4, analysed by Stern, *Hertfordshire Demesne*, pp. 150–1; and see the wider discussion on pp. 145–56 for a comparison between the values assigned to a *valor* or *proficuum* and an analysis of the elements that might have contributed to it.

[80] WAM 25464, mem. 3r: 'Levabilis preter terras, prata, pasturas, lanam et proficuum in stauro xxv li. xij s. vij d. qua. Sic gaineria valet xx li. viij d. ob. qua.'

recurring elements: building works financed by manorial funds should be counted as part of the overall product of the estate, as this money was not remitted to Westminster; in the same way, goods or produce remitted to Westminster or to the abbot's household which had no cash value entered on the manorial account effectively diminished the cash value of the estate, and it had therefore to be reimbursed in some guise. Any wool collected from the manor and sold centrally had also to be given a value—or an estimate—or a note that it had not been included in the calculation. In this way in 1370–1 (II 23), the *valor* of Feering had 'lana appreciata' added to it; in 1374–5 (II 24), the value of the wool for Aldenham was estimated; and in the abbot's state for 1362–3 (I 5), the *valor* has 'preter xl petras lane' in the case of Todenham, with different amounts for the other manors. Other variations might include an increase in stock, perhaps a cash purchase by the estate centre, as at Kinsbourne in 1374–5 (II 24). In 1366–7 (I 7), at Staines, the *valor* was £25 10s. 'preter respectuaciones', that is, the sums put in respite, allowances made in the auditing process for elements that might in this instance have been considered part of the true worth of the manor. Cash payments directly from the manor for legitimate charges were also considered to have been a part of the *valor*. In 1369–70 (II 23), at Feering, this was the case with a payment of a pension to the abbot of Colchester; and in 1371–2 (I 10) foreign payments of £34 7s. 2¼d. directly from Pershore were also considered part of the *valor*, in an insertion made late in the accounting process.

The states of both the abbot and convent from the mid-1360s offer, at their conclusion, a series of grand totals. These were intended to allow some overall understanding of the financial position of the estate, as well as its resources in terms of corn and stock. On the abbot's manors, there are grand totals of livestock across the estate first in 1355–6 (I 4). The grand totals for 1364–5 (I 6) cover finance as well: for arrears, isolating the desperate debts; the combined total of the *valor* for the manors; totals of each type of stock; and totals of the cash rents, by term and overall. The rolls for 1366–7 (I 7) and 1367–8 (I 8) have similar totals. That for 1370–1 (I 9) goes further and compares the total *valor* of the abbot's lands with the previous year, noting that in the year of the roll it was £83 6s. 0½d. more; a similar reckoning was also performed for the totals of stock and rent. These comparisons became standard, continuing to feature in rolls up to 1382–3 (I 17). On the roll for 1373–4 (I 11), the totals in places have been written in a second ink, as have the totals and comparisons with previous year at the end of the document. This helpfully confirms their place at the very end of the of writing up the roll and the sequence of calculations made in relation to the year's audit.

Grand totals also appear on the convent's states. In 1351–2 (II 10) and 1352–3 (II 11) there are grand totals of stock; in the latter year there are cash totals of arrears, of excess on the accounts, of leviable rent, and of the farms of the manors at lease. The following account, for 1353–4 (II 12) has a total of the estimated amount of corn. The roll for 1358–9 (II 15) has a brief note of the total arrears, but it is not then until the dockets for 1362–3 (II 16) that there is again a total at the end of the roll: a listing of the remainders of all the stock, live and dead, and of the cash total of the arrears. This is the first account to include a brief statement of the financial position of each of the principal obedientiaries, a note of debt, balance or excess. The following annual dockets are similar: 1363–4 (II 17), 1365–6 (II 18)—from 1366–7 (II 20) there is a cash total of the *valor* for all the estates as well as the remainders of livestock. The 1368–9 dockets (II 21) are more thoughtfully totalled: all entries of the *valor*, all cash deliveries to the treasurer, all corn received by the granger, all arrears, and all remainders of stock. The obedientiaries also have statements of their overall financial positions. This pattern is repeated in 1369–70 (II 22); 1374–5 (II 25) and 1376–7 (II 26) have grand totals of stock and corn, but not of cash; 1378–9 (II 28) has totals of livestock, corn, and arrears and excesses in the dockets, as well as cash totals for the obedientiaries. 1380–1 (II 29), with its grand totals of corn and stock, is the last of the states for the convent to make some attempt at an overall picture until the dockets for 1397–8 (II 40), when sum totals of stock, corn and malt, cash deliveries, arrears—and leviable arrears—once again appear, extending in 1399–1400 (II 42) once more to encompass the *valor* of all the manors and rectories. What these states show is that the auditing process for the convent's accounts did at times produce overall figures in a form that was thought worth recording, but that this was not a *sine qua non* of the convent's states at this date and that there was a good deal of variation. This does not mean that those managing the finances of the convent overall did not know the complete financial position, but that they did not choose to record it in this way. Nor did they at any point—unlike the abbot—choose to record in these documents a comparison between years; but this does not mean that it did not happen. Likewise when the states of the obedientiaries reappear in 1409–10 (II 49), we can be sure that their accounts had been prepared and summarised elsewhere in the interim.

The compilation of the states in draft form would have produced documentation that was a work in progress, added to as sections came to hand. Yet most of the states we have are not like this: they are fair copies written by a single hand, in one operation—and some of them are very fine productions, which in itself tells us a little about the purpose of the engrossment.[81] Just a handful of documents show us the states as a work in progress,

[81] This happens even with the earlier material, e.g. II 4. It is not uncommon with medieval accounts for fair copies, after audit, to be made, for preservation; and they seem at times to have

where particular pieces of information had not yet come to hand and were added subsequently.[82] Even fewer have notes by auditors,[83] which suggests they were not normally part of the documentation considered at the audit—and it is mostly likely that their purpose was a formal one, for example, presentation in chapter; or definitive copies for the conventual treasurers or the abbot. We can see they are copies, not only from their finished form, but also from the way in which information is handled, repeated, omitted or simply miscopied.[84] There are many small instances of this, what might be considered carelessness from one point of view, but it may also have its origins in the documents that preceded the fair copy. If the interim documents were scrappy, informal or too indefinite to constitute the permanent record, they may well also have required a good deal of attention for a copyist to render them completely faithfully. Some of this may also represent a lesser degree of care in the preparation of the manorial accounts, particularly where information was repeated from year to year. There is a reflection here, too, on general standards of estate administration.[85]

Although the abbot and convent had separate administrative systems for their estates, there was a good deal in common in the ways that their records were prepared and functioned. All the documents in the sequences of views, states and dockets edited in this volume are parchment rolls—with one exception, I 20, which is written on paper. Almost all the rolls were made up Chancery fashion, that is, with each succeeding membrane sewn to the foot of the preceding one. The principal exception were the engrossments of the convent's views for 1321–3 (II 6–8), which were Exchequer fashion rolls, with all the membranes fastened together at the head (like a book viewed from the side). Most of the membranes were laid out to a similar pattern, with vertical folds setting out the left margin on the recto, and in some instances the centre as well and a right margin, or at least a point to align text at the right-hand side. The sole paper document (I 20) is a fair copy: although paper, as a less expensive medium, was used for preparing drafts, it might in some instances by the later fourteenth century be used for making engrossments or for clear digests of material.

---

a momentum of their own. Clerks too sometimes perceived that the documents had less purpose, as, for example with II 14: no one took the trouble to sew together the membranes of the engrossed roll.

[82] See p. 19 above.

[83] For example, *probatur* ('it is approved'): II 44, mem. 1 dorse, cash deliveries to Westminster; II 49, against the grand cash total.

[84] On I 23, Pershore, the list of stock remaining at the audit started with 'viij boves', which was subsequently struck out; the 8 oxen appear later in the list, i.e. here the copyist's eye has skipped down the document he was copying. There are many mistakes in the copying of rents, and the totalling of the states is therefore eccentric at times: e.g. I 14, rents for Castlemorton.

[85] See the comments in Harvey, *Estates*, pp. 290–3.

The states had their own distinctive appearance and layout. From the 1350s on, the convent's documentation was written on narrow, Chancery fashion rolls, usually between 110 and 145 mm wide—unlike the manorial accounts, which were usually around 200 mm in width. From the 1360s and subsequently there is more evidence that the documentation was produced in duplicate[86]—sometimes with rolls separating out the royal manors—and this may reflect the fact that there were two conventual treasurers, the senior of whom was frequently the warden of the royal manors and sometimes warden of the churches as well. Later states continue to demonstrate this pattern: in 1382–3 (II 30), the roll contains the states of the convent's manors and those of the royal manors; in 1383–4 and 1385–6 (II 31–2), the rolls contain the convent's manors only; and in 1386–7 (II 33), there are two separate rolls, both fair copies, one for the convent's states and one for the royal manors. It is possible that this same arrangement obtained in the 1350s: two of the rolls (II 12, II 15) include royal manors, both on the dorse and in the latter case headed separately—and the other rolls do not mention them. At this point, however, none of the convent's rolls has a heading beyond the regnal year.

The documentation for both the abbot and convent exhibits some changes from 1362–3, but they are mainly more accomplished in form rather than there being a substantial difference in content. This coincides with the start of the abbacy of Nicholas Litlyngton (1362–86), although there is no direct evidence that he was responsible for the changes. From 1362–3 (I 5), the abbot's documents are clearly titled 'states'—'status terrarum et porcionum domini abbatis Westm''. They are then called 'states' up to and including the roll for 1397–8 (I 22); the roll for 1398–9 (I 23) employs the title used by the convent—'dockets'—but its form is essentially unchanged. From 1362–3 (II 16), the convent's documents, which had previously been untitled, are called dockets—*dogerellus*. As well as the states of the convent's manors, they contain the states of the obedientiaries as a separate element from 1362–3 to 1368–9, and again from 1409–10 to 1414–15.

A small group of clerks wrote these rolls: their hands recur on states and dockets of close date, and on other account rolls of the period, working for both abbot and convent; and their work is typical of those writing accounting documentation at this point.[87] For example, II 35, the convent's dockets for 1391–2, were written by the clerk who wrote II 37, the dockets for 1393–4; this clerk also wrote a set of dockets for 1392–3 (ERO, D/DM M157: Plate 1), a near duplicate of II 36, which was however written by a different, if similar,

[86] A second, fair copy also survives of the dockets for 1358–9 (II 15).

[87] These forms are not significantly different in style or preparation from those produced by other clerks trained to write administrative documents: *Household Accounts from Medieval England*, ed. Woolgar, i, pp. 47–8.

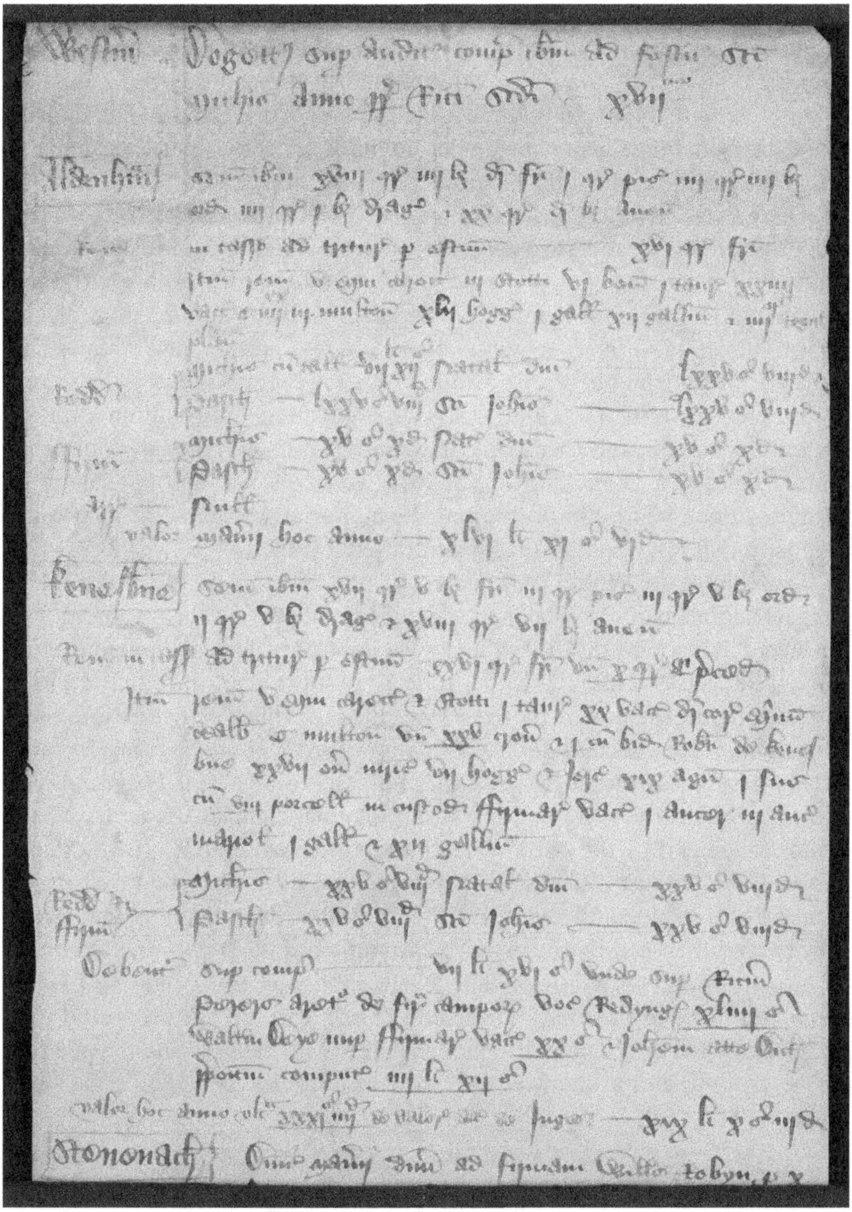

Plate 1. The manors of Aldenham and Kinsbourne, from the dockets of the manors of convent of Westminster for 1392–3 (Essex Record Office, D/DM M157, mem. 1 recto). This roll is a fair copy, written in one operation, laid out with a vertical fold for the left margin on the recto. It is a near duplicate of II 36, but has the entries for the royal manors precede those for the convent's rectories. Reproduced by courtesy of the Essex Record Office.

hand. Both abbot and convent developed their own layouts for their documents, especially the states and dockets, and these were evidently well known at the Abbey—much as other administrations developed their own forms beyond those in common use like the manorial account. These forms of the views and the states were familiar to the clerks at the Abbey, presumably from individual training and copying in the institution.

There were two groups of personnel especially associated with the accounts. Firstly, there was a cadre of professional auditors and estate administrators of some distinction, whose main interests lay in working with these documents, checking the detail of the financial position and making calculations to understand the functioning of the estate—and we have already seen some of the capabilities they possessed. They were supported by a second group, clerks whose principal tasks were collating information, drafting routine documents and then copying them out fair—by the late fourteenth century there were at any one time at least two clerks, perhaps more, engaged on these duties.[88] The composition of the manorial accounts was sometimes in other hands, especially if they were drafted locally.

The change to leasing of manors, of smaller parcels of land, and of animals and probably poultry had a significant impact on the information in the states. It may be that the states were important for estate managers in coming to decisions about whether to lease property; but once that decision had been made, the fact of the lease introduced a degree of fiction into these documents. The accountants on manors—and those writing up the states—produced inventories of corn and stock on each of the properties, and these quantities were in some instances then totalled up across all the estates at the end of the year. When manors were leased out—for example, Yeoveney, in August 1379—the lessees had included in their lease precise numbers of livestock and quantities of corn.[89] They paid their rent in the year, which was duly noted on the manorial account and the state—but the quantities of stock and corn did not change in these documents from year to year, remaining those in the lease. At the end of the lease the farmer would have reckoned for the difference between the quantity in the lease and the position on the ground, and a financial settlement would have been made, but with

[88] An example of the 'micro-communauté graphique' discussed by P. Bertrand, *Les écritures ordinaires. Sociologie d'un temps de révolution documentaire (1250–1350)* (Paris, 2015), pp. 293–352. For other 'micro-communities' of this sort, found in administrations with their own forms of accounts, see, for a seigneurial lordship, *Elizabeth de Burgh, Lady of Clare (1295–1360): Household and Other Records*, ed. J. Ward (Suffolk Records Society, 57; 2014), p. iv, and listing on pp. 151–4 of different forms; and for a monastery, the records of Norwich Cathedral Priory, discussed in Saunders, *Introduction to the Obedientiary and Manor Rolls of Norwich Cathedral Priory*, and Dewez, 'Connaître par les nombres'.

[89] WAM, Muniment Book 17, ff. 41v–42r.

some modifications written into each lease. At Yeoveney in 1379, five of the cows in the stock originally leased out were evidently in calf, and an increment in cattle was therefore expected in the final balance at the end of the farm, albeit thirty-one years down the line. In documentary terms, this led, in instances where the demesnes were leased out, to the quantities of corn and stock being repeated year after year, with little or no relation to the position on the manor. There is scarce evidence that from time to time the Abbey checked on lessees to see what stock there was in fact on the manor, and one or two instances in the states note a difference; but this does not seem to have been a common practice.[90] Leases were made in different ways: by indenture, by court roll and possibly simply by informal arrangements.[91] The numbers of some livestock, especially poultry, remain unchanged in the states over long periods when there is no evidence now of a formal lease. At Ashford, for example, the demesne was farmed to John Clerk of Staines for corn rents and for a twelve-year term, probably in 1356–7 (II 14). The numbers of cart-horses, oxen and sheep vary through the second half of the fourteenth century, but there is either a direct equivalence or a simple omission in the numbers of ganders, breeding geese, cocks, capons and hens from *c.*1370, around the end of Clerk's lease, as far as the documents in this edition continue. Between 1374–5 (II 24) and 1414–15 (II 51), the state records each year one gander, three breeding geese, twelve capons, one cock and six hens (although the states for 1383–4, 1385–6 and 1386–7 (II 31–3) only record the gander and geese). From 1405–6 (II 48) the numbers of all the other livestock remain the same from year to year too.

A feature of the later states is the length of the lists of arrears.[92] The abbot's memoranda for 1349 (I 2) are important for the way in which they list out debtors, for example, at Denham, where the debts of three serjeants beyond the present incumbent were recorded. This was a precursor of a more complex recording of debt: whereas manorial accounts up to this point had largely contented themselves with a final balance, charging any debt to the official rendering the account, in the second half of the fourteenth century the official's debt was broken down and it was recognised that others were responsible for components of it. This has become known as the *onus* system of accounting. After the cash balance, there would be a note of *Et debet* ('and he owes'), followed by a list introduced by the words *Unde super* ('whence [charged] upon'). There might be a further section here noting items put in

[90] II 34, Battersea, '24 cows, of which according to the number farmed 1 is missing'.

[91] Leases by indenture: Harvey, *Estates*, pp. 152–63; lease of the demesne by court roll to a villein: II 14, Greenford, 1357–8.

[92] *Manorial Records of Cuxham*, ed. Harvey, pp. 69–71; Harvey, *Manorial Records*, p. 36.

respite, that is, forgiven or held over, often preceded by the word *Respectuantur*.[93] This allowed landlords to understand more about the state of indebtedness on their estates—one of the great challenges of late medieval landowning—and it led to the compilation of rolls of arrears, and decisions about which debts were leviable, or not.[94] These debts were listed on the states, with increasing complexity. In the abbot's states in 1387–8 (I 19), one individual, William Huller, is named as having arrears for Ebury; in 1396–7 (I 21), there are five individuals named as responsible for debts from this manor. In turn, the length of these *unde super* sections necessitated abbreviation in the documentation: the states for the convent from 1395–6 (II 38) employ a shortened form, omitting the details of who owed what. Full dockets, listing who was responsible for the arrears, continued to be produced, however: in 1405–6, rolls survive in both the full and abbreviated forms (II 47; WAM 6131, 6136). Thereafter the convent's dockets only contained the total of arrears, manor by manor, not the listing of those responsible for them; but they did include totals of overall amounts of arrears and of leviable arrears (e.g. II 50–1). While there are no dockets surviving for the abbot's manors between 1398–9 (I 23) and 1421–2 (I 24), a similar transition was made. Those owing arrears were noted in the docket for 1398–9, but a total for each manor was all that was given in 1421–2—although we do not know if there were fuller listings that were prepared in parallel with the abbreviated form.

* * * * *

The states and dockets of Westminster document one of the most important changes in land management in the later Middle Ages, the transition from demesne farming back to leasing, on the two parts of one of the greatest monastic estates in the country. They demonstrate some of the calculations and assessments estate managers made during this period of transition. This documentation may have developed out of the views of manors, and it can be situated at the conclusion of the process of auditing manorial accounts.

[93] Cf. a similar pattern in household accounts: *Household Accounts from Medieval England*, ed. Woolgar, i, pp. 43–4.

[94] There was a parallel to this debt owing to landlords: found less often in estate accounts, rather than household documentation or the records of purchasing officials and receivers, where it was the lord, rather than his agents, who was in debt to others—and accounts of household officials, for example, conclude with lists headed *Debentur*, 'there are owed'. In turn this led to the creation of 'debentures', documents containing a statement of debt, which might be transferred or traded. For the position of the royal wardrobe, E. Wright, 'Henry IV, the Commons and the Recovery of Royal Finance in 1407', in *Rulers and Ruled in Late Medieval England: Essays Presented to Gerald Harriss*, ed. R. E. Archer and S. Walker (London, 1995), pp. 65–81, at p.72. Other households did this as well: see debentures for household purchases of Richard Plantagenet, duke of York, *c.*1446, BL, Egerton Charters 7360–4.

Notes and calculations show that those making the decisions were highly numerate and capable of bringing into the equation considerations of some complexity. Yet the documents themselves are an opaque record of this process. Most of them are fair copies and show little sign of having been used directly to make decisions, although that must have been the purpose of their immediate precursors, the drafts and the auditors' working documentation which we no longer have. The preservation of the states and dockets in fair copy form may owe more to the ideals of monastic reform rather than estate management—that there should be documents that would demonstrate to the community the financial position of their house.

Method of Editing

The documents published in this volume belong to a period extending from the late thirteenth century to the early 1420s. All of them were written almost entirely in Latin. As far as we know, Latin was the language normally used in documents of this period by Benedictine monks, no less consistently in administering their estates, whether near or far from the monastery, than in the liturgical hours sung daily in their chapels; it was also the language that was employed when they used professional clerks, auditors and administrators to prepare accounting documentation for them. The language of the abbot's household, however, was Anglo-Norman French, and this was probably used into the second half of the fourteenth century for at least some administrative documents like letters and writs, but much more rarely for accounts.[1] On just a few occasions, there are some words of Anglo-Norman in the texts edited in this volume[2]—which have either come from the household or the wider context in which this language was spoken; and there are also some Middle English words, particularly for agricultural terms and crops.

In preparing the documents for publication, the aim has been to present as nearly as possible the original language of the clerk, that is, what each clerk wrote, or what he intended to write had he extended the abbreviated forms of Latin, in all documents up to 1375 (I 12 and II 25). After 1375, the states and dockets are more repetitive in form and language, and two strategies have been adopted. Firstly, they have been calendared in English, with one exception, I 15, the states of the abbot's manors at views held at Easter 1380 and on 25 and 26 March 1381: this document is not in the form common to the others of this period, and it has therefore been presented in its original Latin. Secondly, where sections, particularly rent accounts, are repeated in exactly the same form, reference is made back to the earlier account, but the total of rents is given again. Where documents have been edited in Latin, the intention has been to preserve the original orthography used by each clerk. There is in practice little doubt about what most of the extensions from Latin forms would have been, except in some instances of usage of singular or plural, or gender, and some grammatical constructions where there are several possibilities. The Word List and Glossary has been employed to indicate how words have been extended in these cases, with reference to each document and the

[1] See, for example, many of the writs and household ordinances published in *Walter de Wenlok*, ed. Harvey, pp. 49–154, 241–8.
[2] e.g. I 2B, Longdon rectory, 'ij mulveles pess' sals''.

clerks who wrote it, and to comment on grammatical questions. The general rule has been to follow the patterns of classical grammar, unless there is evidence to the contrary. In rare cases of ambiguity, information is given in the footnotes to the texts, but in most cases to have done so would have obscured the text with a good deal of editorial matter. Italic type has therefore been used to express doubt. Corrections to the text have only been made where slips of the pen or eccentricities would mislead, and in each case the original form is given in a footnote. The Word List and Glossary has been used as well as a guide to Latin forms and their translation, to underpin the choices used in the calendared documents: the variety of word forms from the calendared documents has been preserved here.

In the full transcripts, all abbreviated words that are not from Latin forms have had their extensions placed in italics, taking into account the practice of individual clerks. The Word List and Glossary has been used to explain and define practice and the meaning of early occurrences of these words—and it also takes into account unusual or early forms that occur in the post-1375 documents. Abbreviated forms of place-names have not been extended and retain their final suspensions in documents up to 1375; common English forms for the principal places have been used in the calendars after that date, but lesser place-names have been left in the forms in which they are found in the manuscripts, although italic type has been used to expand forms that are likely, to facilitate the reading of the texts.

All capitalisation and punctuation are editorial. The use of *i*, *j*, *u* and *v* has been standardised: in verbal forms, *j* and *v* have been used where the letter has a consonantal value. In Roman numerals, however, the manuscript usage of *i* and *j* has been retained. The patterns of underlining employed in the texts up to 1375 have been preserved as they have been found in the manuscripts. Italic type has been used for all entries in the margins, with roman for uncertain extensions. The word forms for weights, measures and currency, which occur frequently, have been shortened to standard forms: all appear in the list of editorial conventions, which also explains the ways in which editorial reconstructions of damaged or partial documents have been indicated.

Word List and Glossary

This Word List and Glossary sets out firstly to identify words employed in the texts that are not in *OLD*, *LS*, *DMLBS*, *AND*, *MED* or *OED*. It also includes words that are in *AND*, *DMLBS*, *MED* and *OED* where the usage is different, where the usage here occurs thirty or more years earlier than the first cited use, or where the orthography might lead to confusion. Secondly, the purpose of the list is editorial, to explain the practices that have been employed in expanding abbreviated words, especially Latin words, and to underpin the translations used in the calendars. Finally, the aim has been to explain how particular Latin grammatical constructions have been followed, and to note the principal divergences from classical forms (as outlined in *OLD* and *LS*).

Words are given as they appear in the manuscripts, in their abbreviated forms, not as a standardised *nom. sing.* or first person.

affrus: draught horse, affer (*DMLBS* averus; *Manorial Records of Cuxham*, ed. Harvey, p. 775). Extended to forms in *-us*, *-i*; treated as *m.*, including in the expression *j affrus fe'*, e.g. I 12, Pershore, paralleling examples of *pullanus femellus.*

anas, **anates**, **agnates**, **annates**: duck, usually a female; the texts use *mallardus* for drakes. The manorial stock listings imply that these are managed or domesticated birds rather than wildfowl. Treated as Latin forms from *anas*, *anatis*, *f.*

ancer, **anser**: gander (*LS*, *DMLBS* anser). Extended to forms from *anc/ser*, *-eris*, *m*.

aper: boar. Treated as Latin forms from *aper*, *apri*, *m.*

apriculus: young boar (diminutive form of *aper* not recorded in *DMLBS*); I 17, Hyde. Extended to forms in *-us*, *-i*, *m*.

aracii: see *haras*.

arreragia: arrears. Occurs mainly as *pl.*, from *arreragium*, *-i*, *n.*, and occasionally as *sing.*, from *arreragia*, *-e*, *f*. Extended to forms in *n. pl.* unless evidence to the contrary.

arura: ploughing, plough service (*DMLBS* arura).

auditus: audit (*DMLBS* auditus 1.3, 1448). Extended to forms from *auditus*, *-us*, *m*.

avena, **avene**: oats. Treated as a *pl.* from *avena*, *-e*, *f.*, extended as such unless there is evidence that *sing.* was intended. The *sing.* is uncommon, but occasionally used, e.g. II 4, Stevenage, corn panel, has *sing.* Cf. *Manorial Records of Cuxham*, ed. Harvey, p. 777. Ashford accounts, translated forms, e.g. II 32: *aven' gross'*, coarse oats; *aven' minut'*: fine oats.

averagium: payment in lieu of customary carrying service (*DMLBS* averagium). Extended to forms from *averagium*, *-i*, *n*. There is some confusion in the states for Wheathampstead and Launton about whether the word is *averagium* or *avesagium*, a payment for pannage for pigs, for pasturage. At Wheathampstead, where the payment was made at All Saints, II 10 has *avisag'*, and II 32 has *avesag'*; but the custumal (CUL, MS Kk.5.29, ff. 73v, 76) makes it clear this is carrying service. At Launton, the payment was made at Martinmas; II 23 and II 37 refer to *avesagio* and *aves'*, and pastugare or pannage is probably intended on this manor even though some dockets, such as II 24, clearly intend *averagium* (II 24: *av'ag'*).
avesagium, **avisagio**: a payment for pasturage or pannage (*DMBLS* avesagium). See also the preceding entry, *averagium*.

baven', **bavein**, **baveyne**: bundle of brushwood, bavain (*DMLBS* bavenum; *MED* bavein, 1315; *OED* bavin, *sb*., 1528). Latin forms extended as if from *bavenum*, *-i*, *n*.; cf. principally the manors of Hendon and Hampstead.
billeta: firewood, billets/blocks of wood (*DLMBS* billetum, 1a, *c*.1300; *MED* billet, n. (2), 1437). Extended to forms from *billetum*, *-i*, *n*., in *pl*. II 26, Greenford has 1,000 'for the Thames', i.e. for works on the river bank, suggesting something more substantial than 'firewood'.
bladum: corn. Extended throughout to forms in *sing*. from *bladum*, *-i*, *n*.
bovettus, **bovectus**: bullock. Extended to forms in *-us*, *-i*, *m*.
boviculus: young bullock, young heifer. Extended to forms in *-us*, *-i*, *m*. The presence of heifers is either indicated directly, as in II 4, Teddington, *j boviculus femellus*, or implicitly by repetition in the list, I 14, Pershore, *j boviculus*, *iij boviculi*. For *boviculus* referring to heifers, see *Manorial Records of Cuxham*, ed. Harvey, p. 778.
braseum, **brasium**: malt. Extended to forms in *-um*, *-i*, *n*., following orthography of manuscript. Translation: *cap' bras'*, very good malt (e.g. I 16, Denham).
brott': sweepings of corn. *Manorial Records of Cuxham*, ed. Harvey, p. 778, sub *brot*; also Harvey, *Medieval Oxfordshire Village*, p. 47. Possibly cognate with *OED* brod, *sb*.[1], from OE and ON, *broldr*, a spike on a plant; but the meaning seems to have changed slightly: *MED*, sub *brod* n. (1), a sprout or shoot. II 8, Stevenage, 6 bus. under *multura*; II 9, Turweston, has both *brot'* and a Latin, *gen. sing*. form, *brotti*, referring to wheat and dredge.

calumpnia: in dispute, e.g. I 23, Pershore.
canabis, **canabus**, **cannabis**: hemp. Extended to forms from *-is*, *-is*, or *-us*, *-i*, following the manuscript.
capo, **capones**, **caupones**: capon. Extended to forms from *ca(u)po*, *caponis*, *m*.
carectates: cartloads. Extended as forms from *carectas*, *-atis*, *f*.

cerclac': see *sarclac'*.

cherchshot, cherset: church scot, in origin corn given at Martinmas to support the clergy. Paid at Ashford, e.g. II 21. At Greenford, II 23, a rent at Martinmas, perhaps for gathering stubble on the demense. Neilson, *Customary Rents*, pp. 193–6, especially 195–6.

chirs': a weed, possibly a thistle (*OLD* cirsion); *cirsium* is now the botanical name for genera of thistles, but has not been traced in medieval usage. II 23, Mulsham, 20 qr. rye, full of chirs' and darnel. No apparent reference in T. Hunt, *Plant Names of Medieval England* (Woodbridge, 1989).

cigniculi: cygnets. Extended to forms in *-us, -i, m.*

cignottus: young swan. Extended to forms in *-us, -i, m.*

cignus, cygnus, signus: swan. Extended to forms in *-us, -i, m.*; treated as *m.* even where a female is implied: II 15, Wheathampstead, *j cignus errarius femellus*. Occasionally stock accounts refer to half swans and cygnets, e.g I 17–18, Denham, and I 8 Islip: the most likely explanation is that the abbot in these instances was only entitled to a moiety of the swans on the manor. At Denham, this may relate in some way to the division discussed under I 1, note 30.

clades, clata: hurdle (*DMLBS* cleta). Forms in *clades* treated as if from *clades, -is, f.*; *clat'* extended as if from *clata, -e, f.*

clav': clove, a measure of weight of 7 or 8 lb. avoirdupois (*OED* clove *sb.*[3]), here usually 7 lb. Extended to forms from *clavus, -i, m.*, and *clavis, -is, f.*, following the use of the manuscript.

cobbi: male swans, cob swans (*OED* cob *sb.*[1], 2., 1570; *MED* cobbe (n.)(a), 1476).

compot': account, but in the expression *super compotum* meaning 'at the audit', i.e. the hearing/rendering of the account. Extended to forms from *compotus, -i, m.* In the expression *super auditum compot' ministrorum* extended in the singular.

concavus: used to describe 'hollow tiles'. See L. F. Salzman, *Building in England down to 1540: A Documentary History* (Oxford, 1952), pp. 231–2. Extended as *adj.* to forms in *-us, -a, -um*.

corium, coreum: hide *or* leather. Extended to forms in *corium, -i, n.*, unless evidence on the manuscript for another form.

corium dealbatum: tawed hide.

cornbote: a payment in sheaves of corn or in commuted form in cash for the service of carrying corn (*MED* corn-bote, *n.*); Neilson, *Customary Rents*, pp. 25, 26, 28. Here, e.g. II 6, at Teddington, abbreviated forms extended to *cornbote*.

cornertyl': corner tile, e.g. II 23, Knowle.

crescat': 'crest', referring to *tegule*, ridge tiles (*MED* creste, *n.* (1)) 1468). See L. F. Salzman, *Building in England down to 1540: A Documentary History* (Oxford, 1952), pp. 230-1. Extend as *adj.* to forms from *crescatus, -a, -um.*

cron', cronande, cronarte, ad cronandum, cronura: crone, old, worn out animal (*DMLBS* cronardus 1377). Abbreviated forms extended as if from *cronardus, -i, m.*, or *cronarda, -e, f.*

crud': undressed (of a hide). Extended as *adj.* to forms from *crudus, -a, -um.*

currallum, scur': small corn, wheat unless another corn specified (*DMLBS* curallum; *Manorial Records of Cuxham*, ed. Harvey, p. 782). Extended to forms in *-um, -i, n.*

custus, custis, custu: costs, expenses (*DMLBS* costus). Extended variously as a second declension noun, *custus, -i, m.*; and fourth declension, *custus, -us, m.*; and also in *sing.* or *pl.* depending on the usage of the manuscript.

cyvera: barrow (*DMLBS* civera). II 18, Battersea.

dam': fallow deer, as translated in I 21–2, Pyrford (*DMLBS* damma 1).

darnell: darnel, a type of weed in cornfields (*Lolium temulentum*), II 23 (*MED* darnel (a)).

dauek: dauke, probably the wild carrot or parsnip (*AND* dauk, *sb.*; *MED* dauk(e *n.*, the wild carrot (*Daucus carota*); *DMLBS* daucus, parsnip, (?) carrot, or similar). II 8, Morden: this is a crop that has to be threshed, and which is then used for the liveries of the *famuli.* Just possibly a variant of *drauk*, cf. *draunk* below.

debentur super compotum: owed at the audit.

dies: day. Occurs as *m.* and *f.*

dimidium, di.: half. Used both as an *adj.*, in agreement with the *sb.*, and as a *sb.* followed by a *gen.*, e.g. *di. corei dealbati* (II 7, Launton).

disproficuus: deficit, shortfall, e.g. I 23, Denham.

dogerellus, dogettus: docket (*OED* docket *sb.*[1], 2. 1485; not in *DMLBS*). Extended as forms in *-us, -i, m., sing.* or *pl.* following the evidence of the manuscript. Possibly derived from *docere*, to tell, inform; but equally *OED* dock *v.*[1], 2, to abridge, shorten, may be related.

dominicum: demesne lands. Extended to forms in *-um, -i, n.*

drag': dredge, mixed corn of barley and oats (*DMLBS* dragetum). Extended where no other evidence to forms from *dragetum, -i, n.* (e.g. I 11, Chaceley).

draunk: drauk, a weed in a cornfield, possibly cockle, darnel or wild oats (*MED* drauk *n.* 1325). II 4, Kingsbourne, under wheat (1312).

drogman', dragman: an oat-legume mixture, and sown as such (Campbell, *English Seigniorial Agriculture*, p. 227). II 10 Wheathampstead: acres sown include 6 qr. *drageti* and 1 qr. 2 bus. *drogman'*. Found at Kinsbourne, Stevenage and Wheathampstead.

equa: brood mare (I 22, Denham)
err', **herr'**: nesting/breeding swan (*DMLBS* aerarius). Extended as *adj.* to forms from *(h)errarius*, *-a*, *-um*.
est': summer. Extended as *adj.* to forms from *estivalis*, *-e*.
estrich': board from the Baltic (*AND* estriccheborde, *sb.* 1410). II 33, both manuscripts, Westerham, 1387–8: *iij long' tabule de Estrich'*, three long Eastland boards.

fab': beans. Extended in plural from *faba*, *-e*, *f.*, unless evidence to the contrary.
fag', **fagatus**, **fagattus**, **fagettus**, **fagotus**, **fagottus**: faggots, firewood (*DMLBS* fagotus). Extended to forms in *-us*, *-i*, usually in *pl.*
falc': mowing. Extended to forms from *falcacio*, *-nis*, *f.*
fe', **fem'**, **femella**, **femellus**: female. Forms from *fe'* and *fem'* extended as *adj.* from *femellus*, *-a*, *-um*.

gaineria: land under cultivation (*DMLBS* waineria).
gersyngpans: a customary payment at Battersea at Michaelmas, perhaps from 'gersuma' and 'pence', a customary payment by unfree tenants to a lord for permission for a daughter to marry (Neilson, *Customary Rents*, p. 86; *DMLBS* gersuma, 3).
grenario: granary, i.e. for *granario* (*LS* and *DMLBS* granarium; II 1, Birdbrook).
gross': of wool, coarse, thick, especially referring to fleeces of older sheep (*DMLBS* grossus, 14 d). Extended as *adj.* to forms in *-us*, *-a*, *-um*.
gruti: grout, infusion of malt before and during fermentation (*OED* grout *sb.*[1]).

ham': hooks or forks, as agricultural implements for moving dung (*OLD* hamus; *LS* hamus; *DMLBS* hamus, 1). Replaces *unct'* used in earlier Battersea listings of stock and implements from II 24.
haras, **aras**, **harasii**, **harasio**: a mixture of peas and vetch (*Manorial Records of Cuxham*, ed. Harvey, p. 768; the suggestion in *DMLBS* haracium, 2, a vegetable, orach, is less likely). Forms in Latin, *aras-*, *haras-*, extended to *-ium*, *-ii*, *n.*
hogaster, **hoggaster**: sheep in their second year. Translated as 'hoggs' in the phrase *jercie et hoggastri*. Extended to Latin forms in *-er*, *-ri*, *m.*
hogerellus, **hoggerellus**: translated as 'young sheep'.
holtiel, **holuwerk'**: curved tiles, to go over crests or edges, or other grooves in the roof (*MED* hol(e *adj.* (1) 1. d., 1333).
hurtardiculi: young rams (*DMLBS* hurdardiculus, *c.*1400; II 10, Greenford, 1352). Extended to forms in *-us*, *-i*, *m.*
hurtardus: ram (*DMLBS* hurtardus). Extended to forms in *-us*, *-i*, *m.*

jercia, **gercia**: gimmer, an unmated ewe, usually between the first and second shearing, i.e. in its second year. Extended to forms in *-a*, *-e*, *f.*

jument': mare. Extended to forms in *-um*, *-i*, *n.*, but in some instances the manuscripts use the form *jumenta*, *-e*, *f.* In places it is likely that the word was intended to mean a heifer, e.g. II 49, Greenford, *xxij vacc'*, *j jumenta*, *j juvencula.*

juvenca, **juvencca**: heifer. Extended to forms in *-a*, *-e*, *f.*

juvencula, **juvenccula**, **juvenculus**: young heifer. The first two extended to forms in *-a*, *-e*, *f.*, and the last to forms in *-us*, *-i*, *m.*

lath': lath. Extended in *pl.* as lath*es.*

lavatorium: ewer. Abbreviated forms extended to *lavatorium*, *-ii*, *n.*

levand': [sums of money] to be raised. Extended to forms in *sing.* in the phrase *et levandum sunt ibidem per annum de claro* where *pl.* might be expected.

liberaciones famulorum: allowances of the *famuli*, the wage servants on the manor. Abbreviated forms from *lib'*, e.g. II 3, Westerham, extended to forms from *liberacio*, *-nis*, *f.*: extensions are made in *pl.* where it is clear there is more than one person; but as *sing.* where there is only one.

ligatur': binding, cord (*DMLBS* ligatura), e.g. II 6, Hampstead. Extended to forms in *-a*, *-e*, *f.*

mallardus, **malardus**: drake, a domestic duck, rather than a male wild duck (*DMLBS* mallardus). Extended to forms in *-us*, *-i*, *m.*

malum: apple. Extended to forms from *malum*, *-i*, *n.*; II 21, Birdbrook, has *malar'* as *gen. pl.*, extended to *malarum.*

manus: hands. In the expressions 'in the hands of', 'into the hands of', the manuscripts use both *sing.* and *pl.* forms, some with *acc.*, others with *abl.* Extended to *in manus*, *in manu*, *in manibus* according to the usage of the manuscript.

mariola (*sing.*), **mariole** (*pl.*) **marol'**: a breeding female goose. Extended as a *sb.* to forms from *mariola*, *-e*, *f.* (e.g. II 17); in the expression *auce mariole*, as *adj.* (e.g. I 9, Chaceley), extended to forms in *-us*, *-a*, *-um*, and translated as 'breeding geese'. There are no examples that support *DMLBS* mariola, as an 'unmated female [goose]'. Cf. *Manorial Records of Cuxham*, ed., Harvey, p. 789.

mas', **masc'**: male. Extended to forms from *masculus*, *-a*, *-um.*

maser': mazer, a wooden cup (*MED* maser, 2). II 18, Moulsham, *j ciphus de maser'*, not extended. Appears later as *j ciphus mureus*, of maple wood (*DMLBS* murraeus, 2; *MED* maser 1(a) is the common maple tree), e.g. II 23, Moulsham.

medselver: a payment by villeins for the use of meadow (see Neilson, *Customary Rents*, p. 84). Found at Battersea, Hampstead and elsewhere.

meis: a container, barrel or basket (*MED* meis(e (a); *DMLBS* meisa). I 7: Pyrford, corn *in ij meis plenis*, but these are very substantial containers, as the two of them together held 60 qr. of rye. May also be connected to *DMLBS* mela, a container, basin, bucket.

mixt', mixtilio, mixtilium: maslin, usually a mixed crop of wheat and rye (*DMLBS* mixtilio). Forms extended to *mixtilio, -nis, f.*, and *mixtilium, -ii, n.*, according to the usage of the manuscripts. The abbreviated form *mixt'* has potential for confusion with *mixtura*, below, mixed corn, often from the mill, but there including all types of corn as part of the perquisites and renders of the mill.

mixt', mixtura: mixed corn, sometimes also including legumes, not grown as a mixture but mixed after the harvest, for example, in the renders/perquisites from the mill, or deliberately mixed as part of the food of *famuli*. Forms in *mixt'* extended to *mixtura, -e, f.* To be distinguished from *mixt'*, meaning maslin, above. II 6, Knightsbridge, paragraph for *mixtilium*, i.e. maslin, but also includes *mixtura* which is made by adding beans (paragraph for *fabe*) as well to the maslin for the *liberaciones famulorum*.

molendin': mill. Extended to forms from *molendinum, -i, n.*

muens: two swans at Ashwell (II 23, 1371), aged 1½ years. Manuscript: *ij cigni muens*, rendered as *ij cigni muentes*, as *adj.* form in *-ens*. It is possible that this refers to mute swans, i.e. the common swan: *OED* mute *adj.* and *sb.*[1], 1, 1375, not emitting sound. *OLD*, *LS* and *DMLBS* do not record *muens*; but note *AND* muer[2], *p.pl.* as *adj.*, of a hawk, mewed, moulted, in process of changing plumage, and *AND* mue[1], *n.*, moult, from *muer*, to change—which normally happens with mute swans in July and August.

multur': multure, payment for grinding at the lord's mill, in cash or kind (Neilson, *Customary Rents*, pp. 98–9; *DMLBS* molitura 2). Extended to forms from *multura, -e, f.*

mulveles: cod or similar fish (*AND* milwere; *DMLBS* mulvellus).

mutatus: taken, *p.pl.* (*DMLBS* mutare). II 11, Launton, *mutatus est per latronem*.

nomen: name. Extended to *nominibus* as *dat./abl. pl.*

ordeum, ordium: barley. Extended from *ord'*, where no evidence for the form, to *-eum, -ei, n.*

outhonkesbotcorn': a customary rent at Teddington (II 4 Teddington, 1312), payable at the rate of 1 p. rye and 1 p. barley per virgate at Michaelmas (WAM 27197). *Bote* is usually a privilege for which the villein pays in cash or corn (*MED* bote n. (2); Neilson, *Customary Rents*, pp. 83–4).

oxepans: a customary payment made at Sawbridgeworth (Sayesbury) (e.g. II 23), at Pentecost for grazing oxen (or cattle) on waste land of which the lord claimed ownership (Neilson, *Customary Rents*, pp. 76–7). Possibly related to *shipselver*. See also Harold Fox, 'Lords and wastes', in *Survival and Discord in Medieval Society. Essays in Honour of Christopher Dyer*, ed. Richard Goddard, John Langdon and Miriam Müller (Turnhout, 2010), pp. 29–48.

pallea: straw or chaff (*DMLBS* palea). In I 3, in estimates of corn, e.g. Bourton-on-the-Hill, *in pallea* means threshed corn still with its chaff, i.e. still to be winnowed, or corn that was partway through the threshing process, with stalks, etc., but was no longer in sheaves, *in garbis*, as at Chaceley rectory. II 39 and others talk of *stramen* and *pallea*, straw and chaff, but also intending all the products of threshing except the grain.

pastur': pasture. Extended to forms in *sing*. in *-a*, *-e*, *f.*

pava: peahen (*DMLBS* pava). Extended to forms in *-a*, *-e*, *f.*

pavenna: peahen (*DMLBS* pavenna), an equivalent form to *pava* (II 11, grand totals). Extended to forms in *-a*, *-e*, *f.*

pavicul': a young peahen (*DMLBS* pavicula; I 18, Ebury).

pelles agnorum, **pelles lanute**: lambskins, woolfells. Extensions from *pellis*, *-is*, *f.*, unless evidence to the contrary.

pelletta, **pellecta**: sheepskins, without wool (*DMLBS* pelletta a). Extended to forms in *-a*, *-e*, *f.*

pelvis: basin (*OLD* pelvis). Extended to forms in *-is*, *-is*, *f.*

perquisita curie: perquisites of the manorial court. Extended to forms from *perquisita*, *-orum*, *n. pl.*

pes compoti: the foot of the account, usually referring to the manorial account, where the final cash balance was struck and debts apportioned.

pis': peas. Extended to forms from *pise*, *pisarum*, *f. pl.*

plumbum: a lead, a vat or vessel used for brewing or similar, often of lead but sometimes of other metal (*DMLBS* plumbum 3a, b). Extended to forms in *-um*, *-i*, *n.*

pratum: meadow. Extended to forms in *-um*, *-i*, *n.*

precaria: boon-work (*DMLBS* precarius 4a). Extended to forms in *-a*, *-e*, *f.*

presepia: manger or receptacles for fodder (*DMLBS* praesepe 1b); I 1, Laleham, the equivalent of *rakkes* below.

preter: besides, in addition. Treated as *prep.* with *acc.*

profectus, **proficuus**: profit, advantage. Both extended to forms in *-us*, *-i*, *m.*

pulimong', **pulmang**: a mixture of beans or peas with corn, normally oats, and sown as such. Found at Oakham (e.g. II 2, 11). Cf. Campbell, *English Seigniorial Agriculture*, p. 227; D. Stone, 'The Consumption of Field Crops in Late Medieval England', in *Food in Medieval England: Diet and Nutrition*, ed. C. M. Woolgar, D. Serjeantson and T. Waldron (Oxford, 2006) pp. 13, 17, where the reference is to *bulmong*, at Wellinborough, Northants.

pullanus: foal (*DMLBS* pullanus). Extended to forms in *-us*, *-i*, *m.*; *pull' fe'*: extended to *pullanus femellus*, *m.*, a filly (I 22, Pyrford).
pullus: colt. Extended to forms in *-us*, *-i*, *m*; *pull' fe'*: extended to *pulli femelli*, *m.*
puls': a mixture of peas and beans, but possibly sometimes another legume (*Manorial Records of Cuxham*, ed. Harvey, p. 793, for the mixture; neither *DMLBS* pulsa, nor *MED* puls, *n.*, identifies this as a mixture). Extended to forms from *pulsa*, *-e*, *f.*, where evidence that a Latin form is intended; otherwise not extended. In I 3, Castlemorton rectory, mixed beans and peas are separate from *puls'*.

querc' curv': curved oak timbers, probably for barrels (*DMLBS* quercus 2). Treated as if from *quercus*, *-us*, *f.* (II 10 Paddington).

rakkes: a manger or framework for holding fodder for livestock (*MED* rak *n.* (2), 1343; *OED* rack *sb.*[2], 3. 14--). I 2B, 1349, for sheep.
ray: darnel (*OED* ray *sb.*[7], 1398; *MED* rai n. (2), 1398), although malting it would have been unusual. I 1, Islip, *ij qr. iij bus. brasei de ray.*
receptum, **recepta**: receipt, or receipts. Extended to forms in *-um*, *-i*, *n.*, in *pl.* unless there is evidence on the manuscript (as on II 8) that *sing.* was intended.
redditus: rents. Treated as a collective *sing.* of *redditus*, *-us*, *f.*, except where *pl.* is explicitly intended.
redditus mobilis: moveable goods as rent, e.g. hens, eggs (II 23, Hampstead, Greenford).
rem': remainder, as *sb.*, or to remain, *v.* Extended to forms from *remanencia*, *-e*, *f.*, and from *remanere*, *v.*, depending on context.
repris', **repric'**: accounting term, reprises, those sums that have to be taken off from income as a regular charge (*DMLBS* reprisa); often in the expression 'beyond reprises'. Extended to forms in *-a*, *-e*, *f.*
repyngselvir: a customary rent probably paid in commutation of a boon-work, reaping at the corn harvest (Neilson, *Customary Rents*, p. 55; II 24, Amwell).
respectuacio, **respectus**: accounting term, respite; a sum held over or allowed, usually after a cash balance (*DMLBS* respectuacio; respectus 6b). Extended to forms from *respectuacio*, *-nis*, *f.*; and *respectus*, *-us*, *m.* according to context.
responsurus: to answer for. Only found on the manuscripts as *r'*, never in extended form (e.g. I 3). Cf. *Manorial Records of Cuxham*, ed. Harvey, p. 794.
rhites, **riches**, **riistes**, **riites**, **ryhtes**: a kind of ale and also, by association, the name of the tax levied by the abbot of Westminster, on every barrel sold by

any of his serfs in the weekly market at Pershore in this period: I 1, Pershore, Longdon; I 3, Castlemorton.

rusc', **rusch'**, **russ'**: beehive (*DMLBS* ruscus 5). Extended to forms in *-a*, *-e*, *f.*

ryngels: a measure of hay, possibly a cartload (*MED* ring *n.* 6, a measure of capacity, but at ½ bus. this looks too small for hay; *MED* ringildie *n.*, office of a serjeant or bailiff, may make a connection between the measure and the manorial officer; perhaps the reference is to a level marked by ironwork in a cart, i.e. a ring, and hence a measure of capacity) I 7, Laleham, Pyrford.

saplath': lath made of sapwood (*MED* sap(e, *n.* 2 (b) sap-lathe, *c.*1350; II 25 Westerham).

sarclac', **sarclanc'**, **cerclac'**: hoeing, weeding (*DMLBS* sarculare; *Manorial Records of Cuxham*, ed. Harvey, p. 795). Extended to forms from *sarclacio*, *-nis*, *f.*, or from variant stems.

sauceti: willow, osiers (*DMLBS* salictum 1e). Treated (I 5, Birdbrook) as a form from *saucetum*, *-i*, *n.*

schiphur: a customary payment due on 30 November and 24 June from 10 customary tenants at Kelvedon (e.g. II 4) in lieu of carrying specified quantities of corn and malt, in a boat hired by them for the purpose.

schokkes, **shokk'**: shocks, sheaves of grain placed on end, leaning together, to dry, e.g. I 22 Denham, II 47 Sayesbury (*OED* shock sb.[1]; *MED* shok, n. (a), 1325; *AND* schoke, s.). The use of shock as a unit of measurement, for 60, does not relate to sheaves of corn (*MED* shok, *n.* (b)), but to commodities imported from the Baltic.

scorefe, **scorfe**, **skorfe**: a feudal fee, 'scor fee', in lieu of military service (II 24 Oakham). Cf. F. G. Davenport, *The Economic Development of a Norfolk Manor 1086–1565* (Cambridge, 1906), p. 47, and App. VIII, p. xxx, n. 1, and works cited there.

scur': see *currallum*.

sexus: type or kind of animal, rather than 'sex of animal' (*DMLBS* sexus 5), in grand totals of livestock (e.g. II 23). Extended as if from forms in *-us*, *-us*, *m.*

sherreves3elde: a sheriff's aid, a county tax on geldable land (Neilson, *Customary Rents*, pp. 124–6). II 25, Knowle.

shipselver: a customary payment made at Sawbridgeworth (Sayesbury) (e.g. II 23), at Martinmas. It is less clear what this payment was for: possibilities are for grazing sheep on waste land of which the lord claimed ownership (Neilson, *Customary Rents*, pp. 76–7), similar to the *oxepans* on this manor; it may be the name for the payment made in communtation of the obligation of carrying animals to Westminster by water (Neilson, *Customary Rents*, pp. 62–3); or it may be the equivalent of *un3eld*, paid here along with *oxepans* (II 24), possibly a payment for commuted hunting services (Neilson, *Customary Rents*, p. 112); but note that the *unȝeld* was collected at Michaelmas at the same time as the *oxepans* (II 24).

sicera: probably cider (*DMLBS* sicera; II 21 Sawbridgeworth).

siligo, silligo: rye (*DMLBS* siligo 1c). Extended to forms from *si(l)ligo, -nis, f.*

solutum: paid, preceding sums of money, *p.pl.* of *solvere.*

sprig', sprigetum, sprygeti: rye (*Manorial Records of Cuxham*, ed. Harvey, p. 797; Harvey, *Medieval Oxfordshire Village*, p. 130; only identified generally as a kind of grain/mixed corn in *DMLBS* sprigetum 1333). II 10, 1352, totals of corn; II 11–13 Ashwell. Extended where it is a Latin form to *sprigetum, -i, n.*

squadbots: a type of boat, I 1 and 2B Ebury (perhaps related to *OED* squat *p.pl.*, close to the ground, i.e. low-lying, shallow draught).

stagg', stagges: swan, likely to be of an age between cygnets and *cigni errarii*, perhaps two to two and a half years old (*DMLBS* staggus 3; *MED* stagge *n.* c; II 11–12, Wheathampstead). Abbreviated forms extended in Latin, from *staggus, -i, m.*

stal': stallion (*MED* staloun). Extended to forms from *stalonus, -i, m.*; II 15, Knowle.

stod': stud, a place where horses are kept, or from a group of mares or colts (*MED* stode *n.* 1(a) or (d)). II 15, Knowle, *j pullanus femellus del stod'.*

stodmar': a mare for breeding, a brood mare (MED stode *n.* 1(f), stod-mere); I 23, Denham.

suella: a young sow (*DMLBS* suillus 2b) I 23, Todenham. Extended to forms in *-a, -e, f.*

super: at, on, during, Latin *prep.* used variously with *acc.* or *abl.* Extended according to the usage of each clerk, e.g. II 1, *super visu*; II 4, *super visum.*

super compotum: see *compotum.*

superplus': accounting term, surplus, an excess, a balance remaining (*DMLBS* superplusagium). Extended to forms from *superplusagium, -i, n.*

sus, sues (*pl.*): sow (*OLD* sus; *DMLBS* sus). Extended to forms from *sus, suis, f.*

tabule: boards (*DMLBS* tabula). Extended to forms in *-a, -e, f.* At Allfarthing, the boards seem to be used as part of the process of tile manufacture, for covering them or for propping them up to dry: II 21, Allfarthing, *iiijC di. C tabule pro tegulis cooperiendis*; II 23, Allfarthing, *iiijC di. tablule plane de fago pro tegulis desiccandis*; II 26 Allfarthing, mentions the storehouse for tiles.

talwod', talwode: talwood, cut wood, as billets, for firewood (*MED* tal-wod(e, *n.*; *AND* talwode); e.g. I 21, Pyrford.

tann': tanned (*DMLBS* tannatio). Extended as if from *tannatus, -a, -um.*
tarr': tar, probably intending an English word in many examples (*OED* tar *sb.*), but some Latin forms intended, e.g. I 1, Bourton, *tarre pure*, from *tarra, -e, f.* Extension made in italics, when it is likely to be an English form: tarr*e.*
taurell': translated as bull calf. Extended to forms in *-us, -i, m.*
tegul': tile (*DMLBS* tegula). Extended to forms in *-a, -e, f.* Different types: *angulares*, corner; *crescat'*, crest or ridge; *plan'*, flat. See L. F. Salzman, *Building in England down to 1540: A Documentary History* (Oxford, 1952), pp. 229–32.
tritur': to thresh, *v.*, threshing, *sb.* (*DMLBS* triturare *v.*; trituratio *sb.*). Extended as appropriate to passive forms of *trituare* in *pl.*: *triturantur*; *in tritur'* extended to forms from *trituracio, -nis, f.*, in *sing.*

unc' ferr', **unct' ferr'**: iron hooks, at Battersea (e.g. II 10) as an implement for clearing dung (*DLMBS* uncus 2a); later replaced by the word *hamus.* Extended to forms from *unc(t)us, -i, m.*
unde super: accounting expression, 'charged against', listing people responsible for debt, translated by the phrase 'of this sum .... owes'.
unȝeld: a customary rent at Sayesbury in Sawbridgeworth (II 24). See *shipselver* above for discussion.

vacc': cow, of a cow. Extended as *sb.* to forms in *-a, -e, f.*; and as *adj.*, to forms from *vaccineus, -a, um* (*DMLBS* vaccinus, -eus).
valor: not translated, accounting term, the worth or value of an estate. In later accounts, the expression *valet hoc anno* is used; the calendared translation continues to use *valor.*
vellera: fleeces (*DMLBS* vellus). Extended to forms from *vellus, velleris, n.* For woolfells, see *pelles lanute.*
vend': [to be] sold, verbal forms from *vendere*; *ad vend'* extended to *ad vendendum.*
ventacione, **ventilacione**: winnowing (*DMLBS* ventilatio). Extended to forms in *-io, -ionis, f.*
vincula: chains. In the expression *festum sancti Petri ad vincula*, the feast of St Peter in chains, 1 August, *vincula* (i.e. *n. pl., acc.*) is sometimes abbreviated as if to suggest *vinculam, f. sing., acc.*
virses: possibly birchwood, or birch branches (*AND* birse), or baskets (*AND* berz). II 37, Battersea: *Thomas Mannok' de virses sibi vend' xx s.*

warth': a customary render, known as *wardpenny* or *wardsilver*, commuting the service of guard, ward or watching on geldable land, at royal castles, markets and so on (Neilson, *Customary Rents*, pp. 131–7; II 25, Knowle).

wodepans, **wodeselver**: woodpenny, woodsilver, a customary rent, paid in commutation of the obligation of carrying wood for the lord's fuel (Neilson, *Customary Rents*, pp. 51–2). II 1, Turweston: wodeselver; II 24, Aldenham, wodepans.

Grammar and syntax

Gerunds and gerundives

The texts commonly use a gerundive where an *adj.* or *p.pl.* form might have been more appropriate, e.g. II 4, Wheathampstead, *Denarii de lana vendenda*, rather than *vendita*. In this case gerundive forms following a noun have been extended in the same case, gender and number as the noun. Gerunds following a verb which one might expect to be associated with a preposition sometimes have none: for example, the forms *assignantur ad levandum* and *assignantur levandum* both occur. Sometimes a substantive is used as if it were a gerund, followed by *acc.* rather than *gen.*, e.g. II 4, Battersea (and other manors, *passim*), *in sarclacione bladi et falcacione prata* (on this account extensions to these forms follow the manuscript, but have been placed in italic to distinguish them from the occasions where the word is written out in full).

Verbs and their forms

Tenses: the imperfect, e.g. *mittebantur*, is commonly used for completed rather than continuous actions in the past, i.e. where a perfect might have been expected, as in II 4.

Number: a singular verb is often followed by a plural sum or quantity, and sometimes vice versa. *Liberetur ... lxxvij qr.* etc. occurs in I 15. *Solutum* and *liberatum* likewise occur before and after sums of money, i.e. without agreement in terms of number. II 4 uses both *ordinatur ..... xx marce* and *ordinantur ad vendendum*. Another common construction is *Levandum sunt* ....., the *sunt* referring, presumably to the plural sum following.

Texts
The Abbot's Estates

I 1 Memoranda compiled at the conclusion of the audit of accounts for the abbot's manors and portions for the year ending on 28 September 1348

A parchment roll, made up of two rotulets attached at the foot by white thread, both approximately 150 mm wide. Rotulet 1 consists of one membrane, rotulet 2 of two membranes sewn Chancery fashion with white thread. Rotulet 2 tapers at the top and has a hole which may be a filing hole. Rotulet 1 is a fair copy in a single hand, with some amendments in a second ink. The recto lists the liveries to officials of the abbot's household in the course of the year, the dorse the debts charged to manorial officials at the close of accounts on 28 September 1348.[1] Rotulet 2 was largely written by a single hand in a single operation. The aim had been to write in the totals as part of this operation. There are small corrections and additions made by this hand as it wrote the text and probably soon afterwards. It contains a summary of corn and stock remaining at the conclusion of the audit, with manorial valors and rents due on 29 September 1348.

WAM 6189

[*Rot. 1, recto*] Memoranda de denariis liberatis fratri B. de Ch*er*tis', Ricardo de Ch*er*iton' et Thome Idelcote de maneriis domini abbatis Westm' anno regni regis Edwardi xxij[2]

*Eyb*ur*y* Serviens ibidem liberavit fratri B. de Chertes' xxj li. xv s. vj d. ob. Prepositus de Lalham, xxvj li. ij s. vij d. Serviens de Stan', xlv li. viij s. x d. Prepositus de Periford, xxx li. xvj s. vij d. qua. Serviens de Denham, lxiij li. xix s. ij d. ob. Prepositus de Islep, lj li. vij s. xj d. Prepositus de Sutton', xviij li. xvij s. Prepositus de Todenham, xij li. ix s. vij d. Prepositus de Borton', xij li. xvij s. iiij d.[3] Prepositus de Herdwyk, lij li. iiij s. vj d. De Ad*a* Broun preposito de Chad', in caseis v s. De Thoma Sp*ar*ke servienti de Chadele, iiij li. De preposito de Langedon' cum rectoria, xxij li. De preposito de Morton' cum rectoria, xx li. De preposito de P*er*shor', xxviij li.
Summa tocius recept*i* CCCCx li. iiij s. j d. qua.

Ricardus de Ch*er*iton computavit. Dixit quod mutuavit domino abbati Westm' CCx li.[4] per ij vices.[5] Item mutuavit per manus B. de Ch*er*tes' xxxv li.

[1] Extant ministers' accounts: Bourton, WAM 8281; Ebury, WAM 26903; Islip, WAM 14795; Laleham, WAM 27135; Longdon manor, WAM 21018; Longdon rectory, WAM 21036; Todenham, WAM 25963.

[2] Benedict de Chertsey was the abbot's receiver and steward of his household, Thomas de Idelcote, the abbot's chamberlain (WAM 14795, 8281–2). Richard de Chiriton was active in the wool trade and a member of the abbot's household with a supervisory role in the manors of the Western Parts (WAM 8278–9).

[3] MS: 'iiij d.' inserted.

[4] MS: 'x' inserted in the same hand.

[5] MS: 'per ij vices' inserted in the same hand.

Item eidem per manus fratris B. de Ch*er*tes' alia vice mense Julij Cxx li. Summa CCClxv li.
De quibus recepit de preposito de Todenham xij li. vj s. De preposito de Borton', vij li. De preposito de Morton', vj li. De preposito de Langedon, lxv s. De preposito de Herdwyk, viij li. x s. De preposito de Pershor', C s. De preposito de Sutton', lx s. Summa xlv li. xij d.
Item recepit de lana de anno preterito apud Sutton' vj saccos viij petras xiij lib., precium sacci viij marcas, preter viij petras xiij lib. pro xx s., xxxiij li.[6]
Item recepit de preposito de Todenham anno xxij^{do} xlv petras. De preposito de Borton, xxvj petras. De preposito de H*er*dwyk', xxxiij petras. De preposito de Chadesle, xxj petras. De preposito de P*er*shor', lvij petras. De prepositis de Sutton' et Islep, xxxiij petras.[7]
Summa CCxv petras quod continet viij saccos vij petras, precium cuiuslibet sacci[8] ut supra, preter vij petras in avantagio, quod continet xlij li. xiij s. iiij d.[9]
Summa totalis recept*i* Cxx li. xiiij s. iiij d. Et sic dominus debet dicto Ricardo CCxliiij li. v s. viij d.[10]
Recepta T. Idilcote anno xxij^{do} Idem recepit de preposito de Perifford', vj li. vj s. ij d. De preposito de Lalham, xv s. ix d. De preposito de Islep, viij li. vj d.[11] ob. qua. De preposito de Todenham, vj li. xvj s. x d. De preposito de Borton',[12] lxxix s. vij d. ob. qua. De preposito de Morton', l s. De preposito de Pershor', xvj li. De Ricardo de Cheriton, x li. Et de lx s. receptis de preposito de Herdwyk'.
Summa tocius recept*i* lvij li. viij s. xj d. ob.[13]

[*Rot. 1, dorse*] Debita ballivorum et prepositorum maneriorum domini abbatis[14]

[6] In the mid-fourteenth century and later, a stone for wool of 14 lb. and a sack of 26 st. are widely mentioned on the abbot's wool-producing manors (WAM 8280–1, 8438A, 14794–5, 22122, 25962). For the variability of these weights in the wider scene, see, however, T. H. Lloyd, *The Movement of Wool Prices in Medieval England.* Economic History Review Supplements, 6 (Cambridge, 1973), p. 2.

[7] The entry relates to the wool of 325 fleeces sent from Islip to Sutton-under-Brailes (WAM 14795). Thus two reeves were involved.

[8] MS: 'cuilibet sacc''.

[9] A reference to the so-called merchant's advantage, whereby, in the buying and selling of agrarian produce by weight, the merchant received 21 for every 20 of the units in use: R. H. Britnell, 'Advantagium Mercatoris': A Custom in Medieval English Trade', *Nottingham Medieval Studies* 24 (1980), pp. 37–50. Richard de Chiriton apparently received the advantage in respect of only 140 of the 215 st. of wool collected from the abbot's manors on this occasion.

[10] MS: 'liiij' written in a second ink, probably correcting another figure.

[11] MS: 's.' struck out before 'd.'

[12] MS: a short erasure follows.

[13] This total is written in a small hand, i.e. not the main text hand.

[14] MS: written in a single column, with the entry for each manor on a new line. In verifiable cases, with only one exception, the debts listed in this schedule represent the preliminary balance

Eyeb*ur*y debet ix li. ix. s. iiij d. ob. Pirford debet xxj li. v s. ix d. Stanes Yeveney[15] debet xj li. xij s. xj d. Denham debet xx s. viij d. ob. Islep debet xxxj li. xvij d. Todenham debet vij li. xvij s. vij d. Bourton debet ix li. v s. ij d. Manerium de Morton' cum rectoria debet xxvij li. xiiij s. viij d. Manerium de Langedon' cum rectoria debet xxxiij li. xvij s. ix d. Ballivus libertatis de H*er*dwik'[16] debet xxxiij s. iiij d. Herdwik' debet xiiij li. xj s. ix d. Rectoria de Chadd' cum manerio debet Ciij s. ix d. ob.[17] Pershore debet xxx li. iij s. v d. ob., unde super Ad*am* Hugh' nuper prepositum ibidem xix li. xj d. qua., et super eundem Ad*am* pro ij cignis vj s. viij d. Sutton' debet lxxiiij s. ij d. qua.

Memorandum quod debita ballivorum de Pershore patent in rotulo sequenti.[18]

[*Rot. 2, mem. 1 recto*] Memoranda de remanenciis super compotum maneriorum domini abbatis Westm', arreragiis redditus termini sancti Michaelis et proficibus maneriorum de anno xxij^{do}[19]

*Eyeb*ury*'* Remanent ibidem iiij qr. ij p. avenarum, iij jumenta, iiij affri femelli, j pullanus femellus etatis di. anni, xv boves, ij tauri, lxj vacce, ij hogastri masculi, j sus, vij porculi etatis di. anni et plus, vij porcelli, xv cigni unde iiij herrarii, ij pave, vij auce unde j anser, iij mariole, j gallus, vj galline, di. corei equini,[20] ij vellera lane, iij batille unde ij squadbotes, ij bus. seminis canabi, xj petre canabi, Cxxvj pecie meremii, M^{1}M^{1}M^{1}M^{1} lathes de corde quercuum. Item remanent ibidem xvj carectates feni per estimacionem in stauro, preter fenum de relucro. Et debet cum manerio ut patet in j cedula huic rotulo consuta.[21]

between charge and discharge when the account of the official in question was closed. For this widespread system, see P. D. A. Harvey, *Manorial Records* (London, 1984), pp. 31–5. For Adam Hugh's debt at Pershore, see below, n. 52.

[15] MS: 'Stanes Yeveney' bracketed together.

[16] MS: 'H*er*dwik' inserted, possibly in another hand.

[17] MS: sum inserted in another hand; 'iiij li. vj s. vj d.' struck out.

[18] Below, I 1.

[19] The term referred to here, and in similar contexts in later documents, is the quarter normally beginning on 24 June and ending on 28 or 29 September. The practice of dealing with the rents of this term, not as hitherto at the audit for the current year, but in that for the ensuing one was adopted in the abbot's manors in the late 1340s. Nevertheless, an estimate of rents to be anticipated in this quarter might be included in the account for the current year.

[20] MS: 'di. corei equini' inserted in another hand.

[21] The reference is to the final debt of Robert atte Noke, bailiff of Eye, the official rendering account, and it amounted to £7 19s. 2½d. (WAM 26903). The schedule, said to be sewn to the present document, does not survive.

Valor manerii xlv li. v s. Redditus et firme termini sancti Michaelis liiij s. vj d. ob. qua.

Pirford' Remanent ibidem iij jumenta, vj boves, j vacca, j hurtardus, j multo, j ovis matrix, ij hogastri, iiij cigni, j coreum vituli tannatum, v vellera, l carectates bruerie, xxxvj clades pro falda. Et debet[22]
Valor manerii lj li. iiij s. Redditus et firme termini Michaelis xviij li. vj s. ix d. ob.

Stanes et ʒeoveney Remanent ibidem ij qr. brasei molendini, v equi carectarii, vj affri, xxij boves, j taurus, xxiij vacce, ij apri, ij sues, xxij porci, xij porculi, vj porcelli, xxix auce unde ij anceres v mariole, ij galli, xij galline, xxx lib. canabi in estimacione, j bus di. seminis canabi, di corei equini,[23] vj pecie meremii unde ij quelibet longitudinis xxxv pedum et iiij quelibet longitudinis xxiiij pedum, xxv clades pro falda, lx tegule plane, ix holuwerk'. Et debet
Valor manerii iiij^{xx}iiij li. iiij s.[24] Redditus et firme termini Michaelis xij li. xiiij s. x d.

Lalham Remanent ibidem ij equi carectarii, iiij affri unde j femellus vetus, xij boves, xx multones, xxxiiij hogastri, xlviij jercie, lxxvj agni, j sus, vij porculi, vj porcelli, iiij pave, j paviculus, xij capones, j gallus, vj galline, j coreum equinum dealbatum, xxxij garbe canabi, di. bus. seminis canabi, j borda fag*ina*, CCCC iij quartrone lathes de corde quercuum, lxvij pecie meremii,[25] vij presepia,[26] xxviij clades pro falda.
Et debet
Valor manerii xxxiij li. iij s. Redditus et firme termini sancti Michaelis Cvj s. v d. ob.

[*Rot. 2, mem. 2 recto*][27] *Denham* Remanent ibidem ii qr. ordei, vij equi carectarii, x jumenta, vj affri, iij pullani masculi etatis ij^{or} annorum di., ij pullani masculi etatis j anni di., v pullani etatis di. anni, xx boves, j taurus, xlj vacce, j taurellus, iiij jumenta, v hurtardi,[28] Cxxxij oves matrices, iij jercie, v agni, j aper, iij sues, xix porci, xxj porculi, x porcelli, xvj cigni, j

[22] In this case, and in all similar cases on rot. 2, no sum follows the words 'et debet' or 'debet' following the name of the debtor.
[23] MS: 'j bus. di. seminis canabi, di. corei equini' inserted, probably in the main text hand.
[24] MS: sum altered from 'iiij^{xx} li. iiij s.' by the main hand while writing this for the first time.
[25] MS: 'lxvij pecie meremii' inserted in the margin, either in the main hand or in a second hand that was very similar.
[26] MS: 'p'sep'. For *rakkes* as a vernacular alternative, see I 2B.
[27] Written in a smaller hand, but very similar to rot. 1, mem. 1.
[28] MS: a short erasure follows.

pava, xiij auce unde j anser iij mariole, xij capones, j gallus, vj galline, j pipa cisere pro aceto habendo.
Et debet
Valor manerii hoc anno lxxvj li. vj s. x d. preter xv li. allocatas pro pensione[29] conventus.
De quibus pro participacione regine xxx li. xj s. viij d., et sic valet xlv li. xvj s. ij d.[30]
Redditus et firme termini sancti Michaelis vj li. xiij s. iij d.

Islep' Remanent ibidem xxiiij qr. vj bus. de puls', xix qr. brasei ordei, xx qr. brasei drageti,[31] ij qr. iij bus. brasei de ray, iiij equi carectarii, j jumentum, j pullanus femellus triennalis, j pullanus femellus biennalis, j pullanus masculus etatis j anni et di., xxxiiij boves, Cxxxij multones, ij hogastri, ij jercie, j aper, iiij sues, xxij porci, xxij porculi, xij porcelli unde vj lactantes, vij cigni herrarii, xlij auce unde ij anseres vij mariole, xviij capones, ij galli et xij galline.
Et debet
Valor manerii hoc anno iiij^{xx}xvij li. iiij s. j d. qua.
Redditus et firme termini Michaelis xv li. vij s. j d. qua.

Todenham Remanent ibidem iiij equi carectarii, xxvj boves, viij hurtardi, Cxlvj multones CCvj oves matrices, xxxv hogastri unde ix hurtardiculi, xiiij jercie, vj agni, j aper, iij sues, v porci, xxxiiij porculi, xxix porcelli, xvj auce unde j anser ij mariole, xxiiij capones, ij galli, xviij galline, Cviij clades pro falda, vij borde quercuum,[32] iij algee pro bidentibus.
Et debet
Valor manerii hoc anno l li. viij s.
Redditus et firme termini Michaelis vj li. xv s. ix d. ob.

Bourton' Remanent ibidem iij jumenta, ij pullani etatis j anni et di. unde j masculus et j femellus, j pullanus masculus etatis di. anni, xviij boves, j multo proveniens de extrahura, Cxlij hogastri et liiij[33] jercie, j aper, ij sues, xxiiij porculi, xiiij porcelli, xx capones, ij galli, x galline, l clades de virgis

[29] MS: 'pensione' inserted.
[30] MS: this sentence inserted. On Edward I's grant of Denham to Westminster Abbey in 1292, as part of the endowment of Eleanor of Castile's anniversary, the manor was appropriated by the abbot for his portion. Previously, however, the prior and convent had enjoyed a fee-farm rent of £15 p.a. from this source. The abbot therefore agreed to give them £15 p.a.—the 'pension' of the above entry—and contribute £30 6s. 8d. p.a. (11s. 8d. per week) from the issues, to be divided between alms for the poor and wages for the monks. The latter payment is the *participacio* referred to in the text, but said there to amount to £30 11s. p.a. For these contentious arrangements, see Flete, *History*, pp. 117–19, and Harvey, *Estates*, p. 339.
[31] MS: 'xx qr. brasei drageti' inserted in the main text hand.
[32] MS possibly 'querci'.
[33] The number in the current manorial account is 154 (WAM 8281).

pro falda,[34] lxx lagene in v barillis tarre pure, j lagena uncti et cepa.
Et debet
Valor manerii xxxvj li. x s.
Redditus et firme sancti Michaelis lx s. iiij d. qua.

Rectoria de Morton' Nichil remanet ibidem.
Prepositus ibidem debet
Valor rectorie x li. xviij s. x d. ob. qua.
Manerium de Morton'[35] Remanent ibidem j aper, ij sues, xij porci, xiiij porculi, xiiij porcelli.
Et debet
Valor manerii lx li. v s. iij d. qua. Redditus et firme termini Michaelis x li. v s. ij d. ob. qua.

Manerium de Langdon' Remanent ibidem ij jumenta, ij pullani femelli etatis ij^{or} annorum, viij boves, xvj auce unde j anser ij mariole, xij capones, j gallus, vj galline.
Et debet
Valor manerii xvij li. Redditus et firme termini Michaelis lxiiij s. viij d. ob. qua.

Rectoria de Langedon' Remanent ibidem ij qr. pisarum et ad triturandum in quoddam tasso[36] per estimacionem xvj qr. pisarum unde[37] ij qr. fabarum, ij jumenta, viij boves, iiij bovetti, ij boviculi, j juvencula, viij vituli superannati, ij apri, iij sues, xvj porci, xx porculi, x porcelli, xxiij auce, xviij capones, j gallus, vj galline, iij pecie meremii, j doleum vacuum, j lucerna.
Et debet
Valor rectorie xvij li. xiij s. ij d. ob.
Redditus et firme termini Michaelis nichil.

[*Rot. 2, mem. 1 dorse*] *Herdwik'* Remanent ibidem iiij qr. iiij bus. multure, vj equi carectarii, lij boves, CCxlvj multones, CCClviij agni, iij apri, iiij sues, xxij porci, xlij porculi, xviij porcelli, iij pavones, xx auce unde j anser iiij mariole, j malardus, ij anates, xxiiij capones, j gallus, xv galline, lxij clades de virgis pro falda, j p. seminis canabi, vj lib. canabi, Cxlvj opera.
Et debet

[34] Followed in the MS by an erasure equivalent in length to a line of text.
[35] The so-called rectory of Castlemorton and that of Chaceley, mentioned below, were dependent chapelries of Longdon rectory.
[36] MS omits 'tasso'.
[37] MS repeats 'unde'.

Valor manerii hoc anno Cvij li. x s.
Redditus et firme termini Michaelis xij li. x s. iij d. ob.

Chadd' Adam Bron' prepositus ibidem per xij septimanas post festum sancti Michaelis anno xxj°.[38] Idem Adam debet

Manerium de Chadd' Tempore Thome *S*par*ke servientis ibidem anno xxij° post predictum Ada*m* etc. Rem*anent* ibidem j equus carectarius femellus, j pullanus femellus biennalis, ix boves, j taurus, xxj vacce, iiij vituli, vij hurtardi, j multo, CCiij oves matrices, ij agni, j aper, ij sues, xj porci, xvij porculi, ix porcelli, xxx auce <u>unde j anser iiij auce mariole</u>, xij capones, j gallus, vj galline.
Et debet
Valor manerii xj li. xij s. vj d.
Redditus et firme termini Michaelis xxj s. iiij d. ob.

Rectoria de Chadd' Remanent ibidem xiij qr. iij bus. de puls'.
Et valet hoc anno ix li. iij s. ij d. ob.

Pershore[39] Remanent ibidem j qr. v bus. siliginis, iij qr. pisarum, iiij bus. multure molendini, j qr. brasei molendini, viij equi carectarii, xxxix boves <u>unde iij de</u> bovettis adjunctis, ij tauri quorum <u>j</u> vetus et debilis, xxvij vacce quarum <u>iij</u> adjuncte, unde <u>j hoc anno</u> primo vitulavit et <u>ij</u> de adjunctione non vitulaverunt hoc anno, iij bovetti, iiij juvence, iiij boviculi, iij juvencule, viij vituli, vij hurtardi, CCxxviij oves matrices, CCxvj multones, ij hogastri, iij jercie, x agni, j aper, iij sues, xxvij porci, xxij porculi, xij porcelli, xvj auce <u>unde j anser ij auce mariole</u>, xxv capones,[40] ij galli, xij galline, j petra canabi per estimacionem, j p. seminis canabi.
Et debet
Valor manerii Cxxx li. xj s. ix d. ob. qua.
Redditus et firme termini Michaelis xxvj li. xij s. ob. qua.

[38] 29 September–22 December 1347.
[39] The following passage relates, first, to the multiple manor of Pershore and its members, Pensham and Pinvin, and secondly to the urban rents and the portmoot of Pershore and to the abbot's income from its liberties in Worcestershire and Gloucestershire. The memoranda of arrears are often verbally identical with similar memoranda for rent-collectors and summary accounts for bailiffs, compiled in 1350–1, covering the years 1344 to 1350–1, and surviving as a discrete document (WAM 22126). Together, the two texts suggest that the abbot kept enrolments of the debts, often large, of these officials, each of whom apparently held office for only one year.
[40] MS: 'xxv capones' inserted, probably in the main hand.

Thomas de Badmynton, ballivus de portmot de Pershore, debet de annis xix° et xx°[41] vij d.
Et rhites ij° annorum, preter x s.,[42] quod continet per estimacionem xiiij s.
Alexander Barret, ballivus de portmoot, debet de anno xxj°[43] xxx s. et v bus. brasei, precium bus. vj d., quod continet ij s. vj d.
Et rhites ij^{or} annorum, que continent per estimacionem xxiiij s.
Et remanent in custodia sua j lagena standarda, xij pondera et ij balances.
Johannes Vanpage, ballivus de portmot, debet xxxiij s. iiij d.
Thomas Part*ri*ch', ballivus hundredorum de Pendefen et Defford', debet xxxix s. iij d.
Willelmus Chese, ballivus hundredi de Wik, debet x s. ij d.
[*Rot. 2, mem. 2 dorse*] Ricardus Chileford', Johannes Arwy, et Thomas atte Welle, collectores redditus de Pershore, debent de anno xviij°[44] iiij s.
Adam Gilberd, Willelmus Pally et Johannes Hugh', collectores redditus de anno xix°,[45] xij s. v d.
Willelmus Cromp, Johannes Kentwyne et Stephanus atte Mor'[46] debent xx s. j d.
Johannes Cok, collector redditus de anno xxj°,[47] debet viij li. iiij s. viij d.[48]
Johannes Osebern de Wik, Willelmus Fox de Pendefen et Willelmus Nichole de Pendesham, collectores redditus de anno xxij°,[49] debent x li. xij s. xj d. ob. qua.
Adam Hugh, nuper prepositus de Pershore, debet xix li. xj d. qua. et vj s. viij d. de ij cignis venditis super compotum hoc anno xxij° qui quidem denarii stalliantur, et debuisset[50] solvisse lx s. ad festum Purificacionis Beate Marie proximum preteritum,[51] et sic de anno in annum quousque etc., unde nichil solvit.[52]

[41] 1344–5 and 1345–6.
[42] WAM 22126 adds 'in anno xxj° solutos'. *Rhites*, alias *riistes* or *riites*, was a kind of ale and also, by association, the name of the tax levied by the abbot of Westminster, at a rate said in 1306–7 to be 5d. per barrel, on every such barrel sold by any of his serfs in the weekly market at Pershore in this period. The bailiff of the portmoot, who administered this custom at Pershore, was entitled to a weekly barrel free of tax. The tax is also mentioned at Longdon in 1348–9 and Castlemorton in 1349–50 (WAM 21019; I 3).
[43] 1346–7.
[44] 1343–4.
[45] 1344–5.
[46] Collectors of rents in 1345–6 (WAM 22126).
[47] 1346–7.
[48] MS: 'iiij s. viij d.' inserted.
[49] 1347–8.
[50] MS: 'debuissent'.
[51] 2 February 1348.
[52] Adam Hugh, reeve of Pershore and of its members, Pensham and Pinvin, is said in 1343–4 to have been the predecessor of John Adkyns, the current reeve, and he was probably in office until

Sutton Remanent ibidem j qr. ij bus. brasei ordei et j qr. ij bus. brasei drageti, ij jumenta, ij pullani femelli biennales, j pullanus femellus etatis j anni et di., ix boves, Cxxxiiij multones, j sus, vj porcelli, j cignus staggus, xxxiij auce unde ij anseres v mariole, xij capones, ij galli, xij galline, j p. seminis canabi, j cista, xxx clades de virgis pro falda.

Et debet

Valor manerii xxx li. xj s.

Redditus et firme termini Sancti Michaelis vij li. iij s. v d. ob.

*c.*29 September 1343. His debt on leaving office was adjusted over two or three years, and the penalty of 6s. 8d. for 2 missing swans was part of the final settlement in 1346. Payment in instalments is first mentioned in this case at the audit of Adkyns' account in 1347. By the end of the year 1348–9, the homage of Pershore had become liable for payment of his arrears, and this arrangement suggests that he was by then dead: WAM 22121–4; I 2B and I 3.

I 2A and B Memoranda compiled at the conclusion of the audit of accounts for the abbot's manors and portions for the year ending on 28 September 1349

A parchment roll of two rotulets, sewn Exchequer fashion with green thread, approximately 145 mm wide. The two rotulets are in different hands. Rotulet 1 contains transactions between Robert de Shareshill, who was steward of the Western Parts 1346–51,[1] and manorial officials in the course of the year; it consists of one membrane now numbered 2A. It was written throughout by a single hand, including the totals, but with some alterations and corrections in that same hand. Rotulet 2 contains a statement of corn and stock remaining at the conclusion of the audit, apportionment of arrears and rents due on 29 September 1349. It consists of two membranes, sewn Chancery fashion with light green thread, and is now numbered 2B. Rotulet 2 is a fair copy, written in a single hand throughout, but it is damaged, and the text is incomplete.[2]

WAM 6180

[I 2A, *Rot. 1, recto*] Memorandum quod Robertus de Sharishulle, seneschallus domini abbatis Westm', recepit de Thoma Wylkyn, preposito de Sutton', x s. ex mutuo.

Item idem Thomas liberavit eidem j jumentum de herietto quod sibi vendebatur super compotum pro di. marca, unde a retro iiij s. viij d.[3]

Item idem Robertus habuit de bonis Johannis Robyns, prepositi de Borton',[4] j carectam cum rotis ferratis que allocatur de arreragiis, precium x s.[5]

Item de Andr*ea* Eyloff', preposito de Langedon', j bovem precium v s., et de eodem Andr*ea* vij s. in denariis.[6]

Item de Willelmo Holdi, preposito de Morton', j bovem, precium iiij s. vj d.[7]

Item de Ricardo Crank, preposito de Herdwyk', ij boves et ij boviculos[8] appreciatos ad xix s. viij d.

[1] WAM 8280–2, 20123–5.

[2] Extant ministers' accounts: Ebury, 28 September 1348–13 April 1349, WAM 26904, and 13 April 1349–28 September 1349, WAM 26905; Islip, 13 September 1348–11 April 1349, WAM 14796, 11 April 1349–27 May 1349 and 27 May–29 September 1349, WAM 14797; Laleham, 28 September 1348 –5 December 1348, WAM 27136, and 5 December 1348–28 September 1349, WAM 21020; Longdon manor, 28 September 1348–14 April 1349, WAM 21019, and 14 April 1349–28 September 1349, WAM 21020; Longdon rectory, 28 September 1348–14 April 1349, WAM 21037, 14 April 1349–28 September 1349, WAM 21038; Staines and Yeoveney, 28 September 1348–24 May 1349 and 24 May 1349–29 September 1349, WAM 16873.

[3] See further below, I 2B, rot 2, mem. 2 recto.

[4] MS: 'prepositi de Borton'' inserted in the main hand of the text.

[5] Robyns, who had been reeve at Bourton-on-the-Hill since 1343, died in the course of 1348–9 (WAM 8278–81; and see below I 2B, rot. 2, mem. 2 recto).

[6] For Eyloff, see below, I 2B. The ox was the heriot of a deceased tenant, the cash a loan.

[7] See further below, I 2B.

[8] MS: 'ij bov' et ij boviculi'.

Item de Johanne Bernard, preposito ibidem, in j bove, ix vaccis, ij bovettis, ij boviculis, j vitulo superannato appreciatis ad xxxv s. vj d.[9]
Item de preposito de Pershore pro feodo de[10] terminis natalis Domini et pasche C s. Item de eodem de termino nativitatis sancti Johannis bapth*iste* vj s.[11]
Item pro ij bovettis liberatis Johanni Mochegros, precepto[12] dicti Roberti, qui vendebantur dicto preposito pro vj s.[13]
Item de Ad*a* Broun, nuper preposito de Chadele, xxiij s. iiij d., unde iij s. iiij d. de quodam fine Radulfi le ȝonge.[14]
Item pro Thoma Sp*ar*k, nuper servienti ad Chad',[15] quem manucepit, xxvij s. xj d.[16]
Item pro j jumento, ij bobus, vj vaccis receptis de Johanne Hademor', preposito de Chad', xxv s. vj d.
Item pro iiij vaccis de [*rot. 1, dorse*] eodem de bonis domini Johannis Sapi xvj s.[17] Summa totalis xv li. xiij d.
Item idem Robertus recepit de Johanne Adekyn, preposito de Pershor', pro ratiocinacione inquisicionis apud Wygorn' racione pontis de Pershor' ad festum purificacionis beate Marie[18] xlv s. iiij d. per j talliam sigillatam. Item eidem alia vice pro eodem x s. Summa lv s. iiij d.[19]

[I 2B, *Rot. 2, mem. 1 recto*] Memoranda de diversis remanentibus super compotum omnium maneriorum domini abbatis Westm' anno xxiij^{cio}[20]

[9] Bernard succeeded Crank in the course of this year (WAM 8437–38A and C).
[10] MS omits 'de'.
[11] Shareshill's stipend was normally paid from the issues of the manor of Pershore, and the variable instalments recorded here are credible examples of the system (WAM 22122–4).
[12] MS: 'preceppto'.
[13] See further below, I 2B. Mochegros is mentioned at Castlemorton and Longdon, 1348×53 (WAM 21022; I 3).
[14] Broun was reeve of Chaceley 21 December 1343–22 December 1347 (WAM 21079–82).
[15] MS: 'nuper servienti ad Chad'' inserted in the main text hand.
[16] For the surety system in a manorial context, see *Medieval Society and the Manorial Court*, ed. Z. Razi and R. Smith (Oxford, 1996), pp. 213–14 and 232–3.
[17] Sapi, a landowner in Pershore, was also a customary tenant of the abbot of Westminster in Chaceley and Longdon, and in Pershore itself, and one of his tenants for life there. He died in or before December 1348, when 8 of his cows were delivered as heriots by the reeve of Pershore to the reeve of Longdon (WAM 52016, 21037, 24408).
[18] 2 February 1349.
[19] The latest phase in the long-running dispute between the abbot of Westminster and the abbot of Pershore, about obligations for the repair and maintenance of Pershore Bridge, was marked by the verdict of a jury in Hilary Term in the court of King's Bench that inhabitants of Pershore shared responsibility in this matter with the abbots of Westminster. Shareshill's expenditure on the jury coincided with the beginning of the above term. For the jury's verdict, see *Public Works in Mediaeval Law*, ed. C. T. Flower (Selden Society, 40; 1923), pp. 361–2; and for the bridge itself, D. Harrison, *The Bridges of Medieval England. Transport and Society, 400–1800* (Oxford, 2004), p. 212.
[20] MS repeats regnal year.

Pirford Remanent ibidem super auditum compoti sui iij affri femelli, iiij boves, j vacca, ij multones, j ovis matrix, l carectates bruerie parvi valoris, xl clades[21] unde xx debiles.
Walterus Cosyn, nuper prepositus ibidem, debet xxiij li. vj s. vj d. qua.[22]
Robertus ate Wade, nunc prepositus, debet lxvij s. iij d.
Et valet manerium hoc anno[23]
Memorandum de redditu termini Michaelis cum tallagio, preter decasum redditus, ad minus xviij li.

Lalham Remanent ibidem ad triturandum per estimacionem in garbis xxvj qr. ordei de exitu anni precedentis. Item remanent ibidem ij equi carectarii, viij affri, unde v femelli unde j de stray', xxxvj boves, iij vacce, iij bovetti, ij juvence, v boviculi, j juvencula, j ovis matrix, j agnus de exitu, j sus, vj porcelli lactantes, j pavo, iiij pave, iiij paviculi, xij capones, j gallus, vj galline, j cor*i*um di. equinum dealbatum, ij petre cannabis, petra de viij lib., di. bus. seminis cannabis, j borda fagina, CC et di. xx lathe*s* de corde quercuum, lxviij pecie meremii, vij rakkes pro bidentibus, Cx tal*u*wode.
Et Johannes South' nuper prepositus ibidem debet[24] iiij li. vij s. vj d.
Et Johannes le Heyward' nunc prepositus ibidem debet, cum xxj s. j d. de diversis rebus et catallis nativorum existentibus etc.,[25] lxxix s. j d.
Memorandum de redditu termini Michaelis cum tallagio preter decasum Ciij s.

Stanes Yeveney Remanent ibidem iiij equi carectarii unde j debilis, vij affri unde v masculi, j equus molendini, xix boves unde ix cronardi, j taurus, xxviij vacce unde ij cronardi, ij juvencule, ij apri, ij sues, xvij porci, xvij porculi,[26] vj porcelli, xxxj auce unde ij anseres v mariole, ij galli, xij galline, di. bus. seminis cannabis, v pecie di. meremii, quorum ij longitudinis xxv pedum et iij et di. longitudinis xxiiij pedum, iij coria equina dealbata, xj clades pro falda.
Et Johannes atte Noke nuper serviens ibidem debet xij li. xxj d. qua., unde super Johannem Cosyn messorem xlv s. ij d. ob. qua., super Willelmum

[21] MS omits 'clades'.
[22] Cosyn was reeve of Pyrford 1346–7 and possibly until a point in the year 1348–9 (WAM 27145).
[23] Followed by a blank space in the MS.
[24] MS omits 'debet'.
[25] Cf. the phrase used in the current minister's account (WAM 27136): 'de diversis rebus de bonis nativorum arestatis ut patet per parcellas'.
[26] MS: 'xvij porculi' inserted in main hand.

Takepany messorem vj s. vj d., et super Thomam Cosyn messorem ix li. xij s. vij d. ob.[27]
Et Johannes Crendone nunc serviens excedit xliiij s. vij d. ob.[28]
Memorandum de redditu termini Michaelis cum tallagio preter decasum xj li.

Denham Remanent ibidem xliiij qr. iiij bus. di. brasei drageti, iiij equi carectarii, x jumenta, v affri, iij pullani masculi etatis iij annorum et di., ij pullani masculi etatis ij annorum et di., j pullanus femellus etatis j anni et di., ij pullani de exitu unde j masculus et j femellus etatis di. anni, xxx boves, ij tauri, xliij vacce, iiij hurtardi, Cxxiij oves matrices, j multo,[29] j hogaster, Cij agni, ij apri, iij sues, xiiij porci, xij porculi, xij porcelli, xxj cigni unde iiij errarii vj staggi xj cigniculi j pavo, j pava, xv auce unde j anser iij mariole, xij capones, j gallus, vj galline, j cor*i*um et j qua. equinum dealbatum, Cxxiiij vellera, Cv vellera agnorum, M^{l}DCCiiij^{xx}x talwode, M^{l} bylet'.
Et Nigell*us* de Padyngton' nuper serviens debet lj s. ix d. ob. qua.
Et Robertus atte Noke nuper serviens debet xxxvij s. xj d. qua.[30]
Et Johannes South' nuper serviens debet xxxiij s. ij d. ob.
Et Johannes Hanecok' nunc serviens debet xliij s. iiij d. qua.
Memorandum de redditu termini Michaelis preter decasum etc. iiij li. ij s.

Eyebury Remanent ibidem j qr. siliginis, et ad triturandum per estimacionem in garbis x qr. mixtilionis. Item remanent ij qr. iij bus. pisarum, iiij qr. iiij bus. ordei et ad triturandum, et in pallea per estimacionem xxx qr., unde x qr. ordei[31] in pallea triturand*um* per j hominem existentem in curia. Item remanent iij jumenta, viij pullani quorum iij masculi etatis j anni et di. et iij femelli etatis j anni di. et ij pullani de exitu,[32] ij affri femelli, vij boves, ij tauri, lix vacce, j sus pregnans, ij porculi, xxij cigni unde iij errarii vj staggi xij cigniculi, ij pave, iiij auce unde j anser iij mariole, j cor*i*um

[27] John atte Noke was serjeant of Staines and Yeoveney 28 September 1348–24 May 1349, the date of his death. John Cosyn was collector of rents and estreats as well as reap-reeve at Staines 29 September 1348–19 January 1349, when he was removed from office. William Takepenny was woodward at Yeoveney 29 September 1348–24 May 1349, when he died; and for the greater part of this period, if not the whole, he was also collector of rents and estreats and reap-reeve. Thomas Cosyn was collector of rents and estreats and reap-reeve at Staines 3 March 1349–1 August 1349, when he died (WAM 16872, rots. 1–2).

[28] Crendon was serjeant of Staines and Yeoveney 24 May–8 June 1350. The excess of £2 4s. 7d. relates to his account for the period 24 May–29 September 1349 (WAM 16872–3).

[29] MS: 'multon''.

[30] Robert atte Noke's service at Denham preceded similar service at Ebury which began on 9 January 1342 (WAM 26896).

[31] MS: 'ordei' inserted.

[32] MS: 'viij pullani quorum … ij pullani de exitu' inserted in same hand but in a darker ink.

vacc*ineum* crudum, et iiij batill*i* unde ij squadbots, ij bus. seminis cannab*is*,[33] xj petre cannabis, petra de vij lib., M[1]M[1] M[1] ixC di. lathys.
Robertus atte Noke, nuper serviens, debet xxxj s. vj d. qua.
Et Philippus Ploumtr' excedit[34]
Memorandum de redditu termini Michaelis preter decasum redditus xxix s.

Islepp' Remanent ibidem xiij qr. j bus. iij p. puls', et ad triturandum per estimacionem in ij finibus duorum tassorum xx qr. puls'. Item remanent ibidem xxxj qr. di. bus. ordei, et ad triturandum in quodam tasso per estimacionem xl qr. ordei. Item remanent xx qr. vj bus. drageti. Item remanent vj qr. iij bus. brasei frumenti, xxiiij qr. iij bus. brasei ordei, iiij equi carectarii, ij jumenta, j pullanus femellus triennalis, j pullanus masculus biennalis, xxxix boves, xv vacce unde j juvenca non vitulavit, j bovettus, j multo,[35] ij apri, iiij sues, xx porci, xviij porculi, x porcelli, xiij cigni unde vij errarii, lxiij auce unde ij anseres vij auce mariole, xviij capones, ij galli, xij galline, j doleum cisere, ij batill*i*, vij olle enee, j securis.
Et Cecilia, nuper uxor Willelmi Dolle quondam prepositi ibidem, debet[36] Cij s. unde dominus posuit in respectum, ut patet in pede compoti, xlv s.[37]
Ricardus le Hounte, prepositus ibidem post ipsum, debet vj li. xvj s. ij d. ob.
Thomas Bigge prepositus ibidem post ipsum debet vij li. vj s. v d.[38]
Memorandum de redditu et firmis termini Michaelis preter decasum per estimacionem xiiij li. x s.

Suttone Remanent ibidem ad triturandum per estimacionem vij qr. frumenti. Item remanent ad triturandum per estimacionem viij qr. puls'. Item remanent ibidem iiij qr. ij bus. iij p. brasei ordei, xxix qr. vj bus. brasei drageti. Item remanent ibidem ij jumenta, ij pullani femelli triennales, j pullanus masculus biennalis, j pullanus masculus etatis j anni et di., ij

[33] MS: 'ij bus. seminis cannabis' inserted in main text hand.
[34] MS leaves sum blank. Plumtre succeeded Noke as serjeant of Ebury on 13 April 1349 and served until 28 September 1349. His excess when his account was closed amounted to £1 16s. 3d. But his actual claims were much larger and were subsequently allowed on the intervention of the abbot. See WAM 26905.
[35] MS: 'multon''.
[36] MS: 'debet' omitted.
[37] William Dolle, reeve of Islip since 1332, died on 13 September 1348. The respite of £2 5s. in the outstanding debt of Cecilia, his widow, a year later recognised the depredations of royal purveyors on demesne supplies of grain at Islip in 1345–6 and the respites previously granted to her husband on these grounds. She was left, finally, with a debt of £2 17s. (WAM 14794–6).
[38] Richard Hunte died on 11 April 1349. His posthumous account for the period 13 September 1348–1 April 1349 was not formally audited, but the final debt of £6 16s. 2½d. was approved at the end of the current year. Thomas Bigge, alias Thomas le Hunte, was not so fortunate, and at the same audit, his debt was raised to £15 2s. 8½d. (WAM 14797).

pullani etatis di. anni unde j masculus et j femellus, ix boves, ij vacce, j multo,[39] j sus, v porci, vj porculi, vij porcelli, j cignus staggus, xxxvij auce unde ij anseres v mariole, xij capones, ij galli, xij galline, j p. seminis cannabis, x lib. cannabis, v carcosia et iij qua. unius carcosii bovis.
[*Rot. 2, mem. 2 recto*] Item remanet j cista.
Et Thomas Wylkyns, prepositus ibidem, debet iiij li. x s. j d. qua. De quibus ponuntur in respectu xiiij s. viij d., unde x s. quos mutuavit Roberto Shareshulle et iiij s. viij d. de j jumento eidem Roberto vendito plus quam recepit.[40]
Memorandum[41] de redditu et firmis termini Michaelis, preter decasum, per estimacionem viij li.
Et[42] sic debet de claro xxv s. v d.

Todenham Remanent ibidem ad triturandum per estimacionem xl qr. frumenti. Item remanent ibidem in granario vj qr. ij bus. di.[43] mixtilionis. Et remanent ad triturandum per estimacionem v qr. mixtilionis. Item[44] remanent ix qr. j bus. j p. puls', et ad triturandum per estimacionem xxxviij qr. puls'. Item remanent in granario xxj qr. ij bus. ordei, et ad triturandum per estimacionem xv qr. ordei. Item remanent in granario xvij qr. j bus. avenarum vescosarum, xiij qr. iiij bus. brasei ordei. Item remanent ibidem iiij equi carectarii, xxvij boves, j vacca, vij hurtardi, ij multones, Clxxvj oves matrices, Clxj agni, ij apri, vj sues, viij porci, xxxvij porculi, xxv porcelli, xvj auce unde j anser ij auce mariole, xxiiij capones, ij galli, xviij galline, lx clades pro falda, v bordes quercine, iij algee[45] pro bidentibus, x lagene et di. de tarra in quodam barello.
Et debet de claro xvij s. xj d. ob. qua.
Memorandum de redditu et firmis termini Michaelis preter decasum vj li. x s.

Bourtone Remanent ibidem ij bus. et p. puls', et ad triturandum per estimacionem v qr. puls'. Item remanent ibidem in granario ij qr. ij bus. ordei, et ad triturandum per estimacionem vij qr. ordei. Item remanent

[39] MS: 'multon''.
[40] MS: the whole of this sentence from 'De quibus' is an insertion, probably in the main hand. See I 2A.
[41] MS: preceded by a marginal note, 'ȝ b', i.e. suggesting that it should follow the succeeding entry.
[42] MS: preceded by a marginal note, 'ȝ a'.
[43] MS: 'di.' inserted.
[44] MS: the sentence beginning 'Item remanent' about pulses has been inserted in smaller handwriting, but probably by the main hand.
[45] MS: 'algea'.

ibidem iij jumenta, xviij boves, j vacca, j multo,[46] Cxlv hogastri, x jercie unde iij oves steriles, j aper, ij sues, vj porci, xxv porculi, x porcelli, xx capones, ij galli, x galline, l clades debiles pro falda, ij olle enee, j patella enea,[47] xlix lagene et di. de tarra in iij barellis et in fundo unius alii barelli quorum quodlibet integrum ba[rellum contin]et[48] xiiij lagenas, M^{l}Cviij fagoti.
Et Johannes Robyns debet xxi ..... et non plus quia respectuantur eidem xiiij s.[49] viij d. de avenis c[aptis ad] opus domini regis et x s. de j carecta cum rotis ferratis quem [R. de] Shareshulle abduxit de bonis dicti Johannis.[50] Et Robertus on the Hulle nunc prepositus excedit xj s. j d.
[Memorandum] de redditu et firmis termini Michaelis preter decasum per estimacionem lvj s.

[*Hardwicke*][51] Remanent ibidem xj qr. vj bus. frumenti unde ix qr. vj bus.
.....
Et ad triturandum per estimacionem l qr. iiij bus. frumenti
..... ij qr. fabarum. Et ad triturandum per estimacionem
..... rem' ad triturandum per estimacionem viij .....
.....ur' molendi. Item .....
..... boves iij vac.....
.....r' vj st' .....

[*Rot. 2, mem. 1 dorse*][52] *Rectoria de Chaddeslee* Remanent ibidem ad triturandum per estimacionem x qr. siliginis. Item remanent in granario ibidem xxviij qr. vj bus. di. puls'.
Et nichil debetur quia arreragia ibidem omnino onerantur in compoto suo de manerio.[53]

[46] MS: 'multon''.
[47] MS: 'ij ollas eneas, j patell' eneam'.
[48] Hole in MS: passage in square brackets here and following lines conjectural.
[49] MS: 'iiij s.'; WAM 8278–81, 'xiiij s.'
[50] The first of the two respites granted by the auditors on the last—and as we can assume—posthumous, account relates to the seizure of 7 qr. of oats over a period of three years, beginning in 1345–6 (WAM 8278–81). For Sharehill's seizure of the cart from Robyns' goods, see I 2A.
[51] From this point onwards, the MS is fragmentary, tapering to a point. Each line of text lacks its original beginning and end. On the front, a substantial part of the entry for Hardwicke and the entire entries for Chaceley manor and Deerhurst are now lost. On the back, the concluding entries relating to the bailiffs of the abbot's liberties are lost.
[52] There is a good deal of blank space at the head of the dorse.
[53] A reference to the account of John Hathemere, who had become reeve of Chaceley manor by 28 September 1349 and, in accordance with normal practice, of the rectory as well (WAM 21083).

Rectoria de Longdone Remanent ibidem ad triturandum per estimacionem in garbis xl qr. frumenti. Item remanent ibidem in granario vij qr. v bus. di. mixtilionis humidi, xj qr. vj bus. j p. puls', et ad triturandum per estimacionem xxx qr. j p. puls'. Item remanent iij bus. avenarum.[54] Item remanent ibidem ij jumenta, viij boves, ij vacce, ij apri unde j crassatus, iij sues, xx porci, xv porculi, xxiiij porcelli unde xiiij lactantes, vj auce unde j anser iiij auce mariole, xviij capones, j gallus, vj galline, ij mulveles pess*ouns* sals*e*,[55] iij pecie meremii, j doleum vacuum, j lucerna.
Et nichil debetur ibidem quia omnino patet in compoto suo de manerio.[56]
Memorandum de denariis redditus et firmarum termini Michaelis per estimacionem ij s. viij d.

Manerium de Langedon' Remanent ibidem vj bus. di. scuralli mixtilionis, et ad triturandum per estimacionem in garbis iiij qr. mixtilionis. Item remanent in granario iiij bus. puls' et ad triturandum per estimacionem xvj qr. puls',[57] v jumenta, v pullani unde iij etatis iij annorum, unde j masculus, et ij pullani de exitu femelli etatis di. anni, xvj boves, j vacca, xv auce unde ij anseres v marole, xij capones, j gallus, vj galline,[58] j corium vacceneum crudum.
Andreas Eyloff' nuper prepositus ibidem debet de claro xxxiij s. iij d. ob.,[59] et non plus quia super Willelmum Boteler in respectu xvij li. xviij s. iiij d. qua.[60] Et super Robertum Shareshulle senescallum xj s. vj d., unde iiij s. vj d. de j bove et vij s. in denariis sibi mutuatis.
Et Willelmus But nuper prepositus debet viij li. xvj s. vj d. ob. qua. ad quod debitum Ricardus de Underhulle habet parcellas de nominibus debitorum.
Et Ricardus Underhulle debet viij s. iiij d.

[54] MS: 'Item remanent iij bus. avenarum', an insertion in small script by the text hand.
[55] MS: 'mulveles pess' sals'', probably intended to be French: salted codfish.
[56] A reference to the account of Richard Underhill, now serjeant of Longdon manor and rectory.
[57] MS: 'et ad triturandum per estimacionem xvj qr. puls'' inserted by the text hand.
[58] An erasure 50 mm in length occurs at this point in the MS.
[59] MS: 'iij d. ob.' interlined in the text hand.
[60] Eyloff was reeve of Longdon manor and rectory 28 September 1347–14 April 1349 (WAM 21018–19, 21036). There follows a summary of the allowances and respites recorded in greater detail in his final, posthumous, account for the manor of Longdon for the period 28 September 1348–14 April 1349; these reduced his arrears to the final 'clear' sum of £1 13s. 3½d. mentioned above (WAM 21019). William Boteler was probably bailiff of Longdon manor and rectory 1347–8, and also granger there in the summer of 1348, but left, probably in 1349, to serve at Castlemorton (WAM 21019, 21037–8; and see the present account, below). William But was Eyloff's immediate predecessor as reeve of Longdon manor and rectory and may have held office since 1341–2 (WAM 21017–19). Underhill was serjeant of Longdon manor and rectory 14 April 1349–29 September 1350 and probably since Boteler's departure (WAM 21019–22, 21037–9). He was also collector of court estreats, and in this capacity had duties extending to Castlemorton (I 3).

Memorandum de redditu termini Michaelis cum tallagio et firmis preter decasum lx s.

Rectoria de Mortone[61] Frumentum. Nichil remanet,[62] set memorandum quod mutuat*um* in compoto iij qr. vj bus. frumenti. Et remanent ibidem ad triturandum per estimacionem xvj qr. frumenti. Item remanent ibidem ad triturandum per estimacionem xxx qr. fabarum et puls'.
Et remanent ibidem super compotum iiij qr. vij bus. iij p. puls'.
Et remanent ibidem ad triturandum per estimacionem xx qr. puls', iiij qr. ordei, et ij qr. avenarum. De stauro nec de arreragiis nichil.

Manerium de Mortone Frumentum. De remanencia in granario nichil, sed ad triturandum per estimacionem iij qr. frumenti. Item remanent j bos, iiij vacce in custodia prepositi de Chadd', j aper, ij sues, xij porci, viij porculi, vj porcelli non decimati.
Willelmus Holdy, nunc prepositus, debet xiiij li. xvij s. ix d. et non plus quia super Robertum Shareshulle senescallum respectuatur iiij s. vj d. de j bove sibi vendito.[63] Et super Willelmum Boteler in respectu vij li. xij s. vij d.
Et Thomas Paal, nuper prepositus ibidem, debet adhuc C s. iiij d. ob. qua., ad quod debitum Ricardus de Underhulle habet parcellas fere de nominibus eorum ad levandum etc.[64]

*Pershore, Pendesh*am*, Pendefen* Frumentum. Nichil remanet [in granario]. Set remanet apud Pendesham ad triturandum per estimacionem j qr. frumenti. Item apud Pendefen ad triturandum per estimacionem viij qr. frumenti. Et remanent in granario super compotum j qr. v bus. mixtilionis, iiij qr. ij bus. siliginis. Item remanent apud Persshore ad triturandum per estimacionem v qr. siliginis. Et apud Pendefen ad triturandum per estimacionem j qr. iiij bus. siliginis. Et remanent in granario xxxviij qr. vj bus. di. pisarum. Et apud Pendesham ad triturandum per estimacionem xj qr. pisarum. Et remanent in granario vij bus. ordei. Et remanent apud Pendefen ad triturandum per estimacionem ij qr. ordei. Et apud Pendesham per estimacionem vj qr. ordei. Item remanent in granario v qr. vj bus. iij p. drageti. Et apud Pendesham ad triturandum per estimacionem iij qr. drageti. Et apud Pendefen ad triturandum per estimacionem v qr. drageti. De avenis in granario nichil remanet. Set apud Pendefen ad triturandum

[61] MS: 'mutuatum' inserted above this heading in the text hand.
[62] i.e. no wheat harvested in 1348 remained. The rest of the entry on wheat refers to wheat harvested in 1349; for the 16 qr. not yet threshed, see also I 3.
[63] For this transaction, see I 2A above.
[64] Paal was probably reeve of Castlemorton 1348–9; for his debt see also I 3.

per estimacionem iiij qr. avenarum. Et apud Pendesham ad triturandum per estimacionem x qr. avenarum. Item remanent ij qr. v bus. j p. mixture molendini. De braseo molendini nichil remanet.
[*Rot. 2, mem. 2 dorse*] Item remanent ibidem vj equi carectarii unde j equus molendini,[65] ij affri, xxxvij boves, ij tauri unde j vetus et debilis, xxix vacce, quarum iij steriles et iij de adjunctione hoc anno et non vitulaverunt, vj boves, iij juvence, ix boviculi, vj juvencule, j vitulus, viij hurtardi, Clxvij oves matrices, xxxiiij multones, lv agni, ij apri, iij sues, xxix porci, xxj porculi, xvj porcelli, xvj auce quarum j anser ij auce mariole, xxiiij capones, ij galli, xij galline, C casse bidencium, di. petre cannabis, ij p. seminis cannabis, j olla enea defracta continens ij lagenas sine pede apud Pendesham.
Johannes Adekyns prepositus nunc debet x li. xviij s. iij d., et non plus quia respectuantur eidem iij s. de vj cassis multonum liberatis J. Gloucestr',[66] et vj s. de bovettis liberatis J. Mochegros, precepto R. Shareshulle, pro quo dictus R. est responsurus,[67] et xix li. xj d. qua. currentes super totum homagium pro arreragiis nuper Ade Hugh, prepositi ibidem, quod quidem stallatum fuit solvendum annuatim ad festum purificacionis beate Marie[68] lx s., quousque predictum debitum fuerit solutum.
Memorandum de redditu et tallagio termini Michaelis cum firmis per estimacionem preter decasum redditum xxiiij li.
Ricardus Cherlefford',[69] Johannes Arwy et Thomas atte Welle, collectores redditus de anno xviij^{o},[70] debent[71] ij s. viij d.
Adam Gilberd', Willelmus Palli et Johannes Hugh', collectores redditus de anno xix^{o},[72] debent ij s. v d.

[65] Pershore had three mills, and throughout the fourteenth century the inclusion of a mill horse in inventories of livestock here betrays the continued existence of a mill of this kind; for a late example, see I 23; and for the mills, WAM 22093, 22113, 22211. On such mills, and their frequent use for malt-grinding and in urban situations, see J. Langdon, *Mills in the Medieval Economy: England 1300–1540* (Oxford, 2004), pp. 125–6.
[66] Bailiff and granger in the Western Parts (WAM 22124).
[67] For this transaction, see above, I 2A.
[68] 2 February.
[69] There are holes in the MS here. Editorial insertions, in square brackets, in the remaining text, other than those of a routine character, derive from entries relating to Pershore portmoot in I 1. For the enrolled accounts which were probably the source of the following memoranda relating to the arrears of the abbot's rent-collectors in Pershore and the bailiffs of the portmoot there, see I 1. All the arrears mentioned in the present document were still outstanding when the enrolled accounts for the year 1350–1 were compiled (WAM 22126). Among the rent-collectors named, John Hugh, William Cromp, John Kentwen and John Cok are said to be dead; and the silent omission of Richard Cherlefford suggests that he, too, had died.
[70] 1343–4.
[71] MS omits 'debent'.
[72] 1344–5.

Willelmus C[romp'] de Pendefen, Johannes Kentwen de Pendesham, et Stephanus [atte Mo]re de Wyke, collectores redditus de anno xx^{mo},[73] debent xiiij s. v d.

Johannes Cok, c[ollector] redditus et firm*arum* omnino pro terminis sancti Andr*ee*, pasch*e*, et nativitatis [sancti] Johannis baptiste de anno xxj^{o},[74] debet vj li. ij s. vj d.

Johannes Osebern de Wyke, Willelmus Fox de Pendefen [et] Willelmus Nichole de Pendesham', collectores redditus d[e anno xxij^{o}][75] debent lxviij s. j d. ob. qua.

Thomas de Bad[m]yngton', ballivus de port'mot' [debet de annis] xix^{o} et xx^{o}[76] [vij d.], preter x s. de ryhttes in anno xxj ^{o} [solutos, et] ryhttes ij annorum solv*endum*.[77]

Alexander Baret nuper ballivus de portmot' d[ebet] de annis xix^{o} et xx^{o}, preter x s. de rightes in anno xxj^{o}, [v bus.] brasei, precium bus. vj d., ij s. vj d.[78]

[Et remanent in custodia sua j lagena] standarda, ij balances [et xij pondera.] ..... de portmot' ..... lxxj

[73] 1345–6.

[74] i.e. for the quarters ending, respectively, on 30 November 1346, and 1 April and 24 June 1347.

[75] 1347–8.

[76] 1344–5 and 1345–6.

[77] MS adds: 'x s. ut supra'. 1346–7.

[78] MS: 'vij d., ij s. v d.'

I 3 States of the abbot's manors and portions in the Western Parts for the period 29 September 1349 to 24 June 1350

A parchment roll of four membranes, Chancery fashion. Membranes 1 and 2 are sewn together with green thread; 2 and 3, and 3 and 4, with white thread. A substantial part of the first membrane, measuring 180 mm in width at the top but narrowing to 55 mm at the bottom, was torn away before the dorse was used. On the recto, we should also allow for the loss of the title of the document except for the words *Status super*, and loss of a significant part of each of the first ten lines of the entry relating to Islip. It is, however, impossible to measure exactly the losses in the affected lines. On membrane 1 recto, many of the sums have been crossed out, and some were altered in a second hand. The dorse of membrane 1 is a fair copy, as are membranes 2 and 3 recto and dorse; membrane 4 recto is a fair copy, but in a different hand. Although much of the roll is a fair copy, it has not been laid out with folds or rulings, unlike later states.

The document covers three rental terms: Michaelmas and Christmas 1349, and Easter 1350. But its focus is on the view of the abbot's manors held in principle on 25 March 1350. The final date for the submission of returns to the view from the manors was 1 May 1350, but many even later entries found their way into the final document.[1] Unless otherwise indicated, panels in the document recording anticipated yields of corn or target yields—which of the two is intended is not always clear—relate to corn sown in the winter or spring of the year 1348–9, harvested, if harvested at all, in the summer and autumn of 1349, and threshed, if at all, in the first half of 1349–50, the period covered by the document.

Longdon manor and Longdon rectory are omitted from the document, and this is explained by the assignment of the issues of each to the new work in the cloister and monastic buildings for the years 1349–52.[2]

WAM 24408

[*Mem. 1 recto*] Status super .....

[Islip]

Frumentum. R*esponsurus*[3] minus tercio vij qr. ..... Pise. Responsurus minus semine et di. ..... Ordeum. Responsurus plus se altero et di. ..... Dragetum. Responsurus minus se altero ...... Avene. Responsurus plus se[4] vij° j bus. .....

Seminacio. Seminantur ibidem xxviij qr. v[5] [bus.] ..... s[uper terram] nativorum, iij qr. vj bus. p[isarum super terram nativorum], v qr. iiij bus.

[1] Extant ministers' accounts, each of which, with the exception of Staines and Yeoveney, runs from Michaelmas 1349 to Michaelmas 1350: Bourton-on-the-Hill, WAM 8282; Chaceley, WAM 21083; Ebury, WAM 26906; Hardwicke, WAM 8438A; Pershore, Pensham and Pinvin, WAM 22124; Staines and Yeoveney, 28 September 1349–8 June 1350 and 8 June–29 September 1350, WAM 16873, rots. 1–2.

[2] WAM 23451.

[3] MS: 'R'. In this context, the initial R is never extended in MS. For a similar case, see *Manorial Records of Cuxham*, ed. Harvey, p. 794.

[4] MS omits 'se'.

[5] MS: a further digit may now be lost.

ordei ..... Seminantur ibidem xij qr. vij bus. drageti ....., unde v qr. iij bus. tempore Willelmi Dolle.[6] Item seminantur ..... bus. avenarum.
Remanencia. Et remanent super compotum Thome le Hunte[7] ij qr. iij bus. frumenti, et tritur*abantur* tempore W. Dolle ix qr. ij bus. frumenti, et ad triturandum per estimacionem in garbis vj qr. frumenti. Item remanent super compotum dicti Thome iiij qr. ij bus. pisarum unde j qr. ij bus. humid*e*, et ad triturandum per estimacionem xx qr. veterum pisarum.[8] Item remanent super compotum dicti Thome vj bus. ordei; et tritur*antur* tempore W. Dolle xxij qr. vj bus. ordei, et ad triturandum per estimacionem in pallea xxx qr. ordei,[9] de quibus W. Dolle seminavit xix qr. iiij bus. ordei. Item remanent super compotum dicti Thome vij qr. drageti, unde seminant*ur* tempore W. Dolle v qr. iij bus. drageti. Item remanent ij qr. avenarum unde vij bus. in farina. Item j qr. ij bus. brasei frumenti, xxxvij qr. iiij bus. brasei ordei, viij qr.[10] brasei drageti. Item j qr. iiij bus. et di. p. multure in manibus molendinarii.[11] Item remanent iiij equi carectarii, ij jumenta, j pullanus masculus biennalis, xxxvj boves, j bovettus de extrahura, ... affri debiles, iiij pullani biennalles, j boviculus, et ij vituli superannati, ij apri, iiij sues, xxij porci, iiij porculi, viij porcelli, vij cigni herarii,[12] ij cignotti, ij anseres, vij auce mariole, et xliiij aucule decimate, ij galli, xij galline, j doleum cisere quasi asceti in ij pipis, unde ascetum unius pipe fere expenditum in hospicio domini.
Recepcio De arreragiis ultimi compoti xx li. iiij s. viij d. ob. De redditu assiso xxvij li. xvij d.; de firmis iij terminorum xxx s. j d. ob. qua.; de chevagio xiij d.; de vendicione bladi xvj li. ij s. x d. ob.;[13] de vendicione stauri lxv s. vij d.;[14] de mortuo stauro xiiij s. iij d.;[15] de exitu manerii liij s.

[6] William Dolle the younger, son of William Dolle the elder with Cecilia, his wife. Served as demesne sower, holding the plough in the winter of 1348–9, and as granger in the summer of 1349 (WAM 14797). One of the granger's responsibilities was to supervise threshing.
[7] Reeve of Islip 27 May 1349–28 September 1349 and beyond; his account for this period also includes the short period of office of William Ottele, 27 April–11 May 1349 (WAM 14797).
[8] i.e. peas harvested in 1348.
[9] Cf. the previous estimate of 40 qr. (I 2B).
[10] MS: 'iiij bus. di.' struck out.
[11] MS: 'Item j qr. iiij bus. et di. p. multure in manibus molendinarii' inserted.
[12] MS: 'xiij porculi, x porcelli superannales, vij porcelli de ex*itu*, xij cigni, quorum vij herarii' struck out; 'xxij porci ... vij cigni herarii' inserted in a second hand.
[13] MS: 'xiiij li. xiiij s. ob.' struck out; new sum inserted in a second hand, which also made the other insertions in this paragraph.
[14] MS: 'xj s. x d.' struck out; new sum inserted.
[15] MS: 'xiij s. j d. ob.' struck out; new sum inserted.

iiij d. ob. qua.[16] De bonis nativorum defunctorum venditis lxij s. viij d.[17] ..... De perquisitis curie vj li. iiij s. j d.

Summa totalis recepti cum arreragiis iiij^{xx} li. xix s. ij d. ob.[18]

Expense In allocacionibus redditus iij terminorum lxvj s. v d. ob.[19] In defectu redditus xxxv s. xj d.; in defectu tallagii x s. j d.; in denariis solutis taxatoribus quinte decime[20] pro terra nativorum vij s. viij d.;[21] in defectu redditus pro termino nativitatis sancti Johannis baptisti ultimo preterito, non petito neque allocato iij s. j d. In custu carucarum xiiij s. x d.[22] In custu carectarum xvij s. vij d. ob. In custu domorum xxv s. ij d. ob. qua. In custu molendini liiij s. iiij d. In minutis xxxj s. ij d. qua. In trituracione bladorum xxxix s. vj d. ob. In blado empto ix s. In stipendiis famulorum xxxvj s. viij d.[23] In expensis superveniencium x s. xj d. In expensis forinsecis xliiij s. ix d. ob.[24] In solucionibus forinsecis xxxvj s. viij d. In denariis liberatis xlj li.[25]

Summa omnium expensarum et liberacionum lxiij li. vj s. j d.[26]

Et sic debet xvij li. xiij s. j d. ob.;[27] de quibus in respectu de arreragiis Willelmi Dolle nuper prepositi ut patet in ultimo pede compoti xlv s. Item respectuantur eidem de arreragiis Ricardi le Hunte et Thome le Hunte ut patet in[28] dicto pede xxxj s.[29] Et sic debet xiij li. xvij s. j d. ob.,[30] unde super

[16] MS: a sum ending in 'vij d. ob.' struck out; new sum inserted.

[17] MS: 'De bonis nativorum defunctorum venditis lxij s. viij d.' inserted. The chattels were heriots (WAM 14796–7).

[18] MS: 'Expense' in main body of text. 'lxxvj li. ob.', 'lxxvj li. ob.' and 'lxxvij li. xvj s. vj d. ob.' struck out in succession, and a new sum inserted.

[19] MS: 'Expense' in main body of text. 'lxiiij s. iiij d. ob.' struck out; new sum inserted.

[20] MS: 'xv^{e}'.

[21] The tax, the second of the two fifteenths granted to the king in 1346, was due on 19 April 1348: M. Jurkowski, C. L. Smith and D. Crook, *Lay Taxes in England and Wales, 1188–1688* (Public Record Office Publications, 31; 1998), p. 47. On the liability of villeins of the clergy to lay subsidies in and after 1334, and the responsibility of ecclesiastics for collecting and delivering the tax, see *The Lay Subsidy of 1334*, ed. R. E. Glassock (British Academy, Records of Social and Economic History, new series, 2; 1975), p. 238. The total assessment of the vill of Islip in 1334 was £6 2s. 8d.

[22] MS: 'xij s. viij d.' struck out; new sum inserted.

[23] MS: followed by 'In stipendio capellani xiiij s. x d.', which has been struck out.

[24] MS: sum altered from 'xliiij s. v d.'

[25] MS: 'xxxij li.' struck out; new sum inserted.

[26] MS: 'liiij li. xij s. vj d. ob.' struck out; new sum inserted.

[27] MS: 'xxj li. vij s. vj d.' and 'xiiij li. x s. v d. ob.' entered and struck out in succession; new sum inserted.

[28] MS omits 'in'.

[29] MS: 'xxxij s.' struck out; new sum inserted. The respite related to goods, including 9 swans, taken by royal purveyors and formerly charged to the reeve as fictitious sales (WAM 14797). Richard le Hunte was reeve of Islip 13 September 1348–11 April 1349.

[30] MS: new sum inserted and 'x li. xiiij s. v d. ob.' struck out. The latter sum had been inserted in place of 'xvij li. x s. vj d.' also struck out.

Ceciliam Dolle xvij s. et super dictum Thomam le Hunte super istud visum xiij li. j d. ob.[31]

Pershore Frumentum. Responsurus minus tercio iiij bus. frumenti. Mixtilio. Responsurus plus semine j bus. mixtilionis. Siligo. Responsurus minus semine ij qr. ij bus. siliginis, non plus quia non plus estimat*ur* in pallea nisi vij qr. iiij bus. Ordeum. Responsurus plus se altero et di. iiij bus. cum vij qr. in pallea ad ventilandum per estimacionem.
Pendesham. Frumentum. Memorandum quod seminat*um* fuit ibidem j qr. vj bus. frumenti; nichil de exitu quia nulla messio ibidem. Siligo. Responsurus plus semine j qr. j bus. Pise. Memorandum quod seminat*um* fuerunt ibidem ij qr. vij bus. pisarum, et nullus exitus inde quia nulla messio. Ordeum. Responsurus plus semine j bus. j p. Dragetum. Responsuru*s* minus se altero j qr. iij bus. cum viij qr. ordei ad ventilandum per estimacionem. Avene. Responsurus minus semine ij bus.
Pendeffen. Frumentum. Responsurus plus semine v bus. iij p. cum xij qr. in toto ad triturandum per estimacionem in garbis. Siligo. Memorandum quod seminantur[32] anno preterito[33] [*mem. 2 recto*] ij qr. iiij bus. Et inde responsurus[34] per estimacionem j qr.; et sic minus semine j qr. iiij bus. Pise. Memorandum quod seminantur[35] anno preterito iiij qr. v bus. pisarum, et nichil responsurus de exitu quia nulla messio. Ordeum. Responsurus minus se altero ij bus. quia estimat*ur* ad triturandum in toto v qr. Dragetum. Responsurus minus semine iij bus. Avene. Responsurus plus semine j qr. ij bus. cum v qr. ad triturandum per estimacionem.
Seminacio[36] De frumento seminato apud Pershor', Pendesham et Pendeffen, nichil hoc anno quia nulla terra warectata fuit. De mixtilione seminata apud Pershor' ij qr. iij bus. mixtilionis, iij qr. vj bus. siliginis, viij qr. iij bus. puls', xij qr. iiij bus. ordei, x qr. iij bus. drageti, iij qr. ij bus. avenarum. Item seminat*ur* apud Pendesham iij qr. v bus. siliginis, iiij qr. j bus. puls', v qr. j bus. ordei. Item ad seminandum per estimacionem ij qr. ij bus. ordei et vj qr. j bus. drageti. Item apud Pendeffen vij qr. ij bus. pisarum et v qr. iij bus. drageti.

[31] MS: 'xvj li. xiij s. vj d.' and 'ix li. xvij s. vij d. ob.' struck out in succession; new sum inserted.
[32] MS: 'seminant'.
[33] 1348–9.
[34] MS: 'inde estimat' responsurus'.
[35] MS: 'seminant'.
[36] The following panel relates to sowing 29 September 1349–25 March 1350.

Remanencia Remanent ad triturandum apud Pendeffen per estimacionem anno preterito viij qr. veteris frumenti et xij qr. frumenti de exitu,[37] tamen inde debentur xij qr. vendita in tasso Willelmo Terri, precium qr. iiij s. viij d.[38] Item remanent in granario xxv qr. iij bus. di. pisarum. Et ad triturandum per estimacionem apud Pendesham iij qr. pisarum. Item remanent ad triturandum per estimacionem apud Pershor' vij qr. iiij bus. siliginis et v qr. veteris siliginis ibidem, sed estimat*ur* anno preterito.[39] Item remanent apud Pendeffen ij qr. v bus. veteris ordei, sed estimat*ur* anno preterito. Et apud Pendesham vj qr. veteris ordei, sed estimat*ur* anno preterito. Item estimat*ur* apud Pershor' in pallea per estimacionem ad ventilandum vij qr. ordei. Item apud Pendesham ad ventilandum per estimacionem in pallea viij qr. drageti. Item remanent apud Pendeffen ad triturandum per estimacionem v qr. ordei. Item remanent de veteri grano apud Pendesham iij qr. veteris drageti, sed estimat*ur* anno preterito. Item apud Pendeffen v qr. veteris drageti sed estimat*ur* anno preterito. Item remanent apud Pendeffen per estimacionem ad triturandum iiij qr. veterum avenarum sed estimat*ur* anno preterito. Item apud Pendesham ad triturandum per estimacionem x qr. veterum avenarum sed estimat*ur* anno preterito. Item remanent apud Pendeffen ad triturandum per estimacionem v qr. avenarum de exitu.

Memorandum quod molendinum respond*et* a festo sancti Michaelis usque j diem Maij[40] ij qr. iij bus. frumenti, xij qr. tolcorn, vij qr. v bus. brasei. Et totum expenditur preter v qr. vj bus. brasei. Item remanent j equus molendini, iiij equi carectarii et non plures quia j in morina. De affris nichil quia ij in morina.

Memorandum de vj pullanis de[41] strayo unde j masculus mittebatur usque Sutton', xxxviij boves, xxv vacce, et non plures quia iiij in morina, v bovetti unde j taurellus et non plures quia j in morina. Item[42] ij jumenta et non plures quia j in morina, ix boviculi, v juvencule et non plures quia j in morina, j vitulus superannatus. De bidentibus nullus quia vend*ebantur* et liber*abantur* aliis maneriis,[43] ij sues et non plures quia j in morina, xix

[37] i.e. wheat harvested in, respectively, 1348 and 1349. For the former estimate, see also I 2B.

[38] For this transaction, see later in this document.

[39] For the estimates made in 1348–9 and relating to corn harvested in 1347–8, see I 2B. The care to identify estimates that were not up-to-date is explained by awareness of the hazards of storage, exemplified below in the mice of Castlemorton; see also Campbell, *English Seignorial Agriculture*, p. 416.

[40] 29 September 1349–1 May 1350.

[41] MS omits 'de'.

[42] MS: 'Item' inserted.

[43] 35 ewes were sent to Todenham in October 1349; 60 lambs to Bourton-on-the-Hill in November; 1 ram and 36 wethers to Chaceley in December 1349; 7 rams and 139 ewes were sold in January 1350; and 4 gimmers sold in a month that is not recorded. Only 1 gimmer and 1 wether remained in Pershore, Pensham and Pinvin at the end of the year 1349–50 (WAM 22124). For the great

porculi unde j apriolus et non plures quia ij in morina, xvj porcelli superannati, xvj porcelli de exitu, j anser, iij mariole.

Recepcio De arreragiis ultimi compoti x li. xviij s. iij d. De redditu iij terminorum lxxj li. ij s. v d. qua.; de redditu de Wych' iij terminorum x s. ix d.; de novo redditu iij s. ix d.; de firmis l s. ix d. ob. De vendicione bladi iiij li. xviij d. qua., unde lvj s. de xij qr. frumenti venditis Willelmo Terri in tasso et adhuc remanent in tasso dominico, xvij s. vj d. qua. de v qr. vj bus. iij p. veteris drageti venditis, precium qr. iij s., et viij s. de ij qr. brasei molendini venditis.[44] De vendicione stauri lxix s. ob., unde v s. de j tauro, iiij s. de j alio tauro, l s. de vij hurtardis, Cxxxix matricibus et iiij jerciis venditis, precium capitis iiij d., ij s. de viij porcellis, iij s. iij d. de xiij aucis, ij s. de xij caponibus, et ij s. ix d. ob. de xxvj gallinis et di. venditis. De mortuo stauro iiij s. j d. qua. De operibus venditis iiij s. ij d. qua. De exitu manerii iij s. De perquisitis curie liiij s. iiij d. De forinsecis receptis xxvij s. xj d.[45]

Summa totalis recepti cum arreragiis iiij^{xx}xvij li. ix s.

Expense In allocacione redditus iij terminorum vj s. iiij d. ob. In denariis respectuatis collectori redditus iij terminorum xxxvij s. iij d. ob. qua. In allocacione redditus tenencium[46] in manu domini accedencium nativorum de Pendesham per iij terminos xxxiij s. vij d. ob. In allocacione redditus[47] nativorum tenencium de Pendeffen pro eodem xxxiij s. ix d. In allocacione redditus tenencium nativorum de Wyk pro eodem xxxj s. ix d. qua. In allocacione redditus librorum tenencium xxix s. v d. ob. In denariis de redditu duplicato onerato pro iij terminis x s. vij d. ob. qua.[48] In custu carucarum xxv s. iij d. In custu warectacionis vij s. iiij d. In precariis carucarum iiij s. iiij d. qua. In custu domorum xvj s. iiij d. In custu molendini xxx s. In minutis necesariis xxij s. vij d. In custu bidencium iiij s. In trituracione et ventilacione bladi lj s. x d. ob. In stipendiis pro dimidio anno xlij s. In vadiis ballivi xxx s. In expensis senescalli et superveniencium iiij s. ix d. In expensis forinsecis xxiij s. xj d. In denariis liberatis liij li. xj s. ob.

---

mortality among sheep in 1349, *Knighton's Chronicle, 1337–1396*, ed. and trans. G. H. Martin (Oxford, 1995), p. 101.

[44] For the sale of wheat at Pinvin to William Terry, and for a surplus of malt at the mill on 1 May 1350, see earlier in this document.

[45] The receipts were from the abbot's liberties in Gloucestershire and Worcestershire (WAM 22124).

[46] WAM 22124, which was probably the scribe's source, uses both 'tenementa' and 'tenentes' in the relevant passages.

[47] MS omits 'redditus'.

[48] The allowance corrected an accounting anomaly, whereby the reeve of of this manor was still charged annually with the rents of assize for two customary holdings, despite the fact that they had long been held on leases for lives, and one was now in fact vacant.

Summa omnium expensarum et liberacionum lxxiiij li. xvj s. x d. ob. Et sic debentur xxij li. xij s. j d. ob. Item super totum homagium xix li. xj d. qua. de arreragiis Ade Huwe nuper prepositi ibidem solvendis annuatim xx s. quousque etc.[49]

De Johanne Arvy et Thom*a* atte Well' collectoribus redditus de anno xviij° ij s. viij d.[50]

De Ada Gilberd', Willelmo Palli et Johanne Hugh' collectoribus redditus de anno xix°[51] ij s. v d.

De Willelmo Cro*m*pe, Johanne Kentwen' et Stephano atte Mor' collectoribus redditus de anno xx°[52] xiiij s. v d.

De Johanne Cok' collectore redditus de anno xxj°[53] vj li. ij s. vj d.

De Johanne Osebern', Willelmo Fox et Willelmo Nichole, collectoribus redditus de anno xxij°,[54] lxviij s. j d. ob. qua.

De Thoma de Badmyngton', ballivo de portmot de annis xix° et xx°,[55] vij d. et ryches predictorum duorum annorum preter x s. solutos in anno xxj°[56]

De Alexandro Barat', ballivo de portmot, de anno xxj°, xx s. et v bus. brasei, precium bus. vj d., ij s. vj d., et eciam riches unius anni. Item j lagena standarda, ij balances, xij pondera.

De Johanne Vampage de hoc anno xxiiij°[57] ballivo de portmot lxvij s.

De Thom*a* Patrich' ballivo hundredorum de Pendeffen et Defforde de arreragiis suis anni precedentis [iiij li. viijs.][58]

De Willelmo Chese ballivo hundredi de Wyk xviij s. ix d. [de hoc anno]

De Willelmo Tundi ballivo hundredi de Pendeffen de hoc anno iij s. x d.

De Elia Felawes ballivo hundredi de Defford' de hoc anno pro amerciamentis levandis ij s. ix d.

Summa totalis denariorum debencium xlij li. xvij s. ij d. qua.

De quibus solut*um* post visum Cx s. per j talliam. Item assignatur solvere Willelmo Paleffryman per literam domini di. marca.[59] Item domino Johanni

[49] Cf. I 1 and I 2B, where the instalment owed by the homage is £3 p.a.

[50] The year was 1343–4. On the antiquity of this debt and several others in the following list, and on the decease, among the debtors named, of Hugh', Cromp', Kentwen' and Cok', see I 2B.

[51] 1344–5.

[52] 1345–6.

[53] 1346–7.

[54] 1347–8.

[55] 1344–5, 1345–6.

[56] 1346–7.

[57] 1349–50.

[58] MS omits sum; supplied from WAM 22126, 1348–9. Having completed his year in office, Patrich' was now locum tenens until a successor could be found (WAM 22126). Elias Felawes, whose duty of collecting amercements is noted below, was not in the full sense bailiff of Defford hundred.

[59] The palfreyman had business at Stourton (WAM 22124).

capellano pro stipendio anni precedentis xl s. Item in expensis magistri W. Wapton' et senescalli vj s. xj d.

Bourton Frumentum. Responsurus plus se altero j bus. di. cum iiij qr. in pallea per estimacionem ad ventilandum. Puls'. Responsurus minus semine et dimidio di. bus. cum vj qr. pisarum ad triturandum et ventilandum per estimacionem. Ordeum. Responsurus plus se altero iiij qr. vj bus. cum iiij bus. ad triturandum per estimacionem. Avene. Responsurus plus semine j bus. di.

Seminacio ibidem viij qr. iij bus. frumenti, vij qr. ij bus. puls', xxij qr. ordei, vij qr. iiij bus. avenarum.

Remanencia Item remanent ibidem ad triturandum per estimacionem in pallea iiij qr. frumenti. Item remanent per estimacionem ad triturandum vj qr. puls'. Item remanent ibidem vj bus. ordei. Et ad triturandum per estimacionem iiij bus. ordei. Item remanent ij bus. avenarum. Item remanent ibidem ij jumenta, xviij boves, j vacca, Ciiij^{xx}ix multones, iij matrices, ij sues, j apriolus, xviij porculi, vij porcelli de illis de remanencia, vij porcelli de exitu. Memorandum de j jumento, iij multonibus, iiij ovibus matricibus, xxiij agnis superannatis, ij agnis [*mem. 3 recto*] de exitu, j porco, iij porculis, iij porcellis de illis de remanencia et viij porcelli de illis de exitu sunt in morina.

Recepcio De redditu assiso iij terminorum vj li. x s. j d. qua.; de redditu mobili x d.;[60] de firmis v s. vj d. ob. De vendicione bladi xxij s. v d. ob., unde iiij s. viij d. de j qr.[61] ij bus. et ij partibus unius bus. de che*r*cheschoth', ij s. viij d. de j qr. puls', et xxiiij s. de viij qr. ordei.[62] De vendicione stauri xxj s. iiij d., unde de j jumento viij d., de iiij affris iiij s. j d., de j apro, vij porcis xv s., de iij gallis, viij gallinis xix d.[63] De exitu manerii xvij s. vj d. De perquisitis curie xxvij s. vij d.

Summa totalis recepti xj li. xv s. iij d. qua.

Expense In superplusagio ultimi compoti xj s. j d. In allocacione redditus viij s. ob. qua. In defectu redditus terr*e* nativorum pro iij terminis xxv s. viij d. In custu carucarum viij s. vj d. ob. In custu carectarum ij s. viij d. In minutis xv s. v d. In custu bidencium v s. vj d. ob. In trituracione bladorum xiiij s. qua. In vj bus. puls' emptis iij s. In stipendiis xxx s. iiij d. In expensis

[60] A payment in lieu of a ploughshare.

[61] MS: 'j qr.' inserted.

[62] An inflation of the amount of rye paid as churchscot this year, and of the proceeds from selling it, robs the entry of coherence. At the final audit of his account, the reeve was charged with 1s. 1½d. from the sale of 2⅔ bus. of rye from churchscot, 2s. 8d. from the sale of 1 qr. pulse, and £1 4s. from the sale of 8 qr. barley: a total of £1 7s. 9½d. (WAM 8282).

[63] The mare and affers were strays.

senescalli et superveniencium vj s. x d. In forinsecis expensis ix d. In denariis liberatis Cxv s.

Summa omnium expensarum et liberacionum xij li. vj s. x d. ob. Et sic excedit xj s. vij d. qua.

Herdwick[64] De arando nichil quia non habeatur aliqua noticia ad presens. Seminantur ibidem xvij qr. vij bus. frumenti, xviij qr. v bus. fabarum, v qr. puls', ix. qr. vj bus. ordei, xvj qr. iiij bus. drageti, et ij qr. v bus. avenarum.
Providetur super facturam. Memorandum quod oportet providere super facturam iiij qr. iiij bus. puls' pro liberacionibus, et xxxiij qr. ordei pro liberacionibus in parte, et pro ordeo in parte vendicionis et denariis inde receptis premanibus et domino liberatis.[65]
Remanencia Remanent j qr. iiij bus. frumenti, vij qr. vij bus. fabarum, j qr. puls', iiij qr. iiij bus. avenarum, et iiij bus. multure. Item vj equi[66] carectarii unde iij in custodia Johannis Glouc' apud Pershore, xliiij boves, ij vacce, xxiiij multones, Cxlj oves matrices, ij jercie, xxvj agni de exitu. Item ij apri, iiij sues, xix porci, xxiij porculi, xxvj porcelli, j pavo, j anser, iiij auce mariole et xxv aucule, j maullardus, ij annati, xiij capones, non plures quia xij liberantur Johanni Glouc' usque Pershore, j gallus, xv[67] galline.
Recepcio De arreragiis ultimi compoti anni precedentis xix li. iij s. v d. qua. De redditu iij terminorum xxxvj li. xj s. iij d. qua.; de firmis iij terminorum xxxv s. iiij d. qua.; de blado vendito xix li. xix s. unde xxx s. de ix qr. veteris frumenti, receptis in anno elapso per indenturam, pro timore putredis precium iij s. iiij d.,[68] ix li. de xxxvj qr. frumenti de exitu venditis, precium qr. v s., et ix li. ix s. de xlij qr. ordei venditis, precium qr. iiij s. vj d.[69] De vendicione stauri xij s. j d., unde de ij affris femellis xij d., de j vacca iij s., et de xxvj aucis vij s. vij d., precium cuiuslibet iij d. ob., et de ij annatis vj d., precium cuiuslibet ij d. De mortuo stauro vendito ij s. x d., unde de j coreo boum mortuorum in morina xviij d. et de j coreo boum mortuorum in morina xvj d. De exitu manerii xxiij s. x d., unde xiij s. iiij d. de dimidia

[64] From here onwards, the main text is written in a different hand, probably the hand which wrote I 2B, or a very similar one.
[65] On the sale of barley, see further below.
[66] MS repeats 'equi'.
[67] MS: altered from 'xvj'.
[68] The wheat, harvested in 1348, may be that referred to above, I 2B, where the quantity is given as 9 qr. 6 bus. We can assume that the indenture was that to which, following normal practice, John Bernard, now reeve of Hardwicke, was a party on entering office.
[69] Presumably an estimate: in the event, only 34 qr. 1½ bus. of barley were sold in the course of the year (WAM 8438A).

virgata terre quondam Roberti Penbrugg' dimissa ad seminandum.[70] De finibus et perquisitis cur*ie* xxvij s. viij d.

Summa totalis recepti iiij^{xx} li. xv s. v d. ob. qua.

Expense Primo in allocacione redditus pro iij terminis iiij li. ix s. viij d.; in defectu redditus tenementorum in manu domini pro iij terminis vij li. xvj s. ij d. In custu carucarum xij s. iij d. ob. In custu plaustrorum et carectarum v s. xj d. In minutis necessariis[71] xviij s. ix d. qua., unde xj carucis ad seminacionem frumenti et xj carucis ad seminacionem fabarum de precaria[72] v s. vj d. In custu bidencium ij s. ix d. In trituracione bladi per dietas et ventilacione xliiij s. ij d. ob. In stipendiis famulorum xxvij s. In expensis senescalli et superveniencium iiij s. vij d. In solucionibus forinsecis xv s. In expensis forinsecis xij d. In denariis liberatis xlvj li. vj s. vj d. unde [*mem. 4 recto*] domino Gilberto Chasteleyn[73] per manus Johannis Glouc' C s.

Summa omnium expensarum et liberacionum lxv li. iij s. x d. qua. Et debet xv li. xj s. ob., unde super Robertum Hoppere collectorem redditus et extractarum curie x li. vij s. x d. ob. qua., unde de superoneracione[74] super compotum de ij curiis tent*is* ante festum sancti Michaelis vij li. xviij s. iiij d., ut creditur de onere ballivi libertatis ibidem.[75] Et sic super prepositum de claro Ciij s. viij d. ob. qua.

Souttone Frumentum. Responsurus minus se altero et dimidio iij bus. j p. Siligo. Responsurus plus semine iiij bus. j p. Puls'. Responsurus[76] Dragetum. Responsurus minus tercio et dimidio j qr. iij bus. et di. Avene. Responsurus minus se altero j qr.

Seminacio Seminantur ibidem viij qr. ij bus. frumenti, iij qr. iiij bus. et di. siliginis, vij qr. iiij bus. puls', ix qr. iij bus. drageti, vj qr. iiij bus. avenarum.

[70] The half-virgate of unfree land (*terra nativa*) formerly held by Robert Penbrugg' on customary terms, including labour services as well as a money rent of 13s. 4d. p.a., was now held by William Sley and Edward Gabbe for the identical money rent, and without labour services, but with an undertaking on their part to cultivate the arable belonging to the holding (WAM 8438A).

[71] MS: 'minute neccessarie'.

[72] MS: 'p'ce'.

[73] On 18 October 1348, Chasteleyn, with several others, including Robert Shareshill and Roger de Brugges, met, probably at Longdon, to consider the affairs of Abbot Simon Bircheston (d. 12 May 1349), and Chasteleyn's status on the earlier occasion and in 1349–50 may have been that of counsellor. But it is also possible that the above payment and others mentioned later in the present document represent the repayment of a loan made to Abbot Langham at a difficult moment. See below, and for Brugges, see below, n. 98.

[74] MS: 'superuneracione'.

[75] i.e. the rent-collector and collector of court estreats for Hardwicke in 1349–50 should not have been charged with the proceeds of courts held before the beginning of that year on 29 September 1349, if this had happened.

[76] MS: no details follow.

Remanencia Remanent[77] ibidem vj qr. iiij bus. j p. frumenti, j qr. siliginis, j qr. j bus. j p. multure, iij qr. j bus. brasei ordei, xxxiij qr. iiij bus. brasei unde vij qr. veteris brasei.[78] Item remanent ij jumenta, vij pullani biennales unde ij masculi v femelli, ix boves, j vacca lactans, j juvenca, j vitulus de exitu etatis unius septimane, j sus, vj porci unde iiij suelle porcellate quarum j porcellavit v porcellos, ut patet inferius, iiij porculi, xj porcelli non decimati, ij anseres, v auce mariole, xxxv aucule non decimate, xiiij capones, ij galli, xij galline, x lib. cannabis, xliiij casse bidencium, iij qr. unius corei pullani dealbati, j cista.
Recepcio De arreragiis iiij li. x s. j d. qua., unde ponentur eidem in respectum xiiij s. viij d., unde x s. quos mutuavit R. Sharshull' senescallo et iiij s. viij d. percipiendos de dicto R. Sharshull' pro j jumento eidem R. vendito etc.[79] De redditu assiso pro iij terminis xij li. ij s. vj d. ob. qua.; de firmis xij d.; de chevagio j d. De vendicione bladi iiij li. ij s. ij d. qua. unde v bus. j p. frumenti, precium bus. vij d., j qr. j bus. et di. veteris brasei ordei, precium qr. iij s. x d., et de xxij qr. ij bus. iij p. brasei drageti, precium qr. iij s. iiij d. De vendicione stauri xxxiiij s. viij d. ob.; de mortuo stauro vendito vij d. De operibus venditis x d. ob. De exitu manerii viij s. v d. De finibus et perquisitis curie xxiiij s.

Summa totalis recep*ti* xxiiij li. v s. qua.

Expense Primo compoto.[80] In allocacione redditus iij s. In defectu redditus xix s. x d. In custu carucarum v s. iiij d. ob. In custu carectarum iiij s. iij d. In custu domorum xj s. xj d. In custu molendini vj s. viij d. In minutis necessariis vij s. xj d. ob. In trituracione bladi xxiij s. ij d. ob. In empcione bladorum xij s. viij d. qua. In stipendiis famulorum x s. In expensis superveniencium ij s. ob. In expensis forinsecis xxvij s. vij d. In liberacionibus denariorum xiiij li. xvj s. viij d.

Summa totalium expensarum et liberacionum xxj li. xj s. ij d. qua. Et debet liij s. x d. De quibus ponuntur eidem in respectum ut patet supra in titulo arreragiorum xiiij s. viij d. Et sic debet xxxix s. ij d.

[*Mem. 1 dorse*][81] *Rectoria de Morton'* Frumentum.[82] De toto exitu tritur*antur* xj qr. frumenti de hoc anno de rectoria, que[83] vend*untur*, et libera*ntur*

[77] MS omits 'Remanent'.
[78] i.e. 7 qr. of the remaining malt were malted in 1348–9.
[79] See I 2A.
[80] Perhaps an expression for the first, unrevised, account of expenses, concluded before respites mentioned at the end of the panel were considered.
[81] The dorse is a fair copy, in the first hand. At the foot of mem. 4 dorse, inverted, is the single word: 'Islep'.
[82] MS: 'Frumentum' inserted.
[83] MS omits 'que'.

manerio lij s. Sed tunc remanent adhuc ad triturandum per estimacionem in garbis xvj qr., sicut vetus granum ut estimabat*ur* anno preterito.[84] Mixtilio. Remanent ibidem ad triturandum per estimacionem in garbis ij qr. mixtilionis de exitu huius anni. Fabe et pise mixte. Et pro toto exitu ij qr. v bus. fabarum et pisarum mixtarum que venduntur et expenduntur in compoto. Et remanent ad triturandum per estimacionem j qr. fabarum et pisarum mixtarum et iij qr. de puls' de exitu huius anni. Item tritur*antur* de veteri grano vij qr. iiij bus. fabarum et puls' que expenduntur in compoto. Et remanent ad triturandum per estimacionem de veteri grano xxij qr. di. veterum fabarum et puls', sicut estimabatur anno preterito.[85] Item remanent ad triturandum de veteri grano per estimacionem xx qr. de puls' sicut estimabatur anno preterito. Ordeum. De toto exitu iij qr. iiij bus. ordei et vend*untur* in compoto. Et remanent ad triturandum de veteri grano per estimacionem sicut estimabatur anno preterito iiij qr. ordei. Dragetum. De toto exitu triturantur ij qr. j bus. drageti, et venduntur in compoto. Avene. De toto exitu triturantur vij bus. avenarum et venduntur in compoto. Et remanent ad triturandum de veteri grano sicut est*imabatur* anno preterito ij qr.

Recepcio De redditu assiso vj s. viij d. De vj qr. frumenti venditis xxx s.; de ij qr. v bus. fabarum et pisarum mixtarum venditis vj s. vj d. ob. qua.; de ij qr. puls' venditis iiij s.; de vj qr. ordei venditis xxviij s.; de ij qr. j bus. drageti venditis v s. iij d. ob. qua. De stramine vendito xij d. De pallea vendita ij s. vj d. De pastura et crofta ij d. Summa totalis recept*i* iiij li. iiij s. iij d. ob.
De quibus in trituracione bladi vj s. Et sic debet lxxviij s. iij d. ob.
De quibus liberantur domino post visum j die Maij per manus J. Gloucestr' lxx s. per j talliam. Et debet viij s. iij d.

Manerium de Morton' Frumentum. De parte exitus de terr*a* nativorum tritur*antur* j qr. vij bus. frumenti; et expend*untur.* Et remanent ad triturandum per estimacionem in garbis de terra nativorum ij qr. frumenti. De parte exitus veteris frumenti tritur*antur* et expend*untur* iiij bus. Et remanent ad ventilandum in pallea iiij bus., et sic non respondet ad estimacionem sicut estimabatur anno preterito de ij qr. frumenti quia destructum fuit per mures. *Responsurus.*[86] Fabe et puls'. De toto exitu de terr*a* nativorum tritur*antur* et expend*untur* ij qr. vj bus. fabarum et pisarum.

[84] For this wheat, harvested in 1348, see I 2B.

[85] Cf. I 2B, where the 30 qr. beans and pulse harvested in 1348 are said to be unthreshed. The following entries show that an estimated 20 qr. pulse, 4 qr. barley and 2 qr. oats harvested in the rectory manor at Castlemorton in 1348–9, and now therefore 'old grain', were still unthreshed when this part of the view took place.

[86] MS: 'Responsurus' is a marginal note. See I 2B. We are to understand that 1 qr. of the 3 qr. estimated here had been threshed, but mice had eaten the rest.

Avene et vesce. Remanent ad triturandum de terra nativorum per estimacionem in garbis j qr. avenarum et vescarum.
Seminacio Seminantur ibidem iij qr. ij bus. frumenti et iij qr. j bus. puls'.
Remanencia Remanent ibidem j affrus, j pullanus, xj boves et non plures quia ij in morina et j venditur. Item remanent iij vacce, unde j in custodia R. Sharishull' senescalli.[87] Item remanent ij sues, nullus aper quia j in morina. Item remanent iiij porci, viij porculi, unde j apriolus, vj porcelli superannati, viij porcelli de exitu huius anni.
Recepcio[88] De arreragiis ultimi compoti xx li. ij s. vij d. ob. qua., unde super Thomam Pal' C s. iiij d. ob. qua.[89] De redditu assiso iij terminorum xx li. ix s. ob.; de firmis [*mem. 2 dorse*] iij terminorum xxv s. v d. De j veteri bove vendito iiij s. viij d.; de j veteri vacca ij s.; de viij porcis venditis xvj s.; de xxxij gallinis venditis iiij s.; de CCiiij^{xx}x ovis venditis ix d. ob. qua. De operibus venditis xvij s. ix d. ob. qua. De exitu manerii viij s. ij d. Et memorandum de exitu columbarii pro quo quidem Ricardus Atthull' est responsurus. De perquisitis curie xl s. ix d.

Summa totalis recepti cum arreragiis xlvj li. xij s. iij d. ob. qua.
Expense In acquietanciis redditus iij terminorum x s. v d.; in defectu redditus liberorum ten*ementorum* et quod non potest levari pro tribus terminis xxv s. viij d. ob. qua.; in defectu redditus tenementorum nativorum cum tallagio iij terminorum liiij s. ij d. In custu carucarum ij s. iiij d. In custu carectarum iij s. xj d. In custu molendini ij s. vj d. In j bus. salis empto xij d. In ventilacione blad*orum* ij dol*ia*.[90] In stipendiis pro dimidio anno iij s. x d. In denariis liberatis Johanni de Gloucestr' ballivo ad solvendum domino Gilberto Chasteleyn xv li. per j talliam.[91]

Summa omnium expensarum et liberacionum xxj li. iiij s. j d. qua. Et sic debet xxv li. viij s. ij d. ob., unde super Thomam Pal' nuper prepositum C s. iiij d. ob. qua. debit*um* supra. De Henrico Weylond lxx s. iij d.[92] De Johanne Mochegros xl s. xj d.[93] De[94] Johanne Pagen' xxvj s. iij d., unde

[87] For the cow—or, as on the first mention of this animal, the ox—see also I 2B, and the present document, below.
[88] MS: 'Recept''.
[89] For this debt, see also I 2B.
[90] i.e. ale was provided for those winnowing the demesne corn, as though they were engaged in 'wet' boons.
[91] See above, n. 73.
[92] A tenant of the abbot in Castlemorton, who is said in 1352–3 to owe £1 9s. 1d. in arrears of rent for a carucate of land, now unoccupied, and in 1353–4 to owe double this amount (WAM 21053, 21055). How the above debt of £3 10s. 3d. relates to these debts is uncertain.
[93] For Mochegros, see I 2A and B.
[94] MS: 'debito de W. Holdy' inserted in the margin in another hand against the entries from John Pagen up to and including Robert Sharishull. The exact reference is unclear.

super Johannem Upton xviij s. iij d.[95] De Nicholao Weylond v s. iijd.[96] De Ricardo Underhull', nuper collectore extractarum curie de anno xxiij°,[97] xxx s. viij d. Item debet de ij rythes ix d. De Roberto Sharishull' xij s. vj d. et j vacca in custodia sua. De Rogero de Brugges ix li. v s. viij d. ob.[98] De Johanne Kerdiff nunc messore et collectore estractarum curie xxxv s.

Manerium de Chadesle. Frumentum. Responsurus plus tercio iiij bus. di. Siligo. Responsurus minus semine et dimidio j qr. j bus. iij p. siliginis. Puls'. Responsuru*s* minus semine j qr. ij bus. di. pisarum. Ordeum. Responsurus minus se altero j qr. j bus. ordei. Dragetum. Responsuru*s* minus semine et dimidio ij bus. iij p. drageti. Avene. Responsurus minus semine et dimidio iij bus. j p. avenarum.
Seminantur. Seminantur ibidem ix qr. di. bus. frumenti unde super terram nativorum vij bus. frumenti. Item seminantur v qr. v bus. siliginis unde super terram nativorum j qr. iiij bus. siliginis. Item seminantur iiij qr. ij bus. pisarum, x qr. vj bus. ordei unde super terram nativorum ij qr. iij bus. ordei. Item seminantur iij qr. j bus. drageti et iij qr. ij bus. avenarum.
Remanencia Remanent ibidem iij qr. vij bus. iij p. frumenti, j qr. puls'. j p. ordei, vij bus. di. avenarum. Item ij jumenta, j pullanus femellus triennalis, xiij boves, j taurus et non plures quia j in morina, xx vacce, ij boviculi, j juvencula, v vituli superannati, viij vituli de exitu. De bidentibus nichil.[99] Item remanent ij sues, xv porculi, xij porcelli superannati, xij porcelli de exitu, j auca, iiij mariole.
Recepcio[100] De arreragiis ultimi compoti iiij s. viij d. qua. De redditu iij terminorum xlj s. iij d. qua.; de firmis xxv s. j d. ob. De vendicione blad*i* liij s., unde de ix qr. di. bus. veteris siliginis, precium qr. xx d., de j qr. iij bus. novi siliginis, precium qr. iij s. viij d., de xvj qr. iij bus. j p. veteris puls',

[95] Pagen was probably reeve of Castlemorton 1349–50 and certainly reeve there 1357–8 (WAM 21056); and Upton was probably reeve here for a short period in 1349.

[96] A connection between Nicholas Weylond and Thomas Weylond, mentioned above, is likely; but our sources shed no light on the former's debt to the abbot.

[97] 1348–9.

[98] Brugges held land in Castlemorton and is known to have attended the meeting convened in October 1348 to consider the affairs of Abbot Bircheston (WAM 21053; see also n. 73 above). His large share of the debt to the abbot, noted in this provisional balance of receipts and expenses relating to the rectory of Castlemorton, suggests that he may have been reeve and Thomas Pal's successor in the office.

[99] Cf. the losses from murrain recorded in the reeve's account for the manor of Chaceley for 28 September 1349–28 September 1350 (WAM 21083), which records the death of 1 ram, 41 wethers, 9 ewes, 5 hoggs and gimmers, and 4 lambs at Chaceley and the sale of 9 wethers, 78 ewes, 37 hoggs and gimmers from fear of sheep rot (*putredo*). The ewes, hoggs and gimmers were sold in November 1349.

[100] MS: 'Recept''. In this panel 'old corn' is that harvested in 1348, and 'new' corn is that harvested in 1349 and otherwise known as 'the issues' of corn.

precium qr. xvj d., de j qr. veteris drageti xvj d., et iij qr. drageti de exitu, precium qr. xl d. De vendicione stauri lv s. iij d. ob., unde de ij vaccis vij s., de j vacca iij s., de j vacca iiij s., de ix multonibus, lxxviij matricibus, xxxvij hogastris et[101] jerciis xxxj s., precium capitis iij d., de xliiij aucis, precium cuiuslibet iij d. ob., de vj gallinis, ix d.; de mortuo stauro xj s. ij d. ob., unde xvj d. de xviij pellibus lanutis, vij s. vj d. de xxxvj pellibus lanutis. De exitu manerii xxx s. v d. ob., unde xxv s. vj d. de firma vaccarum.[102] De perquisitis curie xj s. xj d. De forinsecis xxxviij s. x d., unde xxj s. x d. de Elena Broun.[103]

Summa totalis recepti xiij li. xij s. j d. ob.

Expense In allocacione redditus cum Cx s. solutis W. Dernefford vj li. iiij s. ij d. qua.;[104] in defectu redditus tenementorum in manu domini vij s. vij d. ob. In custu carucarum x s. v d. In custu carectarum et plaustri ij s. vj d. In custu domorum ix d. In minutis xlij s. v d. ob., unde in stramine et pallea xiij s. iiij d., in feno xx s. In custu bidencium iij s. viij d. In trituracione bladi xvij s. ob. In stipendiis xv s. In forinsecis expensis x s. ij d. In denariis liberatis Cxv s. x d., unde domino Gilberto Chasteleyn per manus J. Gloucestr' lxviij s.,[105] R. Tymmes preposito de Borton' vj s. v d.,[106] et quasi mutuo per manus R. Sharishill' xlj s. vj d.[107]

Summa omnium expensarum et liberacionum xvij li. ix s. vij d. ob. qua. Et sic excedit lxxvij s. vj d.

Rectoria de Chadesle Frumentum. Tritur*antur* ibidem ix qr. j bus. frumenti; et remanent ibidem ad triturandum per estimacionem in pallea j qr. iiij bus. frumenti de exitu. Siligo. Remanent ibidem ad ventilandum per estimacionem in pallea j qr. iiij bus. siliginis de toto exitu. Item triturantur ibidem de veteri siligini iij qr. vij bus.; et remanent ad triturandum per estimacionem in pallea et in garbis vj qr. j bus. ad respondendum ad estimacionem sicut

[101] MS omits 'et'.

[102] 17 cows were farmed at 5s. per cow p.a., but evidently at only 1s. 6d. per cow for the period covered by the present document. The farmer was entitled to dairy produce and calves (WAM 21083).

[103] Elena was the widow of Adam Broun, reeve of Chaceley, for whom see I 1.

[104] The larger part of this sum represents half the annual pension of £11 p.a. granted to William de Derneford, the younger, by the abbot and convent of Westminster in 1319, in part settlement of his claim to the manor of Deerhurst, then in dispuite between the two parties; see Harvey, *Estates*, p. 174. William was also entitled to a squire's livery yearly.

[105] For other instalments of this payment, see this document, above.

[106] Tymmes was reeve, not of Bourton-on-the-Hill, but of Todenham (WAM 8282, 25962–4).

[107] The quasi-loan mentioned here was in fact Robert Shareshill's debt to the reeve of Chaceley, carried over from the end of the previous year, 1348–9, and consisting of two items amounting to £2 1s. 6d. (I 2A).

estimatur anno preterito.[108] Puls'. Triturantur de[109] toto exitu vj bus pisarum. Ordeum. Triturantur de toto exitu ix qr. v bus. ordei. Dragetum. De exitu nichil quia nullus exitus. Avene. De toto exitu j qr. di bus. avenarum.

Summa totalis quarteriorum de exitu huius anni xxiij qr. iiij bus. di. bladi.

Remanencia Remanent ibidem viij qr. iiij bus. frumenti unde in pallea per estimacionem j qr. di. Item remanent vij qr. v bus. siliginis in pallea et ad triturandum per estimacionem. Item vj bus. di. puls'.

Recepcio De redditu termini Michaelis iiij s. iiij d.;[110] de firmis ij s. ix d. De vendicione bladorum lvj s. vij d. ob., unde iiij s. ix d. ob. de ij qr. vij bus. veteris siliginis venditis, precium qr. xx d., xxxvij s. iiij d. ob. de xxviij qr. veterum pisarum venditis precium xvj d., xiiij s. vj d. de iij qr. v bus. ordei venditis, precium qr. iiij s. De vendicione straminis et pallee ad manerium xiij s. iiij d. De feno vendito ad manerium xx s. preter iij carectates feni liberat*as* Ricardo Underhull', precium ix s. cum quibus dictus R. nondum oneratur.[111]

Summa totalis recepti iiij li. xviij s. ob.

De quibus in custu domorum iij d., in trituracione bladi v s.

Et sic debet iiij li. xij s. ix d. ob. De quibus retrahend*um* pro excessu compoti manerii lxxvij s. vj d. Et sic debet ultra xv s. iij d. ob.

Todenham Frumentum. Responsurus plus tercio et di. j qr. iij bus. j p. cum xxvij qr. ad triturandum per estimacionem in garbis. Mixtilio. Responsurus plus se altero j bus. Puls'. Responsurus plus se altero ij qr. vij bus. j p. cum xvj qr. ad triturandum per estimacionem in garbis. Puls' et avene. Memorandum quod seminantur anno preterito[112] vj qr. j bus. et ex hoc responsurus ij qr. ij bus. Et sic in perdicione de semine iij qr. vij bus. Ordeum. Responsurus plus sexto ij bus.[113] cum vij qr. ordei ad ventilandum in pallea per estimacionem. Avene. Responsurus plus se altero j qr. j bus. j p.

Seminacio Seminantur ibidem hoc anno xv qr. di. bus. frumenti, v qr. j bus. mixtilionis, xv qr. vij bus. puls' unde vj qr. super terram nativorum, vj qr. ordei, [*mem. 3 dorse*] vij qr. vij bus. drageti, xiij qr. avenarum unde iij qr. iiij bus. seminantur super terram nativorum.

Remanencia Remanent ibidem in granario xj qr. vij bus. frumenti. Item ad triturandum de exitu per estimacionem in garbis xxvij qr. frumenti. Item ad triturandum per estimacionem de veteri grano sicut estimabatur anno

[108] For the estimate of 10 qr., see I 2B.
[109] MS omits 'de'.
[110] At Chaceley rectory, all rents for the year were payable at Michaelmas.
[111] For the livery of hay to Underhill, serjeant of Longdon manor and rectory, see WAM 21021.
[112] 1348–9.
[113] MS: 'ij bus.' inserted.

preterito xl qr. frumenti.[114] Item remanent ibidem ix qr. ij bus. mixtilionis, ix qr. iij bus. puls'. Item remanent ad triturandum per estimacionem de exitu xvj qr. puls'. Item ad triturandum per estimacionem de veteri grano xxvij qr. iiij bus. puls' ad respondendum sicut estimabatur anno preterito.[115] Item remanent viij qr. ordei cum vij qr. per estimacionem in pallea. Item remanet j qr. drageti. Item remanent ibidem xv qr. veteris ordei ad ventilandum per estimacionem, sicut estimabatur anno preterito.[116] Item remanent ibidem iij equi carectarii, xxvij boves, vij hurtardi, xxxiij multones, Clxx matrices, Clx agni de exitu, ij apri, iij sues, ix porci, xxv porculi, xx porcelli, j auca, iij mariole, vj capones, ij galli, xviij galline, pro firma.

Recepcio[117] De arreragiis ultimi compoti xvij s. xj d. ob. qua. De redditu assiso x li. vij s. iij d.; de firm*is*. vj s. x d. ob. De vendicione bladi xxij li. xij s. ix d. De vendicione stauri vj li. xv s. iij d. qua. De mortuo stauro vj d. De operibus venditis iiij d. De exitu manerii ix s. vj d. De perquisitis curie xxxj s. iiij d. De forinsecis receptis lxxvj s. v d.

Summa totalis recepti xlvj li. xviij s. ij d. ob.

Expense In allocacione redditus iij s. In defectu redditus pro iij terminis xlj s. xj d. qua. In custu carucarum v s. iiij d. In custu carectarum v s. xj d. ob. In custu domorum vj s. x d. In custu molendini vj d. In minutis x s. ob. qua. In custu bidencium viij s. vj d. In trituracione bladi xxxvij s. j d. qua. In j qr. vij bus. frumenti emptis pro semine ix s. iiij d. ob. In stauro empto Cx s. ob. In stipendiis xxv s. x d. In forinsecis expensis ij s. ij d. In decimis solutis ix s. ob. qua.[118] In denariis liberatis fratri R. M*e*rston xxx li. xj s. iij d.[119]

Summa omnium expensarum et liberacionum xliiij li. xj d. ob. Et sic debet lj s. iij d.

Denham Frumentum. Responsurus minus tercio viij qr. j bus. Mixtilio. Responsurus minus se altero ij bus. Haras. Memorandum quod seminantur anno preterito[120] vj qr.; et inde responsuru*s* j qr. vj bus. Et sic in perdicione de semine iiij qr. ij bus. Dragetum. Responsurus plus semine et dimidio ij qr. vj bus. di. Avene. Responsurus plus semine vj bus. di.

Seminacio Seminantur ibidem xxxvj qr. vj bus. frumenti, v qr. iiij bus.

[114] For this estimate, see I 2B.

[115] We are probably to understand that 27 qr. 4 bus. of pulse harvested in 1348 and 16 qr. harvested in 1349 were to be acccepted as fulfilling the estimate made at the audit in the latter year, that there were 38 qr. of unthreshed pulse in store. See I 2B.

[116] See I 2B.

[117] MS 'Recept''.

[118] The payment represents a retreat on the abbot's part from a claim made in 1347–8 that he did not owe tithe of lambs or wool at Todenham, since he had a portion in the church there (WAM 25963).

[119] Abbot's receiver and steward of his household (WAM 22124, 26907).

[120] 1348–9.

mixtilionis, ij qr. vj bus. haras, xxvij qr. j bus. drageti, xxiij qr. bus. avenarum.

Remanencia Remanent ibidem ad festum annunciacionis beate Marie[121] v qr. iiij bus. scuralli frumenti. Item remanent ibidem iiij equi carectarii, ix jumenta, iiij affri, iij pullani masculi [*mem. 4 dorse*] triennales, ij pullani masculi biennales, v pullani unde iij masculi et ij femelli, etatis unius anni di., xxj boves, ij tauri, xl vacce, xviij agni superannati, ij apri, iij sues, xvj porculi, v porcelli, xiiij cigni unde iiij erarrii et[122] vj staggi quorum j errarius, et v staggi onerabantur per indenturam, sed de eisdem serviens nunquam[123] visum habere potuit, ideo etc., nec adhuc potest,[124] j anser, iij mariole.

Recepcio[125] De arreragiis ultimi compoti xliij s. iiij d. qua. De redditu iij terminorum xiiij li. ix s. iiij d. ob.; de firm*is* xviij s. xj d. De vendicione bladi vj li. xxij d. qua. De vendicione stauri xxij d. ob. qua. De mortuo stauro[126] vij d. De operibus venditis vij s. v d. De firmis. De firma dayerie xxj s. vj d. De perquisitis curie xxix s. vij d. ob.

Summa totalis recepti xxvj li. xiiij s. vj d. qua.

Expense In resolucione redditus xxvj s. iij d. In defectu redditus xix s. iij d. ob. qua. In custu carucarum xxj s. vj d. ob. In custu carectarum ix s. x d. In custu domorum ix s. iiij d. In minutis v s. xj d. In custu bidencium xij d. In trituracione bladi lxix s. j d. qua. In bladis emptis xlj s. vij d. qua. In falcacione prati post festum Michaelis et compoti reddicionem viij s.[127] In stipendiis xxxv s. iiij d. In vadiis servientis[128] xiiij s. vij d. In expensis domini et superveniencium xxiij s. vj d. ob. In vadiis Roberti Russel cum allocacione expensarum xxiiij s. v d. ob.[129] In forinsecis expensis xiiij s. viij d. In denariis perdonatis firmario vaccarum xlix s. j d. In denariis liberatis vj li. x s.

Summa omnium expensarum et liberacionum xxv li. iij s. vj d. ob. qua.

Et sic debet xxx s. xj d. ob.

[121] 25 March 1350.
[122] MS: 'et' inserted.
[123] MS repeats 'de eisdem'.
[124] The serjeant was John Hanecok', 1349–50 and beyond.
[125] MS: 'Recept''.
[126] MS omits 'stauro'.
[127] MS: 'festum Michaelis et' inserted in the main hand. The reference is to the close of the account of the serjeant of Denham for the previous year, on 29 September 1349, and to the fact that the hay harvest was still in progress.
[128] MS: 'servientis' inserted in main hand.
[129] Robert Russel: not otherwise identified.

I 4 Remainders and other memoranda at the conclusion of the audit of accounts for the abbot's manors for the year ending on 28 September 1356

A parchment roll of one membrane, approximately 100–3 mm wide, tapering to filing holes at the top. A fair copy, written in a small, neat hand: it has been written down the front of the roll, and then turned over and written back up the dorse, i.e. inverted. The manuscript is slightly damaged on the right side at the top and bottom.

The quarterly rents recorded in this document for each manor in the Western Parts (Pershore to Deerhurst) do not derive directly from other surviving material of a similar kind and may have been compiled for this occasion or similar ones in the immediate past. Though consisting mainly of rents of assize and contractual rents, they probably comprise every kind of rent to which the abbot was in principle entitled. The absence of yearly totals for rents serves to emphasise the focus of the document on leviable or 'clear' income. But the sum of leviable income also includes—as we must assume—the profits of demesne husbandry, or, where the demesne was farmed, the annual farm.

The entries for the manors in the Eastern Parts (Denham to Ebury) omit the details of quarterly rents and are more varied in format than those relating to the Western Parts. But they serve the same purpose. Here, too, the sum of leviable income includes income from the demesne and on occasion we glimpse the relative importance of this and other sources of income in relation to rental income.[1]

WAM 6183

[*Recto*] Rem*anencia* super compotum maneriorum domini abbatis Westm' ad festum sancti Michaelis anno xxx^{mo}

Pershore[2] Remanent ibidem j equus pro molendino, iij juvence, v pullani, xj boves, j aper, iij sues, xxxvj porci, xiij porculi, xxiiij porcelli, Ciiij^{xx}ix multones, xvj capones, j gallus, et vj galline. Et debet xxxj s. viij d.
Valor manerii hoc anno lvj li.
De redditu termini Michaelis preter decimas, cum tallagio,[3] xv li. iiij s. iiij d.[4]
De redditu termini[5] sancti Thome apostoli lxxix s. viij d.

[1] Extant ministers' accounts: Bourton-on-the-Hill, WAM 8284; Laleham, WAM 16873; Yeoveney, WAM 16878.

[2] In and after 1351–2, Pershore, Pensham and Pinvin were treated as separate units for the purposes of account and audit. Pershore, however, still included the vill of Wick.

[3] MS omits 'preter decasum', present in other entries.

[4] The appropriated tithes of Pershore had long been commuted into a portion of £8 13s. 4d. p.a. in the church of St Andrew, Pershore, and this was assigned to the Abbey infirmary (*TPN*, p. 218; Harvey, *Estates*, p. 389).

[5] MS: omits 'termini'.

De redditu termini annunciacionis beate Marie iiij li. xv s. vj d. qua.
De redditu termini nativitatis sancti Johannis baptiste lxxix s. viij d.
Et levand*um* sunt ibidem de claro per annum preter feodum et pensionem xxvj li. xij s.[6]

Pendesham Remanent ibidem ij jumenta, xij boves, j taurus, j taurellus, xxiiij vacce, iij bovetti, j juvenca, iij boviculi, ij juvencule, vj vituli, vij hurtardi, CCij oves matrices, xxxviij jercie, ix agni, j aper, ij sues, xvij porci, ix porculi, vj porcelli, iij auce unde j anser et ij mariole, xij capones, j gallus, et vj galline.
Valor manerii hoc anno xlvij li.
De redditu termini Michaelis cum tallagio preter decasum vj li. xiiij d. ob. qua.
De redditu[7] sancti Thome apostoli Cxvij s. vj d.
De redditu termini annunciacionis beate Marie Cxvij s.
De redditu termini nativitatis sancti Johannis baptiste vj li.
Et levand*um* sunt ibidem per annum de claro xxxij li.

Pendefen[8] Valor hoc anno xlj li. x s.
De redditu termini Michaelis cum tallagio preter decasum vj li. xv s. iij d.
De redditu termini sancti Andree apostoli vij li.
De redditu termini annunciacionis beate Marie vij li.
De redditu termini nativitatis sancti Johannis baptiste vij li. ij s. vj d.
Et levand*um* sunt ibidem per annum de claro xxxv li.

Herdwyk Remanent ibidem iiij equi carectarii, xxxvij boves, ij vacce, Clxxiiij multones, Cl agni, ij apri, v sues, xxxviij porci, xxxv porculi, xxvj porcelli, vj auce unde ij anseres iiij mariole, xxiiij capones, j gallus, xv galline.
Valor manerii hoc anno xvj li.
De redditu termini Michaelis cum tallagio preter decasum iiij li. x s.
De redditu termini natalis Domini iiij li. x s.
De redditu termini annunciacionis beate Marie iiij li. x s.

[6] The fee, of £10 p.a., was that of the steward of the Western Parts. The recipient of the pension of £10 p.a. is named as Peter de Crete, of whom no further details are recorded (WAM 22125).
[7] MS omits 'redditu'.
[8] The absence of an inventory of livestock in the following entry betrays the fact that the lease of the demesne to the whole vill of Pinvin, at a rent of 40s. p.a., first mentioned explicitly in the surviving sources in 1357–8, had already taken effect (WAM 22286).

De redditu termini nativitatis sancti Johannis baptiste iiij li. x s.[9]
Et levand*um* sunt ibidem per annum xxviij li. Et debet l s.

Todynham Remanent ibidem iiij equi carectarii, xxxij boves unde v cronarti, j vacca, j jumentum, j juvencula, j vitulus, x hurtardi, Clxxiij multones, Clxx oves matrices, Cvij hogastri et jercie unde iiij^{xx}xj jercie et xvj hogastri, ij agni, ij apri, iij sues, xx porci, x porculi, x porcelli, j anser, iij auce mariole, xxiiij capones, ij galli, xviij galline.
Valor hoc anno xxxj li.
De redditu termini Michaelis cum tallagio preter decasum Cij s.
De redditu termini natalis Domini xxvj s. ij d.
De redditu termini annunciacionis beate Marie xxj s. x d.
De redditu termini nativitatis sancti Johannis baptiste xxvj s. ij d.
Et levand*um* sunt ibidem per annum xvj li.

Borton' Remanent ibidem iiij jumenta, j vacca, j juvenca, xij boves, j bovettus, j boviculus, j vitulus, CCClxiij multones, xxxiiij hogastri, Cxlvj agni, ij apri, iij sues, xxiiij porci, x porculi, xiij porcelli, ij galli, x galline, xxij capones.
Valor manerii hoc anno xxxix li.
De redditu termini Michaelis cum tallagio preter decasum xlvj s.
De redditu termini natalis Domini iiij li.
De redditu termini annunciacionis beate Marie iiij li. xv s.
De redditu termini nativitatis sancti Johannis baptiste iiij li.[10]
Et levand*um* sunt ibidem per annum de claro xvj li.

Morton' Remanent ibidem j pullanus femellus etatis ij annorum, viij boves, Cix multones, j aper, j sus, xix porci, x porculi, xj porcelli, xxj carectates feni.
Valor manerii hoc anno xlj li. vj s.
De redditu Michaelis cum tallagio preter decasum Cvj s.
De redditu termini natalis Domini iiij li. xviij s.
De redditu termini annunciacionis beate Marie iiij li. xviij s.
De redditu termini nativitatis sancti Johannis baptiste iiij li. xviij s.
De redditu termini sancti Petri ad vincul*am* ij s. vj d.
Et levand*um* sunt ibidem per annum de claro xxvj li. Et debet iiij s.

[9] That is, £2 more than the *valor*.
[10] MS: 'de redditu termini sancti Petri ad vincul*am* ij s. vj d.' follows, but the sum has been struck out and the intention was probably to cancel the entire entry. In fact the abbot's rents at Bourton-on-the-Hill included Peter's Pence, but at the lower sum of 1s. 11½d.

Longedon Remanent ibidem ij jumenta, j taurus, viij boves, iiij bovetti, j aper, iij sues, xxj porci, xij porculi, xx porcelli, xxix auce unde j anser iiij mariole, xij capones, j gallus, vj galline.
Valor manerii hoc anno xij li.
De redditu termini Michaelis[11] preter decasum lij s. vj d.
De redditu termini natalis Domini xlij s.
De redditu termini annunciacionis beate Marie xlij s.
De redditu termini nativitatis sancti Johannis baptiste xlij s.
Et levand*um* sunt ibidem per annum de claro xiij li.

Islep' Remanent ibidem j qr. iij bus. frumenti, j qr. iij bus. brasei frumenti, xl qr. brasei ordei et drageti, iiij equi carectarii, xxxvij boves, j jumentum, vij hurtardi, CCvij oves matrices, Clv agni, ij apri, iij sues, xlvij porci, xxvj porculi, ix porcelli, lv auce unde ij anseres et vij mariole, xxxiiij capones, ij galli, xij galline, l carectates feni.
Valor manerii hoc anno iiij^{xx}xvij li.
De redditu termini Michaelis cum tallagio preter decasum xv li. iiij s. iiij d.
De redditu termini natalis Domini iiij li.
De redditu termini annunciacionis beate Marie iiij li. xv s. vj d.
De redditu termini nativitatis sancti Johannis baptiste iiij li.
Et levand*um* sunt ibidem per annum xliiij li. Et debet vj li.

Sutton' Remanent ibidem j qr. vij bus. mixtilionis, xiij qr. brasei drageti, j pullanus femellus etatis ij annorum, ij sues, x porci, vj porcelli, j multo,[12] j ovis matrix, j agnus, xij auce unde j anser iij mariole, ij galli, xij galline, ij rusce apium.[13]
Valor manerii hoc anno xxij li.
De redditu termini Michaelis cum tallagio preter decasum viij li. iiij d. qua.
De redditu termini natalis Domini xliij s. xj d. qua.
De redditu termini annunciacionis beate Marie xliiij s. v d. ob.

[11] MS omits 'cum tallagio'.
[12] MS: 'multon''.
[13] For the champarty agreement made in the course of the year 1354–5, which explains the virtual absence of draught animals in this inventory and in similar inventories subsequently until *c.*1380, see GRO, D1099/M50. According to the agreement between Abbot Simon Langham on the one part and William atte Welles, reeve of Sutton and the homage of the vill on the other, the reeve and certain tenants of the vill were to cultivate the arable demesne and to receive half the issues of corn every year during the abbot's lifetime. Langham, abbot of Westminster 1349–62, and subsequently bishop of Ely, archbishop of Canterbury and a cardinal, died at Avignon in 1376. The champarty agreement lasted until 1378–9 (GRO, D1099/M31/44–6).

De redditu termini nativitatis sancti Johannis baptiste xliij s. xj d. qua.
De redditu termini sancti Petri ad vincula xix d.
Et levand*um* sunt ibidem per annum xviij li. preter bladum. Et debet x.....[14]

Chaddisle Remanent ibidem ij jumenta, j pullanus masculus etatis ij annorum, x boves, ij tauri, v bovetti, xxiiij vacce, j juvenc*a*, viij vituli, j aper, ij sues, xxv porci, xvj porculi, xvj porcelli, ix hurtardi, Ciiij^{xx}xiij oves matrices, iiij agni, xj auce unde ij anseres et iiij mariole, xij capones, j gallus, vj galline.
Valor manerii hoc anno xxviij li.
De redditu termini Michaelis cum tallagio preter decasum xx s.
De redditu termini natalis Domini xiiij s.
De redditu termini annunciacionis beate Marie xiiij s.
De redditu termini nativitatis sancti Johannis baptiste xiiij s.
Et levand*um* sunt ibidem per annum xiiij li. x s. Et debet xiij s. iiij d.

[*Dorse*] *Durhurst* Remanent ibidem ij equi, ix boves, iij boviculi, j vacca, iiij juvencule, Ciij hoggastri, iiij^{xx}vj jercie, j aper, ij sue*s*, xix porci, viij porculi, ix porcelli, iij auce unde j anser ij mariole, j gallus, vij galline.
Valor manerii hoc anno xxix li.
De redditu termini Michaelis cum tallagio preter decasum vj li.
De redditu termini natalis Domini iiij li.
De redditu annunciacionis beate Marie Cv s.
De redditu termini nativitatis sancti Johannis baptiste iiij li. iiij s vj d.
Et levand*um* sunt ibidem per annum xxiij li. Et debet super visum vj li. xvj s.[15]

Denham Remanent ibidem xj qr. frumenti, iij bus. pisarum albarum, ij bus. pisarum grisarum, viij qr. iiij bus. avenarum, xxv qr. iij bus. brasei, iiij equi carectarii, ix jumenta, vj pullani quorum iiij masculi, vj affri, xxv boves, lix vacce, j bovettus, ix hurtardi, iij multones, Clxxvj oves matrices, lx[16] jercie, j agnus, ij apri, iiij sues, lviij porci, xxxj porcelli, vij signi, xxvij auce unde j anser iiij mariole, xviij capones, j gallus, vj galline.
Valor manerii hoc anno Cvij li. xiiij s. .....,[17] et sic preter reprisas lx li. xiiij s.[18]
Et serviens ibidem debet iiij li. xvij d.
De redditu levabili per annum xviij li. xvj s. qua.

[14] MS damaged.
[15] MS: a figure for pence may have been lost at the end of the line, which is slightly damaged; a reference to the half-yearly view of account, held in principle in late March.
[16] MS: one or more digits of this number, which is at the end of a line, may have been lost.
[17] MS: a figure for pence may have been lost at this point, which comes at the end of the line.
[18] For these reprises, see I 1.

De firmis viij li. vij s. vj d.
Levabil*e* ibidem de claro xlv li. xviij s. v d.[19]

Pirford' Remanent ibidem vj qr. ij bus. siliginis, viij qr. avenarum, iij affri, j pullanus femellus, iiij boves, Clxj multones, viij hurtardi, Cxxiij oves matrices, xlv agni, x porci, j sus, xv porcelli.
Et prepositus ibidem debet lxiij s.[20] iiij d.
Valor manerii hoc anno liiij li. xvj s.
Levabil*e* ibidem de claro xlix li.

Ȝeveneye Remanent ibidem ij equi carectarii, v affri, xviij boves, j taurus, xxix vacce, iiij taurelli, xxj juvence, xxij boviculi, xj juvencule, xij vituli, j aper, iij sues, xxx porci, xij porcelli, xxxviij auce unde ij anseres v mariole, j gallus, vj galline.
Et prepositus ibidem debet xx s.
Valor manerii hoc anno xxv li.
Levabil*e* ibidem de claro xvj li., unde de redditu levabili per annum Cs.

Lalham Remanent ibidem ij equi carectarii, j pullanus masculus, j taurus, xxix vacce, vj hurtardi, CCxlviij multones, CCiiij oves matrices, iiij^{xx} hogastri et jercie, CCCvj agni, j aper, ij sues, xx porci, xiij porculi, xviij porcelli, xxiiij auce unde j anser iij mariole, xij capones, j gallus, vj galline.
Et prepositus ibidem debet viij li. xviij s. iij d. ob.
Valor manerii hoc anno xlij li. v s.
Levabile ibidem per annum xix li.

Stanes Valet hoc anno xxvij li.
Levabil*e* ibidem per annum preter placita et perquisit*a* xxj li. x s.[21]
Et debet lij s.

*Eyb*ur*y* Remanent ibidem ij jumenta pro carectis, iiij jumenta pro carucis, vj pulli de exitu, x boves, iiij tauri, lxix vacce, j aper, iiij sues, iiij porci, xvij porcelli, vij hurtardi, Clvij oves matrices unde ix cronande.
Valet hoc anno preter asportat*um* per servientem xliij li.[22]

[19] MS omits 'd.'
[20] MS omits 's.'
[21] Comparison with a rental of Staines dated 6 December 1353, when leviable rents amounted to *c.*£20 p.a., suggests that a very high proportion of the above sum consisted of rents (WAM 61786).
[22] A reference to John atte Gate, serjeant of Ebury 1349–55. In 1353–4 and again in 1354–5, Gate paid a fine of £10 to avoid a full audit of his account (WAM 26910–11). A new serjeant had been appointed by 29 September 1356 (WAM 26912).

De redditu et firmis levabilibus per annum viij li. xv s.
Levand*um* sunt ibidem de claro xxvij li. xv s.

Summa levand*a* in maneriis occidentalibus CCiiij^{xx}xj li.
Summa levand*a* in maneriis propinquis preter Denham Cxxxiij li. v s.
Summa frumenti et mixtilionis xx qr. iiij bus.
Summa brasei iiij^{xx}iij qr. vj bus.
Summa equorum carectariorum xxiiij, affri[23] xviij, jumenta xxviij, pullani et pulli xxij, boves CCxlviij, tauri xij, vacce CCxxxix, bovetti et boviculi xlix, juvence et juvencule xlij, vituli de exitu xxix.
Hurtardi lxiiij, multones et hogastri MDCCv, matrices et jercie MDCCxiij, agni de exitu DCCCxij. Summa MMMMCCCij.
Apri xix, sues et suelle xlv, porci CCCiiij^{xx}xvj, porculi CC, porcelli CCvj.

[23] The text switches here from the genitive to the nominative.

I 5 States of the abbot's manors and portions at the conclusion of the audit of accounts for the year ending on 28 September 1363

A parchment roll of four membranes; membranes 1 to 3 are approximately 160 mm wide, and are sewn Chancery fashion, with white thread using a tight oversew; membrane 4 is a small, unattached piece of parchment and may represent one item in an entry for the manor of Hyde—as part of the process of abbreviating the material for the status—that was intended for the unused space, 230 mm in length, at the end of membrane 3, but never entered there. The roll is a well laid out fair copy, and membranes 1 and 2 both have three vertical folds to assist in the layout; membrane 3 has four vertical folds. The dorse of membranes 1 to 3 is blank, with the exception of 'Status terrarum et porcionum domini abbatis Westm' ..... de anno xxxvij°' written on the back of membrane 1 in a later hand. The text of paragraphs recording rent is laid out with the entry for each term on a new line, but is edited here as continuous text.[1]

WAM 6191

[*Mem. 1 recto*] Status terrarum et porcionum domini abbatis Westm' super auditum compoti ministrorum in vigilia sancti Michaelis archangeli anno regni regis Edwardi tercii post conquestum xxxvij°

Islep' Summa terminorum sancti Michaelis xv li. xix s. iiij d., sancti Thome apostoli iiij li. xiij s. vj d., annunciacionis Cxv s. vij d., sancti Johannis baptiste iiij li. xviij s. viij d. Totalis xxxj li. vij s. j d.
Valor manerii hoc anno lij li. xviij s. vj d. preter lanam.[2]
Arreragia Willelmi Dolle prepositi viij li.[3]
Remanent super compotum iij qr. brasei, ij equi carectarii, xxiiij boves, vitulus masculus, v hurtardi, Cxxvij multones, Cxxvij oves matrices, xviij agni, j aper, iiij sues, xxx porci pro lardario,[4] xxx porculi, xxj porcelli, ij

[1] Extant ministers' accounts: Bourton-on-the-Hill, WAM 8291; Chaceley, WAM 21089; Ebury, view of account, 2 March 1363, WAM 26906; Islip, WAM 14802; Laleham, 29 September 1362–18 February 1363, WAM 26906; Pinvin, WAM 22920; Sutton-under Brailes, WAM 28969; Todenham, WAM 25969; Yeoveney, 29 September 1362–25 March 1363, WAM 16882.

[2] 236 fleeces, weighing 23 st. 2 lb., were sent for sale from Islip to Bourton-on-the-Hill, now the collecting centre for wool produced on the abbot's manors in the Western Parts. At Bourton, the total crop from these manors of 2,431 fleeces, weighing 11½ sacks, was sold, under the supervision of Br. John Lakyngheth, the abbot's treasurer, to John Osbern, a London merchant. Of this total, Osbern received merchant's advantage amounting to one sack (WAM 8291, the source for numbers of fleeces noted below; 14802).

[3] Dolle was reeve of Islip 1351–86. As reeve he received half the demesne arable crops at Islip, in accordance with a champarty agreement made in 1360–1 (WAM 14802).

[4] i.e. the 30 'fat pigs' that Dolle, who farmed the piggery, was to deliver to the abbot's household this year (WAM 14802).

anseres, vij mariole, xxviij capones, ij galli, xij galline, iiij rusce apium, j olla enea continens unam lagenam di., j securis et j sarra.

Sutton' Summa terminorum sancti Michaelis vij li. v s. j d., natalis Domini xlvij s. xj d., pasche xlv s. iij d., nativitatis sancti Johannis baptiste xliiij s. ix d. Totalis xiij li. iij s.
Valor manerii hoc anno xxvij li. preter xij petras iiij lib. lane.[5]
Arreragia Thome Welles prepositi ibidem l s.
Remanent super compotum ij apri, j sus, j suella, viij porci, vj porculi, ij porcelli, j hurtardus, lxx multones, lxv oves matrices, x agni, j anser, iiij mariole, ij galli, xij galline, iij capones et lx carectates feni.

Todenham Summa terminorum sancti Michaelis vj li. xviij s. j d. ob. qua., natalis Domini liij s. vj d. ob. qua., annunciacionis Marie et pasche lxj s. ij d., nativitatis sancti Johannis baptiste liij s. iiij d. Totalis xv li. vj s. ij d. ob.
Valor manerii hoc anno xxiij li. xvj s. preter xl petras lane.[6]
Arreragia Rogeri firmarii vij li.,[7] Johannis Blisse prepositi xj li. ij s. viij d. Inde respectuantur xxij s. viij d.
Remanent super compotum ij equi, xxiiij boves, j vacca, j aper, iij sues, xiij hogetti, v porculi, xij porcelli lactantes, viij hurtardi, CCiiij oves matrices, lviij hogastri, iiij^{xx}vij jercie, Cxiiij agni, xviij capones, j gallus, xviij galline, ij anseres, iiij mariole, ij lagene tarre et j barellus continens xij lagenas, et lxiij carectates feni.

Bourton' Summa terminorum sancti Michaelis lxj s. iiij d., natalis Domini xxxix s. vij d., annunciaconis beate Marie xlj s. vij d., nativitatis sancti Johannis xxxix s. x d. ob. qua. Totalis vij li. ij s. vj d.[8]
Valor manerii hoc anno xiij li. vj s. preter lviij petras viij lib. lane.[9]
Arreragia nulla.
Remanent super compotum iiij jumenta, x boves, j vacca, ij juvencule, CCCCxvj multones, j aper, ij sues, xxiiij porci, xij porcelli, ij galli, x galline,

[5] The weight of 153 fleeces. For the champarty arrangement currently in operation on the arable demesne in this manor, see I 4.
[6] The weight of 254 fleeces. At the collecting centre the weight is given as 40 st. 3 lb. (WAM 8291).
[7] Roger de Erdyngton, farmer of the arable demesne, with some meadow and pasture, 1360–74. His farm included 2 cart-horses, 24 oxen and the pigs listed in the following inventory (WAM 25965–6, 25970–1; GRO, D1099/M30/10–11). Until and including 1362–3, John Blisse accounted, as reeve, for the demesne sheep and other stock excluded from Erdyngton's lease (WAM 25966–7, 25969).
[8] Correctly, it may appear, £9 2s. 4¾d. However, the difference between the two sums (£1 19s. 10d.) is identical with the sum of rents for the quarter ending on 24 June, and this was evidently held over until the next year of account.
[9] The weight of 413 fleeces.

xx capones, l clades, ij barelli tarre continentes xxiiij lagenas, et ij lagene in alio veteri barello, et lxx carectates feni.

Pershore Summa terminorum sancti Michaelis xj li. xvj d. ob., sancti[10] Andr*ee* Cxix s. vij d. ob., annunciacionis beate Marie ix li. xvj s. ix d., nativitatis sancti Johannis vj li. xv d. Totalis xxxij li. xix s.
Valet manerium hoc anno xvj li. xix s. preter ij saccos viij lib. lane.[11]
Arreragia Ricardi Darnel prepositi j d. qua.
Remanent super compotum j qr. v bus. brasei, j equus pro molendino, ij pullani, ix boves, ij juvence, iij vituli, j aper, ij sues, xviij porci, iiij porculi, vij porcelli, CCx multones, CCl hogastri, xij capones, j gallus, v galline, lx carectates feni, j olla enea continens ij lagene et j urciolus continens j lagenam.

Pendesham Summa terminorum sancti Michaelis vj li. iiij s. x d., sancti Andr*ee* vj li. xij s. vj d., annunciacionis vj li. xij s., nativitatis sancti Johannis vj li. xv s. Totalis xxvj li. iiij s. iiij d.
Valor manerii hoc anno xxxiij li. xv s. preter xix petras j lib. di. lane.[12]
Arreragia Ade Andrew prepositi iij s. iiij d.[13]
Remanent super compotum ij jumenta, xj boves, iiij boviculi, ij tauri, xxj vacce, ij juvencule, iiij vituli, viij hurtardi, CCv oves matrices, iiij^{xx}xiij agni, j aper, ij sues, xvj porci pro lardario, vj porculi, viij porcelli, j ancer, ij mariole, xij capones, vj galline.

Pendefen Summa terminorum sancti Michaelis viij li. xvij s. ix d., sancti Andr*ee* viij li. ix. s. vj d., annunciacionis viij li. v s. vj d., nativitatis sancti Johannis viij li. iij s. vj d. Totalis xxxiij li. xvj s. iij d.
Nullum remanet ibidem staurum quia terra dominica ad firmam.[14]
Valor manerii hoc anno xxxv li. xviij s. v d.
Arreragia Johannis Broun prepositi xxxvj s. qua.[15] Inde respectuantur v s. xj d. ob. qua. de reddditu de Wyche.

Herdewyk' Summa terminorum sancti Michaelis Cxiij s. ob., natalis Domini Cxiij s. ob., annunciacionis Cxiij s. ob., nativitatis sancti Johannis Cxvviij s. vij d. Totalis xxij li. xvij s. viij d. ob.

[10] MS omits 'sancti'.
[11] The weight of 412 fleeces.
[12] The weight of 205 fleeces.
[13] Andrew was reeve of Pensham 1351–70, bailiff 1370–1, and reeve again 1374–5 (WAM 23213–26).
[14] For this lease, see I 4.
[15] Broun, alias John Baron, was reeve of Pinvin 1361–4 (WAM 22289–91; and see n. 24 below).

Valor manerii hoc anno xxxviij li. vj s. preter xvij petras et x lib. lane.[16]
Arreragia Johannis Bernard prepositi Cxj s. j d. Inde respectuantur xxxviij s., et residuum pro bidentibus emendis.
Remanent super compotum iiij equi, xxvij boves, ij vacce, Cxlij multones, iiij^{xx}xvij agni, ij apri, iiij sues, lij porci unde xxvj pro lardario, xv porculi, xviij porcelli, j anser, vj mariole, xxiiij capones, ij galli, x galline, xxxiiij carectates feni, j barellus tarre continens xij lagenas, iiij vomeres et ij cultre.

[*Mem. 2 recto*] *Durhurst* Summa terminorum sancti Michaelis vij li. viij s. vj d., natalis Domini Cj s. iij d., annunciacionis vj li. viij s. ij d., nativitatis sancti Johannis iiij li. xix s. vj d. Totalis xxiij li. xvij s. v d.
Valor manerii hoc anno xxx li. cum lana appreciata ad viij li.[17]
Arreragia Johannis prepositi ibidem[18] vij li. iiij s. vj d. qua.[19]
Remanent super compotum j affrus, j jumentum, viij boves, j vacca, CCxl multones et vj carectates feni.

Chaddesle Summa terminorum sancti Michaelis xxix s. iiij d., natalis Domini xxiij s. ij d., annunciacionis xxiiij s. ij d., nativitatis sancti Johannis xxiiij s. Totalis C s. viij d.
Valor manerii hoc anno x li. preter xiiij petras lane.[20]
Arreragia nulla.
Remanent super compotum ij jumenta, viij boves, j taurus, xxviij vacce, xij vituli unde vj annales, j aper, ij sues, xxij porci, xiiij porculi, vj porcelli, iiij hurtardi, CCj oves matrices, xj agni, j anser, iij mariole, xij capones, j gallus, vj galline, xl clades, xxx carectates feni et vij lagene tarre.

Longedon' Summa terminorum sancti Michaelis lxxv s., sancti[21] Andr*ee* lxxv s., annunciacionis lxxv s.,[22] nativitatis sancti Johannis lxxv s. Totalis xv li.[23]

[16] The weight of 171 fleeces; at the collecting centre the weight is given as 17 st. 9 lb. (WAM 8291).
[17] MS: 'xxx li. cum lana appreciate ad viij li.' inserted in a second hand. 215 fleeces, weighing 20 st. 2 lb., were sent from Deerhurst to the collecting centre this year (WAM 8291).
[18] Probably John Palmer, reeve of Deerhurst 1362–6 (WAM 8450, 24511; I 6).
[19] MS: the cash sum is in the same additional hand that added the cash sum and valuation of wool in the *valor* statement immediately preceding.
[20] The weight of 205 fleeces. At the collecting centre, the weight is given as 14 st. 2 lb. (WAM 8291, 21089).
[21] MS omits 'sancti'.
[22] MS: followed by 'lx', struck out.
[23] The manor was leased to Robert de Grafton, Alexander de Wynkebourne and Henry Grafton, vicar of Longdon, on 25 June, 1357, with livestock and dead stock, for 20 years, and the lessees owed the rent of £15 p.a. recorded here. Their lease excluded, among other items, perquisites of courts (WAM 32744).

Valet hoc anno xxvj li. xiij s. vij d. cum relevio.
Arreragia Johannis Broun collectoris x li. xvj s. j d.; inde de relevio uxoris Edwardi Kerdiff' viij li. xij s. ij d.[24]

Morton Summa terminorum sancti Michaelis ix li. xvij s. ij d., natalis Domini vj li. v s. vij d., annunciacionis vj li. vj s., nativitatis sancti Johannis vj li. ix s. Totalis xxviij li. xvij s. ix d.
Valet hoc anno xxviij li. xiij s. j d. preter xx petras ij lib. lane.[25]
Arreragia Ricardi Ode iiij li. x s. qua., Johannis Pagene et Henrici Ode xxvj s. v d. qua., Nicholai Gerueys xj li. xvj s. v d. ob. qua., Roberti de Wilyngton' ix s. viij d. ob. qua., Willelmi Haukyns lxxij s. iiij d. ob. qua., eiusdem Willelmi[26] lvij s. iiij d. ob. qua., Ricardi de Bradestok lxxvij s. ix d. ob. qua., Ricardi Mulward Cij s. vij d. qua., Henrici Ode nunc collectoris xl s.[27] Totalis xxxv li. xij s. x d. ob. qua.[28]
Remanent super compotum j bos in calumpnia et Ciiij^{xx}vj multones.

Wyk de hundredo Johannes Staunton ballivus ibidem debet xxxiiij s. j d.
Valet hoc anno xxvij s. ij d.
Pershore portmot' Johannes Glovere ballivus ibidem debet xviij s. vj d.
Valet hoc anno xxxvij s. v d.
Pendefen Johannes Tondy ballivus hundredi ibidem debet x s. vj d.
Valet hoc anno xvj s. viij d.
Defford' Robertus Berald' ballivus hundredi ibidem debet xxvj s. viij d. qua.
Valet hoc anno xxxvj s.
Glouc' Johannes Derneford' ballivus ibidem debet Cj s. iiij d.
Valet hoc anno viij li. viij s.

[24] For Broun, alias John Baron, collector of court estreats at Longdon and Castlemorton, see WAM 21024–5, 24511–14, 24516; and I 12. Kerdyff is now elusive; for his wife's relief, see I 6–7.
[25] The weight of 167 fleeces.
[26] MS: 'eundem Willelmum'; the second letter of 'eundem' has been altered.
[27] Ode was reeve of Castlemorton 28 September 1352–25 March 1353 (WAM 21053). For John Pagene, reeve, and William Haukyns, rent-collector, in 1357–8, see WAM 21056. Robert de Wilyngton, alias Wolyngton, was serjeant at Castlemorton 25 March–28 September 1354 (WAM 21054–5); and, as noted in the text, Henry Ode was currently rent-collector. No office or dates can be assigned to Nicholas Gerveys or Richard Mulward. Since 28 September 1357, Richard de Bradestok had been farmer of the demesne arable and meadow but not the pastures, at a rent of £4 in the first year but rising to £5 p.a. for the rest of his term (WAM 21056).
[28] This sum is misplaced in the MS, where it occurs after the next and last entry for Castlemorton.

Lalham Summa terminorum sancti Michaelis iiij li. viij s., natalis Domini lxj s. vj d., annunciacionis lxij s. iiij d., nativitatis sancti Johannis lxij s. vj d. Totalis xiij li. xiiij s. iiij d.
Valor manerii hoc anno xxix li. xv s. preter iijCiiij^{xx}iij vellera lane.[29]
Arreragia Johannis Heyward' nuper prepositi x li. ij s. qua., inde[30] respectuantur iij s. xj d.[31] Et remanent clare ix li. xviij s. j d. qua. Johannes South' nuper collectoris xxxij s. viij d.[32]
Excessus Johannis Mille ballivi ibidem lxxiij s. ob.
Remanent super compotum v qr. ij bus. brasei ordei, ij equi carectarii, iij stotti, j pullanus, xij boves, ij hurtardi, Ciiij^{xx}vij multones, Cxxxviij oves matrices, Ciij hogastri, xiiij agni, j anser, ix auce, j gallus, vj galline, xij capones, j aper, iij sues, xij porci, xvj porculi, v hogetti, xiiij porcelli, j corium dealbatum, xiij pelles lanute, ix pellette et per estimacionem liiij carectates feni.

Piryford' Summa terminorum sancti Michaelis xviij li. xix s. x d. ob., sancti Thome apostoli viij li. xiiij s. viij d., pentecost*es* vij li. x s. xj d. Totalis xxxv li. v s. v d. ob.
Valor manerii hoc anno xlv li. xiij s. preter iijCiiij^{xx}v vellera lane.[33]
Arreragia Johannis atte Hethe nuper prepositi xxxvij ob. qua., inde respectuantur vij s. v d. ob., et remanent clare xxix s. vij d.;[34] Nicholai Chike lij s. x d. qua., inde respectuantur xv s. j d. ob., et remanent clare xxxvij s. ix d.[35]
Remanent super compotum j qr. brasei, iij affri, vj boves, j vacca, j vitulus,[36] v hurtardi, Clxj multones, Clxx oves matrices, iiij^{xx}xiij hogastri, Cvj agni, ij sues, ij apri, xv porculi, ij pellette, iij cigniculi, j anser, iiij mariole, xvij aucule, xij capones, j gallus, iiij galline et xxix carectates feni, j pavo et j pava.

[29] MS: 'preter iijCiiij^{xx}iij vellera lane' inserted. We can assume that these fleeces were sent to Ebury, now the collecting centre for wool produced on the abbot's manors in the Eastern Parts, and stored for the time being in the outbuilding of the abbot's house at La Neyte, in Ebury, mentioned below.
[30] MS: 'inde respectuantur iij s. xj d. Et remanent clare ix li. xviij s. j d. qua.' inserted.
[31] Heyward, reeve since 29 September 1362, was removed from office on 18 February 1363; Mille was admitted to office as serjeant or bailiff on the same day and served until 1388 (WAM 27146–58, 24531–2, 24536 and 24536*).
[32] South served as reeve 1356–8 and as rent-collector before the current year (WAM 27141–2).
[33] MS: 'xlv li. xiij s. preter iijCiiij^{xx}v vellera lane' inserted.
[34] Hethe was reeve 1361–2 (WAM 27418).
[35] MS: 'inde respectuantur xv s. j d. ob., et remanent clare xxxvij s. ix d.' inserted. Chike may have served as rent-collector and bailiff at Pyrford before his service as bailiff at Yeoveney 1361–3 (WAM 16881–2).
[36] MS: 'j vitulus' inserted.

[*Mem. 3 recto*] *Yevene* Summa terminorum sancti Michaelis liiij s. iij d. ob. qua., annunciacionis xlix s. iij d. ob. qua. Totalis Ciij s. vij d. ob.
Valor manerii hoc anno xxxij li.
Arreragia Nicholai Chike nuper ballivi viij li. xj s. qua., inde respectuantur Cvij s., et remanent clare lxiiij s. qua.[37]
Remanent ibidem in custodia Johannis Clerk firmarii ibidem iiij affri precium xx s., j taurus, x boves precium capitis xiij s. iiij d.

Denham Summa terminorum sancti Michaelis vj li. xj s., natalis Domini vj li. iij s. vij d., annunciacionis vj li. x s. iij d. ob., Johannis baptiste vj li. iij s. vij d., gulam Augusti xij d. ob. Totalis xxv li. ix s. vj d.
Remanent super compotum iij qr. ij bus. frumenti,[38] xx qr. vj bus. brasei ordei, j qr. iij bus. brasei drageti, iiij equi, iiij jumenta, vij affri, viij pullani, ij tauri, xlviij vacce, vj boviculi, xxviij boves, iij juvence, j corium dealbatum, ix hurtardi, Clxviij oves matrices, lxiij agni, iij apri, iij sues, xx porci, xxvj porculi, xx porcelli, x pellette, xiiij cigni, iij cignotti,[39] xviij cigniculi, iiij anseres, viij mariole, xxiiij aucule, lv capones, ij galli et vj galline.
Valor[40] manerii hoc anno lxiiij li. xviij s. preter Clxij vellera lane et lxx vellera agnorum.
Arreragia Roberti Broun ballivi xxj li. v s. x d., inde respectuantur xxj li. iiij s. iij d.,[41] et remanent clare xix d.

Eybur' Summa terminorum sancti Michaelis xliiij s. x d. ob., natalis Domini xxxviij s. iij d. ob., pasche xliiij s. j d. ob., nativitatis sancti Johannis lj s. vij d. ob. Totalis viij li. xviij s. xj d.
Valor manerii hoc anno xxxiij li. viij s.
Arreragia Johannis atte Gate ballivi lxxviij s. j d. ob. qua.[42]
Remanent super compotum iij qr. iij p. siliginis, vj jumenta, j pullanus

[37] MS: 'et remanent clare lxiiij s. qua.' inserted. For Chike, see n. 35. John Clerk, alias John le Clerk, of Staines, was granted a farm of the demesne at Yeoveney on 24 March 1363 and at the same time assumed such responsibilities of the reeve as were not included in the farm. For the indenture between Chike and Clerk in which the demesne livestock and dead stock were listed, but neither the rent p.a. nor a term of years mentioned, see WAM 16882, rot. 2. The livestock listed in the indenture differed in some particulars from those apparently received by Clerk according to the panel above.
[38] MS: 'iij qr. ij bus. frumenti' inserted in main text hand.
[39] MS: 'iij cignotti' inserted.
[40] MS: the section for the *valor*, the arrears and clear value may be an insertion.
[41] Robert Broun is mentioned as bailiff of Denham 1363–8 (WAM 6196–7, 24512). The large respite may represent an early contribution from the abbot's central funds, to which Broun's arrears were in fact owing, to the cost of the new house for Abbot Litlyngton at Denham: the first references to this work occur in 1363–4. See I 7; and for Broun, WAM 24516; I 6.
[42] Gate was bailiff or serjeant of Ebury 6 April 1362–29 October 1364 (WAM 26916–20; I 7–8).

femellus, viij boves, ij tauri, lj vacce, j aper,[43] iiij sues, xiiij porci, xxiiij porcelli, di. corei dealbati[44] et liiij carectates feni per estimacionem.
Item remanent in quadam domo apud La Neyte M^{l}iijCxlix vellera lane.[45]

Stanes Summa terminorum sancti Michaelis vij li. xvj s. ij d. ob. qua., natalis Domini vij li. xvj s. ij d. qua., annunciacionis vij li. xvj s. ij d. qua., sancti Johannis baptiste vij li. xvj s. ij d. qua. Totalis xxxj li. iiij s. ix d. ob. Valet hoc anno xxviij li. iij s. iiij d.
Arreragia Johannis Tangleye nulla.[46]

[*Mem. 4 recto*] *Hyde* Remanent super compotum iij equi carectarii, j affrus, x boves,[47] j taurus, xxxj vacce, ij hurtardi, lvij multones, Ciiij^{xx}xix oves matrices, xiij hogastri, v jercie, ij anseres, iiij mariole, j gallus, v galline, xix capones, ix pavones et pave, ij agni, lxiiij clades, vj pellette, xxiiij carectates feni.[48]

[43] MS: 'j aper' inserted.
[44] MS: 'di. coreum dealbatum'.
[45] To the total of 1,349 fleeces recorded here, Laleham, Pyrford and Denham contributed 1,000 this year; and this year's crop of 236 fleeces at the manor of Hyde, though belonging to the prior and convent and not to the abbot, was to our knowledge delivered to the bailiff of La Neyte. The 113 fleeces needed to make up the total of 1,349 may have been left over from last year's crop. For the wool crop at Hyde, see WAM 27070.
[46] The absence of an inventory of livestock from this entry implies that the demesne was in the hands of a farmer, and it is a safe inference that the farmer was John Tangleye, the rent-collector (WAM 16933, 24511–12; I 6–8).
[47] MS omits 'x boves'; supplied from WAM 27070.
[48] MS: the following entries, in the nature of jottings, are written vertically on the back of mem. 4 but struck out: 'iijCiiij li. v s.; iijCxviij li. x s. iij d.; ijCxxxiiij li. xvj s.' Though assigned to the portion of the prior and convent, Hyde was, from 1363, administered as part of the abbot's portion, and was the responsibility of the abbot's steward in the Eastern Parts. The above panel relating to Hyde is written on a membrane that appears never to have been attached to the three membranes now constituting the rest of WAM 6191, but its contents are demonstrably an inventory of the livestock and dead stock of the manor of Hyde at the end of the year 1362–3, the year to which the other membranes relate (WAM 27070). It seems likely that it represents one item in a 'state' of this manor that was intended for the unused space at the end of the recto of mem. 3, but never entered there, and perhaps never completed.

I 6 States of the abbot's manors and portions at the conclusion of the audit of accounts for the year ending on 28 September 1365

A parchment roll of three membranes, approximately 145 mm wide, sewn Chancery fashion with white thread in a tight oversew. The roll is a fair copy, laid out on all three membranes with two vertical folds.[1] The dorse is blank except for a later note 'Status terrarum abbatis Westm' de anno xxxix^{o}' on membrane 1.

WAM 6197

[*Mem. 1 recto*] Status terrarum et porcionum domini abbatis Westm' super auditum compoti ministrorum suorum in vigilia sancti Michaelis anno regni regis Edwardi tercii xxxix^{o}

Lalham [Rents as in I 5: £13 14s. 4d.]
Valet manerium hoc anno xlij li. v s.[2]
Arreragia diversorum xvij li., unde super Johannem South' xxxij s. viij d., Johannem Haiward x li. ij s. qua., Johannem atte Mille vj li. xxij s. ob. qua.[3]
Remanent super compotum in granario vj qr. j bus. et di. frumenti, et in grangia per estimacionem xij qr. frumenti. Item in tasso xiij qr. puls' per estimacionem. Item v qr. v bus. brasei frumenti. Item xviij qr. brasei ordei. Item iij qr. iij bus. brasei drageti. Item ij equi carectarii. Item iiij stotti, xij boves, lxj multones, vj agni de exitu, iij apri, iiij sues, xij porci pro lardario, xv porculi, xx porcelli, xvj auce unde j anser et tres auce mariole, xxj capones, iij cigni erarii, iiij cigniculi, j gallus et vj galline, xvij carectates feni.

Periford' [Rents as in I 5: £35 5s. 5½d.]
Valet hoc anno liiij li. xvj s.
Arreragia Nicholai Chyke lij s. x d. qua., Willelmi Wippeschot viij li. x s. viij d. ob. qua.[4]

[1] Extant ministers' accounts: Bourton-on-the-Hill, WAM 8293; Chaceley, WAM 21090; Ebury, WAM 26920; Hyde, WAM 2072; Laleham, WAM 27147; Pensham, WAM 22220; Pinvin, WAM 22292; Pyrford, WAM 27419; Yeoveney, WAM 16884.
[2] Including hay and wool. 93 fleeces were sent to Br. Walter de Warfeld, one of two conventual treasurers who evidently marketed the wool from the abbot's manors in the Eastern Parts with wool from conventual manors in this period (WAM 27147).
[3] South was formerly rent-collector at Laleham, Haiward formerly reeve, and Mille currently serjeant.
[4] Wippeschot was reeve at Pyrford 1364–5 (WAM 27419, 24511); for Chyke's earlier service here, see I 5.

Remanent super compotum v qr. avenarum. Item iij affri, viij boves, ij hurtardi, Clxxix multones, Cxxxix oves matrices, iiij^{xx}xv agni de exitu, viij auce unde j anser et ij auce mariole, xv capones, iiij^{xx} carectates feni.[5]

Yeveneye Summa terminorum sancti Michaelis vij li. v s. viij d. qua., annunciacionis vj li. xvij s. viij d. qua. Totalis xiiij li. iij s. iiij d. ob.
Valet hoc anno xvj li. x s.
Excessus. Johannes Clerc firmarius ibidem excedit super compotum v s. xj d. ob.[6]
Remanent super compotum iiij affri, x boves, j gallus et vj galline et xij capones.

Denham [Rents as in I 5: £25 9s. 6d.]
Valet hoc anno iiij^{xx}xj li.
Arreragia Roberti Broun ballivi ibidem vj li. xj s. iij d. ob. qua.
Remanent super compotum xxix qr. iiij bus. frumenti per estimacionem in garbis, iiij qr. j bus. brasei frumenti, xj qr. v bus. brasei ordei, xxx qr. vij bus. brasei drageti, vj equi, iij jumenta, iij pullani, vj affri, ij tauri, xxvij boves, xliiij vacce, v hurtardi, xxij multones, Cxxvj oves matrices, Cxxix agni, iij apri, ij sues, xxviij porci, iiij porculi, xv porcelli, xj cigni et di., ix cigniculi, xlij auce unde v anseres et vij mariole, xl capones, j gallus, vj galline et lx carectates feni.

Eybur' Summa terminorum sancti Michaelis lvij s. vj d., natalis Domini xlj s. x d., pasche xlviij s. v d., nativitatis sancti Johannis baptiste xlj s. ix d. Totalis ix li. ix s. vj d.
Valor hoc anno xliiij li. xiiij s.[7]
Arreragia Nicholai Chike ballivi xij li. ix s. j d. ob., Johannis atte Gate nuper ballivi lx s.[8]
Remanent super compotum ij equi, iij jumenta, ij pullani, ix boves, ij tauri, xlviij vacce, j sus, ij cigni, j cignottus, iij cigniculi, iiij pavones, vj pave, iiij pavicule, xlvj penne pavonum, ij capones, iiij auce et lij carectates feni.

[5] 287 sheep's fleeces were sent to Br. Walter de Warfeld at Westminster this year (WAM 27419).
[6] Since 24 March 1363, Clerk was farmer of the demesne at Yeoveney, without a specified term; said to be of Staines (WAM 16882, rot. 2).
[7] The *valor* included hay delivered to the abbot's household and valued at £4 (WAM 26920).
[8] At the audit in 1365, Gate was given 2 February and 13 April 1366 as dates for payment of this sum, in equal instalments (WAM 26020–1).

Stanes Summa terminorum sancti Michaelis vij li. xv s. ix d. ob., natalis Domini vij li. xiiij s., annunciacionis vij li. xiiij s., nativitatis sancti Johannis vij li. xiiij s. Totalis xxix li. xvij s. ix d. ob.
Valet hoc anno xxxij li. vj s. viij d.
Arreragia nulla, nec staurum aliquod est ibidem, quia terre dominice sunt ad firmam.[9]

Hyde Summa terminorum sancti Michaelis xlvj s. iiij d., natalis Domini xlvj s. iiij d., pasche xlvj s. iiij d., nativitatis sancti Johannis xlvj s. iiij d. Totalis ix li. v s. iiij d.
Valet manerium hoc anno xxxix li.[10]
Arreragia Nicholai Chike nuper ballivi xxvj s. vij d.[11]
Remanent super compotum v bus. fabarum, iiij bus. pisarum, iiij bus. avenarum, ij equi carectarii, iiij stotti, xiij boves, j tauri, xli vacce, viij hurtardi, Cxiij multones, Ciiij^{xx}ix oves matrices, CCiiij^{xx}vij agni, ij anseres, iiij auce mariole, xix aucule, j gallus, vij galline, ix capones, xliiij clades et xxij carectates feni.

Islep' [Rents as in I 5: £31 7s. 1d.]
Valet manerium hoc anno iiij^{xx}ij li. x s.
Arreragia Willelmi Dolle prepositi viij li.
Remanent super compotum vj qr. frumenti, viij qr. iiij bus. pisarum, ij qr. vj bus. avenarum, xxj qr. ij bus. brasei, ij equi carectarii, xxiiij boves, ij bovetti, j hurtardus, CCxiij multones, xxvij oves matrices, xiiij hogastri, xxiij agni, j aper, iiij sues, xxx porci, xxx porculi, xxj porcelli, xxxiiij capones, ij anseres, vij auce mariole, ij galli, xij galline, iij cigni erarii, ij cigni albi et j cignottus.[12]

[*Mem. 2 recto*] *Sutton'* Summa terminorum sancti Michaelis Cvij s., natalis Domini iiij li. vj s., pasche iiij li. iij s., nativitatis sancti Johannis iiij li. ij s. x d. Totalis xvij li. xviij s. x d.
Valet manerium hoc anno xxxiiij li. xj s.
Arreragia Thome Willes nuper prepositi vij s. viij d. ob.,[13] Roberti de Preston' prepositi lx s. ij d.

[9] For John Tangleye, farmer of the demesne, see I 5.
[10] The *valor* included 451 sheep's fleeces and 178 lambs' fleeces delivered to Br. Walter de Warfeld at Westminster, for sale (WAM 27072).
[11] Chike, was bailiff of Hyde 28 September 1363–30 October 1364 (WAM 27170A–27172).
[12] 230 fleeces, weighing 1 sack 2 st. 2 lb., were sent this year from Islip to the collecting centre at Bourton-on-the-Hill (WAM 8293). As will appear in the course of this document, a total of 2,286 fleeces, weighing 10 sacks 17 st. 3 lb., were collected at Bourton and sold this year.
[13] Alias Thomas Welles, reeve at Sutton-under-Brailes 1362–3 (I 5).

Remanent super compotum j aper, j sus, viij porci, vij porculi, viij porcelli, j anser, iij auce mariole, xij capones, j gallus, viij galline et xx carectates feni.

Todenham [Rents as in I 5: £15 6s. 2½d.]
Valet manerium hoc anno xlvij li. x s.
Arreragia Rogeri de Erdyngton' firmarii iiij li.
Remanent super compotum vij qr. bus. multure molendini, ij equi carectarii, xxiiij boves, j aper, iij sues, xiij hogetti, v porculi, xij porcelli lactantes, j vacca, vj hurtardi, CClxxiiij multones, CClvij oves matrices, iij agni, xvj capones, ij galli, xviij galline, ij anseres, iiij auce mariole et xxxvj carectates feni.[14]

Bourton' [Rents as in I 5: £7 2s. 6d.]
Valet manerium hoc anno xlvj li. viij s.[15]
Arreragia Ricardi Alberd prepositi lxvj s. viij d.[16]
Remanent super compotum iiij jumenta, ix boves, j vacca, ij bovetti, j vitulus, CCCC multones,[17] ij apri, ij sues, xx porci, xiiij porculi, xiij porcelli, ij galli, x galline, xx capones, lxxiiij clades, j barellus tarre continens xij lagenas et lxviij carectates feni.

Pershore [Rents as in I 5: £32 19s.]
Valet manerium hoc anno lxvj li.
Arreragia Ricardi Darnel prepositi ibidem ix li. iiij s. viij d.
Remanent super compotum j equus pro molendino, iij equi carectarii, ij pullani, x boves, ij vacce, ij bovetti, iij boviculi, ij vituli, ij apri, ij sues, xxviij porci, xiij porculi, x porcelli, xxxj oves matrices, CCiiij^{xx}x hogastri, j gallus, v galline, Clvij agni et lxvij carectates feni.[18]

[14] 391 fleeces, weighing 1 sack 20 st., were sent from Todenham to the collecting centre at Bourton-on-the-Hill this year (WAM 8293).
[15] The *valor* included the wool of 495 fleeces, weighing 2 sacks 13 st., from the demesne sheep at Bourton-on-the-Hill, and these were added to the wool collected at Bourton from the other manors in the Western Parts this year (WAM 8293).
[16] Alberd was reeve of Bourton-on-the-Hill 1353–74 and 1376–7 (WAM 8283–303, 8305) and since 1363–4 farmer of the demesne pigs.
[17] MS: 'CCCC multones' inserted.
[18] 356 fleeces, weighing 1 sack 24 st. 4 lb., were sent this year from Pershore to the collecting centre at Bourton-on-the-Hill (WAM 8293).

Pendesham [Rents as in I 5: £26 4s. 4d.]
Valet manerium hoc anno xl li. xiiij s.[19]
Arreragia nulla.
Remanent super compotum ij jumenta, j pullanus, x boves, j taurus, xxj vacce, j taurellus, iij bovetti, iiij boviculi, j juvencula, vj vituli, iiij hurtardi, CCxvij oves matrices, j aper, ij sues, xv porci, x porculi, vij porcelli, j anser, j mariola, ix aucule, xij capones, j gallus, vj galline, xxx carectates feni et vij lagene tarre.

Herdewyke [Rents as in I 5: £22 17s. 8½d.]
Valet manerium hoc anno lj li. iij s.
Arreragia Johannis Bernard nuper prepositi vij li.[20]
Remanent super compotum per estimacionem in garbis v qr. puls',[21] iiij equi carectarii, xxiiij boves, ij vacce, ij vituli, CCxxxviij multones, CCxix agni, ij apri, iij sues, xliij porci, xviij porculi, xxv porcelli, j anser, vj mariole, xxiiij capones,[22] ij galli, x galline, x lagene tarri et xxvj carectates feni.[23]

Durhurst' Summa terminorum sancti Michaelis ix li. xviij s. vj d., natalis Domini Cj s. iij d., annunciacionis viij li. xix s. ij d., nativitatis sancti Johannis Cxviij s. vij d. Totalis xxviij li. xvij s. v d.
Valet manerium hoc anno xxxiij li. xviij s.
Arreragia Johannis Stacy nuper firmarii terrarum dominicarum xl s. vij d. ob. qua.,[24] Johannis Palmere prepositi lxxviij s. vij d. ob.
Nullum remanet ibidem staurum quia terre dominice sunt ad firmam.

[19] The *valor* included wool consisting of 222 fleeces sent this year to the collecting centre at Bourton-on-the-Hill. The weight is given as 20 st. 9 lb. at Pensham, but as 20 st. 13 lb. at Bourton: WAM 8293, 22220.

[20] Bernard was reeve at Hardwicke 1362–3 and possibly for a longer term (I 5).

[21] MS: 'per estimacionem in garbis v qr. puls'' inserted.

[22] MS: 'xxiiij capones' inserted.

[23] 225 fleeces, weighing 1 sack 5 st., were sent from Hardwicke this year to the collecting centre at Bourton-on-the-Hill (WAM 8293).

[24] In 1365–6, the year following that of the present entry, the arable demesne at Deerhurst was demonstrably farmed piecemeal, and hay sold in 25 stacks for a total sum of £4 6s. But the change from farming the demesne to a sole farmer, of whom the last for the time being was John Stacy, and piecemeal farming may actually have taken place in 1364–5. Stacy is mentioned as a farmer in 1365–6, of hay belonging to the demesne in a part of Deerhurst known as Cornham (WAM 8450).

Chaceley [Rents as in I 5: £5 0s. 8d.]
Valet manerium hoc anno xviij li. iij s.[25]
Arreragia Ricardi Hathemar' prepositi nulla.[26]
Remanent super compotum ij jumenta, viij boves, j taurus, xxv vacce,[27] j boviculus, j juvencula, vj vituli, j aper, ij sues, xxvij porci, xv porculi, vij porcelli, iij hurtardi, Ciiij^{xx}vij oves matrices, iiij agni, j anser, iij mariole, xij capones, j gallus, v galline, x lagene tarre et xxij carectates feni.

Longedon' [Rents as in I 5: £15]
Valet hoc anno xix li. iiij s.
Arreragia firmarii manerii ibidem C s., Johannis Broun collectoris perquisitorum curie xxviij s. v d., Edwardi[28] Kerdif' de parte relevii uxoris sui xxxij s.

[*Mem. 3 recto*] *Morton'* [Rents as in I 5: £28 17s. 9d.]
Valet hoc anno cum lana xxxv li. vij s.[29]
Arreragia antiqua xxxv li. xviij s. viij d., Henrici Holdy xxx s. ij d. qua.[30]
Remanent super compotum Ciiij^{xx}v multones, j ovis matrix, j agnus.[31]

Pendefen [Rents as in I 5: £33 162. 3d.]
Valet manerium hoc anno xxxvj li. xj s.
Arreragia Johannis Baron' nuper prepositi v s. vij d. qua., Nicholai Mower prepositi ij s. ij d.[32]
Nullum remanet ibidem staurum quia terre dominice sunt ad firmam.[33]

Wyke de hundredo Valet hoc anno xx s. xj d.
Arreragia Johannis Browet et Is' Wilcot ballivorum vij s. iiij d.
Hundredum de Pendesen Valet hoc anno xxx s. ix d.

[25] The *valor* included wool, consisting of 175 fleeces, weighing 14 st. 12 lb., sent this year to the collecting centre at Bourton-on-the Hill (WAM 8293, 21090).
[26] Richard Hathemar was reeve of Chaceley in 1364–6, but in 1365–6 jointly with his brother, John, whom he had in fact succeeded in 1364–5. For the participation of both in administration at Chaceley, see Appendix (WAM 21090–1).
[27] Of the 25 cows in the vaccary 21 were leased; for the terms, see WAM 21090.
[28] MS: 'Edwardu''.
[29] 192 fleeces weighing 21 st. were sent from Castlemorton to the collecting centre at Bourton-on-the-Hill this year (WAM 8293).
[30] The sum of the 'old arrears' is recognisable in, if not identical with, the sum of arrears at Castlemorton in 1362–3 (I 5). For Henry Holdy, see Appendix.
[31] For the lease of the arable demesne at Castlemorton, which explains the confinement of this inventory to sheep, see I 5.
[32] For Baron, alias John Broun, reeve of Pinvin 1361–4, and Nicholas Mower, reeve there 1364–5, 1367–72, see Appendix.
[33] For the lease of the arable demesne at Pinvin to the whole vill, from 1357–8 to 1367–8, see I 4.

Arreragia Willelmi Tundy iij s. iij d.
Hundredum de Defford Valet hoc anno viij s. ix d.
Arreragia Roberti Berald' ballivi xxxij s. iij d.
Portmot' de Pershore Valet hoc anno lxviij s. v d. ob.
Arreragia Johannis Vampage nuper ballivi xvij s. iij d.,[34] Nicholai Glovere nuper ballivi lxv s. iiij d.[35]
Balliva libertatis Glouc' Valet hoc anno ix li. iiij s. vj d.
Arreragia Johannis Derneford' nuper ballivi iiij li. x s. viij d., Johannis Elme et Johannis Parker ballivorum in anno xxxviij^{o} Cviij s. xj d., Johannis Parker nunc ballivi xix s. iiij d.[36]

Summa arreragiorum Clvj li. vj s. vj d., inde desperata plus quam xl li.
Summa totalis valorum hoc anno DCCCxlviij li. iij s., inde La Hide xxxix li.
Sic valent maneria viijCix li. iij s.

Summa equorum et affrorum xxxix, jumentorum et pullanorum xix. Summa istius sexus lviij.
Summa boum et bovettorum Ciiij^{xx}xvij, taurorum viij, vaccarum Ciiij^{xx}iiij, boviculorum et vitulorum xxvij. Summa sexus iiijCxvj.
Summa hurtardorum xxix, multonum M^{l}ixCiiij^{xx}viij, ovium matricum MClxxiiij, agnorum ixCxxiiij. Summa sexus iiijM^{l}Cxv.
Summa aprorum xvij, suum xxvj porcorum CCxj, porculorum et porcellorum CCiiij^{xx}ij. Summa sexus vCxxxvj.

Summa terminorum sancti Michaelis Cxxxviij li. vij s.
natalis Domini iiij^{xx}vj li. xiiij s. ij d. ob. qua.
annunciacionis beate Marie iiij^{xx}xiiij li. xij s. qua.
nativitatis sancti Johannis baptiste iiij^{xx}vj li. xix s. ix d. qua.
Totalis iiijCvj li. xiij s. qua.

[34] Vampage was bailiff of Pershore portmoot 1347–8 and 1349–50 and very likely in the intervening year (I 1, I 3). The arrears of 17s. 3d. mentioned above represent the unpaid residue of a debt of £3 7s. dating from 1350, and this was still unpaid in 1372 (I 10).
[35] Probably bailiff 1363–4; in 1372, still owed £2 12s. 0½d. (I 10).
[36] Derneford was bailiff in 1362–3, Elme and Parker in 1363–4.

I 7 States of the abbot's manors and portions at the conclusion of the audit of accounts for the year ending on 28 September 1367

A parchment roll of three membranes, approximately 160 mm wide, sewn Chancery fashion with blue thread in a tight oversew. The roll is a fair copy, in a single hand, laid out on membrane 1 with two vertical folds, for the left margin and the centre, and on membranes 2 and 3 with a single vertical fold for the left margin. The dorse is blank except for 'Status terrarum abbatis anno xlj^{mo}' written on the back of membrane 1 in a later fourteenth-century hand. There is some water-staining on the roll, which has made some short passages illegible.[1]

WAM 6196

[*Mem. 1 recto*] Status terrarum et porcionum domini abbatis Westm' super auditum compoti ministrorum suorum in vigilia sancti Michaelis anno regni regis Edwardi tercii[2] post conquestum quadragesimo primo

Islep' Summa terminorum sancti Michaelis xv li. xix s. iiij d., sancti Thome apostoli iiij li. xiij s. iiii d., annunciacionis Cxv s. v..., nativitatis sancti Johannis iiij li. xviij s. ..... Summa totalis .....[3]
Arreragia Willelmi Dolle prepositi xv li.
Valet manerium hoc anno cum lana Cv li. x s.[4]
Remanent super compotum ij qr. j bus. et di. frumenti, v qr. iiij bus. puls', iij bus. avenarum, j qr. iiij bus. brasei, j jumentum, iij pullani, xxiiij boves, j boviculus, j hurtardus, CCxiij multones, xij oves matrices, xviij hogastri et jercie, xviij hogerelli, vj agni, j aper, iiij sues, xxx porci pro lardario, xxx porculi, xxj porcelli, xxvij capones, ij anseres, vij auce mariole, vj galli, xij galline, iiij cigni erarii, j cigniculus et di.

Sutton' [Rents as in I 6: £17 18s. 10d.]
Arreragia Roberti de Preston' prepositi de claro l s.
Valet manerium hoc anno xxxiiij li.
Remanent super compotum j qr. mixtilionis, xviij qr. iiij bus. brasei, j aper, j sus, vj porci pro lardario, iij porculi, vj porcelli, j anser, iij auce mariole, vj capones, j gallus, viij galline.

[1] Extant ministers' accounts: Bourton-on-the-Hill, WAM 8295; Ebury, 31 May 1367–29 September 1367, WAM 26921; Pensham, WAM 22222.
[2] MS omits 'tercii'.
[3] MS water-stained. The total would have been £31 6s. 11d., as the rent for the term of St Thomas the Apostle has fallen by 2d. to £4 13s. 4d.; but it may nonetheless have been entered on the rolls as £31 7s. 1d., as in the following account, I 8.
[4] The wool was apparently sold at Islip, and no further details survive.

Todenham [Rents as in I 5: £15 6s. 2½d.][5]
Arreragia Rogeri de Erdyngton' ballivi iiij s. xj d.[6]
Valet manerium hoc anno li li. xiij s.[7]
Remanent super compotum ij equi carectarii, xxiiij boves, j aper, iij sues, xiij hoggetti, xij porcelli lactantes, j vacca, vj hurtardi, CCCxliij multones, CClxij oves matrices, xvj capones, ij galli, xviij galline, ij anseres, iiij auce mariole.

Bourton' Redditus terminorum sancti Michaelis lxj s. iiij d., natalis Domini xxxix s. vij d., annunciacionis xlj s. vij d., nativitatis sancti Johannis xxxix s. x d. ob. qua.
Totalis ix li. ij s. iiij d. ob. qua.
Arreragia Ricardi Alberd' prepositi iiij li. vij s. iiij d. Valet manerium hoc anno cum lana lij li. xiij s.[8]
Remanent super compotum iiij jumenta, j pullanus femellus, x boves, j vacca, j juvenca, j boviculus, ij vituli, vijCx multones, ij apri, ij sues, xx porci unde xviij pro lardario, xiiij porculi, xiij porcelli, ij galli, x galline, xx capones, lxvj carectates feni.

Pershore [Rents as in I 6: £32 19s.]
Arreragia Ricardi Darnell' nuper prepositi vj li. iiij s. viij d.,[9] Ricardi Hugh' collectoris xxx s., Johannis P*a*rker ballivi C s.
Valet manerium hoc anno cum lana lxxv li. xiiij s.[10]
Remanent super compotum iij qr. siliginis, iij qr. mixtilii, j equus pro molendino, iij equi carectarii, x boves, iiij vacce unde j in calumpnia, ij boviculi unde j femellus, ij vituli annales et ij de exitu, ij apri unde j pro lardario, ij sues, xxiiij porci unde xvij pro lardario, xiij porculi, xiiij porcelli, iiijCx hogastri, xiij agni, x capones, ij cigni erarii, lj carectates feni.

[5] MS: water stain, here only 'xv li.' is legible.
[6] Erdyngton's lease of the arable demesne, dating from 1360, was renewed for 7 years on 30 September 1367 (WAM 25971; for the draft lease, see WAM 25966).
[7] 475 fleeces, weighing 2 sacks 5 st. 7 lb., were sent this year from Todenham to the collecting centre at Bourton-on-the-Hill (WAM 8295).
[8] The demesne crop of wool at Bourton-on-the-Hill this year consisted of 625 fleeces, weighing 3 sacks 1 lb. (WAM 8295).
[9] Darnell was reeve of Pershore 1362–5 (I 5–6).
[10] 429 fleeces, weighing 2 sacks 2 st. 10 lb., were sent from Pershore to the collecting centre this year (WAM 8295).

Pendesham [Rents as in I 5: £26 4s. 4d.]
Arreragia Ade Andrewe prepositi xxvj s. vj d. qua.
Valet manerium hoc anno cum lana xlviij li. xiiij s.[11]
Remanent super compotum vj qr. brasei, j equus, ij jumenta, j pullanus etatis ij annorum, j pullanus istius anni, xj boves,[12] iij tauri, xxj vacce, iiij juvence, vj boviculi, v vituli, iiij hurtardi, CCxxix oves matrices, ij apri, ij sues, xij porci pro lardario, vij porculi, vij porcelli, j auca, ij mariole, xiij aucule, xij capones, j gallus, vj galline, xxxij carectates feni.

Herdewyk [Rents as in I 5: £22 17s. 8½d.]
Arreragia Johannis Bernard' nuper prepositi lxvj s. iij d.,[13] Johannis Gery prepositi vij li. xv s. iiij d.
Valet manerium hoc anno cum lana xlv li.[14]
Remanent super compotum per estimacionem lx qr. frumenti, iiij equi carectarii, xxxj boves unde vj ad cronandum, iij vacce, ij boviculi, j vitulus, Cxlvij multones, viij oves matrices, ix hogastri, CCxxij agni, ij apri unde j pro lardario, xiij porci, iij sues, xxj porculi, xx porcelli, j auce, iiij auce mariole, xxiiij capones, ij galli, x galline, xxiiij carectates feni.

Durhurst [Rents as in I 6: £28 17s. 5d.]
Arreragia nulla.
Valet manerium hoc anno xxix li. iiij s. Remanent super compotum j jumentum et j bos provenient*es* de heriettis.

[*Mem. 2 recto*] *Chaddesley* [Rents as in I 5: 6s. 8d.]
Arreragia Johannis Hathemare prepositi lx s.[15]
Valet manerium hoc anno cum lana xxv li.[16]
Remanet super compotum j affrus, j jumentum, j pullanus, x [boves] ..... calumpn*ia*, j taurus, xxiij vacce, j taurellus, iiij juvence, ij sues, xix porci unde xvj pro lardario, ix porculi, x porcelli, ix hurtardi, CCxiiij oves matrices, iij agni, j auca, iij auce mariole, xix aucule, xij capones, j gallus, v galline, xxiiij carectates feni, j bovettus, vj boviculi, vj vituli.

[11] 210 fleeces were sent from Pensham to the collecting centre at this year. The weight is said at Pensham to be 23 st., but at Bourton-on-the-Hill, 22 st. (WAM 8259, 22222).
[12] MS: 'j taurellus' follows, but has been struck out.
[13] Bernard is mentioned as reeve in 1362–3 but the exact length of this, his second term in office, is uncertain (I 5–6).
[14] 241 fleeces, weighing 1 sack 9 st., were sent from Hardwicke this year to the collecting centre (WAM 8295).
[15] This section of the MS is water-stained. A figure for pence may have followed, but is now illegible.
[16] A figure for shillings may have followed, but is now illegible. 173 fleeces, weighing 16 st. 7 lb., were sent from Chaceley to the collecting centre this year (WAM 8295).

Longedon' [Rents as in I 5: £15].
Arreragia Edwardi Kerdyf de parte relevii uxoris sue xxxij s., vicarii de Longedon' firmarii manerii[17] xv li., et Johannis Broun collectoris viij s.
Valet manerium hoc anno xvij li. xv s.

Morton' [Rents as in I 5: £28 17s. 9d.]
Arreragia antiqua xxxv li. xviij s. viij d.,[18] Henrici Holdy prepositi x li. iij s. ix d. ob. qua.
Valet manerium hoc anno cum lana xxxiiij li. vij s.[19]
Remanent super compotum CC multones.

Pendefen [Rents as in I 5: £33 16s. 3d.]
Arreragia Johannis Broun nuper prepositi v s. vij d. qua., Nicholai Mower ij s. ij d., Radulfi Pendefen' prepositi xviij d. ob. qua.[20]
Valet manerium hoc anno xxxvj li. vij s.
Nullum remanet ibidem staurum quia terre dominice sunt ad firmam.[21]
Wyke de hundredo Valet hoc anno xxiij s. ij d. Arreragia ballivorum ibidem xxiij s. ij d. qui debentur adhuc.
Hundredum de Pendefen Valet hoc anno xliiij s. j d.
Arreragia Willelmi Tundy ballivi xxj s. j d.
Hundredum de Defford' Valet hoc anno xvij s. Arreragia Roberti Geraldi prepositi lxxj s. ij d.
Portmot' de Pershore Valet hoc anno lxxix s. vj d.
Arreragia Johannis Vampage nuper ballivi xvij s. iij d., Nicholai Glovere nuper ballivi lxv s. iiij d.[22]
Ballivia libertatis Gloucestr' Valet hoc anno .....[23]
Arreragia Johannis Derneford' nuper ballivi iiij li. x s. viij d.,[24] Johannis Elme et Johannis ballivi anno xxxviij^{o}[25] Cviij s. xj d., Johannis P*ar*ker ballivi anno xxxix^{o}[26] xix s. iiij d.

[17] Henry Grafton (above, I 5, n. 23).
[18] For the last itemised reference to these arrears in these sources, see I 5.
[19] 88 fleeces, weighing 9 st. 7 lb., were sent from Castlemorton to the collecting centre this year (WAM 8295). The arable demesne was in the final year of the 10-year lease granted to Richard de Bradestoke in 1356–7 (WAM 21056).
[20] Mower was reeve of Pinvin: see I 6.
[21] For this farm, see I 4, n. 8.
[22] For these arrears of long-standing, see I 6.
[23] MS blank.
[24] Derneford was bailiff in 1362–3 (I 5).
[25] 1363–4. John *ballivus* was probably John Parker serving the first of two consecutive terms in this office (I 6).
[26] 1364–5.

Lalham [Rents as in I 5: £13 14s. 4d.]
Arreragia Johannis Southe iij s. xj d., Johannis Heyward Cvj s. iij d. qua. Johannes Mille ballivus excedit xliij s. iij d. qua.[27]
Valet manerium hoc anno cum lana xlviij li.
Remanent super compotum viij qr. iiij bus. frumenti per estimacionem in garbis, vij qr. siliginis in granario, et in tasso x qr. siliginis per estimacionem, xx qr. brasei ordei, xij qr. drageti, ij equi carectarii, iij jumenta, j pullanus, j stottus, xij boves, ij apri, ij sues, xvj porci, xvj porculi, vij porcelli, x auce unde j anser iij mariole, xij capones, iiij cigni erarii, v cignotti, j cigniculus, xvj galli et galline, xxv ryngels feni.

Denham [Rents as in I 5: £25 9s. 6d.]
Arreragia Roberti Broun ballivi vij li. xiij s. xj d.
Valet manerium hoc anno cum lana et novo edificio,[28] cum[29] feno expendito in hospicio, et cum proficuo tenementi quondam Jacobi Andrew iiij^{xx}ij li.[30]
Remanent super compotum iiij qr. frumenti in granario et in tasso xxiiij per estimacionem, v qr. mixtilionis per estimacionem in garbis, xv qr. brasei ordei, xl qr. brasei drageti, v equi carectarii, j jumentum, ij pulli, iiij stotti, iij tauri, xxij boves, lij vacce unde v cronarde, ij hurtardi, CCxxvj multones unde xij cronardi, lxxiij oves matrices unde xxv cronarde, xxxvj agni de exitu, ij apri, iij sues, xxij porci, xvj porculi, viij porcelli, x cigni et di. erarii, xiij cigniculi unde ij sub calumpnia, xl auce unde iij anseres vj auce mariole, xxxvj capones, ij galli, xij galline, lj carectates feni.

Periford' [Rents as in I 5: £35 5s. 5½d.]
Arreragia Willelmi Wybschot xlvj s. vij d. ob. qua., Ricardi Bedewynd' iiij li. iij s. viij d.[31]
Valet manerium hoc anno cum lana lxx li.
Remanent super compotum lx qr. siliginis per estimacionem in ij meis plenis, iiij qr. v bus. avenarum, iij jumenta, ij pullani, vj boves, iij hurtardi, CCxxvj multones unde xvij cronardi, Clxxiiij oves matrices unde xiiij cronarde, liij[32] agni, xxvij pelles lanute, iiij^{xx}xij ryngels feni.

[27] For Heyward and Southe, see I 6.
[28] A reference to the new house built for Abbot Litlyngton (1362–86) at Denham in the years 1363–9 and possibly to the new bridge also mentioned at Denham in the 1360s (WAM 24511–13; I 8).
[29] MS: 'cum' inserted.
[30] A reference to the estate in the manor of Denham, purchased by the abbot from James Andrew, a mercer of London, and Matilda, his wife, in 1366 (Harvey, *Estates*, p. 421).
[31] Bedewynd was serjeant at Pyrford, and Wybschot reeve, 1364–5 (WAM 27419, 24511).
[32] MS: 'g' follows, but has been struck out.

[*Mem. 3 recto*] *Stanes* Redditus terminorum sancti Michaelis vij li. xv s. ix d. ob., natalis Domini vij li. xiiij s., annunciacionis vij li. xiiij s., nativitatis sancti Johannis vij li. xiiij s. Totalis xxx li. xvij s. ix d. ob.
Arreragia Johannis Tangeley collectoris xl s. j d., totum de respectuacione.[33]
Valet manerium hoc anno xxv li. x s. preter respectuaciones.
Nullum remanet ibidem staurum quia terre dominice sunt ad firmam.

Yeveneye [Rents as in I 6: £14 3s. 4½d.]
Arreragia .....[34]
Valet manerium hoc anno xvij li. iiij s. ob. ad firmam.[35]
Remanent super compotum iiij affri, x boves, j gallus, vj galline, xij capones.

Eybury [Rents as in I 6: £9 9s. 6d.]
Arreragia nulla.
Valor non potest extendi nisi juxta firmam anni precedentis, videlicet liij li. vj s. viij d.[36]
Remanent super compotum iij qr. iij bus. silignis, iiij jumenta, ij pullani, viij boves, ij tauri, lx vacce, j aper, j sus, ij porcelli, vij auce unde j anser et j auca mariola, ij cigni erarii, v cigniculi, j gallus, vj galline, vj capones, v pavones, iij pave, lxx carectates feni.

Hyde [Rents as in I 6: £9 5s. 4d.]
Arreragia Walteri Page xl s.[37]
Valet manerium hoc anno cum lana lxxj li. xviij s.
Remanent super compotum xix qr. vj bus. siliginis per estimacionem in palea et garbis, v bus. avenarum, iij equi carectarii, iiij stotti, iiij jumenta, xiiij boves, j taurus, xl vacce, iij vituli, j juvenca, viij hurtardi unde ij cronardi, Ciiij^{xx}ix multones unde xvij cronardi, CClxxvj oves matrices unde xxxv cronarde, Cj agni de exitu, j aper, ij sues, vij porci, xxxj porculi, viij porcelli, j anser, iiij auce mariole, xxiiij aucule, xxiiij capones unde xiij albi, ij galli, xij galline, xx carectates feni.

[33] For John Tangley, the farmer, see I 5.
[34] MS: blank.
[35] For John Clerk, farmer of the demesne, see I 6.
[36] The arable demesne at Ebury was in the hands of a farmer, John Milers, from 28 or 29 September 1365 to 31 May 1367, but exploited directly, under the supervision of the bailiff, John Swanne, from 31 May to 29 September 1367 (WAM 26921). Faced with a year of such change, the auditors—as we are to understand—built a sum identical with the farm received by the abbot for the year 1365–6 into their calculation of the *valor* for the present year, 1366–7. That sum is not recorded.
[37] Page was serjeant at Hyde from 30 October 1365 to 29 September 1375 (WAM 27072–81).

Summa arreragiorum Clviij li. viij s. iij d. Inde desp*er*ata plusquam .....[38]
Summa totalis valorum hoc anno ixCxxxj li. xix s. v d. Valor ballive libertatis[39] Gloucestr' non extenditur infra istam summam.
Summa equorum et affrorum lvij, pullanorum vj. Summa istius sexus lxiij.
Summa boum et bovettorum Ciiij^{xx}xiij, taurorum x, vaccarum CCxiiij, boviculorum et vitulorum xxxix. Summa sexus iiijClvj.
Summa hurtardorum xxxij,[40] multonum ijMiiijCiiij^{xx}xj, ovium matricum MijCxlviij, agnorum iiijClij. Summa sexus iiijMCCxxiij.
Summa aprorum xvij, suum xxvij, porcorum Clxix porculorum et porcellorum CCC. Summa sexus vCxiij.

Redditus terminorum sancti Michaelis Cxxxviij li. vij s., natalis Domini iiij^{xx}vj li. xiiij s. ij d. ob. qua., annunciacionis iiij^{xx}xiiij li. xij s. qua., nativitatis sancti Johannis iiij^{xx}vj li. xix s. ix d. qua. Totalis iiijCvj li. xiij s. qua.

[38] MS blank.
[39] MS: 'libertatis' inserted.
[40] MS adds 'li.'

I 8 States of the abbot's manors and portions at the conclusion of the audit of accounts for the year ending on 28 September 1368

A parchment roll of two membranes, approximately 170–3 mm wide, sewn Chancery fashion in a tight oversew with blue thread. Membrane 1 tapers to a point at the top. A fair copy, all in a single hand. The roll is laid out with three vertical folds. There is only one entry on the dorse, on the back of membrane 1 at the top, in a mid to late fourteenth-century hand: 'Dogetus maneriorum abbatis Westm' anno xlij^{o}'.[1]

WAM 6174

[*Mem. 1 recto*] Status terrarum et porcionum domini abbatis Westm' super auditum compoti ministrorum suorum in vigilia sancti Michaelis anno regni regis Edwardi tercii post conquestum quadragesimo secundo

Islep' Redditus terminorum sancti Michaelis xv li. xix s. iiij d., sancti Thome apostoli iiij li. xiij s. iiij d., annunciacionis Cxv s. vij d., natalis sancti Johannis iiij li. xviiij s. viij d. Totalis xxxj li. vij s. j d.[2]
Arreragia Willelmi Dolle prepositi iiij li. vij s. xj d.
Valet manerium hoc anno, cum lana, preter fenum expenditum in hospicio iiij^{xx}xix li. vij s.[3]
Remanent super compotum j qr. v bus. di. avenarum, j jumentum, j pullanus masculus, j hurtardus, CCxxij multones, xxx oves matrices, x hogastri, xxiiij agni, j aper, iiij sues, xxx porci pro lardario, xxx porculi, xxj porcelli, xl capones, ij anseres, vij auce mariole, ij galli, xij galline, iiij cigni erarii, j cignottus et di.

Sutton [Rents as in I 6: £17 18s. 10d.]
Arreragia Thome Hurry prepositi xv li. ix d. ob.[4]
Valet manerium hoc anno preter fenum expenditum in hospicio xxxij li. xvj s.
Remanent super compotum xj qr. ij bus. brasei drageti, vj boviculi, j aper, j sus, vij porci, x porcelli, j auca, iij mariole, xij capones, j gallus, vj galline.

[1] Extant ministers' accounts: Bourton-on-the-Hill, WAM 8296; Castlemorton, with Longdon, WAM 21025; Ebury, WAM 26922; Hyde WAM 27074; Islip WAM 14804; Pensham, WAM 22223; Pinvin, WAM 22294.

[2] The correct total is £31 6s. 11d., the rent for the term of St Thomas the Apostle is 2d. less than on I 5 and I 6; the new rent level for this term appeared on I 7. The total appears correctly in subsequent accounts.

[3] Cf. the current minister's account, where the *valor* omits wool but adds 'cum edifici*o*' after the sum; the addition refers to various building works on the sites of the abbot's two houses in Islip, at a total cost of £21 6s. 1½d.; the main item was work on a large grange (WAM 14804). 273 fleeces, weighing 26 st. 7 lb. were sent this year from Islip to the collecting centre for the Western Parts at Bourton-on-the-Hill (WAM 8296, 14804).

[4] Hurry was reeve at Sutton-under-Brailes 1367–8 to 1378–9 (WAM 24512–20, 25914–15; GRO, D1099/M31/44–5).

Todenham [Rents as in I 5: £15 6s. 2½d.]
Arreragia, nulla.
Valet manerium hoc anno xxxvij li. vj s. vj d.
Remanent super compotum ij equi carectarii, xxiiij boves, j aper, iij sues, xiij hoggetti, v porcelli, xij porcelli lactantes, viij hurtardi, CCiiij^{xx}xij multones, CCliij oves matrices, xiiij agni, xvj capones, ij galli, xviij galline, ij anseres, iiij auce mariole.[5]

Bourton [Rents as in I 5: £7 2s. 6d.]
Arreragia Ricardi Alberd' prepositi iiij s. ix d. qua.
Valet manerium hoc anno preter edificium xxxviij li. et custus grangie xiij li. xiiij s. x d.
Remanent super compotum j qr. di. puls', v jumenta, j pullanus femellus, ix boves, ij vacce, j bovettus, j vitulus, vijCxlviij multones, ij apri, ij sues, xx porci, xiiij porculi, xiij porcelli, ij galli, x galline, xx capones,[6] lx carectates feni.[7]

Pershore [Rents as in I 5: £32 19s. 0d.]
Arreragia Ricardi Darnell' nuper prepositi vj li. iiij s. viij d., Ricardi Hugh' collectoris xxxvij s. v d. qua.
Valet manerium hoc anno cum lana lxv li.[8]
Remanent super compotum xj qr. ij bus. multure, ij equi carectarii, j equus pro molendino, ij pullani, viij boves, ij vacce, j bovettus, j juvenca, ij boviculi, ij vituli annales, j vitulus de exitu, ij apri, ij sues, xxx porci, viij porcelli, CCxxiij hogastri, CCCxxiiij agni, j gallus, v galline, j anser, iij auce mariole, xij capones, ij cigni,[9] lv carectates feni.

Pendesham [Rents as in I 5: £26 4s. 4d.]
Arreragia, nulla.
Valet manerium hoc anno cum lana xxxviij li. xv s.[10]
Remanent super compotum j equus, j jumentum, j pullanus, x boves, ij

[5] 490 fleeces, weighing 62 st., were sent this year from Todenham to the collecting centre (WAM 8296). For the livestock in the hands of Roger de Erdyngton, lessee of the demesne, but included in this inventory, see I 5, n. 7.
[6] MS: 'xx capones' inserted at the end of the panel but marked for insertion here.
[7] The demesne crop of wool at Bourton-on-the-Hill this year consisted of 666 fleeces, weighing 3 sacks 6 st. Including this number, 2,530 fleeces, weighing 11 sacks 18 st. of wool, were collected from manors in the Western Parts this year. These were sold as 12 sacks for £108 (£9 per sack). In addition, the so-called refuse was sold for £1 (WAM 8296).
[8] 435 fleeces, weighing 63 st., were sent this year from Pershore to the collecting centre (WAM 8296).
[9] MS: replaces 'cigngn" struck out.
[10] 202 fleeces, weighing 19 st. 11 lb., were sent this year from Pensham to the collecting centre (WAM 8296, 22223).

tauri, xxiiij vacce, j taurellus, iiij boviculus, j juvenca, v vituli annales, vj vituli de exitu, iiij hurtardi, CClx oves matrices, vij agni, ij apri, ij sues, xij porci, xviij porculi, j anser, ij mariole, xiiij aucule, ij cigni,[11] xij capones, j gallus, vj galline, xx carectates feni.

Herdewyk [Rents as in I 5: £22 17s. 8½d.] Arreragia Johannis Gery prepositi xxx s. xj d.
Valet manerium hoc anno xxxviij li.
Remanent super compotum v equi carectarii, xxvij boves, ij vacce, j juvenca, iij multones, xxxix oves matrices, CCxlviij hogastri, xxj agni,[12] ij apri, iij sues, xix porci, xxxix porculi et porcelli, j anser, iiij mariole, xiij aucule, xxiiij capones, ij galli, x galline, xxvj carectates feni.[13]

Durhurst [Rents as in I 6: £28 17s. 5d.] Arreragia Thome Surpayne prepositi xx s.[14]
Valet manerium hoc anno xxxvj li. xij s.
Remanent super compotum j jumentum et j vacca provenientes de heriettis.

Chaddesley [Rents as in I 5: £5 0s. 8d.] Arreragia Johannis Hathemare prepositi xx s.
Valet manerium hoc anno cum lana et novo edificio xviij li. xxij d.[15]
Remanent super compotum j equus, j jumentum, ij pullani, ix boves, j taurus, xxij vacce, j taurellus, ij boviculi, iij juvencule, vj vituli, ij sues, ij apri, ix porci, xv porculi, x hurtardi, Ciiij^{xx}xiiij oves matrices, Cij agni, j anser, iij auce mariole, xxiiij aucule, xij capones, j gallus, v galline, xxxvj carectates feni.

Longedon' [Rents as in I 5: £15] Arreragia Edwardi Kerdyf' de parte relevio uxoris sue xxxij s., vicarii de Longedon' firmarii manerii xxx li., et Johannis Bron' collectoris xxij s.[16]
Valet manerium hoc anno xxix li.

[11] MS: 'cingni' struck out, 'cigni' inserted.
[12] MS: 'agni' inserted.
[13] 277 fleeces, weighing 1 sack 7 st. 4 lb., were sent this year from Hardwicke to the collecting centre (WAM 8296).
[14] Surpayne was reeve of Deerhurst 1367–72 (WAM 24512–15).
[15] 186 fleeces, weighing 15 st. 10 lb., were sent this year from Chaceley to the collecting centre (WAM 8296). The new building is not further identified.
[16] For Henry Grafton, the perpetual vicar at Longdon, see I 6. The arrears charged to him represented twice the annual rent owed by the three lessees of Longdon manor. By the end of the current year, however, the warden of the abbot's household had received £25 from Robert Grafton, another lessee (WAM 24512).

Morton [Rents as in I 5: £28 17s. 9d.] Arreragia Henrici Holdy prepositi vij li. xvij s. xj d.
Valet manerium hoc anno xxxj li. xvj d.

Pendefen Redditus terminorum sancti Michaelis viij li. xix s. ix d., sancti Andree viij li. xj s. vj d., annunciacionis viij li. vij s. vj d., nativitatis sancti Johannis viij li. v s. vj d. Totalis xxxiiij li. iiij s. iij d.
Arreragia Johannis Broun nuper prepositi v s. vij d. qua., Radulfi Pendefen' nuper prepositi iij s. viij d. ob. qua., Nicholai[17] Mower modo prepositi ix s. j d. ob. qua.[18]
Valet manerium hoc anno xxxviij li. xv s.
Nullum remanet ibidem staurum quia terre dominice sunt ad firmam.[19]

Wyke Valet hoc anno xxx s. j d.[20]
[*Mem. 2 recto*] *Hundredum de Pendefen'* Valet hoc anno viij li. xxj d.
Arreragia Willelmi Tundy ballivi iiij li.
Hundredum de Defford Valet hoc anno xxxv s. x d.
Arreragia Roberti Berald ballivi ij s.
Portmotum de Pershore Valet hoc anno lxxv s. ix d.
Arreragia Johannis Vampage nuper ballivi xvij s. iij d., Nicholai Glovere nuper ballivi lij s. ob.
Balliva libertatis Gloucestr' Valet hoc anno viij li. xvij s. iiij d.
Arreragia[21]

Lalham [Rents as in I 5: £13 14s. 4d.] Arreragia Johannis Southe iij s. xj d., Johannis Heyward Cvj s. iij d. qua. Johannes Mille ballivus excedit lxvij s. ob. qua.[22]
Valet manerium hoc anno preter fenum expenditum pro hospicio xlj li. xix s.
Remanent super compotum vj qr. vij bus. di. brasei ordei, xxij qr. vij bus. brasei drageti, j equus carectarius, iiij jumenta, j stottus, xj boves, ij apri, ij

[17] MS: 'Nicholaum'.
[18] Ralph Pinvin was reeve of Pinvin 1365–7 (WAM 22292; I 6). For Broun, alias John Baron, and Mower, see I 6.
[19] The existing farm of the arable demesne to the homage of the vill was terminated with effect from the end of the current year, and on 19 July 1368 the demesne, including meadow and pasture, was leased for 12 years, for £4 6s. 8d. p.a., to William Cole and Robert Crompe, with effect from the former date (WAM 22294).
[20] For cash liveries amounting to £12 3s. 5d. from bailiffs of the abbot's liberties, excluding the liberty in Gloucestershire, received by the abbot's treasurer this year, see WAM 24512.
[21] Followed by a blank space in the MS.
[22] For South, Heyward and Mille, see I 6.

sues, xvj porci, v porculi, xxx porcelli, xxiij auce, xij capones, viij cigni, j cignottus, ij cigniculi, j gallus, x galline, xxxiij carectates feni.

Denham [Rents as in I 5: £25 9s. 6d.] Arreragia Roberti Broun ballivi C s.
Valet manerium hoc anno cum lana appreciata ad xj marcas[23] et cum novo edificio, preter fenum expenditum in hospicio, iiij^{xx}xv li. xvij s.[24]
Remanent super compotum viij qr. frumenti, v qr. ij bus. brasei ordei, iiij qr. ij bus. brasei drageti, vj equi carectarii, iiij pullani, xxix boves, iiij tauri, lj vacce, ij hurtardi, CCxxxvij multones, l oves matrices, xxv agni, iij apri, iij sues, xxij porci, x porculi, xxxiiij porcelli, viij cigni erarii et ij in Tamis', xv cignotti, lxj auce, xxxiiij capones, ij galli, xiij galline, lx carectates feni.

Periford' [Rents as in I 5: £35 5s. 5½d.] Arreragia Willelmi Wibschot' xlvj s. vij d. ob. qua., Ricardi Bedewynd' Cij s. iij d. ob.[25]
Valet manerium hoc anno cum lana appreciata ad x li. et feno pro hospicio ad x marcas[26] lx li. xvij s.
Remanent super compotum iij jumenta, iij pullanni, vij boves, iiij hurtardi, CCxlvj multones, CCxxviij matrices, Cix agni, xxviij vellera, lxix carectates feni.

Stanes [Rents as in I 6: £29 17s. 9½d.] Arreragia Johannis Tangeley collectoris xxvij s. ij d. ob.[27]
Valet manerium hoc anno xxv li. xiiij d.
Remanent super compotum j bos et j vacca provenientes de heriettis.

Yeveneye [Rents as in I 6: £14 3s. 4½d.] Arreragia[28]
Valet manerium hoc anno xvij li. iiij s. ob. ad firmam.[29]
Remanent super compotum iiij affri, x boves, j gallus, vj galline, xij capones.[30]

[23] £7 6s. 8d.
[24] The abbot's treasurer contributed £57 this year, in instalments, to the continuing work on the abbot's house at Denham and the park there. The sum was nearly equal to the net issues of the manor of Denham after deduction of reprises (WAM 24572; I 1); for the new house at Denham, see I 7.
[25] For Bedewynd and Wibschot, see I 7.
[26] £6 13s. 4d.
[27] For Tangleye, who was probably farmer of the demesnes as well as collector of rents, see I 6.
[28] Followed by a blank space in the MS.
[29] John Clerk, farmer of the demesne at Yeoveney since 1363–4, was, in the course of 1367–8, granted a farm of the manor for a rent of £18 13s. 4d. p.a. (WAM 24512; for the rent, I 9).
[30] As in the inventory of livestock in I 7.

Eybury [Rents as in I 6: £9 9s. 6d.] Arreragia Johannis Swan' ballivi iij s. j d. ob.
Valet manerium hoc anno preter fenum expenditum in hospicio[31] xxiiij li. xviij d. et preter pasturam expenditam cum animalibus hospicii.[32]
Remanent super compotum vij jumenta, iij boves, iij tauri, lj vacce, j aper, ij sues, xij porcelli, j ancer, xij capones, j gallus, v galline, ij cigni erarii, vij cigniculi, iij pavones, iij pave, xxxvj carectates feni.

Hyde [Rents as in I 6: £9 5s. 4d.] Arreragia Walteri Page ballivi xx s.[33]
Valet manerium hoc anno, cum lana appreciata ad xiiij li. di. marc*am*, xlix li. xiiij s.[34]
Remanent super compotum iij equi carectarii, iiij stotti, iiij jumenta, xiiij boves, ij tauri, xl vacce, j juvenca, ij boviculi, vij hurtardi, Clxiiij multones, CClxxvij oves matrices, Cxlvj agni, j aper, j sus, xvj porci, viij porculi, xvj porcelli, xxix auce, xij capones, ij galli, xij galline, xv carectates feni.

Summa arreragiorum C li. xix s. vij d. ob. qua.
Summa totalis valorum hoc anno viijClv li. iij s. xj d. ob., preter fenum expenditum in hospicio[35]

Summa equorum et affrorum liij pullanoruim xiiij. Summa istius sexus lxvij.
Summa boum et bovettorum Clxiiij, taurorum xiiij, vaccarum CCij, boviculorum xxxvij. Summa istius sexus iiijCxvij.
Summa hurtardorum xxxv, multonum ijMiijCiiijxxxiij, ovium matricum M^{l}CCCxxxj, agnorum DCClxij. Summa sexus iiijM^{l}Dxxj.
Summa aprorum xx, suum xxviij, porcorum Ciiij^{xx}xiiij, porculorum et porcellorum CCC. Summa istius sexus Dxlij.

Redditus terminorum sancti Michaelis Cxxxviij li. ix s., natalis Domini iiij^{xx}vj li. xvj s. ij d. ob. qua., annunciacionis iiij^{xx}xiiij li. xiiij s. qua., nativitatis sancti Johannis iiij^{xx}vij li. xxj d. qua. Totalis iiijCvij li. xij d. qua.[36]

[31] MS: 'preter fenum expenditum in hospicio' inserted.
[32] Of 106 cartloads of hay, available in the course of the year, 60 were used for the abbot's mares and cows in winter. Of the 106 cartloads, however, 70 remained from the previous year (WAM 26922).
[33] Page was serjeant at Hyde 1365–70 and bailiff there 1370–7 (WAM 27073–81).
[34] 419 sheep's fleeces and 146 lambs' fleeces, with some woolfells and skins of sheep and lambs which died of murrain, were delivered this year from Hyde to Br. Walter de Warfeld, the Abbey treasurer (WAM 27074).
[35] MS: 'preter fenum expenditum in hospicio' inserted before the previous entry, but intended for this point.
[36] MS: an illegible word occurs at the bottom of mem. 3.

I 9 States of the abbot's manors and portions at the conclusion of the audit of accounts for the year ending on 28 September 1371

A parchment roll of two membranes, approximately 145 mm wide, sewn Chancery fashion with white thread in a tight oversew. The roll is a fair copy written throughout in a single hand. It is laid out with three vertical folds. Membrane1 tapers to a point at the top and is blank on the dorse. Membrane 2 is blank on the dorse except for 'Status terrarum domini Nicholai abbatis Westm' de anno xlv°' which is written at the foot of the membrane in a later hand, and a series of memoranda written in a second hand about corn remaining at Denham, Laleham and Pyrford.[1]

WAM 6186

[*Mem. 1 recto*] Status terrarum et porcionum domini abbatis Westm' super auditum compoti ministrorum suorum in vigilia sancti Michaelis anno regni regis Edwardi tercii post conquestum xlv^{to}

Islep' [Rents as in I 7 and I 8, now with the correct total: £31 6s. 11d.] Arreragia Willelmi Dolle prepositi ibidem xiij li. vj s. viij d.
Valet manerium hoc anno cum lana Cj li. xix s.[2]
Remanent super compotum xx qr. pisarum, j qr. vj bus. brasei, xxiiij boves, j hurtardus, iiij^{xx}xiij multones, xxxiij oves matrices, xiij hogastri, xxxiiij agni, j aper, iiij sues, xxx porci pro lardario, xxx porculi et xxj porcelli, xxxviij capones, ij anseres, vij auce mariole, ij galli, xij galline, j cignus erarius et j cigniculus.

Sutton' [Rents as in I 6: £17 18s. 10d.] Arreragia Thome Hurry prepositi ibidem viij li. iij s.
Valet manerii hoc anno cum feno xxxj li. vij s.
Remanent xvij qr. vij bus. brasei, j aper, j sus, v porci, xiiij porculi, j anser, iij auce mariole, xj aucule, j gallus, vj galline et xij capones.

Todenham [Rents as in I 5: £15 6s. 2½d.] Arreragia Rogeri Erdyngton' ballivi lxvj s. viij d.
Valet manerium hoc anno cum lana lij li.[3]

[1] Extant ministers' accounts: Bourton-on-the-Hill, WAM 8299; Chaceley, WAM 21093; Ebury, WAM 26926; Hyde, 27077; Laleham, WAM 27151; Pensham, WAM 22226; Pinvin, WAM 22297; Pyrford, WAM 27420; Todenham, GRO, D1099/M30/10.

[2] 153 fleeces, weighing 21 st., were sent from Islip this year to the collecting centre for the Western Parts at Bourton-on-the-Hill (WAM 8299).

[3] 278 fleeces, weighing 1 sack 9 st. 8 lb., were sent from Todenham this year to the collecting centre at Bourton-on-the-Hill (WAM 8299). For the current lease of the arable demesne to Roger de Erdyngton, see I 5.

Remanent super compotum ij equi, xxiiij boves, j aper, iiij sues, iij hogetti,[4] v porcelli, xij porcelli lactantes, xvj capones, ij galli et xviij galline, ij anseres, iiij auce mariole, Cxlj multones, Cxij oves matrices, xxij hogastri, lxxv agni et lxxiij carectates feni.[5]

Bourton' [Rents as in I 7: £9 2s. 4¾d.] Arreragia Ricardi Albard' prepositi ibidem xiij li. vj s. viij d.
Valet manerium hoc anno cum lana xliiij li. xij d.[6]
Remanent super compotum v qr. puls', vij qr. vj bus. avenarum, vj jumenta, x boves, ij vacce, j taurus, j bovettus, vj boviculi, iij vituli, CCCCxxxix multones, ij apri, ij sues, xx porci, xiiij porculi, xiij porcelli, ij galli, x galline, xx capones.

Pershore [Rents as in I 5: £32 19s. 0d.] Arreragia Ricardi Darnel nuper prepositi vj li. iiij s. viij d., Willelmi Osbern collectoris xvj s. viij d.
Valet manerium hoc anno cum lana et feno iiij^{xx} li. ij s.[7]
Remanent super compotum vj qr. siliginis, vj bus. multure, iiij bus. brasei, iiij equi, j jumentum, j affrus, j pullanus, viij boves, iij vacce, iij vituli, ij apri, iij sues, xv porci, xxxix porculi, xiiij porcelli, vij hurtardi, Clvij multones, iiij^{xx}x oves matrices, lxvj agni, j gallus et vj galline, xij capones, j anser, iij auce mariole, xiij aucule, ij cigni erarii et lxxiiij carectates feni.

Pendesham [Rents as in I 5: £26 4s. 4d.] Arreragia, nulla.
Valet manerium hoc anno xxxviij li. vj s. viij d.[8]
Remanent[9] in manu firmarii iij qr. vj bus. frumenti, xvj qr. iij bus. siliginis, viij qr. j bus. di. puls', xiij qr. vj bus. ordei, xx qr. drageti, j equus, j jumentum, j pullanus, vij boves, xij vacce, vj juvence, ij bovetti, j taurellus, j anser, ij auce mariole, xij capones, j gallus et vj galline.

[4] Previously, as in Erdyngton's lease, 'xiij hogetti', but the change established itself (WAM 25966; I 10).
[5] MS omits 'feni'.
[6] The demesne wool crop at Bourton-on-the-Hill this year amounted to 523 fleeces, weighing 18 st. Including this number, 1,197 fleeces, weighing 6 sacks 2 st. 1 lb., were collected from the manors of the Western Parts. These were sold at Bourton as 6 sacks 6½ st.—an increment of 4 st. 6 lb.—and for £9 6s. 8d. per sack (WAM 8299).
[7] 243 fleeces, weighing 1 sack 5 st. 7 lb., were sent this year from Pershore to the collecting centre at Bourton-on-the-Hill (WAM 8299).
[8] The lease of the site of the manor and the demesne to John Parker for 12 years, for a farm of £8 p.a., rising to £9 3s. 6d. p.a. after the first year, was now in its first year (WAM 22226).
[9] MS: 'Ram''.

Herdwyk' [Rents as in I 5: £22 17s. 8½d.] Arreragia Johannis Gery prepositi ibidem vij li. xij s. ij d. qua.
Valet manerium hoc anno xliiij li.
Remanent super compotum x qr. puls', iiij equi, j pullanus, xviij boves, ij vacce, j boviculus, j vitulus, j aper, iij sues, xliiij porci, xxviij porculi, viij porcelli, j anser, iiij auce mariole, xxiiij capones, ij galli, x galline, et xxx carectates feni.

Durhurst Redditus terminorum sancti Michaelis ix li. xviij s. vj d., natalis domini Cj s. iij d., annunciacionis viij li. xix s. ij d., natalis sancti Johannis Cxviij s. vij d. Totalis xxix li. xvij s. vj d.[10]
Arreragia Thome S*our*payn vij d. qua.
Valet manerium hoc anno xxix li. xvj s.[11]

Chaddesle [Rents as in I 5: £5 0s. 8d.] Arreragia Johannis Hathemer prepositi x s.[12]
Valet manerium hoc anno x li. xij s.
Remanent super compotum iij equi, ix boves, j taurus, xvj vacce, ix vituli, j aper, j sus, x porci, xvj porculi, j anser, iij auce mariole, xxij aucule, xij capones, j gallus et v galline.

Longedon' [Rents as in I 5: £15] Arreragia Edwardi Keardyf' lxvj s. viij d., Johannis Broun messoris xlij s. vij d. ob.
Valet manerium hoc anno xv li. xix s.
Remanent super compotum j jumentum.

Morton' [Rents as in I 5: £28 17s. 9d.] Arreragia Henrici Holdy nuper prepositi C s. ij d., Ricardi Ode nuper prepositi xxiiij s., Ade Palle prepositi ibidem l s. x d. ob. qua.
Valet manerium hoc anno cum reparacione aule ibidem xxxiiij li.
Reman*et* super compotum j bos.

Pendefen [Rents as in I 5: £33 16s. 3d.] Arreragia Johannis Bron' v s. vij d. qua., Radul*fi* Pendefen' iij s. viij d. ob. qua., Nicholai Mower vj li. xij s.
Valet manerium[13] hoc anno xliiij li. xvij s.

[10] The rents at Deerhurst in I 6, I 7 and I 8 had totalled £28 17s. 5d. The totals for the terms in I 9 come to £29 16s. 6d., rather than the £29 17s. 6d. given in the total.
[11] An apparently sole farmer of the demesne at Deerhurst is mentioned, but not named, by the warden of the abbot's household in his account this year. In the following year, which may have been the farmer's first full year, his farm was £4 p.a. (WAM 24514–15).
[12] John Hathemere's current period in office probably extended from 1366 to 1368, but it was not his first (I 6; Appendix).
[13] MS: 'manerio'.

Wyke de hundredo Valet hoc anno xvij s. iiij d.
Arreragia, nulla.[14]
De hundredo de Pendefen nichil respondendum[15] hic quia Nicholaus Mower ballivus ibidem oneratur de proficuo eiusdem in compoto suo de colleccione reddit*us* de Pendefen.
Hundredum de Defford Valet hoc anno xij s. vj d.
Arreragia, nulla.
Portmot' de Perschor' Valet hoc anno lx s.
Arreragia Johannis Vampage nuper ballivi xvij s. iij d., Nicholai Glov*ere* nuper ballivi lij s. ob.
Balliva libertatis Glouc' Valet hoc anno lxvj s.
Arreragia Johannis Derneford[16] iiij li. x s. viij d., Johannis Elme et Johannis Baily anno xxxviij[o17] Cviij s. xj d., Johannis P*ar*ker ballivi anno xxxix[o18] xix s. iiij d., Johannis Clerk nuper ballivi .....[19] Reginaldi Berkesden' xliij s. ix d.[20]

[*Mem. 2 recto*] *Lalham* Redditus terminorum sancti Michaelis Cix s. j d. qua., natalis Domini lxxiij s. iiij d. ob., annunciacionis lxxiiij s. iiij d., nativitatis sancti Johannis lxxiij s. iiij d. ob. Totalis xvj li. x s. ij d. qua.[21]
Arreragia Johannis South collectoris redditus lxv s. vij d.
Valet manerium hoc anno xxvij li. v s.
Remanent super compotum xiiij qr. avenarum, xiij qr. v bus. brasei ordei, j equus, ij jumenta, ij affri, j pullanus, xij boves, j sus, j aper, xvj porculi, viij porcelli, j gallus, vj galline, xj cigni aerarii, j anser, iij auce mariole, v aucule, vj capones, et lx carectates feni.

Denham [Rents as in I 5, but without Peter's Pence on 1 August: £25 8s. 5½d.]
Arreragia Willelmi Spens' ballivi vij li. xviij s. ix d.

[14] Before the close of his account for the year 1370–1, the abbot's treasurer received £4 6s. 5d. from bailiffs of liberties in the Western Parts: 17s. from John Bruet (Wick hundred), 16s. 9d. from Robert Berald (Defford hundred), and £2 12s. 8d. from Reginald de Berkesdon (the liberty in Gloucestershire) (WAM 24514).
[15] MS: 'r''.
[16] Bailiff 1362–3 (I 5).
[17] 1363–4. Cf. I 7, where John Elme and John Parker are identified as bailiffs in this year.
[18] 1364–5.
[19] MS: blank space, no sum entered. Clerk was bailiff of Deerhurst hundred in 1368–9, when the abbot's treasurer received £6 from him (WAM 24513).
[20] Bailiff 1370–1 (WAM 24514).
[21] The supersession this year of the panel of rents at Laleham that had served since 1362–3 reflects the new custumal and rental made by Br. John de Lakyngheth and Richard de Hayton, his clerk, on a 7-day visit. On the same occasion, a new custumal and rental were made for the manor of Staines (WAM 27151).

Valet manerium hoc anno cum lana et feno iiij^{xx}ij li. iij s.
Remanent super compotum xxxij qr. frumenti, ij qr. j bus. pisarum albarum, viij qr. v bus. brasei ordei, xxiiij qr. vj bus. brasei drageti, iiij equi, iiij stotti, iiij pullani, xxv boves, ij tauri, l vacce, viij vituli, j hurtardus, viij oves matrices, Ciiij^{xx}iij agni, vij vellera bidencium, Ciiij^{xx}iij vellera agnorum, vj apri, iiij sues, xxviij porci, xvj porculi, xxvij porcelli, xj cigni aerarii et di., iiij cignotti, iiij cigniculi, ij anseres, vj auce mariole, xlij aucule, xiiij capones, j gallus et xij galline et Cij carectates feni.

Pyrford' [Rents as in I 5: £35 5s. 5½d.] Arreragia Willelmi Webeschote vj s. vij d. ob. qua., Roberti Broun ballivi iiij li.
Valet manerium hoc anno cum lana xlij li. x s.[22]
Remanent super compotum j qr. ij bus. siliginis, xlviij qr. avenarum, j pullus, vj boves, iiij hurtardi, liij multones, iiij^{xx}j oves matrices, xv boviculi, xvij juvence, ij capones et Cxxvj carectates feni.

Stanes Redditus terminorum sancti Michaelis ix li. iiij s. v d. ob., natalis Domini vj li. vj s. iij d., annunciacionis vj li. xv s. ix d. ob. qua., nativitatis sancti Johannis vj li. xviij s. j d. ob. Totalis xxix li. iiij s. vij d. ob. qua.[23]
Arreragia Alexandri Treso*ur* iiij li.[24]
Valet manerium hoc anno xxix li. xiiij s.

Ȝeven' [Rents as in I 6: £14 3s. 4½d.] Arreragia, nulla.
Valet manerium hoc anno ad firmam, ut in precedenti, xviij li. xiij s. iiij d.[25]
Remanent super compotum iiij affri, x boves, j gallus, vj galline et xij capones.[26]

Eybury Redditus terminorum sancti Michaelis iiij li. vj s. j d. ob. qua., natalis Domini lvj s. viij d. ob. qua., pasche lxiij s. iiij d. ob. qua., nativitatis sancti Johannis lvj s. viij d. ob. qua. Totalis xiij li. iij s.[27]
Arreragia Johannis Swan nuper ballivi xx s.,[28] Willelmi Huller ballivi Cix s. vij d.

[22] 125 fleeces were sent this year from Pyrford to Br. Walter de Warfeld, the conventual treasurer, and sold at 3d. per fleece (WAM 27420).
[23] For the new custumal and rental made for the manor of Staines this year, see Laleham above.
[24] Tresour was rent-collector, but also styled 'bailiff', at Staines 1368–1404 (WAM 16934–6, 24513–20, 24524–5, 24527–32, 24535–6*).
[25] For the lease of the manor of Yeoveney to John Clerk for a farm of this amount, see I 8.
[26] As in the inventory of livestock in I 7.
[27] The new rental underlying the panel for rents used above is dated February 46 Edward III, i.e. 1372, in the surviving copy (WAM 26999). It is, however, clear, that it was already in use for the above panel of rents in preference to the panel for 1364–5 that had served since that year.
[28] Swan was serjeant (*sic*) of Ebury from 28 September 1370 until his death, probably on 14 April 1389 (WAM 26926–40).

Valet manerium hoc anno cum feno lxv li. ij s.[29]
Remanent super compotum iiij jumenta, ij pullani, x boves, ij tauri, lxviij vacce, iij sues, iij porci pro lardario, viij porculi, j anser, j auca mariola, v aucule, xiiij capones, j gallus, vj galline, ij pavones, iij pave, iij paviculi et xlv carectates feni.

Hyde Redditus terminorum sancti Michaelis lviij s. vj d. ob., natalis Domini xlix s. viij d., pasche lvj s. vij d., nativitatis sancti Johannis lj s. Totalis x li. xv s. ix d. ob.
Arreragia, nulla.
Valet manerium hoc anno cum lana xliiij li. xiiij s.[30]
Remanent super compotum iij equi, iiij stotti, xiiij boves, ij tauri, xlj vacce, ij bovetti, j boviculus, iij juvence, iij vituli, x hurtardi, Clxj multones, CCxlvj oves matrices, xxxviij agni, j aper, j anser, iiij auce mariole, xx capones, j gallus, j galline et xix carectates feni.

Summa arreragiorum Cxx li. xvij s. iiij d.
Summa totalis valorum hoc anno DCCCxliiij li. xvj s. x d. plus quam in precedenti per iiij^{xx}xiij li. vj s. vij d. ob.[31]

Summa equorum et affrorum lij, pullorum et pullanorum xj. Summa sexus lxiij, minus quam in precedenti per v capita.
Summa boum et bovettorum Ciiij^{xx}iij, taurorum ix, vaccarum CCiij, boviculorum et vitulorum lxvij. Summa sexus CCCClxij plus quam in precedenti per xxvij capita.
Summa hurtardorum xxiij, multonum M^{l}lxxix, ovium matricum Dlxx, agnorum CCCiiij^{xx}vj. Summa sexus ijM^{l}lviij minus quam in precedenti per iiij^{xx} capita.
Summa aprorum xvij, suum xxvj, porcorum Cliiij, porculorum et porcellorum CCCij. Summa sexus CCCCiiij^{xx}xix plus quam in precedenti per iiij^{xx}iij capita.
Redditus terminorum Michaelis Cxxxix li. xviij s. vij d. ob. qua., natalis Domini iiij^{xx}viij li. v s. iiij d. qua., annunciacionis iiij^{xx}xvj li. iij s. iiij d. ob. qua., nativitatis sancti Johannis iiij^{xx}viij li. x s. j d.
Summa totalis redditus CCCCxij li. xvij s. v d. ob. qua. plus quam in precedenti per iiij li. xiiij d. qua.

[29] The hay was valued at 10 marks (£6 13s. 4d.) (WAM 26926).
[30] 398 sheep's fleeces and 38 lambs' fleeces, valued respectively at 6d. and 2d. per fleece, were sent from Hyde this year to Br. Walter de Warfeld, the treasurer (WAM 27077).
[31] The comparison is with performance in 1369–70, a year for which no comparable state of the manors survives.

Denham Durdent'[32] Redditus ibidem per annum x li. viij s. j d. Arreragia, nulla.
Valet manerium hoc anno vij li. vj s.
Remanent super compotum j qr. frumenti, ij qr. iiij bus. brasei frumenti, xxxvj qr. v bus. brasei drageti, ij equi, v jumenta, iij pullani, xij boves, j gallus, viij galline et xxiiij capones.

[*Mem. 2 dorse*] Memorandum quod remanent in manerio de Denham xxxij qr. frumenti, ij qr.[33] pisarum albarum per estimacionem, viij qr. v bus. brasei ordei, xxiiij qr.[34] brasei drageti.
Item apud Lalham xiiij qr. avenarum, xiij qr. v bus. brasei ordei.
Item apud Pirford xlviij qr. avenarum.
Item apud Denham Durdant[35] j qr. frumenti, ij qr. iiij bus. brasei frumenti, xxvj qr. v bus. brasei drageti.

Summa conjuncta xxxiij qr. frumenti, ij qr. pisarum albarum, lxij qr. avenarum, ij qr. iiij bus. brasei frumenti, xxij qr. ij bus. brasei ordei, lxj qr. iij bus. brasei drageti. Summa brasei[36] iiij^{xx}vj qr. j bus.

[32] Denham Durdent's manor originated as half a knight's fee alienated by the abbot and convent of Westminster, probably in the mid-twelfth century, from Denham, the chief manor. The name, in use by 1327, implies that the Durdent family was by then in possession; and it was from Edward Durdent that the abbot leased Denham Durdent's, initially from 1368–9 to 1371–2, for a down payment of £26. Harvey, *Estates*, p. 339; *VCH Bucks.*, iii, p. 259; and see I 12.
[33] MS: 'ij qr.', but see Denham above.
[34] MS: 'xxiiij qr.', but see Denham above.
[35] MS: 'Durdan'.
[36] MS: 'brasei' added in another hand.

I 10 States of the abbot's manors and portions at the conclusion of the audit of accounts for the year ending on 28 September 1372

A parchment roll of two membranes, approximately 171–4 mm wide, sewn Chancery fashion with a tight oversew, with light blue/green thread. The first membrane tapers to a point at the top. Much of the roll is a fair copy, and it has three vertical folds setting out left and right margins, and the centre. A second hand has worked on the grand totals. There are two titles written on the dorse of the roll in late fourteenth-century hands: 'Dog*erelli* anno xlvj^{o}'; and 'Status terrarum domini Nicholai abbatis Westm' de anno xlvj^{o}'.[1]

WAM 6179

[*Mem. 1 recto*] Status terrarum et porcionum domini abbatis Westm' super auditum compoti ministrorum suorum in vigilia sancti Michaelis anno regni regis Edwardi tercii post conquestum xlvj^{to}

Islep' [Rents as in I 7 and I 8: £31 6s. 11d.] Arreragia Willelmi Dolle prepositi ibidem xl s.
Valet manerium hoc anno cum lana iiij^{xx}v li. xj s.[2]
Remanent super compotum xxiiij boves, j hurtardus, Cxxij multones, xxx oves matrices, xxiiij hoggerelli, xxxvj agni, j aper, iiij sues, xxx porci pro lardario, xxx porculi, xxj porcelli, xxxvj capones, ij anseres, vij auce mariole, ij galli, xij galline, ij cigni erarii, j cignottus, iiij cigniculi.

Sutton' [Rents as I 6: £17 17s. 10d.] Arreragia Thome Hurry prepositi ibidem xx s.
Valet manerium hoc[3] anno cum feno xxviij li. xiiij s.
Remanent super compotum j aper, j sus, iiij porci pro lardario, xiij porculi, xij porcelli, j anser, iij mariole, j gallus, vj galline, xij capones.

Todenham [Rents as I 5: £15 6s. 2½d.] Arreragia Rogeri Erdyngton' ballivi, nulla.
Remanent super compotum ij equi carectarii, xxiiij boves,[4] Cxij multones, Cxxviij oves matrices, xxij hogastri, Cv agni, j aper, iiij sues, iij hogetti, xvij porcelli, xvj capones, ij galli, xviij galline, ij anseres et iiij auce mariole.

[1] Extant ministers' accounts: Bourton-on-the-Hill, WAM 8309; Ebury, WAM 26927; Hardwicke in Elmstone Hardwicke, WAM 8443; Hyde, WAM 27078; Islip, WAM 14807; Laleham, WAM 27152; Pensham, WAM 22227; Pinvin, WAM 22298; Pyrford, WAM 27421.
[2] 228 fleeces, weighing 34 st. 2 lb., were sent from Islip to the collecting centre for the Western Parts at Bourton-on-the-Hill this year (WAM 8300, 14807).
[3] MS: 'cum' rather than 'hoc'.
[4] MS: 'ij equi carectarii, xxiiij boves' inserted.

Bourton' [Rents as in I 7: £9 2s. 4¾d.] Arreragia Ricardi Albard prepositi ibidem xj li. xvj s. iiij d. ob. qua.
Valet manerium hoc anno cum lana xliiij li. ix s.[5]
Remanent super compotum vj qr. brasei, vj jumenta, j taurus, x boves, ij vacce, iiij bovetti, j juvenca, j boviculus, j vitulus annalis, j vitulus de exitu, CCCiiij^{xx}xix multones,[6] ij apri, ij sues, xx porci unde xviij pro lardario, xiiij porculi, xiij porcelli, ij galli, x galline, xx capones, iij qr. iij bus. calceti adusti,[7] lxx clades.

Pershore [Rents as in I 5: £32 9s. 0d.] Arreragia Ricardi Darnel nuper prepositi vj li. iiij s. viij d.,[8] Radul*fi* Pendefen nunc ballivi viij li. xv s. x d. ob.
Valet manerium hoc anno cum lana xlj li. viij s., preter xxxiiij li. vij s. ij d. qua. soluciones forinsecas.[9]
Remanent super compotum ij bus. frumenti, xj qr. siliginis, ij qr. iij bus. multure molendini, vij qr. iiij bus. brasei, j equus pro molendino, iij equi carectarii, ix boves, ij vacce, iij boviculi, iij vituli, j aper, iij sues, xlviij porci unde xxviij pro lardario, xx porculi, vij hurtardi, Ciiij^{xx}xj multones, Ciiij^{xx}iiij oves matrices, Clvj hogastri et jercie, iiij^{xx}iiij agni, j gallus, v galline, xvj capones, j anser, iij mariole, xv aucule, iiij^{xx}x carectates feni.

Pendesham [Rents as in I 5: £26 4s. 4d.] Arreragia, nulla.
Valet manerium hoc anno xxxvij li. xiij s. iiij d.[10]
Remanent in manu firmarii[11] iij qr. vj bus. frumenti, xvj qr. iij bus. siliginis, viij qr. j bus. di. puls', xiij qr. vj bus. ordei, xx qr. drageti, j equus, j jumentum, j pullanus, vij boves, xij vacce, vj juvence, ij boviculi, j taurellus, j anser, ij auce mariole, xij capones, j gallus et vj galline.[12]

[5] The demesne wool crop at Bourton-on-the-Hill this year consisted of 553 fleeces, weighing 3 sacks. 1,437 fleeces, including the 553 and weighing 7 sacks 7 lb., were collected at Bourton for sale from manors in the Western Parts (WAM 8300).
[6] Of the 399 wethers, 140 were purchased in October 1371 (WAM 8299).
[7] MS: 'advsti'.
[8] Darnel is last mentioned as reeve of Pershore in 1364–5 (I 8).
[9] MS: 'preter xxxiiij li. vij s. ij d. qua. soluciones forinsecas' inserted. 394 fleeces, weighing 2 sacks 7 lb., were sent from Pershore to the collecting centre at Bourton-on-the Hill this year (WAM 8300).
[10] The *valor* is identical with the sum delivered by Wolstan Andrew, rent-collector at Pensham, to Richard Fortheye, clerk of the abbot's kitchen, who was in effect, his receiver, in the course of the year (WAM 24515).
[11] John Parker, for whom see I 9.
[12] The panel for 'Remanent' encroaches on the space intended for the manor of Hardwicke, the marginal heading for which occurs at this point. Contents as in the inventory of corn and stock in I 9.

Herdwik [Rents as in I 5: £22 7s. 8½d.] Arreragia Johannis Gery prepositi ibidem xx s.
Valet manerium hoc anno xxix li. ix s.
Remanent super compotum v equi carectarii, xvj boves, iij vacce, j vitulus annalis, j vitulus de exitu, ij apri, iij sues, liiij porci unde xxx pro lardario, xviij porculi, xiij porcelli, j anser, iiij auce mariole, xxiiij capones, ij galli, x galline, ij lagene tarri, xxiiij carectates feni, xl clades.

Durhurst [Rents as in I 9: £29 17s. 6d.] Arreragia Thome *Sour*payn prepositi vj li. iij s. x d. ob.
Valet manerium hoc anno xxvj li. iij s. vj d.
Remanent super auditum compoti j pullanus femellus, j lib. piperis.

Chaddesle [Rents as in I 5: £5 0s. 8d.] Arreragia Johannis Hathemare prepositi xxxvjs.
Valet manerium hoc[13] anno xxv li. iij s.
Remanent super compotum in manu Johannis Hathemare firmarii[14] xvj qr.[15] iiij bus. p. frumenti, viij qr. v bus. siliginis, xiij qr. iiij bus. p. puls', xiiij qr. iij bus.[16] ordei, iij qr. drageti, vij qr. vj bus. avenarum, ij equi carectarii,[17] ix boves, j taurus, xxj vacce, j sus, xv porculi, j anser[18] et iij mariole, xij capones, j gallus, v galline.

Longedon' [Rents as in I 5: £15.] Arreragia Edwardi Keardif lxvj s. viij d., Johannis Broun xxiij s. iiij d. ob. qua.
Valet manerium hoc anno xviij li. iiij s.
Remanet super compotum j jumentum.

[13] MS: 'cum' rather than 'hoc'.
[14] In 1371–2, Hathemare, who had been reeve probably since 1366, obtained a lease of the demesne and the vaccary at Chaceley for 12 years and for a farm of £8 p.a. Later evidence suggests that he completed his term (WAM 21094, 24515; I 11–14, 16–17). The following inventory is of the grain and livestock now in his hands and to be returned to the abbot at the end of his term.
[15] MS: 'qr.' inserted.
[16] MS: 'iij bus.' inserted.
[17] MS: 'ij equi carectarii' inserted.
[18] MS: 'j suem, xv porculos, j anserem'.

Morton' [Rents as in I 5: £28 17s. 9d.] Arreragia Henrici Holdy lx s. ij d., Ricardi Od' x s., Ade Pall' l s. x d. ob. qua., Henrici Ode et Ade Pall' xv s. viij d. ob. qua.[19]
Valet manerium xxxiiij li. vij s.

Pendefen [Rents as in I 5: £33 16s. 3d.] Arreragia Johannis Broun v s. vij d. qua., Radul*fi* Pendefen iij s. viij d. ob. qua.
Valet manerium hoc anno xxix li. xij s.

Wyke de hundredo Valet hoc anno xlij s. v d.[20]
Arreragia, nulla.
Hundredum de Pendefen Valet hoc anno xxxiiij s. iij d.
Hundredum de Defford Valet hoc anno xxxv s.
Arreragia Roberti Berald[21] xxxv s. iiij d.
Portmot de Pershore Valet hoc anno lxxj s.[22]
Arreragia Johannis Vampage nuper ballivi xvij s. iij d., Nicholai Glovere nuper ballivi lij s. ob.
[*Mem. 2 recto*] *Balliva libertatis Glouc'* Valet hoc anno lx s. Johannis Derneford iiij li. x s. viij d., Johannis Clyve, Johannis Bayli anno xxxviij°[23] Cviij s. xj d., Johannis P*ar*kere ballivi anno xxxix^no[24] xix s. iiij d., Johannis Clerk nuper ballivi, Reginaldi Berkesdon'.[25]

Laleham [Rents as in I 9: £16 10s. 2¼d.] Arreragia Johannis atte Mille ballivi xxvj s. viij d.
Valet manerium hoc anno xxxvj li.
Remanent super compotum iiij qr. ij bus. siliginis, viij qr. iij bus. di. brasei ordei, et xxiiij qr. p. brasei drageti, iij jumenta, j pullanus etatis ij annorum, et ij pulli de exitu unde j femellus, xij boves, ij sues, xij porci pro lardario,

[19] Holdy is last mentioned as reeve of Castlemorton in 1367–8 (WAM 24511–12; I 8). Richard Ode was reeve here in 1367–8 (WAM 24513). Henry Ode was rent-collector 1362–3 to 1378 and possibly for a longer period (I 5, 12–13). Adam Pall, who was reeve here 1370–1, was probably, with Henry Ode, rent-collector by the end of the current year (Appendix).
[20] The sum is identical with that delivered this year by John Bruet, bailiff of the hundred, to the abbot's receiver; and, similarly, the *valor* for the hundred of Pinvin that follows in this list is identical with the sum delivered to the receiver by William Hanough, bailiff of the hundred (WAM 24515).
[21] Bailiff of the hundred.
[22] Thomas Rysele and John Parker, bailiffs of the portmoot, delivered £3 11s. 5d. to the abbot's receiver this year (WAM 24515).
[23] 1363–4. MS omits 'Arreragra' after the *valor*.
[24] 1364–5.
[25] MS: no sums are entered after the last two names. Clerk, bailiff of Deerhurst hundred in 1368–9, and Berkesden, bailiff in 1370–1, had discharged most of their several debts by the end of the previous year (I 9).

xv porculi unde j apriculus, v porcelli,[26] viij cigni erarii, iiij cignotti, ij cigniculi, j anser, iij auce mariole et viij aucule, xviij capones, iij coria dealbata, j gallus, vj galline, xx carectates feni.

Denham [Rents as in I 9: £25 8s. 5½d.] Arreragia Willelmi Spens*er* ballivi Cvij s. iiij d.
Valet manerium hoc anno cum feno et lana preter resoluciones xlij li. xv s.[27]
Remanent super compotum v qr. iij p. brasei frumenti, xij qr. vj bus. brasei ordei, xliiij qr. v bus. di. brasei drageti, vj equi carectarii, vij stotti, iij pullani unde ij etatis ij annorum et j etatis j anni, xxj boves, ij tauri, xlix vacce, iij coria dealbata et di. unde j corium pullani, vij hurtardi, Cxxx multones et Cl oves matrices, v apri,[28] iij sues, xx porci pro lardario, xx porculi, xiij porcelli, xj cigni aerarii et di., ij cignotti, et vij cignicule, ij anseres, vj auce mariole, xxviij aucule, xxiiij capones, j gallus, xij galline, Ciij carectates feni, j rusca apium, M^{l}ixC talwode et bavyn.

Pyrford' [Rents as in I 5: £35. 5s. 5½d.] Arreragia Roberti Bron' ballivi x li. ix s. iiij d.
Valet manerium hoc anno cum lana liiij li. xij s.[29]
Remanent super compotum ij qr. vij bus. siliginis, xv qr. vj bus. avene, iij jumenta, j pullanus de exitu anni precedentis, vj boves, xiij boviculi, xiiij juvence, Cv carectates feni, lxiiij clades, Cl talwode, C fagetti, j quartrona tegularum concavarum et ijC tegularum planarum.

Stanes [Rents as in I 9: £29 4s. 7¾d.] Arreragia Alexandri Tresour ballivi lij s. ix d. qua.
Valet manerium hoc anno xxxiij li. iij s.

Ȝeven' [Rents as in I 6: £14 3s. 4½d.] Arreragia, nulla.
Valet manerium hoc anno ad firmam ut in precedenti xviij li. xiij s. iiij d.[30]
Remanent super compotum iiij affri, x boves, j gallus, vj galline, xij capones.[31]

[26] The piggery was leased to the men of the vill, from whom the abbot was to receive 12 fat pigs p.a. (WAM 27152).
[27] For the reprises to be met from the issues of Denham, see I 1.
[28] MS: 'v apri' inserted.
[29] No wool crop is recorded at Pyrford this year, and all demesne sheep were in fact dispersed in the course of the year, no doubt under the threat of murrain. 14 ewes were sold before lambing, 4 rams, 50 wethers and 66 ewes sent to Denham, and 50 lambs sent to Hyde (WAM 27421).
[30] The intended reference does not survive; but see I 8.
[31] As in the inventory of stock in I 7.

*Eyb*ury [Rents as in I 9: £13 3s.] Arreragia Johannis Swan nuper ballivi xx s., Willelmi Huller ballivi ix s. viij d.[32]
Valet manerium hoc anno cum feno xlix li.[33]
Remanent super compotum vj jumenta, j pullanus etatis j anni et iij pulli de exitu femelli, viij boves, ij tauri, lxvij vacce, j apriculus, j sus, j porcus, iiij porculi, vj porcelli, j anser, iiij auce marioles, xix aucule, xviij capones, j gallus, vj galline, ij pavones, vj pave, j paviculus, xlix carectates feni.

Hyde [Rents as in I 9: £10 15s. 9½d.] Arreragia Walteri Page ballivi ibidem xx s.
Valet manerium hoc anno cum lana xxxviij li. xiiij s.[34]
Remanent super compotum ij qr. vij bus. siliginis, xv qr. vj bus. avenarum, iij jumenta, j pullanus de exitu anni precedentis, vj boves, xiij boviculi, xiiij juvence, Cv carectates feni, lxiiij clades, Cl talwode, C fagetti, j quartrona tegularum concavarum et ijC tegularum planarum. Super compotum iiij equi carectarii, iij stotti, xiiij boves, ij tauri, xlvj vacce, iij juvence, iiij vituli, vij hurtardi, Clxv multones, Ciiij^{xx}xiij oves matrices, iiij^{xx}ix agni, j aper, j sus, viij capones et xx carectates feni.

Summa[35] arreragiorum iiij^{xx}ix li. ij s. iij d. qua. Summa totalis valorum hoc anno DCCxxv li. xiiij s. viij d. Minus quam in precedenti per Cxix li. ij s. ij d.[36]
Summa equorum et affrorum lix, pullanorum et pullorum[37] xiij. Summa sexus lxxij. Minus quam in precedenti per j capud.
Summa boum et bovettorum Clxxvj, taurorum ix, vaccarum CCxxvj, boviculorum et vitulorum xxviij. Summa sexus CCCCxxxix. Minus quam in precedenti per xxiij capita.
Summa hurtardorum xxij, multonum M^{l}CCCxxj, ovium matricum Diiij^{xx}v, agnorum CCCxiiij. Summa sexus M^{l}M^{l}Ccxlij. Plus quam in precedenti per Ciiij^{xx}iiij capita.

[32] Swan was bailiff of Ebury 31 March 1367 to 29 September 1370; Huller was his successor.
[33] 42 cartloads of hay were used for horses belonging to the abbot's household or to visitors, and 60 on mares ('jumenta') belonging to the manor. The hay is not valued (WAM 26927).
[34] 404 sheep's fleeces and 181 lambs' fleeces were sent from Hyde to Br. Walter de Warfeld, who is described as the abbot's stockman ('instaurator') (WAM 27078).
[35] MS: this section is in a second hand. The numbers in the totals may have been added separately, possibly in a third hand.
[36] MS: in this and the following entries, the comparisons with the previous year, beginning in each case with the words 'minus quam' or 'plus quam', are insertions.
[37] MS: 'pulor''.

Summma aprorum xvj, suum xxv, porcorum Ciiij^{xx}ix, porculorum et porcellorum CClj. Summa sexus CCCCiiij^{xx}j. Minus quam in precedenti per xviij capita.
Redditus terminorum Michaelis Cxxxix li. xviij s. vij d. ob. qua., natalis Domini iiij^{xx}viij li. v s. iiij d. qua., annunciacionis iiij^{xx}xvj li. iij s. iiij d. ob. qua., nativitatis sancti Johannis iiij^{xx}viij li. x s. j d.
Summa totalis redditus CCCCxij li. xvij s. v d. ob. qua.

Denham Durdent' [Rents as in I 9: £10 8s. 1d.] Arreragia Thome atte Hurst ballivi xx s.
Valet manerium hoc anno vj li. xj s.
Remanent super compotum xj qr. iij bus. brasei drageti, ij equi carectarii, v jumenta, iij pullani, xiij boves, iiij vituli, j gallus et xij galline et xxiiij capones.

I 11 States of the abbot's manors and portions at the conclusion of the audit of accounts for the year ending on 28 September 1374

A parchment roll of two membranes, 173 mm wide, sewn Chancery fashion with white thread in a tight oversew. Membrane 1 tapers at the top. The roll is predominantly a fair copy, but less neat than some, such as I 7; in places, however, the totals have been written in a second ink, and at the end of the account, the comparisons of totals with previous years are additions. Membrane 1 is laid out with three vertical folds, for the left and right margins, and the centre; and membrane 2 has a single, central vertical fold. Membrane 1 is endorsed at the top: 'Status terrarum Nicholai abbatis Westm' de anno xlviij^{o}'; there are no endorsements on membrane 2. 'Arreragia' on this account is entered as a marginal heading throughout.[1]

WAM 6182

[*Mem. 1 recto*] Status terrarum et porcionum domini abbatis Westm' super auditum compoti ministrorum suorum in vigilia sancti Michaelis anno regni regis Edwardi tercii post conquestum xlviij^{o}

Islep' [Rents as in I 7: £31 6s. 11d.]
Arreragia Willelmi Dolle prepositi ibidem vj li. xiij s. iiij d.
Valet manerium hoc anno cum lana iiij^{xx}xviij li.[2]
Remanent super compotum xxiiij boves, j hurtardus, Clxvj multones, xlviij oves matrices, xxix hogastri et jercie, xxxix agni, j aper, iiij sues, xxx porci, xxx porculi, xxj porcelli, xxxj capones, ij anseres, vij auce marioles, ij galli et xij galline.

Sutton' [Rents as in I 7: £17 18s. 10d.]
Arreragia Thome Hurry prepositi ibidem lx s.
Valet manerium hoc anno preter fenum expenditum in hospicio domini xxxvj li.
Remanent super compotum ij bus. brasei capitalis, xvj qr. brasei drageti, j aper, j sus, x porci, xj porculi, vj porcelli, j gallus, vj galline, xij capones, j anser, iij auce mariole et viij aucule.

[1] Extant ministers' accounts: Bourton-on-the-Hill, WAM 8302; Deerhurst, WAM 8451; Ebury, WAM 26929; Hyde, WAM 27080; Islip, WAM 14809; Laleham, WAM 27153; Pensham, WAM 22229; Pinvin, WAM 22300; Todenham, GRO, D1099/M30/11.

[2] 222 fleeces, weighing 1 sack 1 st. 3 lb., were sent from Islip to the collecting centre for the Western Parts at Bourton-on-the-Hill this year (WAM 8302, 14809).

Todenham [Rents as in I 5: £15 6s. 2½d.]
Arreragia, nulla.[3]
Valet manerium hoc anno xxxiij li.
Remanent super compotum ij equi carectarii, xxv boves, j aper, iij sues,[4] xiij hogetti, v porcelli, xij porcelli lactantes, xvj capones, ij galli, xviij galline, ij anseres, iiij auce mariole et iiij^{xx}vj carectates feni.[5]

Bourton' [Rents as in I 7: £9 2s. 4¾d.]
Arreragia Ricardi Alberd prepositi ibidem ix li. xvj s. v d.[6]
Valet manerium hoc anno cum lana xxxij li.[7]
Remanent super compotum iiij jumenta, j taurus, xij boves, iij vacce, j bovettus, j juvenca, ij vituli annuales, ij vituli de exitu, CCxx multones, ij apri, ij sues, xx porci, xiiij porculi, xiij porcelli, ij galli, x galline, xx capones et lx carectates feni.

Pershore [Rents as in I 5: £32 19s.]
Arreragia Ricardi Darnell' nuper prepositi vj li. iiij s. viij d., Radul*fi* Pendefen nuper ballivi xx s., Johannis Glyn collectoris redditus iiij li., Willelmi Wycheford ballivi x li. viij s. ij d. ob.
Valet manerium hoc anno cum lana lxviij li.[8]
Remanent super compotum ix qr. vij bus. di. siliginis, viij qr. brasei, j equi molendini, iiij equi carectarii, j affrus femellus, xj boves, iij vacce, j boviculus, ij juvencule, iiij vituli, j aper, iij sues, xviij porci, x porculi, xv porcelli lactantes, Clxxvj bidentes, lij agni, j gallus, v galline, xvj capones, j anser, iij auce mariole, xij aucule, iiij^{xx} carectates feni et ij cignotti.

[3] The entry applies to Roger de Erdyngton in his capacities as bailiff of Todenham and lessee of the demesne, both of which ended with the current year (GRO, D1099/M30/11–12; WAM 24517).
[4] MS: 'sui'.
[5] The horses, oxen and pigs in this inventory represent stock delivered to the abbot by Erdyngton on the expiry of his lease, although only 24 oxen were specified in his lease. Of the cartloads of hay that are mentioned, 50 were harvested in 1374, and 40 in 1373 (GRO, D1099/M30/11). The absence of sheep is explained by the removal of the entire demesne flock, consisting of 4 rams, 55 ewes, 98 hoggs and 7 lambs, to Pershore in December 1373, probably in the expectation of a local murrain (GRO, D1099/M30/11).
[6] In a private capacity, Alberd had purchased, for £15 6s. 8d., all the corn harvested in the previous year and had been responsible for ploughing and sowing demesne arable in the current year to the following specification: 12 qr. wheat, 15 qr. pulse, 20 qr. barley and 8 qr. oats (WAM 8301).
[7] The demesne wool crop at Bourton-on-the-Hill this year consisted of 342 fleeces, weighing 1½ sacks 1 st. 908 fleeces, weighing 4 sacks 8 st. 9 lb., received at Bourton from manors in the Western Parts, including Bourton itself, were sold as 4½ sacks, with 2 lb. of so-called refuse, and at a price of £9 6s. 8d. per sack (WAM 8302).
[8] 159 fleeces, weighing 19 st., were sent from Pershore to the collecting centre at Bourton-on-the-Hill this year (WAM 8302).

Pendesham [Rents as in I 5: £26 4s. 4d.]
Arreragia Wolstani Andrewe collectoris redditus v s. xj d. qua.[9]
Valet manerium hoc anno xxxviij li.[10]
Remanent in manu firmarii iij qr. vj bus. frumenti, xvj qr. iij bus. siliginis, viij qr. j bus. di. puls', xiij qr. vj bus. ordei, xx qr. drageti, j equus, j jumentum, j pullanus, vij boves, xij vacce, vj juvence, ij bovetti, j taurellus, j anser, ij auce mariole, xij capones, j gallus et vj galline.[11]

Herdewyk' [Rents as in I 5: £22 17s. 8½d.]
Arreragia Johannis atte Halle prepositi ibidem iij d. ob. qua.
Valet manerium hoc anno xxv li. Remanent ibidem[12] in manu firmarii xxix qr. vj bus. di. frumenti, xxvij qr. ij bus. di. pisarum, xij qr. ordei, iiij qr. di. avenarum, iiij equi carectarii, xvj boves, j anser, iiij auce mariole, ij galli, x galline, xxj capones et xiiij carectates feni.[13]

Durhurst' [Rents as in I 9: £29 17s. 6d.]
Arreragia Thome Surpayn nuper prepositi xxvij s. iiij d. ob. qua., Johannis atte Halle collectoris redditus ibidem xij s. xj d.[14]
Valet manerium hoc anno xxix li. vj s.[15]

Chaddesle [Rents as in I 5: £5 0s. 8d.]
Arreragia Johannis Hathemer firmarii xxij s. viij d. ob.[16]
Valet manerium hoc anno xiiij li. viij s.
[*Mem. 2 recto*] Remanent in manu firmarii ibidem xvj qr. iiij bus. p. frumenti, viij qr. v bus. siliginis, xiij qr. iiij bus. p. pisarum, xiiij qr. iij bus. ordei, iij qr. drageti, vij qr. vj bus. avenarum, ij equi caretarii, ix boves, j

[9] MS: cash sum in a second ink.
[10] MS: cash sum in a second ink.
[11] As in the inventory of corn and stock in I 9.
[12] MS: 'ibidem' inserted.
[13] The site of the manor of Hardwicke, with the demesne, was leased to John Monmouth, merchant of Gloucester, and Elizabeth, his wife, for their joint and several lives, at a rent of £8 p.a., on 26 November 1373, but with effect from 30 September 1373 (WAM 32755). With the exception of the capons, the livestock listed above is identical with that to be delivered by the lessees to the abbot at the end of their term. The lessees were also to return the quantities of wheat, pulse, dredge and oats received at the beginning of their term, for sowing and for the manorial servants, and this was the subject of an indenture dated 21 September 1376 (WAM 32759). The quantities in the above list differ from those in the latter indenture but recur in later references to the lease.
[14] MS: cash sums in a second ink.
[15] In 1373–4, the site of the manor of Deerhurst and the demesne were leased to Richard, rector of Wick, for a rent of £4 p.a. (WAM 8451). The term is not recorded.
[16] For Hathemere's lease of the arable demesne and vaccary at Chaceley, see I 10.

taurus, xxj vacce unde j remanet in compoto et non remanet in indentura, j sus, xv porculi, j anser, iij auce mariole, xij capones, j gallus et v galline.[17]

Longdon' [Rents as in I 5: £15]
Arreragia Johannis Broun' collectoris xj s.
Valet manerium hoc anno xviij li. xj s.

Morton' [Rents as in I 5: £28 17s. 9d.]
Arreragia Henrici Holdy nuper prepositi lx s. ij d., Ricardi Ode x s., Ade Pall' collectoris l s. x d. ob. qua., Henrici Odea, Ade Pall' collectoris xvj s. v d. ob. qua.[18]
Valet manerium hoc anno xxxiij li. ix s.

Pendefen' [Rents as in I 5: £33 16s. 3d.]
Arreragia Johannis Broun nuper prepositi ibidem vj s. qua.
Valet manerium hoc anno xl li. xvj s.

Wyk' de hundredo Valet hoc anno xij s. viij d.
Arreragia, nulla.
Hundredum de Defford' Arreragia Roberti Berald ballivi ibidem xix s. viij d.
Valet hoc anno xiij s.
Hundredum de Pendefen' Valet manerium hoc anno xxvj s. xj d.
Arreragia, nonnulla.
Portmot' de Pershore Arreragia Johannis P*ar*ker ballivi viij s. v d.
Valet hoc anno lxviij s. v d.
Ballivus libertatis Glouc' Arreragia Reginaldi[19] Berkeston ballivi ibidem xx s.
Valet hoc anno lx s.

Lalham [Rents as in I 9: £16 10s. 2¼d.]
Arreragia Johannis atte Mille[20] xx s.
Valet manerium hoc anno cum lana xlj li.[21]
Remanent super compotum j qr. vj bus. di. ordei, j qr. ij bus. mixtilii, ij qr. brasei ordei, v jumenta, j pull*anus* de exitu, x boves, iij apri, ij sues, xij porci,

[17] As in the inventory of corn and stock in I 10.
[18] The sum is written against the previous two names, which are bracketed.
[19] MS: 'Riginaldi'.
[20] Serjeant and subsequently bailiff of Laleham.
[21] 140 sheep's fleeces and 78 lambs' fleeces were sent from Laleham to Br. Walter de Warfeld, conventual treasurer, for marketing this year. The lambs' fleeces may have been those of 78 new lambs received from Denham in June 1374 (WAM 27153).

xxix porculi, x porcelli, Clvj hogerelli et jercie, lxxv agni de exitu, viij cigni erarii, iij cignotti, j anser, iij auce mariole, viij capones, j gallus, j galline et xvij carectates feni.

Denham [Rents as in I 9: £25 8s. 5½d.]
Arreragia, nonnulla.
Valet manerium hoc anno cum lana et feno lxij li.
Remanent super compotum ij bus. pisarum albarum, v qr. ij bus. di. brasei frumenti, xxxij qr. ij p. brasei drageti, vj equi carectarii, vj stotti pro carucis, ij pullani, xxviij boves, iij tauri, l vacce, ij bovetti, ix vituli, ix hurtardi, Cviij multones, Cxxviij oves matrices, j hogerellus et xlvj agni de exitu, iij apri, ij sues, xxiij porci, xv porculi, vj porcelli, xj cigni erarii et di., vj cigni albi, vj cigniculi, ij anseres, v auce mariole, xxvj aucule, xxvj capones, j gallus, vij galline et iiij^{xx}xij carectates feni.

Pyrford' [Rents as in I 5: £35 5s. 5½d.]
Arreragia Ricardi Bedewynd ballivi ibidem xlix s. vj d. qua. et cum[22] constructione molendini.[23]
Valet manerium hoc anno cum lana et feno expendito in hospicio domini et[24] reparacione camere domini lxiij li.[25]
Remanent super compotum iiij jumenta, ij pullani femelli, vj boves, vij bovetti, viij boviculi, viij juvence, xj juvenculi, ij hurtardi, xlvj multones, xliij oves matrices, xiij hogerelli et jercie, xiiij agni de exitu, j sus, iiij porcelli et liiij carectates feni.

Stanes [Rents as in I 9: £29 4s. 7½d.][26]
Arreragia Alexandri Tresour ballivi ibidem lxviij s.
Valet manerium hoc anno xxxij li. ix s.

Ȝeveney [Rents as in I 6: £14 3s. 4½d.]
Valet manerium hoc anno ad firmam ut in precedenti xviij li. xiij s. iiij d.
Remanent in manu firmarii iiij affri, x boves, ij galli, vj galline et xij capones.

22 MS: 'cum' omitted.
23 The entry probably records the date of the main work on the new mill at Pyrford. Minor work, including the making of a new weir diverting water to it, continued in 1375–6 (WAM 27422). On techniques in use in this period, John Langdon, *Mills in the Medieval Economy: England, 1300–1540* (Oxford, 2004), Chapter 3.
24 MS: 'et' omitted.
25 Work on the abbot's house at Pyrford, which had a moat and drawbridge, is reported over a decade and more, beginning in 1363–4 (WAM 27421–2); J. Armitage Robinson, *The Abbot's House at Westminster* (Cambridge, 1911), p. 17.
26 The rents for this manor from here on are now ¼d. less than I 9.

Eybury [Rents as in I 9: £14 3s.]
Arreragia Willelmi Huller ballivi lx s.
Valet manerium hoc anno cum feno expendito in hospicio domini lxj li.[27]
Remanent ibidem super compotum ix jumenta, j pullanus, ij tauri, x boves, lxviij vacce, j sus, j porcus, ix porculi, vj porcelli, ij anseres, iij auce mariole, xv aucule, j gallus, vj galline, x capones, iij pave, ij cignotti, xxx carectates feni.

[*Mem. 1 dorse*] *Hyde*[28] [Rents as in I 9: £10 15s. 9½d.]
Arreragia Walteri Page ballivi ibidem .....[29]
Valet manerium hoc anno cum lana xlij li.[30]
Remanent super compotum iiij equi carectarii, iiij stotti pro carucis, xiiij boves, ij tauri, liij vacce, iiij vituli annuales, iij vituli de exitu, v hurtardi, Clxxv multones, CCv oves matrices, Clxvij agni, j aper, j sus et xx carectates feni.

Summa arreragiorum lxiiij li. xij s. ob. qua.
Summa totalis valorum hoc anno DCCiiij^{xx}xv li. xiij s. iiij d., plusquam in precedenti per Cxix li. v s. vij d.[31]
Summa equorum et affrorum lxij, pullanorum et pullorum vij. Summa sexus lxix, plusquam in precedenti per ij capita.
Summa boum et bovettorum Ciiij^{xx}xiiij, taurorum x, vaccarum CCxxv, boviculorum et vitulorum xlvj. Summa sexus CCCClxxv, plusquam in precedenti per xiiij capita.
Summa hurtardorum xvij, multonum ixCxxvj, ovium matricum Diiij^{xx}viij, agnorum CCCiiij^{xx}. Summa sexus M^{l}ixCxxiiij. Inde in partibus occidentalibus DCCxxxj et in partibus australibus M^{l}Ciiij^{xx}xiij.
Summa aprorum xiij, suum xxj, porcorum Cxiiij, porculorum et porcellorum CCxlix. Summa sexus CCCiiij^{xx}xvij, minus quam in precedenti per lxxv capita.
Summa Michaelis Cxxxix li. xviij s. vij d. ob. qua., natalis iiij^{xx}viij li. v s. iiij d. qua., annunciacionis iiij^{xx}xvj li. iij s. iiij d. ob. qua., nativitatis sancti Johannis iiij^{xx}viij li. x s. j d. Summa totalis reddit*uum* CCCCxij li. xvij s. v d. ob. qua.

[27] The hay, consisting of 40 cartloads, was valued at £10 (WAM 26929).
[28] The entry for Hyde starts after a considerable space.
[29] MS: blank space. At the audit of his account, Page was credited with an excess of £1 19s. 9¾d. (WAM 27080).
[30] 349 sheep's fleeces and 167 lambs' fleeces were sent from Hyde to Br. Walter de Warfeld, the conventual treasurer, this year (WAM 27080).
[31] In this and the following entries relating to totals for all manors, the comparisons with the previous year, beginning in each case with 'minus quam' or 'plusquam', were inserted.

Denham Durdent Redditus ibidem per annum ix li. viij s. vij d.
Arreragia Thome atte Hurst ballivi ibidem xl s.
Valet manerium hoc anno xxiij li.
Remanent super compotum j qr. ij bus. brasei frumenti, iij bus. brasei ordei, iiij qr. v bus. p. brasei drageti, ij equi carectarii, v jumenta, ij pullani, xiij boves, ij bovetti, ij juvence, j vitulus de exitu, j corium crudum, j gallus, xij galline, j anser, iij auce mariole, xj aucule, xxj capones.

Stourtone[32] Redditus et firme ibidem per annum xiij li. xvj s. ix d. qua.
Arreragia, nonnulla.
Valet manerium hoc anno cum lana xxij li.[33]
Remanent super compotum xxxix qr. iij bus. p. pisarum grisarum,[34] iij jumenta, ij pullani, x boves, j vacca, Cxxiiij multones, lxvj oves matrices et liiij agni.

[32] The abbot of Westminster acquired possession of Stourton, in Whichford (Warwickshire), through nominees in 1369. Although he appears never to have amortised it, he was in possession until 1376–7 (WAM 8303; Harvey, *Estates*, p. 424, no. 41). The reeve of Sutton-under-Brailes was now responsible for Stourton, for which he apparently rendered a separate account (GRO, D1009/M31/44).

[33] 185 wool fleeces, weighing 1 sack 6 lb., were sent from Stourton to the collecting centre at Bourton-on-the-Hill this year (WAM 8302).

[34] MS: 'pisarum grisarum' inserted in the same hand and ink as the rest of this section.

I 12 States of the abbot's manors and portions at the conclusion of the audit of accounts for the year ending on 28 September 1375

A parchment roll of two membranes, 174 mm wide, sewn Chancery fashion with white thread in a tight oversew. Both membranes are laid out with two vertical folds, for the left margin and the centre. The roll is a fair copy in a single hand. There is a tear at the foot of membrane 2, but no evidence that any further membranes were once attached. The dorse of membrane 2 is blank. The section for arrears in each manor's summary account this year is indicated by a marginal heading.[1]

WAM 6177

[*Mem. 1 recto*] Status terrarum et porcionum domini abbatis Westm' super auditum compoti ministrorum suorum in vigilia sancti Michaelis anno regis Edwardi tercii post conquestum xlix^{no}

Islep' [Rents as in I 7: £31 6s. 11d.]
Liberaciones denariorum ibidem hoc anno iiij^{xx}v li. xviij s. iiij d. ob.
Arreragia, nulla.
Valet manerium hoc anno cum lana iiij^{xx}vj li. xix s.[2]
Remanent super compotum xxiiij boves, j hurtardus, Clj multones, xxxiiij oves matrices, xxix hogastri, xxxviij agni, j aper, iiij sues, xxx porci, xxx porculi, xxxij capones, ij anseres, vij auce mariole, ij galli, xij galline, iij cigni erarii, j cigniculus.

Sutton' [Rents as in I 6: £17 18s. 10d.]
Liberaciones denariorum ibidem hoc anno xxxj li. xiiij s. j d.
Arreragia, nulla.
Valet manerium hoc anno preter fenum expenditum in hospicio domini xxx li.
Remanent super auditum compoti ij bus. brasei capitalis, iij qr. v bus. brasei drageti, j bos, j aper, j sus, xiiij porci, v porculi, vj porcelli, xij capones, j anser, iij auce mariole, xviij aucule, j gallus, vj galline.

Todenham [Rents as in I 5: £15 6s. 2½d.]
Liberaciones denariorum ibidem hoc anno xxx li. iij s. vij d.
Arreragia, nulla.
Valet manerium hoc anno xxxvij li.

[1] Extant ministers' accounts: Bourton-on-the-Hill, WAM 8303; Ebury, WAM 26930; Hardwicke in Elmstone Hardwicke, WAM 8445; Hyde, WAM 27081; Laleham, WAM 27155; Pensham, WAM 22230; Pinvin, WAM 22301; Todenham, WAM 25973.
[2] 224 fleeces, weighing 1 sack, were sent from Islip to the collecting centre for the Western Parts at Bourton-on-the-Hill this year (WAM 8303).

Remanent super compotum iij qr. frumenti, j qr. p. siliginis, xxj qr. brasei drageti, iiij equi carectarii, xxij boves, iij vacce, j aper, iij sues, xxv porci, xv porculi, vij porcelli, lx multones, xx capones, iij galli, x galline, ij anseres, iiij auce mariole, xxvij aucule, lxxviij carectates feni.

Bourton' [Rents as in I 7: £9 2s. 4¾d.]
Liberaciones denariorum ibidem hoc anno xxij li. xvj s. viij d.
Arreragia, nulla.
Valet manerium hoc anno cum lana xxxiiij li. x s.[3]
Remanent super compotum ij qr. frumenti, vj qr. vj bus. puls', xix qr. j bus. brasei ordei, v jumenta, xv boves, vij vacce, j taurellus, iij boviculi, ij juvencule, j vitulus annalis, iiij vituli de exitu, CCxxx multones, ij apri, ij sues, xxv porci, viij porculi, xvj porcelli, ij galli, x galline, xx capones, Ciiij^{xx}xvj vellera, l carectates feni.

Pershore [Rents as in I 6: £32 19s.]
Liberaciones denariorum ibidem hoc anno xlix li. xj s. v d.
Arreragia Ricardi Darnel nuper prepositi vj li. iiij s. viij d., Johannis Glyn collectoris redditus anno xlviij^{o} xl s.
Valet manerii hoc anno cum lana lxvij li. xij s.[4]
Remanent super compotum ij qr. j bus. siliginis, j qr. multure molendini, j qr. brasei drageti, j equus pro molendino, iiij equi carectarii, j affrus masculus,[5] j affrus femellus, xj boves, ij vacce, j vitulus annalis, iiij vituli de exitu, j aper, iij sues, xx porci, viij porculi, xiij porcelli, vj hurtardi, iiij^{xx}ix multones, lxxvj oves matrices, lxv hogerelli, lxvj agni, j gallus, v galline, xvj capones, j anser, iij auce mariole, xj aucule, lx carectates feni et j cignus.

Pendesham [Rents as in I 5: £26 4s. 4d.]
Liberaciones ibidem hoc anno xxxvij li. iiij s. v d.
Arreragia Ad*e* Andrew collectoris redditus xx s.
Valet manerii hoc anno xxxvij li. xviij s.
Remanent in manu firmarii iij qr. vj bus. frumenti, xvi qr. iij bus. siliginis, viij qr. j bus. di. puls', xiij qr. vj bus. ordei, xx qr. drageti, j equus, j jumentum, ij bovetti, j taurellus, j anser, ii auce mariole, xij capones, j gallus et vj galline.[6]

[3] The net wool crop at Bourton consisted of 302 fleeces, weighing 1½ sacks. 978 fleeces, including the 302 and weighing 4½ sacks 12 st. 2 lb., were collected at Bourton, but sold as 4 sacks and for £9 16s. 8d. per sack. The number included 196 fleeces of inferior wool (WAM 8303).
[4] 213 fleeces, weighing 1 sack 4 st., were sent from Pershore to the collecting centre at Bourton-on-the-Hill this year (WAM 8303).
[5] MS: a short erasure follows.
[6] As in the inventory of corn and stock in I 9.

Herdewyk [Rents as in I 7: £32 17s. 8½d.]
Liberaciones denariorum ibidem hoc anno xxx li. viij d.[7]
Arreragia, nulla.
Valet manerium hoc anno xxxvj li.
Remanent in manu firmarii xxix qr. vj bus. di. frumenti, xxvij qr. ij bus. di. pisarum, xij qr. ordei, iiij qr. di. avenarum, iiij equi carectarii, xvj boves, j anser, iiij auce mariole, ii galli, x galline, xxj capones et xiiij caretates feni.[8]

Durhurst [Rents as in I 9: £29 17s. 6d.]
Liberaciones denariorum ibidem hoc anno xxxvij li.
Arreragia Johannis atte Halle collectoris redditus ibidem xiiij s. iiij d.
Valet manerium hoc anno xxxij li. xiij s.
Remanent super compotum j bos.

Chaddusle [Rents as in I 5: £5 0s. 8d.]
Liberaciones denariorum ibidem hoc anno xiij li. ij s. v d.
Arreragia Johannis Hathemar' firmarii ibidem xlij s. ob.
Valet manerium hoc anno xiiij li. ix s. ix d.
Remanent in manu firmarii ibidem xvj qr. iiij bus. p. frumenti, viij qr. v bus. siliginis, xiij qr. iiij bus. p. pisarum, xiiij qr. iij bus. ordei, iij qr. drageti, vij qr. vj bus. avenarum, ij equi carectarii, ix boves, j taurus, xxj vacce, j sus, xv porculi, j anser, iij auce mariole xij capones, j gallus, v galline.[9] Et remanet super compotum j boviculus.[10]

[*Mem. 2 recto*] *Longdon* [Rents as in I 5: £15]
Liberaciones denariorum ibidem hoc anno xviij li. x s.
Arreragia Johannis Broun messoris et collectoris ibidem vij d.
Valet manerium hoc anno xviij li. vj s.

Morton' [Rents as in I 5: £28 17s. 9d.]
Liberaciones denariorum ibidem hoc anno xxviij li. x s.
Arreragia Henrici Ode collectoris x s. v d.
Valet manerium hoc anno xxxiij li. xv s. v d.

[7] This sum, delivered by the rent-collector, John Halle, includes £6 0s. 8d. spent on a pipe of wine at Gloucester and sent to the steward of the abbot's household, then at Sutton-under-Brailes (WAM 8845, 24406).
[8] As in the inventory of corn and stock in I 11.
[9] As in the inventory of corn and livestock in I 10.
[10] The steer was probably a stray.

Pendefen [Rents as in I 5: £33 16s. 3d.]
Liberaciones denariorum ibidem hoc anno xxxix li. iiij d.
Arreragia Johannis Broun nuper prepositi ibidem vj s. qua.
Valet manerium hoc anno xxxix li.

Wyk de hundredo Arreragia Johannis Bruet xv s. j d.
Valet hoc anno xv s. j d.
Hundredum de Defford Arreragia Roberti Barald ballivi xxxviij s.
Valet hoc anno xviij s. iiij d.
Hundredum de Pendefen Liberaciones denariorum ibidem hoc anno xxvj s. x d.
Arreragia, nulla.
Valet hoc anno xxvj s. x d.
Portmot de Pershore Liberaciones denariorum ibidem hoc anno lxv s. v d.
Arreragia, nulla.
Valet hoc anno lvij s.
Balliva libertatis Glouc' Arreragia Reginaldi Berkesdon' ballivi libertatis ibidem xxvj s. xj d.
Valet hoc anno xij s. iij d.

Lalham [Rents as in I 9: £16 10s. 2¼d.]
Liberaciones ibidem hoc anno xxix li. xiij s. j d. ob. qua.
Arreragia Johannis South x s.[11]
Valet manerium hoc anno cum lana xxxiiij li. xvij s.[12]
Remanent super compotum ij bus. avenarum, vij jumenta, j pullanus femellus, ij pullani de exitu, x boves, iij apri, ij sues, xvj porci, xx porculi, xv porcelli, j hurtardus, iiij^{xx}xv multones, xl oves matrices, vj agni, vij cigni erarii, iij cigni albi, ij cigniculi, j anser, iij auce mariole, xij aucule, xix capones, j gallus, vj galline et xviij carectates feni.

Denham [Rents as in I 9: £25 8s. 5½d.]
Liberaciones denariorum ibidem hoc anno lxvj li. xv s. j d.
Arreragia Davidi Soper lxxij s. vij d. ob. qua.
Valet manerium hoc anno cum lana et feno ultra resoluciones redditus xlix li.[13]
Remanent super compotum xxvj qr. j bus. brasei drageti, vj equi carectarii, vj stotti, ij pullani, xxv boves, ij tauri, xlviij vacce, ij bovetti, j boviculus, ij

[11] South was reeve of Laleham 29 September 1374– 20 June 1375 (WAM 27155).
[12] 107 sheep's fleeces and 6 lambs' fleeces were sent from Laleham to Br. Walter de Warfeld, cellarer of Westminster, this year (WAM 27155).
[13] For the *resoluciones* (reprises) chargeable to manorial issues at Denham, see I 1.

juvencule, vj hurtardi, lxix multones, Clxviij oves matrices,[14] iiij^{xx}v agni de exitu, ij apri, ij sues, xxiij porci, xvij porculi, viij porcelli lactantes, xiij cigni erarii et di., iiij cigni albi, ij cignotti, viij cigniculi de exitu, ij anseres, vj auce mariole, xix aucule, j gallus, vij galline, v capones, v rusce apium et iiij^{xx}x carectates feni.

Pyrford [Rents as in I 5: £35 5s. 5½d.]
Liberaciones denariorum ibidem hoc anno xxiiij li. iiij s. x d.
Arreragia Ricardi Bedewynd ballivi ibidem xij li.
Valet manerium hoc anno cum lana, feno et bosco lx li. vj s.
Remanent super compotum ij qr. ij bus. avenarum, v jumenta, j pullanus, j pullus de exitu, viij boves, vj bovetti, x juvence, ij hurtardi, lxx multones, Cj oves matrices, xlvij agni, j sus, iij porcelli et lxxiiij carectates feni.

Stanes [Rents as in I 9: £29 4s. 7½d.]
Liberaciones denariorum ibidem hoc anno xxxviij li. xv s. iij d.
Arreragia Alexandri Tresour ballivi ibidem xiiij s.[15]
Valet hoc anno xxxiij li.

Ȝeveneye [Rents as in I 6: £14 3s. 4½d.]
Liberaciones denariorum hoc anno xviij li. xiij s. iiij d.[16]
Arreragia .....[17]
Valet hoc anno manerium ad firmam ut precedenti xviij li. xiij s. iiij d.
Remanent in manu firmarii iiij affri, x boves, j gallus, vj galline et xij capones.[18]

Eybury [Rents as in I 9: £13 3s.]
Liberaciones denariorum ibidem hoc anno l li. viij s. vij d. ob.
Arreragia Willelmi Huller' ballivi ibidem lx s.
Valet manerium hoc anno cum feno expendito in hospicio lviij li.[19]
Remanent super compotum vij jumenta, ij tauri, x boves, lxx vacce, j sus, x porculi, vj porcelli, j anser, iij auce mariole, xviij aucule, j gallus, vj galline, ix capones, iiij pave, ij cigni albi, iiij rusce apium et xxviij carectates feni.

[14] MS: followed by 'v hogerelli et', struck out, in the same hand as the rest of the entry.
[15] MS: followed by a short erasure.
[16] This sum, delivered by John Clerk, farmer of the manor, to the abbot's household, represents the farm of the manor, which is now also the sum of the *valor* (WAM 24518).
[17] No particulars follow.
[18] Remainder of stock as in the inventory in I 7.
[19] 12 cartloads of hay were provided for the household this year; they are not valued in the bailiff's account (WAM 26930).

[*Mem. 1 dorse*] *Hyde* [Rents as in I 9: £10 15s. 9½d.]
Liberaciones denariorum ibidem hoc anno .....[20]
Arreragia Walteri Page ballivi ibidem vj li.[21]
Valet manerium hoc anno cum lana xx li. x s.[22]
Remanent super compotum iiij equi carectarii, iiij stotti, xij boves, ij tauri, lij vacce, ij bovetti et ij juvence, iij vituli annales et iiij vituli de exitu, vj hurtardi, CCxxxvj multones, CClxj oves matrices, Cxxxiiij agni, j aper, j sus et xv carectates feni.

Summa arreragiorum xlij li. xiiij s. viij d. ob.,[23] minus quam in precedenti per xxj li. xvij s. iiij d. qua. Summa[24] totalis valoris hoc anno DCClix li., minus quam in precedenti per xxxvj li. xiij s. iiij d.
Summa equorum et affrorum lxxviij, pullanorum et pullorum xiiij. Summa sexus iiij^{xx}xij, plures quam in precedenti per xxiij capita.
Summa boum et bovettorum CCxvj, taurorum ix, vaccarum CCxxxv, boviculorum et vitulorum xxvij. Summa sexus CCCCiiij^{xx}vij, plures quam in precedenti per xij capita.
Summa hurtardorum xxij, multonum MCxlij, ovium matricum DCCxliiij, agnorum et hogerellorum Diiij^{xx}v. Summa sexus MMCCCCiiij^{xx}xiij, plures quam in precedenti per Dlix capita.
Summa aprorum xij, suum xxj, porcorum Cliij, porculorum et porcellorum CCij. Summa sexus CCCiiij^{xx}viij, minus quam in precedenti per ix capita.
Summa Michaelis Cxxxix li. xviij s. vij d. ob. qua., natalis iiij^{xx}viij li. v s. iiij d. qua., annunciacionis iiij^{xx}xvj li. iij s. iiij d. ob. qua., nativitatis sancti Johannis iiij^{xx}viij li. x s. j d. Summa totalis redditus CCCCxij li. xvij s. v d. ob. qua.
Summa totalis liberacionum denariorum DClvj li. xiiij s. vj d. ob. qua.

Denham Durdent [Rents as in I 11: £9 8s. 6d.]
Liberaciones denariorum ibidem[25] xvj li. x s. x d. ob.
Arreragia Thome atte Hurst ballivi ibidem ix s. j d. qua.
Valet manerium hoc anno xv li.

[20] MS: followed by a blank space. The surviving copy of the bailiff's account for 1374–5 does not include a panel for *liberaciones denariorum*, and from the foot of the account it appears that few or none were made (WAM 27081).
[21] The bailiff paid this debt in April 1376 (WAM 27081).
[22] 452 sheep's fleeces and 133 lambs' fleeces were delivered to Br. Walter de Warfeld, cellarer, for sale (WAM 27081).
[23] MS: numerals inserted.
[24] MS: from this point onwards, down to and including the sum of *liberaciones denariorum*, all numerals are insertions.
[25] MS: 'hoc anno' follows but has been deleted.

Remanent super compotum iij equi carectarii, iiij jumenta, ij pullani masculi et ij pull*i* de exitu, xiiij boves, j gallus, xij galline, j anser, iij auce mariole, xv aucule, xxiiij capones.

Stourton [Rents and farms as in I 11: £13 16s. 9¼d.]
Liberaciones denariorum ibidem hoc anno xiiij li. xiij s. v d. ob. qua.
Arreragia, nulla.
Valet manerium hoc anno cum lana xxvij li. xiiij s.[26]
Remanent super compotum j qr. frumenti, ij qr. per estimacionem in garbis, iij jumenta, j affrus femellus, j pullanus etatis unius anni, j pull*us* de exitu, ix boves, j vacca, j juvenca, Cxlij multones, lxiiij oves matrices, lviij hogastri, lvij agni.

[26] 239 fleeces, weighing 1 sack 7 st. 2 lb., were sent from Stourton to the collecting centre at Bourton-on-the-Hill this year (WAM 8303; see n. 3 above).

I 13 States of the abbot's manors and portions at the conclusion of the audit of accounts for the year ending on 28 September 1377

A parchment roll of two membranes, 147 mm wide, sewn Chancery fashion with blue thread in a tight oversew. Membranes 1 and 2 are both laid out with two vertical folds, for the left margin and the centre. The roll is a fair copy in a single hand, the hand that wrote I 12. The dorse of membrane 2 is blank. The roll is endorsed 'Status terrarum domini Nicholai abbatis Westm' de anno regni regis Ricardi secundi post conquestum primo' at the top of membrane 1.[1]

WAM 6149

[*Mem. 1 recto*] States of the lands and portions of Dom. Nicholas, abbot of Westminster, at the audit of the account of his ministers at 28 September 1377

Islip [Rents as in I 7: £31 6s. 11d.] Cash liveries: £78 2s. 11d. Arrears: none. Valor, with wool: £80.[2] Remaining at the audit: 24 oxen, 1 ram, 162 wethers, 31 ewes, 12 hoggs and gimmers, ... lambs, 1 boar, 4 sows, 30 pigs, 30 young pigs, 21 piglets, 29 capons, 2 ganders, 7 breeding geese, 2 cocks, 19 hens, 3 breeding swans and 14 cartloads of hay.

Sutton-under-Brailes [Rents as in I 6: £17 18s. 10d.] Cash liveries: £24 10s. 2½d. Arrears: none.[3] Valor: £27. Remaining at the audit: 5 qr. 4 bus. pulse, 25 qr. 2 bus. dredge malt; 1 boar, 1 sow, 9 pigs, 10 young pigs, 7 piglets, 1 cock, 6 hens, 12 capons, 1 gander, 3 breeding geese, 10 goslings, 2 breeding swans and 3 cygnets.

Todenham [Rents as in I 5: £15 6s. 2½d.] Cash liveries: £21 8s. 11d. Arrears: none. Valor, with wool: £29.[4] Remaining at the audit: 17 qr. 3 bus. pulse; 3 cart-horses, 18 oxen, 3 cows, 1 boar, 3 sows, 19 pigs, 25 young pigs, 5 piglets, 2 rams, 180 ewes, 173 hoggs, 97 lambs, 20 capons, 2 cocks, 10 hens, 2 ganders, 3 breeding geese, 15 goslings and 65 cartloads of hay.

[1] Extant ministers' accounts: Bourton-on-the-Hill, WAM 8305; Ebury, WAM 26932; Hyde, WAM 27083; Islip, WAM 14812; Pensham, WAM 22232; Sutton-under-Brailes, WAM 25975; Todenham, GRO, D1099/M30/20.

[2] 252 fleeces were sold this year locally, as it appears, for £9 15s. 11d. (WAM 14812).

[3] Thomas Hurry, reeve of Sutton-under-Brailes, was charged with arrears amounting to £4 19s. 1¼d., but this sum was transferred to the foot of his account as reeve of Stourton for 1376–7 (WAM 25974).

[4] 360 fleeces, weighing 1½ sacks 5 st., were sent from Todenham to the collecting centre for the Western Parts at Bourton-on-the-Hill this year. In addition, woolfells and sheepskins from the victims of a severe murrain yielded £1 12s. 8½d. (GRO, D1099/M30/20).

Bourton-on-the-Hill [Rents as in I 7: £9 2s. 4¾d.] Cash liveries: £5 19s. Arrears: owed by Richard Alberd, reeve, £1 10s. Valor, with wool: £35.[5] Remaining at the audit: 4 qr. pulse, 5 qr. 6 bus. oats; 3 mares, 1 foal of this year's issue, 10 oxen, 3 cows, 2 bullocks, 2 young heifers, 2 young bullocks, 1 year-old calf, one calf of this year's issue, 294 wethers, 1 ewe, 3 boars, 2 sows, 26 pigs, 9 young pigs, 9 piglets, 2 cocks, 10 hens, 20 capons, 30 hurdles and 50 cartloads of hay.

Pershore [Rents as in I 6: £32 19s.] Cash liveries: £48 18s. 8d. Arrears: owed by Richard Darnel, lately reeve, £6 13s. 8d.; by John Glyn, lately rent-collector, £2; and by William, the present bailiff,[6] nothing. Valor, with wool: £73.[7] Remaining at the audit: 3 qr. rye, 4 qr. 1 bus. mill multure; 4 cart-horses, 2 mill-horses, 1 affer, 7 oxen, 2 cows, 1 bull calf, 4 young bullocks, 1 young heifer, 4 year-old calves, 4 calves of this year's issue, 1 boar, 2 sows, 24 pigs, 19 young pigs, 15 piglets, 3 rams, 90 wethers, 92 ewes, 117 hoggs and gimmers, 35 lambs, 1 cock, 5 hens, 16 capons, 1 gander, 3 breeding geese, 13 goslings and 62 cartloads of hay.

Pensham [Rents as in I 5: £26 4s. 4d.] Cash liveries: £37 19s. Arrears: owed by John Parker, 10s. Valor: £37 19s. Remaining at the audit: in the farmer's hands, 3 qr. 6 bus. wheat, 16 qr. 3 bus. rye, 8 qr. 1½ bus. pulse, 13 qr. 6 bus. barley, 20 qr. dredge; 1 horse, 1 mare, 1 foal (*pullanus*), 7 oxen, 12 cows, 6 heifers, 2 bullocks, 1 bull calf, 1 gander, 2 breeding geese, 12 capons, 1 cock and 6 hens.[8]

Hardwicke in Elmstone Hardwicke [Rents as in I 7: £22 17s. 8½d.] Cash liveries: £32. Arrears: none. Valor: £36. 19s. Remaining at the audit: 29 qr. 6½ bus. wheat, 27 qr. 2½ bus. peas, 12 qr. barley, 4½ qr. oats; 4 cart-horses, 16 oxen, 1 gander, 4 breeding geese, 2 cocks and 10 hens, 21 capons and 14 cartloads of hay.[9]

[5] The net demesne wool crop at Bourton-on-the-Hill this year consisted of 300 fleeces, weighing 1 sack 9 st. 13 lb. Including these and the fleeces sent to Bourton from Pershore, Stourton and Todenham, a total of 1,244, weighing 6 sacks 14 st., was sold at the price of £8 13s. 4d. per sack to William Grevel of Camden. Grevel, however, was charged for only 6 sacks 12 st. (WAM 8305).
[6] William Osbern.
[7] 320 fleeces, weighing 1½ sacks 8 st. 1 lb., were sent to the collecting centre at Bourton-on-the-Hill from Pershore this year (WAM 8305).
[8] As in the inventory of corn and stock in I 9.
[9] As in the inventory of corn and stock in I 9. The addition of 'et ij boves hoc anno' as a final entry to the panel on Hardwicke was probably intended for that on Longdon, where it duly appears in 1378–9.

Deerhurst [Rents as in I 6: £29 17s. 6d.] Cash liveries: £25 16s. 8d. Arrears: owed by John Halle, £9 6s. 1½d. Valor: £35.

Chaceley [Rents as in I 5: £5 0s. 8d.] Cash liveries: £13 11s. Arrears: owed by John Hathemar', farmer, £2 16s. 8d. Valor: £14. Remaining at the audit: in the farmer's hands 16 qr. 4 bus. 1 p. wheat, 8 qr. 5 bus. rye, 13 qr. 4 bus. 1 p. peas, 14 qr. 3 bus. barley, 3 qr. dredge, 7 qr. 6 bus. oats; 2 cart-horses, 9 oxen, 1 bull, 20 cows, 1 sow, 15 young pigs, 1 gander, 3 breeding geese, 12 capons, 1 cock, [5] hens.[10]

Longdon [Rents as in I 5: £15] Cash liveries: £23 0s. 10d. Arrears: owed by John Brown, reap-reeve and collector of court perquisites, 6s. 8d. Valor: £22 4s. Remaining at the audit: 1 young heifer.

Castlemorton [Rents as in I 5: £28 17s. 9d.] Cash liveries: £31 4s. Arrears: owed by Henry Ode, rent-collector, £2 13s. 4d. Valor: £32 17s.

Pinvin [Rents as in I 5: £33 16s. 3d.] Cash liveries: £39 4s. 8d. Arrears: none. Valor: £39 4s.

Hundred of Wick by Pershore Cash liveries: £1 13s. 1d. Arrears: none. Valor: 14s.
[*Mem. 2 recto*] *Hundred of Defford* Cash liveries: £1. Arrears: owed by Robert Berald for 1374–5, £1 18s., by John Birtlyngham for 1375–6, £2 11s. 5d., and by Walter Cappe for the present year [1376–7] 3s. 9d.[11] Valor: £1 3s.
Portmoot of Pershore Cash liveries: £3. Arrears: owed by John Parker, £1 14s.[12] Valor: £4 16s. 8d.
Hundred of Pinvin Cash liveries: 10s. Arrears: owed by William Hanow, the present bailiff, 3s. Valor: £1 0s. 8d.

Denham [Rents as in I 9: £25 8s. 5½d.] Cash liveries: £45 15s. 11¾d. Arrears: owed by Thomas atte Hurst, £11 10s.[13] Valor, with wool and hay: £52. Remaining at the audit: 61 qr. wheat, 5 qr. maslin, 3 qr. 3½ bus. barley malt, 20 qr. 4 bus. dredge malt; 6 cart-horses, 6 stots, 21 oxen, 2 bulls, 51 cows, 2 heifers, 2 rams, 102 wethers, 101 ewes, 78 lambs, 3 boars, 1 sow, 16 pigs,

[10] As in the inventory of corn and stock in I 10, but from here onwards with 20 cows rather than 21.

[11] Berald was bailiff of Defford hundred for the exceptionally long period of 1362–75 (WAM 24511–16*). Birtlyngham was almost certainly his immediate successor, serving for a year.

[12] Parker was bailiff of the portmoot 1371–5 (WAM 24406, 24515–17).

[13] Hurst is mentioned as bailiff of Denham Durdent's manor 1369–75 and was very likely bailiff of the head manor of Denham during the same period (WAM 3416, 24515).

7 young pigs, 17 piglets, 2 ganders, 6 breeding geese, 24 goslings, 1 cock, 12 hens, 34 capons, 6 beehives and 67 cartloads of hay.

Laleham [Rents as in I 9: £16 10s. 2¼d.] Cash liveries: £25 1s. Arrears: none. Valor, with wool: £41. Remaining at the audit: 25 qr. rye, 7 qr. 1 bus. 3 p. barley malt, 3 qr. 1 bus. 3 p. vetches; 6 mares, 1 year-old foal, 3 foals (1 a male) of this year's issue, 10 oxen, 2 boars, 2 sows, 12 pigs, 22 young pigs, 9 piglets, 1 ram, 152 wethers, 35 ewes, 33 lambs, 6 breeding swans, 3 white swans, 1 gander, 3 breeding geese, 8 goslings, 20 capons, 1 cock, 6 hens, 12 cartloads of hay.

Pyrford [Rents as in I 5: £35 5s. 5½d.] Cash liveries: £22 15s. Arrears: owed by Richard Bedewynde, £1 4s. 2⅛d.[14] Valor, with wool, hay and wood: £72. Remaining at the audit: 38 qr. rye; 3 mares, 6 oxen, 2 rams, 125 wethers, 84 ewes, 47 hoggs, 47 lambs, 60 hurdles, 25 cartloads of hay, 1,000 bundles of talwood, 4,000 faggots and 760 plain tiles.

Staines Rents for the following terms: [Michaelmas], £9 2s. 8½d.; Christmas, £6 4s. 6d.; the Annunciation, £6 14s. 0¾d.; the nativity of St John the Baptist, £6 16s. 4½d. Total: £28 17s. 7¾d. Cash liveries: £40 9s. Arrears: owed by Alexander Tresour',[15] £4 10s. 1d. Valor: with profit of J. atte Halle's tenement,[16] £43 14s.

Yeoveney [Rents as in I 6: £14 3s. 4½d.] Cash liveries: £12 19s. 5½d. Arrears: none. Valor, with increase of stock: £19.[17] Remaining at the audit: 7 mares, 3 two-year-old foals, 3 foals of this year's issue, 12 oxen, 1 bull, 25 cows, 4 calves, 1 boar, 2 sows, 8 pigs, 12 young pigs, 15 piglets, 2 ganders, 3 breeding geese, 19 goslings, 12 capons, 1 cock, 6 hens and 13 cartloads of hay.

Ebury [Rents as in I 9: £13 3s.] Cash liveries: £61 3s. 0½d. Arrears: owed by William Huller,[18] £1 10s. Valor, with hay: £68. Remaining at the audit: 1 qr. rye, 2 bus. barley, 1 qr. oats; 8 mares, 1 mare foal of this year's issue, 2 bulls,

[14] Bedewynde was successively serjeant and bailiff of Pyrford 1366–81 (WAM 24512–13, 27422–5, etc.).

[15] Rent-collector, also called 'bailiff'.

[16] John Hall's tenement was an agglomeration of property in rural and urban Staines, held by Richard atte Piry after the eponymous J. atte Halle, for rents and farms amounting to £7 11s. 6½d. p.a., but now in the abbot's hands as an escheat (WAM 16934).

[17] A reference to the restocking of the demesne at Yeoveney, on the resumption of direct exploitation in the course of 1375–6 (WAM 16886).

[18] Bailiff.

11 oxen, 70 cows, 1 sow, 11 pigs, 9 young pigs, 6 piglets, 2 breeding swans, 1 gander, 3 breeding geese, 19 goslings, 2 peacocks, 4 peahens, 3 beehives and 23 cartloads of hay.

[Totals]
Sum of cash liveries: £617 19s. 5d., £35 14s. 2¾d. more than in the previous year.
Sum of arrears: £48 18s. 10⅝d., £3 3s. 9¼d. less than in the previous year.
Sum of valors: £765 11s. 3d., £26 19s. 1d. more than in the previous year.
Horses and affers, 66; foals and colts, 14. Sum of this category:[19] 80, 3 fewer than in the previous year.
Oxen and bullocks, 184; bulls, 11; cows, 235; young bullocks and calves, 26. Sum of this category, 456, 4 fewer than in the previous year.
Rams, 18; wethers, 1,287; ewes, 780; lambs and hoggs, 1,092. Sum of this category: 3,177, 152 more than in the previous year.
Boars, 13; sows, 18; pigs, 147; young pigs and piglets, 215. Sum of this category: 383,[20] 11 fewer than in the previous year.
Sum of rents, by term: Michaelmas, £139 17s. 3¾d; Christmas, £84 5s.; Annunciation, £103 2s. 9½d.; St John the Baptist, £86 0s. 5½d. Sum total of rents: £413 5s. 6½d., 8s. 6¾d. more than in the previous year.

[*Mem. 1 dorse*] *Stourton* [Rents as in I 11: £13 16s. 9¼d.] Cash liveries, with wool: £30. Arrears: none. Valor, with wool: £30.[21] Remaining at the audit: 6 qr. 2 bus. 3 p. rye, 7 qr. 2 bus. pulse; 4 mares, 1 male two-year-old foal, 2 foals of this year's issue, 9 oxen, 1 cow, 209 wethers, 44 ewes, 39 hoggs and 28 lambs.

Hyde [Rents as in I 9: £10 15s. 9½d.][22] Cash liveries: £2 13s. 4d. Arrears: none. Valor: £31. Remaining at the audit: 1 qr. pulse; 3 cart-horses, 4 stots, 13 oxen, 2 bulls, 40 cows, 1 bullock, 1 bull calf, 1 young bullock, 2 heifers, 1 year-old calf, 3 calves of this year's issue, 6 rams, 153 wethers, 202 ewes, 57 hoggs, 71 gimmers, 146 lambs, 2 boars, 2 sows, 1 hurdle and 22 cartloads of hay.

[19] MS: 'Summa sexus'.
[20] The actual sum of the numbers given is 393.
[21] 264 fleeces, weighing 1½ sacks 4 st., were sent from Stourton to the collecting centre at Bourton-on-the-Hill this year (WAM 8305).
[22] MS: entry partly obscured by a water stain.

I 14 States of the abbot's manors and portions at the conclusion of the audit of accounts for the year ending on 28 September 1379

A parchment roll of two membranes, 154 mm wide, sewn Chancery fashion with white thread in a tight oversew. Membrane 1 tapers at the top. Both membranes are laid out with three vertical folds, for the left and right margins, and the centre. The roll is a fair copy in a single hand. Membrane 1 is endorsed at the top: 'Status hoc ... anno iij^{o}'; and membrane 2 is endorsed at the foot: 'Visus status terrarum domini abbatis Westm' de anno regni regis Ricardi secundi post conquestum tercio'.[1]

WAM 6169

[*Mem. 1 recto*] States of the lands and portions of Dom. Nicholas, abbot of Westminster, at the audit of the account of his ministers at 28 September 1379

Islip [Rents as in I 7: £31 6s. 11d.] Cash liveries: £47 4s. 2d. Arrears: owed by William Dolle, reeve, £16 18s. 2d. Valor, with wool valued at £13 and profit of £3 14s. 4d. from land in the manor of Noke: £77.[2] Remaining at the audit: 4 qr. 5 bus. wheat, 10 qr. malt; 24 oxen, 1 ram, 84 wethers, 39 ewes, 37 young sheep, 39 lambs, 1 boar, 4 sows, 30 pigs, 30 young pigs, 21 piglets, 30 capons, 2 cocks, 12 hens, 4 breeding swans, 3 cygnets, 2 ganders, 7 breeding geese.

Sutton-under-Brailes [Rents as in I 6: £17 18s. 10d.] Cash liveries: £20 18s. 10d. Arrears: owed by Thomas Hurry, reeve, £5 6s. 8d. Valor: £37 0s. 10d.[3] Remaining at the audit: 1 boar, 2 sows, 39 pigs, 27 young pigs, 1 cock, 6 hens, 12 capons, 1 gander, 3 breeding geese, 7 goslings, 2 breeding swans, 3 cygnets.

[1] Extant ministers' accounts: Hyde, WAM 27085; Islip, WAM 14815; Pinvin, WAM 22304; Sutton-under-Brailes, GRO, D1099/M31/45; Todenham, GRO, D1099/M30/13; Yeoveney, WAM 16889.

[2] The net wool crop at Islip this year consisted of 253 fleeces (WAM 14815). It is likely that this wool was sent to the abbot's household at Westminster to be sold; see also n. 4 below. From November 1375 to 1385, and possibly for a slightly longer period, the abbot of Westminster was seised of two parts of the manor of Noke, Oxon, during the minority of Richard de Williamscote, heir of Thomas de Williamscote. Dolle administered the wardship (WAM 14811, 14813, 14825–6).

[3] The *valor* excluded hay provided for the abbot's household (GRO, D1099/M31/45).

Todenham [Rents as in I 5: £15 6s. 2½d.] Cash liveries: £16 14s. 8d. Arrears: none. Valor, with wool valued at £17 6s. 8d.: £44.[4] Remaining at the audit: 3 cart-horses, 18 oxen, 2 cows, 1 boar, 3 sows, 47 pigs, 3 piglets, 2 rams, 170 ewes, 164 wethers, 145 sheep in their second year, 103 lambs, 20 capons, 2 cocks, 10 hens, 1 gander, 2 breeding geese, 13 goslings, 6 cartloads of hay.

Bourton-on-the-Hill [Rents as in I 7: £9 2s. 4½d.][5] Cash liveries: £21 0s. 4d. Arrears: owed by William Strode, bailiff, £5 13s. 4d. Valor, with wool valued at £12: £41. Remaining at the audit: 26 qr. 4 bus. wheat; 3 horses, 3 mares, 1 foal, 13 oxen, 3 cows, 1 bull calf, 1 young heifer, 1 calf, 1 ram, 183 wethers, 52 ewes, 8 young sheep, 28 lambs, 2 boars, 2 sows, 39 pigs, 12 piglets, 2 cocks, 10 hens, 20 capons.

Pershore [Rents as in I 6: £32 19s.] Cash liveries: £54 17s. 7d. Arrears: owed by William Wycheford,[6] £1 14s. 11d.; Wolstan Andrew,[7] £1 8s.; Richard Darnell,[8] £6 4s. 8d; John Glyn',[9] £2; William Osberne,[10] £1 3s. 2d. Valor: £73. Remaining at the audit: 8 oxen, 1 bull, 2 cows, 2 bullocks, 2 heifers, 1 young bullock, 3 young heifers,[11] 6 calves, 1 boar, 3 sows, 26 pigs, 4 young pigs, 13 piglets, 182 hoggs, 47 wethers, 2 ewes, 6 lambs, 1 cock, 5 hens, 15 capons, 1 gander, 3 breeding geese, 16 goslings, 68 cartloads of hay.

Pensham [Rents as in I 5: £26 4s. 4d.] Cash liveries: £26 2s. 8d. Arrears: owed by John Parker, 10s. Valor: £26 2s. 8d. Remaining in the lessee's hands:[12] 3 qr. 6 bus. wheat, 16 qr. 3 bus. rye, 8 qr. 1½ bus. pulse, 13 qr. 6 bus. barley, 20 qr. dredge; 1 horse, 1 mare, 1 foal, 7 oxen, 12 cows, 6 heifers, 2 bullocks, 1 bull calf, 1 gander, 2 breeding geese, 12 capons, 1 cock and 6 hens.[13]

[4] 485 fleeces, weighing 2 sacks, and of an estimated value for the two of £17 6s. 8d., were sent from Todenham this year to the abbot's household at Westminster. There, the abbot's treasurer sold 5½ sacks 10 cloves 2 lb. of wool from the manors in the Western Parts, including Todenham, for a total of £47 9s. 7½d., that is, £8 6s. 8d. per sack; and 2½ sacks from manors in the Eastern Parts for a total of £13 6s. 8d., that is, £5 6s. 8d. per sack (GRO, D1099/M30/13; WAM 24521).

[5] In fact a reduction from £9 2s. 4¾d., and continuing hereafter at this new rate.

[6] Serjeant 1373–9 (WAM 24517–20).

[7] Reeve 1379–80 and probably in the current year; see I 15A.

[8] Reeve 1362–5. The sum of Darnell's arrears had not changed since 1366–7, and this suggests that he had left the manor or was now dead.

[9] Rent-collector 1373–4.

[10] Bailiff 1376–7.

[11] MS: 'j bovicul*us*, iij bovic*uli*'.

[12] John Parker was the lessee.

[13] As in the inventory of corn and stock in I 9.

Hardwicke in Elmstone Hardwicke [Rents as in I 7: £22 17s. 8½d.] Cash liveries: £32. Arrears: none. Valor: £32 16s. Remaining in the lessee's hands:[14] 29 qr. 6½ bus. wheat, 27 qr. 2½ bus. peas, 12 qr. barley, 4½ qr. oats; 4 cart-horses, 16 oxen, 1 gander, 4 breeding geese, 2 cocks and 10 hens, 21 capons and 14 cartloads of hay.[15]

Deerhurst [Rents as in I 6: £29 17s. 6d.] Cash liveries: £31 16s. 8d. Arrears: owed by John atte Hall',[16] £7 18s. 5½d. Valor: £38 5s.

Chaceley [Rents as in I 5: £5 0s. 8d.] Cash liveries: £13 6s. 10d. Arrears: owed by John Hathermere, lessee, £1 7s. 8d.; and by Nicholas Phillip',[17] 13s. 4d. Valor: £14 2s. 10d. Remaining in the lessee's hands: 16 qr. 4 bus. 1 p. wheat, 8 qr. 5 bus. rye, 13 qr. 4 bus. 1 p. peas, 14 qr. 3 bus. barley, 3 qr. dredge, 7 qr. 6 bus. oats; 2 cart-horses, 9 oxen, 1 bull, 20 cows, 1 sow, 15 small pigs, 1 gander, 3 breeding geese, 12 capons, 1 cock, 5 hens.[18]

Longdon [Rents as in I 5: £15] Cash liveries: £19 10s.[19] Arrears: none. Valor: £18 16s. 8d. Remaining at the audit: 2 oxen.

[*Mem. 2 recto*] *Castlemorton* [Rents as in I 5: £28 17s. 10d.][20] Cash liveries: £34 10s. Arrears: owed by Henry Ode,[21] £1 10s. Valor: £32 18s.

Pinvin [Rents as in I 5: £33 16s. 3d.] Cash liveries: £39 12s. Arrears: none. Valor: £39 12s.

Hundred of Wick by Pershore Cash liveries: 18s. 9d.[22] Arrears: none. Valor: 18s. 9d.

Defford Hundred Cash liveries: £1 12s. 6d. Arrears: owed by Robert Berall', £1 18s.; John Birlyngham, £2 11s. 5d.; and Walter Cappe, 3s. 5d.[23] Valor: 18s. 2d.

[14] The demesne was currently leased to John Monmouth and Elizabeth, his wife.

[15] As in the inventory of corn and stock in I 9.

[16] Bailiff and rent-collector at Deerhurst and Hardwicke 1373–93 (WAM 8451–2).

[17] Rent-collector (WAM 24409).

[18] As in the inventory of corn and stock in I 10, but with 20 cows rather than 21.

[19] MS: 'xxix li. x s.'; but 'xix li. x s.', the reading in the account of the abbot's treasurer for 1378–9, is probably correct (WAM 24521).

[20] From here onwards, the rents total £28 17s. 10d., rather than the £28 17s. 9d. found in I 5–13.

[21] Rent-collector 1362–79.

[22] A cash livery to the abbot's treasurer by Walter Clerk, rent-collector or bailiff of the hundred. In common with other such liveries from the hundredal officials mentioned below, Clerk's was made at the audit of his account in which the treasurer took part (WAM 24521).

[23] Berall was bailiff of the hundred in 1362–75, Biryngham in 1375–6 and Cappe in 1376–7.

Portmoot of Pershore Cash liveries: £2 10s.[24] Arrears: owed by John Parker, £5. Valor: £4 14s.
Pinvin Hundred Cash liveries: 15s. 1d.

Denham [Rents as in I 9: £28 8s. 5½d.] Cash liveries: £62 13s. 9¼d. Arrears: owed by Thomas atte Hurst.[25] Valor: £24. Remaining at the audit: 6 cart-horses, 5 stots, 25 oxen, 2 bulls, 39 cows, 3 rams, 151 wethers, 71 ewes, 67 hoggs and gimmers, 72 lambs, 4 boars, 3 sows, 26 pigs, 24 small pigs, 9 piglets, 2 ganders, 6 breeding geese, 25 goslings, 1 cock, 12 hens, 6 beehives, 116 cartloads of hay.

Laleham [Rents as in I 9: £16 10s. 2¼d.][26] Cash liveries: £29 18s. 5d. Arrears: none. Valor, with wool valued at £5 13s. 4d.: £36 4s. Remaining at the audit: 30 qr. rye; 2 horses, 5 mares, 1 foal, 10 oxen, 2 boars, 25 pigs, 2 sows, 6 small pigs, 6 piglets, 3 rams, 155 wethers, 31 ewes, 22 young sheep, 29 lambs, 5 breeding swans, 2 white swans, 1 young swan, 4 cygnets, 1 gander, 3 breeding geese, 6 goslings and 19 cartloads of hay.

Pyrford [Rents as in I 5: £35 5s. 5½d.] Cash liveries: £35 12s. 3d. Arrears: owed by Richard Bedwynd,[27] £5. Valor: £50 5s. Remaining at the audit: 30 qr. rye; 2 horses, 3 mares, 6 oxen, 2 rams, 157 wethers, 110 ewes, 50 lambs, 50 cartloads of hay, 2,500 faggots.

Staines Rents for the following terms: Michaelmas, £9 0s. 10¼d.; Christmas, £6 2s. 8d.; Annunciation, £6 12s. 2½d.; nativity of St John the Baptist, £6 14s. 6½d. Total: £28 10s. 3¼d. Cash liveries: £37. Arrears: owed by Alexander Tresor,[28] £5. Valor: £37 15s.

Ebury [Rents as in I 9: £13 3s.] Cash liveries: £48 16s. 7¼d. Arrears: owed by William Huller, bailiff, £1 10s. 0¾d. Valor: £54. Remaining at the audit: 8 qr. rye; 8 mares, 7 foals, 2 bulls, 10 oxen, 69 cows, 1 sow, 7 pigs, 7 young pigs, 10 piglets, 1 gander, 3 breeding geese, 1 cock, 6 hens, 2 peacocks, 6 peahens, 3 beehives and 25 cartloads of hay.

[24] A cash livery to the abbot's treasurer by John Parker, rent-collector, but said in the treasurer's account to be of £2 (WAM 24521). Parker had served as bailiff or rent-collector in the portmoot in 1371–6, and the arrears noted in the next entry may date in part from that period.
[25] MS: sum left blank. Hurst was probably bailiff 1369–75.
[26] Given in the MS as £16 10s. 3¼d.
[27] Bailiff (WAM 24520).
[28] Styled variously rent-collector and bailiff.

Yeoveney [Rents as in I 6: £14 3s. 4½d.] Cash liveries: £19 9s. 4d. Arrears: owed by the lessee of the cows, £1 15s. 9d.; Richard Rawlyns, bailiff, £1 6s. 4d.;[29] John Botiel', lessee of the mill, £1 8s. 4d. Valor: reckoned as equivalent to the rent of £21.[30] Remaining in the lessee's hands: 7 mares, 5 foals, 10 oxen, 1 bull, 15 cows, 1 calf, 3 sows, 5 young pigs, 7 piglets, 1 gander, 3 breeding geese, 1 cock, 6 hens.

[Totals]
Sum of cash liveries: £604 10s. 5½d. Sum of arrears: £87 18s. 9d. Sum of valors: £705 13s. 2d.
Horses and affers, 66; foals and colts, 15. Sum of this category: 81.
Oxen and bullocks, 190; bulls, 13; cows, 210; young bullocks and calves, 21. Sum of this category: 428.
Rams, 21; wethers, 1,501; ewes, 742; lambs and young sheep, 1,123. Sum of this category: 3,487.
Boars, 13; sows, 22; pigs, 239; young pigs and piglets, 209. Sum of this category: 463.
Sum of rents, by term: Michaelmas, £139 15s. 5½d; Christmas, £84 3s. 2d.; Annunciation, £103 0s. 11d.; nativity of St John the Baptist, £85 18s. 7½d. Sum total of rents: £412 18s. 2d.

[*Mem. 1 dorse*] *Stourton* [Rents as in I 11: £13 16s. 9¼d.] Cash liveries: £6 6s. Arrears: none. Valor, with wool valued at £13: £28 19s. Remaining at the audit: 8 qr. rye; 3 mares, 4 foals, 9 oxen, 1 cow, 256 wethers, 19 young sheep, 31 lambs.

Hyde [Rents as in I 9: £10 15s. 9½d.] Cash liveries: £16 3s. 8d. Arrears: owed by John Clerk,[31] 18s. 1¾d. Valor, with wool valued at £12 6s. 9d.: £39 4s.[32] Remaining at the audit: 14 qr. rye, 6 qr. 3½ bus. dredge; 3 cart-horses, 4 stots, 12 oxen, 2 bulls, 39 cows, 2 bull calves, 1 young bullock, 8 calves, 9 rams, 204 wethers, 267 ewes, 67 hoggs, 73 gimmers, 145 lambs, 1 boar, 1 sow and 27 cartloads of hay.

[29] Rawlyns was bailiff, 15 April 1379–17 August 1379 (WAM 16889).
[30] For the lease of Yeoveney manor to John Dorman for 31 years on 1 August 1379, see WAM Muniment Book 17, ff. 41–2.
[31] Bailiff 1377–April 1381 (WAM 27084–7).
[32] 591 sheep's fleeces were sent to the abbot's household at Westminster for sale this year, and 155 lambs' fleeces, weighing 6 st., were apparently sold locally (WAM 24521).

I 15A and B States of the abbot's manors and portions at views held at Easter 1380 and 25 and 26 March 1381

A parchment roll of two rotulets, sewn Exchequer fashion with a blue-green thread. Rotulet 1 (marked 'A'), the later of the two rotulets, is 120 mm wide, and is laid out with two vertical folds, for the left margin and the centre; rotulet 2 (marked 'B') is 164 mm wide, and is laid out with three vertical folds, for the two margins and the centre. Each is a fair copy, written by a single (but different) hand. Membrane 1 is endorsed 'Status maneriorum domini abbatis Westm' in partibus occidentalibus super facturam visuum ad festum annunciacionis beate Marie anno quarto'; there are no endorsements on membrane 2. Unless otherwise indicated in the particular case, the corn mentioned in Rotulet 1 (I 15A) had been sown and harvested in the previous year, 1379–80, and would be, as far as possible, threshed in the course of the present year. Reprises, demands on annual income in cash or kind that took precedence over all others, might assume different forms, but the commonest of these was almost certainly the mixed corn needed for liveries to farm servants.[1]

WAM 6152

[I 15A, *Rot. 1, recto*] Status maneriorum domini abbatis Westm' in partibus occidentalibus super facturam visuum ad festum annunciacionis beate Marie anno quarto

Islep' Willelmus Dolle prepositus ibidem debet xxvj li. xvj s.
Estimantur ibidem de frumento, ultra vj qr. iiij bus. ibidem tritur*atum*, xxx qr.; inde pro parte domini xv qr.[2]
Estimantur ibidem de ordio, ultra lvj qr. ibidem tritur*atum*, lx qr.; inde pro parte domini xxx qr.
Remanent ibidem de avenis contra adventum domini iiij qr.
Remanent ibidem de braseo contra adventum domini x qr.

Sutton' Petrus Baron prepositus ibidem debet xl s.
Estimantur ibidem de frumento, ultra ij qr. vj bus. ibidem tritur*atum*, iiij qr.
Estimantur ibidem de drageto ad triturandum xxx qr.

[1] Extant ministers' accounts: Ebury, WAM 26934; Hyde, WAM 27085; Islip, WAM 14818; Sutton-under-Brailes, GRO, D1099/M31/46; Todenham, GRO, D1099 M30/14.

[2] According to the champarty agreement between the abbot and tenants of the manor in the vill of Islip, dating from 1359–60 and underlying this entry and the next, the abbot's half-share of arable crops on the demesne each year was to be identified in the fields, after the harvest had been stacked, and then carried to, and stacked in, the grange at the abbot's expense, to await threshing. The assumption of the present entries that the abbot's share will be an exact half of the total threshed suggests that it was now finalised after threshing. In the event this year the abbot received 22 qr. 2½ bus. of wheat and 80 qr. 0½ bus. of barley. The omission of pulse and oats from the reeve's estimates is probably explained by the fact that, since these were spring crops, it was too soon to forecast yields (WAM 14802, 14818).

Remanent ibidem de braseo contra adventum domini, ultra braseum quod fiet, xx qr.

Stourton Petrus Baron prepositus ibidem excedit x s.
Estimantur ibidem de frumento, ultra xij qr. iiij bus. ibidem tritur*atum*, xx qr. Et totum remanet ad opus domini.
Siligo vix sufficit pro liberacionibus et reprisis ad manerium de Sutton'.[3]
Estimantur ad triturandum in uno tasso pisarum ultra prebendam boum et bidencium, vj qr., et remanent ad opus domini.
Estimantur ibidem de drageto, ultra xxxix qr. ibidem tritur*atum*, xx qr., et totum remanet ad opus domini.
Remanent ibidem de avenis contra adventum domini xx qr.

Todenham Willelmus Spong' ballivus ibidem debet lxx s. Blada ibidem vix sufficiunt pro reprisis.

Bourton' Willelmus ballivus[4] ibidem debet iiij li. v s.
Estimantur ibidem de veteri frumento[5] xxvj qr. Inde pro liberacionibus et aliis reprisis x qr. Et sic remanent ad opus domini xvj qr.
Estimantur ibidem ad triturandum de puls', ultra xxvj qr. ibidem tritur*atum*, x qr., et totum remanet ad opus domini.
Estimantur ibidem de ordio ultra xlij qr. ibidem tritur*atum*, xxx qr. Inde pro liberacionibus et ad reprisas xv qr. Et sic remanent ad opus domini xv qr.
Avene[6] vix sufficiunt pro reprisis.

Pershore Wolfstanus Andrew prepositus ibidem debet, cum xliij s. iij d. qua. de antiquis arreragiis,[7] viij li. xix s. vij d.
Frumentum ibidem vix sufficit pro reprisis.
Deficiunt ibidem de siligine pro liberacionibus famulorum usque festum sancti Michaelis[8] per estimacionem iij qr.
Estimantur ibidem de ordio, ultra xlj qr. ibidem trituratum, xl qr.

[3] The reprises owing to Sutton-under-Brailes were probably the liveries needed for farm servants on that manor: at this time, no provision of this kind for farm servants was made at Sutton itself (GRO, D1099/M31/44–7). For the close connection beteen the abbot's estate at Stourton and the manor of Sutton-under-Brailes, see I 11, n. 32.
[4] William Strode.
[5] i.e. wheat harvested in 1379.
[6] MS: 'avena'.
[7] Cf. the sum of £1 8s. owed by Andrew at the end of the year 1378–9, but before his account had been audited (I 14).
[8] 29 September 1381.

[*Rot. 1 dorse*] *Per computacionem selionum*[9] Memorandum quod vend*untur* apud Sto*ur*ton' xxvj acre di. seminate cum frumento, precium acre ij s., liij s.
Item de mixtilione et siligine xj acre di., precium acre ij s., xxiij s.
Item cum avenis x acre, precium acre xv d., xij s. vj d.
Item cum puls' xxj acre di., precium acre xx d., xxxv s. x d.
Summa vj li. iiij s. iij d.

[I 15B, *Rot. 2 recto*] Visus status terrarum domini Nicholai abbatis Westm' in comitatibus Surr', Mid' et Buk', a vigilia sancti Michaelis anno regni regis Ricardi secundi post conquestum tercio usque in crastinum Pasche proxime sequentis

Pyrford' Ricardus Bedwyne ballivus ibidem debet super istum visum xvj s. ob.
Remanent ibidem de siligine ad opus domini, ultra reprisas manerii usque festum Michaelis[10] per estimacionem ad triturandum xxvij qr.
Remanent ibidem de avenis ad opus domini, ultra reprisas manerii usque festum Michaelis, per estimacionem ad triturandum xxvj qr.

Lalham Johannes atte Mille ballivus ibidem debet super istud visum xxij s. ix d.
De frumento liberatur ad hospicium domini xv qr., et residuum vix sufficit pro reprisis manerii usque festum Michaelis.
Remanent ibidem de siligine ad opus domini ultra reprisas manerii usque festum Michaelis per estimacionem ad triturandum xxxvij qr.
De pisis lib*eratur* ad hospicium domini iiij qr., et residuum vix sufficit pro reprisis manerii usque festum Michaelis.
Remanet ibidem de ordio ad opus domini ultra reprisas manerii usque festum Michaelis j qr.
Remanent ibidem de avenis ad opus domini ultra reprisas manerii usque festum Michaelis xix qr.
Remanent ibidem de braseo ordei ad opus domini xij qr.

Eybury Willelmus Hull*er* ballivus ibidem debet super istud visum lxiij s. xj d. qua.

[9] On first reading, this is a puzzling entry. Yet nothing in the preceding entry for Stourton, which relates to the harvest of 1380, rules out the possibility that in 1381 the abbot decided to sell the growing crops before harvest, and this entry may be a memorandum about his transaction.
[10] 29 September 1380.

De frumento liberatur ad hospicium domini iij qr. iij bus., et deficit pro liberacione ballivi usque festum Michaelis j qr. iiij bus.[11] Deficit de siligine pro liberacione famulorum usque festum Michaelis iiij qr. iiij bus.
Ordium De ordio liberatur hospicio domini lxij qr. j bus., et residuum vix sufficit pro reprisis manerii usque festum Michaelis.
De avenis liberatur hospicio domini xxx qr. et residuum vix sufficit pro reprisis manerii usque festum Michaelis.

Hyde Johannes Clerk ballivus ibidem debet super istud visum vij li. xij s. ix d. qua.
Remanent ibidem de frumento ad opus domini ultra reprisas manerii usque festum Michaelis per estimacionem ad triturandum xxvj qr.
Deficit de mixtilione pro liberacionibus famulorum usque festum Michaelis iiij qr.
De ordio liberatur hospicio domini xxix qr. et residuum vix sufficit pro reprisis manerii usque festum Michaelis.
Remanent ibidem de drageto ad opus domini, ultra reprisas manerii usque festum Michaelis, xxv qr. iiij bus.
De avenis nichil remanet ad opus domini ultra reprisas manerii usque festum Michaelis.

Denham Thomas atte Hurst ballivus ibidem debet super istud visum viij li. ix s. j d. ob. qua.
De frumento liberat*ur* ad hospicium domini lxxvij qr. iiij bus. di. et residuum vix sufficit pro reprisis manerii usque festum Michaelis.
Deficit de mixtilione pro liberacionibus famulorum usque festum Michaelis xiiij qr.
De pisis viridibus, pisis grisis et ordio nichil remanet ad opus domini ultra reprisas manerii.
Remanent ibidem de drageto ad opus domini, ultra reprisas manerii usque festum Michaelis, per estimacionem ad triturandum xiiij qr.
De avenis nichil remanet ad opus domini ultra reprisas manerii.
De braseo ordei liberatur ad hospicium domini v qr. j bus., et remanent ad opus domini vj bus.
Remanent ibidem de braseo drageti ad opus domini xxxiiij qr.

Stanes Alexander Tresor ballivus ibidem debet super istud visum xv li. vj s. vj d. ob.

[11] The bailiff of Ebury received, in addition to a stipend of 13s. 4d. p.a., 1 bus. of wheat per week, that is, 6 qr. 4 bus. p.a. (WAM 26934).

I 16 States of the abbot's manors and portions at the conclusion of the audit of accounts for the year ending on 28 September 1382

A parchment roll of two membranes, 174 mm wide, sewn Chancery fashion with white thread in a tight oversew. Both membranes are laid out with three vertical folds, for the centre and for the left and right margins. Membrane 1 tapers at the top. The roll is in large part a fair copy, but additions were required to complete the roll: the valuations of wool and the totals. Membrane 2 is damaged at the foot, but little has been lost, except part of the title at the foot of the dorse:. 'Visus status terrarum d[omini Nicholai abbatis Westm'] de anno regni regis Ricardi secundi post conquestum [sexto]'.[1]

WAM 6163

[*Mem. 1 recto*] States of the lands and portions of Dom. Nicholas, abbot of Westminster, at the audit of the account of his ministers at 28 September 1382

Islip [Rents as in I 7: £31 6s. 11d.][2] Cash liveries: £78 2s. 11d. Arrears: none. Valor, with wool valued at £8: £64.[3] Remaining at the audit: 24 oxen, 1 ram, 125 wethers .... ewes, 17 hoggs, 18 young sheep, 28 lambs, 1 boar, 4 sows, 30 pigs, 21 piglets, 30 capons, 2 ganders, 7 breeding geese, 2 cocks, 12 hens, 41 [cartloads of hay].

Sutton-under-Brailes [Rents as in I 6: £17 18s. 10d.] Arrears: none. Cash liveries: £16 17s. Valor: excluding forinsec expenditure on the lord's household, £17 18s.[4] Remaining at the audit: 3 mares, 8 oxen, 1 cow, 1 calf, 1 sow, 7 young pigs, 6 piglets, 1 gander, 3 breeding geese.

Todenham [Rents as in I 5: £15 6s. 2½d.] Arrears: of William Spong', bailiff, £2 18s. 0¾d. Cash liveries: £15 12s. Valor, with wool valued at £14 7s.: £32 13s.[5] Remaining at the audit: 4 cart-horses, 18 oxen, 2 cows, 1 young bullock, 1 boar, 3 sows, 30 pigs, 13 young pigs, 3 rams, 201 wethers, 57 ewes,

[1] Extant ministers' accounts: Ebury, WAM 26937; Hyde, 27090; Islip, WAM 14822; Laleham, WAM 27157; Pensham, WAM 22236; Pinvin, WAM 22307; Sutton-under-Brailes, GRO, D1099/M31/48; Todenham, WAM 25975.

[2] Recorded here as £31 6s. 10d., however.

[3] The net wool crop at Islip this year, consisting of 241 sheep's fleeces, weighing 1 sack 5 st., was not sold until 1382–3 and was not sent to the collecting centre at Bourton-on-the-Hill for this purpose until that year (WAM 8309, 14823). The *valor* also includes profit of £3 9s. 3d. from the abbot's wardship in Noke (I 14, n. 2; WAM 14821).

[4] The excluded item was hay, valued at 10s. 7½d. (GRO, D1009/M31/48; WAM 24530).

[5] The net wool crop, consisting of 443 sheep's fleeces, weighing 1½ sacks 24 cloves 6 lb., was sent from Todenham to Bourton-on-the-Hill this year and kept there for a year before sale (WAM 8309, 25975).

126 hoggs and gimmers, 57 young sheep, 102 lambs, 20 capons, 2 cocks, 10 hens, 1 gander, 2 breeding geese, 12 goslings.

Bourton-on-the-Hill [Rents as in I 7: £9 2s. 4½d.][6] Cash liveries: £17 2s. 8d. Arrears: of Richard Alberd, 5s. 5½d.; of William Strode, £1 1s. 6½d.; of Gilbert Whyte, £3 7s. 4¾d.[7] Valor, with wool valued at £15 8s.: £27. Remaining at the audit: 5 horses, 1 mare, 2 foals, 12 oxen, 1 bull, 3 cows, 1 ram, 319 wethers, 11 ewes, 38 hoggs, 23 young sheep, 6 lambs, 1 boar, 2 sows, 19 pigs, 24 young pigs, 10 piglets, 2 cocks, 10 hens, 20 capons, 1,004 fleeces weighing 4 sacks 25 cloves 3 lb.[8]

Pershore [and] Wyke [Rents as in I 6: £32 19s.] Cash liveries: £15 17s. Arrears: of Richard Darnell', £6 4s. 8d.; of John Glyn, £2; of William Wictheford', £1 14s. 11d.; of William Osbarne, 16s. 10d.; of William Balk, £4; and of William Sperhauk', £1 3s. 11½d.[9] Valor, with wool valued at £6: £36 4s. Remaining at the audit: 6 horses, including 1 for the mill, 1 mare, 10 foals, 1 bull, 12 oxen, 3 cows, 8 calves, 2 boars, 3 sows, 10 pigs, 6 young pigs, 14 piglets, 106 wethers, 76 ewes, 6 young sheep, 64 lambs, 16 capons, 1 gander, 3 breeding geese, 18 goslings.

Pensham [Rents as in I 5: £26 4s. 4d.] Cash liveries: £25 5s. Arrears: of John Parker, lessee of the arable demesne, £3 10s.; and of William Aleyn, £2.[10] Valor: £26 5s. Remaining at the audit, in the lessee's hands: 3 qr. 6 bus. wheat, 16 qr. 3 bus. rye, 8 qr. 1½ bus. pulse, 13 qr. 6 bus. barley, 20 qr. dredge; 1 horse, 1 mare, 1 foal, 7 oxen, 12 cows, 6 heifers, 2 bullocks, 1 bull [calf], 1 gander, 2 breeding geese, 12 capons, 1 cock, 6 hens.

Hardwicke in Elmstone Hardwicke [Rents as in I 7: £22 17s. 8½d.] Cash liveries: £32. Arrears: none. Valor: £31 16s. 4d. Remaining in the lessee's hands: 29 qr. 6½ bus. wheat, 27 qr. 2½ bus. peas, 12 qr. barley, 4½ qr. oats;

[6] The change to this amount, from £9 2s. 4¾d., first appears in I 14.

[7] Alberd was reeve of Bourton-on-the-Hill 1353–74 (Appendix); Strode was bailiff here 1377–80 (WAM 8306 and I 14); and Whyte was bailiff 1380–5 (WAM 8205–9, 24586).

[8] The number of fleeces and their weight relate to the wool crops on manors in the Western Parts that were delivered to Bourton-on-the-Hill, the collecting centre this year and to the demesne crop at Bourton itself, of which the details are not known. For the later sale of this wool, with the crop of 1382–3, see I 17.

[9] For Darnell, Glyn, Wictheford' and Osbarne, see I 14. Balk was serjeant of Pershore in 1372–3 and possibly for longer (WAM 24516*). Sperhauk, though in arrears at Pershore, was about to become lessee of the demesne at Pensham (LNQ, f. lxiii).

[10] Aleyn was reeve and rent-collector at Pensham 1376–1412 (WAM 22232–47).

4 cart-horses, 16 oxen, 1 gander, 4 breeding geese, 2 cocks, 10 hens, 21 capons and 14 cartloads of hay.[11]

Deerhurst [Rents as in I 6: £29 17s. 6d.] Cash liveries: £34 19s. 4d. Arrears: of John atte Hall', £5 15s. 8½d. Valor: £33 14s. 8d.

Chaceley [Rents as in I 5: £5 0s. 8d.] Cash liveries: £10 10s. Arrears: of John Hathemer', £5 7s. 5¼d.; of Nicholas Phillip' .....[12] Valor: .....[13] Remaining in the lessee's hands: 9 qr. 4 bus. wheat, 13 qr. 2½ bus. rye, 5 qr. 3 bus. peas, 19 qr. 5½ bus. barley, 4 qr. 6 bus. oats; 1 horse, 1 mare, 1 affer, 3 foals, 9 oxen, 1 bull, 20 cows, 1 gander, 3 breeding geese, 12 capons, 1 cock, 5 hens.[14]

Longdon [Rents as in I 5: £15] Cash liveries: £18. [Arrears]:[15] none. Valor: £17 6s. 10d.

Castlemorton [Rents as in I 14: £28 17s. 10d.] Cash liveries: £30 5s. 0½d. Arrears: of Geoffrey Harberd, the lessee, £1 2s.; and of Henry Ode, 8s.[16] Valor: £32 11s.

Pinvin [Rents as in I 5: £23 16s. 3d.] [*Mem. 2 recto*] Cash liveries: £38 14s. Arrears: of William Rayell',[17] £1 15s. 7½d.; and of Ralph Pendefen,[18] 10s. Valor: £37 3s.

Wick Hundred Cash liveries: 16s. 1d. Arrears: of William Rued', 1s. Valor: 15s. 1d.
Defford Hundred Cash liveries: 15s. 5d. Arrears: of John Birtlyngham, £2 11s. 5d.; and of Robert Berald, £1 18s.[19] Valor: 15s. 5d.
Pinvin Hundred Cash liveries: 14s. 3d. Arrears: none. Valor: 14s. 3d.
Portmoot of Pershore Cash liveries .....[20] Arrears ..... Valor .....

[11] As in the inventory of corn and stock in I 9.
[12] MS blank. Hathemer' was lessee of the demesne at Chaceley, and Phillip' was probably rent-collector.
[13] MS blank. There is a later marginal note, in a small hand, 'nondum comput'' ('not yet reckoned').
[14] Changes in the inventory of corn and livestock since 1378–9 suggest that Hathemer', the farmer, had recently been given a new lease. For the previous inventory, see I 14.
[15] MS omits 'Arreragia'.
[16] Ode was rent-collector at Castlemorton 1362–79.
[17] Rent-collector 1379–82 (WAM 22305–7).
[18] Formerly a lessee of the demesne at Pinvin (WAM 22302–3).
[19] For Birtlyngham and Berald, see I 14.
[20] MS: no sum is entered under this or the two following headings relating to the portmoot. There is a marginal note, in a small hand, 'nondum comput''.

Denham [Rents as in I 9: £25 8s. 5½d.] Cash liveries: £51 7s. 8½d. Arrears: of John Brian, lessee of the cows, 5s.; and of Guy Roberd', bailiff, 11s. 10¼d. Valor, with wool and hay valued at .....:[21] £12 5s. 7d.[22] Remaining at the audit: 2 qr. 5 bus. of very good malt; 4 cart-horses, 2 stots, 21 oxen, 1 bull, 44 cows, 2 rams, 77 wethers, 73 ewes, 2 young sheep, 47 lambs, 3 woolfells, 7 lambskins, 3 boars, 3 sows, 10 pigs, 24 young pigs, 30 piglets, 2 ganders, 5 breeding geese, 6 capons, 1 cock, 10 hens, 9 beehives and 107 cartloads of hay.

Laleham [Rents as in I 9: £16 10s. 2¼d.] Cash liveries: £22 12s. 3½d. Arrears: none. Valor, with wool valued at £3 6s. 8d.: £28 12s.[23] Remaining at the audit: 3 cart-horses, 2 mares, 2 foals, 10 oxen, 1 boar, 2 sows, 13 pigs, 16 young pigs, 6 piglets, 1 ram, 160 wethers, 13 ewes, 7 young sheep, 26 lambs, 7 swans, 6 cygnets, 1 gander, 3 breeding geese, 4 capons and 34 cartloads of hay.

Pyrford [Rents as in I 5: £35 5s. 5½d.] Cash liveries: £24. Arrears: of William Downyng', the reeve, £14. Valor, including wool and hay valued at .....:[24] £55. Remaining at the audit: 1 horse, 2 mares, 4 foals, 7 oxen, 2 rams, 159 wethers, 59 ewes, 2 gimmers, 28 lambs, 24 capons and 80 cartloads of hay.

Staines [Rents as in I 14: £28 10s. 3¼d.] Cash liveries: £32. Arrears: of Alexander Tresor', the bailiff, £5 9s. 0¾d. Valor: £37.

Ebury [Rents as in I 9: £13 3s.] Cash liveries: £29 10s. 0½d. Arrears: none. Valor, with hay: £44.[25] Remaining at the audit: 20 qr. 5 bus. barley; 1 cart-horse, 9 mares, 1 foal, 11 oxen, 2 bulls, 60 cows, 1 sow, 9 pigs, 9 young pigs, 2 white swans, 1 gander, 3 breeding geese, 12 goslings, 4 capons, 1 cock, 6 hens, 2 peacocks, 2 peahens and 34 cartloads of hay.

[21] MS: 'cum lana et feno appreciata' inserted, but without a cash sum; the cash total for the *valor* is in another hand.

[22] The hay, delivered to the abbot's household, is valued in the account of the steward of the household at £4 5s. 9½d. (WAM 24530).

[23] MS: 'cum lana appreciata ad lxvj s. viij d.' and cash total added in another hand. 173 sheep's fleeces were delivered to Br. John Canterbury, described as the abbot's stock-keeper ('instaurator'), by the bailiff of Laleham this year, presumably for sale at Westminster (WAM 27157).

[24] MS: 'cum lana et feno appreciata' and cash total added in another hand.

[25] MS: 'cum feno xliiij li.' inserted in a second hand. At the audit, the hay was valued at £5 11s. 8½d. (WAM 26937).

Yeoveney Rent for the lease of manor: for Michaelmas term £10 10s., and the same for the term of the Annunciation. Total: £21. Cash liveries: £21.[26] Arrears: of John Dermon, the lessee .....[27] Valor: £21. Remaining in the hands of the lessee: 7 mares, 5 foals, 10 oxen, 1 bull, 15 cows, 1 calf, 3 sows, 5 young pigs, 7 piglets, 1 gander, 3 breeding geese, 1 cock, 6 hens.

[Totals]
Sum of cash liveries: £803 5s. 8d. Sum of arrears: £68 17s. 11¼d. Sum of valors: £555 13s. 2d.
Horses and affers, 60; foals and colts,[28] 28. Sum of this category: 88.
Oxen and bullocks, 167; bulls, 8; cows, 165; young bullocks and calves, 11. Sum of this category: 351.
Rams, 10; wethers, 1,147; ewes, 324; lambs and young sheep, 611. Sum of this category: 2,412.
Boars, 9; sows, 21; pigs, 121; young pigs and piglets, 228. Sum of this category: 379.
Sum of rents, by term: Michaelmas, £139 15s. 5½d.; Christmas, £84 3s. 2d.; Annuncation, £103 0s. 11d.; nativity of St John the Baptist, £85 18s. 7½d. Sum total of rents: £412 18s. 2d.

[*Mem. 1 dorse*] *Hyde* [Rents as in I 9: £10 15s. 9½d.] Cash liveries: 19s. 4d. Arrears: of Thomas, the bailiff,[29] 11s. 2¾d. Valor, with wool: £6.[30] Remaining at the audit: 4 horses, 3 stots, 14 oxen, 2 bulls, 35 cows, 2 rams, 197 wethers, 54 ewes, 2 young sheep, 41 lambs, 12 white capons, 1 boar, 1 sow and 18 cartloads of hay.

[26] MS: 'xxj li.' inserted.
[27] MS: no cash sum is entered. The leasehold rents entered here and the cash liveries that follow represent the sum of £21 payable by John Dorman (alias Dermon), the lessee of the manor, in two instalments, on 29 September and 25 March. For Dorman's lease, executed in 1379, see I 14, n. 30.
[28] MS: 'pullan' et pull''.
[29] Thomas Chesgate, bailiff 28 September 1381–18 March 1383, and possibly from 2 April 1381 (WAM 27089–91).
[30] MS: 'cum lana vj li.' added in another hand. 30 sheep's fleeces and 40 lambs' fleeces were delivered by the bailiff to Br. John Canterbury, at Westminster, for sale (WAM 27090).

I 17 States of the abbot's manors and portions at the conclusion of the audit of accounts for the year ending on 28 September 1383

A parchment roll of three membranes, 194 mm wide, sewn Chancery fashion with white thread in a tight oversew. All three membranes are laid out with three vertical folds, one for the centre and one each for the left and right margins. Membrane 1 tapers at the top. The roll was intended as a fair copy, but not all information was to hand when the clerk wrote it, and there are additions towards the end relating to wool sales and other profits which have been added in a second ink (and possibly hand); and some totals, particularly the grand totals, remain blank. Membrane 3 is endorsed at the foot 'Status terrarum et porcionum domini Nicholai abbatis Westm' in vigilia sancti Michaelis anno regni regis Ricardi secundi post conquestum vj^{to}'.[1]

WAM 6147

[*Mem. 1 recto*] States of the lands and portions of Dom. Nicholas, abbot of Westminster, at the audit of the account of his ministers at 28 September 1383

Islip [Rents as in I 7: £31 6s. 11d.] Cash liveries: £52 9s. 6½d. Arrears: of William Dolle, the reeve .....[2] Valor, with wool valued at £7, and with £3 9s. 3½d. profit from a portion of Noke manor: £74.[3] Remaining at the audit: 24 oxen, 3 calves, 1 ram, 140 wethers, 23 ewes, 9 hoggs and gimmers, 28 yearling lambs, 23 lambs, 1 boar, 3 sows, 3 pigs, 30 young pigs, 21 piglets, 30 capons, 2 ganders, 7 breeding geese, 2 cocks, 12 hens, 444 fleeces weighing 2 sacks 5 st. 10 lb.,[4] 4 breeding swans, 2 young swans and 4 cygnets.

Sutton-under-Brailes [Rents as in I 6: £17 18s. 10d.] Cash liveries: £17 11s. 10d. Arrears: none. Valor: £2. Remaining at the audit: 3 mares, 10 oxen, of which 2 are old (*cronardi*), 1 cow, 1 bullock, 1 sow, 1 boar, 11 pigs, 15 young pigs and piglets, 1 gander, 3 breeding geese, 1 cock, 6 hens, 12 capons.

[1] Extant ministers' accounts: Ebury, WAM 26938; Hyde, WAM 27091; Laleham, WAM 27158; Pensham, WAM 22237; Pyrford, WAM 27426; Sutton-under-Brailes, GRO D1099/M31/49.
[2] MS: left blank.
[3] The net wool crop at Islip in 1382–3 consisted of 203 fleeces, weighing 1 sack 10 lb. Together with the net crop in 1381–2, consisting of 241 fleeces and weighing 1 sack 5 st., it was still at Islip in 1383–4, and both crops appear in the reeve's final account for that year (WAM 14823). For the crop in 1381–2, see I 16. For the abbot's wardship in Noke, see I 14.
[4] The sum of the wool crops in 1381–2 and 1382–3.

Todenham [Rents as in I 5: £15 6s. 2½d.] Cash liveries: £17 1s. 7d. Arrears: of William Spong', the bailiff, £3 10s. Valor, beyond £26 lost through a murrain of sheep: £5. Remaining at the audit: 1 qr. 3 bus. pulse; 4 cart-horses, 18 oxen, 2 cows, 1 bullock, 1 boar, 3 sows, 25 pigs, 20 young pigs, 7 piglets, 2 rams, 54 wethers, 81 ewes, 32 hoggs and gimmers in their second year, 102 yearling lambs, 75 lambs, 20 capons, 2 cocks, 10 hens, 1 gander, 2 breeding geese, 2 goslings.

Bourton-on-the-Hill [Rents as in I 7: £9 2s. 4½d.] Cash liveries: £16 5s. 5d. Arrears: of William Strode, lately bailiff, £1 1s. 6½d.; Richard Alberd', lately reeve, 5½d.; and Gilbert Whyte, bailiff, £1 10s. Valor, with wool valued at £8 1s., £25, and no more on account of a murrain of sheep.[5] Remaining at the audit: 5 cart-horses, 1 mare, 2 foals, 12 oxen, 1 bull, 2 cows, 1 calf, 295 wethers, 15 sheep in their second year, 33 pigs of which 15 were for the larder, 10 young pigs and piglets, 2 cocks, 10 hens, 20 capons, 1,710 fleeces weighing 7½ sacks 21 cloves 6 lb.[6]

Pershore [Rents as in I 6: £32 19s.] Cash liveries: £52 14s. 1d. Arrears: of Richard Darnell', £6 4s. 8d.; of John Glyn, £2; of William Wycheford, £1 14s. 11d.; of William Osbarne, 16s. 10d; of William Bulk, £2; of William Sperhauk', £1 3s. 11½d.; of Richard Forthey, bailiff, £3. Valor, with wool valued at £4 6s. 2d.: £55.[7] Remaining at the audit: 1 qr. 4½ bus. wheat, 4 bus. 3 p. rye, 5 qr. 4 bus. pulse, 1 qr. 6 bus. multure from the mill, 2 qr. 6 bus. malt; 6 horses including 1 for the mill, 8 foals, 1 bull, 10 oxen, 3 cows 2 of which are in a dispute about the heriot of John Peleworth, 3 young bullocks, 5 calves, 2 boars, 3 sows, 21 pigs, 10 young pigs, 9 piglets, 5 wethers, 88 ewes, 6 hoggs and gimmers, 58 young sheep, 45 lambs, 1 gander, 3 breeding geese, 19 goslings, 16 capons, 1 cock, 5 hens.

[5] MS: 'et non plus propter morinam bidencium', probably inserted but in the main text hand. The net wool crop at Bourton-on-the-Hill this year consisted of 320 fleeces, weighing 1½ sacks 2 lb. (WAM 8309).

[6] The total given as 1,710 fleeces comprised 1,004, weighing 4 sacks 25 cloves 3 lb., remaming at Bourton-on-the-Hill, the collecting centre for manors in the Western Parts, at the end of the previous year of account (1381–2), and 773, weighing 3 sacks 22 cloves 4 lb., the wool crop of these manors in the current year. It weighed in toto 8 sacks 14 cloves 7 lb., the equivalent of 8 sacks 8 cloves according to measures at the Wool Staple. The wool for both years was sold to a merchant who is not named in our sources and for a price that is not recorded (WAM 8309).

[7] The net wool crop at Pershore in 1382–3, sent to Bourton-on-the-Hill, consisted of 123 fleeces, weighing 0½ sack 2 cloves (WAM 8309).

Pensham [Rents as in I 5: £26 4s. 4d.] Cash liveries: £27 10s. Arrears: of John Parker, £3 10s.; of William Aleyn, £1 4s. Valor: £26 14s. Remaining at the audit in the lessee's hands:[8] 3 qr. 6 bus. wheat, 16 qr. 3 bus. rye, 8 qr. 1½ bus. pulse, 13 qr. 6 bus. barley, 20 qr. dredge; 1 horse, 1 mare, 1 foal, 7 oxen, 12 cows, 6 heifers, 2 bullocks, 1 bull calf, 1 gander, 2 breeding geese, 12 capons, 1 cock, 6 hens.[9]

Hardwicke in Elmstone Hardwicke [Rents as in I 7: £22 17s. 8½d.] Cash liveries: £31 18s. 5d. Arrears: none. Valor: £31 18s. 5d. Remaining in the hands of the farmer: 29 qr. 6½ bus. wheat, 27 qr. 2½ bus. peas, 12 qr. barley, 4½ qr. oats; 4 cart-horses, 16 oxen, 1 gander, 4 breeding geese, 2 cocks, 10 hens, 21 capons and 14 cartloads of hay.[10]

Deerhurst [Rents as in I 6: £29 17s. 6d.] Cash liveries: £37 3s. 8d. Arrears: of John atte Hall', £2 15s. 11¼d, including a fine of £1 owed by John Cassy and 16s. for an ox, a heriot, in the hands of William Baker. Valor: £33 9s. 6¾d.

Chaceley [Rents as in I 5: £5 0s. 8d.] Cash liveries: £17. Arrears: of John Hathemere, £5 6s. 4¼d.; of Nicholas Phillip', £10 10s. 8d. Valor: £15 0s. 9d. Remaining in the hands of the lessee: 9 qr. 4 bus. wheat, 13 qr. 2½ bus. rye, 5 qr. 3 bus. peas, 19 qr. 5½ bus. barley, 4 qr. 6 bus. oats; 1 horse, 1 mare, 1 affer, 3 foals, 9 oxen, 1 bull, 20 cows, 1 gander, 3 breeding geese, 12 capons, 1 cock and 5 hens.[11]

Longdon [Rents as in I 5: £15] Cash liveries: £14 6s. 10d. [*Mem. 2 recto*] Arrears: of Gilbert de Hegg', farmer, £3 4s. 10½d. Valor: £17 15s. 6½d.

Castlemorton [Rents as in I 14: £28 17s. 10d.] Cash liveries: £27 8s. Arrears: of Geoffrey H*ar*berd', the lessee, £1 2s.; of Henry Ode, £3 3s. 6¼d. Valor: £32 11s.

Pinvin [Rents as in I 5: £33 16s. 3d.] Cash liveries: £34 10s. 4d. Arrears: of Ralph Pendefen, 10s.; of William Rayell', £3 10s. Valor: £36 0s. 4d.
Wick Hundred Cash liveries: none, as no account has been rendered.[12] Arrears: of Walter Clerk, £4 1s. 7d. Valor: £4 0s. 7d.

[8] The farmer was now William Sperhauk'. See I 16, Pershore.
[9] As in the inventory of corn and stock in I 9; I 17 gives the quantity of barley as 3 qr. 6 bus.
[10] As in the inventory of corn and stock in I 9.
[11] Inventory of corn and stock as in I 16.
[12] MS: 'nichil quia non comp*utavit*', an addition in a small hand.

Defford Hundred Cash liveries: £1 7s. 4d. Arrears: of John Birlingham, £2 11s. 5d.; of Robert Berald', £1 18s.; of William Shephird, 5s.[13] Valor: £1 12s. 4d.
Pinvin Hundred Cash liveries: £1 10s. Arrears: of William Hanogh', 4s. 1d. Valor: £1 14s. 1d.
Portmoot of Pershore Cash liveries: £5. Arrears: of John Parker, £1 4s. 4d. Valor: £2 14s. 10d.

Denham [Rents as in I 9: £25 8s. 5½d.] Cash liveries: £55 16s. Arrears: none. Valor, with £7 16s. 8d. proft from Medmull',[14] £10 18s. the price of 109 cartloads of hay consumed in the abbot's household, and with wool valued at £2 18s.: £25 12s. Remaining at the audit: 2 bus. wheat malt, 1 qr. dredge malt; 3 horses, 3 stots, 2 bulls, 19 oxen, 42 cows, 6 rams, 96 wethers, 67 ewes, 47 lambs, 2 boars, 3 sows, 22 pigs, 55 young pigs, 14 piglets, 13½ breeding swans, 12 white swans, 2 young swans, 10 cygnets, 2 ganders, 5 breeding geese, 24 capons, 1 cock, 10 hens, 70 cartloads of hay.

Laleham [Rents as in I 9: £16 10s. 2¼d.] Cash liveries: £22 9s. Valor, with wool valued at £2 14s. 8d.:[15] £28 9s. Remaining at the audit: 7 qr. 4 bus. oats, 6 qr. barley malt; 1 horse, 6 mares, 1 foal, 10 oxen, 2 boars, 2 sows, 10 pigs, 17 young pigs, 6 piglets, 1 ram, 120 wethers, 19 ewes, 4 young sheep, 30 lambs, 7 breeding swans, 2 cygnets, 1 gander, 3 breeding geese, 15 capons, 1 cock, 6 hens, 42 cartloads of hay.

[*Mem. 3 recto*] *Pyrford* [Rents as in I 5: £35 5s. 5½d.] Cash liveries: £33 8s. 1d. Arrears: of William Millehurst, £4. Valor, with wool valued at £2: £41 8s.[16] Remaining at the audit: 14 qr. 2 bus. oats; 2 mares, 3 foals, 7 oxen, 1 ram, 124 wethers, 38 ewes, 23 young sheep, 29 lambs, 118 cartloads of hay.

[13] Shephird was probably bailiff of the hundred and, if so, this was the first of his two periods of office; see below, I 23 and I 24. For Birlingham (Birtlyngham) and Berald, see I 14.
[14] MS: 'cum vij li. xvj s. viij d. de proficuo de Medmull'' inserted in another hand. *Medmull'*, a watermill, was one of at least four mills in Denham at this date, and probably older than the so-called 'new mill'. But the fact that the lord of Colham paid a rent of a red rose for it annually suggests that it had formerly been out of the abbot's demesne. The notice taken of it in the *valor* this year may mean that it had recently been recovered by the abbot and thus represented a new source of income (WAM 3409–10).
[15] MS: 'cum lana appreciata ad liiij s. viij d.' added in a second ink. The net wool crop consisted of 164 sheep's fleeces and 20 lambs' fleeces. The former were sent to the conventual treasurer at Westminster, for sale, and the latter were sold locally.
[16] MS: 'cum lana appreciata ad xl s. xlj li. viij s.' added subsequently. The net wool crop consisted of 169 sheep's fleeces and 28 lambs' fleeces. The former were sent to the conventual treasurer at Westminster for sale, and it is probably to these that the estimated value in the text applies; the lambs' fleeces, weighing 1 st. 2 lb., were sold locally for 2s. 4d. (WAM 27426).

Staines [Rents as in I 14: £28 10s. 3¼d.][17] Cash liveries: £26 9s. Arrears: of Alexander Tresor, bailiff, £11 10s. Valor, including £6 4s. 8d. in profit from the lands and tenements of John atte Halle: £35 16s.[18]

Ebury [Rents as in I 9: £13 3s.][19] Cash liveries: £10 16s. 1d. Arrears: of William Huller .....[20] Valor: .....[21] Remaining at the audit: 1 cart-horse, 8 mares, 2 foals, 10 oxen, 2 bulls, 61 cows, 1 sow, 10 pigs, 12 piglets, 2 white swans, 1 gander, 3 breeding geese, 3 goslings, 1 cock, 6 hens, 39 cartloads of hay and 300 bundles of reeds.

Yeoveney [Rents as in I 16: £21] Cash liveries: £21. Arrears, of John Derman, lessee, ...[22] Valor: £21. Remaining in the lessee's hands: 7 mares, 5 foals, 10 oxen, 1 bull, 15 cows, 1 calf, 3 sows, 5 young pigs, 7 piglets, 1 gander, 3 breeding geese, 1 cock and 6 hens.[23]

[Totals]
Sum of cash liveries: £553 16s. 9½d. Sum of arrears: .....[24] Sum of valors: £593 17s. 5½d.
Horses and affers, ...;[25] foals and colts, ... Sum of this category: .....
Oxen and bullocks, ...; bulls, ...; cows, ...; young bullocks and calves, ... Sum of this category: .....
Rams, ...; wethers, ...; ewes, ...; lambs and young sheep, ... Sum of this category: .....
Boars, ...; sows, ...; pigs, ...; young pigs and piglets, ... Sum of this category: .....
Sum of rents, by term: Michaelmas, £139 15s. 5½d.; Christmas, £84 3s. 2d.; Annuncation, £103 0s. 11d.; nativity of St John the Baptist, £85 18s. 7½d. Sum total of rents: £412 18s. 2d.[26]

[17] Given in the MS as £28 10s. 4¼d.
[18] For the tenements of John Halle, see I 13.
[19] But entered here as £13 4s.
[20] MS: no cash amount entered.
[21] MS: no cash amount entered.
[22] MS: no cash amount entered.
[23] As in the stock account in I 16.
[24] MS: no cash amount entered.
[25] MS: no totals are entered for stock.
[26] The totals for rents are the same as in I 16.

[*Mem. 1 dorse*] *Hyde* [Rents as in I 9: £10 15s. 9½d.] Cash liveries: 2s. Arrears: of Walter atte Westende, bailiff, ...[27] Valor: .....[28] Remaining at the audit: 4 cart-horses, 5 stots, 12 oxen, 1 bull, 40 cows, 5 rams, 139 wethers, 160 ewes, 80 lambs, 2 woolfells, 4 sheepskins, 1 young boar, 39 capons and 15 cartloads of hay.

[27] MS: no cash amount entered.
[28] MS: no cash amount entered.

I 18 States of the abbot's manors and portions at the conclusion of the audit of accounts for the year ending on 28 September 1386

A parchment roll of two membranes, 214 mm wide, sewn Chancery fashion with white thread in a tight oversew. Both membranes are laid out with three vertical folds, for the centre and for the left and right margins. Membrane 1 tapers at the top. The roll is a fair copy. It has been partly eaten by rodents down the right-hand side of the recto: some small lacunae occur here and the text has been supplied from other states. Membrane 1 is endorsed at the top: 'Status terrarum domini Nicholai abbatis Westm' in vigilia sancti Michaelis anno regni Ricardi secundi [post] conquestum decimo'.[1]

WAM 6158

[*Mem. 1 recto*] States of the lands and portions of Dom. Nicholas, abbot of Westminster, at the audit of the account of his ministers at 28 September 1386

Islip [Rents as in I 7: £31 6s. 11d.] Cash liveries: £58 13s. 10d. Arrears: none. Valor, including wool valued at £6 and £3 9s. 3½d. profit from land and tenements in Noke manor: £72.[2] Remaining at the audit: 24 oxen, 1 ram, 219 wethers, 16 ewes, 9 young sheep, 15 lambs, 1 boar, 4 sows, 30 pigs, 30 young pigs, 22 piglets, 30 capons, 1 gander, 7 breeding geese, 2 cocks, 12 hens.

Sutton-under-Brailes [Rents as in I 6: £17 18s. 10d.] Cash liveries: £4 19s. 8d. Arrears: of Thomas Hurry the reeve, nothing. Valor: £20 1s. Remaining at the audit: 3 mares, 9 oxen, 1 cow, 1 calf, 1 boar, 1 sow, 18 pigs, 8 young pigs, 1 gander, 3 breeding geese, 1 cock, 6 hens, 43 cartloads of hay.

Todenham [Rents as in I 5: £15 6s. 2½d.] Cash liveries: £10 18s. 4d. Arrears: of William Sponge, lately bailiff, £2 6s. 4½d. Valor, with wool valued at £10:[3] £19 13s. Remaining at the audit: 4 cart-horses, 16 oxen, 7 cows, 1 bull calf, 7 bullocks, 6 calves, 2 boars, 1 sow, 7 small pigs, 10 piglets, 7 rams, 36 wethers, 199 ewes, 53 young sheep, 142 lambs, 1 gander, 3 breeding geese, 11 goslings, 50 cartloads of hay.

[1] Extant ministers' accounts: Deerhurst, WAM 8452; Islip, WAM 14827; Pyrford, WAM 27427.

[2] The net wool crop at Islip this year consisted of 248 fleeces, and it is likely that these were sent to the collecting centre at Bourton-on-the-Hill (WAM 14627). William Dolle, reeve of Islip and keeper of the abbot's portion in Noke, actually accounted for an excess of receipts over expenses of £3 9s. 3¾d. this year (WAM 14826). For Noke, see I 14.

[3] The estimated value of 323 fleeces sent for sale to the collecting centre at Bourton-on-the Hill (GRO, D1099/M30/17).

Bourton-on-the-Hill [Rents as in I 7: £9 2s. 4½d.] Cash liveries: £23 2s. 8d. Arrears: of Robert Wroxton, lately rent-collector, 14s. 8d.; of Richard Alberd, £1 14s. 9½d.; of Walter Parham, £3 0s. 8d.; of Gilbert Wyte, £5 16s. 0¼d. Valor, including wool valued at £9: £33. Remaining at the audit: 5 horses, 8 oxen, 363 wethers, 1,136 fleeces,[4] 1 brass pot and 10 qr. 5 bus. .....[5] pulse.

Pershore [Rents as in I 6: £32 19s.] Cash liveries: £41 7s. 6d. Arrears: of Richard Darnell, £1 10s.; of John Glyn, 10s.; of William Wicheford, £1 14s. 11d.; of William Balke, £1; of William Sperhauke, £1 3s. 11½d.; of John Child, £1; of William Osberne, £2 17s.; of Richard Fortheye, £5. Valor, including wool valued at £6 13s. 4d.: £43 10s. Remaining at the audit: 6 horses, 2 foals, 11 oxen, 3 cows, 1 bull, 4 bullocks, 1 heifer, 5 young bullocks, 5 calves, 3 boars, 3 sows, 44 pigs, 18 young pigs, 26 piglets, 3 rams, 138 ewes, 10 wethers, 75 hoggs and gimmers, 78 lambs, 1 gander, 3 breeding geese, 20 goslings, 16 capons, 1 cock, 5 hens, 26 cartloads of hay.

Pensham [Rents as in I 5: £26 4s. 4d.] Cash liveries: £26 8s. 9d. Arrears: of William Sperhauk, the lessee, £3. Valor: £26 8s. Remaining at the audit, in the lessee's hands: 3 qr. 6 bus. wheat, 16 qr. 3 bus. rye, 8 qr. 1½ bus. pulse, 13 qr. 6 bus. barley, 20 qr. dredge; 1 horse, 1 mare, 1 foal, 7 oxen, 12 cows, 6 heifers, 2 bullocks, 1 bull calf, 1 gander, 2 breeding geese, 10 capons, 1 cock and 6 hens.[6]

Hardwicke in Elmstone Hardwicke [Rents as in I 7: £22 17s. [8½d.]] Cash liveries: £31 9s. Arrears: of John Hall', the bailiff, nothing. Valor £32 7s. Remaining in the lessee's hands: 29 qr. 6½ bus. wheat, 27 qr. 2½ bus. peas, 12 qr. barley, 4½ qr. oats; 4 cart-horses, 16 oxen, 1 gander, 3 breeding geese, 2 cocks, 10 hens, 21 capons and 14 cartloads of hay.[7]

Deerhurst [Rents as in I 6: £29 17s. 6d.] Cash liveries: £26 13s. 4d. Arrears: of John atte Hall, the bailiff, £12 13s. 7½d. Valor: £33 10s.

Chaceley [Rents as in I 5: £5 0s. 8d.] Cash liveries: £12 9s. 6d. Arrears: of John Hathemere, lately farmer, £2; of Nicholas Phillip', now farmer, £6 13s.

[4] The fleeces represent the total number collected at Bourton-on-the-Hill this year for sale, from Bourton itself and Pershore, where, in each case, the number is not recorded, and from Todenham (323 fleeces) and probably from Islip (248).

[5] MS: edge eaten away.

[6] As in the inventory of corn and stock in I 9.

[7] As in the inventory of corn and stock in I 9, but only 3 breeding geese are recorded this year rather than 4.

4d. Valor: £14 6s. Remaining at the audit, in the farmer's hands: 16 qr. 4 bus. 1 p. wheat, 8 qr. 5 bus. rye, 13 qr. 4 bus. peas, 14 qr. 3 bus. barley, 3 qr. dredge, 7 qr. 6 bus. oats; 2 cart-horses, 9 oxen, 1 bull, [20] cows, 1 sow, 15 young pigs, 1 gander, 3 breeding geese, 12 capons, 1 cock, 5 hens.

Longdon [Rents as in I 5: £15] Cash liveries: £16 17s. 6d. Arrears: of John Broun, reap-reeve, £1 13s. 4d.; of Hugh atte Hegge, £6 13s. 4½d. Valor: £16 18s.

[*Mem. 2 recto*] *Castlemorton* [Rents as in I 14: £28 17s. [10d.]] Cash liveries: £26 13s. 6d. Arrears: of Henry Ode, £2 6s. 8d.; of the farmer, 18s. 8d.[8] Valor: £28 3s.

Pinvin [Rents as in I 5: £33 16s. 3d.] Cash liveries: £35 6s. Arrears: of William Raiell', £1 6s. 8d.; of Richard Pigon, 13s. 4d. Valor: £35 7s.

Wick Hundred Cash liveries: £1 4s. Arrears: of John Aston' and Henry Bruwer, bailiffs, £2 16s. 4d. Valor: £2 17s. 1d.
Defford Hundred Cash liveries: 17s. 8d. Arrears: of John Birlyngham, £2 11s. 5d.; of Robert Berald, £2 18s. Valor: £1 14s. 11d.
Portmoot of Pershore Cash liveries: £3 6s. 8d. Arrears: of John Parker, lately bailiff, £1. Valor: £3 6s. 8d.
Pinvin Hundred Cash liveries: £2. Arrears: of William Hanogh, 11s. 6d. Valor: £2 7s.

Denham [Rents as in I 9: £25 8s. [5½d.]] Cash liveries: £42 4s. 10½d. Shortfall: £6.[9] Arrears: nothing. Remaining at the audit: 6 horses, 4 stots, 19 oxen, 1 bull, 36 cows, 6 rams, 103 wethers, 73 ewes, 56 lambs, 3 boars, 3 sows, 15 pigs, 19 young pigs, 13½ breeding swans, 12 white swans, 2 young swans, 4 cygnets, 2 ganders, 5 breeding geese, 6 goslings, 5 capons, 1 cock, 12 hens, 40 cartloads of hay.

Laleham [Rents as in I 9: £16 10s. 2¼d.] Cash liveries: £25 12s. 4d. Arrears: nothing. Valor, including wool: £33. Remaining at the audit: 6 mares, 7 foals, 12 oxen, 1 boar, 2 sows, 10 pigs, 10 young pigs, 2 rams, 135 wethers, 74 ewes, 39 lambs, 8 swans, 4 geese, 15 capons, 1 cock, 6 hens, 40 cartloads of hay.

[8] Possibly Geoffrey Herberd, as in 1382–3, I 17.
[9] MS: 'Disproficuum manerii hoc anno vj li.' The probable meaning of this entry is that the *valor* of the manor this year fell short by £6 of the reprises; for these unavoidable charges, amounting to £45 6s. 8d. p.a. on the issues of the manor at Denham, see I 1, n. 30.

Ebury [Rents as in I 9: £13 3s.][10] Cash liveries: £46 5s. 11d. Arrears: of William Hull', bailiff, nothing. Valor: £49. Remaining at the audit: 3 horses, 1 foal, 10 oxen, 2 bulls, 47 cows, 1 sow, 2 pigs, 15 piglets, 5 swans, 1 gander, 3 breeding geese, 1 cock, 6 hens, 2 peacocks, 3 peahens, 1 young peahen, 38 cartloads of hay.

[*Mem. 2 dorse*][11] *Pyrford* [Rents as in I 5: £35 4s. 11½d.][12] Cash liveries: £33 5s. 5d. Arrears: nothing. Valor: £38 10s. Remaining at the audit: 3 mares, 4 foals, 7 oxen, 1 ram, 107 wethers, 45 ewes, 98 hoggs and gimmers, 57 lambs, 250 [bundles of] talwood, 3,350 faggots and 87 cartloads of hay.

Staines [Rents as in I 14: £28 10s. 3[¼]d.] Cash liveries: £32. Arrears: of Alexander Tresor', the bailiff, £1 10s. Valor: £36 13s. 4d.

Yeoveney Rents by term, for Michaelmas, £5 5s.; Christmas, £5 5s.; Easter, £5 5s.; and the nativity of St John the Baptist, £5 5s. [Total:] £21. Cash liveries: £21. Arrears: of John Derman, farmer, nothing. Valor: identical with the leasehold rent of the manor. Remaining in the hands of the farmer: 7 mares, 2 foals, 1 bull, 10 oxen, 15 cows, 3 sows, 5 young pigs, 7 piglets, 1 gander, 3 breeding geese, 1 cock and 6 hens.[13]

[Totals]
Sum of cash liveries: £532 14s. 5½d. Sum of arrears: £77 4s. 7¾d. Sum of valors: £547 12s.
Horses and affers, 55; foals and colts,[14] 17. Sum of this category: 72.
Oxen and bullocks, 150; bulls, 7; cows, 148; young bullocks and calves, 29. Sum of this category: 334.
Rams, 18; wethers, 838; ewes, 471; lambs and young sheep, 528. Sum of this category: 1,755.
Boars, 11; sows, 21; pigs, 117; young pigs and piglets, 190. Sum of this category: 339.
Sum of rents, by term: Michaelmas, £139 15s. 5½d.; Christmas, £84 3s. 2d.; Annunciation, £103 0s. 11d.; nativity of St John the Baptist, £85 18s. 7½d. Sum total of rents: £412 18s. 2d.[15]

[10] But entered here as £13 4s.
[11] The text is now written up the dorse from the foot of the roll; the layout of the membrane with three folds facilitates the use of the margin on the dorse.
[12] Excepting only a fall of 6d. in rents for Whitsun, which proved to be temporary; the total is incorrectly given on the roll as £35 5s.
[13] Inventory of stock as in I 16 and I 17, excepting only the foals of which there were now 2 rather than 5.
[14] MS: 'pull' et pull''.
[15] This is the sum of the abbot's rental income by term as in I 16 and I 17, despite the small fluctuations and errors that occurred in the accounts.

I 19 States of the abbot's manors and portions at the conclusion of the audit of accounts for the year ending on 28 September 1388

A parchment roll of two membranes, sewn Chancery fashion with white thread in a tight oversew. Membrane 1 is 218 mm wide; membrane 2 is 231 mm wide. Both membranes are laid out with three vertical folds, for the centre and for the left and right margins. Membrane 1 tapers at the top. The roll is a fair copy, written down the recto and then back up the dorse. Some words and phrases on the right-hand side of the recto are now illegible owing to water-staining. Writing on the outside of the roll, at the top, is also now illegible.[1]

WAM 6165

[*Mem. 1 recto*] States of the lands and portions of William by the grace of God abbot of Westminster at the audit of the account of his ministers at 28 September 1388

Islip [Rents as in I 7: £31 6s. 11d.] Cash liveries: £80 ..... 3½d.[2] Valor, including wool valued at £7 11s.[3] and wood at £32 16s. 11d.: £103. Arrears: of William Dolle, the reeve .....[4] Remaining at the audit: 10 qr. pulse; 24 oxen, 1 ram, 236 wethers, 16 ewes, 13 hoggs and gimmers, ..., 1 boar, 4 sows, 30 pigs, 30 young pigs, 21 piglets, 30 capons, 1 gander, 7 breeding geese, 2 cocks, 11 hens and ..... white swans.

Sutton-under-Brailes [Rents as in I 6: £17 18s. 10d.][5] Cash liveries: £18 0s. 8d. Arrears: of Thomas Hurry, the reeve there, nothing. Valor: £19 10s. Remaining at the audit: 4 mares, 9 oxen, 1 young bullock, 2 boars, 1 sow, 15 .....[6] breeding geese, 1 cock, 6 hens, 11 capons, 48 cartloads of hay.

Todenham [Rents as in I 5: £15 6s. 2½d.][7] Cash liveries: £16 18s. 2d. Arrears: of William Sponge,[8] £1 18s. 4¼d; of Robert Bryan, rent-collector, £2 13s. 4d.; of William Mede, the present bailiff, 13s. 4d. Valor, including wool valued at £10 16s. 4d.:[9] £26. Remaining at the audit: 3 cart-horses, 15 oxen,

[1] Extant ministers' accounts: Hyde, WAM 27097; Staines, WAM 16934.

[2] MS damaged. The accounts of the steward and clerk of the abbot's household record the receipt of £84 10s. from the reeve of Islip in 1387–8 (WAM 24536*, 24537).

[3] The net wool crop at Islip this year, 251 fleeces, weighing 1 sack 3 st. 6 lb., was sent to the collecting centre at Todenham (GRO, D1099/M30/18). See also n. 9 below.

[4] MS: no cash sum is entered.

[5] MS: total obscured by stain.

[6] MS: the next 60 mm are illegible.

[7] MS: total partly obscured by stain—'xv li. .....'

[8] Bailiff 1376–85.

[9] The net wool crop at Todenham this year consisted of 407 fleeces, weighing 1 sack 2 st. With

1 cow, 1 bull, 4 young bullocks, 3 mares, 1 sow, 1 boar, 1 young sow, ... 7 piglets, 26 capons, 1 cock, 9 hens, 1 gander, 3 breeding geese, 6 goslings, 44 cartloads of hay .... 3 gallons [of tar].[10]

Bourton-on-the-Hill [Rents as in I 7: £9 2s. 4½d.][11] Cash liveries: £12 16s. 6d. Arrears: of Robert Wroxton', the former rent-collector, 14s. 8d.;[12] of Richard Alberd, £1 10s. 9½d; of Walter Parham, £3 0s. 8d.; of Gilbert, the bailiff,[13] £1. Valor, including wool valued at £8 15s. 8d.:[14] £17 6s. Remaining at the audit: 4 bus. pulse; 9 oxen, 4 cart-horses, 2 cows, 4 young bullocks, 3 heifers, 1 calf, 2 sows, 12 pigs, 8 piglets, 2 qr. 1 bus. of burned lime (*calceti adusti*), 1 brass pot weighing 14 lb.[15]

Pershore [Rents as in I 6: £32 19s.] Cash liveries: £61 14s. 4d. Arrears: of John Glyn, 10s.; of William Wychford, £1 14s. 11d.; of William Sperhauk, £1 3s. 11½d.; of William Ball', 13s. 4d.; of John Child', £1; of William Osbarn', 15s., of Richard Fortheye, 17s. 4½d. Valor, including the sale of wood and wool valued at £3 16s. 10d.[16] Remaining at the audit: 5 cart-horses, 1 horse for the mill, 12 oxen, 3 cows, 1 bull, 4 calves, 1 boar, 3 sows, 2 pigs, 32 piglets, 4 rams, 8 wethers, 140 ewes, 14 hoggs and gimmers, 101 lambs, 1 gander, 3 breeding geese, 15 goslings, 1 tawed horse hide, 16 capons, 1 cock, 5 hens, 28 cartloads of hay.

Pensham [Rents as in I 5: £26 4s. 4d.][17] Cash liveries: £27 6s. 4d. Arrears: none. Valor: £26. Remaining at the audit in the hands of William Sperhauk, the lessee: 3 qr. 6 bus. wheat, 16 qr. 3 bus. rye, 8 qr. 1½ bus. pulse, 13 qr. 6 bus. barley, 20 qr. dredge; 1 horse, 1 mare, 1 foal, 7 oxen, 12 cows,

---

wool from Bourton-on-the-Hill and Pershore, in addition to that from Islip, 1,095 fleeces, weighing 4 sacks 11 st. 13lb., were collected this year. John Rogers, the stockman, alias sheep-reeve, now in charge of the collection of wool, kept 4 st. The rest, consisting of 4 sacks 6 st., he sent to the steward of the abbot's household at Westminster (GRO, D1099/M30/18; WAM 24537).

[10] The inventory omits sheep, now the responsibility of the stockman. On or about 28 September 1388, the following were in his charge at Todenham: 2 rams, 79 wethers, 180 ewes, 164 hoggs and 108 lambs (GRO, D1099/M30/18).

[11] MS: total obscured by stain.

[12] Wroxton probably held the office in 1383–5, or in one or other of these years.

[13] Gilbert Whyte.

[14] 296 fleeces, weighing 17 todds, were sent from Bourton-on-the-Hill to the collecting centre at Todenham this year (GRO, D1099/M30/18).

[15] In December 1387, 331 wethers were sent by the bailiff of Bourton-on-the Hill to the stockman and, later in the year, a further 74 (GRO, D1099/M30/18).

[16] 143 fleeces, weighing 7 todds 1 clove (14½ st.) were sent from Pershore to the collecting centre at Todenham this year (GRO, D1099/M30/18).

[17] However, the sum total given in the MS is £35 4s. 4d.

6 heifers, 2 bullocks 1 bull calf, 1 gander, 2 breeding geese, 12 capons, 1 cock and 6 hens.[18]

Hardwicke in Elmstone Hardwicke [Rents as in I 7: £22 17s. 8½d.] Cash liveries: £32 14s. 3d. Arrears: of William Gilberd' and John atte Stok', 18s. 2d.;[19] of the lessee of the manor, £2, which he delivered to Alexander Besford as agreed (*ut dicit*).[20] Valor: £32. Remaining in the lessee's hands: 29 qr. 6½ bus. wheat, 27 qr. 2½ bus. peas, 12 qr. barley, 4½ qr. oats; 4 cart-horses, 16 oxen, 1 gander, 4 breeding geese, 2 cocks, 10 hens, 21 capons and 14 carts of hay.[21]

Deerhurst [Rents as in I 6: £29 17s. 6d.] Arrears: of Richard Broun and Richard Heope, £1 5s. 11¼d.;[22] of John Halle, £12 13s. 8¼d. Valor: £37

Chaceley [Rents as in I 5: £5 0s. 8d.] Cash liveries: £14 8s. Arrears: of John Hathemare, £2; of Nicholas Philipp, £5 9s.[23] Valor: £13 14s. Remaining in the lessee's hands: 16 qr. 4 bus. 1 p. wheat, 8 qr. 5 bus. rye, 13 qr. 4 bus. 1 p. peas, 14 qr. 3 bus. barley, 3 qr. dredge, 7 qr. 5 bus. oats; 2 cart-horses, 9 oxen, 1 bull, 20 cows, 1 sow, 15 young pigs, 1 gander, 3 breeding geese, 12 capons, 1 cock and 5 hens.[24]

Longdon [Rents as in I 5: £15] Cash liveries: £13 16s. 2d. Arrears: of William Reeve, rent-collector, £1 15s. 1½d.; of Hugh atte Hegge, lessee, £13 17s. 3d., of which £5 has been delivered to Alexander Besford in payment for 21 farm animals (*bestiarum*) as agreed. Valor: £17

[*Mem. 2 recto*] *Castlemorton* [Rents as in I 14: £27 17s. 10d.] Cash liveries: £26 10s. 8d. Arrears: of Adam Pal, 18s. 8d., of which 10s. has been delivered to Alexander Besford; of Br. John Lakyngh', 9s.;[25] of the lessee of the manor, £3; of Henry Ode, £3 16s. 8d. Valor: £29 8s.

[18] As in the inventory of corn and stock in I 9.
[19] The two names are bracketed together in the MS; both men were rent-collectors.
[20] Steward of the Western Parts, 28 September 1387–*c*.25 March 1400. This payment to Besford and that mentioned below, at Castlemorton, probably represent instalments of his annual fee of £4 (WAM 24410–11, 24537).
[21] As in the inventory of corn and stock in I 9.
[22] The two names are bracketed, and both men were probably rent-collectors.
[23] For Hathemare and Philipp, see I 16.
[24] Inventory of corn and stock as in I 18, but only 7 qr. 5 bus. oats (rather than 6 bus.) are recorded this year.
[25] John Lakyngheth was monk-bailiff for part of this year (WAM 24537), but his involvement in affairs at Castlemorton may be explained by his role as keeper of the temporalities in the vacancy between the death of Nicholas Litlyngton on 29 November 1386 and the delivery of these to William Colchester on 11 September 1387 (WAM 5446).

Pinvin [Rents as in I 5: £33 16s. 3d.] Cash liveries: £35 16s. 0½d. Arrears: of William Rayel, £1 13s. 6d.; of Ralph Pendefen, £1 0s. 2½d. Valor: £36 10s.
Defford Hundred Cash liveries: 11s. 10d. Arrears: of John Birlyngham, £2 11s. 5d.; of Robert Berald, £1 18s.; of William Scheperd, 6s. 6d.[26] Valor: 18s. 4d.
Wick Hundred Cash liveries: 11s. 10d.[27] Arrears: of William Hanow, £1 6s. 9d., of Walter Clerk, 4s. 8d.[28] Valor: £1 3s. 9d.
Pinvin Hundred Cash liveries: 19s. Arrears: of William Hanow, 12s. 10d.
Portmoot of Pershore Cash liveries: £3 11s. 8d. Arrears: of John Parker, £1. Valor: £3 11s. 8d.

Denham [Rents as in I 9: £25 8s. 5½d.][29] Cash liveries: £36 10s. 4¾d.[30] Arrears: of Thomas Durdent, £22 12s. 10¼d.[31] Valor, with wool valued at £1 18s. 9d. and hay used in the abbot's household, and after deduction of the reprises noted above: £11.[32] Remaining at the audit: an estimated 1 qr. of wheat in sheaves, 12 qr. rye in sheaves, 40 qr. barley malt, 26 qr. rye in sheaves; 6 cart-horses, 5 stots, 20 oxen, 2 bulls, 38 cows, 5 bullocks, 7 calves, 2 rams, 85 wethers, 58 ewes, 16 young sheep, 13 lambs, 4 boars, 3 sows, 10 pigs, 17 young pigs, 20 piglets, 2 ganders, 5 breeding geese, 21 goslings, 42 capons, 1 cock, 12 hens, 74 cartloads of hay.

Laleham [Rents as in I 9: £16 10s. 2¼d.] Cash liveries: £19 1s. 4½d. Arrears: none. Valor, with wool valued at £1 5s. 6d.: £24. Remaining at the audit: 16 qr. rye; 3 horses, 7 mares, 6 foals, 12 oxen, 2 sows, 1 boar, 20 pigs, 11 young pigs, 2 rams, 108 wethers, 51 ewes, 19 lambs, 5 breeding swans, 6 cygnets, 1 gander, 3 breeding geese, 15 capons, 1 cock, 6 hens, 32 cartloads of hay.

Staines [Rents as in I 14: £28 10s. 3¼d.] Cash liveries: £31 10s. Arrears: of Alexander Tresour, £1 14s. 4d. Valor: £36 10s.

[26] MS: the three names in this entry are bracketed together.
[27] MS: the sum is preceded by 'xliiij s. vj d. ob.', which has been struck out.
[28] MS: the two names in this entry are bracketed together.
[29] MS: the total given here is £25 8s. 5d.
[30] MS: the sum is preceded by 'xxix li. xxij d. qua.', which has been struck out.
[31] Durdent was bailiff of Denham 1385–7 and in the first few months of 1387–8 (WAM 3409, 24536, 24536*).
[32] 150 fleeces were sent from Denham to the steward of the abbot's household at Westminster this year for sale. With fleeces from Pyrford (251), Laleham (146) and Ebury (204), the total number of fleeces sent to the steward from the wool-producing manors in the Eastern Parts this year was 751. With 1,095 fleeces from manors in the Western Parts, the total number received by the steward of the household was 1,846. Of these, 1,041, weighing 4 sacks, were sold for £28 8s. 4d. (WAM 24537–8).

Yeoveney [Rents as in I 18: £21] Cash liveries: £21. Valor: £21 4s. Remaining in the lessee's hands: 7 mares, 2 foals, 1 bull, 10 oxen, 15 cows, 3 sows, 5 young pigs, 7 piglets, 1 gander, 3 breeding geese, 1 cock, 6 hens.[33]

Pyrford [Rents as in I 5: £35 5s. 5½d.] Cash liveries: £35 2s. 4d. Arrears: of William Mullehurst, £2 10s. 3d.[34] Valor, with wool valued at £1 10s., wood delivered to Westminster and valued at £9 16s. 4d., and hay valued at £5 15s.: £56. Remaining at the audit: 18 qr. of rye in sheaves and 3 qr. in the granary, 59 cartloads of hay; 3 mares, 4 foals, 6 oxen, 2 rams, 192 wethers, 80 ewes, 21 lambs, 5 foals from Laleham.

Ebury [Rents as in I 9: £13 3s.] Cash liveries: £39 4s. Arrears: of William Huller, £1.[35] Valor, with wool valued at £3 8s. and hay consumed in the abbot's household and valued at £6 13s. 4d.: £43. Remaining at the audit: 14 qr. of rye in sheaves, 11 qr. 5 bus. of barley at Westminster; 3 cart-horses, 5 mares, 1 colt (*pull' mas'*), 12 oxen, 2 bulls, 55 cows, 1 sow, 1 boar, 6 piglets, 4 rams, 76 wethers, 129 ewes, 60 lambs, 3 woolfells, 1 lambskin, 2 breeding swans, 3 cygnets, 1 gander, 3 breeding geese, 17 goslings, 2 capons, 1 cock, 6 hens, 1 peacock, 3 peahens, 43 cartloads of hay, 1,450 bundles of reeds (*garbe arundinarum*).

[Totals]
Sum of cash liveries: £569 7s. 11¼d. Sum of arrears: £104 13s. 7½d. Sum of valors: £617 16s. 1d.
[*Mem. 2 dorse*][36] Horses and affers, 58; foals and colts,[37] 19. Sum of this category: 77.
Oxen and bullocks, 168; bulls, 9; cows and heifers, 158; young bullocks and calves, 16. Sum of this category: 351.
Rams, 16; wethers, 1,084; ewes, 654; lambs and young sheep, 533. Sum of this category: 2,287.
Boars, 11; sows, 18; pigs, 95; young pigs and piglets, 175. Sum of this category: 299.
Sum of rents, by term: Michaelmas, £139 15s. 5½d.; Christmas, £84 3s. 2d.; Annunciation, £103 0s. 11d.; nativity of St John the Baptist, £85 18s. 7½d. Sum total of rents: £412 18s. 2d.[38]

[33] Inventory of stock as in I 16 and I 17.
[34] Mullehurst was reeve 1382–6 (WAM 27426–7).
[35] Huller, bailiff of Ebury, died in the course of the year and was briefly succeeded by Janyn, his widow.
[36] The text is now written up the dorse from the foot of the roll.
[37] MS: 'pull' et pull''.
[38] This sum of the abbot's rental income by term is the same as in I 16, I 17 and I 18, despite the small fluctuations and errors that occurred in the accounts.

I 20 States of the abbot's manors and portions in the Western Parts at the conclusion of the audit of accounts for the year ending on 28 September 1393

A roll made up of two sheets of paper, 150 mm wide, sewn Chancery fashion with white thread, in long loops. Both papers were probably laid out with a vertical fold up the centre and possibly one for the left margin. The dorse of both sheets is blank. The roll is a fair copy, laid out in the same manner as the parchment rolls, but the use of paper instead of parchment suggests that the document was made for an official whose needs were immediate rather than long-term and for whom the details of the abbot's rental income, which are here reduced to an annual total, were not of the first importance. The date of the document is established by the entries of the *valor* for, respectively, the manors of Bourton-on-the-Hill and Pensham, which concur with those in the ministers' accounts for these manors for the year 1392–3. Both sheets of paper have been damaged, the document lacks a heading and is incomplete at the foot.[1]

WAM 9304

[*Mem. 1 recto*] *Islip* Rents of assize and leasehold rents: £39 15s. 3d. Cash liveries: £47 16s. 3d. Arrears: none. Valor: £66. Remaining at the audit: 20 qr. wheat, 11 qr. 4 bus. barley malt; 6 cart-horses, 27 oxen, 1 ram, 217 wethers, 16 ewes, 10 sheep in their second year, 16 lambs, 2 boars, 4 sows, 36 pigs, 24 piglets, 30 capons, 1 gander, 7 breeding geese, 8 goslings, 42 cartloads of hay and, in addition, wooden vessels (*ultra staurum vasarum lignearum*).

Sutton-under-Brailes Rents of assize and leasehold rents: £17 7s. 1½d. Cash liveries: £22 10s. 11d. Arrears: of Peter Baron, 16s.[2] Valor, excluding wool: £21 16s. Remaining at the audit: 1 mare, 1 cock, 6 hens, 12 capons, 18 cartloads of hay.

Todenham Rents of assize, leasehold rents and tenements in the abbot's hands: £20 4s. 7½d.[3] Arrears: of Henry Hakkes and Philip Taylor, £2 11s.;[4] of Roger Vernay, 10s.;[5] of Robert Bryan, 6s. 8d.; of Richard Morhouse, £2

[1] Extant ministers' accounts: Birlingham, WAM 22393; Bourton-on-the-Hill, WAM 8311; Pensham, WAM 22240; and Pinvin, WAM 22310.

[2] Probably reeve of Sutton-under-Brailes, 1392–5 (GRO, D1009/M31/51); for his earlier term of office, I 15.

[3] The reference, unique in this document, to vacant tenements or holdings as a source of income is corroborated by annual, piecemeal, sales of arable and meadow belonging to vacant holdings in this manor in the years around 1390 (GRO, D1099/M30/9–10).

[4] Hakkes and Taylor, whose names are bracketed together in the MS, were probably rent-collectors at Todenham.

[5] Vernay, said to be of *Lemyngton* in Todenham was lessee of the site of the manor and the demesne at Todenham, 1391–1400 (LNQ, f. lxix; GRO, D1099/M30/21–3).

10s. 11d.[6] Valor, excluding wool: £21 3s. 3d. Remaining in the hands of the lessee: 30 qr. 7½ bus. wheat, 10 qr. 2½ bus. peas, 62 qr. 7 bus. 1 p. barley; 3 cart-horses, 1 bull, 15 oxen, 1 cow, 1 gander, 3 breeding geese, 1 cock, 6 hens.

Bourton-on-the-Hill Rents of assize and leasehold rents: £18 11s. 2¼d. Cash liveries: £23 17s. 1d. Arrears: of Robert Wroxton', 14s. 8d.; of John Mawnsel, £1 7s. 9d.; of Richard Alberd, £10 9s. 5d.[7] Valor, excluding wool: £38 18s. Remaining at the audit: 30 qr. 7½ bus. wheat, 21 qr. 6 bus. 1 p. peas, 61 qr. 7 bus. barley, 15 qr. 3 bus. 3 p. oats; 5 cart-horses, 12 oxen, 3 cows, 2 sows, 10 young pigs.

Pershore Rents of assize and leasehold rents: £61. Cash liveries: £61 14s. 5d. Arrears: of Richard Hale, £3 19s. 4½d.;[8] of William Ball, 6s. 8d.; of Alexander Besford, £2 16s. 8d.; of John Baron', 3s. 8d.[9] Valor: £94 2s. 5¼d. Remaining at the audit: 5 qr. 1 bus. 1 p. wheat, 12 qr. 3 bus. rye, 41 qr. 2 bus. barley; 3 cart-horses, 10 oxen, 2 sows, 1 horse for the mill, 1 gander, 3 breeding geese, 12 cartloads of hay, 1 cow, 4 lambs.

Pensham Rents of assize and leasehold rents: £23 17s. 8d. Cash liveries: £28 16s. 8d. Arrears: of William Sperhauk, £1.[10] Valor: £25 10s.

[*Mem. 2 recto*] *Pinvin* Rents of assize and leasehold rents: £36 9s. 9½d. Cash liveries: £39 4s. 4d. Arrears: of Richard Sell, 10s. 4d.; of Henry Warde, 9¾d.;[11] of Richard Pygon, 5s.[12] Valor: £39 19s.

Birlingham[13] [Rents of assize] and leasehold rents: £20 0s. 10½d. Cash liveries: £14 10s. 3d. Arrears: none. Valor: £17 4s. Remaining .....

[6] Bryan was rent-collector here in 1384–8 (GRO, D1099/M30/17; I 19); and Morhouse was bailiff here 1 December 1390–28 September 1391 (WAM 25981).
[7] For Wroxton' and Alberd, see above I 17–19; Mawnsell may have succeeded Wroxton' as rent-collector in the mid-1380s.
[8] Lessee of the demesne at Pinvin, with a life-interest; he continued here until 1398–9 (WAM 22310, 22316).
[9] Baron is now elusive; for Ball and Besford, see I 17–19.
[10] Lessee of the demesne at Pensham.
[11] Lessee, with others, of a grange and cattleshed at Pinvin, 1387–96 (WAM 22309).
[12] Currently rent-collector at Pinvin (WAM 22310).
[13] For the acquisition in 1388 of this manor, of which the reversion had been purchased by the Abbey in 1378, see Harvey, *Estates*, p. 421, no. 29.

Deerhurst Rents of assize and leasehold rents: £30 1s. 1¾d. Cash liveries: £54 12s. Arrears: of John Halle, £6 15s. 5¾d.;[14] of Walter Hawrik', £6 3s. 7¾d. Valor: £37 4s.

Hardwicke in Elmstone Hardwicke [Rents of assize and leasehold rents]: £34 10s. 2d. Cash liveries: £18 5s. 6d. Arrears: of Richard Stoke, 5s. Valor: £35 2s.

Longdon [Rents of assize and leasehold rents] .....

[14] Rent-collector.

I 21 States of the abbot's manors and portions in the Eastern Parts at the conclusion of the audit of accounts for the year ending on 28 September 1397

A parchment roll of two membranes, 175 mm wide, sewn Chancery fashion with white thread in a tight oversew. Membrane 1 was laid out with a single vertical fold to create a left margin; there are no folds for the layout of membrane 2. The roll is incomplete and there are many blanks: these allow us to follow the roll's compilation—the roll was written in a single hand, and the variations in the ink suggest the following order. The first stage was for the roll to be laid out with the headings for each manor; then the rents of assize and leasehold rents were written in; then the arrears, the *valor* and remaining corn and stock were entered.[1]

WAM 6139

[*Mem. 1 recto*] States of the manors of Dom. William Colchester, Lord Abbot of Westminster ..... [28 September] 1397

[*Ebury*] Rents of assize £3 12s. 3½d. Leasehold rents: £4 17s. 10½d. Arrears: of Henry Kyrkeby,[2] 17s; of Janyn,[3] £13 11s. 10½d; of Jordemayn,[4] £31 11s. 8d.; of Rubbe,[5] £5 1s. 3d.; of John Huller,[6] 8s. 2½d. Cash liveries: £33 18s. Valor, excluding wool:[7] £46 11s. 0½d. Remaining at the audit: 3 cart-horses, 4 mares, 2 young foals, 12 oxen, 2 bulls, 70 cows, 2 boars, 2 sows, 3 rams, 37 wethers, 120 ewes, 48 young sheep, 72 lambs, 208 coarse fleeces (*vellera lane grosse*), 72 lambs' fleeces, 2 nesting swans, 1 cygnet, 1 gander, 3 breeding geese, 20 goslings, 1 cock, 6 hens, 12 capons and 36 cartloads of hay.

Laleham Rents of assize: £6 2s. 1¼d. Leasehold rents: £25 3s. 3d. Arrears: of Richard Longe,[8] 15s. 10d.; of Tylnye,[9] £1 10s.; of William, rent-collector,[10]

[1] Extant ministers' accounts: Ebury, WAM 26949; Laleham, WAM 27161.

[2] Bailiff 17 April 1389–9 February 1390 (WAM 26941–3).

[3] Alias Joan, widow of William Huller, bailiff, who died in the course of the year 1387–8. Joan succeeded to his duties if not to his title as bailiff, and performed them until 14 April 1389 (WAM 26939–40).

[4] Farmer of the demesne vaccary 1393–4 (WAM 26047).

[5] Richard Rubbe, farmer of the demesne vaccary 1388–93 (WAM 26942, 26948–50).

[6] Bailiff, 28 September 1395–1407; also farmer of the demesne 1399–1407 (WAM 26948–54).

[7] The net wool crop at Ebury this year consisted of 208 fleeces of *lana grossa* and 77 lambs' fleeces; and 67 woolfells represented the casualities of a murrain. The woolfells were sold locally. In 1397–8, the lambs' fleeces were sold locally and the *lana grossa* delivered to Henry Norton at Westminster (WAM 26948–50).

[8] Farmer of the demesne 1388–99 (WAM 16886–9).

[9] In 1400, mentioned as farmer of Billet's manor in Laleham (WAM 27159, 24545).

[10] William Fry, rent-collector at Laleham 1396–8 (WAM 27161).

£3 19s.; of William French, shepherd,[11] £2 5s.; of Nicholas Jakes, £2 7s. 0¼d.; of William Jakes,[12] £2 2s. Cash liveries: £31 11s. 4d. Valor: £33 12s. 8½d. Remaining [at the audit]: 3 qr. wheat, 3 qr. 3 bus. rye, 4 qr. 2 bus. peas, 28 qr. 5 bus. barley, 4 qr. dredge, 6 qr. 3 bus. oats; 2 cart-horses, 15 oxen, 2 boars, 1 sow, 22 young pigs, 4 piglets, 2 cartloads of hay, 2 rams, 122 wethers, 55 ewes, 30 young sheep, 20 lambs, 5 breeding swans, 6 white swans, 4 cygnets, 171 fleeces, 20 lambs' fleeces and 23 woolfells.[13]

Pyrford Rents of assize: £27 15s. 11½d. Leasehold rents: £5 2s. 3½d. Arrears: of William Mulhurst,[14] 13s.; of Richard Baker, 12s.; of Walter Sponge,[15] £1 6s. 2½d.; of John Webbeschot, 6s. 3d. Cash liveries: £32 12s. 7½d. Valor: £36 10s. Remaining at the audit: 2 stots, 1 young foal, 7 oxen, 1 bull, 1 cow, 2 calves, 5 rams, 216 wethers, 40 ewes, 21 young sheep, 12 lambs, 253 fleeces, 6 ploughshares, 3 fallow deer (*dam'*) .....,[16] 250 pieces of talwood, 7,200 faggots at Ham*me*,[17] 40 cartloads of hay.

Denham Rents of assize: £16 2s. 6d. Leasehold rents and customary works (*firme cum operibus*):[18] £29 19s. 3d. Arrears: of the lessee of the cows, for the arrears of the previous year, £1 8s. 9d.;[19] of Wawberd' and Sawer,[20] for arrears of the previous year, £1 2s. 6d.; of William Donsford', collector of the perquisites of courts, £2 1s. 4d.; of the rector, lately lessee of the demesne arable, £5;[21] of Nicholas, the present accountant,[22] £4. Cash liveries: £54 3s. 5d. Valor, excluding wool: £24 0s. 4d. Remaining at the audit: 169 qr. 1 bus. wheat, 8 qr. 2 bus. maslin, 94 qr. 4 bus. barley and

[11] Probably at one time the abbot's stockman for sheep; but the failure of his arrears to change in this year or the next may signify that his service was over (WAM 26161–3; I 23).

[12] Rent-collector 1395–6 (WAM 27160).

[13] The wool crop of the current year, stored at Laleham until 1397–8, but then probably sent to Westminster for sale. The woolfells mentioned above were sold locally in the same year (WAM 27162).

[14] Reeve 1382–6.

[15] Bailiff 1391–2.

[16] 20 mm repaired by stitching follow and, in consequence, an entry may have been lost.

[17] Woodham in Pyrford.

[18] i.e. the rents for contractual tenancies, with the money rents in lieu of labour services which were no longer performed. In 1395–6 the abbot received £1 3s. 5½d. for the so-called sales of works.

[19] The entry relates to the previous farmer of the vaccary, and it shows that he had discharged the greater part of a debt of £4 18s. 9d. in the course of the current year (WAM 3410).

[20] Walter Wauberd' and Thomas Sawer.

[21] The rector, who is named in 1390 as John Draxfield, leased the major part of the demesne arable in a crop-sharing agreement with the abbot, or cash in lieu (WAM 3409). The arrears of £5 charged above to the rector probably dated from 1396–7; if so, they suggest that the cash option operated in this year.

[22] Nicholas Stilman, bailiff 1387–1402 (WAM 3409–10, 3012–13, 24536*, 24539, 24546).

dredge, 20 qr. oats; 1 stot,[23] 3 cart-horses, 6 stots, 15 oxen, 33 cartloads of hay, 2 bulls, 33 cows, 227 fleeces, 16 breeding swans, 12 white swans, 7 cygnets, 2 ganders, 4 breeding geese, 6 capons, 1 cock, 12 hens.

Yeoveney The manor is leased for £21 p.a. to be paid in equal instalments at the four terms and for 12 capons payable at Easter. Valor: £21 4s. Remaining: as appears in the indenture made between the lord and John Dorman, the lessee.[24]

[*Mem. 2 recto*] *Staines* Rents of assize .....[25] Leasehold rents ..... Arrears: of Alexander Tresor' .....

Aldenham rectory Remaining at the audit: 1 sow, 11 pigs, 1 wether, 1 cock, 3 hens, 20 sheepskins; and an estimated 30 qr. of wheat in sheaves.

[Totals]
Sum of rents of assize and leasehold rents .....[26] Sum of arrears ..... Sum of cash liveries ..... Sum of valors .....
Horses and stots, 24; bulls, 6; oxen, 49; cows, 106; boars, 4; sows, 4; small pigs, 37.
Rams, 12; wethers, 412; ewes, 295; young sheep, 194.
Sum of these categories: 1,122.

[23] A word written above 'stottus' in the MS at this point may be 'morina' (murrain).
[24] A reference to the inventory of stock in Dorman's lease, for which see I 14, I 16–18.
[25] MS: blank space here and in the following entries.
[26] MS: blank space here and in the following entries.

I 22 States of the abbot's manors and portions at the conclusion of the audit of accounts for the year ending on 28 September 1398

A parchment roll of two membranes, 122 mm wide, sewn Chancery fashion with white thread in a tight oversew. Membrane 1 is laid out with three vertical folds, for the centre and for the left and right margins; membrane 2 probably had none. The roll is almost entirely a fair copy largely written in a single operation, but with two small additions in a second hand. There is a filing slit at the head of membrane 1. The dorse of membrane 1 is blank; membrane 2 is endorsed at the foot: 'Dogettus abbatis Westm' anno regni regis Ricardi xxij^{to}' in a late fourteenth- or early fifteenth-century hand.[1]

WAM 6159

[*Mem. 1 recto*] States of the [manors] of the venerable father Dom. William Colchester by divine permission abbot [of Westminster, 28 September] 1398

Ebury Termly rents: £8 10s. 2d. Cash liveries: £31 17s. 9½d. Arrears:[2] of Henry Kyrkeby, 17s.; of Janyn, lately bailiff, £22 14s. 10½d.; of Joredmayn, lately lessee of the vaccary, £31 11s. 8d.; of Rubbe, £7 10s. 5¾d.; of John Huller, bailiff, £3. Valor, excluding hay and wool: £25 14s. 0¾d.[3] Remaining at the audit: 4 cart-horses, 4 mares, 3 foals, 12 oxen, 1 bullock, 2 bulls, 67 cows, 3 boars, 2 sows, 4 rams, 33 wethers, 100 ewes, 58 young sheep, 96 lambs, 2 breeding swans, 2 cygnets, 1 gander, 3 breeding geese, 25 goslings, 1 cock, 6 hens, 10 capons, 72 cartloads of hay.

Denham Termly rents: £38 12s. 4d. Cash liveries: £39 16s. Arrears:[4] of Wauberd and Sawer, lately rent-collectors, £1 2s. 6d.; of Donsford', £1 6s. 8d.; of the rector of Denham, lately lessee of the arable demesne, £5; of the lessee of the vaccary, £1 11s. 10d;[5] of the official rendering account, £3. Valor £43 15s. Remaining at the audit: 203 qr. 1 bus. wheat, 8 qr. 2 bus. maslin, 100 qr. 4 bus. barley, 27 shocks,[6] 20 qr. oats; 1 brood mare (*equa*), 1 male foal (*pull' mas'*), 4 cart-horses, 5 stots, 16 oxen, 2 bulls, 34 cows,

[1] Extant ministers' accounts: Bourton-on-the-Hill, WAM 8317; Deerhurst, WAM 8453; Ebury, WAM 26950; Laleham, WAM 27162; Pinvin, WAM 22315; Sutton-under-Brailes, GRO, D1099/M31/53.

[2] For the individuals listed here, see I 21.

[3] 51 cartloads of hay were delivered to the abbot's household this year. The net wool crop probably consisted of 230 fleeces of *lana grossa* and 96 lambs' fleeces (WAM 26950).

[4] For those mentioned by name or office in this panel, other than the lessee of the vaccary, see I 21.

[5] Named as Gore in I 23.

[6] The shocks probably represent an agreed amount of mixed corn selected for tithe in the field and then collected on behalf of the rector, or delivered to him; see the reference in 1396 to 27 *schokkes* of barley and dredge delivered to the rector (WAM 3412).

1 bullock, 4 rams, 31 wethers, 106 ewes, 98 young sheep, 122 lambs, 16 breeding swans, 12 white swans, ...[7] cygnets of this year's issue, 2 ganders, 3 breeding geese, 1 cock, 12 hens, 43 cartloads of hay.

Staines Termly rents: £10 10s. 6d. Cash liveries: £36 1s. 4d. Arrears: none. Valor: £38 8s. 11d.

Laleham Termly rents: £31 13s. 7d. Cash liveries: £28 1s. 8d. Arrears: of Richard Longe,[8] £2 13s. 0½d.; of Tylneye, for Michaelmas term 1397, £1 10s.;[9] of William French, the shepherd, £2 5s.; of Nicholas Jakes, lately rent-collector, £2 7s. 11¼d; of William Jakes, rent-collector, £2 2s.; of William Frye, the minister accounting, £4 10s. Valor: £31 9s. 8d.[10] Remaining at the audit:[11] 4 qr. wheat, 3 qr. 3 bus. rye, 4 qr. 2 bus. peas, 28 qr. 5 bus. barley, 4 qr. dredge, 6 qr. 3 bus. oats; 3 cart-horses, 14 oxen, 2 boars, 1 sow, 22 young pigs, 4 piglets.

Yeoveney Leased for 12 capons and £21 p.a. Valor: £21 4s.

Pyrford Termly rents: £35 10s. 0¾d. Arrears: of Walter Sponge, £1 6s. 2d.; of William Mulhurst, 13s.; of Robert Hone, the official accounting,[12] £7 14s. 4¼d. Valor: £33 6s. 6½d. Remaining at the audit: 2 stots, 1 young filly (*pull' fe'*), 8 oxen, 1 bull, 2 cows, 2 calves, 5 rams, 195 wethers, 42 ewes, 14 young sheep, 70 lambs, 6 ploughshares, 4 fallow deer (*dam'*), 25 capons, 900 pieces of talwood, 1,500 faggots and 500 more in Alexander Tresour's keeping, 48 hurdles, 60 cartloads of hay.

[7] MS: blank space.

[8] Lessee of the demesne, 1388–99 (WAM 16886–9).

[9] That is, for the term ending on 29 September 1397. For Tylneye and for others mentioned in this panel, see I 21.

[10] The *valor* excludes 4 cygnets from the issues of the previous year (1396–7) and 9 from the issues of the current year (1397–8). It also excludes the wool crops of the 2 years: 171 fleeces of *lana grossa* and 20 lambs' fleeces from the previous year, and 191 fleeces of *lana grossa* from the current year (WAM 26171–2).

[11] The following inventory relates to corn and stock in the hands of the lessee of the arable demesne. The rent-collector's account shows that there were also at Laleham at the end of the year 1397–8 2 rams, 108 wethers, 70 ewes, 20 young sheep and 30 lambs (WAM 27162).

[12] Reeve 1397–1400 (WAM 27432–3). For Walter Sponge and Mulhurst, see I 21.

Islip Termly rents: £39 18s. 5d. Cash liveries: £47 17s. 2½d. Arrears: of John the chaplain,[13] £2 3s.; of Bastvill' and his wife, the rent-collectors, £3 8s. 4d., including £1 18s. in wages for Dolle's wife.[14] Valor, excluding wool: £61 1s. 10½d. Remaining at the audit: 5 cart-horses, 18 oxen, 1 boar, 2 sows, 20 pigs, 10 young pigs, 8 suckling piglets, 1 ram, 223 wethers, 22 ewes, 9 sheep in their second year, 20 lambs, 30 capons, 51 cartloads of hay.

Sutton-under-Brailes Termly rents: £17 7s. 1½d. Cash liveries: £19 15s. 9d. Arrears: of John Handes,[15] 8s.; of the official accounting,[16] 5s. 4d. Valor, excluding wool and hay:[17] £19 17s. 3d. Remaining at the audit: 2 wethers, 1 cock, 6 hens, 12 capons, 16 cartloads of hay.

Todenham Termly rents: £20 4s. 7½d. Cash liveries: £20 10s. 4d. Arrears: of Richard Morhouse, £2 15s. 11d.; of Roger Verney, £6 17s. 4d.; of Henry Colyn, 13s. 8d.[18] Valor: £16 7s. 4d.[19] Remaining at the audit: 4 cart-horses, 16 oxen, 2 bulls, 1 cow, 1 boar, 1 sow, 8 piglets, 2 rams, 127 wethers, 198 ewes, 121 lambs, 1 cock, 5 hens, 1 gander, 2 breeding geese, 80 cartloads of hay.

Bourton-on-the-Hill Termly rents: £18 11s. 2¼d. Cash liveries: £22 18s. 5½d. Arrears: none. Valor, excluding wool: £18 8s. 7d.[20] Remaining at the audit: 5 cart-horses, 9 oxen, 1 bull, 3 cows, 4 bullocks, 2 calves, 1 boar, 1 sow, 4 pigs, 4 young pigs, 531 wethers, 67 cartloads of hay.

[13] John Darby, chaplain serving St Edward the Confessor's chapel at Islip since 1380 and, from 1395–6, lessee of the site of the manor and the demesne at Islip, with a 12-year lease, but, in the event, for only a short period (WAM 14830–1).

[14] MS: 'Bastvill' et uxoris collectoris lxiij s. iij d. vadia xxxviij s. uxoris Doll'.' The words 'vadia xxxviij s. uxoris Doll'' are an insertion. The reference is, first, to Richard Basteville, reeve of Islip, 1390–4, and subsequently reeve and, with his wife's help, rent-collector, 1395–1405. But there is also a reference to the widow, who is not named, of William Dolle the younger, formerly reeve, but evidently rent-collector at the time of his recent death (WAM 14798–833).

[15] A tenant of the abbot at Sutton-under-Brailes, *c.*1400 (GRO, D1099/M31/53; WAM 25983).

[16] Robert Hurry, reeve.

[17] The net wool crop at Sutton-under-Brailes this year consisted of 152 fleeces weighing 17 st. 4 lb. (8 todds 18 lb.) and delivered to the collecting centre at Bourton-on-the-Hill. The hay taken into account will have included 6 cartloads of hay expended on horses belonging to the abbot's household on visits to Sutton-under-Brailes, and a further, unspecified quanity delivered to the household as a fictitious sale, for 2s. 1d. (GRO, D1099/M31/53).

[18] Rent-collector at Todenham, 1389–90, and possibly for a longer period (WAM 25978). For Morhous and Verney, see I 20.

[19] The *valor* probably excludes the net wool crop of 203 fleeces weighing 16 st. 13 lb. (i.e. 8 todds 13 lb.) sent this year from Todenham to the collecting centre at Bourton-on-the-Hill (WAM 8317).

[20] The net wool crop at Bourton-on-the-Hill this year consisted of 470 fleeces weighing 24 todds 24 lb. (1 sack 23 st. 10 lb.)

Pershore Termly rents: £61 3s. 8d. Cash liveries: £66 9s. Arrears: of John Mason',[21] £4; of the abbot of Pershore, 3s. 10d. Valor: £67 1s. 8d. Remaining at the audit: 5 qr. 1 bus. 1 p. wheat, 12 qr. 3 bus. rye, 41 qr. 2 bus. barley; 3 cart-horses, 10 oxen, 2 sows, 1 horse for the mill, 1 gander, 3 breeding geese, 1 cow, 4 lambs, 12 cartloads of hay.

Pensham Termly rents: £23 17s. 8d. Cash liveries: £27 10s. Arrears: of William Sperhauk,[22] 9s. Valor: £29 19s. Remaining: as appears in the indenture.[23]

Pinvin Termly rents: £36 9s. 9½d. Cash liveries: £36. [*Mem. 2 recto*] Arrears:[24] of Richard Selk', 10s. 4d.; of Henry Ward', 14s. 9¾d.; of Pygon', 5s.; of Richard Hale,[25] £5 16s. 8d.; of John Cole, lately rent-collector,[26] 7s. 9¼d.; of the minister accounting,[27] £1 10s. Valor: £39 4s. 4d.

Birlingham Termly rents: £20 0s. 10½d. Cash liveries: £19 16s. 0½d. Arrears: none. Valor: £18 16s. Remaining: 15 cartloads of hay.

Deerhurst Termly rents: £13 13s. 0¾d.[28] Cash liveries: £31 17s. 8d. Arrears: none. Valor: £30 10s. 9d.

Hardwicke in Elmstone Hardwicke Termly rents: £34 10s. 2d. Cash liveries: £36 6s. 3d. Valor: £35 6s. 4d. Arrears: none.

Longdon Termly rents: £15 2s. 9¾d. Cash liveries: £24 8s. Arrears: of Richard Webbe, 3s. 7½d. Valor: £25 9s. 7d.

[21] With John Vampage, lessee of the demesne at Pershore, for a term of 12 years beginning on 29 September 1391 (LNQ, f. lvii).

[22] Lessee of the demesne.

[23] A reference to the indenture of lease between the abbot and convent of Westminster and William Aleyn, lessee of the demesne at Pensham. Aleyn, reeve and rent-collector at Pensham, is also mentioned as lessee of the demesne there from 1398 (WAM 22243–7; GRO, D1099/M30/20).

[24] For those mentioned in the following panel, in addition to Hale and Cole, see I 20.

[25] Since 1392, lessee of the site of the manor and the demesne, with a life-interest, last mentioned in this capacity in 1398–9 (WAM 22310, 22316).

[26] Cole was reeve and rent-collector at Pinvin 1395–6 (WAM 22313).

[27] Thomas Irlond, reeve and rent-collector (WAM 22315).

[28] This figure represents rents of assize and contractual rents received by John Pecock, the abbot's collector of rents, when his account was closed on 28 September 1398. Before the clerk of the abbot's household, his receiver, closed his own account for the year, £22 4s. 4d. had been received from Pecock; and payments totalling £10 from John Halle, bailiff of the abbot's liberty in Gloucestershire and lessee of the demesne at Deerhurst, raised liveries of cash to the sum shown (WAM 8453, 24410).

Chaceley Termly rents: £16 3s. 3½d. Cash liveries: £14 10s. 8d. Arrears:[29] none. Valor: £13 18s. 10½d. Remaining at the audit: 9 qr. 4 bus. wheat, 13 qr. 2½ bus. rye, 5 qr. 3 bus. peas, 19 qr. 5½ bus. barley, 4 qr. 6 bus. oats; 1 horse, 1 mare, 9 oxen, 1 bull, 20 cows, 1 gander, 3 breeding geese, 12 capons.

Castlemorton Termly rents: £29 18s. 3¾d. Cash liveries: £22. Arrears: of John Lankyngh', £1 8s. 2½d.; Werkmon', £2 10s.; Adam Pal,[30] 15s. 7½d. Valor: £29 16s. 11d.

Forinsec bailiffs Cash liveries: £8 1s. 3d. Arrears: of William Scheperd,[31] 8s.; of John Aston and Browet,[32] 6s. 8d.; of Margaret Toney,[33] 3s. 8d.; of William Sperhauk,[34] £1 15s. 3d.

Sheep stockman Cash liveries, £6 16s. 8d. Valor: £6 16s. 8d. Arrears: of John Rogers,[35] £1 18s. 1½d.

Bailiff of the liberty in Gloucestershire[36] Cash liveries: £8 16s. 8d. Valor: £8 16s. 8d.

Bailiff of the liberty in Westminster Account not yet rendered. Arrears: of Richard Fortheye, the abbot's receiver, £9 14s. 5½d.

Aldenham The rector has not yet rendered account.[37]

[Totals]
Sum of rents: £502 16s. 4¾d. Sum of cash liveries: £594 0s. 0½d. Sum of arrears: £150 11s. 10¼d. Sum of valors, excepting wool and wood:[38] £615 11s. 11½d.

[29] The heading 'Arreragia' is in a second hand.
[30] Pal's current office, if any, is unknown, but it is of interest that he was currently receiving 6d. a week in alms from Abbot William Colchester (WAM 8317).
[31] Currently rent-collector at Bourton-on-the-Hill (WAM 8317).
[32] Aston and Henry Bruet served as bailiffs of Wick Hundred in 1385–6 and possibly for a longer period (I 18).
[33] Alias Margaret Tundy, rent-collector at Pinvin in 1399–1400 (WAM 21422).
[34] Sperhauk was probably bailiff of the Pershore portmoot, with which he is associated in 1399 (I 23).
[35] Sheep stockman in the Western Parts 1387–8 to 1393–4, and 1397–9 (GRO, D1099/M30/18; WAM 25977, 25982, 22128).
[36] For John Halle, bailiff of this liberty, see n. 28 above.
[37] In accordance with Boniface IX's mandate, the appropriation of Aldenham church did not take effect until the death of the present incumbent in or about 1399. When therefore the church was assigned to Abbot Colchester's anniversary, he received at first only the pension of 13s. 4d. p.a. which the Abbey had possessed in the church since the thirteenth century. It was presumably for this sum that the rector had to still to render account (*TPN*, f. xx; Harvey, *Estates*, p. 403); see also p. 191 above.
[38] The note excepting wool and wood is in a second hand.

I 23 Dockets of accounts for the abbot's manors and portions at the conclusion of the audit for the year ending on 28 September 1399

A parchment roll of two membranes, 149 mm wide, sewn Chancery fashion in a tight oversew with blue thread. Both membranes have been laid out with three vertical folds, for the centre and for the left and right margins. The roll is a fair copy, but there has been some limited reworking noted below. The roll is endorsed at the foot of membrane 2 'Dogettus abbatis Westm' anno regni regis Ricardi secundi xxiij°' in a further late fourteenth- or early fifteenth-century hand. There is some damage to the document through water-staining in places.[1]

WAM 6161

[*Mem. 1 recto*] Dockets of the venerable father Dom. William by divine[2] permission abbot of Westminster at 28 September 1399

Islip Termly rents: Michaelmas, £21 13s. 7d.; St Thomas the Apostle, £5 6s. 7¼d; the Annunciation, £8 0s. 4½d.; the nativity of St John the Baptist, £5 6s. 7¼d. Total: £40 7s. 2d. Cash liveries: £49 7s. 2d. Arrears: of John the chaplain,[3] £2 3s.; of Richard Bastevile, nothing; of John Bryan, nothing. Valor, excluding wool and wood: £53 4s. 2½d.[4] Remaining at the audit: 5 cart-horses, 1 colt, 22 oxen, 1 boar, 2 sows, 10 pigs for the larder, 8 young pigs, 12 piglets, 1 ram, 216 wethers, 20 ewes, 13 young sheep, 21 lambs, 30 capons, 1 gander, 7 breeding geese, 1 tawed hide, 32 cartloads of hay.

Sutton-under-Brailes Termly rents: £17 3s. 4½d. Cash liveries: £22 17s. 4d. Arrears: of John Handes, 8s.; of John Godwyk, 5s. 4d. Valor, excluding wool: £22 16s. 4d.[5] Remaining at the audit: 1 horse, 1 ox, 1 cock, 6 hens, 12 capons, 25 cartloads of hay, 1 brass pot containing 2½ gallons, 174 sheep of both sexes.

[1] Extant ministers' accounts: Bourton-on-the-Hill, WAM 83151; Deerhurst, WAM 24300; Ebury, WAM 26951; Laleham, WAM 27163; Pensham, WAM 22243; Pinvin, WAM 22316; Sutton-under-Brailes, GRO, D1099/M31/54.

[2] MS: 'domini' rather than 'divina'.

[3] John Darby.

[4] The net crop of wool at Islip this year consisted of 12 todds 26 lb. of wool (25 st. 12 lb.); and, in common with every other such crop in the Western Parts, this was sent to the collecting centre at Bourton-on-the-Hill (WAM 8318). The sales of wood envisaged in this entry may have been of undergrowth and fallen branches sold by the acre or other superficial area; for an example in 1402–3, see WAM 14832.

[5] The net wool crop at Sutton-under-Brailes consisted of 166 fleeces, weighing 6 todds 7 lb. (12½ st.) (GRO, D1099/M31/54; WAM 8318).

Todenham Termly rents: £19 2s. 5d. Cash liveries: £21 11s. 2d. Arrears: of Richard Morehouse, £2 15s. 11d.; of Roger Verney, £6 17s. 4d.; of Richard Forthey, 12s. 8d.; of John Olkyn and the shepherd,[6] £1 10s. Valor, excluding wool: £24 3s. 6d.[7] Remaining at the audit: 3 horses, 17 oxen, 1 bull, 1 cow, 1 young boar, 2 young sows, 1 ram, 77 ewes, 161 sheep in their second year, 136 lambs, 1 cock, 5 hens, 1 gander, 2 breeding geese, 40 cartloads of hay.

Bourton-on-the-Hill Termly rents: £15 11s. 4d. Cash liveries: £25 5s. 2d. Arrears: of Walter Hwet, £2 5s. Valor, excluding wool: £28 1s. 2d.[8] Remaining at the audit: 3 cart-horses, 9 oxen, 1 bull, 3 cows, 2 bullocks, 4 young bullocks, 2 calves, 1 boar, 1 sow, 7 young pigs, 382 wethers, 56 cartloads of hay, 2 brass pots, 1 basin[9] and 1 ewer.

Pershore Termly rents: £61 10s. 6d. Cash liveries: £79 11s. 8d. Arrears: of the abbot of Pershore, 3s. 10d. Valor: £71 1s. 8d. Remaining at the audit:[10] 2 qr. 4 bus. wheat, 6 qr. 1 bus. 2 p. rye, 20 qr. 5 bus. barley; 2 cart-horses, 8 oxen, 1 sow, 1 horse for the mill, 1 gander, ...[11] breeding geese, 6 cartloads of hay, 1 cow in dispute (*in calumpnia*).

Pensham Termly rents: £25 1s. 9d. Cash liveries: £29 12s. 4d. Arrears: of William Sperhauk', 12s. Valor: £29 15s. 4d.

Pinvin Termly rents: £36 10s. 1d. Cash liveries: £42 15s. 7d. Arrears: of Richard Selk, 10s. 4d.; of Henry Warde, 14s. 9¾d.; of Pygon', 5s.; of Richard Hale, £4 10s. Valor: £39 11s. 1¾d.

Birlingham Termly rents: £19 19s. 11½d. Cash liveries: £17 10s. Arrears: none. Valor: £17 10s. Remaining at the audit: 16 cartloads of hay.

Deerhurst Termly rents: £30 12s. 7½d. Cash liveries: £30. Arrears: of Thomas Lytsot, rent-collector, 19s. 11½d. Valor: £29 19s. 11½d.

[6] The 'shepherd' may have been the sheep-reeve for the Western Parts, who was at this time John Rogers (WAM 22128).
[7] The net wool crop at Todenham this year consisted of 251 fleeces weighing 11 todds 16 lb. (23 st. 2 lb.) (WAM 8318).
[8] The net wool crop at Bourton-on-the-Hill this year consisted of 385 fleeces weighing 19 todds 1 st. (39 st.) (WAM 8218).
[9] MS: 'pell'' for 'pelv'', 'pelvis'.
[10] MS: followed by 'viij boves', struck out.
[11] MS: blank.

Hardwicke in Elmstone Hardwicke Termly rents: £34 8s. 8d. Cash liveries: £35 0s. 2d. Arrears: none. Valor: £35 0s. 2d.

Chaceley Termly rents: £15 3s. 2½d. Cash liveries: £14 16s. 8d. Arrears: of Nicholas Philipp', 8s. 3d. Valor: £15 11s. 10½d. Remaining at the audit: 9 qr. 4 bus. wheat, 13 qr. 2½ bus. rye, 5 qr. 3 bus. peas, 19 qr. 5½ bus. barley, 4 qr. 6 bus. oats; 1 horse, 1 mare, 1 bull, 20 cows, 1 gander, 3 breeding geese, 12 capons, 1 cock, 5 hens.[12]

Longdon Termly rents: £14 19s. 5¾d. Cash liveries: £19 3s. 4d. Arrears: none. Valor: £20 1s. 7½d.

Castlemorton Termly rents: £30 2s. 0½d. Cash liveries: £21 17s. Arrears: of William Werkman, £2 10s. Valor: £28 12s. 3¼d.

Bailiff of the hundred, liberty and county of Worcester Cash liveries: £3 12s. 10d. Arrears: none. Shortfall (*disproficuus*) of this bailiff .....[13]
Defford Hundred Cash liveries, 9s. 10d. Arrears of William Scheperd, 29s. 8d. Valor: 26s. 6d.
Wick Hundred Cash liveries: £4 12s. 6d. Arrears: of John Aston' and John Brywet, 6s. 8d.[14] Valor: [15] £6 11s. 6d.
Pinvin Hundred Cash liveries: £2 4s. 9d.[16] Arrears: of John Tondy 11s. 2d. Valor: £12.
Portmoot of Pershore Cash liveries: £5 5s. Arrears: of William Sperhauk, £1 17s. 3½d. Valor: £5 7s. 0½d.
Bailiff of the liberty of Gloucestershire and collector of court dues at Deerhurst and Hardwicke in Elmstone Hardwicke [*mem. 2 recto*] Cash liveries: £5 6s. 8d. Arrears: of William Thomas: £2 19s. 10½d. Valor: £5 3s. 4½d.

Sheep stockman[17] Cash liveries: £2. Arrears: of John Roggers, £2 11s. 7½d. Valor: the wool has not yet been sold; it is not entered in the sum total.[18]

[12] Inventory of corn and stock as in I 22, but with 4 qr. 6 bus. oats rather than 4 qr. 5 bus.
[13] MS: 'illius balivi' inserted over an erasure; no sum follows.
[14] The sum applies to Aston and Brywet jointly, and their names are bracketed. Cf. the similar entry above, I 22 (under 'forinsec bailiffs').
[15] MS: 'Valet hoc anno' inserted, but in main text hand.
[16] MS: 'xliiij s. ix d.' inserted in main text hand; 'xxiiij s. ix d.' struck out.
[17] This panel refers not only to the account of the sheep stockman, but also to that of the bailiff and rent-collector at Bourton-on-the-Hill, who accounts for the unsold wool of the Western Parts. This amounted to 3 sacks 11 todds 7 lb. (3 sacks 22½ st.), and in addition 3 todds of refuse wool remained from the previous year (WAM 22128).
[18] MS: 'non intratur in summa totali', in another hand; it may refer to the entry below.

Account of Richard Forthey Cash liveries: to R. Whatle, £33;[19] to T. Carbonell', £2 13s. 6½d. Arrears: of Richard Forthey, £10.[20]

Denham Termly rents: £39 0s. 3½d. Cash liveries: £20 6s. 6½d. Arrears: of Wauberd and Sawer, £1 2s. 6d.; of Donsford', £1 6s. 8d.; of the rector, £5; of Gore, lately lessee of the cows, £1 11s. 10d.; of Godfrey the accountant,[21] £9 11s. 9d. An exceptional shortfall (*disproficuus exceptivus*) because the wool and wood were not valued, £15 6s. 4d.[22] Remaining at the audit: 16 qr. 3 bus. wheat; 3 cart-horses, 4 stots, 2 stud-mares (*stodmar'*), 3 colts (*pull'*), 15 oxen, 2 bulls, 22 cows, 4 rams, 52 wethers, 146 ewes, 99 young sheep, 69 lambs, 2 sows, 6 young pigs, 8 piglets, 16 breeding swans, 2 ganders, 3 breeding geese, 6 capons, 1 cock, 3 hens, 50 cartloads of hay, 1 tawed hide.

Laleham Termly rents: £28 15s. 7d. Cash liveries: £29 5s. 10d. Arrears: of French, the shepherd, £2 5s.; of N. Jakes, £2 7s. 11¼d.; of William Jakes, £2 2s.; of Richard Longe, £1 14s. 5½d.; of William Frye, £3; of the accountant,[23] £1. Valor, excluding wool: £26 10s. 2½d.[24] Remaining at the audit: 3 qr. 3 bus. rye, 4 qr. 2 bus. peas, 28 qr. 5 bus. barley, 4 qr. dredge, 6 qr. 3 bus. oats by heaped measure (*mensura cumulata*); 2 cart-horses, 4 mares, 13 oxen, 1 boar, 1 sow, 9 pigs, 13 young pigs, 26 wethers, 27 ewes, 9 young sheep, 5 lambs, 5 breeding swans, 5 white swans, 4 cygnets, 8 cartloads of hay.

Pyrford Termly rents: £35 1s. 1d. Cash liveries: £38 4s. 10¾d. Arrears: of Walter Sponge, £1 6s. 2d.; of William Mulhurst, 13s.; of John Hampton', 13s.; of the accountant,[25] £5. Valor, excluding wool and wood as below: £37 17s. 9d. Remaining at the audit: 2 stots, 7 oxen, 1 bull, 2 cows, 1 calf, 4 rams, 160 wethers, 38 ewes, 77 young sheep, 34 lambs,[26] 3 swans in the keeping of the prior of Newark, 6 ploughshares, 4 fallow deer (*dam'*), 48 hurdles, 175 talwood, 1,000 faggots, 70 cartloads of hay.

[19] A monk of Westminster, currently pursuing higher studies at Oxford, who, as it appears, might be asked to carry cash liveries from Western manors to the abbot's household if returning to Westminster for a period.
[20] MS: 'xv li. xiiij s.' struck out; 'x li.' inserted in a new ink, but in the main text hand.
[21] Godfrey, a chaplain; see Appendix.
[22] MS: 'Disproficuus .... iiij d.' written over an erasure, possibly a later addition in the main text hand.
[23] William Snow, reeve (WAM 27163).
[24] MS: the cash sum may have been written in a second ink. 64 fleeces of *lana grossa* were sent from Laleham to Westminster, the collecting centre for the Eastern Parts this year; as was customary for such entries in these manors, the weight is not recorded (WAM 27163).
[25] Robert Hone, reeve.
[26] MS: 'xxxiiij agni' inserted in the main text hand.

Staines Termly rents: £42 10s. 2¼d. Cash liveries: £36 16s. 8d. Arrears: of John Dod, 6s. 8d.; of Dorman, 11s. 3d. Valor: £42 0s. 8¾d.

Yeoveney Leased at £21 and 12 capons valued at 4s. p.a.[27] Cash liveries: £21. Valor: £21 4s.

Ebury Termly rents: £6 14s. 7½d. Cash liveries: £154 13s. 10d. Arrears: of Henry Kyrkeby, 17s.; of Janyn, £22 14s. 10½d.; of Jordemayn, £31 11s. 8d.; of Richard Rubbe, £3 12s. 7¾d.; of the purveyor of the duke of Lancaster,[28] £4; of the accountant, £30 16s. 9¼d.[29] Remaining at the audit: 40 qr. wheat, 2 qr. 4 bus. 2 p. peas, 46 qr. 3 bus. 1 p. barley, 8 qr. oats; 3 cart-horses, 6 mares, 10 oxen, 2 bulls, 56 cows, 1 young boar, 2 sows, 3 rams, 39 wethers, 128 ewes, 49 young sheep, 87 lambs, 2 breeding swans, 5 cygnets, 1 gander, 3 breeding geese, 1 cock, 6 hens, 33 cartloads of hay. Valor, excluding wool: £54 12s. 9¼d.[30]

Bailiff of the liberty of Westminster He has not yet accounted.

[Totals]
Sum of rents: £533 14s. 3½d. Sum of cash liveries: £600 18s. 5d. Sum of arrears: £185 3s. 9¼d. Sum of valors, excluding wool not valued: £628 3s. 1½d.
Sum of both sexes of horse, 43; colts (*pull'*), 4; oxen, 102; bulls, 8; cows, 105; bullocks, 6; calves, 3. Total: 271.
Boars, 5; sows, 11; [young] pigs, 43; piglets, 25. Total: 83.
Rams, 13; wethers, 1,000; ewes, 436; young sheep, 408; lambs, 351. Total: 2,258.

[27] MS: 'et xij capones appreciati ad iiij s.' added, possibly in a second hand.
[28] The payment due from purveyors for Henry, duke of Lancaster, was in return for 16 cartloads of hay, and the debt was apparently paid in 1399–1400 (WAM 26952).
[29] John Huller, bailiff.
[30] The net wool crop at Ebury this year consisted of 219 fleeces of *lana grossa*, and these were delivered to Henry Norton at Westminster (WAM 26951).

I 24 Dockets of accounts for the abbot's manors and portions in the Western Parts at the conclusion of the audit for the year ending on 28 September 1422

A parchment roll of three membranes, 194 mm wide, sewn Chancery fashion in a spaced oversew with blue thread. The roll, although a copy in a single hand, was written up on several occasion; the layout is much less painstaking than the fair copies of the late fourteenth century. The manorial headings appear in the centre of the roll, rather than in the margin. Although each manorial panel provides a space and heading for the *valor*, the sum is, in each case, omitted; and in the panel relating to Islip, several other sums are omitted; there are some other idiosyncracies in the writing and spelling.[1] At the foot of the dorse of membrane 3 the roll has been titled, inverted: 'Islep'. Dogettus factus ibidem super compotum anno regni regis Henrici sexti primo.'[2]

WAM 6125

[*Mem. 1 recto*] *Islip* Dockets made there at the audit [of the account] of the manors in the Western Parts of Richard [Harwden], abbot of Westminster [at 28 September] 1422

Pershore Termly rents of assize: £25 16s. 1¼d. Leases of Wyke at the four terms: £7 2s. 2d. Leases of the demesne lands of Pershore: 17s. 1d.[3] Profit (*proficuum*) of the tenements in the lord's hands: £2 3s. 8d. Lease of the manor and demesne lands of Pershore: £12. Lease of the mills: £6 10s.[4] Sale of stock: 3½d. Sale of works: 11s. 5½d. Cash liveries: £54 16s. 8d. Owing at the audit (*Debentur super compotum*): £8 14s. 4d. Put in respite (*Respectus*): £4 14s. 4d. Charged against (*Unde super*): John Hambury, the lessee, £4; the accountant:[5] nothing. Valor: .....[6]

Pinvin Termly rents of assize: £27 0s. 10¾d. Leases at the four terms: £8 19s. 8d. Cash liveries: £35 15s. Owing at the audit: 18s. Put in respite: 18s. Charged against: the accountant,[7] nothing. Valor: .....

Pensham Termly rents of assize: £11 19s. 2d. Leases at the four terms: £14 14s. 10d. Works sold: 9s. 8d. Cash liveries: £19 3s. 10d. Owing at the audit:

[1] Throughout the document 'quatuour' is spelt thus.

[2] Extant ministers' accounts: Todenham, GRO, D1099/M30/35, and WAM 25985.

[3] i.e. the demesne that was leased piecemeal as distinct from the more extensive area at present leased with the site of the manor.

[4] A watermill for corn and a fulling mill that may have been a windmill are mentioned in this period (WAM 22129).

[5] Possibly John Hayward, who is mentioned as rent-collector in 1423–4 (WAM 24429).

[6] MS: blank space.

[7] Possibly Ralph Hanow.

£16 13s. 4d. Put in respite: 18s. Charged against: the lessee of the demesne lands,[8] £3 12s. 11d.; Bartholomew, lately the accountant, £4 9s.; the accountant, £8 2s. Valor: ......

Birlingham Termly rents of assize: £18 10s. 1½d. Leases at the four terms: 14s. 3d. Cash liveries: £19 1s. 5d. Owing at the audit: £2 2s. 7½d. Put in respite: £1 1s. 9½d. Sale of wood: £1 0s. 10d. [Charged against]: John Brokke, the accountant, nothing. Valor: .....

Deerhurst Termly rents of assize: £22 15s. 2½d. Leases at the four terms: £7 13s. 4d. Works sold: 8s. 10d. Cash liveries: £24 10s. Owing at the audit: £6 15s. 0¼d. Put in respite: £1 11s. 8d. Charged against: the prior of Deerhurst, the lessee, 13s. 4d.;[9] the accountant, £4 10s.[10] Valor: .....

Longdon Termly rents of assize: £11 5s. 1d. Leases at four terms: £3 14s. 9d. Sale of stock: 6½d. Cash liveries: £13 11s. 8d. Owing at the audit: £7 15s. 4½d. Put in respite: £2 0s. 4d. [*Mem. 2 recto*] [Charged against]: Robert Goodman, lately accountant for the preceding year, £3 14s. 8d.; the accountant of the present year, £2 0s. 4½d.[11] Valor: .....

Castlemorton Termly rents of assize, £23 18s. 4¼d. Leases at four terms: £6 4s. 2d. Works sold: £1 3s. 4d. Foreign liveries: £8 12s. 2d. Cash liveries: £16 14s. 6d. Owing at the audit: £8 18s. 1d. Put in respite: £2 18s. 1d. [Charged against]: Richard Palle, the accountant, £6. Valor: .....

Hardwicke in Elmstone Hardwicke Termly rents: £12 15s. 6d. Leases at four terms: £20 17s. 10¾d. Cash liveries: £38 10s. 5d. Owing at the audit: £9 6s. 8d. [Charged against]: John Solas, the lessee, £1 6s. 8d.; the accountant, £8. Valor: .....

[*Mem. 3 recto*] *Chaceley* Termly rents of assize: £1 2s. 8¼d. Leases at four terms: £10 14s. 10d. Cash liveries: £12 9s. 4d. Owing at the audit: 6s. 8d., charged against (*pendentes super*) John Curry the younger, the accountant. Valor: ......

[8] Thomas Rowe.

[9] The prior of Deerhurst farmed the site of the manor of Deerhurst and the demesne and *Brodemede* meadow from 1419–20 or 1420–1 to 1438–9 and possibly beyond, for a rent of £5 13s. 4d., falling to £5 6s. 8d. (WAM 8456–60; *VCH Gloucs*., ii, pp. 103–5).

[10] Probably Edward Floke, who is mentioned as rent-collector at Deerhurst, 1420–1×1423–4 (WAM 8456, 24429).

[11] Probably the current rent-collector.

Bourton-on-the-Hill Termly rents of assize: £15 15s. 3¼d. Leases at four terms: £4 11s. 8d. Sale of corn: 1s. 10½d. Sale of stock: 1s. 9d. Cash liveries: £22 1s. 1½d. Owing at the audit: £23, charged against John Hogges the accountant there. Valor: .....

Todenham Termly rents of assize: £16 8s. 2½d. Leases at four terms: £10 11s. 4d. Cash liveries: £24. Owing at the audit: £5 12s. 4d. Put in respite: £1 15s. 8d. [Charged against]: the accountant, £3 16s. 8d.; against the tenants, £1 6s. 8d.; and the accountant[12] owes £2 10s. Valor: .....

Sutton-under-Brailes Termly rents of assize: £15 18s. Leases at four terms: £3 6s. 8d. Cash liveries: £17 17s. 5d. Put in respite: £2 14s. 1d. Owing at the audit: £9 17s. 5d. [Charged against] John Duraunt, the lessee, £5 6s. 8d.; John Leonard, £1 3s. 4d.; the accountant,[13] 13s. 4d. Valor: .....

[*Mem. 1 dorse*] *Islip* Termly rents of assize: £31 19s. 0¾d. Leases at four terms: £21 0s. 7d. Profits of the tenements in the hands of the lord: 4d. Cash liveries: .....[14] Foreign liveries:[15] ..... Foreign payments: £4. Owing at the audit: ..... Put in respite: £3 13s. 4d. [Charged against]: ..... lately [lessee of] the mill,[16] 6s. 8d.; Thomas Wynter, lately lessee of the demesne lands, ...; Gurdon', lately farmer of the mill,[17] 10s.; the accountant,[18] .....

[12] William Hakkes.

[13] John Baron.

[14] MS: cash sums left blank at a number of points in the Islip entry.

[15] Section struck out.

[16] The missing name is probably that of William Millward, farmer of the watermill, the fishery and other appurtenances of the mill for a rent of £3 10s. p.a., who is mentioned in 1416–17 (WAM 14834).

[17] Richard Gurdon, named as farmer of the watermill in 1400–1 and as 'lately' farmer in 1416–17 (WAM 14831, 14833–4).

[18] Very likely John Lake, who accounted as reeve and rent-collector in 1423–4; the substantial arrears with which he was then charged show that he was not a newcomer to the offices (WAM 14835).

Appendix

Appendix
The Abbot's Manorial and Estate Officials

Adekyn, John. Reeve of Pershore, 1343–4 and 1346–51 (WAM 22121, 22123–5).

Alberd, Richard (I). Reeve of Bourton-on-the Hill, 1353–74 and 1376–7 (WAM 8283–303, 8305).

Alberd, Richard (II). Probably reeve of Bourton-on-the-Hill in or shortly before 1392–3; see I 20.

Aleyn, William. Reeve and rent-collector at Pensham, 1376–1412. Farmer of the demesne, probably 1394–1412 (WAM 22232–47; GRO, D1099/M30/20).

Andrew, Adam. Reeve of Pensham, 1351–70; bailiff, 1370–1; reeve, 1374–5 (WAM 22213–26, 22230). For the delivery of manorial stock to him on his election by the homage in 1351, see WAM 22212.

Andrew, Wolfstan. Reeve and rent-collector at Pensham, 1371–4 (WAM 22227–9). Reeve of Pershore, 1379–80 and probably in 1378–9 (I 14 and I 15).

Arwy (Arvy), John. Rent-collector at Pershore, 1343–4 (I 1, 2B, 3). Reeve of Pinvin, 1360–1 (WAM 22288).

Aston, John. Bailiff of Wick hundred, 1385–6 (I 18).

Badmyngton, Thomas. Bailiff of Pershore portmoot, 1340–1 (I 1, 2B, 3).

Baily (Bayli), John. Bailiff of the abbot's liberty in Gloucestershire, 1363–4 (I 6, I 9–10).

Balk (Ball, Bulk), William. Serjeant of Pershore, 1372–3, and possibly for the longer period 1372–7 (WAM 24516*; I 13).

Baron (alias Broun, Bron), John (I). Reeve of Pinvin, 1361–2 (WAM 2289–91). Reep-reeve and collector of the perquisites of the court for the manors of Longdon and Castlemorton, 1361–75 (WAM 21024–5; WAM 24511–14, 24516*; I 12). Rent-collector at Longdon, 1371–4 (WAM 24514–15, 24517).

Baron, John (II). Rent-collector at Sutton-under-Brailes, 1414–31 (WAM 24426–30; GRO, D1099/M31/55–6).

Baron, Peter. Reeve of Sutton-under-Brailes, 1379–81. A second term, comprising the years 1392–5, is well attested; if, however, Baron was the immediate successor of Thomas Hurry (below), it probably began in the late 1380s. Following the normal arrangement for these 2 manors, Baron combined the reeveship of Sutton-under-Brailes with that of Stourton (GRO, D1099/M31/46–7, 51; I 15).

Barret (Barat), Alexander. Bailiff of Pershore portmoot, 1344–7 (I 1, 2B, 3). Held a messuage of the abbot of Westminster in the town of Pershore, for a rent of 12d. p.a. (WAM 32742).

Basteville, Richard. Reeve of Islip, 1390–4; reeve and rent-collector, 1395–1405 (WAM 14828–33). His wife was associated with him in the collection of rents (I 22).

Bedwynd, Richard. Bailiff/serjeant of Pyrford, 1366–70 and 1372–81 (WAM 24512–13, 27422–4; I 7). The abbot's stockman for sheep 1371–2 (WAM 27421).

Berald, Robert. Bailiff of Defford hundred, 1362–75 (WAM 24511–16*; I 5–7, where Berald is described as 'reeve'; I 8 and 12).

Berkesden (Berkesdon), Reginald. Bailiff of the abbot's liberty in Gloucestershire, 1370–1 (I 9).

Bernard, John. Appointed reeve of Hardwicke in succession to Richard Crank/Cronk, in the course of 1348–9 and demitted office for the first time on 24 October 1350 (WAM 8437A, 8438C; I 2A). Is known to have served again as reeve in 1362–3, but may have begun this, his second term, several years previously and continued for a further year (I 5–6).

Besford, Alexander. Steward of the Western Parts, 28 September 1387–*c.*25 March 1400; received a fee of £4 p.a. (WAM 24410–11, 24537; I 19–20). Owned as a free tenant the site of the abbot's former manor house in Pinvin, but we are not told what he built for himself on this site (WAM 22514).

Birlingham (Birlyngham, Birtlyngham), John. Bailiff of Defford hundred, 1375–6 (I 13).

Blisse, John. Reeve of Todenham, 1360–3 (WAM 25966–9).

Boteler, William. Probably bailiff of Longdon manor and rectory 1347–8, and granger there in the summer of 1348; also concurrently bailiff and granger at Castlemorton (WAM 21019, 21037–8; I 2B).

Bradestok', Richard de. Lessee of the demesne arable and meadow at Castlemorton, in accordance with a lease for 10 years, dated 28 September 1357, and specifying a rent of £4 for the first year and £5 p.a. thereafter (WAM 21056).

Bradewell, Adam, described as 'chaplain'. Granted, in or about 1358–9, a 20-year lease of the manor of Chaceley. The lease was terminated in 1361–2; no reason is given in our sources (WAM 21087–8).

Brian (Bryan), John (I). Lessee of the vaccary at Denham, 1381–2 (I 16).

Brian (Bryan), John (II). Lessee of the demesne at Islip, with dovecot and with multure from the mill, 1398–1405 and possibly for a longer period (WAM 14831–3; I 23).

Broun, Adam. Reeve of Chaceley, 21 December 1343–22 December 1347 (WAM 21079–82; I 1). For Elena, his widow, see I 3.

Broun, Richard. Mentioned at Deerhurst, 1387–8, probably as 1 of 2 rent-collectors acting jointly (I 19).

Broun, Robert. Bailiff of Denham, 1362–8 (WAM 24512; I 5–8).

Broun, Robert. Bailiff of Pyrford, 1370–3 (WAM 27420–2, 24514–15).

Bruwet (Bruwer), Henry. Bailiff of Wick hundred, 1385–6 (I 18).

Bruwet (Browet, Bruet, Brywet), John. Mentioned as bailiff of Wick hundred 1364–74, and probably served continuously in this period (WAM 24511–12, 24514–16*; I 6, 10).

Bryan, Robert. Rent-collector at Todenham, 1384–8 (GRO, D1099/M30/17; I 19).

But, William. Reeve of Longdon manor and rectory, certainly in 1341–2, the year of his one surviving account, but very likely for a longer period. He was the immediate predecessor of Andrew Eyloff (below), and the attention paid in the latter's account for 1347–8 to arrears owed by But suggests that the latter had not long been out of office (WAM 21017–19; I 2B).

Cappe (Carpe), Walter. Bailiff of Defford hundred, 1376–7 (I 13).

Carter, Gilbert, see Whyte, Gilbert.

Cherchewyne, John, see South, John (II).

Cherlefford, Richard, see Chileford', Richard.

Chese, William. Bailiff of Wick hundred, 1347–8 or earlier; 1349–50 (I 1, 3).

Chesgate, Thomas. Bailiff of Hyde, 28 September 1381–18 March 1383, and possibly from 2 April 1381 (WAM 27089–91).

Chike (Chyke), Nicholas. First mentioned in surviving records in 1362–3, when he was charged at the audit at Pyrford with modest arrears, of which a significant portion was respited (I 5). He had probably been rent-collector and bailiff here. But his attention was already given to Yeoveney, where he was bailiff, 1361–3 (WAM 16881–2). From Yeoveney it moved to Hyde, where he was bailiff 1363–4 (WAM 27170A–27172), and then to Ebury, where he replaced John atte Gate as bailiff on 29 October 1364 (WAM 26920). He may have continued at Ebury until the end of 31 May 1367, when John Swan, the next bailiff known to us by name, was appointed (WAM 26921). Chike's career pattern suggests that he was the locum for whom the steward in the Eastern Parts, if not the abbot himself, sent in emergencies.

Child, John. An official at Pershore in or shortly before 1385–6; exact office unknown (I 18–19).

Chileford' (Cherlefford), Richard. Rent-collector at Pershore, 1343–4 (I 1, 2B).

Clerk (Clerc, Le Clerc), John (I). Rent-collector at Staines, 1352–3 (WAM 16932). Lessee of the demesne at Yeoveney from 24 March 1363, without a specified term; Clerk is said on this occasion to be of Staines (WAM 16882, rot. 2). Lessee of the manor of Yeoveney from a date in 1367 for a now unrecorded term (I 8). Lessee of the now residual demesne at Staines from 1367 or 1368, with a term of 20 years (WAM 16934). Bailiff of Deerhurst hundred, the abbot of Westminster's liberty in Gloucestershire, in 1368–9 (I 9–10).

Clerk (Clerke), John (II). Bailiff of Hyde, 1377–2 April 1381 (WAM 27084–7).

Cok (Cook), John. Rent-collector in Pershore, 1346–7 (I 1).

Cole, William. With Robert Crompe, lessee of the demesne at Pinvin from 1368–9. In 1375–6, with 2 years of the 12-year lease to run, his share of the lease passed, presumably by sale, to Ralph Pinvin (WAM 22294–303; for further details, see I 8 and 16).

Colyn, Henry. Rent-collector at Todenham, 1389–90, and possibly for a longer period (WAM 25978). Still alive in 1406, when he held a messuage and half-virgate of unfree land at Todenham (GRO, D1099/M38).

Cosyn, John. Reap-reeve and collector of rents and estreats in Staines and Yeoveney, 29 September 1348–19 January 1349 (I 2B).

Cosyn, Thomas. Reap-reeve and rent-collector at Staines, 3 March 1349–1 August 1349 (WAM 16872). With Richard Boweles and John le Clerk, rent-collector at Staines, 1352–3 (WAM 16932).

Cosyn, Walter. Known to have been reeve of Pyrford 1346–7, a year from which his account survives (WAM 27145). A subsequent steep rise in the clear debt charged to him at the end of this year shows that his reeveship lasted for more than 1 year and quite possibly into the year 1348–9 (I 2B).

Crank (Cronk), Richard. Reeve of Hardwicke, 1348–9 (I 2A).

Crendone (Crendon), John. Serjeant/bailiff of Staines and Yeoveney, 24 May 1350–8 June 1350 (WAM 16872, rot. 2; 16873, rot. 1).

Crompe, Robert, see Cole, William; Pinvin, Ralph.

Crompe, William. Rent-collector at Pershore, 1345–6 (WAM 22125; I 1).

Curry, John (I), known as John Curry the elder. Rent-collector at Chaceley, 1410–18 (WAM 24410–28). From this date, he was less conspicuous than his son, John Curry (II), in the administration of the abbot's principal manor in Chaceley. Nevertheless, in 1401, he and Alice, his wife, with John Curry (II) and Joan his wife, were granted a lease of the demesne for their joint and several lives (WAM 21107).

Curry, John (II), known as John Curry the younger, and the son of John Curry the elder, occurs as lessee of the demesne at Chaceley from 1417 and as rent-collector from the following year. During the next 2 decades, the combination of the 2 offices in his hands, though not invariable, may have been normal. WAM 21100–5, and for the prominence of both father and son in the history of the demesne at Chaceley in the fifteenth century, see Barbara Harvey, 'The Leasing of the Abbot of Westminster's Demesnes in the Later Middle Ages', *EconHR*, 2nd series, 22 (1969), pp. 20–1.

Darby, John, alias John the chaplain. Chaplain serving St Edward the Confessor's chapel at Islip (Oxon) since 1380 and possibly for a longer period, for a stipend of £4 p.a. Lessee from 1395–6, with a lease for 12 years, of the site of the manor and the demesne of Islip. By 1400–1, he had been succeeded as lessee by John Brian (above) (WAM 14819–32, 15175).

Darnell, Richard. As an unfree tenant, held a virgate of land in Wick, the rural member of Pershore manor. Reeve of Pershore, 1354–5 and 1362–5, and at each juncture, possibly for a longer period (WAM 327421, 22214; I 5).

Derneford (Dernefford), John. Bailiff of Deerhurst hundred, 1362–3 (I 5).

Dod (Dodde), John. Mentioned in 1392–3 as tenant of a plot of land, probably in urban

Staines, for a rent of 10d. p.a. By 1398–9, probably lessee, for a rent of £9 6s. 8d. p.a., of lands and tenements formerly belonging to Nicholas Brembre and granted by Richard II to Abbot William Colchester. He also leased part of the estate formerly belonging to John Hall, for a rent of £2 10s. per annum. We do not know in which office he had incurred the arrears mentioned in I 23.

Dolle, Cecilia, wife and subsequently widow of William Dolle (I). Within a year of her husband's death, and probably sooner rather than later in that period, Cecilia was charged with the unpaid residue of the arrears of £15 with which he had been charged posthumously. Our sources imply that she paid a substantial part of this within 2 years (WAM 14795–7; I 2B).

Dolle, William (I). Reeve of Islip, 1332–48; the role included responsibility as rent-collector in the vill of Fencot, Murcot and Noke. His last account was closed on 28 September 1348 and later audited in the normal way. But his successor, Richard Le Hunte, assumed office on 13 September 1348, and we can assume that this was the actual date of Dolle's death (WAM 14790–5).

Dolle, William (II), son of William Dolle (I) and Cecilia Dolle. As demesne sower (*seminator*), held the plough in the winter sowing of wheat in 1348–9 (WAM 14796). In the summer of 1349, and as granger, supervised the threshing of demesne corn (WAM 14797). Was reeve of Islip 1351–86. In this capacity he was probably the leading figure among the tenants of the manor who participated in the champarty arrangement relating to the arable demesne: this was in operation 1362–86, the year of his retirement as reeve. Mentioned as rent-collector in 1390–1, and probably appointed as such on his retirement as reeve. An entry in I 22, relating to 1397–8, implies that he was dead but that his wife, mentioned but not named, survived him (WAM 14798–828).

Donsford, William. Collector of perquisites of the court at Denham, 1396–9 (I 21–3). Probably to be identified with John Donsford, described as bedel in 1401–2 (WAM 3413).

Dorman (Derman, Dermon), John. Lessee of Yeoveney manor for 31 years and for a rent of £21 and 12 capons p.a. The lease was executed on 19 August 1379, but the term ran from the preceding 24 June. It is implied that Dorman was also lessee of the demesne vaccary at Staines in 1387–8. Died shortly before 1400–1, when his executors paid a year's rent to the abbot (WAM, Muniment Book 17, ff. 41v–42; WAM 16934–5, 24545).

Downyng, William. Reeve of Pyrford, 1381–2 (I 16). The indenture, dated 29 September 1381, in which Richard Bedwynd, bailiff in charge of Pyrford since 1375–6, delivered the manor's livestock and dead stock to Downyng, included the unusual provision that he should be answerable in all matters to the abbot of Westminster.

Draxfeld, John. Rector of Denham. In the early and/or mid-1390s, leased the major part of the arable demesne in a crop-sharing arrangement with the abbot, or for cash in lieu; for the system in operation in 1395–6, see WAM 3410. The arrears of £5 charged to the rector in 1397 probably dated from 1396–7 and show that the cash option operated in that year (I 21–2).

Duraunt, John. Lessee of the site of the manor with the demesne and fulling mill at Sutton-under-Brailes, for a rent of £2 13s. 4d. p.a., in accordance with a lease for 15 years, probably executed in 1418. By 1428–9, however, Duraunt had vacated the lease. He may have been identical with a member of the Warwickshire gentry family which flourished 1409×46 (GRO, D1099/M31/55–6; C. Carpenter, *Locality and Polity: A Study of Warwickshire Landed Society, 1401–1499* (Cambridge, 1992), p. 654).

Durdent, Thomas. May be identified by circumstantial evidence as bailiff of Denham for the years 1385–7 and the first few months of 1387–8. Thus he succeeded John atte Hurst, bailiff 1384–5, and was himself succeeded by Nicholas Stilman, who was bailiff by 28 December 1387 (WAM 24536, 24536*, 3409).

Elkyn, see Olkyn.

Elme, John. Bailiff of the abbot of Westminster's liberty in Gloucestershire, 1363–4 (I 6–7).

Erdyngton, Roger de. Serjeant/bailiff of Todenham, 1356–66. Lessee of the arable demesne, with some demesne pastures, 1360–74, in accordance with a 7-year lease executed on 30 September 1360 and renewed for a further 7 years on 30 September 1367. Erdyngton died near the date of expiry of the second lease, and possibly while the audit of his last account as bailiff was in progress (WAM 25965–6, 25970–1; GRO, D1099/M30/10–11).

Eyloff, Andrew. Reeve of Longdon manor and rectory, 28 September 1347–14 April 1349 (WAM 21018–19, 21036–7).

Felawes, Elias. Bailiff of Defford hundred, 1349–50 (I 3).

Fortheye, Richard. A secular clerk, who first appears in our sources as the so-called clerk of the abbot's kitchen, an office which he held 1371–9, and thus in the middle years of Nicholas de Litlyngton's abbacy (1362–86) (WAM 24515–16, 24516*, 24518–20). Though originally subordinate to the steward of the abbot's household, who also acted as the abbot's treasurer and was invariably a monk, the clerk was now himself steward or treasurer in all but name. By 1382–3, however, he had moved out of the household, to become bailiff of Pershore. He probably held this office 1382–7, and thus in the last years of Litlyngton's abbacy and the first of William Colchester (1386–1420) (WAM 22127; I 17). In 1393–5, he was rent-collector at Pinvin (WAM 22311–12). By 1397–8, he was the abbot's collector, alias receiver, in the Western Parts and held this office until 1414–15 (WAM 24410–26).

Fox, William. Rent-collector in Pershore, 1347–8 (I 1, 2B, 3).

French, William. Described as a, or the, shepherd. He had probably been one of the abbot's stockmen for sheep in the Eastern Parts, but the failure of his arrears of £2 5s. to change in the course of the three years 1397–9 implies that his service was in the past (WAM 27161–3; I 21–3).

Fry, William. Rent-collector at Laleham, 1396–8 (WAM 27161).

Gate, John atte. Bailiff/serjeant of Ebury, 1349–55, and 6 April 1362–29 October 1364 (WAM 26906–12, 26916–20).

Gery, John. Reeve of Hardwicke, 1364–72 (WAM 8442–3, 24511–14; I 8).

Gilbert, Adam. Rent-collector at Pershore, 1346–7 (I 1, 2B).

Gilbert, William. Probably, with John atte Stoke (below), rent-collector at Hardwicke in 1387–8 (I 19).

Gilbert, see also Whyte, Gilbert

Gloucester, John. Described variously as 'bailiff and granger' and 'supervisor and granger', in manors in the Western Parts in 1349–50. Received wages of 1s. per week throughout the year, and ½ bus. of wheat per week (WAM 22124). It is possible that Gloucester already held these positions in 1348–9 (I 2B).

Glovere, John. Bailiff of Pershore portmoot 1362–3 and possibly later (I 5).

Glovere, Nicholas. Said in 1365 to have served 'recently' as bailiff of Pershore portmoot, and may have done so in 1363–4 in succession to John Glovere, bailiff 1362–3 (I 5–6).

Glyn, John. Collector of rents at Pershore and Wick, 1372–4 (WAM 24516*, 24517; I 11).

Godfrey the chaplain. Serjeant at Denham, probably in 1398–9 (WAM 3431; I 23).

Godwyk (Godwy), John. Rent-collector at Sutton-under-Brailes in 1395–6, and reeve in 1396–7 (GRO, D1099/M31/51–2).

Goodman, Robert. Rent-collector at Longdon, 1411–18 (WAM 24421–28). Reeve of Longdon, 1420–1 (WAM 21026).

Gore. Lessee of the demesne vaccary at Denham, 1397–8 (I 23).

Grafton, Henry. Perpetual vicar at Longdon. On 25 June 1357, received, with Robert de Grafton and Alexander de Wynkebourne, a lease of the manor for 20 years (WAM 21293, and for a further indenture relating to the lease, dated 27 June 1357, see WAM 32744).

Henry died in 1389, seised of a holding in Longdon for which the abbot of Westminster now claimed an ox valued at 13s. 4d. as heriot (WAM 21127, court held on 17 April 1389).

Grafton, Robert. With Henry Grafton and Alexander Wynkebourne, received a lease of Longdon manor for 20 years on 25 June 1357 (WAM 21293, and 32744 for an indenture of 27 June 1357; I 8).

Gurdon, Richard. In 1400–1 mentioned as lessee of the watermill (i.e. the corn mill) at Islip and its apppurtenances in 1400–1, and in 1416–17 said to have been 'lately' (*nuper*) the lessee. In the latter year, his arrears amounted to £5 10s. 2d. (WAM 14831, 14834).

Hakkes, Henry, and Philip Taylor. Probably rent-collectors at Todenham in 1392–3 and, since the names are bracketed together, we can assume that they held the office jointly. Mentioned in 1388–9 and in 1395–6 among those holding at will piecemeal acres belonging to vacant holdings (GRO, D1099/M30/19, 21).

Hale, Richard. At Pershore, where he owed arrears of £3 19s. 4½d. in 1393, Hale may have been a rent-collector (I 20). At Pinvin, from 1392, he was lessee of the site of the manor and the demesne, with a life-interest; he is last mentioned in this capacity in 1398–9 (WAM 22310, 22316).

Halle, John atte (I). Bailiff and rent-collector at Deerhurst and Hardwicke, and probably in each case from 1373 to 1393 (WAM 8445–7, 8451–2; I 12–14). Bailiff of the liberty in Gloucestershire, 1396–1401 (WAM 24298–302).

Halle, John atte (II), the younger. Lessee of the demesne at Deerhurst, 1397–8 (WAM 8453).

Handes, John. A tenant at Sutton-under-Brailes, who in the late 1390s held 2 messuages and 1½ virgates by farm, and in 1406 messuages and 3 virgates variously, on free and customary terms. What office he held, we do not know (GRO, D1099/M31/51–3; WAM 25983).

Hanecok', John. Serjeant at Denham, 1348–50. In each year, the exact date must be regarded as uncertain (I 2B–3).

Hanow (Hanough, Havenoth), William. Bailiff of Pinvin hundred, 1371–7 (WAM 24515, 24516*, 24517, 24406; I 13).

Harberd, Geoffrey. Lessee of the demesne at Castlemorton, 1381–3, and possibly until 1386 (I 16–18).

Hathemere (Hathemare, Hademor'), John. With his brother, Richard, was a figure in manorial administration at Chaceley for four decades and perhaps more. Reeve, 1349–50, 1361–3, jointly with Richard in 1365–6, and sole reeve again in 1368–9 and 1370–1 (WAM 21083, 21088–9, 21091–3, 24514; I 6). In 1371–2, obtained a lease for 12 years and for a rent of £8 p.a., of the demesne and the vaccary, and apparently completed his term (WAM 21094, 24515; I 11–14, 16–17).

Hathemere, Richard. Reeve of Chaceley, 1364–5, and reeve jointly with his brother, John, in 1365–6 (WAM 21090; I 6). Rent-collector in 1373–6 and possibly from 1371 (WAM 21094, 24517).

Haukeshot, Walter. Bailiff of the abbot's liberty in Gloucestershire, 1393–4, 1402–10 and 1416–21 (WAM 24297, 24303–6, 24308–9).

Haukyns, William. Rent-collector at Castlemorton, 1357–8. A longer term or a further term is possible (WAM 21056; I 5).

Hegg' (atte Hegg', de Hegg'), Gilbert. Lessee of the demesne at Longdon, 1382–3 (I 17).

Hegg', Hugh. Lessee of the demesne at Longdon by 23 January 1384, when ordered by the court of Longdon to clear ditches for which he was responsible; still lessee in 1387–8 (WAM 21124, mem. 2; I 17–18).

Heope, Richard. Occurs at Deerhurst 1387–8, probably as one of two rent-collectors acting jointly (I 19).

Hethe, John atte. Reeve of Pyrford, 1361–2 (WAM 27418, I5).

Heyne (Heynes), William. Reeve of Bourton-on-the-Hill, 1374–6 (WAM 8303–4).

Heyward (Heyword), John. Reeve of Laleham, 5 December 1348–28 September 1356, and 29 September 1362–18 February 1363; removed from office on the last date for reasons not explained in our sources (WAM 27136–40, 27145–6).

Hogges (Hegges, Heehges), John. Rent-collector at Bourton-on-the-Hill, 1414–24, and possibly for a longer period (WAM 24426–9).

Holdy (Oldi), Henry. Reeve of Castlemorton, 1364–8 (WAM 24511–12; I 6–8).

Holdy (Oldi), William. Reeve of Castlemorton manor by the end of 1348–9 (I 2A). Reeve of Castlemorton rectory, 1350–1, an appointment normally combined with the reeveship of Castlemorton manor (WAM 21046). It is therefore likely that William Holdy also held the reeveship of the manor in 1350–1.

Hone, Robert. Reeve of Pyrford, 1397–1400 (WAM 27432–3).

Hoppere, Robert. Rent-collector of estreats of the court at Hardwicke, 1349–50 (I 3).

Hughes (Hugh'), Adam. Reeve of Pershore and probably the immediate predecessor of John Adekyn in 1343. The liability of the homage of Pershore for payment of his arrears, which had taken effect by the end of the year 1348–9, suggests that he was by then dead (WAM 22121–4; I 2B).

Hughes, John. Rent-collector at Pershore, 1344–5. Deceased by the end of 1350–1 (I 2B–3).

Hughes (Hugh'), Richard. Rent-collector at Pershore, 1366–8 (I 7–8).

Hulle, Robert on the. Reeve of Bourton-on-the-Hill from an uncertain date in the course of 1348–9 to the end of 1349–50 (WAM 8282; I 2B).

Huller, John. Bailiff of Ebury, 1395–1407; rent-collector, 1400–7 (WAM 26948–54).

Huller, William. Bailiff of Ebury, 28 September 1370 until his death in the course of 1387–8. It is clear that Joan (Janyn), his widow, acted as bailiff from his death until 14 April 1389, when Henry Kyrkeby was appointed to this office (WAM 26926–42).

Hurry, Robert. Reeve of Sutton-under-Brailes, 1397–8; reeve and rent-collector, 1398–9 (GRO, D1099/M31/53–4).

Hurry, Thomas. Reeve of Sutton-under-Brailes, 1367–79 (WAM 24512–20, 25914–15; GRO, D1099/M31/44–5; and for Hurry's first year as reeve, see also I 8). As reeve of Sutton-under-Brailes, Hurry was *ex officio* reeve of Stourton from the abbot's acquisition of this property in 1369 until 1376, the last year in which it is mentioned as one of his manors. For Stourton, see I 11 and 13.

Hurst, Thomas atte. Bailiff of Denham Durdent's manor, 6 March 1369–1375 (WAM 3416, 24515; I 11–12). Bailiff of Denham, 1379–25 March 1380 (I 15).

Hwet (Huet), Walter. Bailiff of Bourton-on-the-Hill, 1396–8 (WAM 8316–18).

Idilcote (Idulcote, Idulkote), T. Abbot's chamberlain, 1346–8 (WAM 14794, 21082, 27133, 27135). Occurs frequently in the ministers' accounts of these years as one who visited the abbot's manors in the course of the year and departed with cash which he subsequently delivered to the household (WAM 14795; I 1).

Jakes, Nicholas. Rent-collector at Laleham before he is first mentioned in the text, and probably in 1394–5 (WAM 27159–62; I 21–3).

Jakes, William. Rent-collector at Laleham, 1395–6 (WAM 27160).

Jordemayn. Lessee of the vaccary at Ebury, 1393–4 (WAM 26947).

Kentwine (Kentwen), John. Rent-collector at Pershore, 1345–6; said to be of Pensham; died before 28 September 1351 (WAM 22515; I 1, 2B).

Kerdiff (Kerdyf, Keardif, Keardyf), John. Reep-reeve and collector of estreats of the court at Castlemorton (I 3).

Kyrkeby, Henry. Bailiff of Ebury, 17 April 1389–9 February 1390 (WAM 26941–3). Bailiff of Todenham, 29 December 1388–28 September 1390 (GRO, D1099/M30/19; WAM 25979).

Lake, John. Reeve and rent-collector at Islip, 1423–4 (WAM 14835; I 24).

Lakyngheth, Br. John, monk of Westminster, abbot's treasurer. Supervises sale of wool (I 5). Makes new custumal and rental for, respectively, Laleham and Staines (I 9); keeper of temporalities (I 19); monk-bailiff (I 19).

Le Hunte, Richard. Reeve of Islip, 1348–9: see the next entry.

Le Hunte, Thomas, also known as Thomas Bigge. Reeve of Islip from 27 May 1349, the third person to hold the office in the year 1348–9, the others being Richard Le Hunte (13 September 1348–11 April 1349) and William Ottele (11 April 1349–27 May 1349) (WAM 14796–7; I 3).

Leonard (Leynard), John. Rent-collector at Sutton-under-Brailes, probably in 1420–2 (I 24).

Leteman, John. Bailiff of Yeoveney, 23 June 1376–15 April 1379 (WAM 16886–9).

Longe, Richard. Lessee of the demesne at Laleham, 1388–99 (WAM 16886–9).

Lovecock, Thomas. Said in 1364–5 to have been 'lately' (*nuper*) reeve of Sutton-under-Brailes (WAM 24511). Probably reeve in 1363–4.

Lytsot, Thomas. Mentioned in 1399 as rent-collector at Deerhurst (I 23).

Mason, John. With John Vampage (below) lessee of the demesne at Pershore, in accordance with a lease for 12 years, dated 29 September 1391. Both lessees are said to be 'of Pershore', a description that may refer in each case to the town of Pershore (LNQ, f. lvii; I 22).

Mawnsel, John. Unidentified except by name, but perhaps one of Robert Wroxton's successors as rent-collector at Bourton-on-the-Hill (I 20).

Mede, William. Bailiff of Todenham, 1387–8 (GRO, D1099/M30/18).

Mille, Gilbert atte. Reeve of Laleham, 20 June 1375–29 September 1375 (WAM 27155). Became reeve on the removal from office of John South (q.v.), and may have served for a longer term than our sources demonstrate. He is erroneously described in WAM 24518 as serjeant of Laleham.

Mille (Mulle, Mylle), John atte. Bailiff/serjeant of Laleham, 18 February 1363–29 September 1388 (WAM 24531–2, 24536–24536*, 27146–58).

Miller, John. Lessee of the arable demesne at Ebury, 28 or 29 September 1365–31 May 1367 (WAM 26029–1).

Millward, William. Lessee of watermill at Islip (I 24).

Mochegros, John. Occurs at Castlemorton in 1349 and 1350. His identity as a manorial servant, probably reeve, is clearer on the second occasion than on the first (I 2B–3).

Monmouth, John. Merchant of Gloucester. In 1373, with Elizabeth, his wife, later Elizabeth Bruys, received for their joint and several lives a lease of the site of the manor of Hardwicke, with the demesne. Elizabeth was the survivor, and as Elizabeth Bruys, after remarriage, was still in possession in 1396–7 (WAM 8445–9, 32775; for details of the lease, I 11).

More, Stephen atte. Rent-collector in Pershore, 1345–6 (WAM 22126).

Morhouse (Morehouse), Richard. Bailiff of Todenham, 1 December 1390–28 September 1391 (WAM 25981).

Mower, Nicholas. Reeve of Pinvin, 1364–5, 1367–72 (WAM 22292, 22294–7). Bailiff of Pinvin hundred, 1370–1 (I 9).

Mulward, Richard. Occurs at Castlemorton in 1362–3 among 8 manorial officials, including the current lessee of the demesne, all of whom owed arrears, and these were in some cases apparently 10 years old. It seems likely that Mulward was a rent-collector or reeve at some point in this period (WAM 21089).

Nichole (Nicholes), William. Rent-collector at Pershore, 1347–8; said to be of Pensham (WAM 22515; I 1, 2B, 3).

Noke, John atte. Serjeant of Staines and Yeoveney, 28 September 1346–24 May 1349, the latter date being the probable date of his death (WAM 16931, 16872).

Noke, Robert atte. Serjeant of Ebury, 9 January 1342–13 April 1349, the latter date being the probable date of his death. Noke had previously served as serjeant of Denham (I 2B).

Norton, Henry. Took delivery of the *lana grossa* in the demesne wool crops at Ebury in 1397–9 (I 21, 23). Probably an official of the abbot's household.

Ode (Odea), Henry. Rent-collector at Castlemorton, 1362–79, and possibly until 1388 (I 5, 12–13, 18–19). Perhaps identical with Henry Ody; said in 1384 to be a serf (*nativus domini*) (WAM 21124, mem. 12, court held on 21 April 1384).

Ode (Hod'), Richard. Reeve of Castlemorton, 28 September 1352–25 March 1353, also in 1368–9 (WAM 24513). Said in 1384 to be a serf (*nativus domini*) (WAM 21124, mem. 12, court held on 21 April 1384).

Olkyn (Elkyn), John. Rent-collector at Todenham, 1397–1404; reeve and rent-collector, 1404–16 (GRO, D1099/M30/24–31).

Osbern, John (I). London wool merchant (I 5).

Osbern, John (II). Rent-collector at Pershore, 1347–8; said to be of Wick (I 1, 2B).

Osbern (Osbarne, Osberne), William. Rent-collector at Pershore, 1370–1 (WAM 24514; I 9). Bailiff of Pershore, 1376–7 (I 13–14).

Ottele, William. Bailiff of Todenham, 1374–5 (WAM 24518, 25973; I 12).

Padyngton, Nigel. Said in 1349 to have been 'lately' serjeant of Denham. If, as seems likely, he was the most senior of the three former serjeants owing arrears on this occasion, a date before *c*.1340 is likely (I 2B)

Page, Walter. Serjeant/bailiff of Hyde, 1365–75 (WAM 27073–81).

Pagene, John de. Possibly reeve of Castlemorton in succession to John Upton in 1349–50 (I 3). Reeve here in 1357–8 (WAM 21056).

Pal (Paal), Thomas. Probably reeve of Castlemorton in 1348–9 or for part of that year (I 2B, 3). Perhaps to be identified with the namesake who was reeve of Castlemorton in 1331–2 and 1336–7, and perhaps until 1348–9 (WAM 21050, 21052).

Palle (Palli, Pally), Adam. Reeve of Castlemorton, 1370–1; rent-collector at Castlemorton, at first alone, but before the end of the year, with Henry Ode (WAM 24514; I 9, 11).

Palle (Palli, Pally), William. Rent-collector at Pershore, 1344–5 (I 1, 2B, 3).

Palmer (Palmere), John, on occasion just called 'John'. Reeve of Deerhurst, 1362–5 (WAM 24511; I 5–6).

Parham, Walter. Said in 1354 to be bailiff of the abbot's liberties in Gloucestershire (WAM 8441). Also exercised a wider supervisory role over the abbot's manors in the Western Parts, where in 1370–1 he was styled 'supervisor', but possibly by 1379 'steward'; in the latter capacity, he had a fee of £4 p.a. (WAM 24514, 24406, 24409). Said to be 'of Bourton'; also held land in Stourton, but probably as a nominee of the abbot of Westminster, who never amortised his land here (WAM 640–1, 643, 8203). In 1383, the abbot granted Parham a pension of £2 p.a. for life, payable from Bourton-on-the-Hill, and a squire's robe, with fur, to be received as often as the abbot's squires received such robes (WAM 8202).

Parker, John (I). Bailiff of the abbot's liberty in Gloucestershire, 1364–5 (I 9–10); bailiff of Pershore, 1366–7 (I 7). In accordance with a lease dated 28 September 1370, became lessee of the site of the manor of Pensham and the demesne for 12 years, at a rent of £8 p.a. (LNQ, f. lxiv). Bailiff of the portmoot of Pershore, 1371–5 (WAM 24406, 24515–17).

Parker, John (II). Bailiff of Pyrford, 1389–90 (WAM 24541).

Patrich', Thomas. Bailiff of Pinvin and Defford hundreds, 1348–9, and subsequently locum tenens until a successor could be found (WAM 22126; I 3).

Phillip, Nicholas. Lessee of the demesne at Chaceley, 1385–1410 and for part of the year 1410–11; by the end of this year, Margaret Phillip, his widow, had become sole lessee. To our knowledge, Nicholas was rent-collector at Chaceley in 1378–9 and in 1400–11, and it is likely that he was so throughout his years as lessee (WAM 21095–7, 24010–20, 24409; I 18).

Pigon (Pygon), Richard. Rent-collector at Pinvin, 1392–3, but an earlier period of service, in or about 1385–6, is a possibility (WAM 22310; I 18).

Pinvin, Ralph. Reeve of Pinvin, 1365–7 (WAM 22293; I 7). Bailiff of Pershore, 1371–2 (I 10). With Robert Crompe (above), farmer of the demesne at Pinvin, 1375–8 (WAM 22302–3).

Plumtre, Philip. Serjeant of Ebury, 29 September 1333–21 April 1337 (WAM 26883–6). Serjeant/bailiff of Laleham, 21 April 1337–29 September 1337 (WAM 27128). Lessee of 53 acres, probably of demesne, at Ebury, 1342–51 (WAM 26897–907). During the last period, Plumtre served again as serjeant of Ebury, 13 April 1349–28 September 1349, thus tiding the administration of the manor over the difficult period following the death of Robert atte Noke, a long-serving serjeant, on 13 April (WAM 26904–5).

Preston, Robert. Reeve of Sutton-under-Brailes, 1364–7 (I 6–7).

Pychford, William. Bailiff/serjeant of Pershore, 1373–8 (WAM 24517–19).

Rawlyns, Richard. Succeeded John Leteman as bailiff of Yeoveney on 15 April 1379 and held office until 17 August. The termination of his appointment may be explained by the beginning of John Dorman's lease of the manor (WAM 16889, rot. 2).

Rayel (Rayell' Raiell'), William. Rent-collector at Pinvin, 1379–82 (WAM 22305–7).

Reeve, William. Rent-collector at Longdon, 1387–8 (I 19).

Richard, rector of Wyche. Lessee of the site of the manor and demesne at Deerhurst, 1373–4. Said to be rector of the church 'del More' (WAM 8451).

Roberd' (Robert), Guy. Bailiff of Denham, 1381–2 (I 16).

Robyns, John. Reeve of Bourton-on-the-Hill, 1343–8; died in office in the course of the following year (WAM 8278–81; I 2B).

Rogers, John. Stockman for sheep, responsible for management of sheep on the abbot's manors in the Western Parts, and for their sale and purchase, as necessary. Though not responsible for the actual sale of *lana grossa*, he had an important role in ensuring that it reached the chosen centre for sale. The earliest of his three surviving accounts covers the period 8 December 1387–28 September 1388, and the latest, the year 1393–4. He may have served continuously between these dates; and he served again in 1397–8 (GRO, D1099/M30/18; WAM 25977, 25982; I 22–3).

Rubbe, Richard. Lessee of the vaccary at Ebury, 1388–93, 1395–8 (WAM 26942, 26948–50).

Rysele, Thomas. Bailiff of the portmoot of Pershore, 1370–2 (WAM 24514–15).

Sawer (Sawier), Thomas. See Wauberd, Walter, below.

Selk (Sell), Richard. The arrears of 10s. 4d. attributed to him annually at Pinvin in 1393–9 inclusive indicate that he had once held office; the repetition of the same sum may mean that he had moved away from the manor (I 20, 22–3).

Shareshill (Shareshull'), Robert. Steward in the Western Parts, 1346–51. The size of his stipend of £10 p.a. indicates that he was chief steward (WAM 8280–2, 22123–5; and for his stipend, see also I 2A).

Shepherd (Scheperd, Shephird), William. Served twice as bailiff of Defford hundred: the first time, probably in 1382–3, the second, in or before 1397–9 (I 17, 22–3). Rent-collector at Bourton-on-the-Hill, 1397–9 (WAM 8317–18).

Snow, William. Reeve of Laleham, 1398–9 (WAM 27163).

Solas, John. The earliest reference in the surviving sources to Solas is as lessee of the demesne at Hardwicke; he obtained a 40-year lease in 1427, with the names of Joan, his wife, and Thomas, his son, in the lease (WAM 8466–7).

Soper, David. To be identified with the serjeant named David holding office at Denham, 1373–5 (WAM 24517–8).

South, John (I). Reeve of Denham for an unknown period before 1348–9 (I 2B).

South, John (II), alias John Cherchewyne. Reeve of Laleham for four discrete terms. The first may have lasted for only one year, 1327–8 (TNA, SC 6/916/20). On 12 October 1331, however, he succeeded Thomas Gyles now removed from office, and served until 1336 (WAM 27121–6). His third term extended only from 29 September 1341 to 8 June 1342, and his fourth from 30 March 1347 to 5 December 1348 (WAM 27130, 27133–6). It is likely that South died on the last date.

South, John (III). Served as reeve of Laleham, 1356–8, and as rent-collector there before 1362–3, when the arrears that he owed are noted in auditors' memoranda (WAM 27141–2; I 5). Served as rent-collector in 1370–1, and as reeve for the greater part of 1374–5 (I 9; WAM 27155).

Spark (Sparke), Thomas. Appointed serjeant/bailiff of Chaceley, 22 December 1347 (I 1) on the death of the reeve, Adam Broun; his tenure of this position was over by 28 September 1349 (I 2B).

Spenser, William. Serjeant/bailiff of Denham, 1368–73 (WAM 24513–15, 24516*).

Sperhauk, William. Charged with arrears of £1 3s. 11½d. at Pershore from 1381 to 1388 (I 16, 19). Lessee of the site of the manor and the demesne at Pensham for 12 years, and at a rent of £8 p.a., in accordance with a lease dated 28 September 1382; said on this occasion to be of Pensham (LNQ, f. lxiii). The lease was renewed for a further 12 years in 1394 (WAM 22241). The forinsec bailiwick that he held in 1397–8 was probably that of the portmoot of Pershore, with which he is explicitly associated in the following year (I 22–3). Probably died before 28 September 1398, when a new lessee, William Aleyn, is mentioned at Pensham (WAM 22243).

Sponge, Walter. Bailiff of Pyrford, probably in 1391–2, the year to which his long-lasting arrears of £1 6s. 2d. can be traced (WAM 27429–33).

Sponge, William. Bailiff of Todenham, 1376–85 (GRO, D1099/M30/12–17; WAM 24519, 25975).

Stacy, John. Mentioned in 1365–6 as lessee of the arable demesne at Deerhurst (WAM 8450).

Stilman, Nicholas. Bailiff of Denham 1387–1402 (WAM 3012–13, 3409–10, 24536*, 24539, 24546).

Stoke, John atte. Rent-collector at Hardwicke, 1394–5, and possibly since 1387–8 (WAM 8448).

Stoke, Richard. Possibly the current rent-collector and, if so, the official rendering account at Hardwicke in 1392–3 (I 20).

Strode, William. Bailiff of Bourton-on-the-Hill, 1377–9 (WAM 8306; I 14).

Surpayne (Surpayn, Sourpayne), Thomas. Reeve of Deerhurst, 1367–72 (WAM 24512–15; I 8).

Swanne (Swan'), John. Serjeant of Ebury, 31 May 1367–29 September 1370 (WAM 26921–4). Swanne's appointment as serjeant coincides with the resumption of direct exploitation of the arable demesne, after a period of leasing, John Miler (above) being the last lessee.

Takepenny (Takepany), Walter. Reap-reeve and collector of rents and estreats at Staines and Yeoveney, 1349 (I 2B).

Takepenny, William. Woodward at Staines and Yeoveney, 1348–9 (I 2B).

Tangleye, John. Tangleye was rent-collector at Staines, 1362–8. He was lessee of the demesne 1363–7, and probably in this position for the entire period for which he was rent-collector (WAM 16933, 24511–12; I 6–8).

Taylor, Philip, see Hakkes, Henry.

Thomas, William. Bailiff of the abbot's liberty in Gloucestershire, and probably in 1394–6, when a gap occurs in the known succession of bailiffs in this period. If so, for his predecessor, see Haukeshot, Walter, and for his successor, Hall, John.

Tilney (Tilneye, Tylney), John. Lessee of Billet's manor in Laleham, probably from 29 September 1400 to 25 December 1400 at a rent of £6 p.a. (WAM 24545, 27159).

Tondy (Tundi, Tundy), John. Bailiff of Pinvin hundred, 1362–3 (I 5). Perhaps identical with John Tundy, bailiff of this hundred in 1398–9 (I 23).

Tondy, Margery, wife of William Tondy, whose lands she held in widowhood (WAM 22524). Probably identical with Margery Toney, bailiff of Pinvin hundred, 1397–8 (I 22). Rent-collector at Pinvin, 1399–1400 (WAM 24412).

Tondy (Tundi, Tundy), William. Bailiff of Pinvin hundred, 1364–5 and 1368–9 (WAM 24511–13; I 7). Of servile status, but, as noted in 1382, after his death, held, in addition to a customary half-virgate, 16 acres of free land acquired by inheritance (WAM 22514). Reeve of Pinvin, 1344–52 (WAM 22284–5).

Tresour (Tresor), Alexander. Rent-collector alias bailiff of Staines, 1368–1404 (WAM 16934–6, 24513–20, 24524–5, 24527–32, 24535–6*).

Tymmes, Robert. Reeve of Todenham, 1346–53 (WAM 25962–4).

Underhill, Richard de. It is likely that Richard de Underhill was serjeant of Longdon manor and rectory from 28 September 1348 and in succession to William Boteler (above), and certain that he held this office from 14 April 1349 to 29 September 1350 (WAM 21019–22, 21037–9). As collector of estreats in 1348–9, his responsibilities were wider and extended to Castlemorton (I 2B–3).

Upton, John. Probably reeve of Castlemorton for a short period in 1349, and as the predecessor of John Pagen' (I 3).

Vampage, John (I). Bailiff of Pershore portmoot, 1347–8 and 1349–50, and very likely in the intervening year (I 1, 3). At about the time he relinquished office, in 1350, he owed the abbot income from the portmoot amounting to £3 7s. The persistent arrears of 17s. 3d. recorded from 1365–72, inclusive, represent the unpaid residue of this debt. Appointed keeper of Tidesley Park, with life-tenure, in 1351.

Vampage, John (II), known in due course as John Vampage the elder. Clerk to the steward of the Western Parts, alias clerk of the courts in the Western Parts, 1387–9. Received a fee of £1 6s. 8d. p.a. (WAM 24537–9). With John Mason, obtained, in 1391, a lease of the demesne at Binholme (rural Pershore), at a rent of £10 p.a., and for 12 years (LNQ, f. lvii). Vampage the elder was already a substantial freeholder in Binholme (WAM 32820). In later leases, his son John, known as John Vampage the younger, was the sole lessee, and the term was 20 years (WAM 22130–1). Vampage the elder died in 1451 or 1452 (WAM 24450–1).

Vampage, John (III), known as John Vampage the younger. In the abbot's employment by 1431–2. Steward of the Western Parts and in receipt of a fee of £2 p.a., with livery or 13s. 4d. p.a. in lieu (WAM 24429–30). Chief steward of the Western Parts 1410–16, with a fee of £5 p.a. and livery (WAM 24437; GRO, D1099/M31/61). By 1454–5, lessee of the abbot's demesne in Binholme.

Verney (Vernay), Roger. Lessee of the site of the manor and the demesne at Todenham, 1391–1400; said to be of *Lemyngton*, in Todenham (LNQ, f. lxix; GRO, D1099/M30/21–3).

Wade, Robert atte. Reeve of Pyrford during the latter part of 1348–9, and possibly for the whole year (I 2A).

Warde, Henry. Lessee, with parcenars, of a grange and cattleshed (*boveria*) at Pinvin, 1387–96 (WAM 22309).

Warfeld, Walter, monk of Westminster. Abbot's stockman, 1371–2.

Wauberd, Walter, and Sawer (Sawier), Thomas. Rent-collectors at Denham, 1395–9 (WAM 3410; I 21–3).

Webbe, Richard. Owed 3s. 7½d. at Longdon in 1398 (I 22). Office not known.

Welles, Thomas (I). Rent-collector at Pershore, 1343–4 (I 1, 2B).

Welles (Willes), Thomas (II). Reeve of Sutton-under-Brailes, 1362–3 (I 5).

Werkman (Werkmon), William. An office holder at Castlemorton before *c.*1397 but otherwise unidentified (I 22–3).

Westende, Walter atte. Bailiff of Hyde, 18 March 1383–28 September 1384 (WAM 27092, 27094).

Weyland, Henry. Owing a debt at Castlemorton as if a former office holder at the end of the account in 1349–50 (I 3).

Weyland, Nicholas. Owing a debt at Castlemorton as if a former office holder at the end of the account in 1349–50 (I 3).

Whateley (Whatley), Robert. A monk of Westminster and currently a student at Oxford. We should understand that Forthey, now receiver in the Western Parts, employed the student returning to Oxford on vacation to deliver cash and/or supervise the delivery of victuals to the abbot's household. Whateley also participated in the audit of ministers' accounts in the Western Parts (WAM 24410–11; for Whateley's career, see *BRUO*, iii, p. 2030).

Whyte, Gilbert, alias Gilbert Carter. Bailiff of Bourton-on-the-Hill, 1380–5 (WAM 8207–9, 24586; I 17).

Wilcot, Is[aiah]. Bailiff of Wick hundred, 1364–5 (I 6).

Wilyngton (Wolyngton, Wollyngton), Robert de. Woodward and reap-reeve at Bourton-on-the-Hill, 10 June 1350–29 September 1350 (WAM 8282). Serjeant of Castlemorton, 25 March 1353–28 September 1354 (WAM 21054–5). Serjeant of Longdon manor, 1352–4, and of Longdon rectory, 1361–2 (WAM 21022–3, 21042).

Wippeschot (Wippeschott, Webschot), William. Reeve of Pyrford, 1364–5 (WAM 27419, 24511).

Wroxton, Robert. Wroxton was probably rent-collector in 1383–5 or one or other of these years, the only recent years for which the surviving sources do not record the name or names of the rent-collector at Bourton-on-the-Hill (I 18).

Wycheford (Wicheford, Wictheford), William. Serjeant of Pershore, 1373–9 (WAM 24517–20).

Wylkyn, Thomas. Reeve of Sutton-under-Brailes, 1348–9 (I 2A–B).

Wynkebourne, Alexander. Serjeant of Longdon rectory, 11 June 1352–25 June 1353, and 1 August 1353–29 September 1353 (WAM 21043–4). Serjeant of Longdon, Castlemorton and Chaceley rectories, 1354–5 (WAM 21045). With Henry and Robert Grafton, participated in a 20-year lease of the manor of Longdon from 25 June 1357 (WAM 32744).

Wynter, Thomas. Mentioned in 1416–17, when he leased the demesne of Islip, with meadow and pastures, dovecot and multure from the mill, for a rent of £13 6s. 8d. By 1430–1, the rent had been reduced by £8 p.a. (WAM 14837; I 22).

Texts

The Convent's Estates

II 1 View of the states of the convent's royal manors, *c.*25 March 1300

A roll of two membranes, 170 mm wide, Chancery fashion, with modern sewing with white thread. Membrane 1 has been laid out with a fold across the top for the title and a fold for a left margin on the recto. The roll is a fair copy, with some alterations to totals possibly in a second ink. The main hand of this document wrote membrane 1 recto and dorse, with some erasures and additions, and also membrane 2 dorse, which was added to continue the account on the dorse (the recto of membrane 2 is blank). There is a title at the head of the dorse of membrane 1, in a mid- to late fourteenth-century hand: 'Status maneriorum A' regine anno regni regis Edwardi j xxviij°', with the 'j' after 'Edwardi' inserted. The document has been edited here as two separate items, II 1–2. II 1, a view of the states of the royal manors—those of Eleanor of Castile's foundation—occcupies membrane 1 recto; the dorse is edited as II 2. Although II 1 and II 2 relate to different obediences, they represent the fruits of a single itinerary by three appointed monks. In each case, the dominant figure was probably Alexander de Neuport, who operates in II 1 as warden of Eleanor of Castile's manors, responsible for their administration, and in II 2 as pittancer, though with similar duties. His dual capacity may explain why the need was felt for a copy of two distinct documents on the same piece of parchment.[1]

WAM 23630

[*Mem. 1 recto*] Status maneriorum domine regine visus per fratres A. de Neuport, A. de Persore et R. de Aldenham anno regni regis Edwardi xxviij°

Torveston Willelmus Patesti prepositus eiusdem manerii debet super visu suo anni xxviij[2] liiij s. x d. Thomas de Wedon' serviens eiusdem manerii debet super visu finalis compoti sui de annis xxvj et xxvij[3] Cxij s. Et sunt ibidem levand*um*[4] de redditu tallagio hydagio et wodeselv*er* de terminis sequentibus Ciij s. vij d. ob. Et sunt ibidem in granario j qr. vij bus. drageti, ij bus. avenarum. Et estimantur ibidem in tasso iij idus Marcii[5] C qr. frumenti, xlij qr. drageti. Inde in semine iiij qr. di. drageti; in liberacionibus famulorum usque festum sancti Michaelis[6] xiij qr. vj bus. frumenti, xj qr. di. drageti; in farina pro potagio famulorum, prebenda equorum, affrorum, vitulorum, pro adventu custodis, xij qr. di. avenarum. Pro stipendiis famulorum assignantur ad vend*endum* x qr. drageti, precium qr. iij s. iiij d. Pro aliis vero expensis et reprisis manerii necnon et pro adventu custodis

[1] Extant ministers' accounts: Birdbrook, 29 September 1299–24 November 1299, and 25 November 1299–29 September 1300, WAM 25402–3; Turweston, WAM 7761; Westerham, WAM 26392. On Eleanor's foundation, see Harvey, *Obedientiaries*, pp. 139–41.

[2] 1299–1300.

[3] 1296–7 and 1297–8.

[4] MS: 'ibid'' follows but has been struck out.

[5] MS: 'iij idus Marcii' inserted; 13 March 1300.

[6] 29 September 1300.

assignantur[7] exitus daerie, perquisita curie, cum aliis minutis exitibus manerii preter lanam. Et sic remanent ad vendendum iiij^{xx}vj qr. ij bus. frumenti, xvij qr. vij bus. drageti. De quibus assignantur ad vend*endum* xij qr. drageti pro xij qr. ij bus. avenarum deficientibus ad prebendam.
Et sunt ibidem ij equi carectarii, viij affri, xv boves, ix vacce, ij boviculi, ij annales, ij vituli, xxxvij multones et matrices, iij agni, vij auce, xiiij capones, ix galline.
Et seminantur ibidem de frumento xxij qr. iiij bus. di., v qr. pisarum, iij bus. vescarum,[8] xxxj qr. drageti preter iiij qr. di. que nondum seminantur, xix qr. j bus. avenarum.

Summa denariorum remanencium xxxij li. xij s. ij d., cum lana estimata ad xviij s. vj d. Memorandum quod respectuantur eidem xlv s. de lana liberata Thome de Wedon' donec inter eosdem discussum fuerit.[9]

Grafton Ricardus de Westiney serviens eiusdem manerii debet super visu compoti sui anni xxviij vj s. x d. ob. Et memorandum quod Ricardus le Hunte serviens ante ipsum nondum reddit compotum de annis xxiiij, xxv et xxvj.[10] Et sunt ibidem levandum de redditu, tallagio et averagio, subtractis acquietanciis de redditu debito aliis, v s. j d. ob. Et fuerunt ibidem ij idus Marcii[11] in granario ij bus. frumenti, iij bus. pisarum et vescarum. Et estimantur ibidem in tasso xv qr. ij qr. avenarum, j qr. di. pisarum et vescarum. Inde in liberacionibus servientis et famulorum usque festum sancti Michaelis v qr. ij bus. di. frumenti, ij qr. ij bus. di. pisarum et vescarum. Et sic deficiunt vj bus. di. pisarum et vescarum pro quibus assignantur iij bus. di. frumenti. In prebenda affrorum et boum, in farina pro potagio famulorum, j qr. avenarum. Pro custu autumpni in denariis, stipendiis famulorum et aliis minutis reprisis et expensis manerii assignatur residuum bladi superius remanentis, cum arreragiis servientis et redditu levando ut supra.
Et sunt ibidem j affrus, viij boves, vj capones, vij galline.
Et seminantur ibidem xiij qr. frumenti, iij qr. j bus. pisarum et vescarum, iiij qr. ij bus. drageti, vj qr. avenarum. Et nichil remanet.

Knoll' Radulphus de Perham serviens eiusdem manerii debet super visu compoti sui anni xxviij vij li. ij s. vij d. ob. qua.[12] Et sunt ibidem levand*um*

[7] MS: 'vend'' follows but has been struck out.
[8] MS: 'fabarum' struck out; 'vescarum' inserted.
[9] 53½ fleeces, weighing 6½ st., were sold. The final price is not recorded (WAM 7761).
[10] 1295–6, 1296–7 and 1297–8.
[11] MS: 'ij idus Marcie' inserted; 14 March 1300.
[12] MS: 'ob. qua.' inserted in the same hand.

de redditu, tallagio et firmis, xvij li. iiij s. v d. ob.[13] Et fuerunt ibidem in granario j qr. vj bus. di. frumenti,[14] j qr. j bus. fabarum, x qr. di. avenarum. Et estimantur ibidem in tasso die sanctorum martirorum Cyriaci et sociorum eius[15] xl qr. frumenti, vj qr. mixt*ilionis*, xij qr. siliginis, iiij qr. ordei,[16] v qr. pisarum, xliiij qr. avenarum. Inde in semine xxxv qr. avenarum; in liberacionibus famulorum usque festum sancti Michaelis viij qr. frumenti, vj qr. mixt*ilionis*, iiij qr.[17] v bus. siliginis, v qr. pisarum; in expensis custumariorum falcancium, arancium et metencium de consuetudine, iij qr. ij bus. frumenti;[18] in farina, prebenda equorum, affrorum, boum et pro adventu custodis et servientis xvij qr. avenarum. Pro stipendiis famulorum et custu autumpni in denariis[19] assignantur vendendum vij qr. iij bus. siliginis precium qr. iij s. iiij d., iiij qr. ordei precium qr. iiij s., ij qr. di. avenarum precium qr. ij s. iiij d. Pro aliis expensis et reprisis manerii necnon et pro vadiis servientis et adventu custodis assignantur vend*endum* viij qr. frumenti precium qr. iiij s., una cum perquisitis curie et aliis exitibus manerii preter daeriam, que valebit per estimacionem iiij li. x s. Et sic remanent ulterius ad vendendum xxij qr. iiij bus. di.[20] frumenti, j qr. j bus. fabarum,[21] precium ut supra.

Et sunt ibidem j equus, iij jumenta, iiij pullani iij annorum, ij pullani ij annorum, xxviij boves, xx vacce, xv bovetti quorum vij juvence, xiij boviculi, xj annales, ij pavones, v pave, v auce, vj capones, xxviij galline.

Et seminantur ibidem de frumento xxj qr. di., de siligine iiij qr. di., de fabis j qr. iij bus., de pisis et vescis ij qr., de albis pisis v bus., xxxix qr. vij bus. avenarum, preter id quod nondum seminatur.

Summa denariorum remanencium custodi solvendorum xxxiij li. xj s. x d. qua.

Bridebrok' Thomas atte Tounesende prepositus eiusdem manerii debet super finali compoto suo anni xxvj[22] xv li. iiij d. Robertus de Neuport serviens post ipsum debet super finali compoto suo anni xxviij vj li. xix s.

[13] MS: 'v d. ob.' inserted in the same hand.
[14] MS: 'frumenti' inserted.
[15] 16 March 1300, according to the kalendar of Westminster Abbey: *English Benedictine Kalendars After AD1100*, vol. 1, *Abbotsbury–Durham*, ed. F. Wormald (Henry Bradshaw Society, 77; 1939), pp. 182–3. It seems likely that the three monks went from Knowle to Oakham, where they conducted the view on or about 21 March.
[16] MS: followed by 'in', but struck out.
[17] MS: 'iiij qr.' inserted.
[18] MS: a short erasure follows.
[19] MS: several words have been erased at this point, and lines have been drawn over the erasure.
[20] MS: 'di.' inserted.
[21] MS: 'j qr. j bus. fabarum' inserted.
[22] MS: a short erasure follows; 'anni xxvj', 1297–8.

iij d. ob. qua. Clemens de Beygham prepositus post ipsum debet super visu suo anni xxviij^{i} xlij s. vj d.[23] Et sunt levand*um* ibidem de redditu et firmis iij terminorum subsequencium xiij[24] li. iij d. Et fuerunt ibidem in grenario in crastino annunciacionis beate Marie[25] vj qr. vj bus. frumenti, ij qr. ij bus. mixt*ure*, iij qr. di. fabarum, xvj qr. v bus. avenarum, cum blado mutuato. Et estimantur ibidem in tasso de frumento veteris grani C qr.,[26] de frumento novi grani Cxx qr., de mixt*ure* viij qr., de fabis et pisis ix qr., de avenis xj qr. Et sunt levand*um* de firma[27] molendini vj qr. vj bus. mixt*ure*.[28] Inde in liberacionibus famulorum usque festum sancti Michaelis v qr. frumenti, x qr. di. mixtilionis. In farina prebenda equorum, affrorum, boum et pro adventu custodis, xxviii qr. vj bus. De quibus deficit j qr. j bus. avenarum, pro quibus assignatur vend*endum* j qr. fabarum et pisarum. Pro custu autumpni in denariis et stipendiis vaccarii et warennarii ix qr. frumenti precium qr. v s. iiij d., xij qr. mixt*ure* precium qr. iij s., xj qr. di. fabarum et pisarum precium qr. iij s. iiij d. Pro nova grangia hoc anno levand*um* assignantur xl qr. frumenti precium qr. v s. iiij d. preter meremium nunc emptum ad eandem pro vj li. xiij s. iiij d. per fratrem A. de Neuport et Robertum de Neuport servientem.[29] Pro aliis reprisis et expensis manerii et pro adventu custodis assignantur vj qr. frumenti precium ut supra una cum perquisitis curie et aliis exitibus manerii preter daeriam, que valebit deductis reprisis Cvij s. de certa firma. Et sic remanent ad vendendum Clxvj qr. vj bus. precium ut supra.

Et sunt ibidem ij equi, xij affri, ij pullani ij annorum, j pullanus unius anni, xiij boves, j taurillus, iij bovetti, xx vacce, xj boviculi, xj annales, j agnus, j pavo, j pava, vj auce, xix capones, xviij galline.

Et seminantur ibidem de frumento liij qr. di., de fabis v qr. v bus., de avenis iiij^{xx}ij qr.

Summa denariorum remanencium custodi solvendorum iiij^{xx}vij li. iiij s. viij d. ob. qua., preter xxxv li. v s. in quibus W. le Englys quondam serviens eiusdem manerii tenetur per scriptum suum obligatorium quod remanet penes fratrem A. de Neuport de blado per ipsum mutuato ut patet in compoto anni xxvj^{i}, que allocantur preposito in compoto anni xxvj^{i}.[30] Et

[23] Robert de Neuport's account covered the period 29 September 1299–24 November 1299 (WAM 25402). As appears below, the view of the manor in Beygham's first year as reeve took place on or about 26 March 1300. 'Anni xxviij': 1299–1300.

[24] MS: 'vij' struck out; 'xiij' inserted.

[25] 26 March 1300.

[26] The stack contained corn harvested in 1298; and in this context we should assume that the 'new grain' mentioned in the next entry was harvested in 1299.

[27] MS: 'exitu' struck out; 'firma' inserted.

[28] MS: 'mixt*ure*' inserted.

[29] MS: 'per fratrem ... servientem' written over an erasure but in the main hand of the account.

[30] MS: 'Et sic est summa clari' struck out; 'que allocantur preposito in compoto anni xxvj^{i}'

memorandum quod sunt[31] vend*endum* ibidem lx acre bosci per estimacionem pro Clx li. precium cuiuslibet acre liij s. iiij d. de quibus frater A. de Neuport tenetur respondere. Et sic est summa clari remanens Cxxij li. ix s. viij d. ob. qua. preter denarios de quibus frater A. de Neuport debet respondere ut supra.[32]

---

inserted. The entry is puzzling. The earlier of the two accounts, which between them cover the year 1297–8, that of Thomas atte Tounesend, the reeve for the period 30 September 1297–13 April 1298, refers to a *scriptum obligatorium* executed by William le Engleys for debts amounting to the sum of £3 17s. incurred in the previous year, 1296–7; and for this sum Thomas was allowed a respite (WAM 25399, 25400; and see also below, II 3).

[31] MS omits 'sunt'.

[32] See also II 3.

II 2 View of the states of the convent's manors assigned to the pittancer, *c.*25 March 1300

A roll of two membranes, described under II 1 and in the same hand as II 1. Br. Alexander de Neuport's position as pittancer is betrayed by the four visits that he paid to Oakham in the course of the year.[1] Br. Richard de Waltham and Br. Robert de Burl', alias de Bures, mentioned below, were evidently his immediate predecessors in this office.

WAM 23630

[*Mem. 1 dorse*] Status pitanciarie Westmon' visus per fratres A. de Neuport, A. de Persor' et R. de Aldenham anno regni regis Edwardi xxviij circa festum annunciacionis beate Marie

Okham Willelmus de Chynniton' serviens eiusdem manerii debet super finali compoto suo anni xxvj[2] lxxix s. ix d. de tempore fratris R. de Waltham. Alwynus prepositus post ipsum debet super finali compoto suo anni eiusdem xxviij s. v d. ob. de tempore fratris Roberti de Burl'. Et memorandum quod idem computans liberavit fratri A. de Neuport lxvij s. de arreragiis suis de tempore dicti Roberti. Willelmus Bell prepositus post ipsum debet super finali compoto suo anni xxvij[3] iiij li. ij s. ij d., unde xxxij s. vij d. qua. sunt de tempore dicti W. Thomas Germeyn prepositus post ipsum debet super visu suo anni xxviij[4] x li. xj s. xj d. ob. Et sunt levandum ibidem de redditu, firmis et tallagio iij terminorum subsequencium xij li. ij s. et j d.
Et fuerunt ibidem in granario die lune in festo sancti Benedicti[5] ij qr. di. frumenti, iij bus. siliginis, xxv qr. ordei, xij qr. drageti et brasei drageti, vij bus. mixture molendini, iij bus. fabarum, ij qr. de pulimong', ij qr. di. avenarum. Et estimantur ibidem in tasso Cx qr. frumenti, iiij qr. siliginis, lxxij qr. ordei, iiij^{xx} qr. fabarum et pisarum, lxxv qr. pulim*ong'*, j qr. avenarum; et apud Langham xxxv qr. frumenti, xiiij qr. siliginis, l qr. pulimong', lxiiij qr. ordei et drageti, xij qr. fabarum et pisarum, v qr. avenarum. Et sunt levand*um* de molendino usque festum sancti Michaelis[6] v qr. mixture. Inde in semine di. qr. avenarum; in liberacionibus servientis,

[1] WAM 20228, the extant minister's account for Oakham.
[2] 1297–8.
[3] 1298–9.
[4] 1299–1300.
[5] 21 March 1300. For the position of the visit of Neuport, Pershore and Aldenham to Oakham in their itinerary, see II 1 above, n. 15.
[6] 29 September 1300.

prepositi et daye usque festum beati Petri ad vincula[7] iiij qr. j bus. j p. frumenti, j qr. vj bus. di. j p. mixture; in liberacionibus famulorum usque festum beati Michaelis vij qr. vj bus. frumenti et mixture proportionaliter. Item pro expensis domus in autumpno ij qr. ij bus. frumenti, vj qr. ij bus. pulimong', ix qr. di. drageti pro braseo cum j doleo sicere ibidem remanenti, v bacones et di. remanentes, unacum exitu daerie.[8] In farina, prebenda equorum, affrorum, boum et pro adventu custodis xiiij qr. avenarum. Et sic deficiunt v qr. di. avenarum pro quibus assignantur vendend*um* viij qr. pulimong'. Et pro custu autumpni in denariis assignantur vendend*um* iiij^{xx}j qr. pulim*ong'*; et pro stipendiis famulorum continue commorancium in curia iiij qr. di. pulim*ong'*. Pro aliis minutis reprisis manerii et pro adventu custodis assignantur perquisita curie cum exitibus manerii preter daeriam. Et sic remanent ad vendendum Cxxxvj qr. j bus. di. frumenti precium qr. iiij s. vj d., xviij qr. di. siliginis precium qr. iij s. vj d., Clxiij qr. di. ordei precium qr. iiij s. vj d., iiij^{xx}xij qr. iij bus. fabarum et pisarum precium qr. ij s. vj d., xxvij qr. ij bus. pulim*ong'* precium qr. ij s.
Et sunt ibidem vij equi et affri, vj boves, iiij vacce, ij annales, x hogastri, v porci, vj porcelli, vij auce, xiij capones, xv galline.
Et seminantur ibidem xj qr. frumenti, ij qr. j bus. di. siliginis, iij qr. vij bus. ordei, vj qr. vj bus. drageti, xviij qr. vj bus. avenarum, preter id quod nondum seminatur.

Summa denariorum levandorum Cxvij li. iij s. xj d. qua. preter lxvij s. liberatos fratri A. de Neuport de quibus superius fit mencio, et de quibus idem tenetur respondere conventui,[9] una cum vij li. ix d. ob. et qua. debitis eisdem de temporibus R. de Wautham et R. Bur'.

Bemflet[10] Memorandum quod debentur super visu Johannis Blosime iiij li. xvij s. ob. qua.[11] Et sunt levand*um* ibidem de redditu, firmis et tallagio ij terminorum subsequentium xij li. vj s. xj d. qua. Et estimantur ibidem dominica in Ramispalma[12] de frumento xij qr., de fabis vij qr., de avenis xiiij qr. Et sunt levand*um* ibidem de firma molendini iiij qr. vij bus. mixture. Inde in liberacionibus famulorum usque festum sancti Michaelis et famulorum in autumpno[13] xxvj qr. v bus. mixt*ure*; in farina pro potagio,

[7] 1 August 1300.
[8] MS: 'v bacones et di. remanentes, unacum exitu daerie' inserted.
[9] MS: 'conventus'.
[10] MS: followed by, struck out, 'Johannes Blosme serviens eiusdem manerii debet super visu suo anni xxviij'.
[11] The reference is to the view at Benfleet in March or April of the previous year, 1299, and to John Blosme as serjeant there at the time, as he was in the current year.
[12] 3 April 1300. Since the view could not be completed without the estimates of corn, this date serves to refine the date (*c.*25 March) in the heading of this document.
[13] MS: 'et famulorum in autumpno' inserted. There is also a marginal note possibly in a new hand

prebenda equorum, affrorum et pro adventu ballivi, iiij. qr. avenarum. Et sic deficiunt ij qr. et vj bus. mixture pro quibus assignantur vend*endum* iij qr. vj bus. avenarum precium qr. .....[14]
Pro falcacione, sarclacione, stipendiis famulorum et pro custu autumpni in denariis, assignantur C agni vendendi, de centena .....,[15] cum lxvij s. v d.[16] de exitibus daerie qui estimantur ad xij li. iiij s.,[17] cuius superplusagium assignatur solvendum pitanciario. Et[18] appreciatur lana per estimacionem ad xvj li. xiij s. iiij d. Pro minutis rebus manerii et pro adventu custodis et senescalli sui assignantur minuti exitus manerii cum perquisitis curie. Et sic remanent ad vendendum vj qr. ij bus.[19] avenarum precium qr. iij s.
Et sunt ibidem ij equi carectarii, xij affri, viij boves, j taurus, xiiij vacce, xxvj hurtardi, CCCCxxviij oves matrices, lxviij gercie, iij auce, xij capones, vij galline.
Et seminantur ibidem xvij qr. di. frumenti, ij qr. v bus. j p. siliginis, di. qr. vescarum, xl qr. iij bus. avenarum.

Summa denariorum remanencium pitanciario solvendorum, deducto superplusagio, xxxiij li. xviij s. vj d. ob. Et memorandum quod debentur ibidem v s. v d. ob. qua. tempore fratris R. de Bures.

Fanton' Johannes Blosme serviens eiusdem manerii debet super visu suo anni xxviij[20] iiij li. xviij s. Et estimantur ibidem de frumento xxx qr., de mixt*ilione* xx qr., de aveni*s* C qr. Inde in liberacionibus famulorum usque festum sancti Michaelis, expense famulorum in autumpno et servientis x qr. frumenti, ix qr. mixt*ilionis*, j qr. avenarum pro braseo; in farina pro potagio famulorum, prebenda equorum, affrorum et pro adventu pitanciarii v qr. di. avenarum. Pro falcacione, sarclacione, stipendiis famulorum et custu autumpni in denariis assignantur vendend*um* xx qr. frumenti, xj qr. mixtilionis, et iiij qr.[21] avenarum. Pro aliis reprisis et minutis expensis manerii assignantur vendendum arrure cum aliis exitibus manerii preter daeriam et lanam que apreciantur per estimacionem ad x li. xvj s.
Et sic remanent ad vendendum iiij^{xx}ix qr. di. avenarum precium qr. iij s. Et sunt ibidem iij equi carectarii, xij affri, viij boves, iij tauri, xxxiiij vacce, xiij annales, vij multones, xlij matrices, Cxx hogastri, j sus, ij porci, xiiij hogetti,

at this point: 'Memorandum de agn''.
[14] MS: no sum is entered.
[15] MS: no sum is entered.
[16] MS: 'cum lxvij s. v d.' in the margin but evidently intended for insertion at this point.
[17] MS: a short erasure follows.
[18] MS: 'estimatur lana' follows but has been struck out.
[19] MS: 'ij bus.' inserted.
[20] i.e. the current view, no doubt held, as at Benfleet, in April 1300.
[21] MS: repeats 'qr.'

xj auce, x capones, xij galline.
Et seminantur ibidem xxxvij qr. di. frumenti, vj bus. fabarum, vij bus. vescarum, ij bus. de harasio, lxij qr. vj bus. avenarum.

Summa denariorum remanencium pitanciario solvendorum, xxix li. ij s. vj d. Et debentur ibidem xxx s. ij d. de tempore fratris R. de Bur'.

[*Mem. 2 dorse*] Summa tocius clari remanentis Ciiij^{xx} li. iiij s. xj d. ob.
De quibus debentur conventui xij li. iij s. v d. ob. de arreragiis debitis eidem apud Okham, Bemflet' et Fantone de temporibus fratrum R. de Waltham et R. de Bures. Et sic remanent de claro Clxviij li. xviij d. solvend*um* pitanciario.
Summa equorum et affrorum xxxvj.
Summa boum xxij, summa taurorum iiij, summa vaccarum lij, summa annalium xv. Summa capitum iiij^{xx}xiiij.
Summa hurtardorum et multonum xxxiij, summa matricum CCCClxx, summa hogastrorum et gerciarum Ciiij^{xx}xviij. Summa capitum DCCj.
Summa porcorum xxij, unde j sus; summa porcellorum vj. Summa capitum xxviij.
Summa aucarum xxj, summa caponum xxxv, summa gallinarum xxxiiij.

II 3 View of the states of the convent's royal manors, *c.*25 March 1305

A roll of three membranes, approximately 193 mm wide, glued Chancery fashion. The recto has been ruled in ink and a margin has also been laid out. The document is a fair copy and all the totals are in the same hand as the main text. On membrane 3 dorse, a hand of *c.*1305–30, has written, inverted, 'Status maneriorum regine visus anno xxxiij° per Reginaldum de Hadham, Rogerum Aldenham, W. Chalk'; and a hand probably of the late fourteenth century has written at the top of membrane 1 dorse, 'Status maneriorum regine anno regni regis E. xxxiij°'. Of the three monks named, Hadham served as warden of Eleanor's manors 30 November 1301–29 May 1302, and possibly from an earlier date in 1301; Aldenham was one of six auditors appointed for her foundation by Abbot Wenlok on 30 November 1304; and Chalk was warden 29 May 1302–17 April 1305, but with leave of absence probably extending from May 1303 to May 1304. In the last period, Chalk led attempts to secure the release of monks of Westminster in custody for complicity in the burglary of the royal treasury in the Abbey in April 1303.[1] The view itself, which relates to four manors of Eleanor of Castile's foundation, comprises, in addition to the estimates normal in such a document, two further items. The first is a comparison of the state of each manor, in summary form, at the conclusion of the wardenship of Hadham on 29 May 1302 with the state of each at the conclusion of Chalk's wardenship on 17 April 1305, followed by a summary of the state of all four together at these two dates. The second rehearses the findings of an enquiry conducted on behalf of the abbot and convent of Westminster by the two auditors, augmented on occasion by other monks, and using local inquests, into allegations of faulty accounting and misappropriation of funds by Chalk. The sums of money deemed chargeable to Chalk by the auditors, after consideration of the evidence, were added to the *onus* at the foot of his final account, covering the period 30 November 1304–17 April 1305.[2] This had already been done when the auditors made their report.[3]

WAM 23640

[*Mem. 1 recto*] Status maneriorum regine visus per fratres R. de Hadham, R. de Aldenham et W. de Chalk custodem eorundem circa festum annunciacionis beate Marie anno regni regis Edwardi tricesimo tercio

*Wes*terh*am'* Philippus quondam serviens de Westerham debet super finali compoto suo anni xxxij lxxiiij s. vj d. qua.[4] Willelmus Godard bedellus

[1] WAM 23631B, 23632–3; WD, f. 417v.

[2] WAM 23638, mm. 12–13; 23939.

[3] Extant ministers' accounts: Birdbrook, 29 September 1304–3 March 1305, WAM 25409; 3 March 1305–14 June 1305, WAM 25410; 14 June 1305–29 September 1305, WAM 25412; Knowle, WAM 27704; Turweston, WAM 7760; Westerham, 29 September 1304–24 June 1305, WAM 26400; 24 June 1305–29 September 1305, WAM 26401. The accounts of the wardens of the manors of Eleanor of Castile for the years 1302–5, enrolled in WAM 23638, are also relevant. For full references, see Harvey, *Obedientiaries*, pp. 145–6. These documents use a year of account beginning on 30 November, two days after Eleanor's anniversary.

[4] The account was for the period 29 September 1303–4 February 1304 (WAM 26397).

ibidem debet super eodem compoto xiij s. vij d. ob. Elias nunc serviens debet super visu compoti sui anni xxxiij vj li. iiij s. qua.[5] Et debentur ibidem de debito Ricardi Broncok pro quodam equo sibi vendito per fratrem R. de Hadham xxvj s. viij d.[6] Item sunt levand*um* ibidem de certis redditibu*s*, firmis et diversis consuetudinibus, minutis exitibus et perquisitis curie per estimacionem citra festum sancti Andree proximo futuro[7] xlvj li. x s. vij d. ob. qua. Item sunt levand*um* ibidem de quatuor veteribus bobus, xxx multonibus, xx matricibus, xxx hogastris et xxxviij agnis vend*endum* assignatis vj li. xviij s. Item sunt levand*um* ibidem de firma xliij vaccarum, iiij^{xx}x matricum xij li. vij s. ix d., videlicet pro qualibet vacca cum vitulo v s. vj d. et pro matrice j d. ob. Item sunt levand*um* ibidem de xxx petris lane que estimantur per servientem et bedellum provenire de CCxxix ovibus l s. precium petre per vij lib. xx d. Item sunt levand*um* ibidem xvj s. de viij porcis ingrassandis in stipula post autumpnum. Item sunt levand*um* ibidem x li. vj s. v d. ob. de xxij qr. frumenti, xxv qr. v bus. avenarum mutuatis diversis gentibus patrie precium qr. frumenti vj s. viij d., precium qr. avenarum ij s. iiij d.

Inde assignantur pro custu carucarum, carectarum, domorum, molendin*i*, falcacionis, sarclacionis, autumpni, stipendiis, feodo servientis, trituracionis, mutacionis stauri et pro adventu custodis xix li. iiij s. ix d. qua. de denariis supra levandis.

Et fuerunt ibidem in granario in festo annunciacionis beati Marie[8] vj qr. j bus. mixt*ilionis*, ij qr. di. avenarum. Et estimabantur ibidem in grangia ibidem eodem die xiiij qr. frumenti, ij qr. siliginis, vij qr. ordei, xxvj qr. avenarum. Inde in semine ij qr. ordei, xxxj qr. di. avenarum. Et assignantur pro liberacionibus famulorum, bedelli, servientis et pro expensis autumpni usque festum sancti Michaelis[9] ix qr. vij bus. frumenti, ij qr. scur*alli*, et xviij qr. mixt*ilionis*. Item assignantur pro potagio famulorum, prebenda equorum carectariorum, affrorum vaccarum tempore vitulacionis et pro adventu custodis xij qr. di. avenarum. Et sic deficiunt de prebenda et liberacionibus predictis ij qr. vij bus. mixtil*ionis* precium qr. iij s. iiij d., xv qr. di. avenarum precium qr. ij s. iiij d., pro quibus emendis assignantur xlv s. xj d. de denariis superius levandis.

Et fuerunt ibidem die supradicto ij equi carectarii, v affri, xiiij boves, ij tauri, xliij vacce, iiij bovetti, v juvence, vij boviculi, viij annales, xxiij

[5] A reference to Elias de Tothey's view of account for the period 29 September 1304–24 June 1305 (WAM 26400).

[6] For Broncok's successful claim to have paid Chalk for the horse, see below, mem. 1 dorse, Westerham.

[7] 30 November 1305.

[8] 25 March 1305.

[9] 29 September 1305.

multones, lxxviij matrices, xlviij hogastri et gercie, lxj agni, j sus, viij porcelli, iiij auce, v galli et galline. Et seminantur ibidem xxvij qr. vj bus. frumenti, ij qr. iiij bus. di. siliginis, xxxiij qr. vij bus. avenarum.

Summa denariorum levand*um* de predicto manerio contra anniversarium de claro lxiiij li. xv s. ix d. ob. qua., preter Cj s. ij d. qua. de debito Philippi servientis et Ricardi Broncok, qui non creduntur levari contra anniversarium predictum.

Turveston' Johannes Mauncel quondam prepositus de Turveston' debet super finali compoto suo anni xxxij[10] iij s. v d. ob. qua. Willelmus Patesti quondam prepositus ibidem debet super finali compoto suo anni precedentis[11] xl s. Petrus Adham nunc prepositus debet super visu compoti sui anni xxxiij[12] xj s. x d. qua. Et sunt levand*um* ibidem citra festum sancti Andree apostoli[13] de redditu, firmis et consuetudinibus Cx s. v d., de minutis exitibus manerii xviij s. iij d., de lactagio ix vaccarum et xx matricum xxxviij s. vj d., de vij petris lane proveniendis per estimacionem de lxix ovibus xxviij s. precium petre xiiij lib. iiij s., de vj qr. j bus. frumenti, ij qr. vj bus. mix*ture*, xiij qr. di. drageti vendendis vel mutuandis lxxix s. viij d., precium qr. frumenti v s., precium qr. mixt*ure* iiij s., precium qr. drageti ij s. viij d., de uno veteri bove et vij hogettis ingrassandis ac eciam de iij vitulis vendendis xxvj s. vj d., de finibus et perquisitis curie xxiij s. ix d. per estimacionem. Inde assignantur pro custu carucarum, carectarum, domorum, falcacionis, carclacionis, autumpni, minutorum, stipendiorum, trituracionis et pro adventu custodis ix li. xvij s. ix d., ut patet alibi per particulas de predicta assignacione confectas.

Et fuerunt ibidem in granario die dominico proximo post festum annunciacionis beate Marie[14] j bus. frumenti, j bus. pisarum,[15] xviij qr. drageti, ij bus. brasei de exitu molendin*i*. Et estimabantur ibidem die supradicto xxij qr. frumenti, x qr. drageti, iiij qr. di. pisarum. Et sunt levand*um* ibidem de exitu molend*ini* x qr. mixture pro liberacionibus famulorum. Inde sunt seminandum xvij qr. drageti. Et assignantur pro expensis autumpnalibus et pro liberacionibus famulorum usque festum sancti Michaelis xvj qr. frumenti, x qr. mixture, ij bus. brasei et j qr. vij bus. drageti. Item assignantur pro farina ad potagium famulorum, prebenda equorum carectariorum, affrorum, boum, sustentacione et separacione

[10] 1303–4.
[11] 1302–3
[12] 1304–5. Peter Adam demitted office on 16 July 1305 and was succeeded by William Arkesden (WAM 7766).
[13] 30 November 1305.
[14] 28 March 1305.
[15] MS: 'ipis".

porcorum et porcellorum, et pro adventu custodis usque festum predictum ix qr. vj bus. avenarum extrahendis de drageto supradicto.
Et fuerunt ibidem die supradicto duo equi carectarii, vj affri, xiij boves, j bovettus, j taurus, x vacce, xix oves, xxx matrices, xxx hogastri et gercie, xix agni, j verrus, j sus, vij porcelli, iiij auce, xiij capones, viij anates, j gallus et v galline.
Et seminantur ibidem xxv qr. frumenti, xx qr. iij bus. drageti.

Summa denariorum levand*um* de claro de predicto manerio contra anniversarium ix li. ij s. viij d.

Knolle Ricardus Warde nunc prepositus de Knoll' est in superplusagio super visu compoti sui anni xxxiij[16] de xvj s. qua. Et sunt levand*um* ibidem de redditu, firmis et consuetudinibus citra festum sancti Andree apostoli[17] xvij li. xj s. qua., de pannagio porcorum, tolneto servisie, arrur*is*, herciatur*is*, averag*io* et operibus vendendis una cum aliis minutis exitibus manerii lxxix s. viij d. ob. qua., de firma xx vaccarum iiij li. x s. qualibet dimissa cum vitulo pro iiij s. vj d., de finibus et perquisit*is* curi*e* citra festum sancti Andree per estimacionem Cxiiij s., de toto blado manerii vend*endo* hoc anno in grosso ultra semen et liberaciones famulorum lx s. Et memorandum quod frater Willelmus de Chalke custos eiusdem manerii vendidit servienti eiusdem manerii totum bladum predictum in grosso pro lx s., ita quod idem serviens a die huius vend*icionis* inveniat totum semen seminandum, liberaciones famulorum, et prebendam equorum usque diem dominicum proximum ante festum sancti Bartholomei.[18] Item sunt levand*um* de firma hameletti de Grafton' de anno preterito in parte et de toto anno presenti[19] vij li. vj s. viij d. Inde assignantur pro custu carucarum, carectarum, domorum, falcacionis, cerclacionis, autumpni, minutorum, vadio servientis, stipendiis, stauro mutando et emendo, superplusagio prepositi, blado emendo, pro expensis autumpni, liberacionum famulorum in autumpno et pro adventu custodis xj li. xviij s. qua.
Et fuerunt ibidem in crastino sancti Ambrosii[20] ij equi carectarii, ij affri, xxiij boves, j taurus, xx vacce, v bovetti, j juvenca. ij annales, vij auce, xij capones. xiij galli et galline. Et seminantur ibidem xvij qr. iij bus. frumenti, iij qr. vij bus. siliginis et mixt*ilionis*, iij qr. v bus. fabarum, ij qr. ij bus. di. vescarum, xxix qr. vij bus. avenarum. Et memorandum quod assignantur

[16] 1304–5.
[17] 30 November 1305.
[18] 22 August 1305. The serjeant was Ralph de Parham.
[19] i.e. for part of 1303–4 and the whole of 1304–5.
[20] 5 April 1305.

vendend*um* iiij vacce steriles in subsidium sustentacionis manerii predicti si forte assignacio predicta sufficere non valebit.

Summa denariorum levand*um* de claro de predicto manerio contra anniversariam xxx li. iij s. iiij d. ob. qua.

Bridebrok' Johannes ate Parkgate quondam prepositus de Bridebrok' debet de veteribus arreragiis compoti sui vj s. viij d. Thomas ate Tounesend' quondam prepositus ibidem debet de veteribus arreragiis compoti sui Cxj s. iiij d. Robertus de Neuport quondam serviens ibidem debet de veteribus arreragiis compoti sui iiij li. iij s. x d. ob. qua. Clemens de Beytham' nuper prepositus ibidem debet de arreragiis compoti sui ix s. j d. Galfridus de Fering nuper serviens ibidem debet super visu compoti sui anni xxxiij[21] preter denarios eidem certis ex causis respectuatos xlij s. ij d. ob. qua. Robertus Whirich nunc prepositus est in superplusagio super visu compoti sui anni xxxiij de iij s. ob. Et sunt levand*um* ibidem de redditu, consuetudinibus, averagi*o* et aliis diversis operibus vendendis ibidem viij li. vj s. viij d. ob. qua., de pasturis ovium vendendis in certo hoc anno l s., de firma xvij vaccarum Cij s., qualibet dimissa cum vitulo pro vj s., de firma gardini et columbarii de anno preterito[22] lxvj s. viij d. De firma vero gardini de anno presenti non est confidend*um*, eo quod Johannes Arnold' firmarius eiusdem et plegii sui predictam firmam ulterius solvere omnino recusant. Dicunt enim quod eandem firmam solvere non possunt nec tenentur quia tres partes arborum in gardino radicitus extirpantur et cultura eiusdem parvum vel nichil ultra reprisam poterit valere.[23] Item sunt levand*um* ibidem de perquisitis curie et viij acris subbosci vendendis hoc anno in parco lxiij s. vij d. ob. qua., de xxvij qr. di. frumenti, iiij qr. j bus. siliginis, j qr. di. mixt*ure*, ij qr. vij bus. di. fabarum, xiij qr. pisarum, v qr. j bus. di. ordei, lxiiij qr. iij bus. avenarum remanentibus ultra semen, prebendam et liberaciones famulorum mutuantis et venditis, xxiiij li. ij s. viij d. qua., precium qr. frumenti vj s. viij d., precium qr. siliginis, mixt*ure* et fabarum v s., precium qr. pisarum et ordei iiij s. viij d., precium qr. avenarum ij s. viij d. Inde assignantur pro custu carucarum, carectarum, molendini, domorum, autumpni, minutorum, feodis servientis et Willelmi clerici,[24] stauro emendo et mutando, trituracioni et pro expensis custodis xvij li. xvj s. ij d. ob., ut patet alibi per parcellas de predicta assignacione confecta.

[21] The reference is to Fering's view of account for the period 30 September 1304–3 March 1305 (WAM 25409). Fering was succeeded by Robert Whirich *alia*s Wolrich on 3 March 1305.
[22] 1303–4.
[23] For the destruction of vines and trees in the garden at Birdbrook in the current year, see WAM 25409. John Arnold's farm of the garden dated from 1299 or 1300 (WAM 25403).
[24] William de Islip, clerk to the auditors serving Eleanor of Castile's foundation (WAM 25409–12).

Et fuerunt ibidem in granario, in festo sancti Gutlaci confessoris,[25] xix qr. iij bus. frumenti, iiij qr. j bus. siliginis, ij qr. di. mixt*ure*, di. qr. scuralli, ij qr. vj bus. di. fabarum, xiij qr. vj bus. pisarum, v qr. j bus. di. ordei, j qr. vj bus. drageti, liij qr. vij bus. avenarum. Et estimabantur ibidem eodem die xvj qr. frumenti, vj bus. drageti, xxviij qr. avenarum. Et sunt levand*um* ibidem de firma molendini vj qr. ij bus. mixt*ure*. Inde assignantur pro liberacionibus famulorum usque festum sancti Michaelis[26] vij qr. vij bus. frumenti, vij qr. ij bus. mixt*ure* et vj bus. pisarum. Item assignantur pro farina ad potagium famulorum, prebendam equorun carectariorum, affrorum, boum et pro adventu custodis xvij qr. avenarum.

Et fuerunt ibidem die supradicto ij equi carectarii, xiiij affri, xj boves, xviij vacce, iiij bovetti, j juvenca, iiij boviculi, vj annales, j pavo et j pava, v auce, viij capones, v galli et galline. Et seminantur ibidem liij qr. frumenti, v qr. vij bus. fabarum, j qr. iiij bus. di. pisarum, iij bus. di. ordei, lx qr. di. avenarum.

[*Mem. 2 recto*]

Summa denariorum levand*um* de claro de predicto manerio contra anniversarium[27] xxxj li. xiij s. vj d., preter ix li. xv s. ij d. ob. qua. de arreragiis Thome ate Tounesend' quondam prepositi et Roberti de Neuport quondam servientis ibidem de quibus denariis non est confidendum contra anniversarium predictum eo quod idem Thomas omnino est insufficiens et de predicto Roberto nisi per viam placiti nichil creditur esse levandum. Et est summa denariorum in dubio po*s*itor*um* qui non creduntur levari contra anniversarium futurum[28] xiiij li. xvj s. v d. Et memorandum de xx li. debitis per Johannem de Watevile de tempore fratris Alexandri de quibus nichil omnino est confitendum contra annunciacionem.[29]

Summa tocius peccunie levand*um* de claro de quatuor maneriis predictis citra festum sancti Andree[30] Cxxxv li. xv s. iiij d. ob., de quibus assignantur pro expensis custodis garcionum et equorum suorum usque festum predictum in universo x li. Item assignantur x li. solvend*um* conventui quas frater W. de Chalke recepit de redditu de Wychio et solvit pro denariis mutuatis ad distribucionem pauperum in anniversario proximo elapso.[31]

[25] 11 April 1305.
[26] 29 September 1305.
[27] 28 November 1305.
[28] MS: possibly a word omitted, 'nisi'.
[29] A reference to Br. Alexander de Neuport's period as warden of Eleanor of Castile's manors (1297–1301).
[30] 30 November 1305.
[31] 28 November 1304. A rental income from Wych (Wychio, alias Wiz) is mentioned in this period as part of the endowment of Eleanor of Castile's anniversary at Westminster and intended

Item assignantur pro quatuor centenis cere emendis pro cereis renovandis et faciendis contra anniversarium proximo futurum xj li. Item debentur conventui de predictis maneriis xvij li. xiij s. iiij d. quos frater Willelmus de Chalk' recepit in manerio de Bridebrok de bosco vendito ibidem, qui quidem denarii assignabantur fabrice ecclesie. Item assignantur pro feodo domini Roberti de Bardeby de annis preteritis et presenti et pro feodo Gerini de anno presenti xxviij s. iiij d.[32] Et sic remanent iiij^{xx}v li. xiij s. viij d. ob. de quibus dominus Henricus elemosinarius exigit pro quodam prato xvj li.[33] Et sic remanent de claro lxix li. xiij s. viij d. ob. Et memorandum quod frater W. liberavit fratri Reginaldo custodi post ipsum CCiiij^{xx} di. lib.[34] j quartr*onum* cere in xxix grossis cereis.

*Wes*ter*ham'* In alio visu reprisa xiiij li. xvj d. nunc, xxj li. x s. viij d. tunc, et plus assignatur levand*um* de minutis exitibus et perquisitis curie nunc quam post Reginaldum Cvj s. ix d. Et plus deficit de liberacionibus famulorum et avenarum pro prebenda de xvij s. v d., et pro stauro mutando nichil tunc sed nunc xxx s. vij d. Et sic plus assignabatur tunc pro reprisa quam nunc habito respectu ad levandum de exitu de iiij s. iiij d. ob. qua. Item tunc debuit Philippus serviens xj li. ij s. et Henricus le Skinnere xxiij s. j d. ob., Ricardus Bronkoc lxvj s. viij d. Summa debiti omnium tunc xv li. xj s. ix d. ob. Summa debiti omnium nunc xj li. xviij s. x d., et sic minus debetur nunc de lxxij s. xj d. ob. Et non sunt nunc ibidem tot capita de grosso stauro sicut in recessu fratris Reginaldi de xx capitibus. Et minus seminatur ibidem nunc de semine hiemali quam seminatum fuit in recessu predicti fratris de xiij qr. iiij bus. di. Et non sunt ibidem nunc tot capita bidencium quot tunc de vj capitibus. De minuto instauro nunc minus de xxxv capitibus.

*Tur*v*eston'* Assignatur pro reprisa nunc plus quam tunc de lxxij s. j d., set tunc minus assignabatur levand*um* de exitu manerii et perquisitis curie quam nunc de xiij s. iiij d. Et nunc assignantur pro mutacione stauri xxxix s. vij d. Et sic nunc plus assignatur pro reprisa in omnibus quam tunc de xix s. ij d., et hoc quia plus restat futuro de anno. Et sunt ibidem de grosso stauro

---

for the poor on that occasion, but also claimed by the monks of Westminster for their wage fund (WAM 23638, 23641).

[32] The convent contributed half the annual fee of 3 marks (40s.) p.a. which Robert de Bardeby, a royal clerk, had enjoyed from a date before 1277 (*Walter de Wenlok*, ed. Harvey, p. 31). Gerin de S. Egidio, frequently employed at this time by the monks of Westminster in litigation to secure the Abbey's rights in Eleanor of Castile's manors, received a fee of 6s. 8d. p.a. and a stipend of £1 5s. p.a. from the warden, but also ad hoc payments in particular cases (WAM 23638, mem. 10; 23639).

[33] Henry de Bluntesdon, the king's almoner.

[34] MS: 'cere' follows but has been struck out.

iij capita plus quam tunc, [*mem. 3 recto*] de bidentibus iij, de minuto stauro minus nunc de xiiij s., de semine hyemali plus seminatur nunc de j bus.

Knolle Assignatur nunc plus pro reprisa quam tunc de lxiij s. ij d. ob. qua. Set nunc plus assignatur levand*um* de exitu manerii et perquisitis curie de C s. ij d. ob. qua. Item nunc assignantur pro blado deficienti xxiiij s. iij d., pro superplusagio prepositi xvj s. qua., ut pro stauro emendo et mutando xliiij s., et sic tunc plus pro reprisa quam nunc de ix li. iiij s. vj d. De grosso stauro tunc plus de xxiiij capitibus, de minuto stauro tunc plus xxvij. Et tunc plus de semine hiemali quam nunc de iiij qr.

Bridebrok Assignatur plus nunc pro reprisa de ix li. xiiij s. ij d. ob. Set assignatur plus nunc levand*um* quam tunc de exitu et perquisitis curie de lxxix s. iij d. qua., et sic plus assignatur nunc quam tunc in universo de Cxiiij s. xj d. qua., et hoc pro maiori tempore. Et fuerunt tunc de grosso stauro plus quam nunc de ij, de minuto instauro plus tunc quam nunc de iiij. Et seminabantur tunc plus de semine hiemali de iiij qr. iij bus. di.

Et memorandum quod[35] habito respectu in omnibus ad visum stauri post fratrem Reginaldum et istud, plus assignatur pro repris*is* iiij maneriorum tunc quam nunc[36] de liiij s. ix d. qua. Et fuerunt de grosso stauro tunc plus quam nunc de xliij capitibus de bidentibus, nunc deficiunt iij capita. De minuto stauro deficiunt nunc xlv capita. Et nunc minus seminatur de semine hiemali de xxj qr. vij bus. De semine vero quadragesimali non fit mencio in isto visu utrum plus seminatur nunc quam tunc quia in confectione istius visus semen[37] quadragesimale non perseminabatur.

[*Mem. 1 dorse*] *West*er*ham'* Compertum est per inquisicionem quod[38] idem frater Willelmus de Chalk iussit vendere C arbores de fago in bosco de Westerham pro quibus recepit xl s. per manus Willelmi Godard bedelli de quibus denariis idem frater non respondet in compoto suo nec ponuntur in compoto manerii. Et idem frater dicit quod predictos denarios talliavit inter ceteros denarios quos recepit de manerio predicto set Philippus de Henle serviens ibidem et Willelmus Godard bedellus parati sunt contrarium probare.[39]

[35] MS: 'Et memorandum quod' inserted.
[36] MS: 'tunc quam nunc' inserted.
[37] MS: 'semine'.
[38] MS: 'quod' omitted.
[39] The references to Godard and Henle date this episode to 1303–4.

Item compertum est quod idem frater recepit xx s. de Ricardo atte Rivere capitali plegio de Westerham pro quodam amerciamento de quibus denariis idem frater non respondet in compoto suo nec ponebantur in rotulo curie nec in compoto servientis. Et respondet idem frater ut prius et ceteri contradicunt.
Item compertum est quod idem frater recepit duas marcas argenti de quadam muliere atachiata ut permitteret eam esse sub manucapcione usque ad proximam assisam de quibus denariis non respondetur in aliquo compotorum. Et idem frater respondet ut prius et ceteri contradicunt.
Item compertum est quod idem frater recepit xiiij s. de Willelmo Goddard bedello pro $M^{l}D$ fagottis factis in bosco de Westerham de quibus denariis idem bedellus habuit talliam contra eundem fratrem W. scriptam de manu eiusdem quam contradicere non potest. Sed de denariis non respondet in compoto suo nec respondetur in compoto servientis.[40]
Item compertum est quod idem frater recepit xx s. de Johanne Bloundel pro catallis Nicholai Berdcok et Willelmi Berdcok incarceratorum apud Westm'. Et idem frater dicit quod predictos denarios expendidit pro deliberacione eorundem incarceratorum et ideo dicit quod non respondet de denariis in compoto suo.[41]
Item compertum est quod idem frater recepit xvj s. viij d. de Johanne Andreu et Galfrido le vineter appellatis per quemdam probatorem in carcere Cantuar', de quibus denariis non respondetur in compoto custodis nec in compoto servientis, set de istis respondet idem frater sicut de xx s. predictis.
Item Ricardus Broncok de West*er*ham dicit quod solvit eidem fratri xl s. pro quodam equo vendito eidem Ricardo per fratrem Reginaldum de Hadham tunc custodem. De quibus denariis frater W. non respondebat in compoto suo set nunc oneratur per auditores.[42]
Item compertum est quod idem frater fecit prosternere plusquam Cxl quercus in bosco de West*er*ham pro quadam domo ibidem edificanda que nondum edificatur, de quibus dedit xl quercus de melioribus.
Item compertum est quod idem frater emit decimas ecclesie de West*er*ham unius anni, de quibus habuit de claro lucro iiij li. argenti, de quibus denariis non respondet conventui. Et Philippus serviens clamat versus

[40] For the *onus* of 14s. charged to Chalk at the audit of his final account in 1305 as a consequence of this finding, see WAM 23638, mem. 13. All such penalties are apparently recorded here, and after due allowances they amounted to £28 15s. 9½d.

[41] The gaol was the abbot of Westminster's in the Abbey's gatehouse on Tothill Street, which served the manor of Westminster: G. Rosser, *Medieval Westminster 1200–1540* (Oxford, 1989), pp. 233–4.

[42] Cf. above, the start of the Westerham account, mem. 1 recto, where 26s. 8d. of the debt is said to be outstanding.

predictum fratrem W. alias iiij li. pro parte sua de lucro ecclesie predicte, quia asserit se participere fuisse de empcione predicta. Dicit e*cia*m et concedit quod conventus habeat predictas iiij li., et quod frater W. respondeat conventui de eisdem, quod si non fecerit idem Philippus nichil relaxabit de eisdem set arreragia compoti sui in quibus conventui tenetur proprietatem retinere.
Item compertum est per tallias scriptas de manu eiusdem fratris quod idem recepit de serviente de West*er*ham ix qr. ij bus. frumenti, xxv qr. v bus. avenarum, de quibus non respondebat in compoto suo, set nunc oneratur per auditores.[43]

*Tur*v*eston'* Compertum est per compotum manerii quod Willelmus Patesti prepositus liberavit Rogero bedello lvij s. pro lana emenda ad opus fratris Willelmi, de qua quidem lana idem frater non respondebat in compoto suo nec de eius precio.
Item compertum per unam talliam scriptam de manu predicti fratris quod idem recepit xxx s. de preposito de T*ur*veston' pro quodam fine facto pro combustione cuiusdam bercarie tempore fratris Alexandri de Neuport, de quibus denariis idem frater non respondebat in compoto suo, set nunc oneratur per auditores quia manum suam contradicere non potest.[44]
Item compertum est quod Rogerus quondam bedellus de T*ur*veston fecit finem x s. cum predicto fratre W. pro pace habenda et pro custodia unius pullani, de quibus solvit eidem fratri v s., de quibus non respondet in compoto suo set dicit quod predictos v s. expendidit in custodia predicti pullani.
Item compertum est per sacramentum vij nativorum domini quod in predicto manerio de T*ur*veston' est quidem warennarius et grangiarius dictus Johannes de Camville positus per custodem qui permittit diversos homines de Bralkel' piscari et destruere piscariam domini in absencia custodis. Et recepit ab eisdem pecuniam pro dicta permissione et licencia, set quantum recepit nesciunt, que quidem pecunia non pervenit ad utilitatem domini nec prepositus inde[45] oneratur in compoto manerii nec ponitur in compoto fratris W. Et quod idem bedellus vendidit qua*n*dam placeam de subbosco pro xxiiij s. vj d., preposito interim quadam infirmitate domo languente, de quibus denariis idem bedellus solvit preposito xx s. et residuum concelavit.[46]

[43] The *onus* consisted of £1 9s. for the wheat and £1 16s. 3¾d. for the oats (WAM 23838, mem. 12).
[44] For the *onus* of £1 10s. charged to Chalk by the auditors, see WAM 23638, mem. 12.
[45] MS: 'inde' inserted.
[46] The reference to the servile status of the jurors on this occasion suggests that the auditors may have had difficulty in finding free men who would serve. Cf. 'the inquest of all the tenants' referred

Item compertum est quod garcio eiusdem bedelli furabatur in autumpno xvij garbas de frumento domini quas idem bedellus fecit receptari in domo cuiusdam vidue native eiusdem ville. Quibus intellectis de predicto bedello, fratres R. de Hadham et R. de Aldenham, ex parte abbatis et conventus, dixerunt eidem fratri Willelmo ut talem bedellum, qui tot mala et dampna in predicto manerio fecit,[47] quam[48] cicius ammoveret, qui respondit eisdem quod propter eos neminem voluit ammovere, sed domodo[49] staret in illo officio tales sub se constitueret ministros secundum quod sibi placuerit et viderit expedere.

Et memorandum quod fratres Reginaldum de Hadam et R. de Aldenham intellexerunt per quosdam de nativis domini quod Johannes filius Ade le clerc' de T*ur*veston contra Deum et justiciam exheredatur de tenemento quod fuit patris sui, nulla super hoc habita inquisicione, et frater Willelmus non permisit predictos R. de Hadham et R. de Aldenham plenam facere inquisicionem de tenentibus domini nativis secundum quod eis injunctum et demandatum fuit per literas domini abbatis, propter quam injuriam dicitur dominum abbatem et totum conventum in magnum incidere periculum nisi predictam exheredacionem dirige faciant indilate.[50]

Knolle Compertum est per diversas tallias super compotum manerii de Knoll' scriptas de manu fratris Willelmi quod idem frater recepit de preposito eiusdem manerii[51] lxxvj s. vij d., de quibus idem frater non respondebat in compoto suo, set nunc oneratur per auditores.

Item compertum est per compotum eiusdem manerii quod idem frater recepit in predicto manerio xxxiiij capita grossi instauri que fecit fugari usque Westm', et ea vendidit ibidem. Set invenitur per compotum manerii quod de predictis xxxiiij capitibus fuerunt ix boves, set non respondet in compoto suo nisi de vij, precium cuiuslibet ix s., ut patet in compoto eiusdem. Item fuerunt de predicto instauro vj vacce, de quibus non respondet in compoto suo nisi de duabus et coreo unius, precium cuiuslibet vj s. viij d. Item recepit duos boviculos cuiuslibet vj s., ut patet in compoto

to below, in a case involving another Camville; and for the legal issues involved, see P. Brand, *The Origins of the English Legal Profession* (Oxford, 1992), p. 30. For the increasing use of juries in manorial proceedings in this period, see *Select Cases in Manorial Courts, 1250–1550: Property and Family Law,* ed. L. R. Poos and L. Bonfield (Selden Society, 114; 1998), pp. lx–lxi.

[47] MS: 'in predicto fecit manerio'.

[48] MS: 'qua'.

[49] MS: for 'dummodo'.

[50] We should understand that Adam held by customary tenure and that John, his son, nevertheless claimed the right to inherit. On the legal context, see P. R. Hyams, *King, Lords and Peasants in Medieval England: The Common Law of Villeinage in the Twelfth and Thirteenth Centuries* (Oxford, 1980), pp. 68–9.

[51] MS omits 'manerii'.

suo predicto. Item recepit v bovettos, v juvencas et vij boviculos, de quibus vendidit Gerino de Sancto Egidio xvj capita, videlicet quodlibet capud pro ij s. iiij d., et non respondet in compoto suo nisi de xvj d. pro quolibet capite, et sic concellantur conventui de predictis xvj capitibus xxxij s., videlicet de quolibet capite ij s. Item concelantur in compoto predicti fratris de predictis animalibus venientibus de manerio de Knoll' ij boves, iij vacce precium cuiuslibet bovis ix s., precium cuiuslibet vacce vj s., et sic concelantur conventui de vendicione dictorum animalium lxx s. Et memorandum quod expenduntur circa fugacionem eorundem de Knoll' usque Westm' x s. Et sic minus respondetur conventui quam valebant apud Knoll'.[52]

Et memorandum quod tempore fratrum Alexandri de Neuport et Reginaldi de Hadham[53] fuit in eodem manerio magnum instaurum de jumentis et pullanis euntibus in parco et boscis manerii, quod quidem instaurum tempore fratris Willelmi totaliter venditur, ita quod nichil inde remansit nec tantum aumentatur[54] set diminuitur numerus alterius instauri.

Bridebrok' Compertum est quod Clemens de Beytham, Willelmus de Neuman' et Willelmus le Gardiner de Bridebrok fecerunt finem cum fratre W. de Chalk' pro xxxiij s. iiij d. quos idem frater recepit per manus Galfridi servientis sine tallia secundum quod idem Galfridus paratus est probare. De quibus idem frater non respondet in compoto suo nec ponebatur in rotulo curie eo quod finis factus fuit extra curiam. Set predictus Willelmus dicit quod talliavit eidem Galfrido predictos denarios inter ceteros denarios quos recepit de manerio et serviens contradicit.

Item compertum est quod idem frater recepit xviij s. iiij d. per manus Galfridi servientis predicti de Willelmo le Engleis, Roberto Melksop, Petro Brian et Roberto Collin pro virida cera sine tallia.[55] De quibus denariis frater Willelmus non respond*et* in compoto suo set dicit quod eosdem talliavit, et serviens contradicit.

Item compertum est quod frater Willelmus recepit vj s. viij d. per manus dicti Galfridi de una sue et iiij porcis venditis ibidem, quos eidem Galfrido noluit talliare et de quibus non respondebat in compoto suo, set nunc inde oneratur per auditores quia non contradicit.

Item compertum est quod idem frater recepit iiij s. iiij d. per manus predicti Galfridi de fine cuiusdam vidue ibidem et de uno ligno de quercu vendito

[52] The auditors imposed an onus of £3 6s. 8d. at the audit of Chalk's account in 1305 for the sale of animals from Knowle (WAM 23638, mem. 13; 23639).

[53] Wardens of Eleanor of Castile's manors in, respectively, 1297–1301 and 1301–29 May 1302.

[54] MS: i.e. 'augmentatur'.

[55] 'Green wax' was a method of enforcing the payment of debts through the king's courts.

Simoni de Henham, de quibus denariis non respondebat in compoto suo, set nunc inde oneratur per auditores quia contradicere non pot*est*.
Item compertum est per compotum eiusdem fratris in quo idem comp*utavit* se soluisse l s.[56] Alicie relicte Eborardi le Parker de Bridebrok, nec ei solvit unicum denarium secundum quod reperitur per recognicionem predicte Alice et mariti sui secundum quod invenitur per compotum predicti Galfridi servientis, qui quidem serviens solvit predictos denarios de exitu manerii de Bridebrok, videlicet xl s. precepto fratris Reginaldi, tunc custodis, et x s. [*mem. 2 dorse*] precepto fratris Willelmi.[57]
Item comp*utavit* idem frater x s. in una roba empta et data Philippo marito Alicie la Parker de Bridebrok et venit idem Philippus in presencia fratrum Jordani, Roberti de Bur', Reginaldi de Hadham et R. de Aldenham, et contradixit expresse, et dixit quod ipse vel uxor sua nunquam receperunt robam nec unicum denarium de predicto fratre Willelmo nec de aliquo alio nisi xl s. in denariis et x s. in blado de Galfrido serviente de Bridebrok.
Item compertum est et inventum oculatafide quod idem frater fecit extirpare tres partes tocius gardini de Brideb*rok*', ita quod quarta pars arborum vix remansit. De quibus arboribus sic eradicatis fieri fecit iiij^{M}C duo quarteria fagotorum vend*endum* per centenam pro Cxviij s. ob., precium cuiuslibet centene pro parte iij s., precium cuiuslibet residui ij s. vj d., quod quidem gardinum cum columbario tradebatur ad firmam pro v marcis annuatim. Et dicunt firmarius illius gardini et plegii sui quod exquo arbores gardini sic eradicantur non tenentur, nec volunt ulterius predictam firmam solvere nec decetero tenere.[58]
Item compertum est quod idem frater recepit de Willelmo le Engleis xvij li. xiij s. iiij d., quos denarios expendidit in officio suo predicto, qui quidem denarii assignabantur ad reparacionem domorum Westmon' solvend*um* fratri Ricardo de Waltham,[59] de quibus denariis predictus frater W. tenetur respondere conventui de maneriis regine.
Item compertum est per inquisicionem omnium tenencium de Bridebrok' quod fuit ibidem quidam Ricardus de Camville bedellus et grangiarius positus per fratrem W., qui asportavit et fecit asportari bladum domini in garbis de grangia de Bridebrok' usque Bumsted in absencia servientis, et idem Galfridus in recessu suo vestigia predicti furti invenit et vicinis intimavit.

[56] MS: 'l s. solidos'.
[57] For a longer view of the monastery's dealings with Alice, the widow of Eborard le Parker, which extended to the taking into the demesne at Birdbrook of part of Eborard's customary holding on his death in or before 1299–1300, see WAM 25403, 25407 and 2363, mm. 8–9 and 13.
[58] John Arnold's farm of the garden at Birdbrook dated from 1299 or 1300.
[59] In common with Jordan de Wratting, Waltham was an auditor for Eleanor of Castile's manors (Pearce, *Monks*, pp. 55–6).

Item compertum est per eandem inquisicionem quod idem bedellus furabatur piscem in vivario manerii, serviente existente apud Westm' ad reddendum compotum suum.
Item compertum est per eandem inquisicionem quod idem bedellus fecit asportari de grangia ij bus. frumenti trituratos et ventilatos, quod quidem frumentum dedit cuidam mulieri de villa serviente hoc ignorante.
Et memorandum quod in istis tribus annis nichil augmentatur[60] in predictis quatuor maneriis de vivo instauro, set diminuitur de xliij capitibus grossi instauri, iij capitibus bidencium et xlv capitibus de minuto instauro. Et minus seminatur in isto anno in quatuor maneriis predictis de semine hiemali quam seminatum fuit cum frater Reginaldus dimisit officium de xxj qr. vij bus. De semine vero quadragesimali non fit mencio in isto visu quia in confectione eiusdem non totum seminabatur.
[*Mem. 3 dorse*] Memorandum quod idem frater comp*utavit* empc*ionem* CCCC lib. cere, precium cuiuslibet centene liiij s., et dicit dominus Henricus de Luthefeld' custos fabrice capelle sancte Marie de sancto Paulo quod idem frater emit de eodem per unam vicem CCCxiij lib. cere, videlicet centenam de v^{xx} lib. pro xl s., precium lib. iiij d. ob. qua. et plus in toto v d., et sic valet centena per v^{xx}xij lib. xliiij s. ix d., si lib. valeat iiij d. ob. qua. Item dicit idem dominus Henricus quod idem frater emit de eodem Cxxxv lib. cere pro lvj s. iij d., precium lib. v d., et sic valet centena per v^{xx}xij lib. xlvjs. viij d., et emit totam ceram pro ix li. xvj d. ob. qua.,[61] et computat x li. xvj s., et sic plus de xxxiiij s. vij d. qua. in toto.[62]
Item computavit idem frater solutum Gerino duobus annis, ut patet per particulas eiusdem fratris, lxxv s. et idem Gerinus contradicit expresse et dicit quod non recepit de eodem nisi xlviij s. viij d., et hoc paratus est probare. Et sic nimis comp*utavit* de xxvj s. iiij d.
Et sic nimis computavit in predictis ij particulis de lx s. xj d. qua.

[60] MS: 'aum''.
[61] MS: 'xvj d. ob. qua.' repeated but struck out.
[62] This finding relates to Eleanor of Castile's anniversary, on 28 November 1304, and the sum of £1 14s. 0¼d. was charged to Chalk at the audit of his account in 1305 (WAM 23636; 23638, mem. 13).

II 4 View of the states of the convent's manors, December 1312

A roll of eight membranes, approximately 210 mm wide, sewn Chancery fashion with white thread– – –. Membrane 4 is narrower, approximately 195 mm wide. Membrane 1 tapers at the top: it is laid out with a fold for the left margin on the recto, and there may also be a vertical fold to the same end on membrane 8. The roll is a finely written fair copy, with the totals all written in the main text hand—that is, it was written in a single operation.[1] The entry for Hampstead on membrane 3 recto includes a lacuna, which the scribe did not understand, but those who had prepared the earlier documentation from which the present roll was copied clearly did, as they made calculations that complete the missing passage, estimating in this case the amount of mixed corn (*mixtura*) needed to make up for the deficit. The inclusion at this point of a beaver-tailed S, distinctive and unusual in this account, and probably an abbreviation for *Summa*, suggests that the lacuna may also have been in an intervening document, i.e. that the present document is a copy of a copy.[2] All the membranes, except membrane 1, have been numbered in a small hand, to keep the membranes in order when it came to sewing them together. The dorse of the whole roll is blank except for a single note on membrane 1, 'Status maneriorum conventus Westm' anno regni regis Edwardi', written at right-angles to the text on the recto, in a sixteenth- or seventeenth-century hand.[3]

WAM 9298

[*Mem. 1 recto*] Status maneriorum conventus Westm' per fratres Henricum de Byrchiston' et Robertum de Beby et Johannem de Neweport, clericum, anno regni regis Edwardi filii regis Edwardi sexto

Batrich' Die sabbati proxima post festum sancti Andree apostoli anno supradicto[4]
De frumento in granario vj qr. Item estimantur in grangia xij qr. de quibusdam[5] molendinis xx qr., deducta decima.[6] Summa xxxviij qr. De quibus in expensis falcacionis prata, domus in autumpno, una cum liberacione servientis et medietate liberacionis bedelli viij qr. Liberabantur apud Westm' super visum iiij qr. Summa xij qr. Et remanent xxvj qr. ad mittendum apud Westm'.

[1] See the Word List and Glossary for comments on the grammar of this document.

[2] See note 29 below.

[3] Extant ministers' accounts: Aldenham, WAM 26063; Ashford: 29 September 1312–25 March 1313, WAM 26704; 25 March 1313–29 September 1313, WAM 26706; Feering and Pattiswick, WAM 25628; Kelvedon, 26 March 1313–30 September 1313, WAM 25798; Kinsbourne, WAM 8801; Knightsbridge, WAM 16402; Launton, WAM 15324; Morden, WAM 27304; Teddington, WAM 27174; Wheathampstead, HALS, DE/Lw/M91.

[4] 2 December 1312.

[5] MS: 'quibus'.

[6] Of Battersea's three mills, Lamput mill and Adkyns mill were water-driven corn mills, and the third, to which no name is attached, a windmill for fulling; see the extent of this manor dated 4 October 1312, CUL, MS Kk.5.29, ff. 44v and 48.

De siligine in grangia estimantur ad triturandum l qr. Summa l qr. De quibus in consuetudine passagii de Chelchhuth',[7] in expensis falcacionis prata, sarclancionis bladi, ad precarias ad bladum metendum in autumpno, domus in autumpno, una cum medietate liberacionis bedelli, xvj qr. v bus. In liberacionibus famulorum, xxix qr. ij bus. In vendicione iiij qr. j. bus. Et nichil remanet.
De ordeo in granario viij qr. Item estimantur in grangia ad triturandum xl qr. De chersett' iij qr. ij bus.[8] Summa lj qr. ij bus. De quibus in semine xxxv qr. Summa xxxv qr. Et sic remanent ad mittendum apud Westm' xvj qr. ij bus.
De fabis estimantur in grangia ij qr. Summa ij qr. Et totum in semine.
De pisis et vescis estimantur in grangia viij qr. Summa viij qr. Et totum in semine et liberacionibus famulorum.
De avenis in granario iiij qr. Item estimantur in grangia xxv qr. Summa xxix qr. De quibus in semine xxx qr. In farina ad potagium famulorum, prebenda iij equorum carectariorum et vj affrorum, et prebenda boum, per estimacionem in garbis, xxxiiij qr. iij bus. In prebenda ballivi et[9] Rogeri atte Doune per suos adventus iij qr. et di. Summa lxvij qr. vij bus. Et sic ordinantur ad emendum xxxviij qr. vij bus. avenarum ad suplendum defectus earundem.
De mixtura de exitu molendinorum xxiij qr. et di. per estimacionem deducta decima. Et totum computatur in liberacionibus famulorum.

Staurum Sunt ibi iij equi carectarii, vj affri, xx boves, j taurus, xvj vacce, ij bovetti, ij juvencce, j juvencula, ij vituli superannati qui ordinantur ad vendendum, xx porci unde j verrus, ij sues, ix porcelli de exitu, ij auce.

Denarii Willelmus de Aysseby serviens ibidem debet super visum compoti sui xxxvij li. v s. x d. Et sunt levandum de redditu terminorum natalis Domini, beate Marie in Marcio, nativitatis sancti Johannis baptiste, et sancti Michaelis, de medselver et tallagio, xxiiij li. xj s. iiij d. ob. qua. De diversis firmis vij li. vij s. xj d. De feno, pastur*is* et animalibus agistandis in pastura una cum fructu gardini xj li. v s. iiij d. De fagottis per estimacionem deducta factura xl s. De tolneto brasei ad molendinos xxj s. De firma vaccarum et juvencarum iiij li. v s. De siligine vendendo xvj s. vj d. De ij vitulis superannatis vendendis viij s. De perquisitis curie xj li. vj s. viij d.

[7] Chelsea. For the customary payment of 1 qr. rye p.a. to the ferryman here, see WAM 27506, 27508.
[8] MS: 'ij qr. ij bus.' For the annual total from churchscot at Battersea, see CUL, MS Kk.5.29, f. 51v; for the individual rate of 1 bus. barley per customary virgate, payable on Hock Day, the second Tuesday after Easter, MS Kk.5.29, f. 48, and WAM 27507.
[9] MS: 'et' omitted. The bailiff is the monk-bailiff of Westminster.

Summa totalis denariorum levandorum C li. vij s. vij d. ob. qua. *Expense* De quibus in diversis acquietanciis redditus xiiij s. ij d. In custis carucarum viij s. j d. In custis carectarum x s. v d. In custis molendinorum aquaticorum et molendini fullonarii iiij li. In custis domorum et clausture circa curiam xxvj s. viij d. In sarclacione bladi et falcacione prat*a* xj s. vij d. In custis autumpni lx s. In minutis neccessariis xiij s. iiij d. In feodo Rogeri servientis xiij s. iiij d. In stipendio Willelmi servientis et aliorum famulorum xxix s. vj d. In trituracione bladi xxiij s. xj d. In xxxviij qr. vij bus. avenarum emendis ad suplendum defectus avenarum ut supra iiij li. iij s. In expensis ballivi per estimacionem xl s.

Summa tocius reprise xx li. xiiij s. Et sic remanent xxix li. xiij s. vij d. ob. qua.

Mordon' Die dominica post festum sancti Andree apostoli anno supradicto[10] De frumento in granario vij bus. frumenti, v bus. scuralli frumenti. Item estimantur in grangia xvj qr. unde vj qr. debilis frumenti. Summa xvj qr. vj bus. De quibus in expensis domus in autumpno, expensis precariarum circa bladum metendum cum liberacione servientis, v qr. et di. In mixtura ad liberaciones famulorum vj qr. v bus. debilis frumenti et scuralli. Item liberabantur apud Westm' super visum vj bus. Summa xij qr. vij bus. Et sic remanent ad vendendum iiij qr. v bus.

De mixtura estimantur in grangia ij qr. Summa ij qr. Et totum in liberacionibus famulorum.

De ordeo estimantur in grangia x qr. Summa x qr. Et totum computatur in semine.

De fabis estimantur in grangia vij qr. Summa vij qr. De quibus in semine iij qr. Et sic remanent ad vendendum iiij qr.

De pisis estimantur in grangia xij qr. Summa xij qr. De quibus in semine iiij qr. In liberacionibus famulorum v qr. Summa ix qr. Et sic remanent ad vendendum iij qr.

De drageto estimantur in grangia viij qr. Summa viij qr. De quibus in semine ij qr. Et sic remanent ad vendendum vj qr. drageti.

De avenis remanent in granario j qr. ij bus. Item estimantur in grangia xl qr. Summa xlj qr. ij bus. De quibus in semine xl qr. per estimacionem. In farina ad potagium famulorum, prebenda equorum carectariorum, prebenda boum et vitulorum, xxj qr. In prebenda ballivi et Rogeri atte Doune j qr. et di. Summa lxij qr. et di. Et sic ordinantur ad emendum ad suplendum defectus earundem xxj qr. ij bus. ut patet inferius.

De mixtura de exitu molendini per estimacionem xviij qr. Et totum computatur in liberacionibus famulorum.

[10] 3 December 1312.

Staurum Sunt ibidem ij equi carectarii, iiij affri, j pullanus etatis ij annorum, xvj boves, v vacce, ij boviculi unde j masculus, ij annales masculi, vij auce unde ij anseres iiij mariole, xij capones, ij galli, x galline, x pulcini.

Denarii Robertus Fabian serviens ibidem debet super visum compoti sui die predicto nichil. Et sunt levandum de redditu terminorum natalis Domini, beate Marie in[11] Marcio, nativitatis sancti Johannis, et sancti Michaelis una cum tallagio ad idem terminum, iiij li. ij s. v d. De arrur*is* vendend*is*, animalibus agistandis in pastura, agnis separandis, pastura vendenda, feno et stramine vendendis, xxiij s. De firma vaccarum xxv s. De ovis vendendis x d. De iiij qr. fabarum vendendis xvj s. Et de iij qr. pisarum vendendis x s. De perquisitis curie xl s. Et de iiij qr. v bus. frumenti vendendis xxv s. iiij d. Et de vj qr. drageti vendendis xvj s.

Summa totalis denariorum levandorum xj li. xvij s. vij d.

Expense De quibus in superplusagio visus compoti die predicto xlj s. vj d. ob. In diversis acquietanciis redditus una cum resolucione redditus vij s. ij d. In custis carucarum x s., carectarum viij s. iiij d. In molendino perficiendo ut in carpentria et plastura parietum xvj s. iiij d. In ferro et ere et aliis neccessariis pro molendino xiiij s. iij d.[12] In sustentacione domorum et clausture circa curiam v s. In sarclacione bladi et falcacione prat*a* viij s. In custis autumpni lxx s. In minutis expensis viij s. In feodo Rogeri servientis et stipendiis diversorum famulorum lxv s. viij d. In trituracione bladi xiij s. iiij d. In xxj qr. ij bus. avenarum emendis ad suplendum defectus earundem ut patet supra xlix s. vij d. In expensis ballivi per estimacionem ix s.

Summa tocius reprise xvj li. vj s. ij d. ob. Et sic deficiunt ad sustentacionem manerii hoc anno iiij li. viij s. vij d. ob.

Thodynt' Die dominica post festum sancti Andree apostoli anno supradicto[13]
De frumento in grangia nichil.
De siligine in granario j qr. ij bus. Item estimantur in grangia xvj qr. Item de iij bus. et di. de outhonkesbotcorn'.[14] Summa xvij qr. v bus. et di. De quibus in semine ij qr. vij bus. In expensis domus in autumpno et expensis circa precarias autumpnales ij qr. j bus. In mixtura ad liberaciones

[11] MS: 'in' inserted.
[12] In Fabian's final account as serjeant for the year 1312–13, he was charged with the entire cost, £16 4s. 3d., of the new mill and its transport from Aldenham, where it was constructed, to Morden, by way of Chelsea and Battersea (WAM 27304).
[13] 3 December 1312.
[14] A customary rent, for which at Teddington 1 p. rye and 1 p. of barley were due per virgate at Michaelmas (WAM 27197).

famulorum ix qr. ij bus. Summa xiiij qr. ij bus. Et sic remanent ad vendendum iij qr. iij bus. et di.
De ordeo in grangia per estimacionem xxvj qr. Item de iij bus. et di. de outhonkesbotcorn'. Item de j qr. vij bus. de chersett'.[15] Summa xxviij qr. ij bus. et di. De quibus in semine xvj qr. In braseo facto pro cervisia ad expensas autumpni j qr. Summa xvij qr. Et sic remanent ad mittendum apud Westm' xj qr. ij bus. et di.
De fabis estim*atur* in grangia j qr. Summa j qr. De quibus in plantacione v bus. In mixtura ad liberaciones famulorum iij bus. Et eque.
De pisis estimantur in grangia xij qr. Summa xij qr. De quibus in semine ij qr. vj bus.[16] In mixtura ad liberaciones famulorum ix qr. ij bus. Et eque.
De vescis estimantur in grangia ij qr. Summa ij qr. De quibus in semine vj bus. In mixtura ad liberaciones famulorum j qr. ij bus. Et eque.
De avenis estimantur in grangia xxx qr. Summa xxx qr. De quibus in semine per estimacionem xviij qr. In braseo facto pro cervisia ad expensas autumpn*ales* j qr. et di. In farina ad potagium famulorum, prebenda j equi carectarii, iiij affrorum et boum, xij qr. et di. In prebenda ballivi et Rogeri atte Doune j qr. et di. Summa xxxiij qr. et di. Et sic ordinantur ad emendum ad suplendum defectus earundem iij qr. et di.

Staurum Sunt ibi j equus carectarius, iij affri unde j assignatur vendendum, ut patet inferius, iiij boves, j taurus, vj vacce unde j assignatur ad vendendum ut patet inferius et alius ad emendum ut patet inferius, j bovettus, j boviculus femellus, ij annales femelli, xlij multones, xlix oves matrices, xxviij hogastri, j sus, j verrus, iij porci, ij hogetti, j anser, iij mariole, iij capones, ij galli, vij galline, vij pulcini.

[*Mem. 2 recto*] *Denarii* Walterus le Notier prepositus ibidem debet super visum compoti sui die predicto iiij s. qua. Et sunt levandum de redditu terminorum natalis Domini, pasche, nativitatis sancti Johannis et sancti Michaelis una cum tallagio ad eundem terminum vj li. vj s. iij d. De agnis euntibus in pastura in estate, animalibus agistatis et stipula vendenda vj s. iij d. De lactagio vj vaccarum cum vitulis et lactagio ovium matricum xlj s. De lana ovium vendenda lxij s. De j affro debili vendendo ij s. De j veteri vacca vendenda v s. vj d. De iij qr. iij bus. et di. siliginis vendendis xiij s. ix d. De perquisitis curie xxj s.

Summa totalis denariorum levandorum xiiij li. xxj d. qua.

[15] For churchscot at Teddington, 1 bus. of barley per virgate was due at Michaelmas (WAM 27197).
[16] MS: followed by 'de' expunged.

Expense De quibus in acquietancia redditus prepositi ij s. ix d. In custis carucarum x s. iij d. In custis carectarum iiij s. viij d. In reparacione diversarum domorum ij s. In bercaria vento prostrata relevanda in omnibus expensis xviij s. In falcacione prat*a* xvij d. ob. In custis autumpni xiij s. vj d. In minutis neccessariis xiij s. iiij d. In feodo Rogeri atte Doune servientis una cum stipendiis diversorum famulorum xxxv s. iiij d. In trituracione bladi vj s. viij d. In iij qr. et di. avenarum emendis ad implendum defectus earundem ut patet supra v s. x d. In j affro emendo x s. In j vacca emenda ix s. In expensis ballivi per estimacionem x s.

Summa tocius reprise vij li. ij s. ix d. ob. Et sic remanent ad mittendum apud Westm' vj li. xviij s. xj d. ob. qua.

Echelefford' Die lune proxima post festum sancti Andree apostoli anno supradicto[17]

De frumento in granario vj bus. scuralli frumenti. In grangia per estimacionem j qr. Inde in liberacionibus famulorum vj bus. scuralli. In expensis domus in autumpno et in liberacione servientis manerii v qr. iij bus. Summa vj qr. j bus. Et sic ordinantur ad emendum ad suplendum defectus frumenti iiij qr. iij bus. ut patet inferius.

De siligine in grangia ij qr. j bus. Et in grangia ad triturandum per estimacionem xl qr. Summa xlij qr. j bus. De quibus in expensis domus in autumpno et precariarum iij qr. et di. In liberacionibus famulorum xx qr. v bus. Summa xxiiij qr. j bus. Et remanent ad vendendum xviij qr.

De ordeo per estimacionem in grangia xxx qr. De cherssett' nichil quia nichil receptum.[18] Summa xxx qr. Inde ad seminandum xxiij qr. iiij bus. Summa xxiij qr. et di. Et remanent ad mittendum apud Westm' v qr. et di.

De fabis et pisis estimantur in grangia ad triturandum iij qr. et di. Inde in semine vj bus. fabarum, iiij bus. pisarum. In liberacionibus famulorum ij qr. ij bus. Et eque.

De avenis per estimacionem in grangia lx qr. Inde in semine xxxiij qr. In potagio famulorum, prebenda j equi carectarii et iiij affrorum et boum xvj qr. et di. In prebenda ballivi et[19] Rogeri atte Doune ij qr. Summa lj qr. et di. Et sic remanent ad mittendum apud Westm' viij qr. et di.

[17] 4 December 1312.

[18] For churchscot at Ashford, 4 bus. of barley per virgate were due at Michaelmas. The above entry relates to payments due at the previous Michaelmas and amounting to 9 qr. 6 bus. barley (WAM 26703–4).

[19] MS: 'et' omitted.

Staurum Sunt ibi j equus carectarius, iiij affri, v boves, j taurus, x vacce unde j assignatur ad vendendum pro alia emenda ut patet inferius, ij bovetti, j juvenca,[20] ij juvencule, j annalis, liij multones, iiij^{xx}xiij oves matrices, xlvij agni, j verrus, j sus, v porci, xliiij porculi, vij auce unde j anser iiij mariole, ij galli, iiij galline et vj pulcini.

Denarii Radulfus de Bernewell' serviens ibidem debet super visum compoti sui iiij li. xvij s. j d. qua. Levandum sunt de redditu de terminis natalis Domini, beate Marie in Marcio, nativitatis sancti Johannis baptiste, cum tallagio, vj li. ix s. ij d. De diversis firmis x s. x d. De diversis pasturis et stipula vendendis cum fructu gardini vij s. vj d. ob. qua. De lana vendenda lx s. De lactagio vaccarum et ovium matricum lxxiij s. v d. De xviij qr. siliginis vendendis lxxij s. De j veteri vacca viij s. De perquisitis curie l s. De firma de Scheperton' x li. De redditu de Haleweford xj li. x s. vj d.[21] De perquisitis curie xiij s. iiij d.

Summa totalis denariorum levandorum xlvij li. xj s. xj d.

Expense Inde in acquietanciis redditus viij s. viij d. In custis carucarum xv s. viij d. In custis carectarum ij s. In falcacione prat*a* et custis autumpni xl s. In minutis expensis cum unccione bidentium[22] xx s. In reparacione domorum vj s. viij d. In grangia manerii de novo facienda quia ruinosa vj li. xiij s. iiij d. In feodo[23] Rogeri atte Doune servientis cum stipendiis servientis manerii et aliorum famulorum lvij s. ij d. In trituracione bladi et ventacione xviij s. ix d. In j vacca emenda x s. In expensis ballivi per suos adventus xvj s.

Summa tocius reprise xvj li. viij s. iij d. Et sic remanent ultra reprisam xxxj li. iij s. viij d. preter relevacionem molendini omnino ruinosi.

Greneford' Die lune proxima post festum sancti Andree apostoli anno supradicto[24]

Sunt levandum ibidem de redditu x li. xv s. qua. De firma per annum xviij s. x d. De iij bus. siliginis de cherssett' vendendis xviij d. precium bus. vj d. Et sunt levandum ibidem de finibus et perquisitis curi*e* xix s.

Summa xij li. xiiij s. iiij d. qua.

[20] MS: 'jumenta'.

[21] For the fee-farm rents owing to the Abbey from Shepperton and Halliford, which the serjeant or reeve of Ashford was responsible for collecting, see Harvey, *Estates*, pp. 351–2, 354. From Halliford, 15 hens were also due.

[22] MS: 'bidend''.

[23] MS: 'fedo'.

[24] 4 December 1312.

Expense De quibus in diversis acquietanciis redditus xx s. ix d. ob. In factura vM[1] fagottorum xx s. x d. precium M[1] iiij s. ij d. In expensis ballivi per suos adventus iiij s. xj d.

Summa lxvj s. vj d. ob. Et sic remanent pro Westm' x li. vij s. ix d. ob. qua. una cum M[1] fagottorum qui ordinantur pro Westm'.

Ecclesia de Stanes[25]
Sunt in granario scuralli frumenti iij qr. v bus. Et estimantur in grangia xviij qr. precium qr. v s. vj d. Et expendebantur in autumpno de frumento iiij qr. ij bus.
De siligine j qr. De avenis viij qr. iiij bus. j p.
De siligine estimantur ad triturandum xxxv qr. precium qr. iiij s.
De ordeo estimantur ad triturandum xxvj qr. precium qr. iiij s. Et mittebantur apud Westm' viij[xx] j qr.
De fabis et pisis estimantur xvj qr. precium qr. xl d. ad foragium.
Inde ordinatur pro trituracione et ventacione, de custis autumpni, pro decimis colligendis et intrandis xx marce.

Knygtbrugg' Die martis proxima post festum sancti Andree apostoli anno supradicto[26]
De frumento in granario v qr. vj bus. frumenti. In grangia ad triturandum per estimacionem x qr. Summa xv qr. vj bus. De quibus in liberacione servientis, expensis domus in autumpno, v qr. Liberabantur fratri Guidoni[27] super visum iiij qr. Summa ix qr. Et sic remanent ad mittendum apud Westm' vj qr. vj bus.
De mixtura in grangia ad triturandum per estimacionem xv qr. Summa xv qr. Et totum in liberacionibus famulorum. Et eque.
De ordeo estimantur in grangia ad triturandum xl qr. Summa xl qr. De quibus in semine xx qr. In liberacionibus famulorum vj qr. iij bus. et di. Summa xxvj qr. iij bus. et di. Et sic remanent ad mittendum apud Westm' xiij qr. iiij bus. et di.
De fabis et pisis xv qr. estimantur in grangia. Summa xv qr. De quibus in semine ij qr. In liberacionibus famulorum xiij qr. Et eque.
De avenis estimantur in grangia l qr. Summa l qr. De quibus in semine xxvj qr. In farina ad potagium famulorum, prebenda equorum carectariorum,

[25] The church at Staines was assigned to the convent's portion, and at this date in particular to the treasurers for the use of the bailiff. For its unusual wealth, see J. Blair, 'The Minsters of the Thames', in *The Cloister and the World: Essays in Honour of Barbara Harvey*, ed. J. Blair and B. Golding (Oxford, 1996), pp. 5–28, at p. 24, and references given there.
[26] 5 December 1312.
[27] Guydo de Ashwell, treasurer 1311–13 (Pearce, *Monks*, p. 71).

affrorum et boum xviij qr. ij bus. In prebenda ballivi ij bus. Summa xliiij qr. et di. Et sic remanent ad mittendum apud Westm' v qr. et di.

Staurum Sunt ibidem ij equi carectarii, vj affri et j assignatur ad emendum ut patet inferius, ix boves, xiiij vacce, ij bovetti, j juvencca, iij boviculi unde j juvencula, ij annales unde j masculus, xij multones, iiij^{xx}vij matrices, lxxiiij hogastri, j verrus, ij suelle, vj porcelli de exitu lactantes, j anser, ij mariole, iij capones, j gallus, iij galline, ij pulcini, j coreum dealbatum, iiij rusce apium, iiijC fagotti.

Denarii Johannes Boneyr' serviens de Knyghtbrugg' die predicto.
De redditu et tallagio iiij li. xix s. qua. De diversis firmis xxij s. De feno et litera, arrur*is*, diversis pasturis, stipula, rosis, lino, porettis et fructu gardini vij li. viij s. v d. De lana vendenda lxiiij s. vij d. De firma vaccarum iiij li. xj s. De lactagio ovium matricum xiij s. iiij d. De finibus et perquisitis xl s.

Summa totalis denariorum levandorum xxiij li. xviij s. iiij d.

Expense De quibus in superplusagio compoti xxx s. vij d. ob. qua. In acquietanciis diversorum reddituum viij d. In custis carucarum xxviiij s. In custis carectarum xxiij s. In custis domorum sustinendarum viij s. In sarclacione bladi et falcacione prat*a* xij s. In custis autumpni viij li. x s. In minutis expensis xxxv s. In stipendiis diversorum famulorum lxiij s. iiij d. In trituracione bladi xvij s. x d. In j affro emendo ad suplendum defectus affrorum xij s. In expensis ballivi per suos adventus iiij s.

Summa totalis reprise xx li. iiij s. v d. ob. qua. Et sic remanent ad mittendum apud Westm' lxxiij s. x d. ob.

[*Mem. 3 recto*] *Hamstede* Die mercurii in festo sancti Nicholai anno supradicto[28]
De frumento in granario ij bus. Et assignantur ad vendendum ut patet inferius.
De siligine in granario iij bus. Item estimantur in grangia ad triturandum iiij qr. Summa iiij qr. iij bus. Et totum in liberacionibus famulorum. Et eque.
De ordeo estimantur in grangia ad triturandum iiij qr. et di. Summa iiij qr. et di. De quibus in semine j qr. et di. In liberacionibus famulorum iij qr. Et eque.
De pisis et vescis estimantur in grangia ad triturandum ij bus. Et totum assignatur in semine. Et eque.

[28] 6 December 1312.

De avenis estimantur in grangia ad triturandum xxx qr. Summa xxx qr. De quibus in semine xxx qr. In farina ad potagium famulorum, prebenda j equi carectarii, iiij affrorum, boum et vitulorum, per estimacionem in garbis xiiij qr. et di. In expensis ballivi et Rogeri servientis vj bus. Summa xlv qr. ij bus. Et sic assignantur ad emendum ad suplendum defectus earundem xv qr. ij bus. ut patet inferius.
[De mixtura de exitu molendini ....][29]
Memorandum quod assignantur ad emendum ad suplendum defectus liberacionum famulorum xj qr. v bus. mixture ut patet inferius.

Staurum Sunt ibidem j equus carectarius, iij affri unde j assignatur ad vendendum et j alius ad emendum ut patet inferius, vj boves unde j assignatur ad vendendum pro alio emendo quia debilis, j taurus, xij vacce unde j assignatur ad vendendum pro alia emenda, ij juvencce, j boviculus, ij hurtardi, xiij multones, iiij^{xx}xiiij oves matrices, lxiiij hogastri, iiij auce unde j anser et ij mariole, j gallus, iiij galline, j coreum equinum dealbatum.

Denarii. Radulfus le Mai serviens ibidem debet super visum die predicto xj s. v d. ob. Et Thomas Broun prepositus ibidem habet levare de redditu et tallagio per tempus predictum x li. viij s. vj d. De diversis firmis lxvj s. vj d. Et de quadam consuetudine que vocatur medselver,[30] colleccione bruerie, diversis pasturis, animalibus agistatis, feno et arrur*is* vendendis, consuetudinibus trituracionis, cariagii fimorum, feni, frumenti et avenarum, et precariis in autumpno iiij li. v s. De firma vaccarum cum vitulis et lactagio ovium matricum iiij li. ix s. ij d. De lana bidentium et agnorum vendenda lv s. De j affro debili vendendo iij s. De j bove debili vendendo viij s. De j veteri vacca debili vendenda v s. De ij bus. frumenti vendendis xvj d. De finibus et perquisitis curie xl s.

[29] A lacuna, probably affecting one or two lines of the original text, occurs in the MS at this point. It is clear that the missing text recorded receipts of mixed corn from the mill, and the editorial insertion provides the likely heading for such an entry. The missing text was known to the author of the ensuing memorandum, and it enabled him to estimate how much mixed corn should be purchased to complete the total amount needed for the year's liveries to the famuli. Between the lacuna which we must envisage and the memorandum occurs a capital S, probably intended as the first letter of 'Summa'. But the capital is a beaver-tailed S, a form of this letter seldom used in the present document, itself the work of one scribe. Moreover, no space occurs between the S and the memorandum, although originally one must have been intended, to accommodate the final sum of mixed corn remaining. These circumstances suggest that the scribe of the present document did not fully understand his immediate exemplar, which itself had the lacuna at this point, but did his best to follow it by copying its beaver-tailed S and continuing with the memorandum.

[30] At Hampstead, according to the extent of 1312, the tenants of two holdings, each of a messuage and five acres, owed, in each case, 5d. p.a. in *medselver*, on 24 June (CUL, MS Kk.5.29, ff. 34v, 35).

Summa totalis denariorum levandorum xxviij li. xj s. vij d. ob. De quibus in defectu redditus et tallagii quia tenement*a* in manu domini vj s. x d. In custis carucarum xvij s. vj d. In custis carectarum ix s. In custis molendini nichil. In custis domorum sustinendarum ut in domibus cooperiendis et aliis neccessariis earundem reparandis viij s. In sarclacione bladi et falcacione prat*a* x s. In custis autumpni lxxj s. In minutis expensis xiij s. iiij d. In feodo Rogeri servientis et stipendiis diversorum famulorum vij s. vj d. In trituracione bladi v s. v d. In xv qr. ij bus. avenarum emptis ad suplendum defectus earundem xxxiij s. j d. In xj qr. v bus. mixture emptis ad suplendum defectus liberacionum famulorum xxxviij s. ix d. In j affro emendo xij s. In j bove emendo xvj s. In j vacca emenda xij s. In expensis ballivi vj s. viij d. In factura viijM^{l} fagottorum cum cariagio vijM^{l} de eisdem apud Westm' C s., et cariagium jM^{l} assignatur pro carecta de manerio.

Summa totalis reprise xviij li. vij s. j d. Et sic remanent x li. iiij s. vj d. ob. De quibus dominus Henricus de Blontesdon' percipiet de redditu et tallagio dicti manerii x li.[31] Et sic remanent de claro ultra reprisam manerii iiij s. vj d. ob.

Aldenham Die mercurii predicto et anno supradicto[32]
De frumento estimantur in grangia ad triturandum viij qr. Summa viij qr. De quibus in stipendio fabri pro ferramento carucarum et ferramento equorum et affrorum de convencione, allocacione prandii sui in advent*ibus* ballivi, expensis domus in autumpno una cum expensis circa precarias autumpnales ij qr. ij bus. et di. Summa ij qr. ij bus. et di. Et sic remanent ad mittendum apud Westm' v qr. v bus. et di.
De pisis et vescis estimantur in grangia ij qr. De quibus in semine iiij bus. In liberacionibus famulorum j qr. et di. Et eque.
De avenis estimantur in grangia ad triturandum lxx qr. Summa lxx qr. De quibus in semine lx qr. In farina ad potagium famulorum, prebenda equorum carectariorum, vj affrorum et boum xxiiij qr. In expensis ballivi et servientis j qr. et di. Summa iiij^{xx}v qr. et di. Et sic ordinantur ad emendum xv qr. et di.
De mixtura de molendino adhuc habet levare xxiij qr. Et totum in liberacionibus famulorum. Et assignantur ad emendum ad suplendum defectus liberacionum famulorum ut patet inferius xj qr. iij bus.

Staurum Sunt ibidem ij equi carectarii, vj affri, iiij boves, j taurus, viij vacce, j boviculus, ij juvenccule, iiij vituli superannati unde j masculus, iij

[31] Formerly Edward I's almoner, and probably a source of loans to the convent. For a hint of a transaction of this kind in 1301, see WAM 29081–2.
[32] 6 December 1312.

hurtardi, xxxvj multones, lix matrices, xxxix hogastri, j verrus, ij sues, xiiij porci, vj auce unde j anser ij mariole, xxiiij capones, j gallus, x galline.

Denarii Thomas Boydyn ibidem prepositus debet super visum suum v s. Et sunt levandum ibidem de redditu et tallagio una cum firma piscarii xix li. ij s. vj d. ob.[33] De M[l] fagottorum vendend*o* deducta factura xxvj s. viij d. De lana vendenda xlj s. iiij d. De firma vaccarum et lactagii ovium matricum xlvij s. iiij d. ob. De finibus et perquisitis curie Cxij s. vj d.

Summa totalis denariorum levandorum xxx li. xv s. x d.

De quibus in acquietanciis diversorum reddituum xij s. v d. ob. In custis carucarum xxiiij s. In custis carectarum vij s. viij d. In custis molendini xij d. In custis domorum sustinendarum et clausture circa curiam x s. In falcacione prat*a* et custis autumpni lv s. vj d. In minutis expensis xviij s. In feodo Willelmi Eron' et stipendio j porcarii per annum xxiiij s. vj d.[34] In trituracione bladi vj s. x d. In xv qr. et di. avenarum emptis ad suplendum defectus avenarum ut patet supra xl s. In xj qr. iij bus. mixture emptis ad suplendum defectus liberacionum famulorum xxxvij s. xj d. In expensis ballivi per suos adventus xxvj s. viij d.

Summa totalis reprise xiij li. iiij s. vj d. ob. Et sic remanent ad mittendum apud Westm' xvij li. xj s. iij d. ob.

Kenesberne Die jovis post festum sancti Nicholai anno supradicto[35]
De frumento in granario v qr. Item estimantur in grangia ad triturandum l qr. unde iij qr. de draunk. Summa lv qr. De quibus in expensis domus in autumpno j qr. et di. In mixtura ad liberaciones famulorum xiiij qr. ij bus. Liberabantur apud Westm' super istud visum iij qr. In vendicione xxxvj qr. ij bus. Summa ut supra. Et eque.
De pisis iiij qr. estimantur in grangia ad triturandum. Summa iiij qr. De quibus in semine di. qr. Summa di qr. Et sic remanent ad vendendum iij qr. et di. Et eque.
De pisis et vescis estimantur in grangia ad triturandum ij qr. et di. Summa ij qr. et di. De quibus in semine di. qr. Summa di. qr. Et sic remanent ad vendendum ij qr. Et eque.
De drageto estimantur in grangia ad triturandum xxiiij qr. Summa xxiiij qr. De quibus in semine iiij qr. et di. Et sic remanent ad vendendum xix qr. et di. Et eque.
De avenis estimantur in grangia ad triturandum xxiiij qr. Summa xxiiij qr. De quibus in semine l qr. In farina ad potagium famulorum, prebendam xij

[33] To which sum the farm of the fishery apparently contributed 2s. p.a. (WAM 26063).
[34] William Eron, currently serjeant at Aldenham.
[35] 7 December 1312.

affrorum, una cum sustentacione agnorum et vitulorum xxx qr. In prebenda equi ballivi per suos adventus iiij bus. et di. Summa iiij^{xx} qr. iiij bus. et di. Et sic ordinantur ad emendum ad suplendum defectus earundem ut patet inferius lvj qr. iiij bus. et di.
[*Mem. 4 recto*] De preposito de Wathamsted' de mixtura de exitu molendini ad suplendum defectus liberacionum famulorum huius manerii xiiij qr. ij bus. Et eque.

Staurum Sunt ibi xiij affri[36] unde iij debiles assignantur ad vendendum pro ij reemendis, quia tot sufficiunt pro manerio, j taurus, x vacce, iij bovetti, iij juvencce, j boviculus, j juvencula, iij vituli superannati quorum ij masculi, xviij multones, xxj oves matrices, xiiij hogastri, xxiiij jercie, xxxviij agni superannati, j verrus, j sus, xij porculi, v porcelli de exitu, j anser, ij mariole, vj capones, j gallus, vj galline, j pulcinus.

Denarii[37] Willelmus Enfemme prepositus habet levare die predicto de arrur*is* vend*endis* et agnis separandis in pastur*a* dominici v s. Et de feno manerii et pastur*a* tenementi Lovekyne le Hathknetter quod est in manu domini xvj s. Et de lana vend*enda* xl s. De firma lactagii vaccarum, juvenccarum et ovium matricum lxij s. vij d. ob. Et de xxxvj qr. ij bus. frumenti vendendis vij li. v s. Et de iij qr. et di. pisarum vendendis xj s. viij d. Et de vj s. de ij qr. pisarum et vescarum vendendis. Et de lviij s. vj d. de xix qr. di. drageti vendendis. Et de v s. de iij veteribus affris vendendis. Et de xxx s. de operibus[38] custumariis vend*endis*.

Summa totalis denariorum levandorum xviij li. xix s. ix d. ob.

De quibus in superplusagio visus compoti die predicto Cv s. vj d. ob. qua. In custis carucarum et ferracione affrorum xxxiiij s. In custis carectarum ix s. In custis domorum sustinendarum x s. In blado sarclando, pratis falcandis et levandis vj s. In custis autumpni Cx s. In minutis expensis xij s. In stipendio j daie in hieme xij d. Et alii famuli ad bladum. In trituracione bladi xij s. In lvj qr. iiij bus. di. avenarum emendis ad suplendum defectus earundem ut patet supra vj li. xj s. xj d. ob. precium qr. ij s. iiij d. In ij affris emendis xxvj s. viij d. In expensis ballivi per suos adventus v s.

Summa tocius reprise xxiij li. iij s. ij d. qua. Et sic deficiunt ad suplendum reprisam manerii hoc anno iiij li. iiij s. v d.

[36] MS omits 'affri'.
[37] The rents and tallage of Kinsbourne were collected by the reeve of Wheathampstead, who accounted for them with the rents and tallage of Wheathampstead itself. For the configuration of the two manors and close administrative connection between the two, see Stern, *Hertfordshire Demesne*, pp. 47–58, and Fig. 1.4.
[38] MS: 'empc''.

Langeton' Die sabbati proxima post festum sancti Nicholai anno supradicto[39]
De frumento estimantur in grangia ad trituracionem xx qr. Summa xx qr. De quibus in expensis circa precarias autumpnales, expensis domus in autumpno ij qr. In mixtura ad liberaciones famulorum iij qr. et di. Summa v qr. et di. Et sic remanent ad vendendum xiiij qr. et di. ut patet inferius.
De siligine estimantur in grangia ad triturandum xviij qr. Summa xviij qr. De quibus in expensis circa precarias autumpnales, expensis domus in autumpno j qr. vij bus. Summa j qr. vij bus. Et sic remanent ad vendendum xvj qr. j bus.
De fabis et pisis in granario ij qr. j bus. Item in estimacione in grangia ad triturandum xij qr. Summa xiiij qr. j bus. De quibus in semine iiij qr. In mixtura ad liberaciones famulorum x qr. j bus. Et eque.
De drageto estimantur in grangia ad triturandum xxiiij qr. Summa xxiiij qr. De quibus in semine vij qr. Summa vij qr. Et sic remanent ad vendendum xvij qr. Et eque.
De avenis in granario iiij qr. Item estimantur in grangia ad triturandum lxxiiij qr. Summa lxxviij qr. De quibus in semine xl qr. In prebenda ij equorum carectariorum, iiij affrorum et boum, per estimacionem in garbis xxiij qr. In prebenda herciatorum ville de consuetudine j qr. ij bus. In prebenda ballivi j qr. Summa lxv qr. ij bus. Et sic remanent ad vendendum xij qr. vj bus.
De mixtura de exitu molendini estimantur xv qr. vj bus. et di. deducta decima. Et totum assignatur in liberacionibus famulorum.
De braseo de exitu molendini estimantur ij qr. et di. deducta decima. Et totum assignatur ad vendendum.
De farina avenarum de exitu molendini estimantur ij bus. deducta decima. Et totum assignatur ad vendendum.

Staurum Sunt ibidem ij equi carectarii, iiij affri, xiiij boves unde ij assignantur ad vendendum et alius ad emendum, xiij vacce <u>unde j assignatur</u> ad vendendum et alie ad emendum, j taurus, j juvenca, j boviculus, iiij annales, lxj multones, lxxj matrices, xxiiij hogastri, j sus, j porcus, xv hogetti, xiij porcelli, v auce <u>unde j anser</u> iij mariole, xij capones, j gallus et v galline.

Denarii Ricardus de Ambresdon' prepositus ibidem debet super visum suum ij s. iiij d. ob. Et sunt levandum ibidem de redditu xvj li. x s. j d. De diversis pasturis et stramine venditis vj s. ix d. De lana vendenda per estimacionem C s. De lactagio vaccarum et ovium matricum iiij li. xxij d. Et de liij s. ij d. de xiiij qr. et di. frumenti vendendis <u>precium qr. iij s. viij d.</u>

[39] 9 December 1312.

Et de xliij s. de xvj qr. j bus. siliginis vendendis precium qr. ij s. viij d. Et de lvj s. viij d. de xvij qr. drageti vendendis precium qr. iij s. iiij d. Et de xxv s. vj d. de xij qr. vj bus. avenarum vendendis. Et de ix s. ij d. de ij qr. et di. brasei de exitu molendini. Et de xij d. de ij bus. farine avenarum vendendis. De perquisitis curie Cvj s.[40]

Summa totalis denariorum levandorum xl li. xv s. vj d. ob.

De quibus in acquietanciis diversorum reddituum ix s. iiij d. In custis carucarum xx d. In custis carectarum iij s. In custis molendini nichil. In boveria boum de novo facienda xl s. In aliis domibus emendendis v s. In falcacione prat*a* de consuetudine iij s. In custis autumpni xviij s. In minutis expensis xiij s. iiij d. In trituracione bladi xv s. j d. In ij bobus et j vacca mutandis ultra vendicionem eorundem vj s.[41] In expensis ballivi per suos adventus x s.

Summa tocius reprise vj li. iiij s. v d. Et sic remanent ad mittendum apud Westm' xxxiiij li. xj s. j d. ob.

[*Mem. 5 recto*] *Wathamsted'* Die martis proxima post festum sancti Nicholai[42] anno supradicto[43]

De frumento in granario xx qr. Item estimantur in grangia ad triturandum lx qr. et di.[44] Summa iiij^{xx} qr. et di. De quibus in expensis domus in autumpno, ferracione equorum et affrorum de convencione iij qr. ij bus. In liberacionibus bedelli et eiusdem wodewardi ij qr. et di. In mixtura ad liberaciones famulorum[45] xix qr. vj bus. Item liberabantur apud Westm' super visum xx qr. Summa xlv qr. iiij bus. Et sic remanent ad mittendum apud Westm' xxxv qr.

De ordeo estimantur in grangia ad triturandum v qr. ordei. Summa v qr. De quibus in semine ij qr. Summa ij qr. Et sic remanent ad mittendum apud Westm' iij qr.

De pisis estimantur in grangia ad triturandum j qr. et di. Summa j qr. et di. De quibus in semine vj bus. Summa vj bus. Et sic remanent ad vendendum vj bus. ut patet inferius. Et eque.

[40] MS: 'de' erased before 's.'

[41] i.e. the purchase price of two oxen and one cow is expected to exceed the selling price of the stock to be replaced. In the event at Launton, no cow was sold or purchased; but an ox and a cow were slaughtered and the hides sold for 6s. (WAM 15324).

[42] MS: 'Michaelis'.

[43] 12 December 1312.

[44] Customary renders of wheat, probably totalling a little over 2 qr. 2 bus., were apparently omitted from this panel; for these, see HALS, DE/Lw/M129, and CUL, MS Kk.5.29, ff. 73v–76v.

[45] MS: 'fam' fam'', i.e. word repeated.

De drageto estimantur in grangia ad triturandum viij qr. Summa viij qr. De quibus in semine ij qr. et di. Summa ij qr. et. di. Et sic remanent ad mittendum apud Westm' v qr. et di.
De avenis sunt in granario x qr. ij bus. Estimantur in grangia ad triturandum xlv qr. Et de x qr. et di. de redditu.[46] Summa lxv qr. vj bus. De quibus in semine iiij^{xx}iiij qr. In diversis acquietanciis redditus iiij bus. In farina ad potagium famulorum, prebenda iij equorum carectariorum, xiiij affrorum et iiij equorum trium carucarum iiij^{xx}j qr. v bus. In expensis ballivi per suos adventus et servientis iiij qr. Summa Clxx qr. j bus. Et sic ordinantur ad emendum ad suplendum defectus earundem Ciiij qr. iij bus.
De mixtura in partem solucionis firme iij molendinorum xlviij qr. Summa xlviij qr. De quibus in liberacionibus famulorum xix qr. vj bus. et di. Item liberand*um* sunt preposito de Kenesb*er*ne pro liberacionibus famulorum ibidem xiiij qr. ij bus. Summa xxxiiij qr. di. bus. Et sic remanent ad vendendum xiij qr. vij bus. et di.
De braseo de firma j molendini ij qr. Et assignantur ad vendendum.

Staurum Sunt ibidem vij equi carectarii, xiiij affri unde ij assignantur ad vendendum et alius ad emendum, j taurus, viij vacce, ij taurilli, iij juvencce, iij boviculi unde ij masculi j femellus, iij annales, lxvij multones, lxiij matrices, xix agni superannati, ij verri, ij sues, xxij alii porci et hogetti, iij porcelli, iij cigni unde j errarius, vij auce unde j anser iij mariole, xiij capones, j gallus, j gullus, ij galline.

Denarii Simon in le Lane prepositus de Wathamstede habet levare de redditu et talliagio[47] xxxviij li. xv s. xj d. qua. De arrur*is* custumar*iis* ij s. vj d. De lana vendenda xlix s. viij d. De firma exitus et lactagii vaccarum et lactagii ovium matricum xlvj s. x d. ob. De vj bus. pisarum vendendis ij s. vj d. De xiij qr. vij bus. et di. mixture vendendis xlvj s. v d. ob. De ij qr. brasei de exitu molendini vendendis vj s. De ij affris vendendis iiij s. De perquisitis curie vj li. xiij s. iiij d. De operibus vend*endis* iiij li. xiij s. iiij d.

Summa totalis denariorum levandorum lviij li. vij d. qua.

Expense De quibus in superplusagio visus compoti die predicto xxiiij s. ob. In diversis acquietanciis redditus et averagiorum xxvj s. xj d. ob. In custis carucarum iiij li. In custis carectarum xl s. In custis molendinorum cum molis emendendis vij li. xiij s. iiij d. In custis domorum xx s. In falcacione prat*a* ij s. iij d. In custis autumpni viij li. x s. In minutis expensis cum

[46] For customary renders of oats at Wheathampstead, due on 1 November, see CUL, MS Kk.5.29, ff. 76v, 78v.
[47] MS: the second 'a' in 'talliagio' is written over another letter which may have been 'g'.

unccione bidentium xl s. In feodo servientis[48] et stipendiis famulorum xlj s. iiij d. In trituracione bladi xiij s. viij d. qua. In Ciiij qr. iij bus. avenarum emendis ad suplendum defectus earundem xij li. iij s. vj d. ob. In ij affris emendis xxvj s. viij d. In mutacione j vacce ultra valorem eiusdem iij s. In expensis ballivi xxxviij s.

Summa tocius reprise xlvj li. xxj d. ob. qua. Et sic remanent ad mittendum[49] apud Westm' xj li. xviij s. ix d. ob.

Harpenden' Memorandum quod ecclesia de Harpeden'[50] vend*endum* ante autumpnum.[51]

Stith' Die mercurii in festo sancte Lucie virginis anno supradicto[52]
De frumento ix qr. iij bus. in granario. Item remanent in grangia ad triturandum per estimacionem l qr. Summa lix qr. iij bus. De quibus in expensis domus in autumpno, consuetudine bedelli in autumpno ij qr. et di. In mixtura ad liberaciones famulorum xx qr. Summa xxij qr. et di. Et sic remanent ad mittendum apud Westm' xxxvj qr. vij bus.
De ordeo estimantur in grangia ad triturandum viij qr. Et totum computatur in semine. Et eque.
De pisis estimantur in grangia ad triturandum xxx qr. Summa xxx qr. De quibus in semine vj qr. In mixtura ad liberaciones famulorum ij qr. j bus. Summa viij qr. j bus. Et sic remanent ad vendendum xxj qr. vij bus.
De drageto estimantur in grangia ad triturandum x qr. Summa x qr. De quibus in semine ij qr. Summa ij qr. Et sic remanent ad vendendum viij qr.
De avena[53] in granario ij qr. Item estimantur in grangia ad triturandum l qr. Summa lij qr. De quibus in semine xl qr. In farina ad potagium famulorum, prebenda iiij equorum carectariorum et xij affrorum xxxvj qr. In expensis ballivi et servientis per suos adventus ij qr. Summa lxxviij qr. Et sic ordinantur ad emendum ad suplendum defectus earundem xxvj qr.
De mixtura de exitu molendini xviij qr. Et totum computatur in liberacionibus famulorum. Et eque.

[48] Roger atte Doune.
[49] MS: followed by 'ad', but struck out.
[50] MS: possibly omits words such as 'ordinatur ad'.
[51] Correctly, the chapel of St Nicholas at Harpenden. But the memorandum is concerned only with the Abbey's moiety of the greater tithes of the parish of Wheathampstead; this comprised the vills of Harpenden, Kinsbourne and the vill of Wheathampstead itself (Stern, *Hertfordshire Demesne*, pp. 51–2).
[52] 13 December 1312.
[53] The MS (and probably the scribe's exemplar) uses the collective singular, although other parts of the document use a plural form.

Staurum Sunt ibidem iiij equi carectarii unde j assignatur ad vendendum et alius ad emendum, xij affri unde ij assignantur ad vendendum et alii ad emendum, j taurus, ix vacce, j taurillus, j boviculus, v juvencule, ij annales, lj multones, xlix matrices, xl hogastri, j verrus, ij sues, xvj alii porci et hogetti, ix porcelli, ix auce unde j anser iiij mariole, x capones, j gallus, vj galline, j coreum, v rusche apium.

Denarii Rogerus atten Hopend' prepositus de Stith' debet super visum compoti sui nichil. Et sunt levandum ibidem de redditu xxix li. xiij s. viij d. ob. De diversis firmis iiij s. iiij d. De diversis pasturis, equis euntibus in bosco, agnis euntibus in pastur*is*, melle apium, firma tolneti fori et fructu gardini vendendo xiij s. De firma exitus et lactagii vaccarum et lactagii ovium matricum xlix s. j d. De xxj qr. vij bus. pisarum vendendis lj s. ob. De viij qr. drageti vendendis xxvj s. viij d. De j equo carectario vendendo iij s. De ij affris vendendis v s. vj d. De perquisitis curie Cxvj s.

Summa totalis denariorum levandorum xliij li. ij s. iiij d.

De quibus in superplusagio visus compoti sui xxxvij s. vij d. ob. In acquietanciis diversorum reddituum ix s. iij d. qua. In custis carucarum xliij s. vij d. In custis carectarum xxij s. x d. cum una carecta de novo emenda. In custis domorum vj s. viij d. In sarclacione bladi et falcacione prat*a* v s. In custis autumpni xliiij s. In minutis expensis xvj s. In feodo servientis et stipendiis diversorum famulorum xxxiiij s. In trituracione bladi xvij s. iiij d. In xxvj qr. avenarum emendis ad suplendum defectus earundem lx s. viij d. In j equo carectario emendo xxvj s. viij d. In ij affris emendis xxvj s. viij d. In expensis ballivi xxiiij s.

Summa tocius reprise xviij li. xiiij s. iij d. ob. qua. Et sic remanent ad mittendum apud Westm' xxiiij li. viij s. qua. Et memorandum quod molendinum est ruinosum et factura eiusdem estimatur ad v marcas preter j molam de stauro et j molam emendam.

Ayswell' Die jovis post festum sancte Lucie virginis anno supradicto[54]
De frumento in granario xij qr. v bus. Item estimantur in grangia ad triturandum lij qr. De exitu molendinorum vj qr.[55] Summa lxx qr. v bus. De quibus in expensis domus in autumpno et liberacionis servientis v qr. iij bus. et di. Et sic remanent ad mittendum apud Westm' lxv qr. j bus. et di.
De mixtura estimantur in grangia ad triturandum lx qr. De quibus in mixtura ad liberaciones famulorum xx qr. Et sic remanent ad vendendum xl qr.

[54] 14 December 1312.
[55] Ashwell's two mills, one a watermill and the other a windmill, were to be valued together at £8 p.a. in the extent of 1315 (CUL, MS Kk.5.29, f. 83v).

De pisis et vescis estimantur in grangia ad triturandum xxx qr. De quibus in semine xj qr. et di. In mixtura ad liberaciones famulorum vj qr. j bus. et di. Summa xvij qr. v bus. et di. Et sic remanent ad vendendum xij qr. ij bus. et di.
De drageto in grangia xj qr. ij bus. Item estimantur in grangia ad triturandum xxx qr. Summa xlj qr. ij bus. De quibus in semine xxx qr. Summa xxx qr. Et sic remanent ad mittendum apud Westm' xj qr. ij bus.
De avenis remanentibus in granario j qr. j bus. et di. Item estimantur in grangia ad triturandum xl qr. Summa xlj qr. j bus. et di. De quibus in semine xlv qr. in farina ad potagium famulorum, prebenda ij equorum carectariorum et xvj affrorum xlix qr. j bus. In expensis ballivi et servientis per suos adventus ij qr. et di. Summa iiij^{xx} xvj qr. v bus. Et sic ordinantur ad emendum ad suplendum defectus earundem lv qr. iij bus.
De mixtura de exitu [*mem. 6 recto*] molendin*orum*[56] xx qr. Et totum assignatur in liberacionibus famulorum. Et eque.
De braseo de exitu molendinorum xxxv qr. Et totum assignatur ad mittendum apud Westm'. Et eque.

Staurum Sunt ibidem iij equi carectarii, xvj affri unde iij assignantur ad vendendum et alii iiij affri ad emendum, xix multones, j verrus, ij sues, xxvj hogetti, iiij cigni unde iij errarii, j anser, ij mariole, v capones, j gallus, ij galline, xxiiij pulcini.

Denarii Sunt levandum ibidem de redditu de terminis natalis Domini, pasche et sancti Johannis baptiste et sancti Michaelis xxxviij li. xx d. De operibus precariis vendendis in autumpno xxiiij s. xj d. De diversis firmis xx d. De diversis pasturis vend*endis*, et columbellis, et stramine, et stipula, et terra arabili dimittenda,[57] et lana xix ovium, Cxviij s. De blado vendendo vij li. xvij s. x d. De iij affris vendendis ix s. De finibus et perquisitis curie x li. xv s. De tolneto fori et stallagio[58] xxxix s. iiij d.[59]

Summa lxvj li. vij s. v d.

Expense De quibus in superplusagio Thome nunc servientis[60] vij li. xvij s. ix d. In diversis acquietanciis redditus et tallagii lxiij s. vj d. ob. In custis carucarum xxv s. In custis carectarum xxj s. iiij d. ob. In emendacione

[56] MS: 'molendini', but the plural is probably appropriate.

[57] In 1311–12, 25 acres of demesne arable were at farm piecemeal for rents amounting to £1 19s. 3d. p.a. (WAM 26260).

[58] MS: 'tallagio'.

[59] In his final account for 1311–12, the serjeant of Ashwell was charged with toll of £1 and stallage of 19s. for this Saturday market. In the extent of 1315, each item was valued at £1 p.a. (WAM 26260; CUL, MS Kk.5.29, f. 89v; *VCH Herts.*, iii, p. 200).

[60] Thomas de Lincolnia.

grangie feni et aliarum domorum xxxiij s. iiij d. In emendacione ij molendinorum preter j molam emendam xx s. In j mola emenda l s. In falcacione et sarclacione xvj s. In custis autumpni xvj li. In minutis expensis xvj s. In feodo servientis libertatis, capellani beate Marie,[61] et pro ij magnis comitatibus, et stipendiis servientis manerii, j bercarii, j daie, j porcarii, molendinarii, j ripereve et j tassatoris in autumpno lxxvij s. viij d. In trituracione bladi xxvj s. iiij d. In ventilacione medietatis tocius bladi ij s. ij d. In lv qr. iij bus. et di. avenarum emendis ad suplendum defectus vj li. ix s. iiij d. In iiij affris emendis lx s. In expensis ballivi per suos adventus xl s.

Summa lij li. xviij s. vj d. Et sic remanent pro Westm' xiij li. viij s. xj d.

Amewelle Die sabbati proxima post festum sancte Lucie virginis anno supradicto[62]
Sunt in granario j qr. ij bus. siliginis. Et estimantur in grangia ad triturandum de siligine xx qr. De exitu molendini, de arreragiis anni v^ti^ una cum firma eiusdem de anno vj^to^ xij qr. et di.[63] Summa xxxiij qr. vj bus. De quibus in liberacionibus j tenentis carucam capientis <u>qr. per x septimanas</u> et j fugatoris, j daye capiencium <u>qr. per xij septimanas</u>, et j herciatoris capientis <u>vj bus per ix septimanas</u>, xij qr. vj bus. Et sic remanent ad vendendum xxj qr. ut patet inferius.
De drageto estimantur in grangia ad triturandum vj qr. Summa vj qr. Inde in semine viij qr. Et sic ordinantur ad emendum ij qr. drageti ad suplendum defectus ut patet inferius.
De avenis sunt in granario j bus. et di. Et estimantur in grangia ad triturandum vj qr. et xij qr. et di. de redditu. Summa xviij qr. v bus. et di. De quibus in semine xx qr. In prebenda iiij affrorum, iiij boum, et farina pro potagio famulorum x qr. ij bus. et di. Et sic deficiunt xj qr. v bus. qu*e* ordinantur ad emendum ut patet inferius.

Staurum Sunt ibi iij affri, iiij boves, j taurus, xij vacce, iij annales, ij galli, iij galline.

Denarii Walterus Wasselyn serviens eiusdem manerii debet super visum compoti sui lxxiij s. x d. ob. Et sunt levandum ibi de redditu vj li. xviij s. xj d. Et de xxvj s. viij d. de tallagio. Et sunt levandum de pastura, pratis et

[61] By an agreement with the rector of Ashwell, antedating the appropriation of the rectory by the Abbey in 1225, the monks of Westminster were bound to find a chaplain to celebrate a daily Mass of the BVM in Ashwell parish church. His stipend at this time was 18s. p.a. (WAM 26260; Harvey, *Estates*, p. 404 and n.)
[62] 16 December 1312.
[63] The reference is to the years of account 1310–11 and 1311–12.

consuetudinibus vendendis xv li. xij s. ix d. De firma vaccarum lxvj s. Et sunt levandum xlij s. de xxj qr. siliginis precium qr. ij s. Et sunt levandum de finibus et perquisitis curie xliij s. Et de[64] iiijM[1] fagottorum vendendis deducta factura lxv s. precium M[1] xvj s. iij d.

Summa denariorum xxxviij li. viij s. ij d. ob.

Expense De quibus in resolucione redditus iij s. In custis carucarum xiij s. iiij d. In custis carectarum iij s. In custis domorum xiij s. iiij d. In falcacione prat*a* et sarclacione bladi ix s. In custis autumpni xliiij s. In minutis expensis xiiij s. In stipendiis servientis et daie xviij s. iiij d. In v qr. et iij bus. frumenti pro liberacione servientis, ij qr. drageti pro semine, xiij qr. vj bus. et di. avenarum emendis, liij s. j d. ob. In expensis ballivi per suos adventus xiij s. iiij d.

Summa ix li. iiij s. v d. ob. Et sic remanent pro Westm' xxix li. iij s. ix d.

*Kell*eveden' *Berewik*[65] Die lune proxima post festum sancte Lucie virginis anno supradicto[66]

De frumento estimantur in grangia ad triturandum xliij qr. Et de firma molendini iiij qr. vij bus. Summa xlvij qr. vij bus. Inde in liberacione servientis, mixtura ad[67] liberaciones famulorum, expensis domus in autumpno, diversis consuetudinibus et liberacione wodewardi de Wolde Wode ex consuetudine xviij qr. v bus. j p. et di. Et sic remanent ad vendendum xxix qr. j bus. di. j p. et di. ut patet inferius.

De mixtura in granario v bus. Et estimantur in grangia ad triturandum ij qr. Et de firma molendini viij qr. v bus. Et totum assignatur pro liberacionibus famulorum. Et eque.

De pisis estimantur in grangia ad triturandum xij qr. Summa xij qr. Inde in semine j qr. et di. In mixtura ad liberaciones famulorum vij qr. et di. Et sic remanent ad vendendum iij qr. ut patet inferius.

De avenis in granario j qr. Et estimantur in grangia ad triturandum l qr. Summa lj qr. De quibus in semine, in potagio famulorum, prebenda j equi carectarii, xviij affrorum, boum et agnorum Clxx qr. v bus. et di. Et sic deficiunt Cxix qr. v bus. et di. avenarum qu*e* ordinantur ad emendum ad suplendum defectus.

[64] MS: 'de' omitted.

[65] 'Kelleveden' is normally the only component of the name; 'Berewik' draws attention to Kelvedon's dispersed character as a settlement (P. H. Reaney, *The Place-Names of Essex* (English Place-Name Society, 12; 1935), pp. 58–9, 290–2).

[66] 18 December 1312.

[67] MS: 'ad' omitted.

Staurum Sunt ibidem j equus carectarius, xv affri et deficiunt iij qui ordinantur ad emendum ut patet inferius ix boves, xxvj multones, iiij^{xx}xiiij oves matrices, lx agni, j verrus, j sus, xiiij porculi, xvj auce unde iij mariole et ij anseres, vj capones, ij galli, xvj galline.

Denarii Johannes serviens eiusdem manerii debet super visum compoti sui xxxvj s. iiij d. Et sunt levandum ibidem de quadam consuetudine vocatur schiphur[68] et redditu natalis Domini, pasche, sancti Johannis baptiste et sancti Michaelis x li. xvj s. ob. Et sunt levandum de diversis firmis xv s. Et sunt levandum de diversis pasturis vendendis viij li. ij s. Et sunt levandum de lana vendenda lxx s. Et de lactagio iiij^{xx}xiiij ovium matricum xv s. viij d. Et sunt levandum de xxix qr. j bus. di. j p. et di. frumenti Cxvj s. x d. ob. Et sunt levandum de iij qr. pisarum vendendis ix s. De finibus et perquisitis curie lxij s. vj d.

Summa xxxv li. xix d. ob.

De quibus in resolucione redditus xl s. In acquietanciis reddituum diversorum ij s. v d. In expensis carucarum xxix s. viij d. In custis carectarum x s. viij d. In custis domorum iij s. In j mola emenda lxvj s. viij d. In falcacione prat*a* et sarclacione bladi xiij s. xj d. In custis autumpni iiij li. xx d. In minutis expensis xxj s. In stipendiis j servientis, j spergentis sulcos, clerici facientis compotum, carectarii, daie, j ripereve, j tassatoris, iij furcatorum et ij hominum euncium ad carucas in autumpno xlij s. viij d. In trituracione frumenti, mixture, pisarum et avenarum xiij s. xj d. qua. In medietate frumenti, mixture et pisarum vannanda ix d. ob., videlicet iij qr. pro j d. In medietate avenarum vannanda, videlicet iij qr. per x bus., vij d. ob. In Cxix qr. v bus. et di. avenarum emendis xvij li. xix s. ob. qua., precium qr. iij s. In iij affris emendis xlv s. In expensis ballivi per suos adventus vj s.

Summa expensarum xxxvj li. xvij s. j d. Et sic deficiunt pro sustentacione manerii xxxv s. v d. ob.

[68] A payment, due on 30 November and 24 June from 10 customary tenants (2s. from each on each occasion), in lieu of carrying specified quantities of grain and malt, in a boat hired by them for the purpose, to Salcott, Heybridge or Maldon, the tenants having first threshed the corn and made the malt. From these three places, grain and malt might be transported by water to Westminster, though not at the tenants' expense (CUL, KS Kk.5.29, ff. 114v, 115v; and for a glimpse of tranporting corn from Salcott to Westminster at the Abbey's expense, below, n. 76).

Feering et Pateswick[69] Die martis proxima post festum sancte Lucie virginis anno supradicto[70]

Sunt in granario ij bus. frumenti. Et estimantur in grangia ad triturandum de frumento viij^{xx} qr. Summa viij^{xx} qr. ij bus. frumenti. De quibus in liberacionibus diversorum famulorum, et mixtura liberacionum famulorum, et diversis consuetudinibus falcancium, et expensis domus in autumpno xxxvj qr. v bus. di. Et sic remanent ad mittendum apud Westm' vj^{xx}iij qr. iiij bus. di. Et eque.

De mixtura in granario di. qr. Et estimantur de exitu molendinorum xxxiiij qr.[71] Summa xxxiiij qr. di. Et totum assignatur in liberacionibus famulorum.

De pisis sunt in granario j qr. Et estimantur in grangia ad triturandum xj qr. Summa xij qr. Inde in semine v qr. Et sic remanent ad vendendum vij qr. ut patet inferius.

De avenis estimantur in grangia ad triturandum C qr. Summa C qr. De quibus in semine iiij^{xx}xviij qr. In prebenda equorum carectariorum, affrorum, vitulorum et agnorum, adventus ballivi et Rogeri de Stalham forestarii lxxviij qr. Et sic deficiunt lxxvij qr., que ordinantur ad emendum ad suplendum defectus.

Staurum Sunt ibidem ij equi carectarii, xxj affri, et sic deficiunt j ad emendum et iij ad mutandum ut patet inferius, xij boves, j taurus, j taurillus, xxij vacce, vij vituli, xxv multones, v hurtardi, lxvj oves matrices, xviij agni. Et sunt ibidem j sus, ix porcelli, xiij auce unde iiij mariole et ij anseres. Et sunt ibidem xij capones, ij galli, xvj galline, xij annates.

Denarii Et sunt levandum ibidem de redditu de terminis natalis Domini, pasche, sancti Johannis baptiste et sancti Michaelis, et tallagio xxix li. ix s. iiij d. Et sunt levandum de diversis exitibus manerii xiiij li. x s. x d. In vij qr. pisarum vendendis xxj s., precium qr. iij s. In iij veteribus affris vendendis xij s. Et sunt levandum de finibus et perquisitis curie Cxvj s. xj d.

Summa lj li. x s. j d. qua.

Expense De quibus in superplusagio compoti Willelmi prepositi[72] lxiiij s. iiij d. ob. In diversis acquietanciis redditus iij s. In expensis carucarum xv s.

[69] The manor of Feering comprised the vills of Feering and Pattiswick and dispersed lands in Kelvedon. The rectory of Feering was appropriated by Westminster Abbey in 1249, and at an uncertain date the Abbey also acquired the tithes of Pattiswick and control of the free chapel there. In the early fourteenth century, the reeve of Feering accounted for the tithes of Pattiswick in his account for the manor of Feering, but separately for the tithes of Feering, and these duly appear in a distinct part of the whole entry for Feering and Pattiswick in the present document.

[70] 19 December 1312.

[71] For Feering's two watermills, valued in 1289 at £4 p.a., see CUL, MS Kk.5.29, f. 97v.

[72] William Seman.

vj d. In custis carectarum xxxj s. v d. In custis domorum[73] xxvj s. viij d. In custis molendinorum v s. In falcacione prata et sarclacione bladi viij s. viij d. In custis autumpni vj li. xj s. iij d. In minutis expensis iiij li. xxiij d. In feodo Johannis de Bours C s.[74] In stipendiis famulorum xxvij s. ij d. In trituracione bladi estivalis[75] et vannacione iiij li. ob. qua. In lxxvj qr. avenarum emendis xj li. viij s. precium qr. iij s. In iiij affris emendis lxvj s. viij d. In expensis ballivi per suos adventus xxxix s. vj d. ob. qua. In diversis forinsecis expensis in locacione domus pro blado apud Saldcotes,[76] et in conduccione navis apud Westm' lxiij s. vj d.

Summa l li. iij s. ix d. Et sic remanent de claro pro Westm' xxvij s. iiij d.

De decima[77] Eodem die apud Feering[78] estimantur in grangia ad triturandum de frumento xxxiij qr. frumenti. Inde in custis autumpni et liberacionibus famulorum iij qr. Et sic remanent ad vendendum xxix qr.
De ordeo estimantur in grangia ad triturandum iij qr. et di. Et totum ordeum computatur ad vendendum.
De pisis estimantur in grangia ad triturandum iij qr. Summa iij qr. Inde in liberacionibus famulorum j qr. et di. Et sic remanent ad vendendum j qr. et di.
De avenis in granario iiij qr. Et estimantur in grangia ad triturandum xvj qr. Summa xx qr. Inde in prebenda in autumpno v qr. iij bus. et di. Et sic remanent ad vendendum xiiij qr. et di.

Denarii Sunt levandum ibidem de arreragiis compoti prepositi precedentis vij d. In xxix qr. frumenti vendendis Cxvj s., precium qr. iiij s. In iij qr. et di. ordei vendendi*s* xiiij s. precium qr. iiij s. In j qr. et di. pisarum vendendi*s* iiij s. vj d. precium qr. iij s. In xiiij qr. iiij bus. et di. avenarum vendendis xliij s. vij d. ob.

Summa viij li. xviij s. viij d. ob. Et sic remanent pro Westm' xxiij s. v d. ob.

Fanton' Die jovis in festo beati Thome apostoli anno supradicto[79]
Sunt in granario de frumento ij bus. Et estimantur in grangia ad triturandum xv qr. vj bus. Summa xvj qr. Et totum computatur in liberacionibus

[73] MS: 'domo', followed by 'xxx s.', but this has been erased.
[74] John de Bours', alias le Burser, or de Bousser, is mentioned as bedel at Feering 1295–1301 and was still receiving a fee of £5 p.a. in 1320–4 (WAM 25597–601, 25638–9).
[75] MS: 'est''.
[76] Salcott, the building for corn waiting to be transported to Westminster.
[77] There follows the 'state' of the tithes of Feering, exclusive of Pattiswick.
[78] MS omits 'Feering'.
[79] 31 December 1312.

famulorum pro debilitate frumenti. Et sic deficiunt ad emendum ix qr. pro liberacionibus famulorum ut patet inferius.
De pisis et fabis estim*atur* in grangia ad triturandum j qr. Et totum computatur in semine. Et eque.
De avenis sunt in granario j qr. et di. Et estimantur in grangia ad triturandum C qr. Summa Cj qr. et di. De quibus in semine l qr. In prebenda equorum carectariorum, affrorum, boum, vitulorum,[80] agnorum et adventus ballivi xxix qr. vij bus. j p. Et sic remanent ad vendendum xxj qr. di. di. bus.[81] et j p. ut patet inferius.

Staurum Sunt ibidem ij equi carectarii, xij affri, viij boves, j taurus, ij taurilli, xxj vacce, vij boviculi unde iij masculi et iiij femelli, vij annales unde iiij masculi et iij femelle. Et sunt ibidem ij hurtardi, iij multones, iiij^{xx}xviij oves matrices, xxv agni superannati, vj auce unde iiij mariole ij anseres, j gallus, v galline, xiij pulcini.

Denarii Et sunt levandum ibidem de diversis pasturis vendendis, feno vendendo et fructu vendendo xiiij s. x d. Et estimantur ibidem de denariis levandis de lactagio vaccarum Cxv s. vj d. precium vacce v s. vj d. Et sunt levandum ibidem de lactagio iiij^{xx}xviij ovium matricum xxiiij s. vj d. precium capitis iij d. Et sunt levandum ibidem de lana ovium lx s. iiij d. videlicet vellus veterum ovium vj d. et agnorum iiij d. Et sunt levandum ibidem de lana agnorum nove natorum ij s. iiij d. per estimacionem vellus j d. qua. In xxj qr. di. di. bus. et p. avenarum vendendis liij s. xj d.

Summa xiij li. xvij s. vj d.

De quibus in superplusagio Roberti servientis xvj s. viij d. qua. In expensis carucarum xxvj s. iiij d. ob. In custis carectarum xviij s. xj d. In custis domorum xx s. In falcacione prat*a* et sarclacione bladi xviij s. vj d. ob. In custis autumpni Cxij s. vj d. In minutis expensis xx s. x d. ob. In trituracione tocius bladi x s. x d. qua. In vadiis servientis xliiij s. In stipendio eiusdem xiij s. iiij d. In tunica estivali eiusdem ij s. In stipendiis j carectarii, ancille, vaccarii, iiij famulorum carucarum et j hominis spergentis sulcos, et clerici facientis compotum xxvij s. vj d. In ix qr. frumenti emendis pro liberacionibus famulorum xxxvj s. In expensis ballivi per suos adventus xij s.

Summa xix li. vj d. ob. qua. Et sic deficiunt pro sustentacione manerii Ciij s. j d. ob. qua.

[80] MS: 'vituli'.

[81] MS: two full points separate 'di.' and 'di.'

Bemflet' De frumento estimantur in grangia ad triturandum xx qr. Summa xx qr. Et totum computatur in liberacionibus famulorum. Et eque.
De mixtura de firma molendini vj qr. et di. Et totum computatur in liberacionibus famulorum. Et eque.
De fabis sunt in granario j qr. Et estimantur in grangia ad triturandum j qr. ij bus. Et totum computatur in liberacionibus famulorum. Et eque.
De pisis sunt in granario di. qr. Et estim*atur* in grangia ad triturandum di. qr. Et totum in liberacionibus famulorum. Et eque. Et deficiunt pro liberacionibus famulorum iij qr. ut patet inferius.
De avenis sunt in granario j qr. Et estimantu*r* in grangia ad triturandum l qr. Summa lj qr. De quibus in semine, farina pro potagio famulorum, prebenda equorum carectariorum, affrorum, boum per estimacionem in garbis et agnorum lix qr. vij bus. Summa lix qr. vij bus. et sic deficiunt ad emendum viij qr. vij bus. avenarum[82] ut patet inferius.

Staurum Sunt ibidem ij equi carectarii, ix affri et sic deficiunt j affrus ad emendum ut patet inferius, vj boves. Et sunt ibidem xxiiij hurtardi, iiijClxxj oves matrices, iiij^{xx} agni superannati. Et sunt ibidem iij auce unde ij mariole j anser, iij capones, j gallus, ij galline, v pulcini.

Denarii Sunt levandum ibidem de redditu de terminis natalis Domini, pasche, sancti Johannis baptiste et sancti Michaelis cum tallagio incerto xix li. xiij s. ix d. ob. qua. Et sunt levandum ibidem de diversis firmis iiij s. Et sunt levandum ibidem de diversis pasturis vendendis et frustra aque vendenda, et ovis vendendis xxxvij s. iiij d. ob. In lactagio ovium matricum vij li. xvij s. precium cuiuslibet iiij d. Et sunt levandum ibidem de lana ovium matricum, hurtardorum, agnorum superannatorum, et agnorum nove natorum ix li. xij s. vj d. Et sunt levandum ibidem de diversis operibus vendend*is* xxiij d. Et sunt levandum de CCClxx agnis vendendis vj li. iij s. iiij d. precium cuiuslibet iiij d. Et sunt levandum de finibus et perquisitis curie xlj s. viij d.

Summa xlvij li. xj s. vij d. qua.

De quibus in diversis resolucionibus redditus lxix s. vj d. In custis carucarum xxv s. v d. In custis carectarum xvij s. In custis domorum xxx s. In j mola emenda xlvj s. viij d. In custis molend*ini* xvj s. iiij d. In falcacione [*mem. 8 recto*] prat*a* et sarclacione bladi xvj s. In custis autumpni lxx s. ij d. In minutis expensis xxxiiij s. vij d. ob. In stipendiis diversorum famulorum xxxvij s. In trituracione tocius bladi viij s. ob. qua. In iij qr. bladi emendis pro liberacionibus famulorum xij s. In viij qr. vij bus. avenarum emendis xxj s. x d. In j affro emendo xv s. In diversis forinsecis expensis x s.

[82] MS: 'viij qr. avenarum vij bus.'

Summa xxj li. ix s. vij d. ob. qua. Et remanent xxvj li. xxiij d. ob.

Item sunt levandum hoc anno de diversis feodis firmis lxvij li. Summa lxvij li.
Summa tocius frumenti mittendi apud Westm' CCiiij^{xx}xix qr. et di bus.
Summa tocius ordei mittendi apud Westm' xlix qr. v bus.
Summa tocius drageti mittendi apud Westm' xvj qr. vj bus.
Summa tociarum avenarum mittendarum apud Westm' xiiij qr.
Summa omnium denariorum levandorum remanecium pro Westm' CCClviij li. xvij s. ij d.

De quibus ordinantur ad suplendum defectus reprise manerii de Morden iiij li. viij s. vij d. ob. Item ad suplendum defectus manerii de Kenesberne iiij li. iiij s. v d. Item ad suplendum defectus manerii de Kelleveden' xxxv s. v d. ob. Item ad suplendum defectus manerii de Fanton Ciij s. j d. ob. qua. Et in expensis fratrum Henrici de Bercheston', Roberti de Bebi et Johannis de Neweport clerici euncium per singula maneria conventus pro visu compoti faciendo lxix s.

Summa xix li. vij d. ob. qua.

Et sic remanent de claro CCCxxxix li. xvj s. vj d. qua.

II 5 View of the states of the convent's royal manors, January 1318

A roll of one membrane, 210 mm wide. Originally, at least one further membrane was attached Chancery fashion, and it is likely that the missing part of the manuscript contained entries relating to Knowle or Westerham or to both. The document is well written in a single hand, with totals in the same hand, but with some crossings out and insertions in this hand. There are no folds to guide layout. The dorse is blank except for the heading 'Compotum fratris J. Wytney custodis maneriorum regine de anno regni regis Edwardi ij xj^{o}', written in a late fourteenth- or early fifteenth-century hand.[1]

WAM 23646

[*Mem. 1 recto*] Status maneriorum domine regine visus per fratrem J. de Wytteneye custodem et fratrem Henricum de Bercheston' die lune proxima post festum sancti Hillarii anno regni regis Edwardi xj^{o} [2]

Torveston' Die lune supradicto Johannes Rayson serviens ibidem debuit super finalem compotum suum Cxij s. j d.[3] Et sunt ibidem denarii levand*um* de redditu terminorum annunciacionis beate Marie cum le wodeselver ad eundem terminum, pasche, beati Johannis baptiste, sancti Petri advincula et sancti Michaelis cum tallagio ad eundem terminum, hydagio et torno vicecomitis ad le hokeday, Cvij s. vij d. ob. Item de firmis v s. Item de exitu manerii videlicet de firma v vaccarum, ij juvencarum,[4] xj ovium matricum et columbarii et de aliis minutis exitibus liiij s. iiij d. ob. Item appreciatur lana istius anni de xxvj capitibus xiij s. Et estimantur fines et perquisita xl s. Et estimantur in grangia xxx qr. frumenti, de quibus in liberacione servientis a purificacione beate Marie usque festum sancti Michaelis[5] iij qr. et di., in expensis autumpni j qr., in liberacionibus famulorum a dicto die[6] usque festum sancti Michaelis x qr. vj bus. j p. Et sic restant ad vendendum xiiij qr. v bus. et di.[7] j p. Et valuerit circa festum sancti Hillarii[8] Cxvij s. ix d.,

[1] Extant ministers' accounts: Turweston, two accounts, 30 September 1317–12 May 1318, and 12 May–29 September 1318, WAM 7775, rots. 1–2.
[2] Witney served as warden of Eleanor of Castile's manors 25 March 1315–30 November 1318, when he was succeeded by Henry de Bircheston. Bircheston may have been an auditor of the accounts of these manors, an important office at this time. The view is dated 16 January 1318.
[3] The reference is to Rayson's last account, which closed at Michaelmas 1317 and probably covered the entire year of account 1316–17.
[4] MS: 'ij juvencarum', inserted.
[5] MS: 'a purificacione beate Marie usque festum sancti Michaelis' inserted. 2 February to 29 September 1318.
[6] MS: 'a dicto die' inserted.
[7] MS: 'et di.' inserted.
[8] 13 January 1318.

precium qr. viij s.[9] Item lx qr. drageti, de quibus in semine xxxvj qr., in mixtura cum avenis pro prebenda equorum iiij qr., in gallis, gallinis et caponibus et aucis sustinendis iij bus., in liberacionibus famulorum per predictum tempus[10] x qr. iij bus. j p. Et sic restant ad vendendum ix qr. j bus. et di. j p. Et valuerit circa predictum festum xl s. v d.
Item xiiij qr. pisarum precium qr. iiij s. vj d.,[11] de quibus in semine v qr., in liberacionibus famulorum a purificacione beate Marie usque annunciacionem eiusdem[12] ij qr. Et sic restant ad vendendum vij qr., et valuerit xxxij s. viij d. Item xiij qr. vj bus.[13] avenarum, de quibus in semine ix qr., in farina ij qr., in prebenda equorum viij qr. vj bus., in prebenda boum iij qr. vj bus. Et sic deficiunt ix qr. vj bus. que ordinantur ad emendum, preter iiij qr. drageti ut supra ad prebendam equorum.

Summa tocius levand*i* xxvj li. ij s. xj d.

Inde defectus redditus et acquietanciarum viij s., in custu carucarum xvj s., in custu carectarum viij s. ideo magis hoc anno pro necessariis emendis ad unum par rotarum legandarum, in custu domorum xiij s. iiij d., in minutis expensis x s. viij d., in falcacione et sarclacione iiij s., in custu autumpni xxxij s., in trituracione bladi cum medietate ventilacionis dicti bladi xviij s. viij d. qua., in feodo Willelmi de Kynebell' senescalli xvj s.,[14] in v qr. vj bus. avenarum emendis xix s. ij d. pro quibus ordinantur ad vendendum iiij qr. et di. drageti, in iij vitulis emendis iij s. quia vacce ad firmam, in stipendiis lij s. iiij d. cum stipendio servientis, in expensis fratris J. custodis et fratris H. de Bercheston' facientium visum manerii cum expensis custodis usque festum sancti Michaelis et aliorum superveniencium xlvij s. ij d., in expensis .....[15]

Summa reprise[16] Cxij li. viij s. iiij d. Et sic reman*ent* de claro ad levandum contra distribucionem ultra reprisam xiij li. xiiij s. vij d.[17]

Et remanent ij equi carectarii, vj affri, xiij boves, v vacce, ij juvence, ij tauri, iij boviculi, iij annales, j multo, xj matrices, xiiij hogastri, ij apri, vj hogetti, iij auce unde j anser, iij mariole, vj capones, j gallus, iij galline.
Memorandum quod potuerunt esse ibidem xiiij vacce, ijC bidentium.

[9] MS: 'precium qr. viij s.' inserted.
[10] MS: 'per predictum tempus' inserted.
[11] MS: 'precium qr. iiij s. vj d.' written above the previous four words but not marked for insertion.
[12] MS: 'a purificacione ... eiusdem' inserted.
[13] MS: 'vj bus.' written above the previous two words but not marked for insertion.
[14] Kynebell, alias Kymbell, was steward of Eleanor of Castile's foundation in Buckinghamshire (WAM 23645).
[15] Blank in MS.
[16] MS: 'rep'c'.
[17] The anticipated distribution was that to the poor and to the monks themselves at the anniversary of Eleanor of Castile on 28 November 1318.

Bridebrok' Willelmus de Duddingh*ur*st nuper serviens ibidem debuit super finalem compotum suum de anno Edwardi ix° C s.[18] Willelmus Paternoster prepositus subsequens debet super compotum suum finalem de anno Edwardi x^{mo} xj li.[19]

Facto visu compoti Henrici Lucas servientis ibidem die lune proxima post festum sanctorum Fabiani et Sebastiani anno regni regis Edwardi xj^{mo},[20] debentur eidem eodem die lxv s. vj d. ob. in quibus excedit.

Et sunt ibidem denarii levand*um* de redditu de terminis nathalis Domini preteriti,[21] pasche, nativitatis sancti Johannis baptiste et sancti Michaelis de claro vij li. xvij s. x d. ob. qua., de arrur*is* custumariorum vendend*is* hoc anno per estimacionem x s., de averagi*is* eorundem custumariorum relaxat*is* xviij s. iiij d., de minutis operibus eorundem vendendis per estimacionem j marc*a*, de subbosco ibidem vendendo per estimacionem xxiiij s., de exitibus gardini per estimacionem x s., de virgis sauceti vendendis x s., de firma vaccarum viij li., de perquisitis curie per estimacionem xl s., de C gallinis de redditu venditis xxv s., et de exitu columbarii di. marc*a*.[22] Et estimantur ibidem in grangia eodem die, preter sustentacionem manerii usque festum sancti Michaelis,[23] lxiiij qr. vij bus. frumenti que val*uerint* eodem die xxij li. xiiij s. j d. ob. precium qr. vij s. Item estimantur ibidem preter semen ix qr. fabarum que val*uerint* eodem die lxxij s. precium qr. viij s., et de pisis j qr. qu*od* valuerit vij s.

Summa denariorum levandorum xlviij li. xvj s. xj d. ob. qua. Item xxxj s. viij d.

De quibus oportet pro cust*u* carucarum xviij s. vj d. usque festum sancti Michaelis, et pro cust*u* carectarum videlicet pro j carecta ferrata de novo facienda et aliis carectis pro fimo iterum harnes*iatis* xv s. Item pro dom*ibus* reparand*is* in coopertura ij marc*as*. Item pro custu molendini ij s. Item pro custu autumpni iiij li. Item pro sale emend*o* et aliis minutis di. marc*am*. Item pro vij affris pro carucis emendis plus quam affri qui nunc ibi sunt, modo valent iiij li. x s. Item pro viij^{xx} bidentibus emendis qui bene possint sustineri in pastur*is* domini per annum xxiiij li. precium capitis iij s. Et si non habeant bidentes manerium valebit per annum minus quam solebat de x li. Item oportet pro feodo et expensis servientis ij marc*as*. Item pro lv qr. avenarum emendis que deficiunt pro sustentacione et semine huius anni

[18] 1314–15. Duddinghurst was serjeant at Birdbrook 1307–15 (WAM 25414–22).

[19] 1315–16.

[20] 23 January 1318.

[21] MS: 'nath' dni' dni''.

[22] MS: 'et de exitu columbarii di. marca' written above the next entry, but not marked for insertion.

[23] 29 September 1318.

xij li. vj s. viij d. precium qr. iiij s. viij d.[24] Item pro stipendio servientis, unius daye, unius ripereve et unius piccherii in autumpno xxij s. iiij d. Item pro expensis custodis et supervenientium per estimacionem xl s.

Summa tocius reprise liij li. iiij s. vj d. Et sic oportet providere pro sustentacione manerii hoc anno vj li. xvj d. ob.[25]

Et remanent in stauro ibidem eodem die[26] jumenta pro carectis iij, affri xiiij, boves xv, vacce xxiiij, tauri[27] ij, boviculi iij, vituli[28] superannati iiij, porci,[29] verrus j, sues ij, porc*uli* de dimidio anno viij, porcelli vj, auce iiij et ij anseres, capones vj, galline et galli vj.

[24] MS: 'Item pro lv qr. avenarum ... qr. iiij s. viij d.' written above the next entry but is not marked for insertion.

[25] MS: corrected from 'vj li. xiij s. ob.' in the same hand.

[26] 23 January 1318.

[27] MS: 'taurii'.

[28] MS: 'vitulii'.

[29] MS: 'porcii'. The word is used as a sub-heading for the next four items.

II 6 View of the states of the convent's manors, November–December 1321

A parchment roll of two membranes, approximately 200 mm wide, sewn Chancery fashion with white thread in a tight oversew. Membrane 1 has a diamond shaped filing hole at the head, and this membrane was also laid out with a vertical fold for the left margin on the recto. Membrane 2 was attached to accommodate the stock entry for Hampstead, continuing down the dorse and for which there was not enough space on membrane 1; the recto of membrane 2 is blank. The roll is a fair copy, written in a single hand, including totals, albeit there are a few corrections. It has been slightly damaged by rodents down the left side of the recto, and it is incomplete.

The roll contains the views and associated estimates for the manors of Teddington, Knightsbridge and Hampstead only. It was once part of a larger, Exchequer fashion roll of states for the convent's manors. It is undated, but the serjeant's account for Hampstead for 1321–2 contains some of the same transactions for wheat and maslin.[1]

WAM 9289, rot. 3.

[*Mem. 1 recto*] *Todintone Frumentum* De frumento de empcione ij bus. Et seminantur. Et nichil remanet.

[Silig]o Triturantur ibidem xix qr. v bus. siliginis. Et sunt ad triturandum per estimacionem xij qr.[2] Et de iij bus. di. j p. de cornbote. Summa xxxij qr. di. bus. j p. Inde in semine ix qr. vj bus. Liberantur preposito de Greneford iij qr. In mixtura ad liberaciones famulorum xv qr. iiij bus. di. j p. Et ordinantur ad vendendum iij qr. vj bus. Et nichil remanet.

[Or]deum Triturantur ibidem xxxvij qr. ordei. Et sunt ad triturandum per estimacionem xx qr.[3] Et de ij qr. ij bus. di. j p. de churchschot et cornbot*e*. Summa lix qr. ij bus. di. j p. Inde in semine per estimacionem xix qr. di. Liberantur granetario Westm' xxxvij qr. Et remanent ad mittendum ad granarium Westm' ij qr. vj bus. di. j p.

Fabe Sunt ad triturandum per estimacionem j qr. Et ordinantur ad seminandum. Et nichil remanet.

Pise Sunt ad triturandum per estimacionem iiij qr. Inde in semine per estimacionem ij qr. vj bus. In mixtura ad liberaciones famulorum j qr. ij bus. Et nichil remanet.

Vesce Sunt ad triturandum per estimacionem j qr. Et ordinantur ad seminandum. Et nichil remanet.

[1] II 6 is now filed with four other membranes as WAM 9289, but this is a modern archival arrangement. Extant minister's account: Hampstead, WAM 32406, with the matching entries in its corn account on the dorse.

[2] MS: 'Summa xxxj qr. v bus.' struck out.

[3] MS: 'Summa lvij qr.' struck out.

Avene Triturantur iij qr. avenarum. Et sunt ad triturandum per estimacionem xxx qr. Summa xxxiij qr. Inde in semine per estimacionem xx qr. In farina avenarum et prebenda equorum et affrorum vij qr.[4] Summa xxvij qr. Et remanent vj qr. que ordinantur ad mittendum apud Westm' pro prebenda equ*orum* ballivi.
Liberaciones famulorum De xv qr. iiij bus. di. j p. siliginis et j qr. ij bus. pisarum receptis supra. Summa xvj qr. vj bus. di. j p. Inde in liberacionibus j carectarii, ij carucariorum et j bercarii per annum et daie per idem tempus xvj qr. vj bus. di. j p. Et nichil remanet.
Denarii Sunt ibidem levandum de redditu et tallagio vj li. vj s. vij d. Et de exitu manerii et operibus iij s. Et de iij qr. vj bus. siliginis xxv s. precium qr. vj s. viij d. Et de perquisitis curie xv s. De lana et pellibus[5] nichil, quia ordinantur ad emendum staurum.

Summa receptarum viij li. ix s. vij d.

Inde in acquietanciis redditus per annum ij s. In custu carucarum xiij s. In custu carectarum iiij s. x d. In custu domorum iiij s. In minutis expensis ij s. In falcacione ij s. ix d. In custu autumpni xviij s. In empcione ij bus. frumenti ij s. iiij d. In trituracione bladi iij s. ix d. In stipendiis famulorum xxij s. ix d.[6] In expensis ballivi et Willelmi Bissop per suos adventus x s.

Summa iiij li. v s. v d. Et remanent ultra reprisa*m* iiij li. iiij s. ij d.

Staurum Sunt in eodem manerio j equus carectarius, iiij affri, iij multones, v matrices, iiij agni, j verrus, j sus, vij porci, v porcelli, j ancer,[7] iij mariole, vj capones, viij galline.

Knytebrugg' Frumentum Triturantur ibidem lxj qr. j bus. frumenti et coralli. Et v qr. vj bus. recip*iuntur* de Whatha*m*stede. Summa lxvj qr. vij bus. Inde in semine xiiij qr. iiij bus. In liberacione servientis per annum exceptis v septimanis in autumpno et in expensis autumpni vj qr. v bus. In mixtura ad liberaciones famulorum iij qr. coralli. Liberantur ad granarium Westm' xliiij qr. In vendicione j qr. Et sic deficiunt j qr. vj bus. frumenti.
Mixtilio Triturantur ibidem ix qr. mixtilionis. Et sunt ad triturandum vj qr. per estimacionem. Et de vj qr. receptis de manerio de Batricheseye. Summa xxj qr. Inde in semine vj qr. In mixtura ad liberaciones famulorum xv qr. Et nichil remanet.
Fabe Triturantur ibidem viij qr. vj bus. fabarum. Summa viij qr. vj bus. Inde in semine per estimacionem ij qr. di. In mixtura ad liberaciones famulorum vj qr. ij bus. Et nichil remanet.

[4] MS: 'In prebenda equorum ballivi per estimacionem', written in main hand, struck out.
[5] MS: 'et pellibus' inserted in main text hand.
[6] MS: 'xviij s. iij d.' struck out; 'xxij s. ix d.' inserted in main hand.
[7] MS: 'ancere'.

Ordeum Triturantur ibidem xxx qr. di. bus. Et sunt ad triturandum per estimacionem xxxvj[8] qr. vj bus. Summa lxvj qr. vj bus.[9] di. bus. Inde in semine per estimacionem xxiiij qr. Liberantur ad granarium Westm' xxvij qr. In mixtura ad liberaciones famulorum xv qr. vj bus. di.[10] Et nichil remanet.
Dragetum Triturantur ibidem ix qr. drageti. Et liberantur ad granarium Westm'. Et nichil remanet.
Avene Triturantur ibidem xxx qr. di. avenarum. Summa xxx qr. di. Inde in semine per estimacionem xxv qr. In farina ad potagium famulorum ij qr. Et totum residuum remanet ad prebendam equorum et affrorum. Et nichil remanet.
Liberaciones famulorum iij qr. coralli frumenti, xv qr. mixture, vj qr. ij bus. fabarum et xv qr. vj bus. ordei. Summa xl qr. di. bus. Inde in liberacionibus j carectarii, iiij carucariorum et j bercarii per annum, j vaccarii, j daie et j custodis agnos[11] tempore separacionis et agnellacionis, et j spergentis sulcos xl qr. di, bus. Et nichil remanet.

Adhuc respice in tergo de Knytebrugg'

[*Mem. 1 dorse*][12]

Knytebrugg'

Recepta denariorum Sunt ibidem levandum de redditu et tallagio et firmis Cv s. qua. De lactagio ovium domini et extraneorum[13] et vaccarum per estimacionem xlij s. iiij d.[14] De separacione agnorum, melle et aliis exitibus per estimacionem x s. De lana vendenda per estimacionem lxvj s. viij d. De coriis affrorum et pellibus ovium vendendis viij s. ix d. De perquisitis curie xxx s. per estimacionem.

Summa receptorum xiij li. ij s. ix d. qua.

Expense Inde in decasu redditus viij d. In custu carucarum, ferura equorum carectariorum, boum et affrorum per estimacionem xxxiij s. In custu carectarum hoc anno viij s. In custu domorum iij s. iiij d. In minutis necessariis vj s. viij d. In sarclacione bladi et falcacione pratorum xviij s. In

[8] MS: 'vj' of 'xxxvj' is written over an erasure.
[9] MS: 'vj bus.' inserted in the main hand.
[10] MS: 'xiiij qr. di. bus.' struck out; 'xv qr. vj bus. di.' inserted in main text hand.
[11] MS uses this form in preference to 'custodis agnorum' and also, later in the same line, similarly in preference to 'spergentis sulcorum'.
[12] Mem. 2 recto is blank as it was added probably unexpectedly, after the rest of the Knightsbridge account had been written, simply to contain the material for Hampstead that would not fit on mem. 1 dorse; mem. 1 dorse is written from the head of the roll downwards, i.e. suggesting that this document was part of an Exchequer fashion roll.
[13] MS: 'domini et extraneorum' inserted.
[14] MS: 'xxxix s.' struck out, 'xlij s. iiij d.' inserted.

custu autumpni vij li. In trituracione bladi xxxij s. vj d. In stipendiis servientis et famulorum lix s. x d.

Summa expensarum xv li. ij s. Et sic deficiunt xxxix s. ij d. ob. qua.

Staurum Remanent in eodem manerio ij equi carectarii, x affri, iiij boves, iij vacce, iij juvence, iij juvencule, j vitulus superannatus, liiij oves matrices, viij hogastri. xxxviij agni, j auca, ij mariole, v galline.

Hamstede

Frumentum Triturantur ibidem vj qr. ij bus. frumenti et j bus. j p. coralli. Et de vj qr. frumenti de empcione. Summa xij qr. iij bus. Inde in semine vj qr. In liberacione servientis per annum preter iiij septimanas in autumpno vj qr. In mixtura ad liberaciones famulorum j bus. j p. coralli. In expensis ballivi per suos adventus ij bus. Et nichil remanet.

Mixtilio Triturantur ibidem vj qr. mixtilionis. Et sunt ad triturandum per estimacionem ij qr. di. Et de iiij qr. receptis de manerio de Batricheseye. Summa xij qr. di.[15] Inde in semine iiij qr. In mixtura ad liberaciones famulorum viij qr. di. Et nichil remanet.

Fabe De di. bus. fabarum per estimacionem de exitu. Et computatur in mixtura ad liberaciones famulorum. Et nichil remanet.

Pise Triturantur ibidem ij bus. pisarum. Summa vij bus. Inde in semine per estimacionem ij bus. In mixtura ad liberaciones famulorum v bus. Et nichil remanet.

Ordeum Sunt ad triturandum j qr. ordei per estimacionem. Summa j qr. Inde in semine per estimacionem iiij bus. In mixtura ad liberaciones famulorum iiij bus. Nichil remanet.

Avene Triturantur ibidem xxx qr. avenarum. Et sunt ad triturandum per estimacionem j qr. di. avenarum. Summa xxxj qr. di. Inde in semine per estimacionem xxiiij qr. In farina pro potagio famulorum j qr. In prebenda equorum et affrorum iij qr. di. In prebenda equorum ballivi et W. Bissop per suos adventus ij qr. Liberantur ad granarium Westm' viij qr. di. Summa xxxix qr. Et sic deficiunt vij qr. di. que ordinantur ad emendum.

Liberaciones famulorum De j bus. j p. coralli frumenti, viij qr. di. mixture, di. bus. fabarum, v bus. pisarum et iiij bus. ordei receptis supra. Et de vj qr. j bus. j p. de empcione. Summa xvj qr. Inde in liberacionibus ij carucariorum per annum, j daie per annum et j carectarii per xxiiij septimanas xvj qr. Et nichil remanet.

Recepta denariorum Sunt ibidem levandum de redditu et firmis xij li. xiij s. x d. qua. Et de[16] pastura, pannagio, brueria et feno,[17] et ijM[1] fagottis cum ij

[15] MS: 'viij qr. di.' struck out; 'xij qr. di.' inserted.

[16] MS: 'exitu manerii' struck out.

[17] MS: 'brueria et feno' inserted.

ligaturis vendendis per estimacionem vj li. xiiij s. vij d. Et de vendicione operum per estimacionem xvij s. Et de perquisitis curie per estimacionem xxx s.

Summa xxj li. xv s. v d. qua.

Expense Inde in defectu redditus xlij s. viij d. per annum. In custu carucarum per estimacionem xv s. In custu carectarum vij s. iiij d. In custu molendini, domorum et minutis expensis xv s. In vj qr. frumenti emptis lvj s. precium qr. ix s. iiij d. In vij qr. di. avenarum emptis xxv s. precium qr. iij s. iiij d. In vj qr. j bus. bladi ad liberaciones famulorum emptis xlj s. ob. precium qr. <u>vj s. viij d.</u> In falcacione pratorum xxiij s. In custu autumpni xl s. In trituracione bladi vj s. v d. In stipendiis servientis et famulorum xxxiij s. iiij d. In expensis ballivi et aliis expensis forensecis xiij s. iiij d.

Summa expensarum xv li. xviij s. j d. ob. Et sic remanent ultra reprisa*m* Cxvij s. iij d. ob. qua. que ordinantur pro fagottis faciendis et cariandis ad bracinum Westm'.

[*Mem. 2 dorse*] *Staurum* Sunt in eodem manerio j equus carectarius, v affri, v pullani, xij boves, j ancer, j mariola, ij capones, j gallus et iij galline, x pulcini.

II 7 View of the states of the convent's manors, November–December 1322

A roll of one membrane, approximately 240 mm wide. There is no filing hole at the head of the roll; there may be one at the foot, but this could equally be a flaw in the parchment. The roll is a fair copy, in a single hand, but with some updating in that hand. It was intended to be part of a larger, Exchequer fashion roll of the views of the states of the convent's manors—but it is likely the roll was not completed in its final form (it may be that the membranes were engrossed fair, but were never filed together).[1]

WAM 9289, rot. 5

[*Recto*] *Hwathamsted* Estimacio ibidem facta per sacramentum[2] Thome le Hunte, Roberti Alisaundre, Johannis Kyng', Willelmi Gale et Willlelmi Enfemme[3]

Frumentum Triturantur ibidem de frumento v qr. iij bus. Et sunt ad triturandum per estimacionem CC qr. de dominico. Et de decima iiij qr. frumenti.[4] Et de redditu ij qr. ij bus. et ij partes di. bus. Summa CCxj qr. v bus. et ij partes di. bus. Inde in expensis anni precedentis v qr. iij bus.[5] In semine per estimacionem lxx qr. In liberacione bedelli v qr. iiij bus. In allocacione prepositi di. bus. In expensis autumpni ij qr. di. In mixtura ad liberacionem xxv qr. In expensis ballivi et servientis .....[6] bus. Summa Ciij qr. vj bus. di. Et remanent Cij qr. iij bus.[7]

Ordeum Sunt ad triturandum per estimacionem x qr. ordei. Inde in semine ij qr. Et remanent viij qr.

Dragetum Sunt ad triturandum per estimacionem vj qr. Inde in semine iiij qr. Et remanent xij qr.

Avene Sunt ad triturandum per estimacionem iiij^{xx}x qr. avenarum et trituratur j qr. Et j qr. di. de decima. Et de ix qr. iij bus. et ij partes di. bus. de redditu. Summa Cj qr. vij bus. Inde in semine iiij^{xx} qr. per estimacionem. In farina pro potagio, prebenda equorum, affrorum et superveniencium iiij^{xx}iiij qr. vj bus. Et sic deficit lxij qr. j bus. que ordinantur ad emendum.

[1] II 7 is now filed with four other membranes as WAM 9289, but this is a modern archival arrangement. The date of the roll is established by comparison with the extant ministers' accounts: Feering, WAM 25641; Stevenage, TNA, SC 6/871/7; Wheathampstead, HALS, DE/Lw/M105.

[2] MS omits 'sacramentum'.

[3] Enfemme was reeve of Wheathampstead 24 February 1320–29 September 1328 (HALS, DE/Lw/M132–9).

[4] For the Abbey's claim to a moiety of the greater tithes of Wheathampstead, including those of Harpenden and Kinsbourne, see II 4, n. 51.

[5] MS: 'Inde in expensis anni precedentis v qr. iij bus.' inserted; 'v' corrected from 'vij'.

[6] MS: 'vj' deleted; the correct figure has not been inserted.

[7] MS: an erasure occurs between 'C' and 'ij' and another before the first digit of 'iij'.

Pise Sunt ad triturandum per estimacionem ij qr. pisarum. Que ordinantur ad vendendum precium qr. iiij s.
Exitus molendinorum Sunt ibidem de firmariis molendinorum xl qr. Inde in mixtura ad liberaciones famulorum xxv qr. vj bus. di. Et remanent xiiij qr. j bus. di. precium qr. iiij s. que ordinantur ad vendendum.
Liberaciones Ordinantur ad liberaciones famulorum xxv qr. frumenti, xxv qr. vj bus. di. de exitu molendini.
Recepta denariorum Oneratur de xxxvij li. xv s. j d. qua. de redditu.[8] Et de viij li. de exitu manerii. Et de lxiiij s. ix d. de vendicione bladi. Et de xxxiij s. iiij d. de x porcis vend*itis* precium cuiuslibet xl d. Et de iiij li. per perquisitis curie. Et de vj li. ij s. de vendicione operum.

Summa lx li. xv s. ij d.

Inde in allocacione vij s. viij d. In custus carucarum et carectarum iiij li. x s. In expensis domorum et[9] molendinorum xx s. In minutis necessariis xx s. In sarclacione et falcacione viij s. In custus autumpni vj li. x s. In trituracione per estimacionem xl s. In feodo et stipendiis xxiiij s. In expensis ballivi et superveniencium xl s. In vj affris emendis xxij s. In lxij qr. j bus. avenarum emendis vij li. iiij s. xj d. ob. precium qr. ij s. iiij d.[10]

Summa xxix li. xvj s. vij d. ob. Et remanent xxix li. xviij s. vj d. ob.[11] qua.

Staurum Sunt ibidem de stauro ij equi carectarii, xv affri, j bos, v vacce, j bovettus, j juvenccus, j boviculus, j juvencula, iij vituli, lxv multones, lviij matrices, iiij hoggastri, vj jercie, xxxviij agni, j verrus, ij sues, j suella,[12] x[13] porci, vj[14] porculi, vij porcelli,[15] viij auce, ij galli, vij galline.

Kenesberne Estimacio facta per sacramentum[16] Willelmi ate Hurne,[17] Symonis de Kenesb*er*ne, Ade de Kenesb*er*ne, Edmundi ate Dych et Willelmi Grondwyne
Frumentum Triturantur ibidem de frumento ij qr. j bus. Et sunt ad triturandum Cxxviij qr. de dominico. Et de decima x qr. Et sunt de redditu

[8] MS omits 'de redditu'.
[9] MS omits 'et'.
[10] MS: 'In lxij qr. j bus. avenarum emendis vij li. iiij s. xj d. ob. precium qr. ij s. iiij d.' inserted in main text hand.
[11] MS: 'ob.' inserted.
[12] MS: 'j suella' inserted.
[13] MS: 'viij' struck out; 'x' inserted.
[14] MS: 'vj' corrected from 'xiij'.
[15] MS: 'vij porcelli' inserted.
[16] MS: 'sacramentum' omitted.
[17] Possibly to be identified with the reeve of Kinsbourne of this name 1300–8 (WAM 8790–8).

ij bus.[18] Summa Cxl qr. iij bus. De quibus in semine xxxiij qr. In expensis anni precedentis iiij qr. ij bus.[19] In liberacione servientis per annum v qr. iij bus. In mixtura ad liberaciones famulorum xvj qr. frumenti iij qr. vj bus. scuralli frumenti. In expensis autumpni j qr. di. In expensis ballivi per suos adventus vj bus. Summa lxiiij qr. v bus. di. Et remanent lxxv qr. v bus. di.
Ordeum Sunt ad triturandum per estimacionem de dominico viij qr. ordei. Et de decima ij qr. Inde in semine ij qr. Et remanent viij qr. ordei.
Dragetum Sunt ad triturandum per estimacionem v qr. drageti de dominico. Inde in semine iij qr. Et remanent ij qr. drageti.
Pise Sunt ad triturandum per estimacionem j qr. pisarum. Inde in semine vj bus. In mixtura ad liberaciones famulorum ij bus.
Avene Sunt ad triturandum per estimacionem de dominico lx qr. avenarum. Et de decima vj bus. Inde in semine l qr. In potagio famulorum, prebenda equorum, affrorum, ballivi et superveniencium xlvj qr. Et sic deficiunt xxxv qr. ij bus. que ordinantur ad emendum.
Exitus molendini Sunt de firma molendini xvj qr. que ordinantur ad liberaciones cum xvj qr. frumenti, iij qr. vj bus. scuralli, ij bus. pisarum.
Recepta Oneratur de viij li. per estimacionem de exitu manerii. Inde in custus carucarum et carectarum xxxviij s. In custus domorum et molendini xiij s. iiij d. In minutis necessariis x s. In sarclacione et custus autumpni iiij li. In trituracione xxviij s. In stipendiis xiiij s. iiij d. In expensis superveniencium x s. In xxxv qr. avenarum emendis per estimacionem iiij li.

Summa xiiij li. iij s. viij d. Et sic deficiunt vj li. iij s. viij d.

Staurum Sunt ibidem xij affri, v vacce, j juvenc*c*a, ij boviculi, j juvenculus, iiij vituli, xxvij multones, xlviij matrices, x hoggastri, viij jercie, xlj agni, j verrus, j sus, v porculi, x porcelli, xvij auce.

Stivenach' Estimacio ibidem per sacramentum Rogeri Trot,[20] Ricardi de Saundorne, Eustacii ate Dene, Roberti Dymers, Johannis ate Hurne et Rogeri prepositi[21]

[18] A reference to the render of wheat owed by the customary tenants of Kinsbourne manor annually on 29 September, and valued at 12d. in the extent of 1315; they also owed 1 qr. 6 bus. of oats p.a. on 1 November, valued at 3s. 6d. in 1315 (CUL, MS Kk.5.29, f. 78v).

[19] MS: 'ij bus.' inserted.

[20] Possibly to be identified with Roger Trot, who demitted office as reeve of Stevenage on 26 November 1298 (TNA, SC 6/870/14).

[21] Roger atte Upend, reeve of Stevenage 1322–3 and probably for a longer period. At the end of the year 1322–3, he paid a fine of £4 to avoid an examination by the auditors of his final account for this year (TNA, SC 6/871/7).

Frumentum Triturantur ibidem iij qr. v bus. Et sunt ad triturandum per estimacionem vj^{xx}viij qr. Et de ix qr. vj bus. de firma et redditu.[22] Summa Cxlj qr. iij bus. Inde in expensis anni precedentis iij qr. v bus. Item in semine lvj qr. In custus autumpni iij qr. v bus. In expensis ballivi vj bus. In mixtura ad liberaciones famulorum xix qr. frumenti v bus.[23] Summa iiij^{xx}ix qr. Et remanent lij qr. iij bus.
Ordeum Sunt ad triturandum xx qr. Inde in semine per estimacionem v qr. Et remanent xv qr.
Dragetum Sunt ad triturandum xv qr. drageti. Inde in semine vj qr. In mixtura ad liberaciones famulorum ix qr.
Pise Sunt ad triturandum viij qr. pisarum. Inde in semine v qr. In mixtura ad liberaciones iij qr.
Avene Triturantur ibidem vj bus. Et sunt ad triturandum per estimacionem l qr.[24] Inde in semine l qr. In farina pro potagio, prebenda equorum, affrorum et expensis ballivi et superveniencium, l qr. et di. Et deficiunt xlvij qr. vj bus. que ordinantur ad emendum precium qr. ij s. iiij d.
Exitus molendini Sunt de exitu molendini xiij qr. que ordinantur ad liberaciones simul cum xix qr. v bus. frumenti, ix qr. drageti, ij qr. pisarum.
Recepta denariorum Oneratur de xxix li. iij s. xj d. ob. de redditu et tallagio. Et de lxxix s. iiij d. ob. qua. de exitu manerii.[25] Et de xlij s. viij d. de j verro, xij porcis et porculis venditis.[26] Et de iiij li. vj s. viij d. de perquisitis curie. Et de xlviij s. j d. ob. de operibus vend*itis*.

Summa xlij li. ix d. ob. qua.

Inde in allocacione xij d. In custus carucarum et carectarum lxx s. x d. ob. In custus domorum xl d. In xlvij qr. vj bus. avenarum emendis Cxj s. v d. precium qr. ij s. iiij d. In minutis necessariis xviij s. In falcacione et custus autumpni per estimacionem xl s. In trituracione bladi xl s. per estimacionem. In stipendiis famulorum xj s. In feodo xxiiij s. In expensis ballivi et superveniencium xxx s.

Summa xvij li. ix s. vij d. ob. Et remanent xxiiij li. xj s. ij d. qua.

Staurum Sunt ibidem ij equi carectarii, xj affri, iiij boves, j taurus, iiij vacce, j juvencca, ij boviculi, ij vituli, iiij multones, x matrices, xxx hoggastri, xj jercie, ix agni, ij verri, ij sues, vij porci, xiij porculi, x porcelli, j anser, ij mariole, xj auculi, x capones,[27] j gallus, v galline, xiiij pulcini.

[22] MS: 'Et de ix qr. vj bus. de firma et redditu' inserted in main text hand.
[23] MS: 'v bus.' inserted.
[24] MS: 'Et ij qr. de redditu' struck out.
[25] MS: 'de exitu manerii' inserted.
[26] MS: 'porcis et porculis venditis' inserted.
[27] MS: 'capones' inserted.

[*Dorse*] *Feryng'* Estimacio ibidem per sacramentum Johannis Prokenot, Willelmi Col, Johannis ate Pyrie, Petri Coman, Johannis Broc, Johannis Gore

Frumentum Triturantur ibidem v qr. Et sunt ad triturandum per[28] estimacionem de dominico Cxl qr. Et de decima l qr. Summa Ciiij^{xx}xv qr. Inde in semine per estimacionem lx qr. In expensis anni precedentis vij qr. In expensis domus in[29] autumpno et precariarum vj qr. di.[30] per estimacionem. In liberacione custodis bosci de Nunchey j qr. In liberacione unius grangiarii quasi per di. annum iij qr. ij bus. In expensis servientis iij qr. In mixtura ad liberaciones famulorum xxiij qr. di. frumenti. Summa Ciiij qr. ij bus. Et remanent iiij^{xx}x qr. vj bus.

Pise Sunt ad triturandum per estimacionem viij qr. de dominico. Et de decima vj qr. Summa xiiij qr. Inde in semine vij qr. In mixtura ad liberaciones famulorum vij qr.

Mixtilio Triturantur ibidem ij qr. iij bus. Et expenduntur in anno precedenti.

Avene Sunt ad triturandum per estimacionem lx qr. de dominico. Et ix qr. de decima. Summa lxix qr. Inde in semine per estimacionem lxx qr. In potagio famulorum,[31] prebenda equorum, affrorum et boum et superveniencium per estimacionem lx qr. Et sic deficiunt lxj qr. que ordinantur ad[32] emendum precium qr. .....[33]

Exitus molendinorum Sunt ibidem de exitu molendinorum xxxij qr. que ordinantur ad liberaciones simul cum xxiij qr. di. frumenti, vij qr. pisarum.

Recepta denariorum Oneratur de redditu et tallagio xxix li. xj s. vj d. ob. Et de ix li. de exitu manerii. Et de C s. de perquisitis curie. Et de x s. de iiij affris vend*itis* quia debiles.

Summa xliiij li. xviij d. ob.

Inde in defectu redditus et aquietanciis x s. vj d. In custus carucarum et carectarum lx s. In custus domorum per estimacionem v s. In custus molendinorum per estimacionem l s. In minutis necessariis xxx s. In trituracione et ventilacione[34] bladi l s. per estimacionem. In falcacione iij s. In custus autumpni iiij li. xv s. per estimacionem. In stipendiis famulorum x s. In feodo J. Bousser C s.[35] In expensis ballivi et superveniencium per

[28] MS: 'per' omitted.
[29] MS: 'domus in' inserted.
[30] MS: 'di.' inserted.
[31] MS: 'fam'' inserted.
[32] MS omits 'ad'.
[33] MS: no amount is mentioned.
[34] MS: 'et ventilacione' inserted in the main text hand.
[35] In 1322–3, Bousser received two instalments of his fee: one, overdue for the previous year, and one for the current year (WAM 25639, 25641).

estimacionem lx s. In iiij affris emendis lx s. In lxj qr. avenarum emendis x li. iij s. iiij d. precium qr. xl d.

Summa xxxvj li. xvj s. x d. Et remanent pro conventu vij li. iiij s. viij d. ob.

Staurum Sunt ibidem ij jumenta ad carectas, ij pullani, xviij affri, ix boves, iiij bovetti, ix vacce, iij juvencc*e*, j boviculus, j juvencula, iiij vituli, ij hurtardi, xxxv multones, xxxvj matrices, xxj hoggastri, x jercie, xxxj agni, ij sues, xiiij porci vendendi, j verrus, vij porculi, x porcelli, xviij auce unde j anser iiij mariole.

Kelleved' Estimacio per[36]

Frumentum. Triturantur ibidem ix qr. v bus. frumenti. Et sunt ad triturandum per estimacionem C qr. Et sunt de exitu molendini iiij qr.[37] Summa Cxiij[38] qr. v bus. Inde in expensis anni precedentis ix qr. v bus. In semine per estimacionem l qr. In liberacione servientis v qr. vj bus. In expensis autumpni iiij qr. In mixtura ad liberacionem famulorum xxxj qr. In liberacione wodewardi j qr. Et remanent xij qr. ij bus.

Pise Sunt ad triturandum per estimacionem viij qr. Et ordinantur pro semine.

Avene Sunt ad triturandum per estimacionem xxxvj qr. Inde in semine per estimacionem l qr. In farina pro potagio famulorum, prebenda equorum, affrorum, boum et superveniencium per estimacionem xxxvj qr. Et sic deficiunt l qr. que ordinantur ad emendum precium qr. xl d.

Exitus molendini Sunt de exitu molendini xiiij qr. que ordinantur ad liberacionem famulorum simul cum xxxj qr. frumenti.

Recepta denariorum Oneratur de x li. xviij s. viij d. de redditu. Et de vj s. viij d. de firmis. Et de vj li. de exitu manerii. Et de iiij li. de perquisitis curie per estimacionem. Et de xvj s. de operibus venditis. Et de xxiiij s. de viij porcis venditis.[39]

Summa xxiij li. v s. iiij d.

Inde in expensis carucarum et carectarum per estimacionem liij s. iiij d. In custus molendini xl d. In minutis necesariis x s. In sarclacione et falcacione xiij s. iiij d. In custus autumpni per estimacionem iiij li. In trituracione per estimacionem xxviij s. In stipendiis famulorum per estimacionem xxx s. In

[36] MS: the heading is incomplete.
[37] MS: 'Et sunt de exitu molendini iiij qr.' inserted in main text hand.
[38] MS: 'Cxiij' corrected from 'Cix'.
[39] MS: 'Et de xxiiij s. de viij porcis venditis' inserted in main text hand.

expensis ballivi et superveniencium xiij s. iiij d. In l qr. avenarum emendis viij li. vj s. viij d. precium qr. xl d.

Summa xix li. xviij s. Et remanent pro conventu lxvij s. iiij d.

Staurum Sunt ibidem ij equi carectarii, xvij affri, vj boves, iij multones, v matrices, vj hoggastri, j jercia, vj agni, j verrus, ij sues, vij porci, vj porculi, vj porcelli, xxiiij auce, ij galli, viij galline. Item de catallis felonum ij equi, xj multones, vj matrices, j hoggaster, j jercia, vj agni.

Amewell' Estimacio ibidem facta per[40]

Frumentum Sunt ad triturandum per estimacionem v qr. Inde in semine ij qr. ij bus. Et remanent iij qr. vj bus.

Silligo Triturantur ibidem x qr. ij bus. silliginis. Et sunt ad triturandum per estimacionem xxij qr. Summa xxxij qr. ij bus. Inde in semine xiiij qr. In mixtura ad liberaciones famulorum v qr. Et remanent xiij qr. ij bus. silliginis.

Dragetum Sunt ad triturandum viij qr. drageti. Inde in semine iij qr. ij bus. Et remanent iiij qr. vj bus. drageti.

Avene Sunt ad triturandum per estimacionem xx qr. avenarum. Et sunt de redditu xij qr. di. Inde in semine xiiij qr. In allocacione prepositi j qr. In prebenda equorum, affrorum et superveniencium et potagio famulorum x qr. Et remanent vij qr. di. avenarum.

Exitus molendini De ix qr. bladi de exitu molendini que ordinantur ad liberaciones famulorum simul cum v qr. silliginis.

Recepta denariorum Oneratur de vij li. x s. de redditu et tallagio. Et de xiiij li. de exitu manerii. Et de xliiij s. ix d. ob. de operibus vend*itis*. Et de xl s. de perquisitis curie.

Summa xxv li. xiiij s. ix d. ob.

De quibus in redditu soluto et aquietanciis x s. In custus carucarum et carectarum xx s. In expensis molendini xl d. In minutis necessariis v s. In custus sarclacionis, falcacionis et levacionis xxxiij s. iiij d. In custus autumpni per estimacionem xl s. In trituracione bladi ix s. v d. In stipendiis famulorum x s. vj d. In expensis ballivi et superveniencium xxx s.

Summa viij li. xix d. Et remanent xvij li. xiij s. ij d.

Staurum Sunt ibidem[41]

[40] MS: the heading is incomplete.

[41] MS: blank.

II 8 View of the states of the convent's manors, November–December 1323

Three parchment rotulets formerly from an Exchequer fashion roll, now filed together as part of a modern archival regrouping of loose membranes. Rotulet 1 is a roll of one membrane, with a diamond-shaped filing hole in the centre at the head. The parchment is approximately 220 mm wide, with a fold for the left margin on the recto. The roll is largely a fair copy, but with additions to some sections in the main hand which show some updating, for example, in the entry for Morden, the sale of barley there and sending the remainder to Westminster. The text was written down the recto and then down the dorse from head to foot. A further membrane, a smaller parchment schedule, is sewn to the dorse, part of the way down, with white thread, – – –, in the middle of the roll. It relates to the manor of Stevenage in the previous manorial year. Rotulet 2 is also a roll of one membrane, 240 mm wide, laid out with a fold for the left margin. There is a diamond-shaped filing hole at the head, and there are further holes for sewing. The roll is a fair copy, written down the recto and then back up the dorse, i.e. not in the same pattern as rotulet 1. It is endorsed at the foot of the roll 'Visus maneriorum de anno xvij°'. Rotulet 4 is a roll of one membrane, 236 mm wide. Although there is no diamond-shaped filing hole at the head, there are sewing holes at this point. The roll is a fair copy: it seems to have been written one manor at a time; it is written down the recto, and also down the dorse, i.e. in the same manner as rotulet 1. Parts of this rotulet are now damaged by water-staining and cannot be read.[1]

WAM 9289, rots. 1, 2 and 4

[*Rot. 1 recto*]

Batricheseye

Estimacio facta ibidem per R. Opi, Willelmum Godwyne, Johannem Playt*ere*, Johannem Bissop, die jovis in vigilia sancte Katerine virginis anno regni regis Edwardi xvij°[2]

Frumentum Triturantur ibidem xxxviij qr. v bus. frumenti unde vj bus. onerantur anno xvj°.[3] Et sunt ad triturandum per estimacionem xviij qr. Et iiij qr. de firma molendini. Summa lx qr. v bus. De quibus ordinantur pro semine xx qr. In mixtura ad liberaciones famulorum ij qr. scuralli. In pane

[1] Extant ministers' accounts, 1323–4: Aldenham, WAM 26072; Ashwell: WAM 262621; Feering manor: 29 September 1323–8 January 1324, WAM 25643; 8 January 1324–29 September 1324, WAM 25646; Feering rectory: 29 September 1323–8 January 1324, WAM 25644; Hendon: WAM 32541; Kinsbourne: WAM 8810; Knightsbridge: WAM 16412; Launton: WAM 15333; Stevenage: LMA, DL/D/D/049/MS25404/022; Wheathampstead: HALS, DE/Lw/M137.

[2] 24 November 1323. Opi was reeve of Battersea, 26 April 1300–29 September 1300, and Playtere reeve here 30 September 1304–30 September 1305 (WAM 27505–6).

[3] 1321–2.

pro autumpno v bus.[4] In expensis anni precedentis vj bus.[5] Et remanent xxxvij qr. ij bus. pro expensis.[6]

Silligo Triturantur ibidem xx qr. ij bus. De quibus iiij qr. onerantur anno xvj°. Et sunt ad triturandum per estimacionem xx qr. Et lx qr. de exitu molendini. Summa C qr. ij bus. De quibus ordina*ntur* pro semine xvj qr. In expensis anni precedentis iiij qr. In mixtura ad liberaciones famulorum lvij qr. In liberacione wodewardi ij qr. In consuetudine passatoris j qr.[7] In expensis sarclacione bladi vij bus. Et pro precariis xij qr. Et remanent vij qr. iij bus. que ordinantur ad vendendum precium qr. v s. iiij d.

Fabe Triturantur ibidem iij qr. et di. que ordinantur ad vendendum precium qr. iij s. vj d.

Albe pise Sunt ad triturandum per estimacionem iij qr. Et ordinantur pro semine.

Nigre pise et vesce Sunt ad triturandum per estimacionem iij qr. Et ordinantur pro semine ij qr. Et pro liberacionibus j qr.

Ordeum Triturantur ibidem xlv qr. iij bus. Et sunt ad triturandum lx qr. per estimacionem. Et iij qr. ij bus. de chershet. Summa Cviij qr. et di. De quibus in semine xl qr. Et totum residuum ordei pro Westm'.

Dragetum Triturantur ibidem vj qr. Et mittuntur ad Westm'.

Avene Triturantur ibidem x qr. avenarum. Et sunt ad triturandum per estimacionem xxv qr. Summa xxxv qr. que ordinantur pro semine et prebenda.

Receptum Oneratur de xix s. de arreragiis compoti sui. Et de xxv li. xv s. iiij d. de reddit*u*. Et de xxviij s. viij d. de firma. Et de xij li. de exitu manerii cum molendino fullon*ario* et feno[8] vendendo. Et de lj s. viij d. de vendicione bladi ut supra. Et de viij s. de equo carectario vendendo per estimacionem. Et de ix li. xj s. ix d. de vendicione operum. Et de Cx s. de perquisitis curie per estimacionem.[9]

Summa lvij li. iiij s. v d.

De quibus pro diversis aquietanciis, custu carucarum, carectarum, domorum lix s. iiij d. Et pro minutis xxiiij s. Et pro xx qr. avenarum emendis pro semine pro frisca terra lx s. Item pro j equo carectario emendo xiij s. iiij d. Item pro sarclacione et trituracione per estimacionem xl s. Item pro falcacione et custu autumpni lxiij s. Item pro stipendiis x s.

Summa xiij li. ix s. viij d.

[4] A reference to the loaves of which every customary tenant performing harvest boons probably received one on each occasion.

[5] MS: 'In expensis ..... vj bus.' inserted in the main hand.

[6] MS: 'xxxvij qr. ij bus. pro expensis' inserted in another hand.

[7] The recipient was the ferryman at Chelsea.

[8] MS: 'feno' inserted.

[9] MS: a short marginal entry opposite this entry is now illegible.

Et remanent pro conventu xliiij li. xiiij s. ix d. Item xxx li. de arreragiis Roberti Fabian.[10]
Staurum Sunt ibidem iij equi carectarii, vij affri unde j jumentum, j pullanus j anni et di., xij boves. Item ij boves qui calumpn*iantur*, iij vituli, j sus, iiij[or] porculi, xij porcelli de exitu ante festum sancti Michaelis, Cij porcelli post festum sancti Michaelis.

Mordon' Estimacio facta ibidem in crastino sancte Katerine virginis anno supradicto[11] per Walterum ate Wode, Henricum atte Hegh', Henricum ate Cherche[12]
Frumentum Triturantur ibidem de dominico xxxvij qr. j bus. Et sunt ad triturandum per estimacionem x qr. Et ij qr. ij bus. scuralli.[13] Item triturantur de decima x[14] qr. vj bus. frumenti. Et de scurallo v bus.[15] Summa lx qr. vj bus. Inde in semine xviij qr.[16] In consuetudine seminatoris j bus. In mixtura pro liberacionibus famulorum iiij qr. In expensis autumpni j qr. scuralli. In expensis anni precedentis v bus. Item ordinantur ad vendendum v qr. precium qr. vj s. viij d. Et residuum pro Westm' videlicet xxxj qr. vij bus.[17]
Mixtillio Triturantur ibidem j qr. Et sunt ad triturandum per estimacionem v qr. Summa vj qr. Inde in semine j qr. et di. In mixtura ad liberaciones famulorum iiij qr. et di.[18]
Fabe Triturantur ibidem de dominico ij qr. ij bus. Et sunt ad triturandum vj qr. Et triturantur de decima j qr. vij bus. Et sunt ad triturandum ibidem per estimacionem v qr. Summa xv qr. j bus.[19] Inde in semine iij qr. et di. In mixtura ad liberaciones famulorum iiij qr. et di.[20] Et ordinantur ad vendendum viij qr. j bus. precium qr. v s.
Pise et vesce Sunt ad triturandum de dominico per estimacionem iiij qr. Et de decima iiij qr. Summa viij qr. Inde in semine ij qr. In mixtura ad liberaciones famulorum vj qr.

[10] MS: 'Expense auditorum vij s.' inserted in margin. 'Item xxx li. de arreragiis Roberti Fabian' added in a second ink, but probably in the main hand. Fabian was serjeant at Batterrsea 30 September 1315–30 September 1316, and previously serjeant at Morden (WAM 27508; II 4). The sewing for the schedule attached to the dorse appears at this point.
[11] 26 November 1323.
[12] MS: 'Expense auditorum iiij s.' inserted in margin.
[13] MS: 'Et ij qr. ij bus. scuralli' inserted in a second ink.
[14] MS: 'iiij' struck out; 'x' inserted.
[15] MS: 'Et sunt ad triturandum per estimacionem' follows without a sum and has been struck out. The appropriation of the rectory of Morden by the Abbey included, initially, all the tithe; see Harvey, *Estates*, p. 411.
[16] MS: 'In semine mixt' cum sill'' follows without a sum and has been struck out.
[17] MS: 'Et residuum .... vij bus.' in a second ink.
[18] MS: 'iiij qr. et di.' in a second ink.
[19] MS: 'xv qr. j bus.' in a second ink.
[20] MS: 'In mixtura ..... iiij qr. et di.' in a second ink.

Avene Triturantur ibidem xx qr. de dominico. Et sunt ad triturandum ibidem l qr. Item sunt ad triturandum de decima xxvj qr. Summa iiij^{xx}xvj qr. Inde in semine xxx qr. In farina pro potagio famulorum ij qr. In prebenda equorum et boum per estimacionem ita quod non excedit[21] xij qr. In prebenda affrorum vj qr. Et ordinantur ad vendendum xviij qr. precium qr. iij s. Et remanent pro Westm' xxviij qr.[22]
Ordeum Sunt ad triturandum de dominico vij qr. Et triturantur de decima vj qr. Summa xiij qr. Inde in semine ij qr. Et remanent pro Westm' xj qr.[23]
Dauek Sunt ad triturandum de decima ij qr. Et ordinantur ad liberaciones famulorum.
Exitus molendini Estimantur de exitu molendini hoc anno x qr. et non plus quia deficit j mola. Et totum ad liberaciones famulorum.[24]
Receptum Oneratur de iiij li. iij s. v d. ob. de redd*itu*. Et de viij s. de exitu manerii per estimacionem. Et de vj li. viij s. de v qr. frumenti, viij qr. j bus. fabarum, xviij qr. avenarum et ordei ad vendendum. Et de xx d. de averagio per estimacionem. Et de xxiiij s. de perquisitis cur*ie*.

Summa xij li. v s. j d. ob.

Inde in superplusagio anni precedentis lxxiiij s. vj d. In redditu soluto et aquietanciis[25] vj s. ij d.[26] In custu de caruc*is* et[27] carectis xx s. In custu domorum manerii et domorum rectorie xx s. In custu molendini videlicet in j mola de novo emenda et redditus aquietanci*a* fact*a* lxvj s. viij d. In expensis minutis per estimacionem viij s. In sarclacione et falcacione iiij s. In custu autumpni per estimacionem de dominicis ls. In trituracione per estimacionem tam dominicorum quam decime xxix s. iij d. In stipendiis famulorum xxxij s.

Summa xv li. x s. vij d. Et sic deficiunt lxv s. v d. ob.

Et memorandum quod nichil ordinatur pro blado decime intrando. Item sunt levandum de arreragiis Roberti de Nunthey lx s.
Staurum Sunt ibidem ij equi carectarii, vij affri unde ij debiles, iij pullani, x boves.

[21] MS: 'ita quod non excedit' inserted.
[22] MS: 'xxviij qr.' in a second ink.
[23] MS: 'Summa xiij qr. .... Et remanent pro Westm' xj qr.' inserted.
[24] MS: 'Et totum ad liberaciones famulorum' in a second ink.
[25] MS: 'et aquietanciis' inserted.
[26] MS: 'Inde in semine ij qr.' follows at this point, and to this entry 'Et remanent pro Westm'' was later added. Identical entries were subsequently added to the Ordeum panel, to which they properly belong, but not deleted here. 'Dauek' is repeated as a heading after 'Et remanent pro Westm'.'
[27] MS: 'et' omitted.

[*Rot. 1 dorse*] *Amwell'* Estimacio facta ibidem die sabbati proxima post festum sancti Nicholai[28] per Walterum Wexmong*er* prepositum[29]

Frumentum Triturantur ibidem et sunt ad triturandum per estimacionem iij qr. di. Et de ij qr. ij bus. de empcione pro semine. Inde in semine ij qr. ij bus. Et remanent pro Westm' iij qr. di.

Silligo Triturantur ibidem xiiij qr. ij bus. Et sunt ad triturandum per estimacionem xviij qr. Summa xxxij qr. ij bus. Inde in semine xviij qr. j bus. In mixtura ad liberaciones iiij qr. v bus. Et remanent ix qr. di. que ordinantur ad vendendum precium qr. iiij s.

Dragetum Triturantur ibidem xij qr. drageti. Et mittuntur apud Westm'.

Avene Triturantur ibidem xl qr. v bus. Et sunt ad triturandum per estimacionem ij qr. Et de xij qr. di. de redd*itu*. Summa lv qr. j bus. Inde in semine per estimacionem xv qr. In farina j qr. In prebenda jumentorum, boum et vitulorum per estimacionem viij qr. In expensis superveniencium per estimacionem j qr. In allocacione prepositi j qr. Et mittuntur apud Westm' xl qr. Et sic deficiunt x qr. vij bus. que ordinantur ad emendum precium qr. per estimacionem ij s. viij d.

Multura De frumento de exitu molendini x qr. Que ordinantur ad liberaciones cum iiij qr. di bus. silliginis.

Receptum Oneratur de xliiij s. iiij d. ob. de arreragiis. Et de vij li. iij s. xj d. de reddit*u*. Et de xiij li. vj s. viij d. de exitu manerii. Et de xxxviij s. de silligine vend*enda*. Et de xxxviij s. de perquisitis cur*ie* per estimacionem. Et de xliiij s. ix d. ob. de operibus vendendis.[30]

Summa xxviij li. xv s. ix d.

De quibus in acquietanciis xj s. iiij d. ob. qua. In custu carucarum et carectarum xxvj s. viij d. In custu domorum per estimacionem ij s. In custu molendini v s. In minutis xix s. In x qr. vij bus. avenarum emendis per estimacionem xxix s. In sarclacione et falcacione xxxiij s. iiij d. In custu autumpni xl s. In trituracione bladi xiiij s. iiij d. In stipendiis vij s. vj d. In expensis forinsecis per estimacionem xxx s.

Summa x li. xviij s. ij d. ob. qua. Et remanent pro Westmon' xvij li. xviij s. vj d. qua.

Staurum Sunt ibidem v jumenta, ij pullani etatis ij annorum et di., ij pullani etatis j anni et di., ij pullani de exitu, iij boves, v vituli.

[28] 10 December 1323.

[29] MS: 'Expense auditorum xiij s. iij d.' inserted in margin. Wexmonger was reeve of Amwell 21 December 1318–10 March 1349 (BL, Add. Rolls 66738–56).

[30] MS: 'vendendis' omitted.

Stivenach' Estimacio facta ibidem die lune proxima post festum sancti Nicholai[31] per[32]

Frumentum[33] Triturantur ibidem xxxij qr. j bus. frumenti. Et sunt ad triturandum per estimacionem xxxvj qr. Et de ix qr. vj bus. de redditu et firmis. Summa lxxix qr. Inde in semine xlix qr. j bus. In expensis anni precedentis viij qr. v bus. In mixtura per estimacionem xx qr.[34] Et remanent j qr. vij bus. Que ordinantur ad vendendum precium qr. vj s.[35]

Pise Triturantur ibidem iij qr. vj bus. pisarum. Et sunt ad triturandum per estimacionem xiiij qr. Inde in semine per estimacionem vij qr. Et in mixtura ad liberaciones viij qr. vj bus. Et ordinantur ad mittendum apud Whathamsted ij qr. Et eque.[36]

Ordeum Triturantur ibidem j qr. j bus. ordei. Et sunt ad triturandum per estimacionem xxiiij qr. Inde in semine vij qr. In expensis anni precedentis j qr. j bus. Et remanent pro Westm' xvij qr.[37]

Dragetum Sunt ad triturandum per estimacionem xiiij qr. Inde in semine v qr. Et remanent pro Westm' ix qr.[38]

Avene Triturantur ibidem xv qr. vij bus. Et sunt ad triturandum per estimacionem xlvj qr. Et de iiij qr. per estimacionem in garbis. Et de iij qr. per estimacionem comest*ibilibus* ante autumpnum crescentibus cum affris.[39] Et de ij qr. de firma. Summa lxxj qr. vj bus. Inde in semine l qr. In farina, prebenda equorum, affrorum, boum, per estimacionem xxxvj qr. Et deficiunt xxvj qr. j bus.[40] Ordinantur ad emendum per visum et ordinacionem ballivi.[41]

Multura De firma molendini xij qr. Et triturantur de brott' vj bus.[42] Que ordinantur ad liberaciones cum xx qr. frumenti, viij qr. vj bus. pisarum. Et deficiunt viij qr. iiij bus. Inde recipiet de Hwathamstede ij qr. Et iij qr. de novo grano. Et de iij qr. de empcione.[43]

[31] 12 December 1323.

[32] MS blank: no names are entered.

[33] MS: 'Expense ibidem ix s. v d. qua.' inserted in margin.

[34] The passage from 'Summa lxxix qr.' to this point has been added in a second ink.

[35] MS: 'Et remanent ... precium qr. vj s.' added in another hand.

[36] MS: 'Et ordinantur ... Et eque.' in another hand.

[37] MS: 'Et remanent pro Westm' xvij qr.' in another hand.

[38] MS: 'Et remanent pro Westm' ix qr.' in another hand.

[39] For a clearer reference to the cultivation of oats as fodder for draught horses at Stevenage in 1316–17, see TNA, SC 6/871/6.

[40] MS: 'bus.' omitted.

[41] MS: 'Ordinantur ad emendum per visum et ordinacionem ballivi' inserted in another hand.

[42] MS: 'Et triturantur de brott' vj bus.' inserted.

[43] MS: 'Inde recipiet de Hwathamstede ... de empcione' in another hand and ink.

Receptum Oneratur de xiiij li. xvij s. xj d. ob. de arreragiis per visum compoti.[44] Et de[45] xxix li. iij s. xj d. ob. de redd*itu*. Et de C s. de exitu manerii per estimacionem. Et de vj li. xiij s. iiij d. de perquisitis cur*ie* per estimacionem. Et de xj s.[46] vij d. de vendicione frumenti. Et de xl s. de operibus vendendis per estimacionem.

Summa lviij li. v s. x d.

De quibus in aquietanciis iij s. ij d. In custu carucarum lv s. per estimacionem. In custu carectarum xiij s. iiij d. per estimacionem. In custu domorum xiij s. iiij d. In custu molendini videlicet j mola et alio opere emendo xx s. In blado emendo ad liberaciones iij qr. pro xij s. In minutis xij s. In falcacione et sarclacione ij s. In custu autumpni lx s. per estimacionem. In stipendiis xj s. In feodo ballivi libertatis xxiiij s. In trituracione bladi xxviij s. vj d. In expensis servientis xl s.

Summa xiiij li. xiiij s. iiij d. Et sic remanent pro conventu xliij li. xj s. vj d.

Staurum[47]

[*Rot. 1 recto: attached schedule*][48]

Visus compoti prepositi de Stivenach' de anno xvj^{mo}

Receptum Idem oneratur de xj li. xvij s. ob. de arreragiis. Et de xxix li. iij s. xj d. ob. de redditu. Et de iiij li. xviij s. vij d. de exitu manerii. Et de iiij li. x s. de vendicione bladi. Et de xliiij s. vij d. de vendicione stauri. Et de vj li. vij s. j d. de perquisitis curie. Et de lx s. xj d. qua. de operibus vendendis.

Summa recept*i* lxij li. ij s. ij d. qua.

Expense In acquietanciis iij s. viij d. ob. qua. In custu carucarum lvj s. In custu carectarum xvij s. vij d. ob. In custu domorum ij s. ix d. In custu molendini ix s. iij d. In minutis xx s. xj d. In blado empto xxiiij s. In stauro empto xlv s ob. qua. In falcacione ij s. iiij d. In custu autumpni iiij li. iij s. ob. In trituracione xxxix s. iij d. qua. In stipendiis xj s. In feodo ballivi libertatis xxiiij s. In expensis forinsecis lj s. iij d. In liberaciones suas xxvj li. xiiij s.

[44] The view cited here is a summary account of the reeve of Stevenage (Roger atte Upend) for the year 1322–3, and probably represents an agreement with the convent that his final account for the latter year should not be examined in detail (for this account, TNA, SC 6/871/7). The view, however, was stiched to the view of the states for 1323–4, the present document, and so made available to the auditors in 1323–4. This schedule is edited at the end of the dorse of this rotulet.

[45] MS: at this point, a new hand takes over writing the account for the remainder of the dorse. 'de' was omitted in the handover to the new clerk.

[46] MS: 's.' inserted.

[47] No details follow.

[48] The following view of the reeve of Stevenage's account for 1322–3 is attached as a schedule to the dorse of rot. 1, at approximately the point where the estimates for the manor of Stevenage made in December 1323 appear.

Summa expensarum et liberacionum xlvij li. iiij s. ij d. ob. qua. Et debet xiiij li. xvij s. xj d. ob.

Memorandum quod deficiunt de estimacione xl qr. j bus. frumenti, xij qr. ij bus. avenarum.

[*Rot. 2 recto*] *Bemflete* Per sacramentum Sewalli Wodegare et W. Wodegare et Salamonis filii Johannis diebus veneris et sabbati ante festum sancti Nicholai[49]

Frumentum. Triturantur ibidem de frumento xx qr. v bus. unde ij qr. scuralli. Item triturantur ibidem de decima x qr. v bus.[50] Summa xxxj qr. ij bus. Inde in expensis anni precedentis j qr. v bus., in semine xvij qr. vj bus. et di. In oblatis contra pascham j bus. In mixtura ad liberaciones iiij qr. Et sic remanent pro conventu vij qr. v bus. et di.

Mixtilio Sunt ad triturandum per estimacionem de decima ij bus. Que ordinantur ad liberaciones famulorum.

Fabe Sunt ad triturandum per estimacionem de dominicis ij qr. et di. Item triturantur ibidem de decima iij qr. Et sunt ad triturandum per estimacionem de eadem decima iij qr. Summa viij qr. iiij bus.[51] Inde in expensis anni precedentis vij bus. In mixtura ad liberaciones j qr. vj bus. Et remanent v qr. vij bus. que ordinantur ad vendendum precium qr. iiij s. viij d. [52]

Harasium[53] Sunt ad triturandum per estimacionem j qr. Item sunt ad triturandum de dec*ima* iiij bus. Summa j qr. et di. que ordinantur ad liberaciones famulorum.

Avene Sunt ad triturandum per estimacionem de dominicis xx qr. Item triturandum de decima vij qr. Summa xxvij qr. Inde in semine per estimacionem xv qr. In farina pro potagio j qr. et di. In prebenda affrorum et boum per estimacionem v qr. et di. Et remanent pro conventu v qr.

Exitus molendini[54] Sunt ibidem de firma molendini ix qr. Que ordinantur ad liberaciones famulorum videlicet v qr. pro isto manerio et iiij qr. pro Fanton.

Liberaciones Memorandum quod ordinantur pro liberacionibus famulorum xij qr. et di.[55] ut patet supra.

[49] 2–3 December 1323.

[50] The appropriation of the rectory at Benfleet by the Abbey, in the late twelfth century, gave a share of the greater tithes to the vicar; this was probably collected in the field with the Abbey's share. For the appropriation, see Harvey, *Estates*, p. 405.

[51] MS: the sum has been altered from 'viij qr. v bus.'

[52] MS: 'ordinantur ad vendendum precium qr. iiij s. viij d.' inserted possibly in a second hand.

[53] MS: 'et vesch*e*' struck out.

[54] A windmill (CUL, MS Kk.5.29, f. 116v).

[55] MS: 'et di.' inserted.

Receptum Oneratur de xx li. ix s. vj d. ob. de reddit*u*. Et de xxix s. ij d. de firmis. Et de vj li. xiij s. iiij d. de diversis exitibus manerii. Et de viij s. de ij affris vendendis in estate per estimacionem. Et de xxxiij s. iiij d. de perquisitis curie per estimacionem. Et de ij s. de vendicione operum. Et de xxvij s. v d. de fabis vendendis. Et de ij s. de vendicione operum.

Summa xxxij li. iij s. iij d. ob.[56]

Inde in diversis resolucionibus redditus lxxij s. vj d. In custu carucarum et carectarum per estimacionem vj s. In custu molendini et j mola emenda lxxiij s. iiij d. In custu domorum et murorum[57] per estimacionem xiij s. iiij d. In minutis expensis v s. In sarclacione et falcacione xiij s. iiij d. In custu autumpni et decima intranda xx s. In ij affris emendis xxij s. In trituracione bladi vj s. viij d. In stipendiis famulorum et vadiis servientis iiij li. v s.

Summa expensarum xv li. xvij s. ij d. Et sic remanent pro conventu xvj li. vj s. j d. ob.

Staurum Summa ibidem vj affri, iiij boves, ix auce, j gallus, v galline.

Fanton Estimacio facta per Robertum Typhayne et Willelmum Syward

Frumentum Triturantur ibidem de frumento et scurallo xxix qr. v bus. Et sunt ad triturandum per estimacionem iiij qr. Summa xxxiij qr. v bus. Inde in semine xxij qr. v bus. In liberacione grangie j qr. ij bus. Item miss*a* usque Westm' vj qr. ij bus. et di. In mixtura ad liberaciones iij qr. iij bus. et di.[58]

Fabe Sunt ad triturandum per estimacionem viij qr. Inde in semine j qr. et di. In mixtura ad liberaciones famulorum vj qr. et di.

Avene Triturantur ibidem lxviij qr. j bus. Et sunt ad triturandum per estimacionem xl qr. Summa Cviij qr. j bus. Inde semine xxx qr. In farina ad potagium j qr. In prebenda equorum, affrorum et boum x qr. In expensis superveniencium ij qr. Et remanent pro Westm' lxv qr. j bus.

Liberaciones Memorandum quod ordinantur pro liberacionibus famulorum xv qr. unde iiij qr. debet recipi de Bemflet et j qr. de empcione.

Receptum Oneratur de arreragiis xliij s. Et de iiij li. xiiij s. iiij d. de pastura et feno et fructu vendendis[59] per estimacionem.

Summa vj li. xvij s. iiij d.

Expense Inde in custu carucarum et carectarum xvj s. vj d. per estimacionem. In custu domorum per estimacionem x s. In minutis per estimacionem x s. In custu sarclacionis et falcacionis xviij s. In custu autumpni xlv s. In trituracione bladi xvj s. In stipendiis v s. In j qr. bladi empto ad liberaciones.

Summa expensarum vj li. v s. vj d. Et sic remanent xj s. x d.

[56] MS: 'iij s. iij d. ob.' written over an erasure.

[57] MS: 'et murorum' inserted.

[58] MS: 'et di.' inserted.

[59] MS: 'de pastura et feno vend' et fructu'; 'et fructu' is an insertion.

Staurum Sunt ibidem ij equi carectarum, vj affrorum, ij boves, xiiij auce, j gallus, v galline.[60]

Kelleved' Estimacio ibidem facta die sancti Nicholai[61] per Johannem Silkeneside, Johannem Mot et Johannem Vynour et Willelmum Mauncel servientem[62]

Frumentum Triturantur ibidem xxxvj qr. vj bus. frumenti. Et sunt ad triturandum per estimacionem lx qr. Summa iiij^{xx}xvj qr. vj bus. Inde in semine[63] liij qr. j bus.[64] In expensis anni precedentis x qr. iij bus. j p. In liberacione servientis v qr. vij bus. In liberacione custodis bosci j qr. In expensis autumpni iiij qr. j bus. et di. per estimacionem. In mixtura ad liberaciones ix qr. Et remanent pro Westm' xiij qr. j bus. j p.

Pise Sunt ad triturandum per estimacionem xij qr. De quibus in semine vj qr. per estimacionem. In mixtura ad liberaciones vj qr.

Avene Triturantur ibidem xij qr. avenarum. Et sunt ad triturandum[65] per estimacionem lxv qr. Inde in semine per estimacionem l qr. In farina pro potagio, prebenda equorum, affrorum et boum xxvj qr. In expensis superveniencium j qr. Et eque et nichil remanet.

Exitus molendini De exitu molendini xviij qr. que ordinantur ad liberaciones. Et memorandum quod ordinantur ad liberaciones xxxvj qr. Et deficiunt de liberacionibus iij qr. que capiuntur de novo grano.

Receptum Oneratur de arreragiis xxxj s. ij d. qua. Et de x li. xviij s. viij d. de redd*itu*. Et de xl d. de firmis. Et de vj li. xiij s. iiij d. de exitu manerii per estimacionem. Et de iiij li. de perquisitis curie per estimacionem. Et de xvj s. de operibus per estimacionem.

Summa xxiiij li. ij s. vj d. qua.

De quibus in custu carucarum et carectarum per estimacionem xxx s. et non plus quia carecte nove. In custu domorum per estimacionem vj s. viij d. In custu molendini xl d. In minutis xij s. In sarclacione et falcacione xiij s. iiij d. In custu autumpni lx s. In stipendiis xxxj s. iiij d. In trituracione bladi xij s. per estimacionem. In expensis servientis xx s.

Summa ix li. viij s. viij d. Et sic remanent pro conventu xiiij li. xiij s. x d. qua.

[60] MS: 'Expense auditorum x s. v d.' in margin in another hand. It is unclear to which manor or manors this entry relates; South Benfleet with Fanton Hall is a possibility.

[61] 6 December 1323.

[62] William Mauncel is also named as serjeant at Kelvedon in 1318–19 (TNA, SC 6/844/37).

[63] MS: 'per estimacionem' follows but has been struck out.

[64] MS: 'Memorandum quod semen frumenti de Fering'' in the margin at this point.

[65] MS: 'avenarum ... triturandum' written over an erasure.

Staurum Sunt ibidem ij equi carectarii, xij affri, v boves, viij multones, xxviij matrices, viij hoggastri, vij jercie, xxvij agni, j verrus, j suus, iij porci, x porcelli.

Fering' Estimacio ibidem factura die sancti Nicholai[66] per Johannem ate Pyrie, Petrum Coman servientem et messorem

Frumentum Triturantur ibidem de dominico iiij^{xx}viij qr. iij bus. frumenti. Et de decima lxxj qr. j bus. Et sunt ad triturandum per estimacionem de dominico Clx qr. frumenti. Summa CCCxix qr. et di. Inde in semine lx qr. iij bus. In expensis arrur*e*, falcacionis, precariarum in autumpno et panum acrarum[67] iiij qr. j bus. j p. In expensis domus in autumpno et pro aucis autumpnalibus ij qr. et di. In liberacionibus serviencium v qr. iij bus. et di. In liberacione custodis bosci j qr. In liberacione grangiarii quasi per di. annum iij qr. ij bus. In expensis superveniencium per estimacionem ij qr. In mixtura ad liberaciones xij qr. Et remanent pro conventu CCxxviij qr. vj bus.

Fabe Triturantur ibidem de decima j qr. et di. fabarum. Que ordinantur ad liberaciones famulorum.

Pise Triturantur ibidem de dominico ij qr. pisarum. Et de decima v bus. Et sunt ad triturandum per estimacionem xij qr. de dominico. Et de decima viij qr. Summa xxij qr. v bus. Inde in semine per estimacionem iiij qr. In mixtura ad liberaciones xiiij qr. In vendicione iiij qr. v bus. precium qr. iiij s.[68]

Ordeum Sunt ad triturandum de dominico per estimacionem vj qr. In mixtura ad dragetum faciendum ij qr. In vendicione iij qr. precium qr. v s.

Avene Triturantur ibidem de dominico xx qr. et di. Et sunt ad triturandum de dominico C qr. Et de decima xx qr. per estimacionem. Summa Cxl qr. iiij bus. Inde in semine iiij^{xx} qr.[69] In farina, prebenda jumentorum et affrorum, boum et vitulorum, superveniencium,[70] totum residuum avenarum.

Exitus molendini De exitu molendini xxxvj qr. que ordinantur ad liberaciones famulorum cum xij qr. frumenti, j qr. et di. fabarum, xiiij qr. pisarum.

[66] 6 December 1323.

[67] A reference to harvest services at Feering, formerly rewarded with one wheat loaf per person, morning and evening, and other comestibles. By the early fourteenth century, customary tenants performing harvest services received 4d. and one loaf per acre (CUL, MS Kk.5.29, f. 99; TNA, SC 6/841/6–7).

[68] MS: 'precium qr. iiij s.' inserted.

[69] MS: 'qr.' omitted.

[70] MS: 'superveniencium' inserted.

Receptum Oneratur de xiij li. de arreragiis. Et de xxix li. xj s. vj d. ob. de redditu. Et de ix li. de exitu manerii per estimacionem. Et de xxxviij s. vj d. de ordeo et pisis vendendis per estimacionem. Et de iij s. iiij d.[71] de j affro vendendo per estimacionem. Et de C s. de perquisitis curie per estimacionem.

Summa lviij li. xiij s. iiij d.

Inde in aquietanciis x s. vj d. In custu carucarum et carectarum liiij s. per estimacionem. In custu cum muro faciendo minuto lx s. per estimacionem. In custu domorum et murorum xx s. In custu molendini per estimacionem vj s. viij d. In ij affris emendis quia j nullius valoris et alter debilis xxvj s. viij d. In falcacione per estimacionem iiij s. vj d. In custu autumpni per estimacionem lxviij s. In trituracione bladi per estimacionem l s. In feodo J. de Bousser C s. In stipendiis xlij s. vj d. In expensis superveniencium per estimacionem lxvj s. viij d.

Summa xxv li. ix s. vj d. Et remanent pro Westm' xxxiij li. iij s. x d.

Staurum Sunt ibidem ij jumenta, xx affri, iiij^or boves, x vacce, ij bovetti, iiij boviculi, viij vituli, iij hurtardi, xv multones, lviij matrices, xxxj hoggastri, x jercie, liiij agni, j verrus, ij sues, xv porci, xxj porcelli.

Ecclesia de Feryng' Oneratur de ix li. vj s. viij d. de firma de Pateswyk. Et de vj s. viij d. de stramine et palea vendendis per estimacionem.

Summa ix li. xiij s. iiij d.

Inde solutum vicario de Fering' lxvj s. viij d. In trituracione bladi l s. In custu autumpni per estimacionem iiij li. xvj s.

Et remanent pro Westm' lxxx s. viij d. preter bladum quod oneratur in manerio de Fering'.

[*Rot. 2 dorse*] *Whathamsted'*[72] Estimacio ibidem die mercurii in crastino sancte Lucie virginis[73] per sacramentum Symonis le Couherd, Johannis fabri, Willelmi Gale et Willelmi ate Mulle

Frumentum Triturantur ibidem C qr. j bus. iij p. de dominico. Et de decima iij qr. di.[74] Et sunt ad triturandum lxxv qr. Item sunt ibidem ad levandum de redd*itu* ij qr. ij bus. et ij partibus di. bus.[75] Summa Ciiij^xx j qr. et di. p. In expensis anni precedentis xiij qr. iij p.[76] Inde in semine lx qr. vj bus. In liberacione grangiarii per estimacionem j qr. et di. In liberacione Galfridi

[71] MS: 'iiij d.' inserted.

[72] MS: 'Expense auditorum x s. iiij d.' in the margin.

[73] 14 December 1323.

[74] For the Abbey's claim to a moiety of the greater tithes of Wheathampstead, including those of Harpenden and Kinsbourne, see II 4, n. 51.

[75] A customary render due on 29 September; for references to this and to the render of oats due on 1 November, see II 4.

[76] MS: 'In expensis anni precedentis xiij qr. iij p.' inserted.

le Rous per annum v qr. iij bus. di.[77] In expensis superveniencium per estimacionem iiij bus. In expensis autumpni per estimacionem ij qr. di. In mixtura ad liberaciones famulorum xx qr. Summa Ciij qr. vj bus. di. p.[78] Et remanent pro conventu lxxvij qr. ij bus.
Ordeum Sunt ibidem ad triturandum xvj qr. Inde in semine v qr. Et remanent pro conventu xj qr.
Dragetum Sunt ibidem ad triturandum xx qr. Inde in semine v qr. Et remanent pro conventu xv qr.
Pise Sunt ad recipiendum de Styvenache ij qr. pisarum ad semen.[79] Et ordinantur pro semine.
Avene Triturantur ibidem de dominico xv qr. j bus. avenarum. Et de decima iij qr. iij bus. Item sunt ibidem de redditu ix qr. iij bus. et ij partibus di. bus. Et sunt ad triturandum Cl qr. Summa Clxxvij qr. vij bus. In semine lx qr. In farina pro potagio famulorum iij qr. In prebenda ij equorum, xviij affrorum et boum per estimacionem lxv qr. In expensis superveniencium et ballivi libertatis per estimacionem v qr. Summa Cxxxiij qr. Et remanent pro conventu xliiij qr. vij bus.
Exitus molendini Sunt ibidem de firma molendini xl qr. cum xx qr. frumenti.[80] Summa lx qr. Inde ordinantur pro liberacionibus lij qr. Et ordinantur ad mittendum apud Stevenach' ij qr. Et apud Kenesberne vj qr. Et eque.[81]
Receptum Oneratur de iiij s. ij d. ob. qua. de arreragiis compoti sui. Et de[82] xxxvij li. xv s. qua. de redditu assiso per annum. Et de iiij li. xiiij s. de exitu manerii per estimacionem. Et de vj li. ij s. iiij d. ob. de vendicione operum. Et de iiij li. ij s. de perquisitis cur*ie* per estimacionem.

Summa lij li. xvij s. vij d.[83]

Inde in allocacione vij s. viij d. In custu carucarum et carectarum per estimacionem iiij li. x s. In expensis domorum et[84] molendini per estimacionem cum j mola emenda[85] xxiiij s. In minutis expensis xxx s. In expensis sarclacionis et falcacionis viij s. In expensis autumpni per estimacionem vij li. In expensis trituracionis per estimacionem lxij s. In stipendiis et feod*is* xxvj s. In expensis superveniencium per estimacionem l s.

Summa xxj li. xij s. viij d. Et remanent pro conventu xxxj li. iiij s. xj d.

[77] This allowance, amounting to *c*.1½ bus. of wheat per week, probably belongs to the aftermath of the Abbey's recovery of the manor of Hendon from Richard le Rous, the fee-farm tenant, in 1312–15. See Harvey, *Estates*, p. 416, no. 11.
[78] MS: 'di. p.' inserted.
[79] See also above.
[80] For the three mills of Wheathampstead, see II 4.
[81] MS: a marginal note has been erased at this point.
[82] MS: 'de iiij s. ij d. ob. qua. de arreragiis compoti sui. Et de' inserted in main hand.
[83] MS: 'vij d.' inserted in main hand.
[84] MS: 'et' omitted.
[85] MS: 'cum mola emenda' inserted in main hand.

Staurum Sunt ibidem de stauro ij equi carectarii, xviij affri, iij vacce, j jumentum, j juvencula, ij vituli superannales, iij vituli, lxxviij multones, liiij oves matrices, xliij agni, j aper, ij sues, vij porci, vij porculi, xij porcelli.

Kenesberne Estimacio ibidem die jovis post festum sancte Lucie virginis[86] per sacramentum W. Enfeme, Nicholai Crips et Johannis grangiarii[87]
Frumentum Triturantur ibidem xxix qr. ij bus. frumenti de dominico. Et de decima[88] vij qr. vij bus. Et sunt ad triturandum de dominico xxvij qr. Summa lxiiij qr. j bus. Inde in semine xxx qr. vij bus. In liberacione servientis per annum v qr. iij bus. et di. In expensis autumpni j qr. et di. In expensis superveniencium per estimacionem iiij bus. In mixtura ad liberaciones xiij qr. Summa lj qr. ij bus. et di. Et remanent pro conventu xij qr. vj bus. di.
Ordeum Triturantur ibidem de decima[89] j qr. j bus. Et sunt ad triturandum de dominico x qr. Summa xj qr. j bus. Inde in semine ij qr. Et remanent pro conventu ix qr. j bus.
Dragetum Sunt ad triturandum de dominico xvij qr. drageti. Inde in semine iij qr. Et remanent pro conventu xiiij qr.
Avene Triturantur ibidem de dominico xiij qr. v bus. avenarum. Et de decima[90] vij qr. ij bus. Et sunt ad triturandum lxx qr. Summa iiij^{xx}x qr. vij bus. Inde in semine xlv qr. In prebenda equorum, affrorum, agnorum et vitulorum per estimacionem xxxvj qr. In farina pro potagio famulorum ij qr. In expensis superveniencium per estimacionem ij qr. Summa iiij^{xx}v qr. Et remanent pro conventu v qr. vij bus.
Multura De xvj qr. de exitu molendini que ordinantur ad liberaciones famulorum cum xiij qr. frumenti supra[91] et vj qr. frumenti[92] recipiendis de Hwathamsted.
Liberaciones Memorandum quod ordinantur pro liberacionibus famulorum xxxv qr.
Receptum[93] Oneratur de vj li. xiij s. iiij d.[94] de exitu manerii per estimacionem. Et de xliij s. de vendicione operum.
Summa viij li. xvj s. iiij d.

[86] 15 December 1323.
[87] MS: 'Expense auditorum ix s. iiij d.' in margin in another hand.
[88] MS: 'x^{a}'.
[89] MS: 'x^{a}'.
[90] MS: 'x^{a}'.
[91] MS: 'supra' inserted.
[92] MS: 'frumenti' inserted.
[93] MS: 'Memorandum quod non oneratur de x li. vj s. j d. eo quod sunt de superoneracione bladi estivalis', in the margin in another hand.
[94] MS: 'iiij d.' inserted.

Inde in custu carucarum et carectarum per estimacionem xxx s. In expensis domorum et molendini xx s. per estimacionem. In minutis expensis per estimacionem x s. In expensis sarclacionis et falcacionis per estimacionem ij s. In expensis autumpni per estimacionem iiij li. In trituracione bladi per estimacionem xxx s. In stipendiis xiiij s. iiij d. In expensis forensecis per estimacionem xx s.

Summa x li. vj s. iiij d. Et sic deficiunt xxx s.

Staurum Sunt ibidem xiij affri, iiij vacce, j juvenctus, j taurillus, j juvencula, iij vituli superannati, ij vituli, j hurtardus, xxxvj multones, xlviij matrices, viij hoggastri, xvj jercie, xliij agni, j sus, x porculi, xv porcelli.

Aldenham[95] Estimacio ibidem die sabbati ante festum beati Thome apostoli[96] per Thomam Sayer, Rogerum Canep' et Ricardum Neel

Frumentum Triturantur ibidem xxxvj qr. frumenti. Et sunt ad triturandum x qr. Summa xlvj qr. Inde in expensis in anno preterito j qr. j bus. In semine xv qr. vj bus. In expensis in autumpno vj bus. per estimacionem. In mixtura ad liberaciones famulorum ij qr. Summa xix qr. v bus. Et remanent pro Westm' xxvj qr. iij bus.

Ordeum Triturantur ibidem iiij qr. ordei. Que remanent pro conventu.

Avene Triturantur ibidem xlj qr. Et sunt ad triturandum per estimacionem liiij qr. Summa iiij^{xx}xiiij qr. Inde in semine l qr. In farina pro potagio famulorum j qr. In prebenda equorum, affrorum per estimacionem xx qr. In expensis superveniencium per estimacionem ij qr. Summa lxxiij qr.[97] Et remanent pro conventu xxj qr.

Exitus molendini De xviij qr. de exitu molendini pro tribus terminis per tallias et cum ij qr. frumenti et iij qr. de novo grano. Et totum computatur in liberacionibus famulorum.

Receptum Idem oneratur de Cxvij s. ob. de arreragiis compoti sui. Et de vij li. de arreragiis prepositi ante ipsum.[98] Et de xix li. xij s. iij d. de redditu. Et de xlvj s. de exitu manerii. Et de viij li. de perquisitis curie. Et de vj li. de vendicione operum.

Summa xlviij li. xv s. iij d. ob.

Inde in aquietanciis xiij s. In custu carucarum et carectarum xxx s. In custu novi molendini x li. xiij s. iiij d.[99] In custu domorum xiij s. iiij d. In minutis

[95] MS: 'Expense auditorum xvij s. iiij d.' in margin in another hand.

[96] 17 December 1323.

[97] MS: 'Summa lxxiij qr.' inserted.

[98] The arrears were those of, respectively, Thomas Sayer, currently reeve, for the period 13 September 1323–*c*.17 December 1323, and Roger Canep' for his final year as reeve, ending on 13 September 1323 (WAM 26069, 26072).

[99] The actual cost of the mill was £13 6s. 7d. (WAM 26072).

xx s. In sarclacione et falcacione v s. In custu autumpni xlvij s. In stipendiis xxiij s. In expensis superveniencium xl s.

Summa xx li. iiij s. iij d. Et remanent pro Westm' xxviij li. xj s. ob.
Staurum Sunt ibidem iij equi carectarii, vj affri, j pullanus etatis j anni et di., ij vacce, viij vituli, j hurtardus, iij multones, ix matrices, vj hogg*astri*, ij agni.

[*Rot. 4 recto*] *Hendon'* Estimacio ibidem die martis in vigilia sancti Thome apostoli[100] per sacramentum Ricardi Rolf, Godwyn atte Pyrie et Stephani servientis[101]
Frumentum Triturantur ibidem xx qr. ij bus. et di.[102] frumenti, iij qr. scuralli. Et sunt de redditu xxxij qr. iiij bus.[103] Et sunt de remanencia xxij qr. di. Summa lxxv qr. ij bus. di.[104] Inde in semine xxij qr. j bus. p. In liberacione servientis per annum vj qr. di. In defectu terre existentis in manibus domini v qr. In mixtura ad liberaciones famulorum iij qr. scuralli. In pane furnito ad precarias in autumpno ij qr. j bus. In expensis superveniencium j qr. Summa xxxix qr.[105] vj bus. j p. Et remanent pro Westm' xv qr. et di. Et remanent pro anno futuro que non levabuntur in illo anno xx qr. j p.
Fabe Sunt ad triturandum per estimacionem iiij qr. fabarum. Et ordinantur ad semen.
Dragetum Triturantur ibidem xx qr. Inde in adjectione ad avenas ij qr. Et remanent pro Westm' xviij qr.
Avene Triturantur ibidem xxv qr. iij bus. Et sunt ad triturandum per estimacionem xx qr. Et de j qr. vij bus. de redditu.[106] Summa xlvij qr. ij bus. Inde in semine xl qr. Ita quod permutacio est[107] inde de pisis per ordinacionem ballivi. Et totus redditus avenarum ordinatur pro expensis superveniencium et prebenda.
Braseum frumenti et ordei De remanencia xv qr. vij bus. Et de redditu xxij qr. et di. Summa xxxviij qr. iij bus. Que ordinantur ad vendendum pro cariagio fagattorum[108] preter xvj qr. que est remanere pro anno adhuc futuro.

[100] 20 December 1323.
[101] Stephen de Trafford, serjeant at Hendon, 1323–4 (WAM 32539–41).
[102] MS: 'ij bus. et di.' inserted.
[103] MS: 'Et sunt de redditu xxxij qr. iiij bus.' inserted.
[104] MS: 'Summa lxxv qr. ij bus. di.' written over an erasure. 'Expense auditorum xiij s. x d.' written in the margin; 'Hamst' viij s. iiij d. ob.' follows but has been struck out. For the sum of 8s. 4½d. as auditors' expenses at Hampstead, see below n. 131.
[105] MS: 'qr.' omitted.
[106] MS: 'Et de j qr. vij bus. de redditu' in margin.
[107] MS: 'est' omitted.
[108] MS: 'fagattorum' inserted.

Braseum avenarum Sunt ibidem xx qr. brasei avenarum de remanencia. Et de redditu xxxviij qr. vj bus. Summa lviij qr. vj bus. Inde ordinantur pro cariagio busci xx qr.

Exitus molendini De exitu molendini ix qr. cum iij qr. scuralli frumenti et cum xix qr. de empcione et v qr. de novo grano. Et totum computatur in liberaciones famulorum.

Receptum Oneratur de xxiiij li. x s. ij d. qua. de redditu. Et de iiij li. de tallagio per estimacionem. Et de v s. de firmis. Et de x li. de exitu manerii per estimacionem. Et de iiij li. de perquisitis curie per estimacionem. Et de xxviij s. de operibus vendendis. Et de x s. de factura brasei.

Summa xliiij li. xiij s. ij d. qua.

Inde in defectibus xij s. In custu carucarum et carectarum et ferrura equorum[109] xl s. In custu domorum videlicet factura novi columbarii in omnibus ix s. preter opera.[110] In custu molendini vj s. viij d. per estimacionem. In minutis necessariis[111] ordinatis pro cariagio busci, preter braseum gruti et avenarum que estimantur ad xiij li., pro eodem cariagio xviij li. In xix qr. mixture emendis iiij li. xv s. In falcacione per estimacionem xiij s. In custu autumpni xxiiij s. In stipendiis xlvij s. In expensis superveniencium per estimacionem xl s. In superplusagio compoti [sui anni prec]edentis[112] viij li. vj s. xj d. qua.

Summa xl li. vij d. qua. Et remanent pro Westm' iiij li. xij s. vij d.

Staurum Sunt ibidem iij equi carectarii, vj affri quorum ij masculi, iij pullani etatis ij annorum et di., ij pullani etatis j anni et di. et ij pullani de exitu, viij boves, viij vacce, j taurus, iiij[or] bovetti, ij juvence, iiij boviculi, iij juvencule et vj vituli.

Langeton'[113] Estimacio facta ibidem in crastino sancte Lucie[114] per Ricardum de Ambresdon' prepositum,[115] Jacobum Baldewyn, Radulfum le Coupere et Augustinum Neel[116]

Frumentum Triturantur ibidem xiiij[117] qr. ij bus. frumenti. Et sunt ad triturandum per estimacionem xvj qr. Summa xxx qr. ij bus. Inde in semine xij qr. In expensis anni precedentis ij qr. vj bus. In mixtura ad liberaciones

[109] MS: 'et ferrura equorum' inserted.

[110] The sum quoted is the sum later paid to a carpenter for a new dovecot *in grosso* (for the whole work); but other kinds of work were also needed, and the total cost was *c.*£1, although no labour services were used (WAM 32541).

[111] MS: 'cum xviij li.' follows but has been struck out.

[112] Text obscured by water staining.

[113] The whole of the Launton entry is written in a darker ink.

[114] 14 December 1323.

[115] Ambresdon was reeve of Launton 28 January 1293–19 October 1322 (WAM 15303–31).

[116] MS: 'Expense auditorum viij s. ix d.' in margin.

[117] MS: 'xiiij' corrected from 'xiij'.

ix qr. v bus. Et remanent ad vendendum v qr. vij bus.
Silligo Triturantur ibidem de silligine iij qr.[118] Et sunt ad triturandum per estimacionem xiiij qr. Summa xvij qr. Inde in expensis anni precedentis j qr. v bus. In semine iiij qr. di. In mixtura ad liberaciones x qr. iiij bus. ....
Fabe et pise Triturantur ibidem vj bus. Et sunt ad triturandum per estimacionem vij qr. ij bus. Summa viij qr. Inde in semine v qr. di. per estimacionem. In mixtura ad liberaciones ij qr. di. Et eque.
Dragetum Triturantur ibidem di. qr. drageti. Et sunt ad triturandum per estimacionem xij qr. Summa xij qr. di. Inde in semine per estimacionem v qr. Et remanent vij qr. et di. qr. que ordinantur ad vendendum precium qr. iiij s.
Avene Triturantur ibidem iiij qr. di. Et sunt ad triturandum per estimacionem xl qr. Summa xliiij qr. di. Inde in semine xxx qr. Et totum residuum pro prebenda equorum, affrorum, boum, agnorum et [superveniencium].[119] Et eque.
Liberaciones Estimantur de exitu molendini xij qr. preter decimam.[120] Et ordinantur ad liberaciones cum ix qr. v bus. [frumenti, x] qr. vij bus. silliginis, ij qr. di. fabarum.
Receptum Oneratur de xxj s. vij d. [de arreragiis]. Et de xviij li. xv s. vj d. ob. de redditu. Et de xl s. de exitu manerii per estimacionem. Et de lviij s. vij d. de blad*o* vend*endo* precium ut supra. Et de ..... li. x s. de perquisitis curie per estimacionem. Et de x li. de operibus vendendis per estimacionem.[121] Summa receptorum xxxvij li. ..... qua. Inde in aquietanciis ..... s. ij d. In custu carucarum et carectarum per estimacionem xx s. In custu domorum videlicet nove grangie fac*iende*[122] xx marcas.[123] In custu molendini per estimacionem pro custu mol*e*[124] ij marc*as* ..... per estimacionem x s. ....
Summa expensarum .... xij ..... ob. qua.
[*Staurum*] Sunt ibidem ij equi [carectarii], viij affri, ... xj multones, xiij matrices, iij hogastri, ij jercie ..... porculi .....

[118] MS: 'iij qr.' inserted.
[119] MS waterstained. Subsequent passages in this account in square brackets supply text now obscured by water stains. The lacunae that follow in this and manorial entries are also the result of these stains.
[120] Although the Abbey claimed a pension of 2 marks (26s. 8d.) p.a. from the rector of Launton, it had no claim to the tithes there (*VCH Oxon*, vi, p. 240).
[121] MS: 'Et de x li. de operibus vendendis per estimacionem' inserted.
[122] MS: 'fac'' inserted.
[123] i.e. £13 6s. 8d. Actual expenditure on the grange included 9s. 4½d. on wages for a man quarrying stone (*ad fodiendum petras*) for 45 days, at 2½d. per day, and 2s. for a helper for 12 days; but a complete record of expenditure does not survive (WAM 15333).
[124] MS: 'mol*e*' inserted.

Asswelle[125] *Frumentum* Sunt ibidem de firma lx qr. frumenti. Et de redditu xxxv qr. Summa iiij^{xx}xv qr. Inde in allocacione prepositi et bedelli j qr. j bus. Et remanent pro conventu iiij^{xx}xiij qr. vij bus.
Dragetum Sunt ibidem de firma Cxx qr. drageti .....
Braseum .....
Receptum Oneratur de iiij li. viij [s. de] arreragiis compoti precedentis. Et de ..... x s. Et de xxxv li. [iij s.] de redditu. Et de xiij s. viij d. de firmis. Et de ....j s. viij d. de perquisitis curie per estimacionem. Et de xxviij s. de operibus vendendis per estimacionem.

Summa liiij li. xvj s. vj d.

Inde in allocacionibus diversis x s. per estimacionem. In feodis xlij s. ..... In expensis minutis ij s. per estimacionem. In expensis superveniencium per estimacionem l s. Et remanent pro conventu ..... xij s.

[*Rot. 4 dorse*] *Knyttebr'* Estimacio ibidem facta die jovis ante natalem Domini[126] per Petrum Cromhere, Nicholaum Swon, et Reginaldum Child' servientem[127]
Frumentum Triturantur ibidem l qr. v bus. frumenti. Et sunt ad triturandum per estimacionem vij qr. Summa lvij qr. v bus. Inde in semine xj qr. v bus. In liberacione servientis v qr. vij bus. In expensis autumpni iiij bus. In mixtura ad liberaciones j qr. et di. per estimacionem. Et remanent pro conventu xxxviij qr.
Mixtillio Triturantur ibidem xiiij qr. mixtillionis. Et sunt ad triturandum per estimacionem xiiij qr. Summa xxviij qr. di. Inde in expensis anni precedentis v qr. In semine iiij qr. v bus. In mixtura ad liberaciones xviij qr. v bus.
Fabe Ordinantur pro semine fabarum ij qr. que ordinantur ad emendum de preposito de Mordon'.
Pise et vesce Triturantur ibidem iij qr. j bus. Et sunt ad triturandum per estimacionem ix qr. Summa xij qr. j bus. Inde in semine per estimacionem iij qr. In mixtura ad liberaciones ix qr. j bus.
Ordeum Triturantur ibidem xlvj qr. Et sunt ad triturandum per estimacionem xxxij qr. Summa lxxviij qr. Inde in semine per estimacionem xviij qr. In liberacionibus famulorum v qr. di.[128] Et remanent pro conventu liiij qr. et di.
Avene Triturantur ibidem v qr. Et sunt ad triturandum per estimacionem xx qr. Summa xxv qr. Inde in semine xviij qr. Et totum residuum pro expensis manerii.

[125] The entry begins in a new ink.
[126] 22 December 1323.
[127] Child was serjeant at Knightsbridge 1321–8 (WAM 16411, 16416).
[128] MS: 'In liberacionibus famulorum v qr. di.' inserted.

Liberaciones Ordinantur ad liberaciones xxxix qr. bladi, unde j qr. et di. frumenti, xviij qr. v bus. mixtillionis, ix qr. j bus. pisarum, v qr. di. ordei, et iiij qr. ad recipiendum de novo grano.[129]
Receptum Oneratur de iiij li. xix s. qua. de redditu. Et de viij s. de firmis. Et de Cx s. de exitu manerii per estimacionem. Et de xxx s. de perquisitis curie.
Summa xij li. vij s. qua.
Inde in superplusagio anni precedentis xxxj s. v d. qua. In aquietanciis viij d. In custu carucarum xxxv s. In custu carectarum per estimacionem ix s. In custu domorum x s., videlicet pro domo carectarum facienda. In minutis xv s. In sarclacione et falcacione per estimacionem xv s. In custu autumpni vj li. In stipendiis lvij s. In trituracione bladi per estimacionem xxxv s. In expensis superveniencium viij s. x d. ob. qua.
Summa xvj li. xvij s. qua. Et deficiunt iiij li. x s.
Staurum Sunt ibidem iij equi carectarii, ix affri. iiij boves, vj vacce, j juvencca, j boviculus, j juvencula, iiij vituli superannati, iiij vituli de exitu, x multones, xxxv matrices, xvj hogastri, xvj jercie, xxxiiij agni.

Hampsted' Estimacio facta ibidem die jovis supradicta [per Re]gin[aldum][130] Seman servientem[131]
Frumentum. Triturantur ibidem xj qr. j bus. frumenti. Inde in semine vij qr. ij bus. In liberacione servientis ij qr. vij bus.
Silligo Sunt ad triturandum per estimacionem iiij qr. Et de ij [qr.] silliginis de empcione. Summa vj qr. Inde in semine ij qr. In liberaciones famulorum iiij qr.
Pise Semen pisarum ad ordinacionem ballivi.
Avene Triturantur ibidem vj qr. et di. ..... Et sunt ad triturandum per estimacionem xxx qr. Inde in semine per estimacionem xx qr. In farina pro potagio famulorum per estimacionem ..... vij ..... Et remanent pro conventu ix qr. et di.
Liberaciones Ordinantur ad liberaciones xix qr. v bus. ..... deficiunt de liberacione servientis, videlicet iiij qr. silliginis, xij [qr.] bladi empti, et iij qr. v bus. de remanencia.
[*Receptum*] ..... de xl s. de arreragiis Willelmi servientis[132] ...... de x li. xviij s. x d. qua. de redditu. Et de xxx s. ...... Et de vj li. xiij s. iiij d. de exitu manerii

[129] MS: 'unde .... novo grano' all have been added in small handwriting on a second line, in order to fit it in; the hand is probably the main text hand.
[130] Passages in this account in square brackets supply text now obscured by water stains. The lacunae that follow in this and subsequent sections are also the result of these stains.
[131] MS: 'Expense auditorum viij s. iiij d. ob.' in margin.
[132] William de Arkesdene, serjeant at Hampstead; mentioned as such since 1296–7 (WAM 32385, 32401, 32403).

per estimacionem. Et de xxj s. de operibus vendendis per estimacionem. Et de xxx s. de .....

..... xiij s. ij d.

Inde in defectibus et aquietanciis xlij s. viij d. ...... [In custu] carucarum ..... [In custu] carectarum vj s. In custu domorum ij s. In custu molendini iij s. iiij d. In minutis ..... factur*a* fagattorum et in cariagio C s. per estimacionem. In blado emendo lx s. In falcacione pratorum per estimacionem ..... In custu autumpni xl s. In trituracione bladi v s. vj d. In stipendiis xxxij s.

Summa xvj li. ij s. ...... [Et] remanent pro conventu ..... viij li. ......

Staurum Sunt ibidem ..... affri, j pullanus etatis j anni et iij ..... iiij^{or} boves, ij vacce, iiij vituli.

Greneford' Estimacio ibidem facta ..... et R. de Sutbur'.....

Frumentum ..... ad triturandum per estimacionem x qr. Summa ..... Inde ad liberaciones x qr. Et remanent xvij qr. j bus. di.

Silligo ..... per estimacionem vij ...... Et sunt ad triturandum per estimacionem vij qr. et di. Et iij bus. de redditu. Summa viij qr. iij bus. Inde in expensis precariarum in autumpno j qr. In mixtura ad liberaciones vij qr. iij bus.

Ordeum Triturantur ibidem vij qr. et di. ordei que remanent pro conventu et mittuntur.

Avene Triturantur ibidem liij ...... bus. [Et sunt per estimacionem] ad triturandum xlvj qr. Summa iiij^{xx}xvij qr. j bus. Inde in semine per estimacionem ..... In prebenda equorum, affrorum, boum et superveniencium x qr. j bus. Et .....

Liberaciones Estimantur ad liberaciones famulorum ..... de Batrich'.

Receptum Oneratur ...... de arreragiis. Et de x li. xv s. qr. de redditu. Et de xxj s. x d. de firmis. Et de vij li. de exitu manerii per estimacionem. Et de iiij li. de perquisitis curie per estimacionem.

Summa xxiij li. xix s. vj d. qua.

Inde in aquietanciis xxj s. j d. ob. In custu carucarum per estimacionem xix s. In custu carectarum viij s. In custu domorum et camino reparando xx s. In minutis necessariis cum factura et cariagio busci viij li. In blado emendo pro liberacionibus x qr. pro l s. In custu falcacionis pratorum viij s. vj d. In custu autumpni xxx s. In trituracione bladi preter opera v s. ..... In stipendiis xxxviij s. vj d. In expensis supervenvencium per estimacionem xxx s.

Summa xix li. ix s. vij d. Et remanent pro conventu iiij li. ix s. x d. ob. qua.

Staurum Sunt ibidem ij equi carectarii, ix affri, ix boves, ij bovetti, j sus, vj porculi, vj porcelli.

II 9 View of the royal manors, December 1334

A roll of one membrane, indented down the right-hand side of the recto, varying in width between 135 and 140 mm. The document is a fair copy; it may have been written up in blocks, a manor at a time. It is endorsed in a contemporary hand 'De maneriis domine regine', and at the top of the dorse, in a late fourteenth- or early fifteenth-century hand, 'Anno Edwardi iij viij°'.[1] This view of the manors of Queen Eleanor's foundation was occasioned by Henry de Byrcheston's demittal of office as warden of the manors on 7 December 1334—an event soon followed by his death—and the beginning of Simon de Byrcheston's wardenship. Internal evidence suggests that the view of the manor took place at Westerham on or about that same day, 7 December. At Birdbrook, however, the view took place on 16 December, and at Turweston on 19 December. The manors of Knowle and Grafton were at present out of the demesne and were not subject to a view. The view was carried out by Robert de Curtlington, who was one of the two treasurers of Eleanor's foundation, and by Philip de Brightwell, a senior monk, who was apparently appointed ad hoc for the view.[2]

WAM 23668

[*Mem. 1 recto*] Hec indentura testatur de visu maneriorum regine Elianore facta per fratres Philippum de Bryhtwell' et Robertum de Curtlinton inter fratrem Henricum de Byrcheston' custodiam maneriorum dictorum dimittentem et fratrem Symonem de Byrcheston dictam custodiam recipientem septimo die Decembris anno Domini M°CCCxxxiiij^to^ anno vero regni regis Edwardi tercii a conquestu viij°

Westerham

Frumentum[3] In primis Willelmus serviens ibidem[4] oneratur de xx qr. ij bus. frumenti et iiij bus. scuralli de exitu, iij qr. ij bus. de empcione. Et estimantur ad ventilandum v qr., et ad triturandum xlv qr. Item de excessu invento in granario ij bus. Inde in semine seminato tunc xxj qr. ij bus. Et estimantur ad seminandum ij qr. di. In liberacione servientis j qr. ij bus. et pro residuo anni v qr. ij bus. Item pro liberacionibus famulorum iiij qr. vj bus. Et remanent ad vendendum xxxix qr. ij bus.

Mixtura Item de mixtura nichil de exitu. Estimantur ad ventandum ij qr. et ad triturandum xij qr. Et onerat se de iiij bus. siliginis et v qr. de mixtura pro liberacionibus famulorum de empcione. Inde estimantur ij qr. j bus. di. Et pro liberacionibus famulorum xvij qr. ij bus. di.

[1] Extant ministers' accounts: Birdbrook: WAM 25434; Westerham: WAM 26426.

[2] Pearce, *Monks*, pp. 81–2; Harvey, *Obedientiaries*, pp. 141 and 147.

[3] Each of the corn entries for this manor is distinguished by '3'—the mark commonly used by auditors to draw attention to particular points—in the left-hand margin, possibly in another hand. For the mark, *Manorial Records of Cuxham*, ed. Harvey, p. 53.

[4] William Mauncel, serjeant at Westerham 1325–36 (WAM 26421–7).

Ordeum yemale Item respondet de ij qr.[5] de exitu. Et estimantur ad ventandum j qr. ij bus. Et ad triturandum iij qr. Inde in semine ij qr. Et pro liberacionibus famulorum ij bus. Et pro braseo faciendo et vendendo iiij qr.
Fabe Item estimantur ad triturandum ij qr. di. Item estimantur pro semine iij bus. Et ad vendendum ij qr.
Pise Item estimantur ad triturandum v qr. Inde estimantur pro semine ij qr. di. Et pro liberacionibus famulorum ij qr. di.
Vesce Item estimantur ad triturandum iij qr. Inde pro semine j qr. di. Et ad vendendum j qr. di.
Ordeum quadragesimale Idem respondet de j qr. v bus. de exitu. Et estimantur ad tascam x qr. di. Item j qr. de empcione. Et estimantur ad emendum pro semine ij qr. Inde pro semine ij qr. Et pro liberacionibus famulorum xiij qr. ij bus.
Dragetum Item estimantur ad triturandum xij qr. Inde in semine per estimacionem ij qr. Et pro braseo faciendo et vendendo x qr.
Spelt' Item estimantur ad triturandum iiij qr. Et totum ad vendendum.
Avene Item respondet de iij qr. v bus. de exitu. Et de j qr. vij bus. excessu in granario. Et estimantur ad triturandum Cxx qr. Inde[6] in estimacione pro semine xxxv qr. In potagio famulorum nunc j qr. et pro residuo anni j qr. di. In prebendam ij equorum carectariorum per lxx noctes ij qr. j bus. di.[7] et[8] pro residuo anni futuri per estimacionem vj qr. Item pro iiij affris a die epiphanie[9] per estimacionem vij qr. di. et pro bobus in garbis, vaccis, vitulis et agnis cum necesse fuerit per estimacionem viij qr. Item pro prebenda nunc ij bus.[10] custodis, senescalli et aliorum superveniencium ij qr. di. Et ad vendendum lxj qr. vj bus. di.
Liberaciones famulorum Item de scurallo frumenti iiij qr. vj bus. De mixtura xvij qr. ij bus. di., ij qr. de pisis. De ordeo quadragesimali xiij qr. ij bus. Item de excessu invento in granario iij qr. Item de mixtura de empcione ij qr. Et de mixtura emenda vij qr. j bus. di. Et hoc totum sufficit pro liberacionibus famulorum.

Instaurum

Et sunt ibidem ij equi carectarii, iiij affri et j pullanus de remanencia. Item xiiij boves et iiij bovetti jungendi de remanencia. Et ordinantur iiij boves de cronura ad vendendum. Item sunt ij tauri, xxvij vacce et iij juvence jungende

[5] MS: 'qr.' omitted.
[6] MS: 'Inde' omitted.
[7] We should understand that the 70 nights were reckoned from 29 or 30 September 1334, the date of the beginning of the year of account, and ended on or about 7 December 1334, the date of the view at Westerham.
[8] MS repeats 'et'.
[9] 6 January.
[10] MS: 'nunc ij bus.' inserted.

de remanencia et non plures quia j vacca et j juvenc*ca* venduntur in yeme. Item v boviculi et iiij juvencule jungend*i* ad bovettos et juvencas. Et vij vituli jugend*i* ad boviculos quorum iij femelli. Et remanent. Item j sus et xvij hogetti de remanencia et iiij inventi in manerio. Et remanent j sus et xxj hoggetti. Item j anser et iij mariole de remanencia. Et iij mariole et j auca de invencione cum aliis in manerio. Et omnes remanent. Item sunt x capones de remanencia et iij invencione. Et remanent. Item sunt j gallus et xij galline de remanencia. Item de invencione viij galliculi pro caponibus faciendis. Et vj polett*e* pro gallinis. Et omnes remanent. Item sunt lxxij multones, iiij^{xx}xiiij matrices, xlix hogastri et jercie, et xlix agni de remanencia. Et preter h*os* in morina a festo sancti Michaelis iiij matrices, x hogastri et j agnus. Item sunt xv pelles de morina de quibus venduntur xj. Et remanent iiij ad vendendum.

Recepta denariorum per estimacionem

In primis de redditu per annum xl li. xiij s. vj d. ob. Item de firm*is* iij molendinorum vij li. iiij s.[11] Et de aliis firmis minutis ut patet in compoto precedenti lix s. iiij d. Item de firm*a* xxvij vaccarum et iij juvencarum, salva reprisa pro xij vitulis de exitu huius anni ab lactandis, vij li. xix s. Item de lactagio matricum, pannagio, vendicione feni, pastur*e*, foragii, bosci, lane, operibus arur*is* et aliis operibus vendendis sicut in anni*s* precedentibus per estimacionem xiij li. Item de xxx^{ta} M^{l} tegularum de remanencia vendendis lx s. Item de xxxix qr. ij bus. frumenti precium qr. v s. iiij d., iiij qr. ordei yemalis precium qr. iiij s., ij qr. fabarum precium bus. vj d. ob., j qr. di. vescarum precium bus. vj d., x qr. drageti precium bus. iiij d., iiij qr. de spelt' precium bus. iij d., lxj qr. vj bus. di. avenarum precium qr. ij s., per estimacionem ut nunc in patria, xix li. xviij s. iij d. ob. Item de iiij bobus de cronura vendendis liij s. iiij d. per estimacionem. Item de j vacca et j juve*nca* nunc vendendis xj s. Item de xxj porcis vendendis per estimacionem lxiij s. Item de perquisitis curie per estimacionem sicut in anno precedenti iiij li. x s.

Summa receptorum et recipiendorum per estimacionem Cvli. xj s. vj d.

Expense et reprise per estimacionem

Inde in resolucione redditus et defectu xj s. ix d. ob. qua. In custu carucarum nunc iiij s. ix d., et pro residuo anni xv s. iij d. In custu plaustrorum et carectariorum nunc xiij d., et pro residuo anni xviij s. xj d. In custu molendinorum per estimacionem xx s. In custu domorum nunc xxv s. viij d., et residuum per estimacionem vj s. viij d. In pratis falcandis et blado sarclando xxxij s. In custu autumpni per estimacionem iiij li. x s. Item in minutis per estimacionem xxiiij s. In iij qr. ij bus. frumenti nunc emptis

[11] The mills were watermills for corn (WAM 26426). The fulling mill mentioned *c.*1300 may now have been out of use (WAM 26392).

precium bus. viij d., iiij bus. siliginis precium bus. vij d., v qr. mixture precium bus. vj d., j qr. ordei et ij qr. mixture famulorum nunc emptis precium bus. v d. ob., et pro vij qr. j bus. et di. mixture[12] adhuc emendis precium bus. ut supra per estimacionem lxxvj s. vj d. qua. In blado triturato et triturando per estimacionem xl s. In stipendiis famulorum lxiiij s. iiij d. In stipendiis et expensis senescalli, custodis et aliorum superveniencium per estimacionem iiij li.

Summa expensarum et reprisarum per estimacionem xxv li. xj s. Et remanent ad liberandum thesaurario iiij^{xx} li. vj d.

[*Mem. 1 dorse*]

Bridbrok xvi die Decembris

Johannes le Neuman serviens ibidem[13] respondet de l qr. ij bus. frumenti de exitu. Et estimantur ad triturandum lx qr. Inde in semine xlvij qr. v bus. In liberacione servientis nunc iiij bus., pro residuo anni vj qr. Item pro liberacione grangie nunc v bus. et pro residuo triturando per estimacionem j qr. di. In liberacion*e* famulorum nunc ij qr. vj bus. et pro residuo anni per estimacionem xiiij qr. Et remanent ad vendendum xxxvij qr. ij bus.

Mixtura Item respondet de iij qr. de exitu. Et estimantur ad triturandum j qr. di. Inde in semine j qr. iij bus. et pro liberacionibus famulorum iij qr. j bus.

Fabe et pise Item respondet de iij qr. j bus. de exitu. Et estimantur ad triturandum xxxvj qr. Inde[14] in estimacione pro semine x qr. Et pro liberacionibus famulorum ij qr. Item pro sustentacione j qr. Et ad vendendum xxvj qr. j bus.

Ordeum Item respondet de j qr. ordei ad triturandum. Et totum pro semine.

Avene Item de xxij qr. avenarum de exitu. Et estimantur ad triturandum Cxl qr. Inde estimantur pro semine lx qr., in farina pro potagio iij qr., in prebendam xij affrorum tempore seminis yemalis vj qr. vij bus., j bus. di. per noctem. Et estimatur prebenda eorundem a ij die Januarii usque secundum diem Maij xxij qr. v bus. et di. Et pro ij[15] equis carectariis j p. per noctem per idem tempus iij qr. v bus. j p. Item pro bobus in garbis x qr. Item pro prebenda senescalli, custodis et aliorum superveniencium iij qr. Et ad vendendum lij qr. v bus. et p.

[12] MS: a short erasure follows.
[13] Serjeant at Birdbrook 1334–52 (WAM 25434).
[14] MS: 'inde' omitted.
[15] MS: 'ij' inserted.

Liberaciones famulorum Item respondet de xvj qr. vj bus. frumenti, iij qr. j bus. mixture, ij qr. fabarum et pisarum, x qr. mixture de firma molendini. Et totum nunc pro liberacionibus famulorum.

Instaurum

Item sunt ibidem ij equi carectarii qui remanent. Et xij affri de remanencia et iij emendi. Inde ordinantur vendendum iij ut remaneant xij affri. Item xv boves de remanencia et ij emendi. Inde in morina ij. Et remanent xv. Item j taurus de remanencia et j ad emendum. Inde j ad vendendum. Item sunt xx vacce, vij boviculi, unde j juvencula adjuncta cum juvenculis, vij vituli[16] adjuncti cum boviculis, unde ij femelli, que remanent. Item de vij vitulis iam superannatis computatis iij in morina et remanent iiij adjuncti cum boviculis. Item de ij verris de remanencia. In*de* j in morina. Et remanent j verrus, j sus et vj porcelli de remanencia. Item j anser et iij mariole, ij galli et xij galline de remanencia. Et Clj galline de redditu ad vendendum. Item iij dolea cizere de remanencia ad vendendum.

Recepta denariorum

Item de redditu ix li. xj s. xj d. ob., de firmis xxiiij s. per estimacionem. Item de xxxvij qr. ij bus. frumenti venditis precium bus. vj d., xxvj qr. fabarum et pisarum precium bus. v d., lij qr. v bus. j p. avenarum precium bus. iij d., xvij li. iij s. iiij d. ob. qua. Item de iij stottis venditis iiij s. Item de j tauro vendito vj s. Item de coreis trium vitulorum venditis iij d. Item de[17] vj porculis venditis xij s. Item de xx auculis de exitu huius anni per estimacionem vendendis v s. x d., Cxlix gallinis de redditu vendendis xxiiij s. x d. Item de iij doleis cizere de remanencia venditis xv s. Item de pastura vendita Cvj s. viij d. Item de firma xx vaccarum vj li. xiij s. iiij d. Item de oseris,[18] firma gallinarum et ovis, et firma columbarii xxiij s. viij d. Item de subbosco et hayis, pomis, piris et cizera huius anni per estimacionem lxx s. Item de operibus custumariis lxxij s. Et de perquisitis curie per estimacionem lx s.

In denariis recipiendis per estimacionem liiij li. xiij s. j d. qua.

Expense et reprise per estimacionem

Inde in resolucione redditus v s. vj s. In custu carucarum per estimacionem xx s. In custu carectarum per estimacionem xij s. iij d. In custu domorum per estimacionem xij s. Item pro iij affris, ij bobus et j tauro emendis v marcas per estimacionem. In minutis per estimacionem j marcam. Item in custu molendini per estimacionem di. marcam. In sarclacione et falcacione per estimacionem iij s. x d. In custu autumpni per estimacionem vj li. In stipendiis famulorum xv s. iiij d. In stipendiis senescalli et expensis eiusdem

[16] MS: 'vitulis'.
[17] MS: 'de' omitted.
[18] MS: 'osirs'.

et custodis per suos adventus, et aliorum superveniencium per estimacionem iiij li.

Summa expensarum et reprisarum per estimacionem xvij li. xv s. vij d. Et remanent ad liberandum thesaurario xxxvj li. xvij s. vj d. qua.

Turveston' xix° die Decembris

Frumentum[19] Prepositus ibidem respondet de xxix qr. frumenti de exitu. Et estimantur ad triturandum xxx qr. Item de j qr. vj bus. iij p. de cumulis singulorum qr.[20] Inde in semine xxiiij qr. ij bus. In liberacionibus famulorum nunc iiij qr. vj bus. In liberacione grangiarii nunc v bus. Et estimantur pro liberacionibus famulorum in grangia pro residuo anni xvj qr. vj bus. Et ad vendendum xiiij qr. iij bus. iij p.

Brot'. Item respondet de j qr. brotti de exitu frumenti et drageti. Et remanet ad vendendum.

Dragetum Item respondet de v qr. drageti. Et estimantur ad triturandum lxxv qr. Et ij qr. di. de cumulis ut supra.[21] Inde estimantur pro semine xxxv qr. In liberacionibus famulorum nunc j qr. vij bus. Et estimantur pro residuo anni viij qr. iij bus. Et ad prebendam boum in garbis ij qr. Et ad vendendum xxxv qr. ij bus.

Puls' Item respondet de v qr. ij bus. de exitu. Et estimantur ad triturandum x qr. Et de cumulis iiij bus. nunc inventis in granario.[22] Inde estimantur pro semine iiij qr. di. In liberacione famulorum nunc iij qr. di. Et estimantur pro residuo anni vj qr. vj bus. In vendicione nunc j qr. di. Et oportet emere pro prebenda equorum et superveniencium per estimacionem xij qr. avenarum ij bus. Et inde in prebenda iiij equorum in yeme ij qr. v bus. Et pro prebenda eorum in quadragesima v qr. v bus. Et pro potagio famulorum ij qr. di. Et pro prebenda superveniencium j qr. di.

Liberaciones famulorum Item respondet de xxj qr. di. frumenti supra, x qr. ij bus. drageti, x qr. ij bus. de puls' supra, que sufficient ad liberaciones famulorum.

Instaurum[23] Item sunt ibidem iiij equi carectarii, iiij affri, xiij boves, j taurus, ix vacce et j juvenca adjuncta, iij boviculi adjuncti unde j taurillus, j bovettus et j juvenca. Item ij boviculi adjuncti ad bovettos. Et iij superannati adjuncti ad boviculos. Et in vendicione nunc iiij vacce. Item

[19] The sign '3' has been placed against each corn entry.

[20] MS: 'Item' follows but has been struck out. The heaped measure used in threshing of wheat at Turweston represented approximately 1 additional peck per quarter of grain. For the same measure used in the threshing of dredge, and for the heaped measure representing approximately 1½ additional pecks per quarter used for pulse, see below.

[21] As in note 20.

[22] As in note 20.

[23] This heading appears at the right-hand side.

xxviij multones unde j in morina, xviij matrices et iij agni de remanencia. Item j anser et iiij mariole, xij capones, ij galli et xij galline de remanencia. Item xij pelles lanute et ij pellette, que venduntur.
Denariorum recepta[24] In primis de redditu cum aliis consuetudinibus in toto Cxvj s. viij d. Item de firmis lj s. iiij d. Item de operibus customariis ij s. iiij d. De firma ix vaccarum et j juvence, salva reprisa pro iij vitulis ablatis xliiij s. vj d. De pellis lanutis, vij gallis, xxj gallinis,[25] xxiiij auculis per estimacionem, lactagio matricum, lana de exitu huius anni, exitu columbarii, firma gallinarum, et pomis vendendis per estimacionem lij s. vj d. Item de iiij vaccis venditis xx s. Item de xiiij qr. iij bus. iij p. frumenti precium bus. v d., j qr. brotti precium bus. iiij d., xxxv qr. ij bus. drageti precium qr. ij s. vj d., j qr. di. de puls' precium ut supra, vj li. xv s. ob. qua. Et de perquisitis curie per estimacionem xxx s.

Summa receptarum per estimacionem xxij li. xij s. iiij d. ob. qua.

Expense et reprise per estimacionem

Inde in allocacione et defectu redditus xxiiij s. vj d. In custu carectarum per estimacionem xij s. In ferrura equorum viij s. Et pro xij qr. ij bus. avenarum emendis per estimacionem xxiiij s. vj d. In sale et foragio vij s. xj d. Et in aliis minutis per estimacionem vj s. viij d. In custu domorum per estimacionem j marcam. In trituracionem bladi per estimacionem xxxiiij s. vj d. In sarclacione et falcacione iiij s. ix d. In custu autumpni per estimacionem xij s. In stipendiis famulorum xlj s. ix d. In expensis senescalli, custodis et aliorum superveniencium per estimacionem xl s.

Summa expensarum et reprisarum xij li. vj s. xj d. Et remanent ad liberacionem thesaurario x li. v s. vj d.

Summa totalis levandum per estimacionem Cxxvij li. iij s. vj d. Summa equorum carectarum viij et affrorum xx. Item boum xlij, taurorum iiij, vaccarum et juvencarum lx, boviculorum, bovettorum et superannatorum xliiij. Item j verrus, ij sues et xxvij hogetti. CCCxiij bidentes preter morinam, iij anseres, xiij mariole, j auca, xxv capones, xiij galli et galliculi, et xliij galline.

[24] This heading appears at the right-hand side.
[25] MS: 'vij gallorum, xxj gallinarum'.

www.ingramcontent.com/pod-product-compliance
Lightning Source LLC
LaVergne TN
LVHW011913200926
848484LV00002B/611